THE SURVEYOR IN COURT

THE SURVEYOR
IN COURT

by

P. H. CLARKE
LL.B., F.R.I.C.S., A.C.I.Arb.

1985

THE ESTATES GAZETTE LIMITED
151 WARDOUR STREET, LONDON W1V 4BN

First Published 1985

ISBN 0 7282 0091 0

Printed in Great Britain at The Bath Press, Avon

Table of Contents

	page
Table of Statutes	xiii
Table of Statutory Rules, Orders and Instruments	xix
Table of Cases	xxi
INTRODUCTION	xxxv

PART ONE
PROCEDURE AND EVIDENCE

CHAPTER 1 – PROCEDURE

INTRODUCTION	3
HIGH COURT	4
(1) Constitution and jurisdiction	4
(2) Commencement of proceedings	5
(3) Pre-trial procedure	5
(4) Trial and judgment	7
(5) Costs	8
(6) Appeals	10
COUNTY COURTS	10
(1) Constitution and jurisdiction	10
(2) Commencement of proceedings	11
(3) Pre-trial procedure	12
(4) Trial and judgment	13
(5) Costs	13
(6) Appeals	13
LANDS TRIBUNAL	13
(1) Constitution and jurisdiction	13
(2) Commencement of proceedings	14
(3) Pre-hearing procedure	14
(4) Hearing	16
(5) Decision	17
(6) Proceedings without a hearing	17
(7) Costs	18
(8) Appeals	19

LOCAL VALUATION COURTS 19
(1) Constitution and jurisdiction 19
(2) Commencement of proceedings 19
(3) Pre-hearing procedure 20
(4) Hearing 21
(5) Decision 22
(6) Costs 22
(7) Appeals 22

RENT ASSESSMENT COMMITTEES 23
(1) Constitution and jurisdiction 23
(2) Commencement of proceedings 24
(3) Pre-hearing procedure 24
(4) Hearing 24
(5) Decision 25
(6) Costs 26
(7) Appeals 26

PLANNING INQUIRIES AND HEARINGS 26
(1) Constitution and jurisdiction 26
(2) Commencement of proceedings 28
(3) Pre-hearing procedure 28
(4) Hearing 30
(5) Report and decision 31
(6) Written representations 32
(7) Costs 33
(8) Appeals 34

CHAPTER 2 – EVIDENCE
INTRODUCTION 37

FACTS 38
(1) Law, fact and opinion 38
(2) Relevance, admissibility and weight 40

PROOF 41
(1) Evidence 42
(2) Formal admissions 50
(3) Judicial notice 50
(4) Presumptions 51

FACTS WHICH MAY NOT BE PROVED 52
(1) Estoppel 53
(2) Public policy and privilege 56

CHAPTER 3 – EXPERT EVIDENCE
INTRODUCTION 59

WAYS IN WHICH THE COURT OBTAINS EXPERT
   ASSISTANCE 59

(1) Assessors 59
(2) Court experts 60
(3) Expert witnesses 60

EXPERT EVIDENCE 62
(1) Subjects of expert evidence 62
(2) Competency, compellability and bias 63
(3) Fact and opinion in expert evidence 66

PROCEDURE 83
(1) Before the hearing 83
(2) At the hearing 90

PART TWO
THE EXPERT WITNESS

CHAPTER 4 – THE EXPERT WITNESS: PRINCIPLES AND PRACTICE
INTRODUCTION 95

DUTIES OF AN EXPERT WITNESS 95

QUALITIES OF AN EXPERT WITNESS 97
(1) Expertise 97
(2) Knowledge of evidence and procedure 98
(3) An objective approach 99
(4) The courage of his opinions 99

INSTRUCTIONS AND FEES 100
(1) Instructions 100
(2) Fees 101

WORK OF AN EXPERT WITNESS 102
(1) Before the hearing 102
(2) At the hearing 118
(3) After the hearing 121

CHAPTER 5 – EXPERT WITNESS DOCUMENTS
INTRODUCTION 123

EXAMPLE 1 (INITIAL REPORT) 123

EXAMPLE 2 (DOCUMENTS SUBMITTED UNDER RULE 42 (4) OF THE LANDS TRIBUNAL RULES 1975) 126

EXAMPLE 3 (EXPERT REPORT FOR EXCHANGE) 129

EXAMPLE 4 (PROOF OF EVIDENCE) 135

EXAMPLE 5 (WRITTEN REPRESENTATIONS) 145

CHAPTER 6 – THE ADVOCATE – EXPERT WITNESS:
  COMBINING THE ROLES
INTRODUCTION   155

DUTIES OF AN ADVOCATE   157

ADVOCACY: STYLE AND QUALITIES   158
(1) A logical mind   160
(2) A clear presentation   160
(3) A good memory   161
(4) A calm temperament   161

THE ADVOCATE – EXPERT WITNESS IN PRACTICE   162
(1) Preparation   163
(2) Statement of agreed facts   165
(3) Hearing   166
(4) Decision   190

PART THREE
THE INDEPENDENT EXPERT

CHAPTER 7 – THE INDEPENDENT EXPERT
INTRODUCTION   193

ARBITRATOR OR EXPERT?   193
(1) Clear words of appointment   194
(2) Construction in context or by comparison   194
(3) Indicia of appointment   195

ARBITRATOR AND EXPERT COMPARED   199
(1) Arbitration Acts   199
(2) Liability for negligence   206

PRACTICE AND PROCEDURE   212
(1) Appointment   212
(2) Initial letter   213
(3) Procedure before determination   215
(4) Determination   218

CHAPTER 8 – PROFESSIONAL NEGLIGENCE
INTRODUCTION   221

DUTY OF CARE   221
(1) Duty to client   221
(2) Duty to third parties   223

STANDARD OF CARE   224
(1) General rule   224
(2) Standard of care in valuation   226

DAMAGES 231
(1) Measure of damages 231
(2) Remoteness of loss 233
(3) Contributory negligence and joint defendants 240
(4) Assessment of damages 241

LIMITATION OF ACTIONS 247

EXCLUSION OF LIABILITY 249
(1) Exclusion by operation of law 249
(2) Exclusion under the terms of a contract 249
(3) Exclusion under a notice in tort 253

PART FOUR
ARBITRATION

CHAPTER 9 – LAW OF ARBITRATION I
INTRODUCTION 259

ARBITRATION AND THE COURTS 260

HOW ARBITRATIONS ARISE 261
(1) Arbitration by agreement 261
(2) Arbitration under statute 261
(3) Arbitration by order of court 263

ARBITRATION AGREEMENT 264
(1) Form and effect 264
(2) Content 266

LIMITATION 268
(1) Time limits imposed by arbitration agreement 268
(2) Time limits imposed by Limitation Act 1980 273

APPOINTMENT OF ARBITRATORS 274
(1) Who may be appointed? 274
(2) Methods of apppointment 275
(3) Revocation of appointment and removal 280

STAY OF CONCURRENT PROCEEDINGS IN COURT 285
(1) Arbitration not terminated by action 285
(2) Statutory provisions 286

CHAPTER 10 – LAW OF ARBITRATION II
INTRODUCTION 289

DUTIES OF AN ARBITRATOR 289
(1) Duties imposed by arbitration agreement 289
(2) Duties imposed by Arbitration Acts 291
(3) Duties imposed by rules of natural justice 292

ARBITRATION PROCEDURE   293
(1)   Procedure: before the hearing   293
(2)   Issues of law   303
(3)   Procedure: at the hearing   308

EVIDENCE AND SUBMISSIONS   312
(1)   General rule   313
(2)   Relaxation of general rule   313
(3)   Admissibility of evidence   315
(4)   Arbitrator receiving secret evidence   317
(5)   Arbitrator's use of own expert knowledge   319
(6)   Arbitrator's view of the law   323
(7)   Arbitrator's failure to hear evidence or submissions   323

CHAPTER 11 – LAW OF ARBITRATION III
INTRODUCTION   325

MAKING THE AWARD   325
(1)   Time for making the award   325
(2)   Delegation   325
(3)   The award of several arbitrators   326
(4)   Final and interim awards   326

FORM AND CONTENT OF THE AWARD   327
(1)   Writing or parol   327
(2)   Form to comply with submission   328
(3)   Award must be final and complete   328
(4)   Award must be certain   328
(5)   Award must be consistent   328
(6)   Award must be possible   329
(7)   Recitals   329
(8)   Determination and directions   329
(9)   Declaratory awards   331
(10) Signature and stamping   331

REASONS   332
(1)   Duty to give reasons   332
(2)   When should a reasoned award be given?   334
(3)   Judicial guidance as to reasons   335

INTEREST   342
(1)   Interest for the period before the commencement of
      proceedings   342
(2)   Interest for the period after commencement of proceedings
      and before the award   342
(3)   Interest for the period after the award   343
(4)   Interest in rent review arbitrations   344

COSTS 344
(1) Arbitrator's power regarding costs 344
(2) Arbitrator's discretion regarding costs 345
(3) Payment and taxation of costs 349
(4) Reasons for an award of costs 351
(5) Costs and completeness of awards 352

PUBLICATION, DELIVERY AND CORRECTION OF
AWARD 353
(1) Publication 353
(2) Delivery 353
(3) Correction 353

CHAPTER 12 – LAW OF ARBITRATION IV
INTRODUCTION 355

EFFECT OF AN AWARD 355
(1) Effect on the parties 355
(2) Effect on strangers 358
(3) Effect on the arbitrator 358

CHALLENGING AN AWARD 359
(1) Appeal on a question of law 360
(2) Application to remit or set aside an award 370
(3) Defence to an action on the award 382
(4) Declaration 382
(5) Appeal by agreement 383

ENFORCING AN AWARD 383
(1) Enforcement as a judgment 383
(2) Action on the award 385

CHAPTER 13 – ARBITRATION IN PRACTICE
INTRODUCTION 389

APPOINTMENT 389
Initial letter 391

PRELIMINARY MEETING 391
(1) Notification to the parties 391
(2) Preliminary meeting 392

ORDER FOR DIRECTIONS 393

BEFORE THE HEARING 397
(1) Arbitrator's functions 397
(2) Reading the documents 398

HEARING 399
(1) Arrangements 399
(2) Procedure 400

AWARD   402
(1)   Award with reasons   403
(2)   Award without reasons   422
(3)   Letter to the parties   422
(4)   Correction of award   423

APPENDICES

APPENDIX A – INTERPRETATION OF DOCUMENTS
Introduction   427
Fundamental question   427
Interpretation, rectification and implication   428
Literal approach   431
Purposive approach   433
Interpretration having regard to whole document   436
Interpretation to produce a reasonable result   437
Contra proferentem rule   439
Plans   439

*APPENDIX B – ARBITRATION UNDER THE AGRICULTURAL
    HOLDINGS ACTS*
Introduction   445
Disputes referred to arbitration under the 1948 Act   446
Appointment of an arbitrator   447
Revocation of appointment and removal   448
Procedure   448
Award   450
Costs and remuneration   452
After the award   453
Agricultural Holdings (Notices to Quit) Act 1977   454

*APPENDIX C – STATUTES, STATUTORY INSTRUMENTS AND
    CIRCULARS*
Statutes   459
Statutory rules, orders and instruments   513
Circulars   555

INDEX   569

Table of Statutes

[References in **heavy type** are to the text of the provisions concerned]

1677	Statute of Frauds	268
1698	Arbitration Act	260
1845	Lands Clauses Acts	376
1846	County Courts Act	10
1914	Bankruptcy Act	
	s. 137 (2)	52
1925	Law of Property Act	
	s. 40	268
	s. 84	14
1935	Law Reform (Married Women and Tort-feasors) Act	241
1936	Public Health Act	262
	s. 37	263
	s. 303	263
1945	Law Reform (Contributory Negligence) Act	
	s. 1 (1)	240
	s. 4	240
1947	Town and Country Planning Act	70
1948	Agricultural Holdings Act 11, 262, 277, 336, 445	
	s. 1	445
	s. 2	445
	s. 5 .... 446, 452	
	s. 6 .... 446, 452	
	s. 7 .... 446, 452	
	(1)	445
	s. 8 .... 446, 447	
	(2)	448
	s. 8A	446
	s. 9	446
	s. 10 .... 446, 452	
	s. 11	446
	s. 13 .... 446, 449	
	s. 14	446
	s. 34	447
	s. 47	449
	s. 57	447
	s. 61	452
	s. 68	446
	s. 70 .... 445, 446, 447, 449, **459**	
	(1)	**459**
	(2)–(5)	448
	(2)	**459**
	(3)	**459**
	(4)	**459**
	(5)	**460**
	(6)	**460**
	s. 71	454

s. 72		454
s. 73		454
s. 77 .... 445, 456, **460**		
(1) 447, 449, **460**		
(2)–(6)		451
(2) 448, **460**		
(3)		**460**
(4)		**460**
(5)		**460**
(6)		**460**
4th. Sch.		451
6th. Sch. 445, 449, 456, **461**		
para. 1 (1) 447, **461**		
(1A) 447, **461**		
(2) 448, **461**		
(3) 447, **461**		
2 .... 448, **461**		
2A 448, **461**		
3 .... 448, **461**		
4 .... 447, 448, **461**		
5 .... 453, **461**		
6 .... 449, **462**		
7 .... 450, **462**		
8 .... 449, **462**		
9 .... 450, **462**		
10		450
(1)		**462**
(2)		**463**
(3)		**463**
11 & 12		450
11 (1)		**463**
(2)		**463**
12		**463**
13 .... 451, **463**		
14 .... 450, **463**		
15 .... 451, **463**		
16 .... 451, **463**		
17 .... 451, **464**		
18 .... 452, 453, 454, **464**		
19 .... 453, **464**		
20 .... 453, **464**		
20A 451, **464**		
20B 452, **464**		
21 .... 452, **464**		
22 .... 452, **464**		
23 .... 452, **464**		
24 .... 450, **464**		
25 (1) 448, **465**		
(2) 453, **465**		

	25A 454, **465**	s. 14 .... 326, **471**	
	(1) **465**	s. 15 .... 330, **471**	
	(2) **465**	s. 16 .... 355, **471**	
	(3) **465**	s. 17 .... 359, 374, 423, **471**	
	(4) **465**	s. 18 .... 199, 349, **471**	
	26 .... 453, **465**	(1) 206, 344, 345,	
	27 .... **465**	350, **471**	
	28 .... 447, **465**	(2) 326, 350, **471**	
	29 .... 447, 449, **465**	(3) 344, 345, **471**	
1948	Local Government Act	(4) 352, 359, **471**	
	. ... 19, 513, 515	(5) **472**	
1949	Finance Act	s. 19 (1) 350, **472**	
	s. 35 and Sch. 331	(2) 350, **472**	
1949	Lands Tribunal Act 13	(3) 351, **472**	
	s. 1 (5) 263, 308	(4) 351, **472**	
1950	Arbitration Act 261, 445	s. 19A (1) (a) **342, 472**	
	Pt. I 261	(b) **343, 473**	
	s. 1 .... 262, 282, 283, 290,	(2) 343, **473**	
	303, **466**	s. 20 .... 343, 344, **473**	
	s. 2 .... 265, **466**	s. 21 .... 304, 360, **473**	
	(1) 262, 265, 283, **466**	s. 22 .... 352, 359, 370, 371,	
	(2) 283, **466**	379, **473**	
	(3) 262, 265, 283, **466**	(1) **372,** 382, **473**	
	s. 3 .... 265, 387, **466**	(2) 325, 381, **473**	
	(1) 266, **466**	s. 23 .... 352, 370, 371, 373,	
	(2) 266, **466**	379, **473**	
	s. 4 (1) 262, 266, 286, 287, **466**	(1) 262, 282, 283, 284,	
	s. 5 .... 262, 286, 287, **467**	377, **473**	
	s. 6 .... 276, **467**	(2) 300, 377, 380, **473**	
	s. 7 .... 282, 283, **467**	(3) 377, **473**	
	(a) 276, **467**	s. 24 .... 262, **473**	
	(b) 201, 276, **467**	(1) 275, 282, 283,	
	s. 8 (1) 276, 292, **467**	372, **473**	
	(2) 276, 326, **468**	(2) 282, 285, **473**	
	(3) 262, 277, **468**	(3) 286, 287, **473**	
	s. 9 .... 326, **468**	s. 25 .... 262, 282, **474**	
	s. 10 (1) (a) 278, **468**	(1) 279, 283, **474**	
	(b) 278, **468**	(2) 279, **474**	
	(c) 278, **468**	(3) 279, **474**	
	(d) 278, **468**	(4) 280, **474**	
	(2) 278, **468**	s. 26 .... 262, 383, 384, 385,	
	s. 11 .... 263, 308, **469**	387, **474**	
	s. 12 .... 15, 311, **469**	(1) **383,** 385, **474**	
	(1) 299, 301, 312,	(2) 383, **474**	
	317, **469**	(3) 383, **475**	
	(2) 312, **469**	(4) **475**	
	(3) 312, **469**	s. 27 .... 262, 268, 269, 271,	
	(4) 301, 312, **469**	272, **475**	
	(5) 312, **470**	s. 28 .... 298, 333, 385, **475**	
	(6) 296, 298, **470**	s. 29 .... 262, **475**	
	(a) 298, **470**	(1) **475**	
	(b) 301, 302, **470**	(2) 367, **475**	
	(c) 312, **470**	(3) 367, **475**	
	(d) 312, **470**	s. 30 .... 261, **476**	
	(e) **470**	s. 31 (1) 261, 367, 445, **476**	
	(f) **470**	(2) 261, **476**	
	(g) 318, **470**	s. 32 .... 264, 384, **476**	
	(h) **470**	s. 33 .... **476**	
	s. 13 (1) 225, **470**	s. 34 .... **476**	
	(2) 325, 381, **470**	s. 44 .... **477**	
	(3) 282, 283, 284, 325,	1954	Landlord and Tenant Act
	382, **470**	.... 4, 11, 74, 75	

Pt. II 5,67,107,129
s. 34 133
  (a) & (b) 74
1957 Housing Act 263
  s. 65 263
1958 Agriculture Act
  s. 8 (1) 461
  Sch. 1 461
    para. 21 (1) 450
      (2) 453
1958 Tribunals and Inquiries Act 336
1959 County Courts Act
  s. 6 (b) 274
1959 Rights of Light Act
  s. 2 14
1961 Land Compensation Act
  s. 4 (1)–(3) 117
  s. 5 (2) 127
  s. 14 (3) 127
1963 Agriculture (Miscellan-
      eous Provisions) Act
  s. 20 .... 462, 463
1965 Rent Act 23
1967 General Rate Act 19, 263
  s. 19 .... 168, 169, 173, 177,
                     178, 187
  s. 20 .... 168, 169, 173, 178, 179,
              181, 187, 189
  s. 76 .... 19, **477**
    (1) **477**
    (2) **477,** 513
    (3) **477**
    (4) **477**
    (5) **478**
  s. 78 263
  s. 83 (5) 178
    (6) 21, **478,** 516
    (7) **478**
    (8) 21, **478**
    (9) **478**
  s. 88 (3) 513
    (6) 515
  s. 117 (3) 513
1967 Leasehold Reform Act 23,
                                  26, 40
1968 Civil Evidence Act 45, 70, 82,
                                135, 315
  Pt. I 45, 48
  s. 1 .... , 45, **478**
    (1) **478**
    (2) **479**
  s. 2 .... 45, 46, 47, 48, 49,
                        315, **479**
    (1) **479**
    (2) **479**
    (3) **479**
  s. 3 .... 47, **479**
    (1) **479**
    (2) **480**
  s. 4 .... 45, 46, 47, 48, 49,
                        315, **480**
    (1) **480**
    (2) **480**
    (3) **480**
  s. 5 ...... 45, 46, 47, 48, 315, **480**
    (1) **480**
    (2) **481**
    (3) **481**
    (4) **481**
    (5) **482**
    (6) **482**
  s. 6 .... 47, **482**
    (1) **482**
    (2) **482**
    (3) **482**
    (4) **483**
    (5) **483**
  s. 7 .... 47, **483**
    (1) **483**
    (2) **484**
    (3) **484**
  s. 8 .... 48, **484**
    (1) **484**
    (2) **484**
    (3) **484**
    (4) **485**
    (5) **485**
    (6) **485**
  s. 9 .... 45, 48, **486**
    (1) **486**
    (2) (a) 49, 50, **486**
      (b) 49, 77, **486**
      (c) 49, **486**
      (d) 49, **486**
    (3) 50, **486**
    (4) (a) 50, **486**
      (b) 50, **486**
      (c) 50, **486**
    (5) **487**
    (6) **487**
  s. 10 (1) **487**
    (2) **487**
    (3) 83, 315, **487**
    (3A) **488**
    (4) 83, 315, **488**
  s. 18 (1) 45, 83, **488**
      (b) 315, **488**
    (2) 83, **488**
    (3) **488**
    (4) **488**
    (5) **489**
    (6) **489**
1970 Administration of Justice Act
  Sch. 3 .... 274, 474
    para. 11 474
1971 Fire Precautions Act........... 228
1971 Town and Country Plann-
      ing Act 26, 34
  s. 22 139
    (1) 140
  s. 29 28
  s. 36 139
  s. 53 .... 136, 139
  s. 94 147

	s. 290	140
	Sch. 9 27,	**489**
1971	Tribunals and Inquiries Act	
	s. 12	451
	Sch. 1	451
1972	Agriculture (Miscellan-	
	eous Provisions) Act	
	s. 15 (1)	465
1972	Civil Evidence Act 14, 83,	315
	s. 1 45,	**493**
	(1)	**493**
	(2)	**493**
	s. 2 (1)	**493**
	(2)	**493**
	(3)–(6)	84
	(3)	**494**
	(4)	**494**
	(5)	**494**
	(6)	**494**
	(7)	**494**
	(8)	**494**
	s. 3 61,	**495**
	(1)	**495**
	(2)	**495**
	(3)	**495**
	s. 5 315,	**495**
	(1) 83,	**495**
	(2) 83,	**495**
	(3)	**495**
1972	Local Government Act	
	s. 272 (2)	492
1973	Land Compensation Act	
	Pt. I	318
1975	Arbitration Act	261
	s. 8 (2) (a)	467
	(b)	475
	(c)	476
	(d)	476
	(e)	476
1977	Administration of Justice Act	
	s. 17 (2) 383,	475
1977	Agricultural Holdings	
	(Notices to Quit) Act	445
	s. 2 (2) & (3)	454
	(3)	455
	s. 5	454
	s. 10	455
1977	Rent Act 11,	23
	s. 77 23,	**495**
	(1)	**495**
	(2)	**495**
	(3)	**496**
	(4)	**496**
	s. 78 23,	**496**
	(1)	**496**
	(2)	**496**
	(3)	**496**
	(4)	**496**
	(5)	**496**
	Sch. 11 23,	**497**
	Sch. 12 23,	**501**
1977	Unfair Contract Terms Act	

	.... 210, 211, 250,	253
	s. 1 (1) (a)	250
	(b)	253
	(3)	253
	ss. 2–7	250
	s. 2 (1) 250,	253
	(2) 250,	253
	s. 3	251
	ss. 6 & 7	251
	s. 10	250
	s. 11 (1) 251,	252
	(3) 253,	254
	(4)	251
	(5)	251
	s. 12 (1)	251
	(2)	251
	s. 13	250
	s. 14	251
	Sch. 1	250
	Sch. 2	251
1978	Civil Liability (Contri-	
	bution) Act	241
	s. 1	241
1979	Arbitration Act 260, 261, 332,	
	352,	445
	s. 1 ...... 205, 262, 304, 305, 307,	
	317, 332, 359, 361, 366,	
	367, 368, 369, 370, 395,	
	397, 405,	**504**
	(1) 360, 371, 377,	**504**
	(2) 292, 304, 360,	**504**
	(3) 360,	**504**
	(4) 360, 361, 362, 363,	
	369,	**504**
	(5) 332, 333, 361,	**504**
	(6) 332, 333, 361,	**505**
	(6A) 334, 368, 370,	**505**
	(7) 368,	**505**
	(8) 360,	**505**
	s. 2 .... 216, 262, 303, 304,	
	305, 307, 392, 427,	**505**
	(1) 304,	**505**
	(2) 304,	**505**
	(2A) 305,	**506**
	(3) 305,	**506**
	s. 3 ...... 285, 295, 304, 305, 307,	
	332, 360, 366, 367, 370,	
	392,	**506**
	(1) 367,	**506**
	(2) 367,	**506**
	(3)	**506**
	(4) 305, 366,	**507**
	(5) 262, 367,	**507**
	(6) 367,	**507**
	(7) 367,	**507**
	s. 4 .... 363, 366,	**507**
	(1) 367,	**507**
	(2)	**507**
	(3) 367,	**508**
	(4) 367,	**508**
	(5)	**508**
	s. 5 ...... 281, 296, 300, 310,	**508**

(1) **508**
(2) **508**
(3) **508**
(4) **508**
(5) 296, **508**
(6) **508**
s. 6 .... 278, **509**
(1) 276, 468, **509**
(2) 326, 468, **509**
(3) **509**
(4) 278, **509**
s. 7 (1) 261, 333, 445, **509**
(2) 367, **510**
(3) 264, **510**
s. 8 (1) **510**
(2) **510**
(3) 473, **510**
(4) **510**
1979 Sale of Goods Act
s. 55 252
1980 Housing Act 23
s. 61 (7) 500
s. 72 23
s. 142 23
s. 152 (1) 496
(3) 496, 501
Sch. 25
para 42 496
Sch. 26 .... 496, 501
1980 Limitation Act 247, 268, 270,
273, 274
s. 2 247
s. 5 247
s. 7 385
s. 8 (1) 385
s. 34 (1) 273, **510**
(2) 273, **510**
(3) 273, **511**
(4) 273, **511**
(5) 274, 382, **511**
(6) 274, **511**
(7) **511**
1980 Magistrates Courts Act
s. 154 .... 485, 494
Sch. 7 .... 485, 494
1981 Supreme Court Act 4
s. 70 (1) 59
s. 148 (1) 505, 506
(2) 334, 368, 505
(3) 305, 506
s. 152 (1) 506
(4) 485, 494
Sch. 5 506

Sch. 7 .... 485, 494
1982 Administration of Justice
Act
s. 15 (6) 342, 472
Sch. I Pt. IV 342, 472
1982 Supply of Goods and
Services Act 206, 249
Pt. II 206, 210
s. 12 (1)–(4) 210
(4) & (5) 211
s. 13 .... 210, 222
s. 14 211
s. 15 211
s. 16 (1) & (2) 211
(3) 211
(4) 211
1984 Agricultural Holdings Act .. 445
s. 1 446
s. 8 .... 445, **512**
(1) 447, 451, 453, **512**
(2) **512**
(3)–(5) 448
(3) **512**
(4) **512**
(5) **512**
s. 10 (1) 460, 461, 462,
464, 465
(2) 463, 465
s. 11 (5) (a) 447
(b) 465
Sch. 3
para. 18 460
19 460
(3) 449, 451
28 ... 461, 462, 464, 465
(2) 447
(3) 448
(7) 451, 452
(8) 452
(9) 454
(10) 447, 449
Sch. 4 .... 463, 465
1984 County Courts Act 10
s. 64 263
s. 148 (1) 475, 485, 488,
494, 510
Sch. 2
para. 22 (a) 475
(b) 475
33 485
34 488
43 494
70 510

Table of Statutory Rules, Orders and Instruments

[References in **heavy type** are to the text of the provisions concerned]

— Rules of the Supreme Court 4
   Ord. 14 5
   Ord. 25 r. 8 (1) (b) 84
   Ord. 27 50
   Ord. 38 rr. 20–34 .... 48, 315
    r. 29 (1) 315
    rr. 35–44 .... 84, 315
    r. 35 .... **531**
    r. 36 .... 84, 85, 129, 133, **531**
    r. 37 ..... 84, 85, 86, **531**
    r. 38 .... 84, 85, 86, 129, 133, 135, **532**
    r. 39 .... 86, **532**
    r. 40 .... **532**
    r. 41 ..... 84, 85, 90, **533**
    r. 42 .... **533**
    r. 43 .... 90, **533**
    r. 44 .... **533**
   Ord. 40 60
   Ord. 59 r. 4 382
   Ord. 73 r. 5 (1) (a) & (b) . 370
    (2) 360

1948 Agricultural Holdings (England & Wales) Rules 451
   1st. Sch. Form A 451
   2nd. Sch. 451

1956 Rating Appeals (Local Valuation Courts) Regulations 19, **513**

1971 Rent Assessment Committees (England & Wales) Regulations 23, **516**

1973 Counter Inflation Business Rents Order 435

1974 Town & Country Planning Appeals (Determination by Appointed Persons) (Inquiries Procedure) Rules 27, **520**

1974 Town & Country Planning (Inquiries Procedure) Rules 27

1975 Lands Tribunal Rules . 14, 15, 87
   rr. 10 & 11 87
   r. 10 .... **533**
   r. 11 .... 87, 88, **534**

    (3) 88, **534**
   rr. 12 & 13 89
   r. 12 .... **535**
   r. 13 .... **535**
   r. 14 .... **535**
   r. 33 A 89, **536**
   r. 41 .... 88, 89
   r. 42 .... 88, 90, 91, 99, 107, 110, 119, **537**
    (4) 90, 126, 127, **537**
    (6) 89, **538**
   r. 45 88
   r. 48 (2) 87, 89
   Pt. II 88
   Pt. IV 308

1977 Lands Tribunal (Amendment) Rules 14, 17, 87, 537

1977 Town & Country Planning General Development Order
   art. 3 143
   art. 4 143
   Sch. I Class I 136, 139, 142, 144
    I. 3 143

1978 Agricultural Holdings (Arbitration on Notices) Order 454, **538**
   art. 3 .... 456, **539**
   arts. 5–7 456
   art. 5 .... **540**
   art. 6 .... **540**
   art. 7 .... **540**
   art. 9 .... 454, **541**
   art. 9A 455, **541**
   art. 11 .... 455, **542**
   arts. 12 & 13 ..... 456, **542, 543**

1980 Regulated Tenancies (Procedure) Regulations 23
   reg. 2 .... 497, 498, 499
   reg. 3 .... 502, 504
   Sch. 1 para. 1 497
    2–4 498
    5 498
    6 499
   Sch. 2 para. 1 502
    2 502
    3 504

1980 Rent Assessment Com-
mittees (England &
Wales) (Amendment)
Regulations 23, 517, 518
1980 Rent Assessment Com-
mittees (England &
Wales) (Rent Tri-
bunal) Regulations 23, **545**
1981 County Court Rules   10
Ord. 19 263
Ord. 20 rr. 14–26   48
r. 27 .... 84, 85, **554**
r. 28 .... 84, **554**
1981 Lands Tribunal (Amendment) Rules 14, 87, 534, 538
1981 Lands Tribunal (Amendment No 2) Rules 14, 87,
535
1981 Rent Assessment Com-
mittees (England &
Wales) (Amendment)
Regulations 23, 518, 520
reg. 3 .... 499, 504
1981 Rent Assessment Com-
mittee (England &
Wales) (Leasehold

Valuation Tribunal)
Regulations 23, **547**
1981 Rent Assessment Com-
mittees (England &
Wales) (Rent Tribu-
nal) (Amendment)
Regulations 23, **546**
1981 Town & Country Planning
(Enforcement) (In-
quiries Procedure)
Rules   28
1981 Town & Country Planning
General Develop-
ment (Amendment)
Order 142
1984 Agricultural Holdings
(Arbitration on
Notices) (Variation)
Order 454, 539, 541, 542,
544
art. 5 .... 455, 542
1984 Lands Tribunal (Amend-
ment) Rules 14, 87
1985 Supply of Services (Exclusion of Implied Terms)
Order 211

Table of Cases

AB Marintrans v. Comet Shipping Co Ltd (1985) *The Times* 19th March 1985 ... 241
Abu Dhabi Gas Liquefaction Co Ltd v. Eastern Bechtel Corporation [1982] 2
  Lloyd's Rep 425 279
Adam (W. & R. R.) Ltd v. Hockin (VO) [1966] RA 339; [1966] RVR 431; 13
  RRC 1 156
Agromet Motoimport v. Maulden Engineering Co (Beds) Ltd [1985] 2 All ER
  436 .... 385, 386
Aiden Shipping Co Ltd v. Interbulk Ltd (1984) *The Times* 5th December 1984 ... 375
Ailsa Craig Fishing Co Ltd v. Malvern Fishing Co Ltd [1983] 1 All ER 101 .. 250, 439
Alfred Golightly & Sons Ltd v. Durham County Council (1981) 260 EG 1045,
  1135 & 1199; [1981] RVR 229 111
Allen v. Greenslade (1875) 33 LT 567 374
Allied London Investments Ltd v. Hambro Life Assurance Ltd (1985) 274 EG
  148 343
Amalgamated Estates Ltd v. Joystretch Ltd (1980) 257 EG 489 269
Amalgamated Metal Corporation Ltd v. Khoon Seng Co [1977] 2 Lloyd's Rep
  310 383
Ames v. Milward (1818) 8 Taunt 637; 129 ER 532 328
Amherst v. James Walker Goldsmith & Silversmith Ltd (No. 1) (1980) 254 EG
  123 314
Anns v. Merton London Borough Council [1978] AC 728; [1977] 2 WLR 1024;
  121 SJ 377; 75 LGR 555; [1977] JPL 514; 243 EG 523 & 591 223
Anon (1814) 2 Chit 44 315
Antaios Compania Naviera SA v. Salen Rederierna AB [1984] 2 Lloyd's Rep
  235; [1984] 3 WLR 592 .... 336, 364, 368
Appleton v. Norwich Union Fire Insurance Society Ltd (1922) 13 Ll L Rep
  345 .... 285, 379
Archital Luxfer Ltd v. Henry Boot Construction Ltd [1981] 1 Lloyd's Rep 642 .. 348
Arenson v. Arenson & Casson, Beckman, Rutley & Co [1977] AC 405; [1975] 3
  WLR 815; 119 SJ 810; [1975] 3 All ER 901; [1976] 1 Lloyd's Rep
  179 .... 196, 206, 207, 210
Argyll (Duchess of) v. Beuselinck [1972] 2 Lloyd's Rep 172 225
Ashbridge Investments Ltd v. Minister of Housing & Local Government [1965]
  1 WLR 1320; [1965] 3 All ER 371 361

Babanaft International Co SA v. Avant Petroleum Inc [1982] 1 WLR 871;
  [1982] 3 All ER 244 .... 270, 305, 368
Baber v. Kenwood Manufacturing Co Ltd [1978] 1 Lloyd's Rep 175; 121 SJ 606
  .... 194, 204
Bailey (C.H.) Ltd v. Memorial Enterprises Ltd [1974] 1 WLR 728; 118 SJ 8;
  [1974] 1 All ER 1003; 27 P & CR 188 .... 428, 438
Bailey v. Derby Corporation [1965] 1 WLR 213; [1965] 1 All ER 443; 129 JP
  140; 108 SJ 939; 63 LGR 36; 16 P & CR 192; [1965] RVR 43 238
Baker Britt & Co Ltd v. Hampsher (VO) (1976) 239 EG 971; 19 RRC 62 180
Baker v. Cotterill (1849) 18 LJQB 345; 7 D & L 20; 14 Jur 1120; 82 RR 956 307
Baker v. Hunter (1847) 16 M & W 672; 4 D & L 696; 16 LJ Exch 203; 153
  ER 1360 .... 329, 381
Banin v. MacKinlay [1984] 1 All ER 1116 292
Baron v. Sunderland Corporation [1966] 2 QB 56; [1966] 2 WLR 363; 109 SJ
  1029; [1966] 1 All ER 349 .... 266, 271
Bartle v. Musgrave (1841) 1 Dowl (NS) 325; 5 Jur 1061; 63 RR 838 372
Barton (W. J.) Ltd v. Long Acre Securities Ltd [1982] 1 WLR 398; [1982] 1 All
  ER 465; 262 EG 877 74
Basildon Development Corporation v. J. E. Lesser (Properties) Ltd [1985] 1 All
  ER 20 241

Bates (Thomas) & Son Ltd v. Wyndhams (Lingerie) Ltd [1981] 1 WLR 505;
    125 SJ 32; [1981] 1 All ER 1077; 257 EG 381; 41 P & CR 345 429
Bath (Henry) & Son Ltd v. Birgby Products [1962] 1 Lloyd's Rep 389; 106 SJ
    288 .... 310, 378
Batty v. Metropolitan Property Realisations Ltd [1978] QB 554; [1978] 2
    WLR 500; 122 SJ 63; [1978] 2 All ER 445; 246 EG 43; 7 BLR 1
    .... 222, 241
Baxter v. F. W. Gapp & Co Ltd [1939] 2 KB 271; 108 LJKB 522; 160 LT 533;
    55 TLR 739; 83 SJ 436; [1939] 2 All ER 752 .... 229, 237, 246
Baxters & Midland Ry, Re (1906) 95 LT 20; 70 JP 445; 22 TLR 616 373
Beaumont Property Trust v. Tai (1982) 265 EG 872 436
Beddow v. Beddow (1878) 9 Ch D 89; 47 LJ Ch 588; 26 WR 570 281
Bell Hotels (1935) Ltd v. Motion (1952) 159 EG 496 .... 230, 244
Bellshill & Mossend Co-Operative Society Ltd v. Dalziel Co-Operative Society
    Ltd [1960] AC 832; [1960] 2 WLR 580; 104 SJ 248; [1960] 1 All ER 673;
    1960 SC (HL) 64; 1960 SLT 165 386
Belvedere Motors Ltd v. King (1981) 260 EG 813 .... 202, 227
Bibby (J) & Sons Ltd v. Merseyside County Council (1979) 251 EG 757; 39 P &
    CR 53; [1979] RVR 286 340
Birmingham City Council v. West Midlands Baptist (Trust) Association (Inc)
    [1970] AC 874; [1969] 3 WLR 389; 133 JP 524; 113 SJ 606; [1969] 3
    All ER 172; 20 P & CR 1052; 67 LGR 571; affirming [1968] 2 QB 188;
    [1968] 2 WLR 535; 111 SJ 851; [1968] 1 All ER 205; 19 P & CR 9
    ....54, 228
Birtley Co-Operative Society Ltd v. Windy Nook & District Industrial Co-
    Operative Society Ltd (No. 2) [1960] 2 QB 1; [1959] 2 WLR 415; 103 SJ
    240; [1959] 1 All ER 623 383
Bishopsgate (99) Ltd v. Prudential Assurance Co Ltd (1985) 273 EG 984 370
BL Holdings Ltd v. Robert J. Wood & Partners (1979) 12 BLR 1; 128 SJ 570 227
Black v. Oliver (VO) [1978] QB 870; [1978] 3 All ER 408; [1978] 2 WLR 923;
    142 JP 630; 122 SJ 194; [1978] RA 117; 76 LGR 431; 247 EG 43 40
Blackett v. Bates (1865) LR 1 Ch 117; 35 LJ Ch 324; 2 H & M 610 387
Blackwell v. Derby Corporation (1911) 75 JP 129 287
Blanchard v. Sun Fire Office (1890) 6 TLR 365 275
Blow v. Norfolk County Council [1967] 1 WLR 1280; [1966] 3 All ER 579; 131
    JP 6; 111 SJ 811; 66 LGR 1; [1966] RVR 557 80
Bolam v. Friern Barnet Hospital Management Committee [1957] 1 WLR 582;
    101 SJ 357; [1957] 2 All ER 118 .... 224, 229, 230
Bolton v. Puley (1982) 267 EG 1160 .... 240, 244
Boots The Chemist Ltd v. Street (1983) 268 EG 817 428
Bovis Group Pension Fund Ltd v. GC Flooring & Furnishing Ltd (1984) 269
    EG 1252 .... 148, 306, 307
Boyer (William) & Sons v. Minister of Housing & Local Government (1968) 20
    P & CR 176; 113 SJ 53; 67 LGR 374 337
BP Exploration Co (Libya) Ltd v. Hunt (No. 2) [1982] 1 All ER 925 343
Bracegirdle v. Oxley [1946] 1 KB 349 361
Bracknell Development Corporation v. Greenlees Lennards Ltd (1981) 260 EG
    500 63
Bradley (Edwin H.) & Sons Ltd v. Secretary of State for the Environment
    (1982) 264 EG 926 164
Bradshaw's Arbitration, Re (1848) 12 QB 562; 17 LJQB 362; 12 Jur 998 371
Braid Investments Ltd v. East Lothian District Council (1981) 259 EG 1088;
    [1982] RVR 13 98
Bremer Handelsgesellschaft mbH v. Westzucker GmbH (No. 2) [1981] 2
    Lloyd's Rep 130 335
Bremer Vulcan Schiffbau Und Maschinenfabrik v. South India Shipping Cor-
    poration Ltd [1981] AC 909; [1981] 2 WLR 141; [1981] 1 All ER 289
    281
Brown (Christopher) Ltd v. Oesterreichischer Waldbesitzer R Gmbh [1954] 1
    QB 8; [1953] 3 WLR 689; 97 SJ 744; [1953] 2 All ER 1039; [1953] 2
    Lloyd's Rep 373 .... 302, 386
Brown v. Vawser (1804) 4 East 584 353

Buckland *v*. Watts (1968) 208 EG 969; 112 SJ 841; 118 NLJ 1009 227
Bulk Transport Corporation *v*. Sissy Steamship Co Ltd [1979] 2 Lloyd's Rep
    289 353
Burgess *v*. Purchase & Sons (Farms) Ltd [1983] Ch 216; [1983] 2 WLR 361;
    [1983] 2 All ER 4 204
Burkett Sharp & Co *v*. Eastcheap Dried Fruit & Perara [1962] 1 Lloyd's
    Rep 267 383
Burroughs Machines Ltd *v*. Mooney (VO) (1976) 241 EG 845; 20 RRC 324;
    [1977] RA 45 .... 78, 181
BVS SA & Another *v*. Kerman Shipping Co SA [1982] 1 WLR 166; [1982] 1
    All ER 616; [1982] 1 Lloyd's Rep 62 364
Bwllfa & Methyr Dare Steam Collieries (1891) Ltd *v*. Pontypridd Waterworks
    Co [1903] AC 426; [1900–3] All ER Rep 600; 72 LJKB 805; 89 LT 280;
    52 WR 193; 19 TLR 673 72

Camden (London Borough of) *v*. Secretary of State for the Environment &
    Herweld [1980] JPL 31 388
Camden (Marquis) *v*. CIR [1914] 1 KB 641; affirmed [1915] AC 241 63
Camillo Eitzen & Jewson & Sons, Re (1896) 40 SJ 438 292
Campbell *v*. Edwards [1976] 1 WLR 403; 119 SJ 845; [1976] 1 All ER 785;
    [1976] 1 Lloyd's Rep 522; 237 EG 647 .... 203, 204, 210, 222
Carreras Ltd *v*. D. E. & J. Levy (1970) 215 EG 707 .... 231, 245
Carus-Wilson & Greene, Re (1886) 18 QBD 7; 56 LJQB 530 197
Cassir, Moore & Co Ltd *v*. Eastcheap Dried Fruit Co [1962] 1 Lloyd's Rep 400
    329
Centrovincial Estates PLC *v*. Bulk Storage Ltd (1983) 268 EG 59; 45 P & CR 393 358
Chandris *v*. Isbrandtsen Moller Co Inc [1951] 1 KB 240; 66 TLR (Pt 2) 358;
    94 SJ 534; [1950] 2 All ER 618; 84 Ll L Rep 347 267
Chapman *v*. Charlwood Alliance Properties Ltd (1981) 260 EG 1041 .... 305, 307
Chartered Trust PLC *v*. Maylands Green Estate Co Ltd (1984) 270 EG 845 272
Chinnery *v*. Basildon Development Corporation [1970] RVR 530 .... 54, 90, 91
Christopher Brown Ltd *v*. Oesterreichischer Waldbesitzer R Gmbh [1954] 1
    QB 8; [1953] 3 WLR 689; 97 SJ 744; [1953] 2 All ER 1039; [1953] 2
    Lloyd's Rep 373 .... 302, 386
City of London Corporation *v*. Watneys (London) Ltd [1983] RVR 5 75
Clarke *v*. Findon Developments Ltd (1983) 270 EG 426 .... 267, 268
Clibbett (W) Ltd *v*. Avon County Council [1975] RVR 131; 237 EG 271 54
Clinker & Ash Ltd *v*. Southern Gas Board (1967) 18 P & CR 372; [1967] JPL
    473; 203 EG 735 54
Clippens Oil Co Ltd *v*. Edinburgh & District Water Trustees [1907] AC 291 239
Compton Group Ltd *v*. Estates Gazette Ltd (1977) 36 P & CR 148; 244 EG
    799 .... 148, 434
Cooke-Bourne (E. D. & A. D.) (Farms) Ltd *v*. Mellows [1982] 2 All ER 208;
    262 EG 229; 126 SJ 481 449
Cooper *v*. Shuttleworth (1856) 25 LJ Exch 114 283
Corisand Investments Ltd *v*. Druce & Co (1978) 248 EG 315, 407 & 504 .... 76, 228,
    230, 239, 246
Costa *v*. Georghio (1984) 8 CSW 322 248
Coupland *v*. Arabian Gulf Petroleum Co [1983] 3 All ER 226 222
Coventry City Council *v*. J. Hepworth & Son Ltd (1982) 265 EG 608; 46 P &
    CR 170 435
Crabb *v*. Arun District Council [1976] Ch 179; [1975] 3 WLR 847; [1975] 3 All
    ER 865; 32 P & CR 70 55
Craven *v*. Craven (1817) Moore CP 403; 7 Taunt 644; 18 RR 623; 129 ER 256 .. 317
Cressey *v*. Jacobs (1977) (unreported) Bernstein & Reynolds *Handbook of
    Rent Review* p. [DC 97] 437
Crighton & The Law Car & General Insurance Corporation Ltd, Re [1910] 2
    KB 738; 80 LJKB 49; 103 LT 62 .... 299, 300
Curtis *v*. Potts (1814) 3 M & S 145; 105 ER 565 387
Cutts *v*. Head [1984] 2 WLR 349; [1984] 1 All ER 597 .... 81, 349
Czarnikow Ltd *v*. Koufos (The Heron II) [1969] 1 AC 350 .... 232, 233

Daisley v. B. S. Hall & Co (1973) 225 EG 1553 242
Dalmia Cement Ltd v. National Bank of Pakistan [1974] 2 Lloyd's Rep 98;
    [1974] 3 All ER 189 385
Daniels (H. E.) Ltd v. Carmel Exporters & Importers Ltd [1953] 2 QB 242;
    [1953] 3 WLR 216; 97 SJ 473; [1953] 2 All ER 401; [1953] 2 Lloyd's
    Rep 103 356
Dare Valley Ry, Re (1868) LR 6 Eq 429; 37 LJ Ch 719 385
David Taylor & Sons Ltd v. Barnett Trading Co [1953] 1 WLR 562; 97 SJ 226;
    [1953] 1 All ER 843; [1953] 1 Lloyd's Rep 181 371
Davie v. Edinburgh Magistrates 1953 SC 34 61
Davies v. Pratt (1855) 16 CB 586 374
Davies v. Price (1864) 11 LT 203; 34 LJQB 8; 12 WR 1009 386
Davis v. Witney UDC (1899) 15 TLR 275 353
Dodd Properties (Kent) Ltd v. Canterbury City Council [1980] 1 WLR 433;
    [1980] 1 All ER 928; 124 SJ 84; 253 EG 1335; 13 BLR 45 .... 232, 236,
                                                                                    242, 243, 247
Donoghue v. Stevenson [1932] AC 562; 101 LJPC 119; 147 LT 281; 48 TLR
    494; 1932 SC (HL) 31; 1932 SLT 317; 37 Com Cas 350; 76 SJ 396 223
Dorset Yacht Co Ltd v. Home Office [1970] AC 1004; [1970] 2 WLR 1140;
    [1970] 2 All ER 294; [1970] 1 Lloyd's Rep 453; 33 MLR 691; 114 SJ 375
    223
Dowling v. Pontypool etc Ry Co LR 18 Eq 714 63
Drummond v. Hamer [1942] 1 KB 352; 111 LJKB 385; 58 TLR 156; [1942] 1
    All ER 398 284
Duvan Estates Ltd v. Rossette Sunshine Savouries Ltd (1981) 261 EG 364 .... 74, 361,
                                                                                            368
Dwyer v. Rodrick (1983) *Law Society's Gazette* 23rd November 1983 p. 3003; *The
    Times* 12th November 1983 221

Eads v. Williams (1854) 4 De GM & G 674; 24 LJ Ch 531; 24 LT (OS) 162; 3
    WR 98; 1 Jur (NS) 193; 43 ER 671 .... 314, 387
Eagle Star Insurance Co Ltd v. Gale & Power (1955) 166 EG 37; [1955] JPL
    679 246
Eardley v. Otley (1818) 2 Chit 42; 23 RR 740 375
Eastcheap Dried Fruit Co v. NV Gebroeders Catz Handelsvereeniging [1962] 1
    Lloyd's Rep 283 378
Eastwood v. Ashton [1915] AC 900 440
Edlingham Ltd v. MFI Furniture Centres Ltd (1981) 259 EG 421 269
Edwards, ex p., Re Smith (1886) 3 Morrell's Bank Rep 179 387
Edwards v. Bairstow [1956] AC 14; [1955] 3 All ER 48; [1955] 3 WLR 410; 99
    SJ 558; 48 R & IT 534 361
Edwin H. Bradley & Sons Ltd v. Secretary of State for the Environment (1982)
    264 EG 926 164
Ellison v. Bray (1864) 9 LT 730 307
Elmbridge Borough Council v. Secretary of State for the Environment &
    Baptist (1980) 39 P & CR 543; [1980] JPL 463; 78 LGR 637 337
English Exporters (London) Ltd v. Eldonwall Ltd [1973] Ch 415; [1973] 2
    WLR 435; [1973] 1 All ER 726; 25 P & CR 379; 117 SJ 224; 225 EG
    255 .... 67, 68, 69, 76, 77, 82
Enoch & Zaretzky Bock & Co, Re [1910] 1 KB 327; 79 LJKB 363; 101 LT 801
    .... 309, 311, 313
Erich Schroeder, The [1974] 1 Lloyd's Rep 192 .... 351, 352
Esso Petroleum Co Ltd v. Mardon [1976] 2 WLR 583; [1976] 1 QB 801; 120 SJ
    131; [1976] 2 All ER 5; [1976] 2 Lloyd's Rep 305 .... 222, 225
Essoldo (Bingo) Ltd's Underlease, Re (1971) 115 SJ 967; 23 P & CR 1; 220 EG
    1437 277
European & American SS Co v. Croskey & Co (1860) 8 CB (NS) 397; 29 LJCP
    155; 6 Jur (NS) 896; 8 WR 236; 141 ER 1219 283
European Grain & Shipping Ltd v. Johnston [1982] 3 All ER 989 331
Evans (F. R.) (Leeds) Ltd v. English Electric Co Ltd (1978) 36 P & CR 185;
    245 EG 657 .... 407, 409

Evans v. London Hospital College & Others [1981] 1 WLR 184 64
Evans v. Rees (1839) 10 Ad & El 151; 2 P & D 626; 50 RR 366; 113 ER 58 358
Excomm Ltd v. Bamaodah (1984) *The Times* 17th January 1985 .... 265, 268
Exormisis Shipping SA v. Oonso, The Democratic Peoples Republic of Korea
    & The Korean Foreign Transportation Corporation [1975] 1 Lloyd's
    Rep 432; [1975] 2 Lloyd's Rep 402 300

Fakes v. Taylor Woodrow Construction Ltd [1973] 1 QB 436; [1972] 2 WLR
    161; 117 SJ 13; [1973] 1 All ER 670 .... 287, 375
Falkingham v. Victorian Railways Commissioner [1900] AC 452; 69 LJCP 89;
    82 LT 506 .... 316, 377
Farr (A. E.) Ltd v. Ministry of Transport [1960] 1 WLR 956; 104 SJ 705; [1960]
    3 All ER 88 267
Faure, Fairclough Ltd v. Premier Oil & Cake Mills Ltd [1968] 1 Lloyd's Rep
    237 .... 291, 375, 383
Fawcett v. Newcastle upon Tyne Metropolitan District Council [1980] RVR
    300; 256 EG 615 117
Fidelitas Shipping Co Ltd v. V/O Exportchleb [1966] 1 QB 630; [1965] 2 WLR
    1059; 109 SJ 191; [1965] 2 All ER 4; [1965] 1 Lloyd's Rep 223 .... 327, 357
Finney Lock Seeds Ltd v. George Mitchell (Chesterhall) Ltd [1979] 2 Lloyd's
    Rep 301 .... 78, 314, 316
Fitzsimmons v. Lord Mostyn [1904] AC 46; 73 LJKB 72; 89 LT 616; 20 TLR
    134; 52 WR 337 345
Foakes v. Beer (1884) 9 App Cas 605; 54 LJQB 130; 51 LT 833; 33 WR 233;
    [1881–85] All ER Rep 106 387
Ford v. Clarksons Holidays [1971] 1 WLR 1412; 115 SJ 642; [1971] 3 All ER
    454 287
Ford v. White & Co [1964] 1 WLR 885; 108 SJ 542; [1964] 2 All ER 755 242
Forster v. Outred & Co [1982] 1 WLR 86; 125 SJ 309 248
Fox v. P. G. Wellfair Ltd [1981] 2 Lloyd's Rep 514; 263 EG 589, 657; [1981]
    Com LR 140 .... 61, 202, 284, 310, 313, 320, 379
Freeman v. Marshall & Co (1966) 200 EG 777 .... 225, 242
Fryer v. Bunney (1981) 263 EG 158 .... 240, 243
Fuga AG v. Bunge AG [1975] 2 Lloyd's Rep 192 374

Gallagher Estates Ltd v. Walker (1973) 28 P & CR 113 70
Garland v. Ralph Pay & Ransom & Others (1984) 271 EG 106 & 197 231
Garton v. Hunter (VO) [1969] 2 QB 37; [1969] 1 All ER 451; [1968] 2 WLR
    86; 112 SJ 924; 14 RRC 136 .... 42, 180, 188
Gatliffe v. Dunn (1738) Barnes 55; 94 ER 804 328
Gaze v. Holden (1982) 266 EG 998 73
Gebr Broere BV v. Saras Chimica SpA [1983] 2 Lloyd's Rep 436 304
George Mitchell (Chesterhall) Ltd v. Finney Lock Seeds Ltd [1983] 2 All
    ER 737 251
George v. Secretary of State for the Environment (1979) 38 P & CR 609; 77
    LGR 687; 250 EG 339 292
Gerard (Lord) & London & North Western Ry, Re [1895] 1 QB 459; 64 LJQB
    260; 14 R 201; 72 LT 142; 11 TLR 170; 43 WR 374 283
Gillespie Bros & Co v. Thompson Bros & Co (1922) 13 Ll L Rep 519 379
Givauden & Co Ltd v. Minister of Housing & Local Government [1967] 1
    WLR 250; [1966] 3 All ER 696; 18 P & CR 88 337
GKN Centrax Gears Ltd v. Matbro Ltd [1976] 2 Lloyd's Rep 555; 120 SJ 401 .. 375
Glasgow & South Western Ry & London & North Western Ry, Re (1888) 52
    JP 215 375
Gold v. Patman & Fotheringham Ltd [1958] 1 WLR 697 63
Goldsmid v. Tunbridge Wells Improvement Commissioners (1866) LR 1 Ch
    App 349 68
Golightly (Alfred) & Sons Ltd v. Durham County Council (1981) 260 EG 1045,
    1135 & 1199; [1981] RVR 229 111
Goold v. Evans & Co [1951] 2 TLR 1189 318
GREA Real Property Investments Ltd v. Williams (1979) 250 EG 651 435
Great Atlantic Insurance Co v. Home Insurance Co [1981] 1 WLR 529 58

Gredley (Investment Developments) Co Ltd *v.* London Borough of Newham (1973) 26 P & CR 400 .... 48, 315

Gregson & Armstrong, Re (1894) 70 LT 106; 38 SJ 237; 10 R 408 292

Gudgion (VO) *v.* Erith Borough Council & London County Council (1960) 7 RRC 324; 53 R & IT 360; on appeal 59 LGR 433; 8 RRC 324; [1961] RVR 492 55

Guppys (Bridport) Ltd *v.* Sandoe (1975) 235 EG 689; 30 P & CR 69 339

Guppys Properties Ltd *v.* Knott (1977) 245 EG 1023 339

Guppys Properties Ltd *v.* Knott (No. 2) (1979) 253 EG 907 .... 336, 339

Guppys Properties Ltd *v.* Knott (No. 3) (1981) 258 EG 1083 337

Guys 'N' Dolls Ltd *v.* Sade Bros Catering Ltd (1983) 269 EG 129 .... 431, 432, 439

Hadley *v.* Baxendale (1854) 9 Exch 341; 23 LJ Exch 179; 23 LT (NS) 69; 2 WR 302; 18 Jur 358; 2 CLR 517 232

Haigh & London & North Western & Great Western Rys, Re [1896] 1 QB 649; 65 LJQB 511; 74 LT 655; 44 WR 618 378

Haigh *v.* Haigh (1861) 3 De GF & J 157; 31 IJ Ch 420; 8 Jur (NS) 983; 5 LT 507 309

Hammond & Waterton, Re (1890) 62 LT 808; 6 TLR 302 198

Harding *v.* Cardiff City Council [1971] 219 EG 885; (1971) RVR 238 .... 70, 91, 110

Harewood Hotels Ltd *v.* Harris [1958] 1 WLR 108; [1958] 1 All ER 104; 102 SJ 67; 170 EG 177 74

Harmony Shipping Co SA *v.* Davis [1979] 3 All ER 177 65

Harvey *v.* Shelton (1844) 7 Beav 455; 13 LJ Ch 466; 64 RR 116; 3 LT (OS) 279; 49 ER 1141 292

Hayn Roman & Co SA *v.* Cominter (UK) Ltd [1981] Com LR 239 332

Hayward *v.* Phillips (1837) 6 A & E 119; 6 LJ (NS) KB 110; 1N & P 288; 1 Jur 985; 45 RR 421; 112 ER 46 372

Heather *v.* P. E. Consulting Group [1973] 1 Ch 189 63

Hedley Byrne & Co Ltd *v.* Heller & Partners Ltd [1964] AC 465; [1963] 3 WLR 101; 107 SJ 454; [1963] 2 All ER 575; [1963] 1 Lloyd's Rep 485 ....223, 234, 253

Hellaby *v.* Brown (1875) 1 H & N 729 371

Henry Bath *v.* Birgby Products [1962] 1 Lloyd's Rep 389; 106 SJ 288 .... 310, 378

Heron II, The [1969] 1 AC 350 .... 232, 233

Heyes *v.* Earl of Derby (Pilkingto Bros PLC, Third Party) (1984) 272 EG 935 .. 205

Hibernian Property Co Ltd *v.* Secretary of State for the Environment (1973) 27 P & CR 197 318

Hickmott *v.* Dorset County Council (1977) 35 P & CR 195; [1977] JPL 715; 243 EG 671 318

Hicks *v.* Richardson (1797) 1 B & P 93; 4 RR 768; 126 ER 796 351

Higgins *v.* Willes (1828) 3 Man & Ry KB 382 328

Higgs & Hill Building Ltd *v.* Campbell Denis Ltd [1983] Com LR 34 303

Hiltons Footwear Ltd *v.* Leicester City Council & Culverwell (VO) (1977) 242 EG 213; 20 RRC 350; [1977] RA 28 169

Hogg *v.* Belfast Corporation [1919] 2 Ir Rep 305; 53 Ir LT 62 274

Holdsworth *v.* Dimsdale (1871) 24 LT 360; 19 WR 798 81

Hopper, Re (1867) LR 2 QB 367; 36 LJQB 97; 8 B & S 100; 15 LT 566; 15 WR 443 .... 198, 209, 378

Hughes *v.* Metropolitan Ry Co (1877) 2 App Cas 439; 46 LJQB 583; 36 LT 932; 25 WR 680 55

Huntley, Re (1853) 1 E & B 787; 22 LJQB 277; 17 Jur 571; 1 WR 305; 1 CLR 426; 17 JPJ 294; 118 ER 631 381

Industrial Properties (Barton Hill) Ltd *v.* Associated Electrical Industries Ltd (1976) (unreported) Bernstein & Reynolds *Handbook of Rent Review* p. [DC 171]; on appeal [1977] QB 580; [1977] 2 WLR 726; 121 SJ 155; [1977] 2 All ER 293; 242 EG 955; 34 P & CR 329 .... 56, 72

International Tank & Pipe SAK *v.* Kuwait Aviation Fuelling Co KSC [1975] QB 224; [1974] 3 WLR 721; 118 SJ 752; [1975] 1 All ER 242; [1975] 1 Lloyd's Rep 8 270

IRC *v.* Clay & Buchanan [1914] 3 KB 466 .... 406, 409
Italmare Shipping Co *v.* Ocean Tanker Co Inc (The Rio Sun) [1982] 1 WLR
    158; [1982] 1 All ER 517; [1981] 2 Lloyd's Rep 489 .... 363, 364

Jackson *v.* Barry Ry [1893] 1 Ch 238; 68 LT 472; 9 TLR 90; 2 R 207 372
James Longley & Co Ltd *v.* South West Thames Regional Health Authority
    (1983) *The Times* 14th July 1983 62
JEB Fasteners Ltd *v.* Marks Bloom & Co [1983] 1 All ER 583 .... 224, 235
Jedranska Slobodna Plovidba *v.* Oleagine SA [1983] 3 All ER 602 270
Jefferies *v.* O'Neill (1983) 269 EG 131; 446 P & CR 376 431
Jenkins *v.* Betham (1855) 15 CB 168; 24 LJCP 94; 1 Jur (NS) 237; 100 RR 297 .. 227
Johnson *v.* Lamb 1981 SLT 300 .... 275, 318
Junior Books Ltd *v.* Veitchi Co Ltd [1982] 3 WLR 477; [1983] AC 520 234

K Shoe Shops Ltd *v.* Hardy (VO) [1983] 1 WLR 1273; [1983] 3 All ER 609;
    127 SJ 764; 269 EG 37 .... 171, 190
Kelly *v.* London Transport Executive [1982] 2 All ER 842 66
Kennard *v.* Harris (1824) 2 B & C 801; 4 D & R 272; 107 ER 580 372
Kenney *v.* Hall Pain & Foster (1976) 239 EG 355 & 429 .... 229, 235, 245
Kentucky Fried Chicken (GB) Ltd *v.* Secretary of State for the Environment
    (1977) 245 EG 839; [1977] JPL 727 .... 61, 323
Kenworthy & The Queen Assurance Co, Re (1893) 9 TLR 181 378
Ketteman *v.* Hansel Properties Ltd & Others (1984) 271 EG 1099 248
Kirkup *v.* British Rail Engineering Ltd [1983] 1 WLR 1165; [1983] 3 All ER
    1147; affirming [1983] 1 WLR 190; [1983] 1 All ER 855 86
Kitts *v.* Moore & Co [1895] 1 QB 253; 64 LJQB 152; 12 R 43; 71 LT 676; 43
    WR 84 281
Knott *v.* Long (1735) 3 Stra 1025 350

Langham House Developments Ltd *v.* Brompton Securities Ltd (1980) 256 EG
    719 .... 194, 436
Larchin *v.* Ellis (1862) 11 WR 281 309
Law Land Co Ltd (The) *v.* Consumers' Association Ltd (1980) 255 EG 617 428,
                                                                                        431, 438
Leachman *v.* L. & K. Richardson Ltd [1969] 1 WLR 1129 439
Lees *v.* English & Partners (1977) 242 EG 293 242
Leigh *v.* English Property Corporation Ltd [1976] 2 Lloyd's Rep 298; 120 SJ 64
    .... 194, 196
Lewis Emanuel & Son Ltd *v.* Sammut [1959] 2 Lloyd's Rep 629 284
Lewis *v.* Barnett (1981) 264 EG 1079 437
Lewis *v.* Haverfordwest RDC [1953] 1 WLR 1487; 97 SJ 877; [1953] 2 All ER
    1599; 52 LGR 44 346
Liberian Shipping Corporation "Pegasus" Ltd *v.* A. King & Sons Ltd [1967] 2
    QB 86; [1967] 2 WLR 856; 111 SJ 91; [1967] 1 All ER 934; [1967] 1
    Lloyd's Rep 303 .... 271, 272
Liesbosch Dredger *v.* SS Edison (The Liesbosch) [1933] AC 449 238
Lively *v.* City of Munich [1976] 1 WLR 1004; [1977] 1 Lloyd's Rep 418 65
Liverpool City Council *v.* Irwin [1977] AC 239; [1976] 2 WLR 562; [1976] 2
    All ER 39; 32 P & CR 43 .... 430, 431
Lloyd *v.* Wright [1983] 3 WLR 223 285
London & South of England Building Society *v.* Stone [1983] 3 All ER 105; 267
    EG 69 .... 224, 235, 237, 246
London County Council *v.* Tobin [1959] 1 WLR 354; 10 P & CR 79; 123 JP
    250; 103 SJ 272; [1959] 1 All ER 649; 57 LGR 113 .... 54, 73
London Export Corporation Ltd *v.* Jubilee Coffee Roasting Co Ltd [1958] 1
    WLR 661; 102 SJ 452; [1958] 2 All ER 411; [1958] 1 Lloyd's Rep
    367 .... 284, 378
Longley (James) & Co Ltd *v.* South West Thames Regional Health Authority
    (1983) *The Times* 14th July 1983 62

Lotus & Delta Ltd *v.* Culverwell (VO) & Leicester City Council (1976) 239 EG 287; 21 RRC 1; [1976] RA 141 180
Love *v.* Mack (1905) 92 LT 345 230

Maceaura *v.* Northern Assurance Co Ltd [1925] AC 619; 94 LJPC 154; [1925] WC & Ins R 181; 133 LT 152; 41 TLR 447; 21 Ll L Rep 333 372
Magdalen College, Oxford *v.* Heritage [1974] 1 All ER 1065; [1974] 1 WLR 441; 118 SJ 243; 27 P & CR 169 455
Malmesbury Ry *v.* Budd (1876) 2 Ch D 113; 45 LJ Ch 271 281
Mansfield *v.* Robinson [1928] 2 KB 353; 97 LJKB 466; 139 LT 349; 92 JP 126; 44 TLR 518 452
Marchi-Stevenson Ltd *v.* Edwards (VO) (1958) 3 RRC 289; 51 R & IT 553 88
Margulies Bros Ltd *v.* Dafnis Thomaides & Co (UK) Ltd [1958] 1 WLR 398; 102 SJ 271; [1958] 1 All ER 777; [1958] 1 Lloyd's Rep 250 375
Marsh *v.* Bulteel (1822) 5 B & Ald 507; 1 Dow & Ry KB 106; 106 ER 1276 386
Mathew *v.* Maughold Life Assurance Co Ltd (1985) *The Times* 23rd January 1985 248
Maynard *v.* West Midlands Regional Health Authority [1984] 1 WLR 634; [1985] 1 All ER 635 .... 225, 230
Mediterranean & Eastern Export Ltd *v.* Fortress Fabrics (Manchester) Ltd [1948] 2 All ER 186; [1948] WN 244; [1948] LJR 1536; 64 TLR 337; 92 SJ 362; 81 Ll L Rep 401 .... 313, 377
Melwood Units Pty Ltd *v.* Commissioner of Main Roads [1979] AC 426; [1978] 3 WLR 520; 122 SJ 434; [1979] 1 All ER 161; 19 RVR 99; 38 P & CR 195 .... 38, 71
Metropolitan Properties Co (FGC) Ltd *v.* Good (1981) 260 EG 67 338
Metropolitan Properties Co (FGC) Ltd *v.* Lannon [1969] 1 QB 577; [1968] 3 WLR 694; [1968] 3 All ER 304; 112 SJ 585; 19 P & CR 858; [1968] RVR 490 338
Metropolitan Property Holdings Ltd *v.* Laufer (1974) 29 P & CR 172; 233 EG 1011 .... 336, 338, 340
Metropolitan Tunnel & Public Works Ltd *v.* London Electric Ry [1926] 1 Ch 371; 95 LJ Ch 246; 135 LT 35; 70 SJ 387 287
Micklewright *v.* Mullock (1974) 232 EG 337 379
Midanbury Properties (Southampton) Ltd *v.* Houghton T. Clark & Son Ltd (1981) 259 EG 565 339
Middlemiss & Gould *v.* Hartlepool Corporation [1972] 1 WLR 1643; 116 SJ 966; [1973] 1 All ER 172 384
Midland Bank Trust Co Ltd *v.* Hett, Stubbs & Kemp [1978] 3 WLR 167; [1979] Ch 384; 121 SJ 830; [1978] 3 All ER 571 .... 222, 224, 226
Miliangos *v.* George Frank (Textiles) Ltd [1976] AC 443; [1975] 3 WLR 758; 119 SJ 774; [1975] 3 All ER 801; [1976] 1 Lloyd's Rep 201 247
Miller (T. A.) Ltd *v.* Minister of Housing and Local Government [1968] 1 WLR 992; 112 SJ 522; [1968] 2 All ER 633; 19 P & CR 263; 66 LGR 39; [1969] RPC 91 38
Mitchell (George) (Chesterhall) Ltd *v.* Finney Lock Seeds Ltd [1983] 2 All ER 737 251
Modern Engineering (Bristol) Ltd *v.* C. Miskin & Son Ltd [1981] 1 Lloyd's Rep 135 .... 284, 324, 379
Mole *v.* Mole [1951] P 21 79
Molton Builders Ltd *v.* Westminster City Council (1975) 30 P & CR 182; 119 SJ 627; 238 EG 411 148
Montgomery, Jones & Co *v.* Liebenthal & Co (1898) 78 LT 406; 14 TLR 201 373
Montrose Canned Foods Ltd *v.* Eric Wells (Mercants) Ltd [1965] 1 Lloyd's Rep 597 373
Moorcock, The (1889) 14 PD 64 430
Moore *v.* Lambeth County Court Registrar [1969] 1 WLR 141 90
Moran *v.* Lloyd's [1983] 1 QB 542; [1983] 2 All ER 200; [1983] 1 Lloyd's Rep 472; [1983] Com LR 132 .... 370, 378, 382
Morgan *v.* Perry (1973) 229 EG 1937 242
Moscow V/O Exportkhleb *v.* Helmville Ltd (The Jocelyne) [1977] 2 Lloyd's Rep 121 271

Mountview Court Properties Ltd *v.* Devlin (1970) 21 P & CR 689; 114 SJ 474;
    [1971] JPL 113 338
M'Rae *v.* M'Lean (1853) 2 E & B 946; 2 CLR 391; 18 Jur 244; 2 WR 63; 118 ER
    1020 382
Munday *v.* Bluck (1861) 9 CB (NS) 557; 30 LJCP 193; 7 Jur (NS) 709; 9 WR
    274; 142 ER 219 318
Mutual Shipping Corporation of New York *v.* Bayshore Shipping Co of Mon-
    rovia [1985] 1 Lloyd's Rep 189 .... 359, 374
Myron (The) *v.* Tradax Export SA [1969] 1 Lloyd's Rep 411 375
Myron, The [1970] 1 QB 527; [1969] 1 Lloyd's Rep 411 308

Nagel's Lease, Re, Allen *v.* Little Abbey School (Newbury) [1974] 1 WLR
    1077; [1974] 3 All ER 34; 118 SJ 532; 28 P & CR 158; 232 EG 455 217
Nash *v.* Basildon Development Corporation (1972) 222 EG 221 80
Nash *v.* Phillips (1974) 232 EG 1219 240
National Westminster Bank Ltd *v.* BSC Footwear Ltd (1980) 257 EG 277; 42
    P & CR 90 .... 267, 268
Nauman *v.* Nathan (1930) 37 Ll L Rep 249 290
Neilson *v.* Poole (1969) 20 P & CR 909 441
Nema, The [1982] AC 724; [1981] 3 WLR 292; [1981] 2 All ER 1030; [1981] 2
    Lloyd's Rep 239 .... 307, 362, 363, 364, 365, 368, 369
Nicholson *v.* Little [1956] 1 WLR 829 346
Northampton Gaslight Co *v.* Parnell (1855) 15 CB 630; 224 LJCP 60; 3 CLR
    409; 1 Jur (NS) 211; 3 WR 179 203
Norwich Union Insurance Society *v.* Tony Waller Ltd (1984) 270 EG 42 79

Official Custodian for Charities *v.* Goldridge (1973) 26 P & CR 191; [1973] JPL
    708 40
Oil Products Trading Co Ltd *v.* Société de Gestion d' Enterprises Coloniales
    (1934) 150 LT 475 382
Oliver *v.* Nautilus Steam Shipping Co Ltd [1903] 2 KB 639 79
Ollett *v.* Bristol Aerojet Ltd [1979] 1 WLR 1197; [1979] 3 All ER 544 86
Orion Compania Espanola de Seguros *v.* Belfort Maatschappij Voor Algemene
    Verzekgringun [1962] 2 Lloyd's Rep 257 291
Oswald *v.* Earl Grey (1855) 24 LJQB 69 315
Overseas Tankers (UK) Ltd *v.* Morts Dock & Engineering Co Ltd (The Wagon
    Mound) [1961] AC 388; [1961] 2 WLR 126; [1961] 1 All ER 404 232
Overseas Tankers (UK) Ltd *v.* The Miller Steamship Co Pty (The Wagon
    Mound (No. 2)) [1967] AC 617; [1966] 3 WLR 498; [1966] 2 All ER 709
    232
Owen *v.* Nicholl [1948] 1 All ER 707; [1948] WN 138; 92 SJ 244 319
Oxford Shipping Co Ltd *v.* Nippon Yusen Kaisha [1984] 2 Lloyd's Rep 373 297

Paal Wilson & Co A/S *v.* Partenreederei Hannah Blumenthal [1982] 3 WLR
    1149 .... 281, 300
Pancommerce SA *v.* Veecheema BV [1982] 1 Lloyd's Rep 645 323
Parsons (H) (Livestock) Ltd *v.* Uttley Ingham & Co Ltd [1978] QB 791 233
Pegler *v.* Railway Executive [1948] AC 332; [1948] LJR 939; 64 TLR 212; 92 SJ
    296; [1948] 1 All ER 559 273
Pepys *v.* London Transport Executive [1975] 1 WLR 234; [1975] 1 All ER 748;
    118 SJ 882; 29 P & CR 248 351
Perkins (H.G.) Ltd *v.* Best-Shaw [1973] 1 WLR 975; [1973] 2 All ER 924 .... 326, 350
Perry *v.* Sidney Phillips & Son [1982] 1 WLR 1297; [1982] 3 All ER 705; 263
    EG 888; 126 SJ 626 .... 222, 233, 240, 243, 247
Philipps *v.* Philipps (1878) 4 QBD 127 299
Philips *v.* Ward [1956] 1 WLR 471; 100 SJ 317; [1956] 1 All ER 874 .... 241, 242
Phoenician Express SARL *v.* Garward Shipping Corporation Ltd (1983) *The
    Times* 23rd November 1983 265
Phoenix Timber Co Ltd's Application, Re [1958] 2 QB 1; [1958] 2 WLR 574;
    102 SJ 231; [1958] 1 All ER 815; [1958] 1 Lloyd's Rep 305 287
Phonizien, The [1966] 1 Lloyd's Rep 150 282

Pickering *v.* Sogex Services (UK) Ltd [1982] RVR 225; 262 EG 770; 20 BLR 66
.... 102
Pinion, Re [1965] 1 Ch 85   63
Pioneer Shipping Ltd *v.* BTP Tioxide Ltd (The Nema) [1982] AC 724; [1981] 3
     WLR 292; [1981] 2 All ER 1030; [1981] 2 Lloyd's Rep 239 .... 307, 362, 363,
                                                                                                    364, 365, 368, 369
Pirelli General Cable Works Ltd *v.* Oscar Faber & Partners [1983] 2 AC 1;
     [1983] 2 WLR 6; [1983] 1 All ER 65; 262 EG 879   248
Plumb Bros *v.* Dolmac (Agriculture) Ltd (1984) 271 EG 373 .... 428, 434
Pointe Gourde Quarrying & Transport Co Ltd *v.* Sub-Intendent of Crown
     Lands [1947] AC 565   38
Pointer *v.* Norwich Assessment Committee [1922] 2 KB 471; 91 LJKB 891; 86
     JP 149; 67 SJ 98; 20 LGR 673; 2 RA 965 .... 71, 78
Ponsford *v.* HMS Aerosols Ltd (1976) (unreported) Bernstein & Reynolds
     Handbook of Rent Review p. [DC 241]; [1979] AC 63; [1978] 3
     WLR 241; 122 SJ 487; [1978] 2 All ER 837; 38 P & CR 270; 247 EG
     1171 .... 72, 406, 408, 427, 433
Pool *v.* Pool [1951] P. 470   79
Port Sudan Cotton Co *v.* Govindaswamy Chettiar & Sons [1977] 2 Lloyd's Rep
     5; reversing [1977] 1 Lloyd's Rep 166   379
Poyser & Mills Arbitration, Re [1964] 2 QB 467; [1963] 2 WLR 1309; [1963] 1
     All ER 612 .... 336, 451
Pratt *v.* Swanmore Builders Ltd [1980] 2 Lloyd's Rep 504 .... 284, 285, 379
Prenn *v.* Simmonds [1971] 1 WLR 1381; 115 SJ 654; [1971] 3 All ER 237   434
President of India *v.* La Pintada Compania Navigacion SA [1984] 3 WLR 10   342
Price *v.* Popkin (1839) 10 A & E 139; 2 P & D 304; 8 LJ (NS) QB 198; 3 Jur 433;
     50 RR 362; 113 ER 53 .... 329, 330, 380
Pugh *v.* Smiths Industries Ltd (1982) 264 EG 823 .... 432, 433
Purslow *v.* Bailey (1705) 2 Ld Raym 1039; 1 Salk 76; 87 ER 972   355

R. *v.* A Rent Assessment Committee for London, ex p Ellis-Rees & Others
     (1982) 262 EG 1298   309
R. *v.* Abadom [1983] 1 WLR 126 .... 68, 76, 77, 83
R. *v.* Bingham (1831) 2 C & J 130; 2 Tyr 46; 1 LJ (NS) Exch 62; 149 ER 55   387
R. *v.* Daye [1908] 2 KB 333   43
R. *v.* Deputy Industrial Injuries Commissioner [1965] 1 QB 456   77
R. *v.* London Rent Assessment Panel, ex p. Cliftvylle Properties Ltd (1982) 266
     EG 44   338
R. *v.* Paddington VO & Another ex p. Peachey Property Corporation Ltd
     [1964] 1 WLR 1186 [1964] 3 All ER 200; affirmed [1966] 1 QB 380;
     [1965] 2 All ER 836; [1965] RVR 384 .... 169, 180, 187, 190
R. *v.* Penguin Books Ltd (1961)   90
R. *v.* Secretary of State for the Environment ex p. Mistral Investments Ltd
     [1984] JPL 516   309
R. *v.* Turner [1975] 1 QB 834; [1975] 2 WLR 56; [1975] 1 All ER 70   68
Rabin *v.* Mendoza & Co [1954] 1 WLR 271; [1954] 1 All ER 247   79
Ravee *v.* Farmer (1791) 4 TR 146; 2 RR 347; 100 ER 942   357
Reardon Smith Line Ltd *v.* Yngver Hansen-Tangen [1976] 1 WLR 989; 120 SJ
     719; [1976] 3 All ER 401   434
Reynolds *v.* Manchester City Council (1980) 257 EG 939; [1981] RVR 123   96
Rio Sun, The [1982] 1 WLR 158; [1982] 1 All ER 517; [1981] 2 Lloyd's Rep
     489 .... 363, 364
River Wear Commissioners *v.* Adamson (1877) 2 App Cas 743   433
Rocco Guiseppe & Figli *v.* Tradax Export SA [1983] 3 All ER 598   344
Rogers *v.* Rosedimond Investments (Blakes Markets) Ltd (1978) 247 EG 467 ...   46,
                                                                                                                   67, 75
Rosen (P) & Co Ltd *v.* Dowley & Selby [1943] 2 All ER 172   347
Ross *v.* Caunters [1979] 3 WLR 605; [1980] 1 Ch 297; 123 SJ 605; [1979] 3 All
     ER 580   223
Routh *v.* Central Land Board (1957) 8 P & CR 290 .... 70, 78

Safeway Food Stores Ltd *v*. Banderway (1983) 267 EG 850 195,432,433,437
Schofield *v*. Allen (1904) 116 LTJ 239; 48 SJ 176 285
Scott *v*. Avery (1851) 5 HLC 811; 25 LJ Exch 308; 28 LT (OS) 207; 2 Jur (NS)
    815; 4 WR 746; 10 ER 1121 288
Segama NV *v*. Penny Le Roy Ltd (1983) 269 EG 322 .... 71, 314, 369
Sellar *v*. Highland Ry 1919 56 Sc LR 216; SC (HL) 19 275
Service Welding Ltd *v*. Tyne & Wear County Council (1979) 38 P & CR 352;
    250 EG 1291; [1979] RVR 215, 77 LGR 646; [1979] JPL 612 52
Seyfang *v*. Searle & Co [1973] 1 QB 148 65
Shaylor *v*. Woolf [1946] Ch 320; [1947] LJR 41; 175 LT 170; 90 SJ 357; [1946]
    2 All ER 54 265
Sheen *v*. Bumstead (1862) 1 H & C 358 91
Sheffield (City of) *v*. Meadow Dairy Co Ltd (1958) 2 RRC 395; 51 R & IT 233;
    171 EG 357; 122 JP 274 .... 88, 89
Shelling *v*. Farmer (1725) 1 Stra 646 358
Shephard *v*. Brand (1734) 2 Barnard 463; 94 ER 620 378
Shield Properties & Investments Ltd *v*. Anglo-Overseas Transport Co Ltd
    (1984) 273 EG 69 .... 78, 317, 376
Shirlcar Properties Ltd *v*. Heinitz (1983) 268 EG 362 269
Simmons *v*. Swaine (1809) 1 Taunt 549; 127 ER 947 328
Simpson *v*. Grove Tompkins & Co (1982) *The Times* 17th May 1982 242
Singer & Friedlander Ltd *v*. John D. Wood & Co (1977) 243 EG 212 .... 226, 229,
                                                                                239, 246
SL Sethia Lines Ltd *v*. Naviagro Maritime Corporation [1981] 1 Lloyd's Rep
    18 327
Smith (E. E. & Brian) (1928) Ltd *v*. Wheatsheaf Mills Ltd [1939] 2 KB 302;
    108 LJKB 602; 160 LT 389; 55 TLR 599; 83 SJ 456; [1939] 2 All ER
    251; 44 Com Cas 210 290
Smith ex p. Edwards, Re (1886) 3 Morrell's Bank Rep 179 387
Smith *v*. Martin [1925] 1 KB 745; 94 LJKB 645; 133 LT 196 384
Smith *v*. Pearl Assurance Co [1939] 1 All ER 95; 55 TLR 335; 83 SJ 113; 63 Ll
    L Rep 1 287
Smith *v*. Trowsdale (1854) 3 E & B 83; 2 CLR 874; 23 LJQB 107; 18 Jur 552 387
Smith (W. H.) & Son Ltd *v*. Clee (VO) (1977) 20 RRC 235; [1978] RA 93; 243
    EG 677 & 764 170
Societe Franco-Tunisienne D'Armement-Tunis *v*. Government of Ceylon
    [1959] 1 WLR 787; 103 SJ 675; [1959] 3 All ER 25; [1959] 2 Lloyd's
    Rep 1 .... 323, 375
Society of Medical Officers of Health *v*. Hope (VO) [1960] AC 551; [1960] 1 All
    ER 317; [1960] 2 WLR 404; 104 SJ 147; 58 LGR 165; 5 RRC 388; 53 R
    & IT 102; 175 EG 263 55
Solomon *v*. Solomon (1859) 28 LJ Exch 129 .... 309, 375
South Sea Co *v*. Bumstead (1734) 2 Eq Cas Ab 80; Vin Ab Arb I 39, p. 140 380
South Tottenham Land Securities *v*. R. & A. Millett (Shops) Ltd (1983) 269
    EG 630 353
South Western General Property Co Ltd *v*. Marton (1982) 263 EG 1090 252
Spence *v*. Eastern Counties Ry (1839) 7 Dowl 697; 3 Jur 846; 54 RR 883 290
Spiers *v*. Halliday (1984) *The Times* 30th June 1984 77
St John the Baptist (Hospital of) *v*. Kent County Council (1970) 214 EG 359
    & 505 70
Stevenson *v*. Nationwide Building Society (1984) 272 EG 663 .... 228, 253
Stockbridge Mill Co Ltd *v*. Central Land Board [1954] 1 WLR 886 .... 70, 78
Stokes *v*. Cambridge Corporation (1961) 13 P & CR 77 54
Stotesbury *v*. Turner [1943] 1 KB 370; 112 LJKB 365; 168 LT 355 .... 345, 349
Stringer & Riley Bros, Re [1901] 1 QB 105; 70 LJKB 19; 49 WR 111 .... 358, 373
Succula Ltd *v*. Harland & Wolff Ltd [1980] 2 Lloyd's Rep 381 .... 282, 284
Sudbrook Trading Estate Ltd *v*. Eggleton [1983] 1 AC 444; [1982] 3 All ER 1;
    44 P & CR 153; 265 EG 215 200
Sutcliffe *v*. Thackrah [1974] AC 747; [1974] 2 WLR 295; 118 SJ 148; [1974] 1
    All ER 859; [1974] 1 Lloyd's Rep 318 .... 196, 206, 226
Sutherland & Co *v*. Hannevig Bros Ltd [1921] 1 KB 336; 90 LJKB 225; 125 LT
    281; 37 TLR 102 359

Table of Cases

Taylor (David) & Son Ltd *v*. Barnett Trading Co [1953] 1 WLR 562; 97 SJ 226;
  [1953] 1 All ER 843; [1953] 1 Lloyd's Rep 181 371
Techno Land Improvements Ltd *v*. British Leyland (UK) Ltd (1979) 252
  EG 805 .... 237, 247
Tew *v*. Harris (1848) 11 QB 7; 17 LJQB 1; 11 Jur 947; 75 RR 270; 10 LT (OS)
  87; 116 ER 376 276
Thameside Estates *v*. Greater London Council (1977) 249 EG 346 111
Thomas Bates & Son Ltd *v*. Wyndhams (Lingerie) Ltd [1981] 1 WLR 505; 125
  SJ 32; [1981] 1 All ER 1077; 257 EG 381; 41 P & CR 345 429
Thomas *v*. Official Solicitor (1983) 265 EG 601 309
Thorp *v*. Cole (1836) 1 M & W 531; 1 Gale 443; 5 Tyr 1047; 5 LJ Exch 281; 150
  ER 545; affirming (1835) 2 Cr M & R 367 326
Tillam *v*. Copp (1847) 5 CB 211; 75 RR 720 310
Timber Shipping Co SA *v*. London & Overseas Freighters Ltd [1972] AC 1;
  [1971] 2 WLR 1360; [1971] 2 All ER 599 344
Tomlin *v*. Standard Telephones & Cables [1969] 1 WLR 1378; [1969] 3 All
  ER 201 81
Tomlinson *v*. Tomlinson [1980] 1 WLR 322 90
Top Shop Estates Ltd *v*. Danino & Another (1984) 273 EG 197 .... 319, 322
Torminster Properties Ltd *v*. Green [1983] 1 WLR 676; [1983] 2 All ER 457;
  256 EG 267 386
Tote Bookmakers Ltd *v*. Development & Property Holding Co Ltd [1985]
  2 WLR 603; 129 SJ 153; 274 EG 585 .... 266, 270
Town Centre Securities Ltd *v*. Wm. Morrison Supermarkets Ltd (1981) 263
  EG 435 .... 46, 314, 315, 317, 326
Tradax Export SA *v*. Volkswagenwerk AG [1970] 1 QB 537 276
Tramountana Armadora SA *v*. Atlantic Shipping Co SA [1978] 2 All ER
  870 .... 346, 348
Treml *v*. Ernest W. Gibson & Partners (1984) 272 EG 68 .... 240, 244
Tribe & Upperton, Re (1835) 3 A & E 295; 42 RR 395 380
Trust House Forte Albany Hotels Ltd *v*. Daejan Investments Ltd (1980) 256
  EG 915 .... 344, 431
Tullis *v*. Jacson [1892] 3 Ch 441; 61 LJ Ch 655; 67 LT 340; 8 TLR 691; 41 WR 11 372
Turner *v*. Fenton [1982] 1 All ER 8 287
Turner *v*. Swainson (1836) 1 M & W 572; 2 Gale 133; 5 LJ Exch 266; 46 RR
  202 329

UDS Tailoring Ltd *v*. BL Holdings Ltd (1981) 261 EG 49 76
Underwood & Bedford & Cambridge Ry, Re (1861) 11 CB (NS) 442; 31 LJCP
  10; 5 LT 581; 10 WR 406; 142 ER 868 326
Unione Stearinerie Lanza & Wiener, Re [1917] 2 KB 558; 86 LJKB 1236; 117
  LT 337; 61 SJ 526 298
United Scientific Holdings Ltd *v*. Burnley Borough Council [1978] AC 904;
  [1977] 2 WLR 806; 121 SJ 223; 33 P & CR 220; 75 LGR 407; 243 EG
  43 .... 435, 437
Universal Cargo Carriers Corporation *v*. Citati [1957] 1 WLR 979; 101 SJ 762;
  [1957] 3 All ER 234; [1957] 2 Lloyd's Rep 191 375
University College, Oxford *v*. Durdy [1982] Ch 413; [1982] 3 WLR 94; [1982] 1
  All ER 1108; 43 P & CR 399; 262 EG 338 277
US Shipping Board *v*. St Albans [1931] AC 632 64

Vasso, The [1983] 2 Lloyd's Rep 346 318
Victoria Laundry (Windsor) Ltd *v*. Newman Industries Ltd [1949] 2 KB 528   232
Vyricherla (Raja) Narayana Gajapatiragu *v*. The Revenue Divisional Officer,
  Vizagapatam [1939] AC 304 407

Waddington *v*. Surrey & Sussex Rent Assessment Committee (1982) 264 EG
  717 338
Wade-Gery *v*. Morrison (1878) 37 LT 270 265

WagonMound,The[1961]AC388;[1961]2WLR126;[1961]1AllER404 232
Wagon Mound (No. 2), The [1967] AC 617; [1966] 3 WLR 498; [1966] 2 All
    ER 709 232
Waldridge *v.* Kennison (1794) 1 Esp 143, NP 80
Walford Baker & Co *v.* Macfie & Sons (1915) 84 LJKB 2221; 113 LT 180 316
Walker *v.* Wilsher (1889) 23 QBD 335; 58 LJQB 501; 54 JP 213; 37 WR 723; 5
    TLR 649 .... 81, 349
Warde *v.* Feedex International Inc [1984] 1 Lloyd's Rep 310 .... 333, 334
Waring (F. R.) (UK) Ltd *v.* Administracao Geral Do Acucar E Do Alcool EP
    [1983] 1 Lloyd's Rep 45 322
Waugh *v.* British Rail Board [1980] AC 521; [1979] 3 WLR 150; [1979] 2 All
    ER 1169 58
Wear (River) Commissioners *v.* Adamson (1877) 2 App Cas 743 433
Weedon *v.* Hindwood Clarke & Esplin (1974) 234 EG 121 228
Weld-Blundell *v.* Stephens [1920] AC 956; 89 LJKB 705; 36 TLR 640; 64
    SJ 529 238
Weller & Co *v.* Foot & Mouth Disease Research Institute [1966] 1 QB 569;
    [1965] 3 WLR 1082; 109 SJ 702; [1965] 3 All ER 560; [1965] 2 Lloyd's
    Rep 414 223
West Midlands Baptist (Trust) Association (Inc) *v.* Birmingham City Council
    [1970] AC 874; [1969] 3 WLR 389; 133 JP 524; 113 SJ 606; [1969] 3 All
    ER 172; 20 P & CR 1052; 67 LGR 571; affirming [1968] 2 QB 188;
    [1968] 2 WLR 535; 111 SJ 851; [1968] 1 All ER 205; 19 P & CR 9 .... 54, 228
Westminster City Council *v.* Secretary of State for the Environment & City
    Commercial Real Estates Investments Ltd [1984] JPL 27 337
Whatley *v.* Morland (1833) 2 Dowl 249; 2 C & M 347; 4 Tyr 255; 3 LJ Exch 58;
    39 RR 790 .... 309, 310, 375
Whitehead *v.* Tattersall (1834) 1 Ad & El 491; 40 RR 342 357
Whitehouse *v.* Jordan [1981] 1 WLR 246; [1981] 1 All ER 267 .... 66, 230
Whitley (F. G.) & Sons Co Ltd *v.* Clwyd County Council (1982) 22 BLR 48 293
Wickman Machine Tool Sales Ltd *v.* L. Schuler AG [1947] AC 235; [1973]
    2 WLR 683; 117 SJ 340; [1973] 2 All ER 39; [1973] 2 Lloyd's Rep 53 427,
    434, 438
Wigginton & Milner Ltd *v.* Winster Engineering Ltd [1978] 1 WLR 1462;
    [1978] 3 All ER 436; 122 SJ 826; 36 P & CR 203 440
Wilks *v.* Cawley (VO) (1965) 11 RRC 336; [1965] RVR 792; [1965] RA 632 178
Willday *v.* Taylor (1976) 241 EG 835 356
Willesden Local Board & Wright, Re [1896] 2 QB 412; 65 LJQB 567; 75 LT
    13; 12 TLR 539; 44 WR 676; 60 JP 708 .... 262, 384
William Boyer & Sons *v.* Minister of Housing & Local Government (1968) 20 P
    & CR 176; 113 SJ 53; 67 LGR 374 337
Wimpey Construction UK Ltd *v.* Poole [1984] 2 Lloyd's Rep 499 226
Winchester City Council *v.* Secretary of State for the Environment (1978) 36
    P & CR 455; affirmed (1979) 39 P & CR 1 .... 62, 63, 323
Windvale Ltd *v.* Darlington Insulation Co Ltd (1983) *The Times* 22nd
    December 1983 345
Wood *v.* Adcock (1852) 7 Ex 468; 21 LJ Exch 204; 16 Jur 251; 86 RR 490 330
Wrenbridge Ltd *v.* Harries (Southern Properties) Ltd (1981) 260 EG 1195 ... 277, 302

Yianni *v.* Edwin Evans & Sons [1982] QB 438; [1981] 3 WLR 843; [1981] 3 All
    ER 592; 259 EG 969; 125 SJ 694 224

Introduction

Every working day surveyors are accepting instructions which may take them into court. Negotiations on a rent review may fail to produce agreement and bring the surveyor to arbitration in an entirely different role as an expert witness. A proposal to reduce a rating assessment may take the surveyor to the local valuation court and perhaps on to the Lands Tribunal. Negotiations for the renewal of a business tenancy may result in an appearance in the county court or High Court. Most cases are, of course, settled by agreement but the possibility of some form of litigation is always in the background. If it arises the surveyor must exhibit other and different skills to those which he uses in his everyday professional life. He must have some knowledge of procedure and evidence. He must know how to write a proof of evidence or draft written representations. He may, and probably will, enter the world of the lawyers: attending conferences with counsel, reading pleadings and opinions, preparing expert reports or documents required to be lodged under rule 42 of the Lands Tribunal Rules.

These skills are barely taught in our universities and colleges. Although several books have been published recently on rent reviews and expert evidence and arbitration in general, the profession still lacks a comprehensive book, written specifically for the valuation surveyor and dealing with the wide range of litigation likely to be encountered by him, from planning appeals to the Lands Tribunal, from rent assessment committees to the High Court, from local valuation courts to arbitration.

The Surveyor in Court attempts to fill this gap in professional literature. Although intended mainly for valuers, many of the topics discussed, such as the nature of expert evidence and the law of arbitration, are also of general interest. I hope, therefore, that it will appeal to a wider professional audience, including those lawyers who do not often venture into the field of property litigation but are occasionally required to do so. Above all, it is intended to be a working handbook, a combination of law and practice. It attempts to provide within one pair of covers all that a surveyor may need when he enters upon litigation, using that term in a broad sense to mean proceedings before the many courts and tribunals which exist in the world of property.

Like most textbooks it is not intended to be read from cover to cover but selectively according to the particular problem or job in hand. It may be helpful, therefore, for the reader to know the overall plan. It is divided into four parts with three appendices. Part I contains an outline of procedure and evidence, with a detailed discussion of expert evidence in valuation. This part contains mainly law. Part II is concerned with the surveyor as expert witness. This is a practical section, covering the principles and practice of expert evidence, expert witness documents and the dual role of advocate and expert. Two of the three chapters in this part contain practical examples. Part III deals with the independent expert and his related liability for professional negligence. It is mainly law but with a practical example. The law and practice of arbitration are discussed in detail in Part IV: four chapters of law covering the arbitration process from the appointment of an arbitrator to the challenge and enforcement of his award, with a final chapter containing a practical example of a rent review arbitration. Appendices A and B deal with the interpretation of documents and agricultural arbitrations respectively. Appendix C contains extracts from selected Acts, statutory instruments and circulars.

I would add some words of caution on two matters in connection with the practical examples. First, in many cases it has been necessary to present two opposing viewpoints on matters of law in order to illustrate a practical point. The law stated in these examples may not, therefore, be correct and none of the submissions on the point of law in issue should be taken as accurate. I hope that the law is correctly stated in the remainder of the book. Secondly, the specimen documents are not intended to be definitive, to be slavishly followed in every case. They should only be taken as a guide and must be adapted to the facts and circumstances of each particular case. Typical documents are not a substitute for careful thought on the part of the surveyor, who should always ask himself about the purpose and content of the document and for whom it is written.

This book could not have been written without the following assistance which I gratefully acknowledge. Mr Roger Emeny FRICS FRVA, of the University of Reading, encouraged me to start and suggested the title. Mrs Sandi Murdoch LLM, of the University of Reading and the Estates Gazette, read the whole book in draft and made many helpful suggestions for improving the style and content. I am greatly indebted to Mr W. H. Rees BSc FRICS, a member of the Lands Tribunal, who also read the first draft and made many suggestions for improvement based on his considerable knowledge and experience. I would add that, although I have incorporated the great majority of these suggestions in the text, I am solely responsible for any errors and omissions. Furthermore, the statements of law and practice contained in this book are entirely my own and it should not be thought that the generous assistance given by Mr Rees signifies that he, or any other member of the Lands Tribunal, necessarily agrees with them.

The staff of the Library Information Service of The Royal Institution of Chartered Surveyors dealt speedily with my requests for copies of decisions and other information.

For undertaking the task of typing I would like to thank Elizabeth Church, Janet Bowdery and, in particular, Patricia Peasnell and Rachel Birch. Mr George Kirton of the Estates Gazette showed great patience while this book was in preparation and then efficiently supervised the publication.

On a personal level, this book is dedicated to my daughter Jane, who grew up while it was being written and spurred me on with her frequent question: "What chapter are you on, Dad?". Finally, I thank my wife for her encouragement and understanding during the long period of writing.

I hope that this book will find its way onto the arbitrator's table and into the expert's briefcase and play some small part in easing the burden of the surveyor in court.

The law is stated as at 31st March 1985.

P. H. Clarke
Sevenoaks

PART ONE
PROCEDURE AND EVIDENCE

CHAPTER ONE

Procedure

INTRODUCTION

Part of the essential knowledge of the surveyor in court is an understanding of procedure and evidence. These are the rules of the game. This chapter outlines the procedures of the various courts and tribunals before which a surveyor may appear. Arbitration procedure is discussed in Chapters 9 to 13; the law of evidence is considered in Chapters 2 and 3.

Broadly, the law of procedure regulates the rights, duties and conduct of the parties to a dispute from the commencement of the proceedings to the enforcement or implementation of the final judgment or decision. With the law of evidence, it is part of the body of law called "adjective law", which is contrasted with "substantive law", that concerned with the rights, liabilities and duties of the parties in the subject-matter (substance) of the dispute.

The law of procedure deals with the constitution and jurisdiction of courts and tribunals; the methods of commencing proceedings; the steps to be taken by the parties before a hearing to define the issues of fact and law; the conduct of the trial or hearing; the judgment or decision and its enforcement or implementation; costs; appeals. It is a wide and highly complicated subject, the province of the lawyer in its more technical aspects, but also of importance to the surveyor, particularly when he has the sole conduct of his client's case before an inferior tribunal.

From the viewpoint of the surveyor involved in litigation, the courts and tribunals discussed in this chapter may be divided into two groups. In the first group are those with a formal procedure, where the surveyor's role will normally be limited to that of an expert witness. These are the High Court, county courts and the Lands Tribunal. Here, procedure will be under the control of solicitor and counsel: the surveyor will require a broad understanding of the subject but not a detailed knowledge (except in relation to the procedural aspects of expert evidencie discussed in Chapter 3). Secondly, there are inferior courts and tribunals with relatively simple procedures, where the surveyor often appears, combining the roles of advocate and expert witness. These are local valuation courts, rent assessment committees (including rent tribunals and leasehold valuation tribunals) and planning inquiries. He will require a more detailed knowledge of the simpler and more informal procedures in operation in these tribunals.

To avoid a multiplicity of references in this chapter, I have omitted references to individual sections, paragraphs, orders, rules, cases, etc but have given the names of the principal Acts and rules governing the procedure for each court or tribunal.

HIGH COURT

(1) Constitution and jurisdiction

The High Court is part of the Supreme Court of England and Wales. Its constitution, jurisdiction and procedure are now governed by the Supreme Court Act 1981 and the Rules of the Supreme Court (RSC). The Court sits in London and in provincial trial centres. An action may be started in London or outside in a district registry.

The High Court is divided into three divisions: Queens Bench, Chancery and Family. Although theoretically each division possesses the overall jurisdiction of the Court, in practice certain business is specifically distributed among the divisions and there is considerable specialisation. Thus, the Queens Bench Division is mainly concerned with disputes in the common law fields of contract and tort, applications for judicial review, disputes concerning ships and mercantile litigation. It has two specialised courts: an Admiralty Court and a Commercial Court. This latter Court exercises a supervisory jurisdiction over arbitrations. The Chancery Division deals with the more technical aspects of law, eg mortgages, trusts, company law and taxation. It also has a specialised court: a Patent Court. Applications for new business tenancies under the Landlord and Tenant Act 1954, where the rateable value of the property exceeds £5,000, are heard in the Chancery Division. The Family Division deals with domestic disputes, eg divorce, legitimacy, adoption and wardship.

Each division of the High Court has officers responsible for the preliminary and procedural aspects of a dispute. They are called masters in the Queens Bench and Chancery Divisions, registrars in the Family Division and district registrars outside London.

The jurisdiction of the High Court may be exercised wholly or partly by a person other than a High Court judge. Thus, a dispute of a technical nature may be referred to a circuit judge, deputy circuit judge or Recorder ("official referee's business") or, with the consent of the parties, a matter may be dealt with by a special referee (with specialised knowledge), a master or registrar; a circuit judge, Recorder or other qualified person may be appointed a deputy judge of the High Court.

(2) Commencement of proceedings

There are four ways of commencing proceedings in the High Court: by writ of summons, by originating summons, by originating motion, by petition. Motion and petition may only be used where they are specifically required or authorised; they will not be considered further in this chapter.

The general rule is that actions which include issues of fact should be begun by writ (particularly in the Queens Bench Division), and disputes of law should be begun by originating summons (particularly in the Chancery Division). A plaintiff is free to choose which method to use, subject to three restrictions. First, certain actions *must* be begun by writ, e.g. most claims in tort. Secondly, an application to the court under a statute must usually be commenced by originating summons, e.g. an application under Part II of the Landlord and Tenant Act 1954 for a new business tenancy. Thirdly, an originating summons should be used where the dispute is concerned with the interpretation of a statute or document, or some other question of law, or the proceedings are unlikely to contain a substantial issue of fact.

Where proceedings are commenced by writ it must be indorsed with a full or concise statement of claim, issued by the court and served on the defendant, who must acknowledge service. An originating summons must normally state the question on which the determination or direction of the court is sought, or the relief or remedy claimed, together with the cause of action. It is issued, served and usually acknowledged in a similar manner to a writ.

After commencement (by writ or originating summons), the proceedings will continue in one of three ways: to summary judgment under RSC Order 14 (i.e. where the defendant has no defence), to trial with pleadings or to trial without pleadings (i.e. where there is no substantial dispute of fact).

(3) Pre-trial procedure

(a) *Pleadings*. Where proceedings are commenced by writ the disputed and agreed facts in the action should be defined before the trial. This is the function of pleadings. These are statements of fact exchanged between the parties in order to define the nature and scope of the dispute and to let each party know the case he will have to meet and the evidence he must adduce.

Pleadings consist of some or (rarely) all of the following:

(i) *Statement of claim*. If the writ was not indorsed with a full statement of claim this must now be served on all defendants. It must contain the facts in support of the plaintiff's action and the relief or remedy sought.

(ii) *Defence*. Each defendant must then serve a defence dealing with all the facts in the plaintiff's claim. A defence may include a "counterclaim" or a "set-off". A counterclaim is a cross-action by the defendant, which can be tried in the same action as the plaintiff's claim although not connected with it. A set-off is a particular defence to the plaintiff's claim, e.g. in a land-lord's action for rent a tenant can raise a set-off in respect of defects in the premises which the landlord has undertaken to repair.

(iii) *Reply.* Frequently, pleadings consist of claim and defence only, but where a defendant introduces new facts or a counterclaim, the plaintiff may make a reply and defence to counterclaim.

(iv) *Further pleadings.* These are rare and may only be served with leave of the court. They are rejoinder, surrejoinder, rebut-ter and surrebutter.

Three general points should be noted regarding pleadings. First, there is a prescribed timetable for their exchange. Secondly, they deal with facts and not evidence. Thirdly, they should contain facts and not law. (For the distinction between law and fact and facts and evidence see Chapter 2 p. 38 below).

(b) *Affidavits.* Pleadings are not used in proceedings commenced by originating summons. Evidence is frequently given on affidavit and their exchange before the trial serves as pleadings. For example, in an application for a new business tenancy, affidavits are frequently sworn by the expert witnesses for the parties. These should define the issues and enable the master, on the first hear-ing of the summons, to give appropriate directions regarding evidence (see p. 7 below).

(c) *Discovery of documents.* This takes place after the close of plead-ings. It is a process concerned with evidence to prove the facts in the pleadings. There are two stages: disclosure of the existence of documents and inspection of those documents.

Discovery is usually voluntary ("automatic") but it may be by order of the court. Under automatic disclosure the parties ex-change lists of relevant documents which are or have been in their possession, custody or power. If automatic discovery does not take place, the master may order discovery on the application of any party.

Under the second stage of disclosure, inspection of documents, each party must allow the other parties to inspect and take copies of the documents in their list, except where valid objection has been made, e.g. on the grounds of privilege (see Chapter 2 p. 57 and Chapter 3 p. 84 below).

(d) *Summons for directions.* This is a "stock-taking" exercise. It allows the master to consider the position shown by the pleadings and order further preparations for the trial. The plaintiff in an action commenced by writ is required to take out a summons for directions within one month of close of pleadings. The question of expert evidence is one of the matters dealt with on a summons for directions (see Chapter 3 p. 85 below). Others include consolidation of actions, orders for further and better particulars of pleadings, interrogatories and the place, mode and time of trial.

Where proceedings are commenced by originating summons the first hearing is similar to a summons for directions. This is known as the "master's appointment".

(e) *Interrogatories*. One of the matters which may be dealt with on a summons for directions is an application for leave to administer interrogatories to an opponent. These are questions (approved by the master) which must be answered on oath. Their purpose is to obtain admissions and further information about an opponent's case.

(4) Trial and judgment

A trial will normally take place in open court unless the judge orders a hearing *in camera*, e.g. for reasons of national security. Only members of the Bar and a litigant in person have the right of audience in the High Court.

The party who must prove his case in order to succeed should begin. This is usually the plaintiff, although where the whole burden of proof rests on the defendant, then he should begin. The usual order is that counsel for the plaintiff opens his case by describing the facts. He calls and examines his witnesses, who may be cross-examined and re-examined, submits his documentary evidence and argues the propositions of law on which he relies.

There are then three alternative procedures. First, the usual procedure is that counsel for the defendant outlines his defence, calls his witnesses, submits his documentary evidence and makes his legal submissions and closing speech. Counsel for the plaintiff replies and, if he raises a fresh point of law, the defendant may reply. Or, secondly, counsel for the defendant may state that he does not intend to call evidence. The plaintiff then sums up his case, followed by submissions by the defendant. In both of these procedures, and in the absence of a jury, the judge delivers or reserves his judgment after the close of the parties' cases. Where the trial is before a judge and jury, the judge sums up, the jury gives its verdict and the judge gives judgment. Under the third alternative, the defendant may submit that the plaintiff has not made out his case in law (he must usually also state that he does not intend to call any evidence). The plaintiff may reply. If the judge upholds the defendant's submission, judgment is entered for him. If the judge rejects it, judgment is entered for the plaintiff.

Where proceedings are commenced by originating summons, the hearing of the summons will eventually be adjourned to a judge for determination in open court or in chambers. Where the question for the court is wholly one of law, evidence will usually be on affidavit, read out by counsel and without cross-examination of the deponents. Disputes of, or including, fact are considered on direct oral evidence, as in the writ procedure.

(5) Costs

The term "costs" has two meanings in litigation: first, the costs which a party pays to his own solicitor, called "solicitor and client" costs; secondly, the costs which one party pays to the other party as a result of the litigation, known as "party and party" costs. Thus, a successful litigant must pay his own solicitor but may recover the whole or part of that payment from the other party under an order for costs by the court. The costs of and incidental to all proceedings in the High Court are in the discretion of the court, which may determine by whom and to what extent costs are to be paid. The court has discretion regarding both liability and amount. This must be exercised judicially, not capriciously but for proper reasons connected with the case, having regard to the result of the action, the conduct of the parties and all other relevant circumstances. (An arbitrator's discretion regarding costs is discussed in Chapter 11 p. 345 below)

(a) *Liability*. The first aspect of costs is liability: who is to pay? The general rule is that a party to litigation will only be required to pay the costs of another party where he is ordered to do so by the court. Usually "costs follow the event", that is to say the costs of the successful party are ordered to be paid by the unsuccessful party (this is known as "judgment with costs"). But, for good reason, the judge may make no order as to costs (each party bears his own costs), or he may make an order other than judgment with costs.

Liability for costs may be influenced by a payment into court by the defendant in an attempt to settle the dispute. This may affect the question of costs in one of three ways. First, where the plaintiff accepts the sum paid in, he will be entitled to his costs up to the date of payment. Secondly, where he does not accept the amount paid in, but proceeds with his action and recovers more than that amount, he will usually recover all his costs. Thirdly, where the plaintiff does not accept the payment into court, proceeds with his action but recovers no more than that sum, then he will normally recover his costs up to the date of the payment and the defendant will receive his costs after that date.

(b) *Amount.* The second aspect of costs is amount: how much can a successful litigant recover? Costs may be awarded in a fixed sum, but costs in the High Court are normally awarded on a prescribed scale (the High Court scale), which has no upper limit. In certain circumstances, costs may be awarded on the lower county court scale. Normally a successful litigant will not recover the whole of his solicitor and client costs: they will be "taxed" by a taxing master of the court. The taxation of costs has no connection with income tax, but refers to a process whereby the judge's order of costs is, in effect, quantified by a scrutiny of the successful party's bill of costs and usually the reduction or deletion of some items in accordance with the appropriate basis of taxation. In addition, any party to litigation (successful or otherwise) who is dissatisfied with his own solicitor's charges may have them taxed by the court.

The basis of taxation will determine the extent of costs recoverable. There are five bases in current use:

(i) *The party and party basis.* A successful party will recover all costs necessarily or properly incurred for the attainment of justice or for enforcing or defending his rights. He will not recover any additional costs incurred for the more convenient conduct of his case. This is the usual basis of taxation and will apply unless a special order is made. The existing party and party basis of taxation may be abolished and replaced with one which will give the successful party a reasonable amount in respect of all costs reasonably incurred, i.e. similar to the common fund basis.

(ii) *The common fund basis.* This is a more generous basis than the party and party basis and allows a successful litigant to recover all costs reasonably incurred. It will usually be ordered where the costs of the litigation are to be paid out of a fund, other than one held by a successful party as trustee or personal representative. For example, in proceedings regarding a will, the beneficiaries may be awarded costs on the common fund basis, to be paid out of the residuary estate. Also, an unsuccessful party who conducted his case scandalously or fraudulently may be ordered to pay costs on the common fund basis.

(iii) *The trustee basis.* This may be ordered where a trustee, personal representative or mortgagee recovers his costs from another party. All costs will be allowed except those which should not have been incurred or where there is some other reason why the successful party should bear them himself. When deciding whether costs should or should not have been incurred regard must be had to the duties of a trustee or personal representative.

(iv) *The solicitor and own client basis.* All costs will be allowed in full unless they are unreasonable in amount or were unreasonably incurred. This basis may be ordered by the court as between the parties, and is also used where a party applies to have his own solicitor's bill taxed by the court.

(v) *The indemnity basis.* This is similar to the solicitor and own client basis. All costs incurred will be allowed except those unreasonably incurred or of an unreasonable amount, and in applying these exceptions the party in receipt of costs will be given the benefit of the doubt.

The High Court has power to make other orders as to costs, but should be slow to evolve a new basis of taxation unless there is a real need which cannot otherwise be met. The meaning and effect of any new basis of taxation should be clear.

The costs of an interlocutory application (e.g. for discovery of documents or interrogatories) will either be the subject of a special order of costs or will be treated as "costs in the cause", that is to say the party who is eventually awarded costs will recover his costs in connection with that application.

Where costs are awarded to a litigant in person he may recover on taxation sums in respect of his own work and for any expenses or losses he has incurred.

A party dissatisfied with a taxation of costs may ask the taxing master to review his decision. If either party is still dissatisfied a further review may be requested, which will be carried out by a judge usually with two or more assessors, one of whom must be a taxing master.

(6) Appeals

As a general rule, either party may appeal to the Court of Appeal against a judgment or order of the High Court (usually as of right but sometimes only with leave). Application may also be made for a new trial or to set aside a verdict, finding or judgment. An appeal may be on a question of law or fact or combined law and fact. In exceptional circumstances leave may be given to appeal direct to the House of Lords.

COUNTY COURTS

(1) Constitution and jurisdiction

The modern system of county courts was established by the County Courts Act 1846. Their jurisdiction and procedure are now governed by the County Courts Act 1984 and The County Court Rules 1981.

Modern county courts are not related to counties. The country is divided into county court districts (each with its own court) and circuits with one or more judges in each circuit. Each court has a registrar, clerical staff, bailiffs and other officers. A county court judge is now called a circuit judge; he presides over one or more courts and also hears criminal cases in certain Crown Courts. Registrars perform judicial and administrative functions similar to those of High Court masters. They also deal with taxation of costs and the administration of their courts.

County courts started life as local courts for the recovery of small debts. They now have a wide civil jurisdiction below prescribed financial limits. For example, they deal with claims in contract and tort up to £5,000 (unlimited by agreement); recovery of land up to £1,000 net annual value; equity matters up to £30,000 (unlimited by agreement); claim for possession under the Rent Acts, and for the recovery of arrears of rent; applications for new business tenancies under the Landlord and Tenant Act 1954, where the rateable value does not exceed £5,000, and a supervisory jurisdiction over arbitrations under the Agricultural Holdings Act 1948 (see Appendix B). Small claims (under £500) may be settled by arbitration in the county courts (see Chapter 9 p. 263 below).

(2) Commencement of proceedings

In county court proceedings there must be a geographical connection between the action and the court in which it is to be heard. It must first be decided, therefore, in which court the proceedings are to be commenced. The general rule is that proceedings should be started in the court for the district where the defendant resides or carries on business or where the cause of action arose. For example, an application for a new business tenancy should be made to the court for the district where the landlord resides or carries on business or where the property is situated.

County court proceedings are divided into (a) actions (commenced by summons) and (b) matters (usually commenced by originating application).

(a) *Actions*. These are similar to proceedings commenced by writ in the High Court and form the bulk of county court litigation. In an action the plaintiff seeks relief or wishes to compel the defendant to do or abstain from doing some act, e.g. proceedings to recover a debt, damages or land. Actions (other than Admiralty and rent actions) are sub-divided into *fixed date* actions, for relief other than the payment of money; and *default* actions, all other actions (including recovery of money).

Both forms of action are commenced by plaint. The plaintiff files in the court office two documents: a request to the court to issue a summons against the defendant and particulars of claim. The registrar issues the summons, which is served on the defendant by the court or the plaintiff, and gives the latter a plaint note.

There is also a summary procedure (a "rent action") for the recovery of arrears of rent from a tenant in occupation. Following service of a summons the tenant must either pay the amount claimed, attend the court to contest the claim or suffer judgment by default.

(b) *Matters*. All other proceedings are called matters and are usually commenced by originating application. For example, an application for a new business tenancy is commenced in this way, the tenant being the applicant and the landlord the respondent.

(3) Pre-trial procedure

(a) *Actions*. After service of a summons the future course of the proceedings will depend on the action taken by the defendant. He may make a payment into court, or admit the whole or part of the claim and ask for time to pay, or file a defence (with or without a counterclaim or set-off) or he may simply do nothing. Where a payment into court or offer to settle is accepted, the proceedings are stayed and the plaintiff obtains judgment. Where such a payment or offer is rejected, or a defence is filed or, in a fixed date action only, the defendant does nothing, then the action will proceed to a pre-trial review or a hearing. Where the defendant takes no action following service on him of a default summons or (where the claim exceeds £500) has no proper defence, then the plaintiff may obtain judgment.

(b) *Matters*. A respondent who wishes to contest an originating application must file an answer. Thus, a respondent landlord of business premises must file an answer to the tenant's originating application, stating the grounds on which he opposes the application. There is no pre-trial review for matters commenced by originating application.

(c) *Pre-trial review*. This is similar to a summons for directions in the High Court. The parties appear before the registrar who considers the course of the proceedings and gives directions for securing the just, expeditious and economical disposal of the action or matter. He will seek admissions and agreements from the parties. Applications for interlocutory orders (e.g. further and better particulars of claim, discovery of documents, interrogatories) should be made at the pre-trial review, although these are required less frequently in county court proceedings than in the High Court.

(d) *Transfer of proceedings*. As stated above, the jurisdiction of a county court is limited geographically and by amount. This may result in proceedings being transferred to another county court (e.g. where they were commenced in the wrong court or the case can be more conveniently tried in another court) or to the High Court (e.g. where the claim exceeds the county court limit). Conversely, an action may be transferred from the High Court to a county court, e.g. where the claim is within the county court limit. (e) *Inquiry and report.* Certain matters may be referred to the registrar or an independent referee for inquiry and report, e.g. proceedings which require a prolonged examination of documents or scientific or local investigation. The registrar or referee will not decide the referred matter but will report back to the court.

(4) Trial and judgment

A county court hearing is similar to a High Court hearing without a jury. It may be before the registrar, the judge or, very rarely, the judge and jury. The right of audience in the county court is wider than the High Court. In addition to counsel and litigants in person, solicitors, Fellows of the Institute of Legal Executives (certain applications only) and other persons with leave have a right of audience in the county court.

For the purposes of a possible appeal, the judge must, if requested, take a note of any question of law, the facts relating thereto and his decision on this question. The judge's notes are his own property and will only be produced to the parties if an appeal is lodged. Shorthand notes are rarely taken in county court proceedings and it is the duty of counsel to take a note of the judgment.

(5) Costs

The position in the county court regarding the award and taxation of costs is similar to that in the High Court but with a lower scale of costs on taxation. The registrar is the taxing officer of the court.

(6) Appeals

As a general rule, and subject to leave in certain cases, a party who is dissatisfied with a decision of a county court judge on a point of law or the admissibility of evidence may appeal to the Court of Appeal.

LANDS TRIBUNAL

(1) Constitution and jurisdiction

The Lands Tribunal for England and Wales was created by the Lands Tribunal Act 1949. It now consists of a President, barristers and surveyors all appointed by the Lord Chancellor. He may appoint other officers including a registrar, who occupies a similar

position to a High Court master or county court registrar. Administratively, he receives and processes all appeals, references and applications and, judicially, he deals with interlocutory applications. He is
the taxing officer of the tribunal. The Lands Tribunal has offices and
courts at 5 Chancery Lane, London WC2 but may sit elsewhere in
England and Wales.

The jurisdiction of the tribunal is entirely statutory and may be
divided into four categories:

(a) *Appeals.* These are sub-divided for procedural purposes into
appeals against determinations by government departments,
authorities or other persons (e.g. against a certificate of unexpended balance of established development value issued by the Secretary of State for the Environment); appeals from decisions of local
valuation courts; and other appeals (e.g. from decisions of leasehold valuation tribunals).

(b) *References.* These are disputes other than appeals under (a)
above and applications under (c) below, e.g. disputed compensation for compulsory purchase or valuations for capital gains tax
purposes. The Lands Tribunal may act as an arbitrator under a
reference by consent.

(c) *Applications.* These are applications under section 84 of the Law
of Property Act 1925 for the modification or discharge of restrictive
covenants and for certificates under section 2 of the Rights of Light
Act 1959.

(d) *Absent Owners.* Where land belonging to an absent or unknown
owner is compulsorily acquired the compensation is determined by
a surveyor member of the tribunal.

Procedure in the Lands Tribunal is regulated by The Lands
Tribunal Rules 1975 as amended by The Lands Tribunal (Amendment) Rules 1977, 1981 and 1984 and (Amendment No. 2) Rules
1981.

(2) Commencement of proceedings

Proceedings are commenced by the submission to the registrar of a
notice of *appeal*, a notice of *reference* or an *application*, according to the
nature of the dispute. The Lands Tribunal Rules contain standard
forms for most notices and applications. Prescribed time limits apply
to notices of appeal. The registrar enters details of appeals and references in the appropriate registers and serves copies on interested
parties. Where an application is made the President will decide what
notices shall be served or publicity given in respect of it.

(3) Pre-hearing procedure

(a) *Statements of case and expert evidence.* As will be seen in Chapter 3,
the Civil Evidence Act 1972 and the rules of court made thereunder

provide for the prior exchange of expert reports in High Court and county court proceedings. These provisions do not apply to the Land Tribunal which has its own procedures for the exchange of expert evidence. They are described in Chapter 3 (p. 87) but briefly are as follows:

(i) *Appeals from local valuation courts.* Copies of the notice of appeal are served by the registrar on the valuation officer and all other parties who appeared before the local valuation court (other than the appellant). Notice of intention to appear may then be given by those parties.

Where such a notice has been given, and the appeal is on a point of law or the net annual value of the appeal hereditament exceeds £1,250, the appellant shall send to the registrar and the other parties a statement of case (including facts to be proved and points of law to be relied on), accompanied by a valuation (or agreed values) and a list of comparable hereditaments. Other parties who intend to appear must then each serve a reply in the same form.

(ii) *Appeals against determinations, references and applications in respect of restrictive covenants.* In these cases the exchanges between the parties are restricted to expert evidence. Where more than one party intends to call an expert witness, every such party shall, on request, send to the registrar that witness's plan and valuation of the subject-property, and either a statement of prices, costs or other particulars relating to comparable properties or a statement that no such information will be relied upon. The registrar then distributes copies to the other parties.

(iii) *Other appeals.* Where a notice of intention to appear has been given in respect of an appeal, the appellant and the other parties must send to the registrar and each other their statements of case (or replies) and, if more than one party intends to call an expert witness, the witness's plans, valuations and comparables as in (ii) above.

(b) *Interlocutory applications.* These are made to the registrar who may (or must if required) refer them to the President for decision. There is also a right of appeal to the President or member selected to hear the case against the registrar's decision.

The tribunal or registrar may, on the application of any party or independently, make orders relating to discovery of documents, delivery of pleadings, interrogatories and the delivery of a statement of agreed facts, facts in dispute and the issues to be tried by the tribunal. The Lands Tribunal Rules also provide that section 12 of the Arbitration Act 1950 (Appendix C p. 469 below) shall apply to proceedings before the tribunal. This gives the parties power to apply to the High Court for a variety of interlocutory orders and writs, e.g. *subpoenas* to compel the attendance of witnesses or production of documents, discovery, interrogatories, security for costs.

(c) *Pre-trial review.* The tribunal or the registrar may, on the application of any party or independently, order a pre-trial review. This is similar to a summons for directions in the High Court. The same guiding principle applies, namely that all necessary or desirable directions shall be given "for securing the just, expeditious and economical disposal of the proceedings". Parties seeking specific directions should do so on this review and efforts should be made to obtain all reasonable admissions and agreements.

(d) *Preliminary point of law.* The President may, on application, order that any point of law in issue shall be dealt with at a preliminary hearing. If a decision on this point substantially disposes of the proceedings then the preliminary hearing will be treated as the hearing of the case and orders made accordingly.

(4) Hearing

The Lands Tribunal must sit in public unless it is determining a dispute on written representations (see p. 17 below), or is acting as an arbitrator on a reference by consent or considerations of national security are involved. A hearing may be held before one or more members of the tribunal who may be assisted by assessors if the case calls for special knowledge. Unless the parties agree otherwise the registar must give at least 14 days prior notice of the place and date of the hearing.

The right of audience before the tribunal is restricted to a litigant in person, counsel or solicitor or, with leave, any other person, e.g. wife or husband of a party, but not usually a surveyor.

The tribunal has a discretion regarding the conduct of a hearing but, unless it otherwise directs, the following have a right to begin: an appellant, a party claiming compensation, a party in receipt of an apportioned rent or rentcharge, a party who instituted a reference and a party who has made an application. If an appellant or applicant does not appear the tribunal may dismiss the appeal or application. If any other party to an appeal or application or any party to a reference does not appear, the tribunal may determine the matter in their absence and make an order of costs. The dismissal of an appeal or application and an *ex parte* determination may be subsequently set aside by the tribunal where good reason can be shown for the party's absence.

Evidence before the Lands Tribunal is usually given orally on oath but, where the parties agree or are so ordered, affidavit evidence may be given, subject to the tribunal's right to require the deponent to attend for examination and cross-examination. The tribunal may inspect the subject-property and any comparable properties referred to by the parties, who have a right to be present if the tribunal intends to enter any premises.

(5) Decision

A decision of the tribunal (with reasons) is normally given in writing, but may be given orally where the tribunal is satisfied that this would not cause injustice or inconvenience to the parties. Where the tribunal's decision is dependent on a question of law, it must contain an alternative award based on an alternative decision on that question. In a reference to determine the amount of compensation on compulsory purchase either party may apply to the tribunal to specify the amount awarded for any particular matter. The Lands Tribunal may make an interim award. The tribunal may correct a clerical mistake or error in its decision arising from any accidental slip or omission. Where a decision of the tribunal directs a sum to be paid it shall carry interest from the date of decision at the same rate as a judgment debt, unless the decision directs otherwise or a rate of interest is prescribed by statute, e.g. compensation for compulsory purchase. A decision of the tribunal may, by leave, be enforced as a judgment or order of the High Court or county court to the same effect (see Chapter 12 p. 383 below).

(6) Proceedings without a hearing

A written representations procedure was introduced by the Lands Tribunal (Amendment) Rules 1977 (Appendix C p. 536 below) to allow the determination of disputes without an oral hearing. Any party to proceedings may apply to the registrar for a direction that this procedure be used, but where the proceedings relate to a claim for compensation, such a direction may only be given with the consent of the claimant.

After an order has been made directing the use of this alternative procedure, the parties may submit written representations for the consideration of the tribunal. The tribunal may also, on the application of any party or independently, require any party to provide a statement of case, reply or further and better particulars. These documents must be sent to the registrar who will distribute them to the other parties. A party in receipt of a representation or other document may make a reply, but each party may only submit one set of representations, except with leave. Any party who intends to rely on expert evidence must submit to the registrar the same expert witness documents as would be required for an oral hearing (see p. 15 above). The tribunal may decide at any time and for any reason that the proceedings should proceed to a hearing and not be dealt with on written representations.

In addition to the above written representations procedure, an application for the discharge or modification of a restrictive covenant may be dealt with without a hearing, where the President decides that the applicant is not a proper person to make the application or where no objections to the application have been made or are withdrawn.

(7) Costs

Subject to the special rules relating to sealed offers (set out below) the Lands Tribunal has a discretion regarding costs. It may order one party's costs to be paid by another party; it may tax or settle costs in a lump sum or direct the manner of taxation e.g. by reference to the High Court or county court scales; it may disallow the costs of counsel. For example, in a rating case an award of costs will usually follow the event; on an application for the discharge or modification of a restrictive covenant the former practice whereby the applicant was usually ordered to pay all the costs, unless the objections were frivolous or vexations, has been discontinued and each case is now dealt with on its merits.

A party to a dispute before the Lands Tribunal may make an unconditional offer to pay or accept a sum as compensation. This is called a sealed offer because, although known to the other party, it is kept in a sealed envelope and is not known to the tribunal after until it has made its decision.

A sealed offer relating to compensation for compulsory purchase fetters the tribunal's discretion as to costs. Thus, the award of costs incurred before a sealed offer is in the discretion of the tribunal, although the acquiring authority is usually ordered to pay the claimant's costs. Where an acquiring authority has made a sealed offer of compensation and the award does not exceed that sum, or the claimant has failed to deliver a claim in sufficient time for the authority to make such an offer, the tribunal shall order the claimant to bear the authority's costs after the date of offer or time when a claim should have been made, unless it has special reasons for deciding not to do so. If the amount awarded is equal to or more than the sealed offer the acquiring authority will usually be ordered to pay the claimant's costs. It is unusual for a claimant to make a sealed offer, but if he does so and the tribunal's award is equal to or more than that amount, it shall order the acquiring authority to pay the claimant's costs after the date of offer unless there are special reasons for ordering otherwise.

The registrar may make a recommendation to the tribunal regarding the costs of interlocutory proceedings held before him with a right of appeal to the tribunal or President by a dissatisfied party.

The registrar is the taxing officer of the tribunal. A party dissatisfied with a taxation of costs may ask the registrar to review it, with a further right of review by the President.

(8) Appeals

A decision of the Lands Tribunal is final, but any party aggrieved by it as being erroneous on a point of law may require the tribunal to state a case for the decision of the Court of Appeal. A decision on an interlocutory application (e.g. discovery of documents) is not a decision for the purposes of an appeal to the Court of Appeal.

LOCAL VALUATION COURTS

(1) Constitution and jurisdiction

Local valuation courts were created by the Local Government Act 1948 to serve as tribunals of first instance for rating appeals. Their constitution and jurisdiction are now contained in the General Rate Act 1967 and their procedure is regulated by section 76 of that Act and The Rating Appeals (Local Valuation Courts) Regulations 1956 (Appendix C pp. 477 and 513 below).

Under the Local Government Act 1948 schemes for the constitution of local valuation panels were made and approved. The members of a local valuation court are drawn from the local valuation panel for the area in which the appeal hereditament is situated. Every local valuation panel (or two or more panels) has a full-time clerk, who assists the panel (or panels) and the courts. Other officers may be appointed with the approval of the Secretary of State for the Environment.

A local valuation court usually consists of the chairman or deputy chairman of the panel and two other members, although with the agreement of all persons appearing before the court, it may consist of two members only. Local valuation courts are convened as often as may be necessary to deal with outstanding rating appeals. Sittings usually take place in the offices of a local authority for the area.

The jurisdiction of a local valuation court is limited to the giving of directions for the alteration of the valuation list where the contentions of the appellant have been found to be justified.

(2) Commencement of proceedings

There are three stages leading up to the commencement of proceedings in a local valuation court: the making of a proposal to alter the valuation list, objections to that proposal, an appeal against those objections. An appeal automatically arises by elapse of time after objections to a proposal. There are two circumstances where this occurs. First, an appeal against a proposal to which objection has been made is deemed to have been made by the maker of the proposal on the date when the valuation officer fulfills his obligation to transmit copies of the proposal and objections to the clerk of the local valuation panel. The date of transmission must be during, but not later than, the period of four months from either the date of a proposal by the valuation officer or the date of service of a proposal on him by any other party. Secondly, in the case of a proposal made by a party other than the valuation officer, and to which he makes an objection, the maker of the proposal is deemed to have made an appeal to the local valuation court on the date of the transmission by the valuation officer of the proposal, objection and valuation officer's notice regarding withdrawal to the clerk of the local valuation panel. The maker of the proposal may withdraw it within 14 days of the valuation officer's objection, but, if he does not do so, the valuation officer must transmit the papers to the clerk within a further period of 14 days to constitute the proposer's deemed appeal.

(3) Pre-hearing procedure

There are no provisions requiring the exchange of pleadings or expert evidence prior to a local valuation court hearing. To a limited extent, the proposal and objection define the issues between the parties and serve as pleadings.

The only application to a local valuation court which is of an interlocutory nature concerns the inspection of rent returns to be used as evidence. The procedure is as follows. The valuation officer may require an owner, occupier or lessee to make a return (usually called a "rent return") to assist him in the preparation of a new valuation list or in connection with a proposal. These returns have a special status as evidence. Except where a valuation is made on the profits basis and the return could not be used as evidence apart from these provisions, rent returns are admissible as evidence of the facts stated in them, and certain rebuttable presumptions apply to their validity. They may be used as evidence by a valuation officer provided two conditions are satisfied. First, he must serve on the maker of the proposal and all outstanding objectors, a notice containing a list of the returns he intends to use and the hereditaments to which they refer. This notice must be served at least 14 days before the hearing. Secondly, he must allow the maker of the proposal and objectors to inspect (after notice) and take extracts from those returns.

A valuation officer's notice of intention to use returns as evidence gives the recipient a right to serve a counternotice calling for the inspection and production of other returns, provided the number of hereditaments specified in the counternotice does not exceed the number in the valuation officer's list.

If the valuation officer fails to comply with this counternotice, the person who gave it may apply to the local valuation court. The court, after hearing the parties, may direct the valuation officer to comply with the notice, wholly or in part. An appeal lies against the court's decision to the Lands Tribunal (section 83(6) and (8) General Rate Act 1967, Appendix C p. 478 below).

(4) Hearing

The clerk to a local valuation court must give at least 14 days notice of the date, time and place of a hearing. He must also advertise it.

A local valuation court normally sits in public, but it may hold a hearing *in camera* on the application of any party, where it is satisfied that the interests of one or more parties would be prejudicially affected by a public hearing. The following parties may appear at a hearing: the appellant, the valuation officer, the owner and occupier of the appeal hereditament, the rating authority and the objectors. These parties may still appear at a hearing, although they have not previously taken part in the proceedings and even though the ratepayer and valuation officer may have reached agreement on a reduced assessment. Such an agreement does not remove the jurisdiction of the court nor the rights of the other parties.

A rating authority may be represented at a hearing by their clerk, or another appointed officer, or by counsel or a solicitor. Other parties may appear in person, or by counsel, solicitor or any other representative, except a member of the local valuation panel for the area. All parties entitled to appear at a hearing may themselves give evidence and call and examine witnesses.

Procedure is determined by the court, subject to two restrictions. First, the appellant has the right to begin, unless (with the appellant's consent) the court decides otherwise having regard to the particular circumstances of the case. Secondly, where there are two or more appeals outstanding against objections to proposals in respect of the same hereditament, the court must not hear a later appeal until the earlier appeals have been settled.

Subject to the appellant's right to begin, the court determines the order in which the parties will be heard. The usual procedure is as follows. First, the appellant states his case and calls and examines his witnesses, who may be cross-examined by the objectors and other parties and questioned by the court. The objectors and any other parties may question the appellant on his evidence. Secondly, the objector (or each objector who wishes to state a separate case) states the grounds of his objection and calls and examines his witnesses, who may be similarly cross-examined by the appellant and other parties and questioned by the court. The appellant and any other parties may question the objectors on their evidence. The objectors then conclude their cases. Thirdly, the appellant makes his final submission but must not introduce fresh evidence. Fourthly, any other party (e.g. the rating authority) who wishes to present a separate case may do so after the appellant and objectors have been heard. The onus is on the appellant 'to show that the contention contained in his proposal is well-founded.

Evidence may be given on oath, but this is not the usual practice. The court may inspect (with or without the parties) the appeal hereditament and the comparable properties quoted by the parties. A local valuation court may proceed with a hearing in the absence of any party, provided it is satisfied that the provisions regarding notices etc have been complied with. A party who does not appear may not appeal to the Lands Tribunal. A court may postpone or adjourn a hearing, or may order that different questions in the appeal be heard at different times, in different places or in such order as may be expedient.

(5) Decision

A local valuation court will reach its decision in private. It may be a majority decision where the court consists of three members but it must be unanimous where only two members are present, failure to agree resulting in a rehearing before another court. The decision of the court must be in writing, signed by the chairman, and contain any necessary directions for the amendment of the valuation list. Copies are sent to the parties and to the valuation officer (where he was not a party to the appeal). If requested to do so on or before its decision, a court must state orally or in writing the reasons for its decision.

(6) Costs

A local valuation court has no power to award costs.

(7) Appeals

Any person who *appeared* before a local valuation court and is aggrieved by the decision may appeal within 28 days of that decision to the Lands Tribunal. An appeal may be on grounds of fact or law (or both), but the tribunal has no jurisdiction to quash a decision of a local valuation court or order a rehearing for a procedural irregularity. This is a matter for the High Court on an application for judicial review. An appeal to the Lands Tribunal is a rehearing of the original appeal and the tribunal may give any directions which the local valuation court could have given.

RENT ASSESSMENT COMMITTEES

(1) Constitution and jurisdiction

Rent assessment committees were created by the Rent Act 1965; their constitution and jurisdiction are now governed by the Rent Act 1977 and the Housing Act 1980. The country is divided into registration areas, corresponding with the areas of counties, London Boroughs and the City of London. Within these areas schemes have been made for the appointment by local authorities of rent officers, and rent assessment committees have been appointed, drawn from a panel of persons nominated by the Lord Chancellor and the Secretary of State for the Environment. They were originally created to deal solely with objections to the fair rents determined by the new rent officers but they now function as the following three different tribunals.

First, as a rent assessment committee carrying out their original function as an appellate tribunal from the rent officer. The procedure is contained in Schedules 11 and 12 to the Rent Act 1977 (Appendix C p. 497 below), The Regulated Tenancies (Procedure) Regulations 1980 and the Rent Assessment Committees (England and Wales) Regulations 1971, as amended by The Rent Assessment Committees (England and Wales) (Amendment) Regulations 1980 and 1981 (Appendix C pp. 516 below). Secondly, a rent assessment committee may function, and be known as, a rent tribunal, when exercising the jurisdiction over restricted contracts formerly exercised by those tribunals and now abolished and transferred to rent assessment committees by section 72 of the Housing Act 1980. Their procedure is found in sections 77 and 78 of the Rent Act 1977 (Appendix C p. 495 below) and The Rent Assessment Committees (England and Wales) (Rent Tribunal) Regulations 1980 as amended by the Rent Assessment Committees (England and Wales) (Rent Tribunal) (Amendment) Regulations 1981 (Appendix C p. 545 below). Thirdly, a rent assessment committee will be known as a leasehold valuation tribunal when dealing with disputes under the Leasehold Reform Act 1967 transferred to it from the Lands Tribunal under section 142 of the Housing Act 1980. Procedure is contained in The Rent Assessment Committee (England and Wales) (Leasehold Valuation Tribunal) Regulations 1981 (Appendix C p. 547 below).

A rent assessment committee, in any of its three roles, must usually consist of a chairman, who shall be the president or vice-president of the panel, and one or two other members. Where it sits as a leasehold valuation tribunal it must contain at least one member experienced in the valuation of land. In special circumstances and with the consent of the parties, the chairman may sit alone.

(2) Commencement of proceedings

Proceedings before a rent assessment committee are commenced in one of the following ways, according to the nature of the dispute and the jurisdiction of the committee:

(a) an *objection* to a fair rent to a rent assessment committee is made by written notice to the rent officer by the landlord or tenant under a regulated tenancy;

(b) the *reference* of a restricted contract to a rent tribunal is made by written notice to the rent assessment panel by the lessor, lessee or local authority;

(c) an *application* to a leasehold valuation tribunal in respect of the enfranchisement price, rent on an extended tenancy or compensation for the landlord's overriding redevelopment rights is made by submission to the tribunal of the appropriate form by the landlord or tenant under a long lease of residential accommodation at a low rent.

(3) Pre-hearing procedure

There are no provisions relating to pleadings or the exchange of expert evidence prior to proceedings before rent assessment committees, rent tribunals or leasehold valuation tribunals. But they should in their own interests and those of the parties encourage applicants and respondents to exchange proofs of evidence before a hearing.

There are, however, several provisions in similar form relating to the supply of information, documents and other preliminary matters. A rent assessment committee, rent or leasehold valuation tribunal may require the parties to provide such further information as it may reasonably require. Parties to proceedings before a rent assessment committee or rent tribunal must be asked whether they require a hearing or whether they wish to submit written representations. Where a hearing is to be held before such a committee or tribunal the parties are to be supplied with copies of all relevant documents, including those prepared by the committee or tribunal. Similar provisions apply where an objection referred to a rent assessment committee is to be dealt with by written representations. An objection to the determination of a fair rent by a rent officer may not be withdrawn unilaterally by the objector but only with the consent of all parties and the rent assessment committee.

(4) Hearing

There are many similarities in the hearing procedures of a rent assessment committee, sitting as such or as a rent or leasehold valuation tribunal. All procedures will be dealt with together, therefore, and similarities and differences noted.

Where a hearing is to be held, the minimum periods of notice of the date, time and place of the hearing are 10 days for a rent assessment committee, 7 days for a rent tribunal and 14 days for a leasehold valuation tribunal. A leasehold valuation tribunal may hear several applications together. Hearings must be in public unless there are special reasons for deciding otherwise. A party may appear in person or by another authorised person, whether or not that person is counsel or a solicitor. At hearings before a rent tribunal a party may be accompanied by a person to assist him. If the house which is the subject of a reference to a rent tribunal is under the general management of a local authority, that authority must be given an opportunity of being heard or submitting written representations. If a party does not appear at a hearing before a rent assessment committee or leasehold valuation tribunal, the committee or tribunal may deal with the matter in his absence, provided they are satisfied that notice of the hearing was correctly given.

The committee and both tribunals may determine their own procedures, including the order in which the parties will be heard. A party appearing before a rent assessment committee or leasehold valuation tribunal may give evidence on his own behalf, call witnesses and cross-examine witnesses called by another party.

A rent assessment committee or leasehold valuation tribunal may, at the request of a party, or independently, postpone or adjourn a hearing. But they shall not do so at the request of one party only unless they consider it reasonable, having regard to the grounds, time of request and convenience. A rent tribunal may postpone or adjourn a hearing from time to time as it thinks fit.

A rent assessment committee or leasehold valuation tribunal may or, if requested, must inspect the subject-premises. The parties shall be given an opportunity to attend. An inspection may be made before, during or after a hearing, or during consideration of written representations. Where an inspection is made after a hearing, the committee or tribunal may re-open the hearing having regard to any matters arising during the inspection. These provisions also relate to the inspection of comparable houses in proceedings before a leasehold valuation tribunal. There are no specific provisions regarding inspections by a rent tribunal.

(5) Decision

A rent assessment committee must not reach a decision until it is satisfied that the parties have had an opportunity of commenting upon the documents supplied to them and upon each other's case. A decision of a rent assessment committee, rent or leasehold valuation tribunal must be in writing, signed by the chairman. It may be a majority decision, but a decision of a rent assessment committee or

leasehold valuation tribunal shall not include any reference to it
being by a majority nor to any minority opinion. A chairman may
correct any clerical or accidental error or omission in a decision.
Rent assessment committees and rent tribunals are not required to
state the reasons for their decisions in every case, but must do so
where a request for reasons is made on or before the notification of
the decision. Leasehold valuation tribunals must always give
reasons for their decisions.

(6) Costs

Rent assessment committees, rent tribunals and leasehold valuation
tribunals have no power to award costs.

Under the Leasehold Reform Act 1967 the costs incurred by a
landlord in selling his freehold or granting an extended lease are
borne by the tenant. The landlord cannot include in those costs his
costs of a reference to a leasehold valuation tribunal.

(7) Appeals

A party to proceedings before a rent assessment committee or rent
tribunal, who is dissatisfied with the decision on a point of law, may
appeal to the High Court, or require the committee or tribunal to
state and sign a case for the opinion of that Court or proceed by way
of judicial review. A party to proceedings before a leasehold valuation tribunal may appeal against the tribunal's decision, on law or
fact, to the Lands Tribunal.

PLANNING INQUIRIES AND HEARINGS

(1) Constitution and jurisdiction

The courts and tribunals described above are judicial in appearance
and function. Planning inquiries and hearings are judicial in
appearance but administrative in function. This has two important
consequences. First, the strict rules of evidence do not apply (see
Chapter 2 p. 37 below). Secondly, although the Secretary of State
or inspector may not have regard to irrelevant matters when
reaching a decision, they may have regard to a wide range of material including extra-legal matters such as government or local planning policy.

The Town and Country Planning Acts contain many provisions
allowing or requiring the Secretary of State to hold some form of
inquiry or hearing before exercising his functions under the Acts.
These may be divided into three groups according to subject-matter.
First, those held to consider objections to proposals by a public
authority, e.g. objections to a structure plan submitted to the Secretary of State for approval. Secondly, those held to consider appeals

against decisions of a local authority, e.g. an appeal against refusal of planning permission. Thirdly, those held to consider appeals against notices or orders served by a local authority on a landowner, e.g. an appeal against an enforcement notice.

The particular procedure to be used depends on the relevant statutory provisions. For example, objections to a structure plan will be heard at an examination in public by a panel consisting of a chairman and two other members. But objections to a local plan will be dealt with at a local inquiry held by a single inspector. The Secretary of State may refer certain applications, appeals or proposals to a Planning Inquiry Commission, or he may, and usually will, cause a local inquiry to be held before a single inspector, perhaps assisted by assessors. Otherwise a private hearing will be held or the matter will be dealt with by written representations.

Space prevents a consideration of all the different procedures used at inquiries and hearings held by the Secretary of State. The remainder of this chapter will be concerned only with those governed by Schedule 9 to the Town and Country Planning Act 1971 (Appendix C p. 489 below), the Town and Country Planning Appeals (Determination by Appointed Persons) (Inquiries Procedure) Rules 1974 (Appendix C p. 520 below) and the Town and Country Planning (Inquiries Procedure) Rules 1974.

These two sets of Rules are almost identical. They both apply to local inquiries and hearings in connection with appeals or references to the Secretary of State and references in this chapter to an inquiry will include a hearing unless indicated otherwise. The Appointed Persons Rules apply where the decision is to be made by an inspector under delegated powers. (These now form the majority of appeals against the refusal or conditional grant of planning permission). The other Rules apply where the decision is to be made by the Secretary of State. The appeals and references covered by both sets of Rules are:

(a) planning applications called in for decision by the Secretary of State;
(b) appeals against the refusal, deemed refusal or conditional grant of:
(i) planning permission; or
(ii) a consent, agreement or approval required by a condition in a planning permission; or
(iii) an approval required under a development order;
(c) appeals or references in respect of consent to carry out works under a tree preservation order;
(d) appeals or references in respect of listed building consent or consent for the demolition of a building in a conservation area;

(e) appeals or references in respect of consent for the display of advertisements.

Other inquiries or hearings either have their own rules of procedure, e.g. the Town and Country Planning (Enforcement) (Inquiries Procedure) Rules 1981, which apply to enforcement, listed building enforcement and established use certificate appeals, or no prescribed procedure, e.g. confirmation of a purchase notice.

(2) Commencement of proceedings

With the exception of applications called-in by the Secretary of State, the above appeals are commenced by the submission of an appeal, either on a standard form or by written notice. Thus, an appeal against the refusal, deemed refusal or conditional grant of planning permission or approval, or in respect of refusal of listed building consent or to demolish a building in a conservation area, must be made within six months of the decision on a form obtained from the Secretary of State. An appeal in respect of any other consent, agreement or approval required by a condition in a planning permission (other than reserved matters), or under a tree preservation order or in connection with the display of advertisements must be made by written notice within six months, 28 days or one month respectively of the decision.

An appeal may only be made by an applicant for permission or consent, except in the case of a direction under a tree preservation order, where an appeal may also be made by an aggrieved person. All appeals must be sent to the Secretary of State, who has power to extend the various time limits. In respect of the above appeals (except advertisement appeals) and called-in applications, the appellant (applicant) or the local planning authority may request a hearing. The Secretary of State may decide an advertisement appeal on written representations only, but if he does not do so, he must hold a hearing if requested by the parties.

(3) Pre-hearing procedure

(a) *Third party representations.* After the Secretary of State has notified the parties of his intention to consider an application or appeal, the local planning authority must inform the appellant and Secretary of State of the names and addresses of any persons who made representations under section 29 of the Town and Country Planning Act 1971 in respect of the proposed development or works. (They are referred to as "the section 29 parties"). This provision does not apply to appeals in respect of tree preservation orders and advertisements.

(b) *Directions or expressions of view.* When a local planning authority considers a planning application it may receive expressions of view or directions from the Secretary of State, another local authority or a government department regarding the grant of permission or consent. Where such a view or direction is relevant to an appeal in respect of the application, the authority or department that made it shall give to the local planning authority a written statement of the reasons for it.

(c) *Notification and publicity.* The Secretary of State or inspector must give to the appellant, the local planning authority and the section 29 parties at least 42 days prior written notice of the date, time and place of the inquiry. A shorter period of notice may be given by agreement; there are provisions for varying the time or place. Where a local inquiry (but not a hearing) is to be held, the Secretary of State or inspector may require the local planning authority and appellant to publicise it by newspaper advertisements and notices. Where an appeal is to be determined by an inspector, written notice of the inspector's name shall be given by the Secretary of State to the appellant, the local planning authority and the section 29 parties.

(d) *Statements.* Where an application is called-in for decision by the Secretary of State, he shall serve on the applicant, the local planning authority and the section 29 parties, not less than 28 days before the inquiry, a statement containing:

(i) the reasons for his direction that the application be referred to him;

(ii) any points which seem to him to be relevant to his consideration of the application;

(iii) any views expressed by a government department that the application should be refused or granted subject to conditions.

In respect of the appeals referred to above, the local planning authority must send to the Secretary of State, the appellant and the section 29 parties, not less than 28 days before the inquiry, a written statement (commonly called a rule 6 statement) containing or accompanied by:

(i) the submissions which the authority proposes to put forward at the inquiry;

(ii) any direction to the authority regarding the grant of permission and any view from a government department or another local planning authority stating that the application should be refused or conditionally granted, and on which the authority intends to rely;

(iii) a list of the documents (including maps and plans) to be referred to or put in evidence by the authority and the arrangements for their inspection and copying.

An appellant *may* be required by the Secretary of State or inspector to serve within a specified period a similar statement on him, the local planning authority and the section 29 parties.

(e) *Attendance at the inquiry.* Where the Secretary of State, a government department or local authority have given a direction or expressed a view and this has been included in the rule 6 statement, the appellant may require the attendance at the inquiry of a representative from the department or authority concerned. This application must be made at least 14 days before the inquiry.

(4) Hearing

Where a local inquiry is held (as opposed to a private hearing) oral evidence must be given in public and documentary evidence must be open to public inspection, unless the Secretary of State has placed restrictions on the persons who may hear or inspect such evidence, e.g. for reasons of national security. The following parties may appear at a local inquiry:

(a) the appellant;
(b) the local planning authority;
(c) the county and district councils (outside Greater London);
(d) the section 29 parties;
(e) a parish or community council which has made representations;
(f) at a hearing, interested parties on whom notice of the inquiry has been served at the request of the Secretary of State or inspector;
(g) any other persons allowed to appear by the inspector.

The situation of the appeal site may also allow appearances on behalf of a National Park Committee, a joint or special planning board or a new town development corporation.

A local authority may appear by their clerk or any other appointed officer, or counsel or solicitor. Other parties may appear in person or by counsel, solicitor or any other person. One person may, with the consent of the inspector, appear for other persons with a similar interest in the inquiry.

Subject to any particular provisions in the relevant Rules, the inspector has a discretion regarding procedure. The appellant will begin, unless the inspector decides otherwise with the appellant's consent. The appellant also has the right of final reply. Other parties will be heard in the order decided by the inspector. He has discretion to proceed with the inquiry in the absence of any parties and to adjourn from time to time.

The appellant, the local planning authority and the section 29 parties may call evidence and cross-examine witnesses. Other persons may only do so if permitted by the inspector. The inspector's discretion, however, must be exercised in accordance with the rules of natural justice. For example, where an inspector at an inquiry into an application by the NCB to carry out open-cast coal mining, refused to allow an objector to cross-examine local authority witnesses this was held on appeal to be a contravention of the rules of natural justice. Anyone appearing at a local inquiry with a *bona fide* objection is entitled to cross-examine witnesses giving evidence contrary to his case.

An inspector may admit any relevant evidence, subject to two exceptions. First, he must not admit evidence which is contrary to the public interest. Secondly, where a representative of a government department attends to give reasons for an expression of view, he may not be asked questions about the merits of government policy. But otherwise he shall give his evidence and be subject to cross-examination like any other witness. A witness from a local authority who attends to explain a direction is in the same position as any other witness. An inspector may take evidence on oath or affirmation. He may require any person to attend to give evidence or to produce documents, other than those relating to private title to land, and provided that person's expenses are paid or tendered.

Where documents are tendered in evidence the inspector may give directions regarding inspection and copying by other parties. The inspector may take into consideration any written representations or statements received by him before the inquiry, subject to disclosure at the inquiry.

The local authority and appellant may amend their rule 6 statements as may be necessary for determining the questions in dispute. The inspector may adjourn the inquiry to allow the other parties time to consider the amendments and may make recommendations regarding the payment of additional costs as a result of such adjournment.

An inspector *may* make an unaccompanied inspection before or during an inquiry without informing the parties. He may, or *must* if requested to do so by the appellant or local planning authority, make an accompanied inspection after the close of the inquiry. He must confirm the date and time of this inspection during the inquiry. The appellant, the local planning authority and the section 29 parties are entitled to be present at this inspection, but the inspector need not defer it due to the absence of any party.

(5) Report and decision

Where the decision is to be made by the Secretary of State, the inspector is required to make a written report to him containing his findings of fact and recommendations (or reasons for not making any recommendations).

Where an inspector with delegated powers of decision proposes to take into consideration any new evidence or any new issue of fact (other than government policy), which he considers material to his decision, he shall not make a decision until he has notified the appellant, the local planning authority and the section 29 parties. They may make written representations or ask for the inquiry to be reopened. An inspector also has a general power to reopen an inquiry if he thinks fit. Similar provisions apply where the decision is to be made by the Secretary of State. But in addition, where he differs from his inspector on a finding of fact and therefore dis- agrees with his recommendation, he shall notify the above three parties and give them an opportunity to make written representa- tions thereon.

A decision of an inspector or Secretary of State must be in writing, with his reasons. It must be sent to the appellant, the local planning authority, the section 29 parties and any other person who appeared at the inquiry and asked for notification of the decision. A decision of the Secretary of State must be accompanied by the inspector's report or a summary of his conclusions and recommendations. A party entitled to a copy of such a decision may request a copy of the in- spector's report within one month. A party notified of an inspector's decision may apply to the Secretary of State within six weeks to inspect any documents, photographs or plans listed in this notifica- tion and shall be given an opportunity to do so.

(6) Written representations

An inspector with delegated powers or the Secretary of State are required to hold a local inquiry or hearing if requested to do so by the appellant or local planning authority. Both parties may, how- ever, agree to the appeal being decided on the basis of written representations. This procedure may be used in simple cases to produce a swift decision at less cost to the parties.

Circular 38/81 (Appendix C p. 561 below) deals with this pro- cedure and Table 2 of the Circular sets out the following target timetable:

(a) submission of appellant's appeal and statement of case (appeal form and any necessary documents) to the Department of the Environment;
(b) notification of the appeal by the Department to the local planning authority within one week of receipt, with request for the completion of a questionnaire (one week) and submission of the authority's statement of case (four weeks);

(c) notification of the appeal by the authority to local residents and other affected persons with arrangements for their comments to reach the Department within the period allowed for submission of the authority's statement of case;

(d) return of the questionnaire by the authority within one week of notification of appeal;

(e) consultation by the Department with other bodies (if necessary) after receipt of the questionnaire;

(f) submission of a written statement of case by the authority to the Department within four weeks of notification of appeal;

(g) copies of third party representations sent by the Department to the authority and the appellant within three days of receipt;

(h) copy of the authority's statement sent by the Department to the appellant within three days of receipt;

(i) submission to the Department within a two week period of the appellant's comments on the authority's statement;

(j) copy of the appellant's comments on the authority's statement sent by the Department to the authority within three days of receipt;

(k) further representations after this stage will only be required in exceptional circumstances;

(l) site visit by the inspector;

(m) issue of decision by the inspector or submission of his report to the Department, both within four weeks of the site visit or conclusion of the written exchanges.

Circular 38/81, unlike its predecessor Circular 32/65, does not contain a target date for the issue of a decision by the Secretary of State following receipt of his inspector's report.

Where the written representations procedure is used there is no requirement that the decision must be accompanied by reasons (in contrast to a decision given after an inquiry or hearing) but reasons must be furnished on request.

(7) Costs

Where a local inquiry is held in connection with the planning appeals discussed above, the Secretary of State has the power to award costs. This power does not apply to a hearing or the written representations procedure, although the Secretary of State may award costs in certain other appeals, e.g. against an enforcement notice, even though the matter is dealt with at a hearing or by written representations. An inspector has no power to award costs but he may make recommendations to the Secretary of State.

In Circular 73/65 (Appendix C p. 555 below) the Secretary of State has stated that he will exercise his power to award costs in accordance with the recommendations in the Report of the Council on Tribunals on The Award of Costs at Statutory Inquiries 1964. Under paragraph 9 of the circular it is recommended "that costs should normally be awarded against a party who behaves unreasonably, vexatiously or frivolously in favour of a party who, being legally entitled to appear at the inquiry, has duly appeared thereat and has not so behaved". Thus, costs do not follow the event, as in the case of litigation, but are dependent on unreasonable behaviour by one of the parties, a policy approved by the courts as perfectly sensible and unobjectionable as a matter of law.

The Secretary of State applies the following general principles when considering whether to make an award of costs for unreasonable behaviour. First, the main criterion is whether one party has been put to unnecessary or unreasonable expense because:

(a) the matter should never have come to inquiry (e.g. where a previous decision of the Secretary of State has made it clear what his decision will be); or

(b) where the appeal and inquiry could not reasonably have been avoided, the other party so conducted itself as to cause unnecessary trouble and expense (e.g. where a reason for refusal or ground of appeal was introduced at a late stage necessitating an adjournment).

Secondly, a higher standard of behaviour is expected from a local planning authority than from an appellant.

The above principles apply to persons *legally* entitled to appear at an inquiry. In the case of third parties and persons who appeared at the inquiry with the consent of the inspector, the general rule is that they should only be eligible for costs where another party has behaved unreasonably in exceptional circumstances, e.g. where an adjournment was caused by such unreasonable behaviour.

(8) Appeals

The local planning authority concerned or any person who is aggrieved by any action of an inspector or the Secretary of State in connection with an application, appeal or consent discussed above may challenge it by application to the High Court. If the court is satisfied:

(a) that the action was not within the powers of the Town and Country Planning Act 1971; or

(b) that certain procedural requirements were not complied with, resulting in substantial prejudice to the applicant;

then it may quash the decision.

An action is outside the powers of the 1971 Act where, for example, the Secretary of State acts on no evidence, or comes to an unreasonable conclusion on the evidence or takes into consideration an irrelevant matter. A failure to comply with the statutory rules of procedure will fall within ground (b) above, provided the applicant has thereby suffered substantial prejudice.

The High Court is not concerned with the planning merits of the case and cannot substitute its own decision for that of the inspector or Secretary of State. It may only quash the decision and remit the matter for a fresh determination.

CHAPTER TWO

Evidence

INTRODUCTION

A surveyor cast in the role of expert witness, advocate or arbitrator, requires a working knowledge of the law of evidence, particularly expert evidence. As an expert witness he must know how to prove the facts on which his opinion is based and what to include in expert witness documents. As an advocate he must know how to prove his case and when to object to his opponent's evidence. As an arbitrator he must know what evidence he may admit and what weight to give to it. The law of evidence is always present when the surveyor is in court. This chapter contains a brief outline of the law of evidence in civil proceedings, as a framework for the more detailed discussion of expert evidence in Chapter 3. Evidence in arbitration forms part of Chapter 10 (p. 312 below). To avoid a multiplicity of references in this chapter, particularly of cases, I have not given the authority for every statement of law.

A law of evidence, allied to a law of procedure, is needed to regulate the material admissible as the basis for judicial decision. It is a complex body of rules and principles, common law and statutory, ancient and modern. It is a particularly difficult branch of the law and the reader may find the diagram on p. 39 helpful when reading this chapter. Evidence has been likened more to a heap of builder's rubble than a rational edifice of law. It suffers from confusion in its vocabulary: many terms have several meanings and some are difficult to define. It lacks a coherent plan and no two writers adopt the same arrangement of topics.

The law of evidence has five main functions: to decide *what* facts may be proved, *how* they may be proved, *who* must prove them, what *standard* of proof is required, and what *weight* shall be given to them.

It should be noted that the law of evidence applies only to judicial proceedings; it does not apply to administrative or quasi-judicial tribunals, e.g. a local planning inquiry. Furthermore, although the rules of natural justice apply to these tribunals, the law of evidence forms no part of natural justice and is, therefore, still inapplicable. An administrative or quasi-judicial tribunal must base its decisions on "evidence", that is to say they must be founded on material which tends logically to show the existence or non-existence of relevant facts, or the likelihood or unlikelihood of relevant future events, but it is not restricted to evidence which would be admissible in a

37

court of law. It is for the tribunal to decide what weight to give to material which has some probative value. Thus, in *T. A. Miller Ltd v Minister of Housing & Local Government* (1968) 19 P & CR 263, the inspector at a local inquiry into an enforcement notice admitted hearsay evidence of past retail sales from the land in the form of a letter from the previous owner. It was held that the admission of this evidence was a matter for the inspector and it was not contrary to the rules of natural justice.

FACTS
(1) Law, fact and opinion
Facts are common to every judicial dispute, whether it is one of law, or mixed fact and law or only fact, and whether it is heard by the High Court, the Lands Tribunal or an NHBC arbitrator holding a hearing in the claimant's dining room. Facts are the raw material of judicial decision and the basis of the law of evidence. A fact is easy to recognise but difficult to define. To a surveyor it is the rent of a shop, the area of a building, the crack in a wall. Broadly, it is something seen or felt or heard. Fact is distinguished from law and from opinion. At first glance it is not difficult to draw these distinctions; this is a deception. In judicial proceedings a question of fact may become one of law due to lack of evidence or to an error in interpreting the supporting framework of law. It may be difficult for a witness to give evidence of fact without straying into opinion: a witness will say that he saw a car travel *slowly* along a road, thus combining fact and opinion (see Chapter 3 p. 61 below).

The difficulties of separating law, fact and opinion may be illustrated by reference to value. Value is a question of fact; in a legal context (e.g. a rent review, rating, compulsory purchase) it is a question of fact determined within a framework of law. Thus, in compulsory purchase the value of the acquired land may be affected by the underlying scheme of acquisition. The interpretation of the statutory and common law provisions relating to the scheme are questions of law, but the extent of the scheme and its effect on value are both questions of fact.

A determination of value may, however, reveal an error of law. In *Melwood Units Pty Ltd v Commissioner of Main Roads* (1978) 38 P & CR 195, an Australian compensation case, the Full Court of Queensland refused to answer the questions on the case stated from the tribunal of fact, on the grounds that an error in valuation could only be a question of fact and not a question of law. It was held by the Privy Council on appeal that it is an error of law for a tribunal of fact to disregard an underlying principle of valuation for compensation (in this case the *Pointe Gourde* principle that the value of land is not to be increased or decreased by the purchasing authority's "scheme") or to reject a transaction which is some evidence of the value of the acquired land.

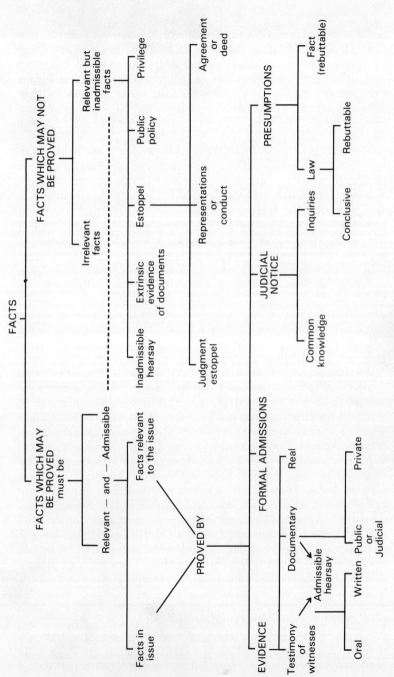

Diagram of Evidence

Similarly, in *Official Custodian for Charities v Goldridge* (1973) 26 P &
CR 191, a decision under the Leasehold Reform Act 1967, the Court
of Appeal held that the Lands Tribunal had erred in law in using a
technique of valuation known as the "adverse differential", applied to
give effect to the statutory exclusion of the sitting tenant's bid from
open market value. There was no justification in law for the application of the "adverse differential" and no evidence in the case to
support this valuation technique. In a rating case, *Black v Oliver (VO)*
(1978) 247 EG 43, the Lands Tribunal held that a flat in beneficial
occupation, but in a very dilapidated condition, could not, as a matter
of law, have a nil assessment. The Court of Appeal did not agree:
whether or not the flat should have a nil assessment was a question of
fact, not a question of law.

Value may also be an opinion. Expert evidence on value is
frequently given in the courts and before the Lands Tribunal. An
expert witness expresses an opinion of value, applying his knowledge,
skill and experience to evidence of fact (comparable transactions). But
in a different context, an opinion of value may be a material fact in
litigation. If an action is brought against a valuer for negligently
preparing a valuation, that opinion of value will be a material fact in
this action. If he denies giving the valuation it will become a fact in
issue; if he admits giving the valuation, but denies that he was negligent, it will be an admitted fact.

The distinction between law and fact is not merely theoretical but is
of practical importance to the surveyor in the witness box or arbitrator's chair. As will be seen in Chapter 3, expert evidence may only be
given on questions of fact, not questions of law (except foreign law
which is a question of fact). An expert witness must take care when
preparing his evidence not to stray into the realms of law, except to
explain the underlying basis of his evidence. The solution to a problem
of mixed fact and law will be helped by an understanding of these
separate fields. For example, a valuer assessing a rent under a rent
review clause in a lease will first ask the question: *what* should I value?
This will be answered by recourse to the law: the terms of the lease will
determine the *subject-matter* of the valuation. His second question: *how*
should I value? is a question of fact and will be answered by recourse to
market evidence and valuation technique. The ability to place a
problem into the correct category of law or fact is a step towards solving
it.

(2) Relevance, admissibility and weight

A fact may be proved if it is (a) relevant and (b) admissible. Both tests
must be satisfied and there is some overlap between them. When a fact
has been proved the weight (probability or importance) to be given to it
must be decided.

A fact is *relevant* when it is material to a party's case. Relevance is not a legal concept but one based on logic. Clearly, facts in dispute, which must be established by the plaintiff to win his case, or by the defendant to succeed in his defence, are relevant. These are called "facts in issue". Facts related to a fact in issue, which render it probable or improbable, are also relevant. These are called "facts relevant to the issue". Facts remote from the substance of a case or which raise side issues are irrelevant and, on that ground alone, are inadmissible.

All facts must be relevant to be *admissible*, but not all relevant facts are admissible. A fact is admissible if the law allows it to be proved by evidence or takes notice of it in some other way, e.g. as a matter of judicial notice (p. 50 below). But a relevant fact may be rendered inadmissible by an exclusionary rule of evidence. Thus, a report prepared by a surveyor for the purposes of litigation is relevant to the dispute but inadmissible on grounds of privilege (p. 57 below). The opinion of an experienced valuer as to the rental value of a shop is admissible but not the opinion of a trader, although he may give admissible evidence about the trading position (see Chapter 3 p. 75 below).

The admissibility of evidence to prove facts is a question of law; the *weight* to be given to admissible evidence is a question of fact. Unlike admissibility there can be no rules: the weight to be given to one piece of evidence as compared to another piece is a matter of commonsense, having regard to the surrounding circumstances and the credibility of witnesses.

Considerations of relevance, admissibility and weight apply whether the dispute is one of fact or of opinion, e.g. a rent review. In the latter case they apply to the facts underlying the opinion or determination of value. For example, in a rent review arbitration, rents agreed after the review date are relevant and admissible unless expressly or impliedly excluded from consideration under the terms of the lease. When assessing compensation for loss or damage, facts relating to the period after the date of assessment may be taken into account. In the case of a valuation at a particular date, the inherent possibilities and prospects in relation to the property at that date may be taken into consideration, but not the events which actually happened after that date and which resolve how those possibilities and prospects in fact turned out. A full discussion of evidence in value disputes is contained in Chapter 3 p. 67 below.

PROOF

A fact is proved when its existence is established to the satisfaction of the tribunal of fact. Proof is the means by which a fact is brought to the attention of the court. A party who must prove his case in order to succeed, whether as plaintiff or defendant, has a burden of proof placed

upon him: "he who asserts must prove." This is called the "persuasive" or "legal" burden. A party who wishes to place a fact before the
court must prove it. This is a different burden of proof (the "evidential"
burden). Under certain circumstances, this latter burden may shift to
the other party during a hearing (e.g. as the result of a presumption,
p. 51 below); the persuasive burden never shifts.

The general rule in civil cases is that the party who must prove his
case must do so on the balance of probabilities. He must show that his
version of the facts is more likely to be true than that of the other party.
This is a lower standard of proof than in criminal cases where the
prosecution must prove its case beyond a reasonable doubt.

There are four ways in which a fact may be proved: (1) by evidence,
(2) by formal admission, (3) by judicial notice, (4) by presumption.
The commonest means of proof is evidence.

(1) Evidence

The word "evidence" has two meanings in the law of evidence. It may
refer to the means whereby a fact is proved, e.g. the production of an
original lease to prove a rent, or it may mean the *fact* itself, the rent. If
the rent is irrelevant and, therefore, inadmissible it is said that it is not
evidence.

The courts have an inherent power to control their own proceedings
and may, at their discretion, exclude any evidence. Also, the parties to
litigation may make their own agreement regarding the admissibility
of evidence, either generally or for a particular purpose. These rules
apply to proceedings before tribunals and arbitrators in addition to
proceedings in the courts.

The law of evidence originally developed around one fundamental
rule, the "best evidence" rule. This states that only the best (or
primary) evidence is admissible; inferior (or secondary) evidence is not
admissible where the best evidence could be given. For example, a
copy of a document is not admissible where the original can be produced. But, by the beginning of the nineteenth century, a reaction
against this old rule had set in and now the trend is towards flexibility in
the admission of evidence. The only surviving example of the rule is
that an original document which is available must be produced in
preference to a copy. The modern approach to evidence allows the
admission of all relevant evidence, the inferior quality of any of that
evidence being dealt with as a question of weight and not admissibility.
For example, in *Garton v Hunter (VO)* [1969] 2 QB 37, the Lands
Tribunal rejected rating valuations of a caravan site made on the
contractor's and profits bases, on the grounds that, as the hereditament
is let at a rack rent, this is the best evidence of value and other evidence
is inadmissible. The Court of Appeal disagreed. It held that the
tribunal had erred in law in rejecting relevant and admissible

evidence, i.e. the contractor's and profits valuations. The case was remitted to the tribunal with a direction to consider all relevant evidence.

Evidence is divided into three categories: (a) testimony of witnesses (usually oral); (b) production of documents (documentary evidence); (c) production or inspection of things (real evidence). Hearsay evidence is now a separate category of evidence with special rules.

(a) *Testimony of witnesses*. Evidence is usually the oral testimony of witnesses given in open court. It is given by question and answer, in examination-in-chief, cross-examination and re-examination. A person may be compelled to appear as a witness by the service on him of a *subpoena ad testificandum*. There are exceptions to these general rules. For example, cases concerning a secret process or national security may be heard *in camera*. Written testimony may be given before trial instead of orally at the trial e.g. on affidavit, or before an examiner appointed by the court or by interrogatories.

(b) *Documentary evidence*. Facts may be proved by the production of documents. A document has been judicially defined as "... any written thing capable of being evidence.... and it is immaterial on what the writing may be inscribed" (per Darling J in *R v Daye* [1908] 2 KB 333 at p. 340). This definition is probably now too narrow and the term has been held to include coffin plates, inscriptions on walls and tape recordings. Documents are classified as either public or judicial, the contents of which may be proved by primary or secondary evidence, or private, which must usually be proved by primary evidence. A public document is one made for public use and to which they are able to refer.

A party producing a document in evidence must prove that it was executed or made by the person stated to have made it, e.g. by the evidence of the person who wrote it or by the production of a certified copy of a public document. The contents must also be proved, e.g. by producing the original document. Documents may also be received in evidence under the special rules relating to hearsay (p. 44 below).

Where a document requires stamping it can only be used in civil proceedings if it has been properly stamped. An objection on stamp grounds can only be taken by the court and cannot be waived by the parties.

A person, including an opponent, may (subject to certain exceptions on grounds of public policy or privilege, p. 56 below) be compelled to produce an original document in his possession by service on him of a *subpoena duces tecum*.

Extrinsic evidence of the contents and meaning of a document is not usually admissible. Extrinsic evidence is written or oral evidence existing outside the four corners of the document. Subject to certain exceptions such evidence will not be admitted as a substitute for a document, nor to contradict, vary or add to or subtract from its contents, nor to interpret it. But extrinsic evidence will be admitted to provide the background to the making of a document as an aid to interpretation. The interpretation of documents is discussed in Appendix A.

(c) *Real evidence.* A tribunal of fact may examine objects produced in court or leave the courtroom to view fixed objects, land and buildings. Thus, a jury may handle Exhibit A, the murder weapon; a "fierce and mischievous dog" may be produced in court to show its "temper and disposition"; a member of the Lands Tribunal may inspect the subject-premises and any comparable properties referred to in evidence by the parties. The demeanour of a witness when giving oral testimony is real evidence.

Although a view is part of the evidence (real evidence) the court or tribunal must ensure that it does not receive or give itself evidence at a view in the absence or without the knowledge of the parties (see Chapter 10 p. 317 below).

Hearsay evidence. In the famous trial of *Bardell v Pickwick*, in *Pickwick Papers*, the following passage appears:

"Now, Mr Weller," said Serjeant Buzfuz.
"Now, sir" replied Sam.
"I believe you are in the service of Mr Pickwick, the defendant in this case. Speak up, if you please, Mr Weller."
"I mean to speak up, sir," replied Sam; "I am in the service o' that 'ere gen'l'man, and wery good service it is."
"Little to do, and plenty to get, I suppose?" said Serjeant Buzfuz, with jocularity.
"Oh, quite enough to get, sir, as the soldier said ven they ordered him three hundred and fifty lashes," replied Sam.
"You must not tell us what the soldier, or any other man, said, sir," interposed the judge; "it's not evidence".

There, in a nutshell, is the fundamental rule of hearsay: what the soldier said is not evidence. As an exclusionary rule of evidence it was more important when Dickens was alive than it is today. It has been justified on the grounds that it is not the best evidence, that the statement was not made on oath and that the person who made it is not in court to be cross-examined.

Hearsay evidence consists of facts, conveyed orally, in writing or by conduct, by a person other than the witness giving evidence. It is contrasted with "direct" or "original" evidence which is given by a person who can speak of the facts from his own knowledge. Unless the hearsay can be brought within a category of admissible hearsay, a third party statement cannot be received by the court to prove the *facts* in it. But, if heard by or made to the person giving evidence, he will be able to give direct evidence that such a *statement* was made. Thus, if B tells A that a shop was recently let at a rent of £1,000 pa, A's evidence will be hearsay as to the amount of the rent but direct evidence that B made a statement regarding that rent.

The rule against hearsay evidence presents particular problems to the valuer who appears as an expert witness. In his everyday work he will probably rely greatly on information obtained from other surveyors, agent's particulars and periodicals. When he changes his role to that of an expert witness this information becomes hearsay, inadmissible unless agreed or admitted under the special procedure in the Civil Evidence Act 1968 (see p. 218 and Chapter 3 p. 68 below).

The inadmissible hearsay rule was originally highly technical, comprising a basic rule of exclusion subject to numerous exceptions, common law and statutory. Hearsay in civil proceedings was reformed by the Civil Evidence Act 1968 (the 1968 Act). This Act applies to "civil proceedings" in any of the ordinary courts of law, before a tribunal where strict rules of evidence apply, e.g. the Lands Tribunal and to arbitrations and references, statutory or otherwise (section 18(1) of the 1968 Act, Appendix C p. 488 below). The hearsay provisions in Part I of the 1968 Act (discussed below) (except computer statements under section 5) have been applied to opinion evidence by section 1 of the Civil Evidence Act 1972 (Appendix C p. 493 below). Hearsay evidence is now a separate category of evidence, subject to conditions which must be satisfied before it can be admitted. A party may now adduce hearsay evidence which would previously have been inadmissible, provided in most cases he suffers the disadvantage of disclosing it to his opponent beforehand.

Hearsay evidence is now admissible in civil proceedings: (a) by express or implied agreement (waiver); (b) under statutory provisions left unaffected by the 1968 Act; (c) under the categories of admissible hearsay created by sections 2, 4 and 5 of the 1968 Act; (d) under the categories of hearsay formerly admissible at common law and now preserved in section 9 of the 1968 Act (section 1 of the 1968 Act, Appendix C p. 478 below).

(a) *Admissible hearsay by agreement or waiver.* As stated above, parties to litigation may make their own agreements regarding the admissibility of evidence, including hearsay evidence. Thus, opposing expert witnesses in a valuation dispute may expressly agree the facts relating to each others' comparable transactions, even though those facts are hearsay from a third party. Strictly speaking, this agreement changes them from hearsay evidence to formal admissions (see p. 50 below).

Hearsay may also become admissible by waiver. This occurs where one party fails to object to the admission of evidence when it is tendered by the other party. It will be assumed that he has waived his right to object and agrees to the admission of this evidence. Thus, in *Town Centre Securities Ltd v Wm Morrison Supermarkets Ltd* (1981) 263 EG 435, both expert witnesses in a rent review arbitration gave hearsay evidence of comparable transactions. Neither party objected at the time, but at the conclusion of the evidence one party objected and the matter came before the High Court under the old special case procedure. It was held that the admissibility of hearsay evidence is now a matter of procedure (rather than substantive law) and that the defendant tenants, having failed to object to the hearsay at the time it was tendered, are to be assumed to have given up their right to insist upon strict compliance with the rules of evidence. The hearsay evidence was therefore admissible under an implied agreement, or waiver, and it was for the arbitrator to assess its weight.

This decision should, however, be contrasted with *Rogers v Rosedimond Investments (Blakes Markets) Ltd* (1978) 247 EG 467, where objections to certain evidence of opinion given by adjoining traders and to hearsay evidence of fact given by an expert witness were not taken until counsels' closing speeches, but the Court of Appeal nevertheless ordered a new trial on the grounds that the deputy county court judge had used the former opinion evidence for an inadmissible purpose (assessing the rental value) and this vitiated his decision. It was not necessary for the Court to deal with the hearsay evidence, although Roskill LJ said *obiter* that he would have hesitated to order a new trial on this ground alone.

(b) *Admissible hearsay under a statute other than the 1968 Act.* Certain statutory exceptions to the rules against hearsay were left unaffected by the 1968 Act. These are few and of minor importance.

(c) *Admissible hearsay under the exceptions created by the 1968 Act.* These are contained in sections 2, 4 and 5 of the Act (Appendix C p. 479 below). The effect of these sections is that hearsay contained (i) in statements made out of court, (ii) in certain records and (iii) in computer statements is now admissible as evidence, provided two conditions are satisfied. First, direct oral evidence of the statements or records would be admissible, i.e. they are not irrelevant or otherwise inadmissible. Secondly, notice has been served on the other party and either he has raised no objection to the proposed hearsay, or the court has determined that this evidence should be admitted (see p. 48 below).

(i) *Out of court statements (section 2)*. This section is wide and far-reaching. It provides that a statement made by *any* person (*whether or not he is called as a witness*) is admissible as evidence of any fact contained in it, subject to the two conditions stated above. The statement may be made orally, or in a document or otherwise (e.g. by conduct), but unless it is made in a document only one-stage hearsay evidence of it will be admissible. Thus, a modern Sam Weller may now tell the court what the soldier said, and he may still do so if the soldier's statement is in a document passed to him by a third party.

(ii) *Records (section 4)*. This section deals with the admissibility of certain records. Subject again to the above two conditions, a statement contained in a document which is, or forms part of, a "record" is admissible as evidence of any fact contained in it. A document is a "record" where it is compiled as a duty from information supplied directly or indirectly by another person (who need not be acting under a duty) and who had, or may reasonably be supposed to have had, personal knowledge of that information. Where the information is passed to the compiler through intermediaries, those intermediaries must be acting under a duty. The circumstances in which a person is acting under a duty include the carrying on of any trade, business, profession or other occupation in which he is engaged or employed, or the holding of any office (paid or unpaid).

(iii) *Computer statements (section 5)*. Computers are now normal business equipment for the storage and processing of information. Statements prepared by a computer were generally inadmissible as evidence at common law; they may now be admitted under section 5 of the 1968 Act. A statement produced by a computer is admissible evidence of any fact contained therein, provided the above two conditions are satisfied together with additional conditions regarding the operation of the computer.

(iv) *Supplementary provisions (section 6) (Appendix C p. 482 below)*. Section 6 contains provisions supplementary to sections 2, 4 and 5. These relate to the production of documents, the drawing of inferences in connection with the admissibility of hearsay evidence, weight of such evidence, corroboration and penalties for false statements in certificates relating to computer statements.

(v) *Credibility (sections 3 & 7) (Appendix C pp. 479 and 483 below)*. Where hearsay evidence is adduced under sections 2 or 4, the maker of the original statement or the original supplier of the information will not be in court to be cross-examined. Provision is made, therefore, in section 7 for the admission of evidence to test the credibility of the absent witness.

(vi) *Rules of court (section 8) (Appendix C p. 484 below)*. The admissibility of hearsay evidence under sections 2, 4 and 5 is subject to rules of court. These are authorised by section 8 and are now found in RSC Order 38 rules 20–34 and The County Court Rules 1981, Order 20 rules 14–26. These rules apply to all "civil proceedings" (see p. 45 above), subject to such modifications as may be agreed between the parties or determined by the particular tribunal. They apply, therefore, to references to the Lands Tribunal and to arbitrations, but they may be modified by the parties, tribunal or arbitrator.

The above rules set out the procedure to be followed where a party wishes to adduce hearsay evidence under sections 2, 4 or 5 of the 1968 Act. He must first serve notice on all other parties, giving details of the hearsay statement. If no objection is made the hearsay evidence may be given, provided it is relevant and admissible. A party in receipt of a hearsay notice may, however, serve a counternotice requiring his opponent to call direct evidence of the facts he intends to prove by hearsay. The determination of the question whether hearsay or direct evidence is to be given will be settled by the court before the trial of the action. A party wishing to call hearsay evidence may resist a counternotice requiring him to call direct evidence, on certain statutory grounds, e.g. that the witness is dead, or unfit to attend or cannot be found. If one of those grounds applies then the court must allow a party to adduce hearsay evidence.

The court has a discretion to admit hearsay evidence at the hearing, even though the requisite notices have not been served on the other parties. Thus, in *Gredley (Investment Developments) Co Ltd v London Borough of Newham* (1973) 26 P & CR 400, the Lands Tribunal exercised this discretion to allow land use records to be produced in evidence in a compulsory purchase case, even though prior notice had not been given.

(d) *Hearsay formerly admissible at common law*. The Civil Evidence Act 1968 abolished all common law exceptions to the hearsay rule, but then preserved some of them as statutory exceptions. These are contained in section 9 (Appendix C p. 486 below) and are divided into two groups.

The *first group* comprises four exceptions. These allow admissible hearsay to be given as evidence of any fact under the common law rules which would have applied to admit these hearsay exceptions. The provisions of Part I of the 1968 Act and rules of court do not apply: it is not necessary, therefore, for prior notice to be given of this evidence. The four exceptions are:

(i) *Informal admissions (section 9 (2)(a))*. A favourable statement made out of court by a party to litigation is not admissible as evidence. But an unfavourable statement by such a party, or by a person with sufficient connection with him, is admissible as evidence against him. These statements are called "informal admissions" in civil proceedings and "confessions" in criminal prosecutions. Informal admissions must not be confused with formal admissions made expressly for particular litigation (p. 50 below). Formal admissions are made for the purpose of agreeing facts and relieving the other party of the burden of proving those facts. Informal admissions may be made at any time, even before any litigation has commenced or is contemplated. An informal admission is not conclusive evidence against the maker: it may be rebutted by other evidence. Formal admissions are conclusive.

An informal admission may be made orally, in writing or by conduct. Where an admission is tendered in evidence against a party he is entitled to have all relevant parts of the statement, etc. put in evidence, including those parts favourable to him (the "whole statement" rule). Admissions made "without prejudice" in an attempt to settle a dispute, are not usually admissible on grounds of public policy (see Chapter 3 p. 78 below).

An admission which does not fall within this common law rule may be admissible under sections 2 or 4. The common law rule has the advantage of allowing double hearsay and dispensing with prior notice.

(ii) *Published works (section 9(2)(b))*. Published works dealing with matters of a public nature (e.g. histories, scientific works, dictionaries and maps) are admissible as evidence of the facts of a public nature stated in them. For example, an expert witness may include an Ordnance Survey map in his evidence without the necessity of calling the maker of the map to give evidence. (Maps and plans used by expert witnesses are often agreed and, therefore, come before the court as formal admissions).

(iii) *Public documents (section 9(2)(c))*. Public documents (e.g. public registers and returns made under public authority) are admissible as evidence of the facts contained in them.

(iv) *Records (section 9(2)(d))*. Records (e.g. the records of certain courts, treaties, Crown grants, pardons and commissions) are admissible as evidence of the facts contained in them.

The *second group* of hearsay evidence, formerly admissible at common law and now preserved by section 9 of the 1968 Act, differs from the first in its relationship to sections 2 and 4. The three exceptions in this second group are only admissible under section 9 if they are not admissible under section 2 or 4. Thus, if the hearsay evidence in question can be brought within the ambit of one of those sections, then it must be presented under that section, including the requirement of prior notice. Only if the hearsay is not admissible under those sections will it be admitted and governed by the common law rules preserved in section 9(3) and (4).

The three former common law exceptions in this second group are:

(i) *Reputation and character (section 9(4)(a))*. Hearsay evidence of a persons's reputation is admissible for the purpose of establishing his good or bad character.

(ii) *Pedigree or marriage (section 9(4)(b))*. Where an issue in civil proceedings involves matters of a blood relationship or marriage, certain hearsay evidence of reputation or family tradition will be admissible to prove or disprove those matters.

(iii) *Public or general rights; identification of persons or things (section 9(4)(c))*. Hearsay evidence of reputation or family tradition will be admissible to prove or disprove public or general rights (e.g. rights to a highway or the boundaries of a manor) or to identify any person or thing.

(2) Formal admissions

A fact which has been formally admitted (agreed) need not be proved by evidence. A formal admission is one made during litigation in order to agree facts in that litigation so that the parties may be released from the burden of proving them. Thus, where two expert witnesses agree a schedule of floor areas or details of comparable transactions, each of them is, in effect, making a formal admission regarding those facts. Formal admissions are not evidence: they are conclusive and cannot be rebutted by contradictory evidence. They must be distinguished from informal admissions, namely unfavourable statements admissible as hearsay evidence under section 9(2)(a) of the Civil Evidence Act 1968 (p. 49 above). Formal admissions may be made during the pleadings prior to trial, by answers to interrogatories, in reply to a notice to admit specific facts or documents under RSC Order 27, and in correspondence or orally before or at the trial. An admission made expressly or impliedly "without prejudice", in an attempt to settle a dispute, will not usually be treated as a formal admission (see Chapter 3 p. 78 below).

(3) Judicial notice

Certain facts may be received by the court as matters of judicial notice. These need not be proved by evidence. Matters of judicial notice fall into two categories: (a) those which the judge knows as part of his common knowledge; (b) those of which the judge is generally aware but where he needs to "refresh his memory" by inquiry or evidence.

In the first category are facts which are so well-known that it would be pointless and time-consuming to require them to be proved by evidence. They are received by the judge without further inquiry. Examples are: the great difference in the value of money in 1189 and 1868, that cats are ordinarily domestic animals and the number of days in the months. A judge may use his *general* knowledge of a well-known fact as a substitute for evidence to prove it, or such knowledge may be used to explain, interpret or draw inferences from a fact proved in evidence. Generally, however, he may not use any *particular* knowledge he possesses as a substitute for evidence, e.g. a medically qualified judge must not substitute his own medical knowledge for expert medical evidence. An expert tribunal may use its expertise to evaluate and interpret technical evidence, but it must not reach a decision based on that expertise, unsupported by or contradictory of the evidence presented to it (see Chapter 10 p. 319 below).

The second category of judicial notice comprises those matters of which the judge is generally aware but where he needs to "refresh his memory" by making inquiries, listening to expert "evidence" or consulting a Secretary of State. For example, he may consult a reference book to remind himself of the date of an important historical event, or he may receive a certificate from a Secretary of State on a constitutional, political or administrative matter, or he may listen to expert evidence before deciding whether a particular class of animals is wild or domestic. When an expert witness gives his opinion he is not, strictly speaking, giving evidence but placing technical information and opinion before the judge so that he may take judicial notice of it when making his decision.

The concept of judicial notice is wide and gives the judge a discretion regarding the facts he may receive without proof. For reasons of convenience and expediency he may take notice of facts that he cannot be required to notice. But a matter should only be judicially noticed if it is so widely known and accepted as true that "no person can raise a question" on it.

(4) Presumptions

In broad terms, a presumption is a conclusion which may or must be drawn, usually from the existence of certain facts. For example, where chattels are found on land it is presumed that they belong to the person in legal possession of that land. A presumption usually operates by shifting the burden of proof from one party to the other, although in some cases it may be conclusive. Presumptions are divided into: (a) presumptions of law, which are further sub-divided into irrebuttable (or conclusive) and rebuttable presumptions; and (b) presumptions of fact, which are all rebuttable.

(a) *Presumptions of law.* These are arbitrary conclusions stated by law and usually attached to particular facts. They are divided into two categories:

(i) *Irrebuttable presumptions of law.* These provide that the conclusion which the law states shall be drawn, whether from particular facts or not, *must* be drawn. They have the character of substantive rules of law. They may be statutory e.g. production of a copy of the "London Gazette" containing details of a receiving order is conclusive proof of the date and making of the order (section 137(2) Bankruptcy Act 1914), or common law, e.g. "every man must be taken to be cognisant of the law".

(ii) *Rebuttable presumptions of law.* These provide that the conclusion required by law to be drawn from particular facts *must* be drawn, *unless* rebutted by contrary evidence. The effect of a rebuttable presumption is, therefore, to shift the burden of proof from the party benefitting from the presumption to his opponent. For example, where land is compulsorily acquired and the occupier re-houses himself in alternative accommodation, it is a rebuttable presumption of law that the purchase price of that accommodation and the cost of any adaptation works represent value for money. Compensation is not, therefore, normally recoverable for this expenditure, unless the claimant can rebut the presumption by showing that he did not receive value for money (*Service Welding Ltd v Tyne & Wear County Council* (1979) 250 EG 1291).

(b) *Presumptions of fact.* A presumption of fact arises where fact A *may* be inferred from the existence of fact B, unless the party against whom the presumption operates can produce contrary evidence. For example, where land has been conveyed and the question of ownership arises at a later date, it is presumed that the ownership continued to vest in the person to whom it was conveyed, unless the contrary can be proved. The importance of a presumption of fact is that the inference *may* be drawn even though there is only a tenuous connection between the two facts.

FACTS WHICH MAY NOT BE PROVED

There are certain facts which may not be proved, even though they are relevant to the issue between the parties. They are rendered inadmissible on the grounds of some overriding public policy or interest. The rule against hearsay evidence (now much reduced in scope) is an example (p. 44 above); where it still applies, the untrustworthy nature of this evidence outweighs the principle that all relevant evidence should be put before the court. Extrinsic evidence of the contents of a document may be relevant but is generally inadmissible (see p. 44 above and Appendix A below). Other categories of exclusion are: (1) estoppel and (2) public policy and privilege.

(1) Estoppel

In broad terms, the doctrine of estoppel prevents a party from proving or denying certain facts in legal proceedings, those facts arising out of a previous judgment, or representations or conduct by the party, or a prior agreement by the party treating the facts as the basis for a transaction. The following are three contrasting examples of the doctrine of estoppel. A "borrower" of money for the purchase of a house, who admitted in litigation that the transaction was neither a loan nor money lending, will be estopped from raising this issue again in subsequent proceedings. Where a yearly tenant built on his land in the belief that he had an absolute right to a long lease, his landlord, who was silent and did not point out his mistaken belief, will be estopped from denying the tenant's right to such a grant. An applicant for planning permission, who gave an undertaking in reliance on which permission was granted subject to a condition embracing that under-taking, will be estopped from later denying that implementation of the permission was conditional on compliance with the condition and from asserting that there is no power to require such compliance.

The doctrine of estoppel appears to consist of substantive rules of law rather than rules of evidence. Nevertheless, it has the effect of excluding evidence which would otherwise be relevant and admissible and a discussion of this topic (at least in outline) is usually found in the law of evidence.

All estoppels are subject to one general rule: they cannot override the general law. Thus, an estoppel cannot give to a tribunal a jurisdiction it does not have, nor make legal something that is illegal, nor fetter the exercise of a statutory duty or discretion.

There are three types of estoppel: (a) judgment estoppel, (b) estoppel by representation or conduct, (c) estoppel by agreement or deed. Judgment estoppel is founded on the principle that there should be an end to litigation. Estoppel by representation or conduct rests on the principle that it is unconscionable for a person to deny that which, knowingly or unknowingly, he has allowed another to assume to his detriment. And the foundation of estoppel by agreement or deed is that a person should not be able to deny the truth of statements previously made by him as the basis for a transaction.

(a) *Judgment estoppel.* A party to litigation will be estopped from raising certain issues which have been the subject of a previous judgment. The effect of that judgment must be considered from the viewpoints of: (i) all persons and (ii) the parties to the earlier litigation and connected persons. (Judgment estoppel in arbitration is discussed in Chapter 12 p. 356 below).

(i) *Effect of judgment on all persons.* A final judgment of a competent court operates to raise an estoppel against all persons, but the extent of that estoppel will depend on the nature of the judgment. Where it decides a general issue, such as the status of a person or thing, it is conclusive proof of the matter decided and binding on all persons. For example, a person who was charged with obstructing a highway was estopped by an earlier decision that the highway is subject to a public right of way from calling evidence to show that such a right of way did not exist. But where a judgment decides only the rights of the parties in the subject-matter of the dispute, it has a limited effect on third parties. Thus, where A obtains such a judgment against B, that is the only fact that is binding on all persons. The grounds on which the judgment was given are not binding on third parties, who are free (subject to certain statutory exceptions) to argue the merits of the case again at a later date.

Decisions of the Lands Tribunal are subject to the doctrine of judgment estoppel. Three propositions may be stated.

First, a decision of the tribunal on a *particular* issue of fact is not binding on third parties and is not admissible in evidence in a later case. Thus, a decision that the owner of backland would buy the front land for access at a price equal to one-third of the consequent increase in value of the backland, or that the net profits of a shop should be capitalised at 3 years' purchase to produce the value of goodwill, are particular decisions of fact based on evidence and are not binding on third parties nor admissible in evidence in a subsequent case (*Stokes v Cambridge Corporation* (1961) 13 P & CR 77; *W. Clibbett Ltd v Avon County Council* 1975 RVR 131).

Secondly, a decision of the tribunal which includes a principle of valuation of *general* application may be cited in a later case. For example, observations of the tribunal regarding the defects in the residual method of valuation under conditions of litigation are of general application and may be referred to in a subsequent case (*Clinker & Ash Ltd v Southern Gas Board* (1967) 203 EG 735).

Thirdly, a decision of the tribunal containing a principle of law or procedure, such as the *method* to be used to calculate loss of goodwill (as opposed to the *multiplier* to be used to value that goodwill), or as to the need for expert witness documents to be agreed or produced in evidence before they are properly before the tribunal, may be cited in a later case (*London County Council v Tobin* (1959) 10 P & CR 79; *Chinnery v Basildon Development Corporation* [1970] RVR 530). The Court of Appeal has, however, stated that the tribunal should not regard itself as bound by its earlier decisions on questions of law (*West Midlands Baptist (Trust) Association (Inc) v Birmingham City Council* (1968) 19 P & CR 9).

(ii) *Effect of judgment on the parties.* A previous judgment has a much greater effect on subsequent litigation between the same parties than is the case with third parties. The position of the parties (and connected persons) is fettered by judgment estoppel (or estoppel *per rem judicatam*).

A judgment obtained by A against B affects subsequent litigation between the parties in two ways. First, A cannot bring a second action against B in respect of the same cause, either permanently or for a limited period. This is "cause of action estoppel". Where the previous judgment was given by a court of limited jurisdiction, the resultant estoppel operates for a limited period only. Thus, in *Society of Medical Officers of Health v Hope (VO)* (1960) 175 EG 263, a decision of a local valuation court on a claim for exemption from rating did not create an estoppel in respect of a new valuation list, even though it was shown or agreed that there had been no change of circumstances. The Lands Tribunal subsequently applied this decision to restrict the estoppel to the year of assessment in which the decision or agreement creating the estoppel was made (*Gudgion (VO) v Erith Borough Council & London County Council* (1960) 7 RRC 324).

Secondly, where there is subsequent litigation between the parties in which the cause of action is different but one or more issues are the same, each party will be estopped from raising again issues which were decided, or which he failed to bring forward or he admitted in the earlier litigation. This is "issue estoppel".

(b) *Estoppel by representation or conduct.* An estoppel may arise out of a representation of an existing fact or facts, made by words or conduct (including silence), by A to B and in reliance on which B alters his position. This is proprietary estoppel. For example, in *Crabb v Arun District Council* (1975) 32 P & CR 70, A and B, who were adjoining landowners, reached an oral agreement in principle that B should have a right of way to the nearest road over A's land. A subsequently erected a fence along the boundary between the two plots and put a gate at the agreed access point. In reliance on the agreement and A's subsequent conduct, B sold part of his land without reserving a right of way over it to the road. A subsequently closed the access point and denied that B had any rights over his land. It was held that A's conduct gave rise to a proprietary estoppel in favour of B, giving him a cause of action to enforce his rights.

A promise, unlike a representation of fact, cannot be used to found an action. It may, however, give rise to an estoppel which can be used as a defence in a subsequent action by the promissor. This is promissory estoppel. It arises where A and B have a legal relationship, and A makes an unequivocal express or implied assurance or promise altering that relationship (without consideration), intending that B shall rely on it and B does so rely on it by altering his position. A cannot subsequently enforce his original rights until he has given notice to B that he intends to revert to the former position.

For example, in *Hughes v Metropolitan Railway Co.* (1877) 2 App. Cas. 439, A (a landlord) served in October a notice to repair within six months on B (his tenant). B suggested that A might like to purchase his interest; negotiations started but on 31st December the price offered was rejected by A. Nothing further happened until the following April when B's agents stated that, because agreement had not been reached on price, the repairs would be carried out. A replied that the negotiations were broken off in the previous December and ample time had elapsed since that date for the completion of the repairs. He started forfeiture proceedings on 28th April, a few days after the expiration of the six months period in the original repairs notice. The tenant sought relief in equity. It was held that he was entitled to such relief, on the grounds that the subsequent negotiations for sale suspended the operation of the repairs notice until 31st December; the six months period then started to run from that date and had not expired when the landlord's action commenced.

It will be noted that the doctrines of proprietary and promissory estoppel are similar. Proprietary estoppel, however, relates to an existing position and promissory estoppel relates to a future position. Other terms which are used to describe one or both of these forms of estoppel are: estoppel *in pais*, equitable estoppel, quasi-estoppel and estoppel by silence or acquiescence.

(c) *Estoppel by agreement or deed.* Where facts have been agreed as the basis for a transaction, the parties will be estopped as against each other from denying the truth of those facts. For example, a tenant sued by his landlord for breach of covenant to repair, is estopped from denying his landlord's title, irrespective of whether the tenancy was granted by deed or whether or not the tenant has gone out of possession (*Industrial Properties (Barton Hill) Ltd v Associated Electrical Industries Ltd* (1977) 242 EG 955).

(2) Public policy and privilege

For reasons of a public interest that overrides the principle that all relevant evidence should be put before the court, certain evidence is rendered inadmissible on grounds of: (a) public policy or (b) privilege.

(a) *Public Policy.* This is the public aspect of that interest which excludes relevant and otherwise admissible evidence. For reasons of national security, the proper functioning of the public service, the detection of crime and the administration of the courts, a witness may be prevented from answering certain questions or producing certain documents. Thus, considerations of national security have excluded evidence of the constructional details of a submarine; the need for freedom and candour between officials has excluded a communication between a colonial governor and a Secretary of State; and, in order not to deter informants, a witness will not be allowed to state the sources of information which led to a criminal prosecution. Similarly, a local authority will not be required to produce case-records on boarded-out foster children, and the NSPCC will not be forced to produce a report on the alleged ill-treatment of a child by its parents, following a complaint by a member of the public. The proper administration of law requires that judges, counsel and jurors shall not be required to give evidence of what occurred in court or in the jury room. Journalists will not be required to reveal their sources unless it is established to the satisfaction of the court that disclosure is necessary in the interests of justice, national security or for the prevention of disorder or crime. In all these cases there is an overriding public interest which states that it is more expedient to exclude the evidence in question than to admit it.

Claims for the exclusion of documentary evidence on grounds of public policy are based on either the *nature* of the document (a class claim) or the *contents* (a contents claim). While it is still recognised by the courts that certain classes of documents must remain privileged from disclosure irrespective of their contents, namely those relating to national defence, diplomatic relations and the detection of crime, the policy of the courts is now to look more closely at class claims. The courts will wish to inspect the documents concerned, basing their decision for or against disclosure on the contents, asking the questions: is production necessary for a fair disposal of the case? and, if so, is the balance of public interest for or against disclosure? Thus, the distinction between class and contents claims has become blurred and the former claims are becoming assimilated into the latter.

A claim for exclusion of evidence on grounds of public policy cannot be waived by a party or a witness, and secondary evidence will not be admitted to prove the excluded facts. A party claiming the exclusion of evidence on this ground need not be a party to the litigation.

(b) *Privilege.* This is the private aspect of the interest excluding relevant and otherwise admissible evidence. It is mainly concerned with communications between a litigant and his legal advisers. It differs from the public policy ground of exclusion in that its benefit may be waived by the person who may claim it and secondary evidence may be given to prove the particular facts in issue.

Communications between a client and his legal advisers, and between those advisers and third parties, where litigation is pending or anticipated (including certain reports) are privileged and inadmissible in evidence except with the consent of the client. Thus, where a surveyor is instructed by a solicitor to prepare a report for the purposes of litigation, that report and any communications between them are privileged from disclosure. This rule applies where the report was prepared *predominantly* for the purposes of litigation even though it was also prepared for some other purpose. Thus, in *Waugh v British Rail Board* [1980] AC 521, the House of Lords ordered disclosure by the Board of a report on a fatal accident, prepared for the dual purpose of advising the Board's solicitor in connection with an anticipated action and to prevent further accidents, but not predominantly for the former purpose.

Where part of a privileged report is quoted to another party in the litigation, then the whole of the report thereby loses its privileged status and must be disclosed if it relates to the same subject-matter (*Great Atlantic Insurance Co v Home Insurance Co* [1981] 1 WLR 529). The rules concerning privilege do not conflict with the procedural rules discussed in Chapter 3 p. 83 below, whereby the prior disclosure of an expert report may be required as a condition of the admission of expert evidence in court. If the party who requested the report does not wish to disclose it then he may properly refuse to do so. But if he wishes to adduce expert evidence based on that report then he may be required to disclose it before such evidence can be given at the trial.

Communications between a client, his surveyor and other advisers are not excluded under this class of privilege. Similarly, communications between the surveyor and third parties are not privileged, even though made in the course of litigation, although such communications may be inadmissible on the grounds that they were made expressly or impliedly "without prejudice" in an attempt to settle the dispute, e.g. correspondence between the surveyors to the parties containing offers and counter-offers to settle.

"Without prejudice" statements are sometimes considered under admissions and sometimes under privilege. They have particular reference to expert evidence and are discussed in Chapter 3 p. 78 below.

CHAPTER THREE

Expert Evidence

INTRODUCTION

Where the decision of a court or tribunal requires specialised knowledge which it does not possess, it must obtain that knowledge from experts. It may do this in three ways: by appointing an expert assessor to assist the court, by appointing a court expert to report on a technical matter, by listening to expert witnesses called by the parties. Whichever method is used, the court is remedying the deficiencies in its own knowledge and equipping itself for the task of making a decision.

The evidence discussed in Chapter 2 is mainly evidence of fact: what a witness did or saw or felt or heard. The evidence discussed in this chapter is expert evidence: conclusions drawn by an expert from facts and experience. The chapter commences with a summary of the ways in which a court receives expert assistance; it then deals with expert evidence, and particularly fact and opinion in this evidence and concludes with the procedures for the adduction of expert evidence in the High Court, county courts and Lands Tribunal.

WAYS IN WHICH THE COURT OBTAINS EXPERT ASSISTANCE

(1) Assessors

Under section 70(1) of the Supreme Court Act 1981 the High Court is empowered to hear and dispose of any cause or matter with the assistance of one or more expert assessors. Scientific advisers may be appointed to assist the Patent Court. A county court judge may summon one or more assessors to assist him. The President of the Lands Tribunal may direct that the tribunal shall hear or determine any case calling for special knowledge with the assistance of one or more assessors. Assessors are frequently required in Admiralty cases, to advise the court on matters of nautical skill and seamanship, and scientific advisers are often appointed in patent cases, but they are rarely appointed otherwise.

An assessor is not a member of the court, nor is he an independent expert, an advocate or a witness. His functions are to advise the court on technical matters, to help the judge understand and draw proper inferences from the evidence, to suggest questions which might be put to expert witnesses and to assist the judge to appreciate the differences between expert opinions.

An assessor should not decide a case: that is the function of the court. The judge may properly reject the advice of an assessor and take his own view of the matter. Where the court is assisted by an assessor it has a discretion whether or not to hear expert evidence.

(2) Court experts

The High Court may appoint one or more independent experts to report on a technical matter, either under the Rules of the Supreme Court (RSC) or under its inherent powers.

RSC Order 40 empowers the court in a non-jury case to appoint one or more court experts "to inquire and report upon any question of fact or opinion not involving questions of law or of construction", provided the question is one for an expert witness and application for the appointment is made by one or both of the parties. The name of the expert, the question to be submitted to him and his instructions (if any) are to be agreed between the parties or, failing agreement, nominated or settled by the court. The court has an inherent power to appoint an expert and may do so on its own initiative.

The report of an independent expert must be sent to the court for distribution to the parties. If any part of it is not accepted by all the parties, it is treated as information furnished to the court and given such weight as the court thinks fit. A party may (with leave) cross-examine a court expert, and may also, provided reasonable prior notice has been given to the other parties, call one or (with leave) more expert witnesses to give evidence on the same question. The report of an expert is not an award; it is provided for the information and guidance of the court.

Court experts are rarely appointed in this country: our adversary system of trial is more suited to the use of expert witnesses. Court experts are much used in civil law countries, where the courts adopt a more inquisitorial role.

(3) Expert witnesses

A court or tribunal usually obtains assistance on scientific and technical matters from expert witnesses called by the parties. They are particularly suited to the adversary system of litigation where the onus is on the parties to put all materials for decision before the court.

An expert witness may be defined as a person with skill and experience in a scientific, technical or professional matter who is allowed to give an expert opinion for the assistance of the court. An expert witness may also give evidence of a technical fact perceived by him, which could not have been perceived by a layman, and of the facts on which his opinion is based. He may combine the roles of witness of fact and expert witness. It is for the court to decide whether expert evidence may be adduced on any particular subject and whether a witness is an expert witness.

The fundamental distinction between a witness of fact and an expert witness should be noted. A witness of fact may not express an opinion except where this is necessary to convey facts personally perceived by him. Thus, he may say that he saw A run from a house although what he is really saying is that he saw a man run from the house and formed the opinion that it was A. He may not, however, express an opinion on facts perceived by others, nor, except as a way of conveying facts, on the question to be decided by the court. Such opinions would be irrelevant and inadmissible. An expert witness, however, may express an opinion on any relevant matter on which he is qualified to give expert evidence. This includes an issue in the proceedings (section 3 Civil Evidence Act 1972, Appendix C p. 495 below). His skill and experience in a technical or professional field allow him to express an opinion which would be inadmissible in the evidence of a witness of fact.

The duty of an expert witness:

> "... is to furnish the judge or jury with the necessary scientific criteria for testing the accuracy of their conclusions, so as to enable the judge or jury to form their own independent judgment by the application of these criteria to the facts proved in evidence."
>
> (per Lord President Cooper in *Davie v. Edinburgh Magistrates* 1953 SC 34 at p. 40).

Although called by one of the parties, an expert witness is not an advocate for that party: he has a duty to assist the court or tribunal to find the truth by giving his objective and impartial opinion.

Strictly speaking an expert witness does not give evidence, but places before the court information to enable it to take judicial notice of those matters necessary for its decision. In practice, the testimony of an expert witness is always called "expert evidence".

Expert evidence is not placed in any special category of evidence which is binding on the court: it may be rejected even though the experts are of the highest standing (*Kentucky Fried Chicken (GB) Ltd v Secretary of State for the Environment* (1977) 245 EG 839). A court or tribunal is not bound to accept uncontradicted expert evidence, although an expert tribunal should not reject such evidence and use its own special knowledge to form a different view of the facts without putting that view to the parties and giving them an opportunity of dealing with it (*Fox v P. G. Wellfair Ltd* [1981] 2 Lloyd's Rep 514; Chapter 10 p. 319 below).

Expert evidence is given to remedy the deficiencies in the technical knowledge possessed by a tribunal. The standard for deciding whether expert assistance is required is the general knowledge of that tribunal not the specialised knowledge of a particular member. It follows, therefore, that where a court or tribunal is an expert one the scope for receiving expert evidence is more limited. An expert tribunal may properly decline to hear expert evidence on a matter within its own expertise, but in a complex technical dispute expert evidence may help to reduce the length of a hearing by simplifying the issues to be decided by the tribunal. The fact that a tribunal is an expert one does not prevent it listening to expert evidence: the reason for an expert tribunal is so that it can understand the evidence more easily, not so that it can dispense with it entirely (*Winchester City Council v Secretary of State for the Environment* (1978) 36 P & CR 455 affirmed (1979) 39 P & CR 1; *James Longley & Co Ltd v South West Thames Regional Health Authority* (1983) *The Times* 14th July 1983; Chapter 10 p. 319 below).

EXPERT EVIDENCE

(1) Subjects of expert evidence

The subjects of expert evidence are many and varied, but all have the same characteristics. They are matters of fact or opinion, of a technical nature and usually outside the normal knowledge and experience of the tribunal of fact. Expert evidence may not be given on a question of law (except foreign law), e.g. it may not be given on the interpretation of documents or legislation. The following examples illustrate the characteristics and subject-matter of expert evidence.

Medical evidence is commonly heard in the courts and may have been one of the earliest subjects on which expert evidence was admitted. Expert medical testimony has been received on causes of death, disease and injury, the effects of poisons, the length of a gestation period and the effect of hospitals on the health of a neighbourhood.

Handwriting is a subject on which both evidence of fact and opinion may be given; it illustrates the distinction between these two types of evidence. A witness of fact may identify a person's handwriting provided he is acquainted with that writing, e.g. by having seen him write. This is evidence of fact. A witness with expertise in handwriting, on the other hand, may express an opinion based on his skill and experience as applied to the document in question. He may give his opinion as to whether the writing is natural or imitated, or show points of comparison. Expert testimony may be received on the probable date of ancient writing or to decipher words beneath obliterations, erasures or alterations.

Expert evidence may be given on commercial practice and principles of accounting. In a tax case, an accountant expressed an opinion that, in accordance with accountancy principles, certain expenditure was of a revenue nature. The Court of Appeal held that, although such evidence was of assistance, it was not conclusive, and the decision as to whether expenditure is revenue or capital is not a question of fact but one of law solely for the decision of the court (*Heather v P E Consulting Group* [1973] 1 Ch. 189).

The value of chattels or an interest in land are well established as subjects of expert testimony. Expert evidence was recently given that an aribtrator would be able to determine a single fixed rent for a period of 21 years under an option to renew a lease (*Bracknell Development Corporation v Greenlees Lennards Ltd* (1981) 260 EG 500). A valuer may express an opinion on value, but he may not say whether words dealing with value in a statute ("nominal rent") have any technical meaning to surveyors. This is a question of law and expert evidence is not admissible on the meaning of ordinary English words in a modern statute (*Marquis Camden v CIR* [1914] 1 KB 641 affirmed [1915] AC 241). Similarly, in a dispute regarding the extent of land to be taken for a railway, expert evidence of engineers was not admitted on the interpretation of the authorising Act and deposited plans (*Dowling v Pontypool etc Ry Co* LR 18 Eq 714). And in a case concerned with the interpretation of the RIBA form of contract, evidence of an insurance expert was not admitted to show the practical difficulties which would arise if a building contractor were required to insure the building owner (*Gold v Patman and Fotheringham Ltd* [1958] 1 WLR 697). In these cases the interpretation of the Acts and contract respectively were questions of law, on which expert evidence was inadmissible.

Finally, expert evidence will not usually be admitted on matters of aesthetic taste, particularly where the tribunal is an expert one. Thus, in a planning case, *Winchester City Council v Secretary of State for the Environment* (1979) 39 P & CR 1, an inspector refused to adjourn a public inquiry to allow expert evidence to be given on the architectural merit of a house. It was held on appeal that this was not a scientific or technical matter, but one of aesthetic taste or commonsense, on which the inspector had rightly said that he did not need to hear evidence. But in *Re Pinion* [1965] 1 Ch 85, there was a gift of a studio and its contents to trustees, and the point at issue was whether this gift was of an educational character or for the public benefit. Expert evidence on the aesthetic merits of the proposed exhibits was admitted so that the court could judge whether they were conducive to the education of the public.

(2) Competency, compellability and bias

(a) *Competency*. The competency of an expert witness is a preliminary question for the court to decide. There are no rules and each case must be decided according to the particular circumstances. An expert witness must be skilled by qualification or experience in the subject-matter of his evidence, but he need not have acquired that skill in the normal course of his profession or business. For example, a solicitor has been allowed to give expert evidence on handwriting. The admissibility of expert evidence is a question of law, but the weight to be given to such evidence is a question of fact.

An expert witness must have expertise in the *particular* subject-matter of his evidence. For example, in *US Shipping Board v St Albans* [1931] AC 632, an action rose out of a collision between two ships in Sydney harbour. The exact spot where this occurred was important. Photographs had been taken from a third moving vessel showing the two ships before, during and after the collision and leave was given by the appellate court for evidence to be given by three land surveyors. Based on the alignment of pairs of background objects in the photographs, they fixed the position of the camera when each photograph was taken and then, by reference to the background, localised the spot where the collision took place. It was held by the Privy Council, however, that the skill or science needed to convert a landscape photograph into a map is not that of a land surveyor and, in the absence of expert evidence on this particular matter, a reversal of the trial judge by the appellate court was not warranted.

Although an expert witness should be competent it would appear that, if he is not, he has the same immunity from negligence as any other witness in judicial proceedings. Thus, in *Evans v London Hospital Medical College & Others* [1981] 1 WLR 184, a mother was charged with the murder of her son after an analysis of certain organs of his body revealed the presence of morphine. Following further investigations, however, the prosecution offered no evidence at her trial and she was acquitted. The mother then claimed damages against the defendants in respect of their alleged negligent analysis. The claim was dismissed by a master on the grounds that it disclosed no reasonable cause of action. This was upheld by the judge on appeal. It was held that the immunity from civil actions given to a witness in judicial proceedings in respect of his evidence, extended to statements made prior to the issue of a writ (or commencement of a prosecution) provided they were made for the purpose of a possible action (or prosecution) and where such an action (or prosecution) was being considered. This immunity was not confined to the preparation of a proof of evidence but extended to preliminary work (in this case the collation and analysis of material). The defendants would, of course, have appeared in court as expert witnesses but no distinction was apparently drawn in this judgment between an expert witness and a lay witness in relation to immunity from civil actions. It would appear, therefore, that an expert witness has no liability for negligence in respect of his evidence provided litigation was under consideration.

(b) *Compellability.* A *subpoena* may be served on a witness of fact to compel him to give evidence. It would appear that an expert may also be compelled to give his expert opinion by the same process, although there are conflicting decisions on this point. In *Seyfang v Searle & Co* [1973] 1 QB 148, application was made in civil proceedings in a court in the USA for an order requiring certain medical experts in this country to be examined on oath and to produce the working papers of articles published several years earlier. The order was made by the master but rescinded on appeal by the judge. He held that the court had a discretion in the matter, and that the principles to be applied were those applied to the calling and examination of witnesses in English courts. These were that a witness of fact was generally required to testify; but, as a general rule, an expert was not required to give expert evidence against his wishes in a case where he had no connection with the facts or history of the matter in issue, and especially where he could not give the required evidence without a breach of confidence or considerable time and study.

This decision, and the interlocutory decision to the same effect in *Lively v City of Munich* [1977] 1 Lloyd's Rep 418, were not considered by the Court of Appeal in *Harmony Shipping Co SA v Davis* [1979] 3 All ER 177. In this case, a handwriting expert was served with a *subpoena* to attend and give evidence on behalf of the defendants. He was reluctant to do so because he had already advised the plaintiffs (to their disadvantage) in the same action and his rule was that he would not advise both parties. When he was initially approached by the defendants he overlooked the fact that he had already advised the plaintiffs. He advised the defendants (to their advantage) but then refused to act further when he discovered his previous involvement in the case. It was held that the court could compel an expert witness to give evidence, subject only to any claim he may have to professional privilege. Lord Denning MR said (p. 182):

> "There is no property in a witness as to fact. There is no property in an expert witness as to the facts he has observed and his own independent opinion on them. There being no such property in a witness, it is the duty of a witness to come to court and give his evidence in so far as he is directed by the judge to do so."

It was also argued, but not established, that there was a contract, express or implied, between the plaintiffs and the expert, that he would not voluntarily assist the defendants and would use his best endeavours not to appear on both sides. The court said that a contract by which a witness binds himself not to give evidence before the court, where he could be compelled to do so, is contrary to public policy and unenforceable.

The decision in this case is not entirely satisfactory and may not be as wide as it might appear. An important point is that the application to set aside the *subpoena* was made by the plaintiffs (not by the expert) and was, in effect, an attempt to limit the defendants' evidence by excluding evidence known to be to the plaintiffs' disadvantage.

(c) *Bias*. A criticism of expert evidence is that, because the expert witnesses are retained by the parties, they are biased in favour of their respective clients and will not put their objective opinions before the court. In the nineteenth century there was much outspoken judicial comment on the unsatisfactory nature and bias of expert evidence. Bias will certainly affect the weight to be given to such evidence. There appears to be no recent case where strong words have been spoken on this subject although in *Whitehouse v Jordan* [1981] 1 All ER 267, Lord Wilberforce stressed the need for impartiality in expert's reports. In this case a joint medical report for the plaintiff was prepared as a result of conferences between two professors and counsel: it was actually "settled" by counsel. Lord Wilberforce said (p. 276):

> "While some degree of consultation between experts and legal advisers is entirely proper, it is necessary that expert evidence presented to the court should be, and should be seen to be, the independent product of the expert, uninfluenced as to form or content by the exigencies of litigation. To the extent that it is not, the evidence is likely to be not only incorrect but self defeating."

Similarly, in *Kelly v London Transport Executive* [1982] 2 All ER 842, the Court of Appeal indicated that it would be wrong for an expert's report to be amended at the instigation of his client's lawyers in order to suit their case and to conceal matters detrimental to the client.

(3) Fact and opinion in expert evidence

An expert's opinion may be based on his general professional skill and experience; or it may be (and usually is) based on facts: proved by himself, proved by others, admitted, agreed or hypothetical. An expert witness might not express an opinion at all, but might give evidence of facts that can only be discovered by a skilled person, e.g. by the use of a microscope or as the result of experiments. Thus, an expert witness may be a witness of opinion, or of fact and opinion or fact only.

The leading case on expert evidence of value is *English Exporters (London) Ltd v Eldonwall Ltd* (1972) 25 P & CR 379, subsequently approved by the Court of Appeal in *Rogers v Rosedimond Investments (Blakes Markets) Ltd* (1978) 247 EG 467. This case concerned the fixing of a rent and an interim rent on the renewal of a business tenancy under Part II of the Landlord and Tenant Act 1954. Megarry J considered the position of an expert witness as witness of fact and opinion and discussed the role of hearsay in expert evidence. Several extracts from this important judgment are given below.

(a) *Opinion based on experience.* The opinion of an expert witness may be based solely on his *general* professional knowledge and experience. The fact that this opinion may be founded on matters of which he has no first-hand knowledge does not infringe the rule against hearsay evidence:

> "As an expert witness the valuer is entitled to express his opinion about matters within his field of competence. In building up his opinions about values, he will no doubt have learned much from transactions in which he has himself been engaged, and of which he could give first-hand evidence. But he will also have learned much from many other sources, including much of which he could give no first-hand evidence. Textbooks, journals, reports of auctions and other dealings, and information obtained from his professional brethren and others, some related to particular transactions and some more general and indefinite, will all have contributed their share. Doubtless much, or most, of this will be accurate, though some will not; and even what is accurate so far as it goes may be incomplete, in that nothing may have been said of some special element which affects value. Nevertheless, the opinion that the expert expresses is none the worse because it is in part derived from the matters of which he could give no direct evidence. Even if some of the extraneous information which he acquires in this way is inaccurate or incomplete, the errors and omissions will often tend to cancel each other out; and the valuer, after all, is an expert in this field, so that the less reliable the knowledge that he has about the details of some reported transaction, the more his experience will tell him that he should be ready to make some discount from the weight that he gives it in contributing

to his overall sense of values. Some aberrant transactions
may stand so far out of line that he will give them little or no
weight. No question of giving hearsay evidence arises in such
cases; the witness states his opinion from his general experience."
(*Eldonwall* p. 383).

(b) *Opinion based on facts.* An expert witness will usually base his
opinion on facts, and where he does so he must put before the
court both facts and opinion:

"Before a court can assess the value of an opinion it must
know the facts on which it is based. If the expert has been
misinformed about the facts or has taken irrelevant facts into
consideration or has omitted to consider relevant ones, the
opinion is likely to be valueless. In our judgment, counsel
calling an expert witness should in examination-in-chief ask
his witness to state the facts upon which his opinion is based.
It is wrong to leave the other side to elicit the facts by cross-
examination."
(per Lawton LJ in *R v Turner* [1975] 1 QB 834 at p. 840).

Furthermore, where an expert witness relies on the existence or
non-existence of some fact which is basic to the question on which
he is asked to express an opinion, that fact must be proved by
admissible evidence (see *Eldonwall* p. 69 below and *R v Abadom*
[1983] 1 WLR 126, see p. 76 below).

Where the reports of expert witnesses are exchanged before
trial, they should contain both facts and opinion (see p. 000
below). The facts are also necessary to allow the court to form its
own opinion, or to rely on facts in preference to opinion. Thus, in
Goldsmid v Tunbridge Wells Improvement Commissioners (1866) LR 1
Ch App 349, the court decided a case concerning the pollution of
a stream on the basis of facts proved and not on the conclusions
drawn by expert witnesses from the scientific investigation of
those facts.

The facts on which an expert witness has formed his opinion
may be (i) proved by him, (ii) proved by other witnesses, (iii)
agreed (admitted), (iv) hypothetical.

(i) *Facts proved by the expert witness.* Where an expert witness
bases his opinion on facts, he may be able to prove those facts
himself: he is then a witness of fact and opinion. But he is not in
any privileged position as a witness of fact and must prove his
facts by admissible evidence.

Hearsay. The above rule applies to expert valuation evidence,
a subject on which there was some confusion until the *Eldonwall*

case. The problem mainly concerns the comparable transactions on which an opinion of value is usually based: must
they be proved by direct evidence or is hearsay sufficient? The
position is now clear:

> "... details of comparable transactions upon which a
> valuer intends to rely in his evidence must, if they are to be
> put before the court, be confined to those details which
> have been, or will be, proved by admissible evidence,
> given either by the valuer himself or in some other way. I
> know of no special rule giving expert valuation witnesses
> the right to give hearsay evidence of facts: ..."
> (*Eldonwall* pp. 384–5).

Earlier in his judgment, Megarry J explained the position
where an expert valuation witness gives evidence of fact
(pp. 383–4):

> "On the other hand, quite apart from merely expressing
> his opinion, the expert often is able to give factual evidence
> as well. If he has first-hand knowledge of a transaction, he
> can speak of that. He may himself have measured the
> premises and conducted the negotiations which led to a
> letting of them at £X, which comes to £Y per square foot;
> and he himself may have read the lease and seen that it
> contains no provisions, other than some particular clause,
> which would have any material effect on the valuation; and
> then he may express his opinion on the value. So far as the
> expert gives factual evidence, he is doing what any other
> witness of fact may do, namely, speaking of that which he
> has perceived for himself. No doubt in many valuation
> cases the requirement of first-hand evidence is not pressed
> to an extreme: if the witness has not himself measured the
> premises, but it has been done by his assistant under his
> supervision, the expert's figures are often accepted without
> requiring the assistant to be called to give evidence. Again,
> it may be that it would be possible for a valuer to fill a gap
> in his first-hand knowledge of a transaction by some
> method such as stating in his evidence that he has made
> diligent inquiries of some person who took part in the
> transaction in question but despite receiving full answers
> to his inquiries, he discovered nothing which suggested to
> him that the transaction had any unusual features which
> would affect the value as a comparable. But basically, the
> expert's factual evidence on matters of fact is in the same
> position as the factual evidence of any other witness."

Where only hearsay evidence can be given of a comparable transaction it can now be dealt with by the notice procedure under the Civil Evidence Act 1968 (Chapter 2 p. 48 above). Notice may not be necessary where there has been an exchange of expert reports prior to the trial (see p. 84 below) and the comparable transaction is included in that report. If this is not the case, a party wishing to adduce hearsay evidence of a comparable transaction must first serve notice on the other party, who may require direct evidence to be given. The court has a discretion to admit hearsay evidence, even though the requisite notices have not been served. In practice, expert witnesses frequently agree each other's comparables before the hearing, thus avoiding the need to prove them by evidence. This is to be encouraged and a party who unreasonably refuses to do so may be penalised in costs.

Where an expert witness negotiated a transaction, which he uses as a comparable in subsequent litigation, he may, of course, give direct evidence of that transaction. But if this evidence includes correspondence to establish the state of mind, motives, knowledge, bargaining position or toughness in negotiation of the parties, then the other party to the current litigation may object to the admission of such correspondence, unless the writers of the letters are called to give evidence (see the remarks of Megaw LJ in *Gallagher Estates Ltd v Walker* (1973) 28 P & CR 113, but he did not express a view as to whether or not this documentary evidence should be admitted despite such objection). Similarly, letters written to an expert witness about other negotiations are hearsay and only admissible by consent of the other party to the current litigation or with leave of the court. If such consent or leave is not given the writers of the letters must be called as witnesses (*Harding v Cardiff City Council* (1971) 219 EG 885). Similarly, in *Prior Brothers & Sisters of the Hospital of St. John the Baptist v Kent County Council* (1970) 214 EG 359, it was stated by the Lands Tribunal that letters between a surveyor and client regarding the basis of valuation would not be of assistance in the absence of oral evidence, and even then it seems unlikely that confidential discussions between persons on the same side would carry much weight in the analysis of a transaction.

An agreement with a third party by or on behalf of one of the parties to the current dispute is admissible in evidence. In *Routh v Central Land Board* (1957) 8 P & CR 290 and *Stockbridge Mill Co Ltd v Central Land Board* [1954] 1 WLR 886, determinations of development value agreed by the district valuer under the Town and Country Planning Act 1947 were held to be admissible in evidence, notwithstanding that the register containing the development values was not a public document:

> "Once one comes to the conclusion—and I think it is plainly right in principle—that actual transactions are admissible if sufficiently comparable, then agreed figures must be also admissible if the subject-matter of the agreed figures is comparable land."
>
> (per Somerwell L J in *Stockbridge* at p. 889; see also *Pointer v Norwich Assessment Committee* [1922] 2 KB 471, p. 78 below).

Post-valuation date evidence. Where a value or compensation is to be assessed as at a particular date, the question arises as to whether facts occurring after that date are admissible in evidence. Three propositions may be stated.

First, comparable transactions agreed after the relevant date are admissible as evidence of value unless excluded, expressly or by implication. Thus, in an Australian compensation case, *Melwood Units Pty Ltd v Commissioner of Main Roads* (1978) 38 P & CR 195, the Privy Council held that the Appeal Court had erred in law in rejecting evidence of the price paid on a sale of adjoining land nine months after the valuation date. Lord Russell of Killowen said (p. 204):

> "Now, it is plain that, in assessing values for the purposes of compensation for resumption on a compulsory acquisition, a tribunal is not required to close its mind to transactions subsequent to the date of resumption; they may well be relevant or of assistance to a greater or lesser degree ..."

This principle has been applied to rent review arbitrations although here regard must be had to the words of the lease, which might exclude certain categories of evidence. For example, in *Segama NV v Penny Le Roy Ltd* (1983) 269 EG 322, the arbitrator was required to determine "the market rent" of a shop, defined as "the yearly rental value of the demised premises having regard to rental values current at the relevant time for similar property ... let with vacant possession." He admitted evidence of post-review date comparables, including rents agreed between landlords and sitting tenants. It was held that he was entitled to do so: such evidence was admissible and it was a matter for the arbitrator to assess the weight to be given to a comparable rent, whether agreed before or after the relevant date. Essentially the question was one of the construction of the lease. The phrase "rental values current at the relevant time" meant the current *worth* of the property and it was entirely plausible that the arbitrator should have regard to the worth of similar property, as evidenced by rents agreed before *or after* the review date. This evidence was relevant and admissible, it was not excluded under the terms of the lease and its admission was consistent with the state of the authorities.

Furthermore, the arbitrator was right to have regard to rents agreed between landlords and sitting tenants, despite the requirement of the lease that the shop is assumed to be let with vacant possession. Although "the market rent" was probably a rent which would be paid in the market for vacant premises this did not preclude the arbitrator from considering rents agreed between existing landlords and existing tenants. He must consider how far such evidence assisted him in determining the question before him and he might think it right to adjust such a rent to what it would have been for vacant possession.

Where the market has altered materially after the date of valuation then evidence of transactions in that changed market is unlikely to be admissible: it would be irrelevant to the question of value in a different market at the valuation date. A valuer or arbitrator at that date is not to be assumed to know of the subsequent changes in the market and, therefore, evidence of those change is inadmissible (see the decision of Whitford J in *Ponsford v HMS Aerosols Ltd* (1976) and of Judge Fay QC in *Industrial Properties (Barton Hill) Ltd v Associated Electrical Industries Ltd* (1977), both unreported but referred to in Bernstein & Reynolds *Handbook of Rent Review*, pp. [DC 241] and [DC 171] respectively).

The second proposition regarding post-valuation date evidence is that where compensation for future loss or damage is to be assessed at a particular date, evidence is admissible of facts occurring after that date. In the leading case, *Bwllfa & Merthyr Dare Steam Collieries (1891) Ltd v Pontypridd Waterworks Co* [1903] AC 426, owners of coal mines under and near waterworks were prevented from working the coal and claimed statutory compensation. In an arbitration to determine the amount of this compensation the question arose as to the admissibility of evidence to show that the value of coal rose after the date of assessment. It was held by the House of Lords that this evidence was admissible. Lord MacNaghton said (p. 431):

> "If the question goes to arbitration, the arbitrator's duty is to determine the amount of compensation payable. In order to enable him to come to a just and true conclusion it is his duty, I think, to avail himself of all information at

hand at the time of making his award which may be laid before him. Why should he listen to conjecture on a matter which has become an accomplished fact? Why should he guess when he can calculate? With the light before him, why should he shut his eyes and grope in the dark?''

This principle applies to the assessment of compensation for disturbance on compulsory purchase. In *London County Council v Tobin* (1959) 10 P & CR 79, the Lands Tribunal assessed the loss of goodwill following the claimant's move to alternative premises by deducting from the value of the goodwill at the old premises the value of the goodwill at the alternative premises. When making this assessment the tribunal took into account known profits after the date of assessment and it was held by the Court of Appeal that it was correct to do so.

The third proposition is that post-valuation date evidence is not admissible to show how the inherent possibilitites or prospects attaching to a property at the date of valuation have turned out by the time the valuation is actually made. Thus, in *Gaze v Holden* (1982) 266 EG 998, the principal issue before the court was whether arbitrators valuing a farm subject to a tenancy ought to have regard to the possibility that the lease might be surrendered before its expiration and also to the fact that it had been surrendered, if that had happened by the date when the value was actually determined. There were several factors in this case indicating the likelihood that the tenant would surrender his tenancy.

Judge Finlay QC (sitting as a judge of the Chancery Division) held that the *Bwllfa* principle did not apply to the *value* of a property at a particular date (as opposed to the assessment of compensation for loss or damage) and, therefore, events which had occurred after that date could not be taken into account as known facts. He said (p. 1004):

"... 'valuation in the usual way' means taking into account the events which have happened as at the date when the property falls to be valued ... and taking into account not only the actualities at that date but the possibilities in relation to all the circumstances; and that the valuer has, as best he can, to form his own judgment as to how these possibilities and the various prospects that are inherent in the then existing situation affect the value of the property as at that date; but he is not entitled to take into account events which happened subsequently and which resolve how these various possibilities and prospects in fact turn out. To do so would be to introduce into the valuation a species of foreknowledge which would not be available to any willing buyer or willing seller entering into a contract as at the date upon which the property falls to be valued."

Similarly, in *Duvan Estates Ltd v Rossette Sunshine Savouries Ltd* (1981) 261 EG 364, it was held that the arbitrator in a rent review dispute should not have had regard to trading accounts relating to a period after the review date, which he considered in order to verify whether the misgivings about trading expressed by the tenant at that date turned out to be justified.

Accounts. Trading accounts may be admissible in evidence in a dispute of value, provided they are relevant. Factors to be taken into account on the question of relevance are the nature of the property, the availability of better evidence and the period of the accounts.

Thus, in *Harewood Hotels Ltd v Harris* (1957) 170 EG 177, the county court judge admitted evidence of the trading accounts of an hotel for the previous five years when determining the rent under section 34 of the Landlord and Tenant Act 1954. The Court of Appeal held that, in the circumstances of this particular case, he was right to do so. The accounts were evidence of the earning capacity of the hotel to a potential lessee and were admissible for the purpose of estimating the open market rent, but for no other purpose. They were not admissible, for example, to show that the tenants should have some concession on the grounds of hardship nor, conversely, to indicate that they might pay more rent than an outsider because they did not wish to give up possession nor to show what the particular tenants could afford to pay in rent. Furthermore, the exclusion of the tenants' occupation and goodwill under section 34 (a) and (b) of the 1954 Act did not prevent the judge from taking the accounts into consideration for the limited purpose of fixing the rent to a potential tenant. The type of property in this case should be noted. Also it appears from the report that there was a lack of other comparable evidence.

In another case concerning the renewal of a lease under the Landlord and Tenant Act 1954, *W. J. Barton Ltd v Long Acre Securities Ltd* (1981) 262 EG 877, the Court of Appeal refused to uphold an order for specific discovery of past accounts relating to a shop and flat and another shop occupied by the same tenants some miles away. The *Harewood Hotels* decision was considered and restricted to properties where the ascertainment of the rent may depend on likely profitability, eg petrol filling stations, racecourses or theatres. It was not to be elevated to a general proposition that accounts are relevant and admissible in every application for a new tenancy under the Landlord & Tenant Act 1954. Evidence of trading accounts would be of no assistance when fixing the rent of ordinary shop premises with no peculiar features, in an area with plenty of comparable premises from which the rental can be deduced.

As stated above, accounts relating to a period after the valuation date are inadmissible to verify whether misgivings expressed by the tenant at that date turned out to be justified (see *Duvan Estates* case p. 74 above).

Finally, mention should be made of a recent case relating to the discovery of accounts of public houses for the purposes of a rating appeal to the Lands Tribunal. The tribunal refused to order discovery because, although it was not prepared to find that this evidence was irrelevant, it was of the opinion that the accounts would not be of any real help and it was in the public interest that a trader should be protected from disclosure of confidential documents which could be of assistance to third parties unconnected with the proceedings. Relevance alone was insufficient to require disclosure. Application was then made to the High Court for an order for disclosure of the accounts but this was refused (*City of London Corporation v Watneys (London) Ltd* [1983] RVR 5).

It should be noted that the above statement of the law relating to post-valuation date evidence and accounts applies both to facts proved by an expert witness and a lay witness.

(ii) *Facts proved by other witnesses.* An expert witness may give an opinion based on facts proved by other witnesses:

> "... factual evidence that (the expert) cannot give himself is sometimes adduced in some other way, as by the testimony of some other witness who was himself concerned in the transaction in question, or by proving some document which carried the transaction in question, or by proving some document which carried the transaction through, or recorded it; and to the transaction thus established, like the transactions which the expert himself has proved, the expert may apply his experience and opinions, as tending to support or qualify his views".
> (*Eldonwall* p. 384).

An expert witness may not give an opinion based on facts not before the court nor on inadmissible hearsay. For example, in a case concerning the renewal of a business tenancy, *Rogers v Rosedimond Investments (Blakes Markets) Ltd* (1978) 247 EG 467, evidence was given by adjoining traders that they were disappointed with the trading area and also as to the rents they considered reasonable for their shops. It was held by the Court of Appeal that an expert witness assisting the court with an opinion of rental value could properly take into account the evidence regarding the trading position, but the traders' opinions regarding rent were irrelevant and should not have been considered by the county court judge.

Where a witness is called to prove a comparable rent he should have first-hand knowledge of the agreement of that rent. Thus, in *UDS Tailoring Ltd v BL Holdings Ltd* (1981) 261 EG 49, the judge ignored evidence of a comparable rent because it was given by an estate management assistant who could not say how the rent was calculated but could only state what he was told to do when recording it.

Books, articles and other technical literature may be referred to by an expert witness in support of his opinion. This literature is not itself evidence but by incorporation it becomes part of the expert's evidence. The books or other literature must be of an authoritative nature and treated as such by the profession or trade to which the expert belongs. They may only be used to support the expert's opinion on, or approach to, a technical problem, and not as evidence of the facts on which the expert is currently expressing an opinion. For example, a valuer could properly look for guidance to *Modern Methods of Valuation* (see *Corisand Investments Ltd v Druce & Co* (1978) 248 EG 315 at p. 318), but he may not refer to details of a transaction that he has seen in a journal as the basis of his opinion of value (this would be inadmissible hearsay: see *Eldonwall* p. 385). In *R v Abadom* [1983] 1 WLR 126, A was charged with robbery, during the course of which a pane of glass in a window was broken. An expert witness gave evidence that he had analysed fragments of glass found embedded in A's shoes and also glass from the broken pane and discovered that they all had the same refractive index. He consulted Home Office statistics, found that only 4% of the samples referred to in those statistics had the same refractive index as the glass he had analysed and expressed the opinion that this was strong evidence that the glass in A's shoes had come from the broken pane. It was held that the use of the Home Office statistics by the expert witness was not contrary to the hearsay rule. Kerr LJ said (p. 131):

> "Once the primary facts on which their opinion is based have been proved by admissible evidence, they are entitled to draw on the work of others as part of the process of arriving at their conclusion. However, where they have done so, they should refer to this material in their evidence

so that the cogency and probative value of their conclusion can be tested and evaluated by reference to it."

The primary facts in this case were, of course, the analysis of the glass fragments, direct evidence of which was given by the expert witness himself.

In a personal injuries case it was held that actuarial evidence would rarely be received by the court to determine economic loss, and the judge refused to admit the tables and commentaries contained in an HMSO publication *Actuarial Tables with Explanatory Notes for Use in Personal Injury and Fatal Accident Cases*, unless evidence was adduced as to the correctness of their contents (*Spiers v Halliday* (1984) *The Times* 30th June 1984).

Published works may be admitted as evidence of facts of a public nature under section 9(2)(b) of the Civil Evidence Act 1968 (see Chapter 2 p. 49 above).

Where an *opinion* given by another expert in an earlier case is put to an expert witness and he approves it, that opinion becomes part of his evidence:

> "An expert witness must be allowed, if his opinion is challenged, to say that it is not merely his own opinion but it is harmony with the opinions of other experts in the same field, and for this purpose to cite their opinions in support of his own."
>
> (per Pearson LJ in *R v Deputy Industrial Injuries Commissioner* [1965] 1 QB 456 at p. 483, see also Diplock LJ at p. 490 where he said that this rule also applies to courts of law applying technical rules of evidence).

The fact that the earlier opinion is hearsay in the later case goes to weight and not admissibility.

Where, however, the existence of a *fact* is in issue, a report made by another expert, who is not called to give evidence, is not admissible as evidence of that fact merely by the production of the report (*R v Abadom* (above); see p. 85 below for the admission of hearsay expert evidence).

A decision on a question of fact in an earlier case (other than one of foreign law) is not usually admissible as proof of that fact in a later case: it must be independently proved (see Chapter 2 p. 54 above).

(iii) *Admitted facts.* An expert opinion may be based on facts formally admitted (agreed). In valuation disputes details of the property (floor areas, construction, tenure, etc) and comparable transactions are frequently agreed and thus form the common basis of the experts' different opinions of value:

> "When a list of comparables is being prepared for the trial, as is usual and convenient, it is all too common to include in the list transactions upon which there will be no admissible evidence but only hearsay of a greater or lesser degree of reliability. If the parties exchange lists of comparables at an early date, often much time and money can be saved by the experts on each side agreeing such of the transactions in each list as, after any necessary inquiry, they feel they can accept as being reliably summarised; and in this way the additional expense of proving a favourable comparable not within an expert's own knowledge can be avoided. But if the other side will not accept the facts, then either the transaction must be proved by admissible evidence or it must be omitted as a comparable."

(*Eldonwall* pp. 386–7).

Facts may also be treated as admissions even though they were not specifically agreed between the parties for the purposes of the litigation. For example, entries in the valuation list relating to comparable properties are admissible as evidence of value in a rating appeal; they are in the nature of admissions against the valuation officer (*Pointer v Norwich Assessment Committee* [1922] 2 KB 471 at p. 477). Furthermore, the valuation officer will not be allowed to impugn the assessments in his own list or the list of another area (*Burroughs Machines Ltd v Mooney (VO)* [1977] RA 45. See also *Routh v Central Land Board* (1957) 8 P & CR 290 and *Stockbridge Mill Co Ltd v Central Land Board* [1954] 1 WLR 886, p. 70 above).

"Without prejudice" statements. Statements made expressly or impliedly "without prejudice", in an attempt to settle a dispute, will not usually be received in evidence. They are not admissions. Where a document is claimed to be privileged from disclosure under this rule, the court may look at the contents before ruling on its admissibility. The "without prejudice" rule applies even though the strict rules of evidence do not apply to the particular tribunal. For example, arbitrators who conducted an arbitration under trade rules permitting them "to act upon evidence and/or information as they may think fit" were not allowed to have regard to evidence of "without prejudice" negotiations (*Finney Lock Seeds Ltd v George Mitchell (Chesterhall) Ltd* [1979] 2 Lloyd's Rep 301). Evidence of a "without prejudice" statement will become admissible where no objection is raised when it is put forward (*Shield Properties & Investments Ltd v Anglo-Overseas Transport Co Ltd* (1984) 273 EG 69).

The protection given by this rule only applies to a statement made in an attempt to settle an existing dispute. For example, in *Norwich Union Life Insurance Society v Tony Waller Ltd* (1984) 270 EG 42, it was held that a landlord's notice purporting to institute a rent review and marked "without prejudice" was admissible in evidence because there was no dispute between the parties when it was served. It was an opening shot: no war had been declared and no dispute had arisen.

A "without prejudice" statement may be made by a party to the dispute or his agent, and it may be made to the other party (or his agent) or to a third party acting as an intermediary. For example, where litigation was imminent between a husband and wife and one of them consulted a probation officer regarding a reconciliation, statements made to him (by either party) were held to be privileged and inadmissible in evidence. (*Mole v Mole* [1950] P 21).

Where the first letter in a sequence of correspondence regarding the settlement of a dispute is marked "without prejudice", then the answer and all subsequent letters will also bear that label even though not expressly so marked, unless there is a clear break in the correspondence which indicates that the ensuing letters are open. This rule will also apply to the *whole* sequence of correspondence where the "without prejudice" label is introduced on the second letter. Thus, in *Oliver v Nautilus Steam Shipping Co Ltd* [1903] 2 KB 639, a workman suffered injuries and accepted a payment from his employers on account of statutory compensation. He accepted a second payment "without prejudice" and stipulated that this applied to all future payments. The employers' agent agreed. It was held that the *first* payment and all subsequent payments were received "without prejudice".

The protection given by the term "without prejudice" may arise expressly or by implication. For example, statements made at a meeting may be impliedly "without prejudice". In *Pool v Pool* [1951] P 470, a meeting was held in an attempt to reconcile a husband and wife when matrimonial proceedings were pending. The attempt failed. In later proceedings it was held that statements made at that meeting were privileged, even though the words "without prejudice" were not used at the time. In *Rabin v Mendoza & Co* [1954] 1 All ER 247, a claim for damages was made for the negligent survey of a house. Before the action commenced, the parties met to discuss a settlement and this meeting was "without prejudice". It was agreed that the defendant surveyors would seek insurance cover against defects developing in the house and, for that purpose, they obtained another surveyor's report. The attempt at settlement failed and an application was made to have the report put in evidence. This was resisted and non-disclosure was upheld. The report was obtained as the result of an express or tacit agreement that it would not be used to the prejudice of either party.

Although an offer made "without prejudice" is not usually receivable in evidence, independent facts admitted in this offer may be admissible. Thus, in *Waldridge v Kennison* (1794) 1 Esp. 143, the defendant made an admission of handwriting in negotiations for compromising an action. This was admitted as evidence against him (see also the *Tomlin* case p. 81 below).

The protection of the "without prejudice" label only applies to the action in which it is made, between the same parties and not between them and third parties. However, in a compensation case, *Nash v Basildon Development Corporation* (1972) 222 EG 221, the Lands Tribunal did not follow this rule for reasons of public policy. The claimant's surveyor sought to produce in evidence a "without prejudice" letter from the district valuer, written to him in his capacity as surveyor to *another* owner. This was refused, notwithstanding the above rule, because the letter concerned one of a number of properties which the Development Corporation were acquiring in the new town area, and if the customary privacy of "without prejudice" negotiations were breached in such circumstances, the attempts of all the parties to reach agreement would be severely hampered.

A "without prejudice" statement may become admissible due to a subsequent event. There are three occasions when this will occur. First, where one party withdraws the "without prejudice" label from his statement and converts it into an open one. For example, in *Blow v Norfolk County Council* [1967] 1 WLR 1280, the district valuer, on behalf of the local planning authority, offered to recommend a payment of £11,500 compensation for the service of a notice of discontinuation in respect of a caravan site. This offer was made "without prejudice". The negotiations failed to produce a settlement and at the Lands Tribunal hearing the "without prejudice" label was withdrawn. The member, however, did not give any weight or consideration to the district valuer's recommendation. On appeal Lord Denning MR said (pp. 1283–4):

> "I am afraid that therein he went wrong in point of law. Once the 'without prejudice' letters have become open letters, they disclosed a plain admission by the District Valuer acting on behalf of the compensating authority of the figure he thought proper. I should have thought that his opinion was very fit for the consideration of the

tribunal ... it ought not to have been dismissed as of no weight or not fit for consideration."

Where the protection of the "without prejudice" label is waived in respect of a statement forming part of a sequence, it is important that the extent of the waiver should be clear, otherwise the whole of the sequence may become admissible.

Secondly, a "without prejudice" offer will be admissible where it has been accepted and forms part of a *binding* agreement. For example, in *Tomlin v Standard Telephones & Cables* [1969] 1 WLR 1378, the plaintiff was injured and claimed damages from the defendants. Negotiations were commenced and all letters from the defendants' insurers were marked "without prejudice". The correspondence showed that there was a binding agreement between the parties for a 50/50 basis of liability but no agreement on amount. In the resultant litigation the plaintiff sought to introduce the agreement regarding liability. The defendants objected on the grounds that it was privileged. It was held that this evidence could be admitted to show agreement on liability, which was a step towards settlement of the dispute, complete in itself and, therefore, capable of agreement independently of the overall settlement.

Thirdly, where a conditional "without prejudice" offer is accepted and the condition is later fulfilled, the "without prejudice" label will be removed and evidence of the offer will be admitted. Thus, in *Holdsworth v Dimsdale* (1871) 24 LT 360, the defendant was sued on a bill of exchange and, in a "without prejudice" letter, offered to waive the notice of dishonour of the bill and give a cheque, provided the plaintiff paid his own costs in the action. The plaintiff discontinued the action and later paid his taxed costs. But, before he made this payment, he commenced another action against the defendant on the bill. It was held that the "without prejudice" letter was admissible as evidence of waiver of the notice of dishonour.

Letters marked "without prejudice" are not admissible on the question of costs, except with the consent of *both* parties (*Walker v Wilsher*) (1889) 23 QBD 335). But where an offer to settle a dispute is made "without prejudice", and is also subject to an express reservation of the right to refer to it on the issue of costs (a "Calderbank" letter), then this offer is admissible for that purpose in cases where a payment into court would not be appropriate (*Cutts v Head* [1984] 2 WLR 349, see also Chapter 11 p. 349 below).

(iv) *Hypothetical facts.* Where the facts of a case are in dispute, an expert witness can only give an opinion on the basis of hypothetical (or assumed) facts. If he were allowed to choose the facts he accepts as true and base his opinion thereon he would usurp the function of the court.

The forensic device of asking an expert witness his opinion on assumed facts may be used to allow him to give an opinion based on hearsay. This practice has been criticised as unhelpful and little weight will be given to such an opinion, unless the hypothetical facts coincide with the facts that are subsequently proved:

> "Of course, the long established technique in adducing expert evidence of asking hypothetical questions may also be employed for valuers. It should, I think, be perfectly proper to ask a valuer, 'If in May 1972 No 3, with an area of 2,000 square feet was let for £10,000 a year for seven years on a full repairing lease with no unusual terms, what rent would be appropriate for the premises in dispute?' But I cannot see that it would do much good unless the facts of the hypothesis are established by admissible evidence; and the valuer's statement that someone reputable had told him these facts, or that he had seen them in a reputable periodical, would not in my judgment constitute admissible evidence."
> (*Eldonwall* p. 385).

(v) *Summary*. The position of an expert valuer as a witness of fact and opinion was summarised by Megarry J. in *Eldonwall* as follows (p. 386):

> "Putting matters shortly, and leaving on one side the matters that I have mentioned, such as the Civil Evidence Act 1968 and anything made admissible by questions in cross-examination, in my judgment a valuer giving expert evidence in chief (or in re-examination):
> (a) may express the opinions that he has formed as to values even though substantial contributions to the formation of those opinions have been made by matters of which he has no first-hand knowledge;
> (b) may give evidence as to the details of any transactions within his personal knowledge in order to establish them as matters of fact; and
> (c) may express his opinion as to the significance of any transactions which are or will be proved by admissible evidence (whether or not given by him) in relation to the valuation with which he is concerned; but
> (d) may not give hearsay evidence stating the details of

any transactions not within his personal knowledge in order to establish them as matters of fact.

To those propositions I would add that for counsel to put in a list of comparables ought to amount to a warranty by him of his intention to tender admissible evidence of all that is shown on the list."

In *R v Abadom* (p. 76 above) the Court of Appeal said that the limits of the hearsay rule in relation to expert evidence are that facts relied on by an expert as the basis of his opinion must be proved by admissible evidence, and that facts cannot be proved by the production of a report made by another expert who is not called to give evidence. In other respects expert evidence is not subject to the rules against hearsay in the same way as the evidence of a witness by fact.

(c) *Expert evidence of fact.* An expert witness, although usually a witness of opinion, may give evidence of technical fact, without expressing an opinion thereon. As a person with skill and experience in a particular technical field he may tell of scientific facts he has seen, which could only be perceived by a trained observer. These may be facts discovered by tests or experiments or by study under a microscope. Usually he will draw conclusions from the facts he has found but, if he does not, he will be a witness of fact, different in degree only from the eyewitness of an accident.

PROCEDURE

Chapter 1 contains an outline of the procedure of the courts and tribunals before which a surveyor may appear. Expert evidence has its own procedures and these are now discussed.

(1) Before the hearing

In 1970 the Law Reform Committee issued its Seventeenth Report *Evidence of Opinion and Expert Evidence* (Cmnd. 4489), containing recommendations for procedural changes in the calling of expert evidence in civil proceedings. These recommendations were implemented by the Civil Evidence Act 1972 and the rules of the court made hereunder. They apply to civil proceedings before tribunals where strict rules of evidence apply and to arbitrations and references, statutory or otherwise (section 5(1) Civil Evidence Act 1972, section 18(1) and (2) Civil Evidence Act 1968; Appendix C pp. 495 and 488 below). In proceedings before a tribunal or arbitrator, however, they may be modified by agreement between the parties or as determined by the tribunal or arbitrator (section 5(2) Civil Evidence Act 1972, section 10 (3) and (4) Civil Evidence Act

1968, Appendix C pp. 495 and 487 below). For example, they do not apply to proceedings before the Lands Tribunal which has its own procedures for expert evidence (see p. 87 below) and arbitrators will usually adopt their own procedure for the prior exchange and adduction of expert evidence (Chapter 10 p. 300 below and Chapter 13 p. 394 below).

As explained below, the rules of court governing expert evidence make such evidence inadmissible unless certain conditions are satisfied. These often include the disclosure of a written report of such evidence before the hearing. The rules do not force the disclosure of an expert report against the wishes of a party: they leave unaffected the privilege attaching to such a report (see Chapter 2 p. 57 above), but may make disclosure necessary if this evidence is to be admitted at the hearing.

The procedures for the calling of expert evidence in the High Court, county courts and Lands Tribunal are now discussed. There are no required procedures for expert evidence in local valuation courts, rent assessment committees or at planning inquiries and hearings.

(a) *High Court and county courts.* Section 2 (3)–(6) of the Civil Evidence Act 1972 enable rules of court to be made regarding expert reports and evidence (Appendix C p. 494 below). The substance of the law is found in these rules, namely RSC Order 38 rules 35–44 for the High Court (Appendix C p. 531 below) and Order 20 rules 27 and 28 of The County Court Rules 1981 for county courts (Appendix C p. 554 below). The procedure is substantially the same in both courts.

The basic rule is RSC Order 38 rule 36 for the High Court and Order 20 rule 27 for county courts. They are in similar terms and provide that expert evidence may not be given at the trial except:

(i) with the leave of the court; or

(ii) with the agreement of all parties; or

(iii) where it is given by affidavit; or

(iv) where the party seeking to call such evidence has made application to the court to determine whether a direction requiring prior disclosure should be made and has complied with any such direction; or

(v) in an action for personal injuries in the High Court, where the party has disclosed his expert's report under the provisions for automatic disclosure in RSC Order 25 rule 8(1)(b).

Expert evidence is usually given in accordance with a direction of the court under RSC Order 38 rules 37, 38 or 41 (i.e. under (iv) above). These rules also apply in the county court (Order 20 rule 28 County Court Rules 1981). The procedure is as follows.

In the High Court consideration must be given to the question of expert evidence at the hearing of the summons for directions (see Chapter 1 p. 6 above) and all parties must make any applications for leave to call such evidence and as to the prior disclosure of expert reports (*Practice Direction (Evidence Expert)* [1974] 1 WLR 904). The applications are made under rule 36 (High Court) or 27 (county court), and the appropriate direction will be given under rules 37, 38 or 41 according to the type of action or evidence.

Rule 37 applies (with two exceptions) to expert evidence in actions for personal injuries. Where a party applies to the court to call oral expert evidence then the court *shall* direct that the substance of the evidence be disclosed in the form of a written report to such other parties and within such period that the court may specify, unless it considers that there is sufficient reason for not so doing. In respect of non-medical expert evidence the court may treat as a sufficient reason for *not* giving a direction any of the circumstances summarised below under rule 38.

Rule 38 applies to expert evidence in actions other than actions for personal injuries. It is under this rule that a surveyor is most likely to give his evidence. Where application is made to the court in respect of oral expert evidence in an action other than one relating to personal injuries, the court *may*, if it is satisfied that it is desirable to do so, direct that the substance of the expert evidence to be adduced by a party be disclosed in the form of a written report to such other parties and within such period as the court may specify.

In deciding whether to give such a direction the court shall have regard to all the circumstances and may treat any of the following as sufficient reason for *not* giving a direction. First, that the expert evidence will be based to any material extent on disputed facts; secondly, that the evidence will be based to any material extent upon facts which are neither directly ascertainable by the expert nor within his general professional knowledge and experience. Thus, as a general rule, exchange of expert reports will only be ordered where the facts underlying the experts' opinions are not in dispute.

Rule 41 deals with hearsay evidence. Where application is made to the court in respect of expert evidence contained in a statement (as opposed to oral expert evidence) and the applicant alleges that the maker of the statement cannot or should not be called as a witness, the court may direct that the rules of court relating to hearsay evidence of fact shall apply to the expert evidence, subject to such modifications as the court may think fit (see Chapter 2 p. 48 above). Thus, the party seeking to rely on hearsay expert evidence must then first serve notice on all other parties, counter notices may be served requiring the expert to attend and give direct oral evidence and resistance by the applicant to the calling of the expert on statutory grounds may be made. The court will determine whether an expert must be called to give oral evidence.

The above rules refer to the disclosure of "the substance" of the expert evidence in the form of a written report or reports. In the Law Reform Committee Seventeenth Report this means the expert's opinion and the relevant facts upon which it is based. This meaning was affirmed by Ackner J in *Ollett v Bristol Aerojet Ltd* [1979] 1 WLR 1197. In the context of a case concerning personal injuries due to an accident caused by a machine, he said (p. 1197):

> "When the substance of the expert's report is to be provided, that means precisely what it says, both the substance of the factual description of the machine and/or the circumstances of the accident and his expert opinion in relation to that accident, which is the very justification for calling him."

Under rule 39 the court may order disclosure of part only of expert evidence. A party may put in evidence an expert report disclosed to him by another party in accordance with the above rules. This report then becomes part of the evidence of the party putting it in.

The court may limit the number of expert witnesses who may be called to give evidence at a trial.

The purpose of prior disclosure of expert reports is to encourage pre-trial settlements, to avoid surprise at the hearing due to opposing expert evidence and to encourage agreement of that evidence.

Where the court directs the disclosure of expert evidence under rules 37 or 38 this disclosure is by mutual exchange of reports on or before an "exchange" date. The court may, however, order the sequential disclosure of expert reports. For example, in *Kirkup v British Rail Engineering Ltd* [1983] 3 All ER 147, the Court of Appeal upheld an order in an action for personal injuries requiring the plaintiff to disclose his engineer's report by a specified date and for the defendants to disclose their report within 42 days thereafter. The reason for this sequential disclosure was that the action was for alleged deafness caused by excessive noise at work, where the area of inquiry went back to 1952 (when the plaintiff entered the defendants' employment) and, until the defendants knew what the plaintiff was going to say about his working conditions, their expert could not start preparing his report. Thus, time and costs would be saved by directing sequential instead of mutual disclosure. In exceptional circumstances disclosure by one party only may be ordered.

It should be noted that where no order for disclosure is made by the court the parties may withhold their reports from each other and call expert evidence at the trial.

(b) *Lands Tribunal.* The procedures described above for the disclosure and admission of expert evidence do not apply to the Lands Tribunal. The tribunal has its own rules for expert evidence contained in the Lands Tribunal Rules 1975, as amended in 1977, 1981 (twice) and 1984. There are four procedures for the prior exchange of expert evidence, namely (i) in appeals from local valuation courts; (ii) in appeals against determinations, references and applications in respect of restrictive covenants; (iii) in other appeals; and (iv) where the written representations procedure is used. These procedures do not apply to evidence given by affidavit.

(i) *Appeals from local valuation courts* (rules 10 and 11 Lands Tribunal Rules 1975, Appendix C p. 533 below). An appellant must state in his notice of appeal whether or not he intends to call an expert witness. Where an appeal has been made and notified, any party who intends to appear at the hearing must serve notice of his intention on the registrar and the appellant. This notice must also state whether or not that party proposes to call expert evidence.

Where an appeal is on a point of law or the net annual value of the appeal hereditament exceeds £1,250, rule 11 requires the appellant to send to the registrar and the other parties a statement of case accompanied by a valuation and description of comparable hereditaments. These must be sent within 28 days of the last date for giving notice of intention to appear. The other parties shall, within 28 days of receipt of the appellant's documents, each send to the registrar, the appellant and the other parties their respective replies in the form of a similar statement of case with valuations and descriptions of comparable hereditaments. The time limits for serving a statement of case and reply may be extended by consent of the parties (with notifications to the registrar) for a period not exceeding 2 months on each notification and 4 months in aggregate (rule 48(2) Lands Tribunal Rules 1975).

Each statement of case (and reply) shall include the facts to be proved and any points of law on which the party intends to rely at he hearing. They shall be accompanied by every valuation of the hereditament which it is proposed to put in evidence (including supporting particulars and computations), or a statement of the value or values which the parties have agreed to attribute to the hereditament in the event of the tribunal allowing or dismissing the appeal, together with a

description of any comparable hereditaments to which the
party intends to refer in support of his case.

In *Marchi-Stevenson Ltd v Edwards (VO)* (1958) 3 RRC 289, the
tribunal considered the interpretation of the word "description" in relation to details of comparable hereditaments and
said (p. 297):

> "In my opinion the spirit of that rule is not met by a
> schedule which merely gives the name and addresses of
> certain occupiers and the 'descriptions' taken from the
> appropriate column of the valuation list—e.g. 'workshop
> and premises' or 'factory and premises', etc etc as the case
> may be. The object of rule 11 ... is to enable the other
> party to prepare for the case he has to answer, and looking
> at Part II of the rules as a whole a reasonable 'descrip-
> tion' of the comparable hereditaments, would, in my
> opinion, extend to 'the facts to be proved' relevant to the
> proceedings."

Valuations lodged under these rules do not have the effect of
binding the parties as though they were pleadings containing
some admission of a relevant allegation by another party (*City
of Sheffield v Meadow Dairy Co Ltd* (1958) 171 EG 357).

If at the hearing any party seeks to rely upon any valuation
or other document which appears to the tribunal not to have
been sent to the registrar in accordance with rule 11 the
tribunal may adjourn the hearing on such terms as to costs or
otherwise as it thinks fit (rule 11(3) Lands Tribunal Rules
1975). Also, if it appears to the Tribunal that any party has
failed to supply a copy of a required document, then it may
direct that a copy be sent and adjourn the hearing with costs
against the defaulting party (rule 41 Lands Tribunal Rules
1975).

(ii) *Appeals against determinations, references and applications in
respect of restrictive covenants* (rule 42 Lands Tribunal Rules 1975,
Appendix C p. 537 below). The appellant in an appeal against
a determination and the claimant in a reference must indicate
in their notices of appeal or reference whether or not they propose to call expert evidence. As a general rule not more than
one expert witness on either side shall be heard unless otherwise ordered. But where the proceedings include a claim for
compensation in respect of minerals or business disturbance,
one additional expert witness on either side may be heard on
these matters. Application for leave to call additional expert
witnesses is made to the registrar under rule 45 (interlocutory
applications) or to the tribunal at the hearing.

Where more than one party intends to call an expert witness, every such party shall send to the registrar within 28 days after a request to do so, the following documents relating to the evidence to be given by the expert witness:

(a) every plan and valuation of the subject-property (including supporting particulars and computations) which it is proposed to put in evidence;

(b) either a statement of any prices, costs or other particulars and any plans relating to properties other than the subject-property (comparables), which are proposed to be given in evidence in support of the valuation, or a statement that no such prices, costs etc will be relied upon.

These are known as rule 42 documents. The registrar shall within 7 days of receipt, send to each party copies of the documents supplied by the other parties. The provisions of rule 48(2) of the 1975 Rules, relating to the extension of time for sending documents, apply to the submission of rule 42 documents (p. 87 above).

If application to call an additional expert witness is made and granted at the hearing or if a party seeks to rely on any plans, valuations or particulars which appear not to have been sent to the registrar, the tribunal may adjourn the hearing on such terms as to costs or otherwise as it thinks fit (rule 42(6)). The provisions of rule 41, relating to the failure to supply copies of documents (p. 88 above), and the observations of the Court of Appeal in the *Meadow Dairy* case (p. 88 above), apply to rule 42 documents.

(iii) *Other appeals* (rules 12 and 13 Lands Tribunal Rules 1975, Appendix C p. 535 below). A notice of appeal, other than an appeal against a determination or from a local valuation court, must indicate whether the appellant proposes to call an expert witness to give evidence in support of the valuations to be relied upon at the hearing. Every party who intends to appear at the hearing of the appeal shall give notice of his intention, also stating whether or not he intends to call expert evidence. The subsequent procedure is then a mixture of the procedures described under (i) and (ii) above. Thus, if the registrar so directs, statements of case and replies shall be served and exchanged as in (i) above. Normally only one expert witness on either side shall be heard and, where more than one party intends to call an expert witness, there shall be a prior exchange of rule 42 documents as in (ii) above. Rules 41 (failure to supply documents), 42(6) (leave to call additional expert witnesses) and 48(2) (extensions of time for submitting documents) also apply.

(iv) *Written representations procedure* (rule 33A Lands Tribunal

Rules 1975, Appendix C p. 536 below). Where the tribunal
directs that any appeal, reference or application be dealt with
without an oral hearing (Chapter 1 p. 17 above) and any party
intends to rely upon expert evidence, then the provisions of rule
42, requiring the exchange of valuations and comparables, will
apply (p. 89 above).

(2) At the hearing

Expert evidence is usually given orally in court, by question and
answer, in examination-in-chief, cross-examination and re-examination. It may also be given by affidavit, or it may be contained in a
written report admitted as hearsay evidence under RSC Order 38
rule 41. In exceptional circumstances it may be given on oath before
an examiner appointed by the court.

Where an expert report has been disclosed to the other parties
before the hearing, the report may be put in evidence at the commencement of the expert's examination-in-chief or at such other
time as the court may direct (RSC Order 38 rule 43). A document
lodged with the registrar of the Lands Tribunal under rule 42(4) of
the Lands Tribunal Rules 1975 is not properly before the member
hearing the reference until it has been agreed or produced by the
witness in the normal way in evidence-in-chief (*Chinnery v Basildon
Development Corporation* [1970] RVR 530).

There is no rule of law which provides that a witness must stay
outside the court until he is called to give evidence. The judge has a
discretion whether or not to allow a witness to remain in court
(*Moore v Lambeth County Court Registrar* [1969] 1 WLR 141). In practice an expert witness is always allowed to remain in court
throughout the hearing (see *Tomlinson v Tomlinson* [1980] 1 WLR
322), although in *R v Penguin Books Ltd* (1961) (the obscenity prosecution relating to *Lady Chatterley's Lover*) the numerous expert
witnesses for the defence were excluded from the court until they
had given their evidence).

In the courts and the Lands Tribunal expert evidence is always
given on oath or affirmation and it may also be so given at other
hearings, including arbitrations, local valuation courts and planning inquiries. When the oath is taken the witness holds the New
Testament (or in the case of a person of the Jewish faith, the Old
Testament) in his uplifted hand and says or repeats after the officer
administering the oath:

> "I swear by Almighty God that the evidence which I shall give
> shall be the truth, the whole truth, and nothing but the truth."

A witness may make a solemn affirmation instead of taking the
oath using the following words:

"I, ... do solemnly, sincerely and truly declare and affirm, that the evidence which I shall give shall be the truth, the whole truth, and nothing but the truth."

In *Sheen v Bumpstead* (1862) 1 H & C 358, Bramwell B stated that a valuer who is asked his opinion of the fair price of land may give this opinion in examination-in-chief but may not give his reasons for holding that opinion, e.g. because other land sold for a certain price. His reasons may only be given in answer to questions in cross-examination. This is no longer good law: "... for many years now such evidence has not been rejected in chief when the witness has been speaking from his first-hand knowledge" (per Megarry J in *Eldonwall* p. 386).

Thus, in examination-in-chief an expert should, in answer to questions from his counsel, state the facts which form the basis of his opinion, his opinion and the reasoning which led to it. An expert witness may refer to books, articles and other literature which are recognised as authoritative in his profession. The extracts or articles referred to become part of his evidence by incorporation (see p. 76 above). An expert witness may refer to his proof of evidence to refresh his memory, to verify facts or figures which he cannot be expected to carry in his head, but (except in planning and similar administrative inquiries) he must not read from it. His evidence must be extracted by question and answer (*Harding v Cardiff City Council* (1971) 219 EG 885). Where a witness is allowed to "refresh his memory" when giving evidence, by referring to a document made by him, that document becomes evidence of any fact contained in it of which he could have given direct oral evidence.

As a general rule it is improper for counsel to communicate with his own witness while that witness is giving evidence, except with the consent of opposing counsel or leave of the court. It is recognised that, in the case of an expert witness, there may be good reson for counsel to communicate with him and such consent or leave will always be given in practice.

As stated above, rule 42 documents lodged with the Lands Tribunal are not evidence until they have been agreed or produced by a witness. If they are not so agreed or produced, questions on them cannot be directed to another witness, although he can be examined on matters within his own knowledge, notwithstanding that such matters might also have formed part of the evidence of another witness not before the tribunal (*Chinnery v Basildon Development Corporation* [1970] RVR 530). In cross-examination counsel must put to the expert witness the substance of the evidence of his own expert, in order that the witness may comment on it. The credibility and expertise of an expert witness may be questioned in cross-examination.

PART TWO

THE EXPERT WITNESS

CHAPTER FOUR

The Expert Witness: Principles and Practice

INTRODUCTION

The first three chapters of this book deal with the law of procedure and evidence, that is to say the framework of adjective law within which an expert witness gives his evidence. The next three chapters discuss the practical side of expert evidence. This chapter deals with the principles and practice of expert evidence; Chapter 5 contains examples of expert witness documents; and Chapter 6 discusses, by means of a practical example, the role of the advocate—expert witness.

DUTIES OF AN EXPERT WITNESS

We have seen that the purpose of expert evidence is to assist the court by placing before it technical information and opinion so that it may take judicial notice of these matters when making its decision. The same principle applies to an administrative tribunal (e.g. an inspector holding a planning inquiry), although, of course, the concept of judicial notice does not apply.

An expert witness has a two-fold duty: to the court and to his client. The *duty to the court* is paramount. An expert witness should assist the court by putting before it *all* relevant facts and his true opinion. He must tell the truth, give his honest opinion and not withhold any evidence which might assist the court, even though it may be detrimental to his client. When the tribunal is itself an expert tribunal, expert witnesses can still assist by agreeing, marshalling and simplifying the facts and presenting fact and opinion clearly and logically. An expert's *duty to his client* is to assemble and prepare his evidence in a competent manner, formulate reasoned opinions, co-operate with other professional advisers and present his evidence accurately and clearly. He should be alert to the possibilities of a compromise settlement of the dispute.

If an expert establishes at the outset that his evidence will be of assistance to his client, then there will be no conflict between these two duties. The test is not whether he can produce evidence to support his client's case, but whether his evidence does in fact support that case. This evidence should in substance be the same whichever side calls him. It follows, therefore, that an expert should *never* appear on behalf of a client who requires him to withhold evidence or put forward an opinion that he does not hold. Unlike an advocate, an expert witness is not the mouthpiece of his client. He is an expert who places his objective evidence before the court and is called by one of the parties because that evidence also supports that party's case. This point has caused concern where a planning officer is required to give evidence at a local inquiry in support of a council decision which is contrary to his own opinion and advice. Is he acting properly if he gives evidence in support of that decision? Should he decline to give such evidence, or, if he does so appear, state his own opinion? In November 1979 the Royal Town Planning Institute issued this guidance to its members:

> "... a chartered town planner as a witness at a local inquiry or other hearing ... must not undertake any duties or carry out any instructions of a public or other employer or a client or supervisor which involve making statements purporting to be his own, but which are contrary to his *bona fide* professional opinion."
>
> (Practice Advice Note No. 1).

The remainder of the Note makes it clear that a planning officer appearing as an expert witness has a duty to tell the truth, both as to fact and opinion. Although he need not voluntarily state that his own opinion is at variance with his council's, he must, if challenged, declare his own opinion and the difference which exists between himself and his council. The Note further suggests that this particular officer is unlikely to be the best witness and that his council may be better served by putting forward another officer, or the chairman of the planning committee or, as suggested in later supplementary guidance, an outside consultant.

The fundamental rule for an expert witness is, therefore, that he should give his own evidence, which he has objectively prepared, the opinions honestly and truthfully held. To do otherwise is to seek disaster. A competent cross-examination will soon reveal the flaws in his evidence, his client's case will suffer and his professional reputation will be tarnished. He will have failed in his duty to the court and in his duty to his client. An example of this occurred in a recent compensation case in the Lands Tribunal, *Reynolds v Manchester City Council* (1980) 257 EG 939. The claimant was represented at the hearing by his father who called an expert witness, Mr G. I. Woolard FIAS. The tribunal said this about his evidence (p. 939):

> "Mr Woolard ... relied neither on comparables nor on his own experience: in his evidence-in-chief and also in cross-examination Mr Woolard was explicit not only that he had never seen the subject-property prior to its demolition but also that the

figures appearing in his valuation had been adopted after discussion with Mr Reynolds ... This being the foundation of his valuation, I regret that I can attach no weight to Mr Woolard's evidence. Valuation is a matter of independent uninfluenced judgment. Opinion evidence given at second-hand is not really evidence at all."

Accordingly the tribunal accepted the acquiring authority's valuation with only minor adjustments.

QUALITIES OF AN EXPERT WITNESS

An expert witness should possess at least four qualities. First, expertise in the subject-matter of his evidence, plus a sound working knowledge of the framework of law in which it is set. Secondly, an understanding of the law relating to expert evidence and the procedure of the particular court or tribunal. Thirdly, an objective and unbiased approach to technical problems. Fourthly, the courage of his opinions.

(1) Expertise

It is, perhaps, a truism that an expert witness must be an expert before he can be an expert witness. But it must be stated because it can be overlooked. Expert witness work is not a branch of surveying, in the way that rating, town planning and land agency are. A surveyor should only accept an expert witness appointment because he is an expert in the particular subject-matter of the dispute and not because he specialises in expert witness work. He should not become an all-purpose expert witness: although, of course, the surveyor who specialises in rating or compulsory purchase or town planning is likely to find himself in the witness box more frequently (and therefore more of a specialist expert witness) than a colleague who spends his working life selling houses. But it is a mistake for a practice to look upon Mr X as their expert witness, available to appear in that capacity, whatever the dispute. Mr X should only consider such an appointment if he is expert in the subject-matter of the dispute.

The first and foremost quality needed by an expert witness is, therefore, expert knowledge of the subject-matter of his evidence. He need not always have paper qualifications (although these usually help to establish his expert status): he may be qualified by experience. His expertise may arise out of a hobby and not out of a profession. But he must have that expertise or he should decline the instructions. Furthermore, he should be expert in the *whole* of the subject-matter of his evidence: he should not need to call in another expert to fill the gaps in his own knowledge or experience. Thus, although a second expert witness may properly be called to give planning evidence to form the basis of an opinion of value, a valuer's qualifications to give evidence of value will be diluted if it is found necessary to call further expert evidence of local values in a case where the issue is substantially the assessment of a very local demand for a property (see *Braid Investments Ltd v East Lothian District Council* (1981) 259 EG 1088 and see also p. 116 below). Where an expert has most, but not quite all, the expertise required by the scope of his evidence I suggest that the factors to be considered when deciding whether he can properly give evidence are: the complexity of the other area of expert knowledge, the extent of the expert's experience in the other field, the importance of the other disputed area to his client's case and the policy of the courts and Lands Tribunal which is to limit the number of expert witnesses.

An expert witness should also be skilled in preparing and giving evidence. He should have a clear, analytical mind, able to marshall facts and draw reasoned conclusions therefrom. He should be able to communicate clearly, both verbally and in writing. He should have a good memory, good powers of observation, a conscientious and painstaking approach to problems and an eye for detail. He should be able to work in a team.

In addition to expert knowledge, an expert witness should have a sound working knowledge of the framework of law in which his evidence is set. Counsel will deal with the law, but an expert witness must understand it and recognise its effect upon his evidence. In the factual question of valuation, for example, the law determines the subject-matter of the valuation and the underlying assumptions. Thus, the determination of a rent under a rent review clause in a lease is a question of fact, determined within the framework of law chosen by the parties to the lease. The expert witness should be able to recognise law and fact in this and similar situations. He must understand the law if he is to gauge its effect on value. Expert witness work is not, therefore, a field for the surveyor who has an aversion to the law.

(2) Knowledge of evidence and procedure

An expert witness should have an understanding of the law of evidence, particularly expert evidence, and of the procedure of the court or tribunal in which his evidence is to be given. A detailed knowledge is not required: he can always seek guidance from his client's lawyers. But an expert's credibility will be improved if he is aware of the various procedural steps before and at the hearing and if he has an understanding of the rules governing the admissibility of evidence. For example, if he wishes to refer to a comparable transaction in support of his opinion of value, he must know the rules governing the admissibility of such evidence (see Chapter 3 p. 67 above). If he wishes to include a hearsay statement in his evidence he must be aware of the notice procedure and warn his client's solicitor in sufficient time for notices to be served (see Chapter 2 p. 48 above). He must know the contents of an expert report for exchange (see Chapter 3 p. 86 above), and the documents required under rule 42 of the Lands Tribunal Rules 1975 (see Chapter 3 p. 88 above), in order that he may draft them correctly. Knowledge of the procedure before trial will alert him to the need to produce documents at different times and allow him to plan his preparatory work accordingly. It would be tedious and time-consuming if an expert witness's ignorance of evidence and procedure required him to make continual reference to his client's lawyers.

(3) An objective approach

The approach of an expert witness must be objective and free from bias. His task is not to produce evidence to support his client's case but to give evidence in support of his objective opinion. In substance his evidence should be the same whichever side retains him. Although he will know what his client wishes him to say, he should approach the problem objectively, in a spirit of scientific inquiry. He should seek the truth and form an honest opinion on the basis of all the facts. A surveyor who cannot be objective should not be an expert witness.

(4) The courage of his opinions

An expert witness should have the courage of his opinions. This work is not for the person who vacillates. An expert witness should seek all the relevant facts before forming his opinion, he should consider them carefully and objectively and then form a reasoned opinion. But, having formed that opinion, he should stick to it, unless new facts come to light at a later date. He should recognise that his opinion may be under attack long before the direct assault of cross-examination. It may not be entirely to his client's liking; it may not wholly support a claim or defence that counsel wishes to use; other retained experts may express disagreement. All these criticisms must be resisted by the expert witness. Of course, if his opinion is too unfavourable to his client he should leave the case; but the situation may arise where subtle pressure is applied to persuade him to modify his opinion. If this is not resisted the expert may find himself in the witness box supporting an opinion which is not wholly his own, and becoming increasingly unhappy under cross-examination.

INSTRUCTIONS AND FEES

(1) Instructions

When instructed to act as an expert witness, a surveyor may have
had no prior involvement in the case (an independent surveyor: not
to be confused with an independent surveyor appointed to settle a
dispute, see Chapter 7 below); or he may already be actively involved but in a different capacity, e.g. as a valuer negotiating a rent
review (a pre-involved surveyor). The nature of his instructions,
subsequent action, initial report and fees will differ according to the
role of the surveyor when instructed as an expert witness.

(a) *An independent surveyor.* An independent surveyor will receive
his instructions from one of several sources, e.g. from his client,
from his client's solicitor, from a fellow surveyor or from another
professional adviser. He should not accept those instructions until
he has satisfied himself on the following three points and then
agreed his fees.

First, is the subject-matter of the proposed evidence within his
professional competence? If it is not he should decline the instructions, stating his reasons and, if possible, suggesting another
surveyor who may be able to assist.

Secondly, he should ensure that there is no other reason why he
should not accept the instructions. For example, can he carry out
the work within the time available? Does he have some connection
with the property or the parties which would prevent him carrying out his duties in an independent and unbiased manner? If he
might gain financially from the result of the dispute, even indirectly, he should decline the instructions. For example, a
surveyor in private practice who is also a director of a company
should not accept instructions to give expert evidence on behalf of
that company. A surveyor should not appear on behalf of a relative. An expert witness must be, and be seen to be, wholly
impartial.

Thirdly, before accepting instructions to act as an expert witness,
a surveyor should ensure that his evidence will be of assistance to his
client. He should never accept instructions before making a preliminary investigation and preparing an initial report (see p. 107
below). This report will form the basis of his evidence and will
ensure that the scope and effect of it are known to his client and other
advisers from the beginning. The report can form the basis of instructions to counsel, particularly to advise on evidence. If his client
is satisfied with the proposed evidence then the surveyor can accept
instructions; if his client is not satisfied then he can look elsewhere
and the surveyor can retire from the case.

The problem in practice is that a client is often unwilling to pay a fee for an initial report which might be unhelpful to him. In certain circumstances, it may be possible for the surveyor to give a preliminary opinion before the preparation of a report. It will depend on the complexity of the case and other circumstances, e.g. in an appeal against a refusal of planning permission, where the area, the property and the planning policies are known to the surveyor, he may be able to form a preliminary opinion from studying the application and refusal. Each case must be dealt with according to its particular facts but the surveyor should beware of giving an instant opinion which he might subsequently be unable to support. A client is often unaware of the special nature of expert witness work and looks upon the instruction as one to produce evidence in support of his case. This situation is particularly difficult where he is an old-established client of the firm: considerable tact is required when explaining the true position to him.

(b) *A pre-involved surveyor.* The position of a surveyor already actively involved in a case, differs from that of an independent surveyor. The initiative for changing his role usually rests with him. He will normally decide when negotiations are unlikely to produce a settlement and recommend an appeal or reference to a court, tribunal or arbitrator, thus altering his role from negotiator to expert witness. At this stage he should set aside the biased attitude of the negotiator and look at the position objectively. He should prepare a written report, containing the same information as the initial report of an independent surveyor, with the addition of a recommendation regarding an appeal or reference. This report should contain sufficient information to enable his client's lawyers to give an opinion on any point of law in dispute and enable them to make an appeal or institute other legal proceedings. Again, it can form the basis of instructions to counsel. The report should state clearly the figure the surveyor can support in his new role of expert witness. This is particularly important where he has been arguing for a different figure in his negotiations. After an appeal or reference has been made, negotiations can continue in an effort to reach a settlement. During this period the surveyor will have a dual role as negotiator and expert witness.

(2) Fees

An expert witness should agree the basis of his fees when he accepts instructions. An independent surveyor should do this immediately after the initial approach to him and before any work is carried out. A pre-involved surveyor may have dealt with expert witness fees in his initial fee arrangement, but if not, he should state his fee for this new role in his interim report.

Fees for expert witness work are usually charged on a time basis, the rates varying according to the complexity of the case and the status and qualifications of the surveyor. It may be expedient to quote a fixed fee for an initial report, with a time basis for future work. If a day rate is quoted the length of the working day should be stated. Where extensive travelling will be required it should be made clear to the client whether or not travelling time is included in the time spent on the job. Separate hourly or daily rates are usually quoted for principals and assistants; secretarial costs, other overheads and profit being included in these rates. They are usually quoted exclusive of value added tax, travelling and hotel expenses, copies of plans and documents, disbursements and other reasonable out of pocket expenses. Litigation is often a lengthy process and the fee arrangements should include interim payments.

Fees for expert witness work should never be related to the outcome of the case. This may be contrary to the bye-laws or code of conduct of the expert's professional body; it may also be unenforceable at law on the grounds of champerty. An agreement that a fee shall be related to the success of legal proceedings is champertous and unenforceable on grounds of public policy. It should be noted, however, that the law of champerty applies only to proceedings in a court of law. Thus, in *Pickering v Sogex Services (UK) Ltd* (1982) 262 EG 770, it was held that an agreement was not champertous that provided for a contingency fee if negotiations on a rating assessment produced a saving of rates. There were two reasons for this decision. First, the negotiations resulted in agreement and a subsequent hearing in the local valuation court merely recorded that agreement and was not therefore litigation. Secondly, a local valuation court is not a court of law and, therefore, even if the agreement had contemplated a contest before such a court, it would not have been champertous. It was also stated *obiter* that the same principle would apply to proceedings before a rent tribunal.

WORK OF AN EXPERT WITNESS

(1) Before the hearing

The work of an expert witness before the hearing may be considered under the following headings: (a) preparation of evidence; (b) preparation of documents; (c) relationship with client, other advisers and witnesses; (d) negotiation, settlement and sealed offer.

(a) *Preparation of evidence.* The key word for the expert witness is "preparation". It is essential to the success of his client's case that he should prepare his evidence fully and meticulously, investigating all the facts and leaving nothing to chance. An expert witness usually states an opinion on a technical matter, on the basis of and within a framework of law. He should, therefore, work from law to fact to opinion.

First, he should find out the scope of the dispute and the issues between the parties. He should obtain instructions which set out his role in the litigation and the extent of his evidence. Clearly, he should not prepare evidence on matters outside the dispute. For example, if he is required to give evidence on defects in a recently completed building, he should ascertain from the contract and specification the scope of the contractor's obligations and then direct his evidence to the defects falling within those obligations. He should not deal with matters which, although they may be departures from a notional specification which the witness thinks might or ought to have applied to this particular building, are not defects under the specification under consideration.

Secondly, an expert witness should acquaint himself with the law relating to his evidence of fact and opinion. He should study the pleadings and other pre-trial documents to find out the issues between the parties and the place of his evidence in the dispute. He should read any opinions given by counsel. He should study any leases or agreements which contain definitions of rent or value forming the subject-matter of his evidence. Where his evidence of value is based on statute or common law (e.g. rating or compulsory purchase) he should refresh his memory on the relevant provisions determining the subject-matter of his valuation.

The framework of law, within which an expert opinion is set, may determine the importance of the facts considered at the next stage of the preparation of expert evidence. For example, in a claim for compensation for compulsory purchase where an acquiring authority have entered the land, the date of entry is material because, as a matter of law, this is the date for ascertaining the value of the land taken. It has greater importance than other dates in the acquisition timetable, e.g. confirmation of the compulsory purchase order.

If there is any doubt on the law underlying his evidence the expert should resolve it with his client's lawyers before finalising his opinion. It is essential for an expert witness to get advice on questions of law as early as possible in the preparation of his evidence. It is important that his evidence of fact and opinion should be consistent with the legal basis of his client's case. Where, as sometimes happens, the assumptions of law underlying an expert's evidence have not been considered by his client's lawyers, he should ensure that his report or proof of evidence state clearly the assumptions he has made, e.g. as to the existence of a special purchaser in an assessment of open market value.

Thirdly, an expert witness should ascertain and weigh the facts. When all material facts have been discovered and considered, then (and only then) should he form his opinion. The sources of these facts will vary according to the particular circumstances of the case. They may be given in his instructions and may be actual facts, which are or will be agreed or proved by other witnesses, or that he is required to assume for the purposes of his evidence. They may be contained in documents to which the witness may refer in his evidence, e.g. a structure plan or planning circular at a planning inquiry. They may be facts which the witness will perceive and note from his inspection of a property (e.g. floor areas, construction, defects) or extract from his records (e.g. comparable transactions). But, whatever the source, the golden rule for the expert witness is that he should check the accuracy of his facts before basing his opinion on them. Like the rule of evidence for documents, he should never rely on secondhand (or inferior) evidence where the best evidence is available. He should ask to see copies of documents and not rely on summaries of their contents. He should check measurements and areas and not rely on information given by others. He should find out as much as he can about all material facts, particularly comparable transactions. He should agree as many facts as possible with the opposing expert witness (see p. 110 below).

To what extent can an expert witness properly delegate to an assistant the collection of information and the preparation of evidence? In my view such delegation should be kept to a minimum. There are two reasons for this. First, an expert witness appointment is a personal one and the client should be able to rely on receiving the services of the expert and not those of his assistant. Secondly, an expert who prepares all or most of the evidence himself will have a better grasp of detail and will, therefore, be a more convincing witness. When he is in the witness box he is on his own and cannot look to his assistant to explain some point under examination. The amount of delegation by an expert witness will clearly depend on many factors, including the complexity of the case, the time available for preparation and the quality of his assistant. The expert, however eminent or busy he is, should never leave the preparation of his evidence wholly or even predominantly in the hands of an assistant.

Lastly, an expert witness will prepare his evidence and five points should be borne in mind. These are: (i) the need to recognise weaknesses in his evidence; (ii) the need to guard against exaggeration; (iii) the need to anticipate likely questions in cross-examination; (iv) the need to recognise that a case may not develop at the hearing in the manner originally anticipated; (v) the need to keep his evidence as simple as possible.

An expert witness should recognise that his evidence will contain at least one weakness, however strong it may appear to be. He must not ignore it in the hope that it will not be noticed by his opponents. It almost certainly will be and, if brought out in cross-examination, it will weaken his evidence. The expert should look for the weakness, explain it to counsel at an early stage (and particularly in his proof of evidence) and then deal with it in examination-in-chief. If it is revealed in cross-examination it will have a greater impact on his evidence than if he reveals it voluntarily in examination-in-chief, where he will have ample opportunity to explain it. For example, an unhelpful comparable transaction may be effectively explained in examination-in-chief. It my be outnumbered by other transactions more relevant to the valuation or there may be special circumstances making the transaction unreliable as evidence of open market value. If these facts are brought out in examination-in-chief they will be less detrimental to his evidence than if they are revealed, seemingly unwillingly, in cross-examination.

An expert witness should never exaggerate his evidence in the hope that it will carry more weight with the court or tribunal. If his opinion is objective, formed after a careful study of the facts and supported by sound reasoning, it will carry more weight than an exaggerated one, revealed to be so in cross-examination. The expert should resist pressures to increase or reduce his opinion of value in his client's favour. It is often said that in disputes of value the court usually splits the difference between the opposing valuers' figures. It is argued that the expert valuer should put forward a higher or lower figure than he can objectively support in the hope that, when the court fixes the rent or value midway between the two figures, it will, in fact, be closer to his real opinion of value. This is a dangerous fallacy: a clear exaggeration of value, upwards or downwards, could severely damage a client's case. If the exaggeration is revealed in cross-examination not only will the expert's reputation suffer but his evidence may be completely rejected, leaving the court with only his opponent's evidence as the basis for decision.

An expert witness should anticipate and prepare for the attacks which will be made on his evidence in cross-examination. The late Sir Patrick Hastings KC, brilliant advocate and cross-examiner, took great care when preparing a case. He wrote in his *Autobiography*:

"For weeks before a trial I cross-examined my prospective opponents to myself; mentally I prepared myself for every difficulty. I assumed that they would find means of escape from any pitfall, and I searched for a method with which to block their exit.''

One of his "prospective opponents" would have been an expert witness, who must similarly prepare for such a cross-examination by anticipating the questions, planning the answers and providing information and opinion to enable him to do so competently. He should not be disconcerted by a question or by a novel line of attack. If he has anticipated it and prepared himself in the calm atmosphere of his office, he will be able to give considered answers. His evidence will thus gain in credibility.

Closely allied to the above, an expert witness should recognise that a case may not develop at the hearing as he anticipated it would. He must be flexible. He must have the mental agility to adapt his evidence to new and unexpected directions. The expert will have lived with the case for months or perhaps years. He will have clear views on what he thinks are the important issues. Not so the judge or tribunal who, fresh to the case, may take an entirely different view of the relative importance of the issues. Also, he may find that the other party's case is presented in a different way to that displayed in negotiations before the hearing. The expert must be able to meet these new situations and he will only be able to do so if he has thoroughly prepared his evidence.

Finally, an expert witness should assist the court by keeping his evidence as simple as possible. It is one of his functions to simplify the technical issues and present them clearly. He should resist any temptation to introduce a myriad of minor points but should concentrate on the fundamental issues in the case. In a value dispute he should base his valuation on a few good comparables in preference to a large number of transactions many of which may be of doubtful relevance.

Preparing evidence for a hearing is hard work and some of it may be unnecessary. It requires a painstaking approach with great attention to detail. Evidence must be thoroughly prepared; if properties are valued or building defects reported on, adequate inspections must be made and notes, photographs, drawings and plans prepared. The more this evidence is committed to memory, so that it may be given at the hearing with a minimum of reference to written sources, the more impressive it will be. But memory is fallible and full notes should be made. The information should be stored in a systematic manner and, on the day of the hearing, it must be immediately to hand in the witness box and not on the other side of the court.

(b) *Preparation of documents.* An expert witness usually gives oral evidence but will spend much of the time before the hearing preparing documents. These will vary according to the nature of the dispute and the court or tribunal. Examples of expert witness documents are given in Chapter 5 and a brief summary of their purpose and contents is set out below.

(i) *Initial report* (Chapter 5 p. 123 below). As stated above an expert witness should never agree to appear in a case until he has decided what his evidence will be. An outline of that evidence should be set out in an initial report so that his client can decide whether or not it will assist him. Similarly, where a surveyor is already involved in a dispute which cannot be settled by agreement, he should prepare a report dealing with the present position, advice on future action and the scope of the evidence he can provide. An initial report may form the basis of instructions to counsel, particularly to advise on the law and evidence.

An initial report should be brief. It will be shorter than an expert report for exchange or a proof of evidence. It should contain the basic facts, any necessary assumptions of fact or law, the expert's opinion and, if necessary, recommendations. Secondary facts used in forming an opinion (e.g. comparable transactions supporting an opinion of value) and the reasoning behind an opinion should not be included in an initial report, unless specifically requested, but an indication of their availability or non-availability might be helpful. Similarly, the detailed reasoning behind the expert's opinion should not form part of an initial report.

(ii) *Expert report* (Chapter 5 p. 129 below). An initial report may be followed by a more detailed expert report. This depends upon the type of dispute, the complexity of the expert's evidence and any directions regarding disclosure of expert reports before trial (see Chapter 3 p. 85 above). For example, where an expert is instructed in a dispute regarding compensation for compulsory purchase, he will usually prepare an initial report and then proceed to his proof of evidence and the documents under rule 42 of the Lands Tribunal Rules 1975. But where he is instructed in a case in the High Court (e.g. renewal of a business tenancy under Part II of the Landlord and Tenant Act 1954) and an order is made for mutual exchange of expert reports, then his initial report will be followed by a fuller expert report suitable for exchange and a proof of evidence for use by counsel.

Where an expert report is to be disclosed it should contain "the substance" of the expert's evidence, i.e. his opinion and the relevant facts upon which it is based (see Chapter 3 p. 85 above). For example, where a report deals with the value of an

interest in land, it may contain a factual description of the
property, the interest valued, the date of valuation, details of
comparables and other value evidence used in forming the
opinion of value, any assumptions of fact or law, any caveats to
which the report is subject and the opinion of value. It is unnecessary to set out the reasoning behind an opinion: this will be
included in the expert's proof of evidence and given orally at the
hearing. It is not necessary for an expert report to contain more
than "the substance" of his evidence:

> "The function of an expert in litigation is not limited to
> giving evidence. He will help solicitors and counsel on his
> speciality, warn them of pitfalls, make suggestions as to
> cross-examination of witnesses, factual as well as expert.
> None of this, as distinct from the substance of the evidence
> which he himself proposes to give in chief at the trial if he is
> called, need be disclosed."

(Law Reform Committee, Seventeenth Report para 60).

Although an expert report should be discussed with counsel
before disclosure, an expert should not alter his report unless he
agrees with the alteration. He should not allow counsel to
"settle" his report (see Chapter 3 p. 66 above).

(iii) *Proof of evidence* (Chapter 5 p. 135 below). The purpose of a
proof of evidence is to set out the evidence to be given by the
witness at the hearing. It is usually written in a form to be used
only by counsel, but at certain administrative inquiries (e.g
planning appeals) proofs of evidence are read out by the
witnesses and handed in as evidence. In arbitration proofs are
often exchanged and then tabled as read at the hearing (see
Chapter 13).

A proof of evidence will be based on earlier reports but will
contain more detail, including supporting evidence, calculations
and the reasoning behind an opinion. The contents will vary
according to the nature of the dispute, the expert's evidence and
whether the proof is to be submitted in evidence. All proofs
should progress logically from law to fact to opinion and from
the general to the particular. For example, the proof of evidence
of a valuer who is to give expert evidence before the Lands
Tribunal in a compensation case, should contain the following:

> (a) his qualifications and experience;
> (b) the background to the case, e.g. name of compulsory pur-
>   chase order, relevant dates;
> (c) a factual description of the subject-property and the sur-
>   rounding area;
> (d) the framework of law for the valuation and any assump-

tions (of fact or law) which have been made, e.g. as to the planning permission which might reasonably be expected to be granted; whether there is an underlying scheme of acquisition and, if so, its extent;

(e) the witness's valuations, with reasons and supporting comparables;

(f) criticisms of opposing expert's valuation.

Detailed statistics, lengthy extracts from other documents and similar material should be put in an appendix to the proof. A list of exhibits to be produced by the witness should be included either in the main body of the proof or, if they are numerous, in a separate appendix. A lengthy proof should have an index and may conclude with a summary.

A proof (or perhaps attached notes) may contain a list of the points which the expert witness thinks are irrelevant to the dispute. This will assist counsel who is then given an opportunity to consider whether the witness is right as to the relevance of these points.

A proof of evidence may include or refer to maps, plans, photographs or other exhibits, agreed or to be submitted by the witness. Maps should be no larger in size than is necessary, they should be submitted flat or folded (not rolled) and should always contain a north point, scale and key. Transparent overlays on a base map may be useful, e.g. to illustrate different forms of development. Photographs should contain a reference number and description on the front and be related to a plan. The plan should show the positions from which the photographs were taken with an arrow indicating the direction of the camera. All plans, photographs, documents and other exhibits should be given a number prefixed by the initials of the witness, e.g. JOD/1, 2, 3 etc.

(iv) *Documents for submission to the court or tribunal.* An expert witness may be required to provide a written summary of his evidence in the form of an expert report (see p. 107 above) or, while giving oral evidence, he may assist the court by putting in a plan, report or other exhibit. For example, as we saw in Chapter 3 (pp. 84 and 87 above), in the High Court and county courts the prior exchange of expert reports may be ordered and these will then normally be submitted in evidence at the start of each witness's examination-in-chief. In the Lands Tribunal there are three procedures for the submission and exchange of expert evidence in the form of valuations and comparables, which are not properly before the tribunal until agreed or produced by the witness in examination-in-chief. An expert witness should ensure that his report or valuation is in accordance with the relevant rule. Thus, an expert report for prior exchange in the High Court or county court should contain "the substance" of his evidence (Chapter 5 p. 129 below); a valuation submitted to the Lands Tribunal under rule 42 of the Lands Tribunal Rules 1975 (as amended) should contain only the information specifically required by this rule, that is to say generally only his valuation and comparables (see Chapter 5 p. 126 below).

This was emphasised by the President of the Lands Tribunal in *Harding v Cardiff City Council* (1971) 219 EG 885 at p. 886:

> "... I want to make a few general observations as to the content of what are usually called rule 42 documents ...
>
> The point I want to make is that the rule does not require the filing of a proof of evidence. All it requires are the valuations, plans etc necessary to enable the other side to prepare their answer. The arguments to be adduced in support of the filed documents are properly put into the witness's proof, which should not normally be put in evidence or be read by the witness, who should only refer to it to verify facts or figures which he cannot be expected to carry in his head. His opinions must be extracted by question and answer."

The above documents should be approved (but not settled) by counsel before they are lodged. The facts in them should either be agreed or proved by admissible evidence at the hearing.

The documents submitted by an expert witness should be of a high standard. The following comments were made by the Lands Tribunal in a case a few years ago:

> "... the documentation of the expert witnesses was not up to the standard normally expected by the tribunal. Plans must be given a scale, co-ordinated with one another, and clearly cross-referenced to any schedules; furthermore, in a reference of this type, one composite plan should be agreed by the experts together with as many facts as possible. Schedules should have proper headings to show what they are about and should be well spread out on sheets larger than foolscap if necessary."

It will be convenient for large schedules to be reduced in size when copied for ease of handling and filing.

(v) *Statement of agreed facts* (Chapter 5 p. 145 below, Chapter 6 p. 165 below and Chapter 13 p. 418 below). It is the duty of expert witnesses to agree as many facts as possible. These should be set out in a statement of agreed facts, usually drafted by the experts and settled by counsel. Maps, plans and photographs should also be agreed. A statement of agreed facts may include such matters as floor or site areas, availability of services, values or alternative values on different assumptions, tenure, cost of works, type and date of construction, defects and town planning. Where the case involves the use of a specialised technical vocabulary, this should be agreed between the parties and included in the statement of agreed facts (see e.g. *Thameside Estates v Greater London Council* (1977) 249 EG 346).

The process of agreeing facts should start as early as possible, to avoid a last minute rush and to provide an agreed basis for each expert's evidence of opinion. One of the functions of the pre-trial review is to obtain reasonable agreements and admissions (see Chapter 1 pp. 12 and 16 above). The witnesses should agree not only the facts but also their meaning and basis. For example, in a recent reference to the Lands Tribunal to determine the purchase price of land with spoil heaps containing coal or combustible material, an agreement as to the quantities of such material was found at the hearing not to be a true agreement because one expert treated the agreed amounts as minimum recoverable quantities but the other expert assumed them to be reasonable estimates (see *Alfred Golightly & Sons Ltd v Durham County Council* (1981) 260 EG 1045, 1135 & 1199). Similarly, expert valuers should use the same method of measurement and of expressing values. It is frustrating and time-consuming for one valuer to talk in terms of a price per square foot of net internal area and the other a price per square yard of gross external area, even though the respective areas may have been agreed.

(vi) *Scott Schedule.* The Scott Schedule is a document much used in disputes in the construction industry. It is named after a former official referee of the High Court and is sometimes called an official referee's schedule. The purpose of a Scott Schedule is to bring together in one document all the issues between the parties. It shows in tabular form the items in dispute, the contentions of the parties and the decision on each item.

There is no prescribed form for a Scott Schedule. Each one will be in tabular form but the headings will vary according to the nature of the dispute. For example, in a claim by a contractor (plaintiff) for money due following completion of a building contract, with a set-off by the employer (defendant) for defective work, the Scott Schedule may contain the following headings (reading from left to right across the page):

(a) reference no.—for each item of work;
(b) contract work—a brief description of the work which the employer alleges should have been done to comply with the contract, specification, variation order, etc;
(c) defendant's comments—the employer's allegations regarding defects in the contract works;
(d) defendant's estimate of loss—the employer's claim in respect of each item of work;
(e) plaintiff's comments—the contractor's defence, admission or partial admission of liability in respect of the employer's allegations;
(f) plaintiff's estimate of loss—the contractor's estimate of the employer's loss if liability is admitted or proved;
(g) official referee's (or arbitrator's) comments (two columns)—his comments on each item of claim and the amount awarded.

Before the hearing the employer (defendant) will complete columns (a) to (d) and the contractor (plaintiff) will then complete columns (e) and (f). The official referee or arbitrator will fill in the two columns under (g) during or after the hearing.

(vii) *Written representations* (Chapter 5 p. 145 below). These are used where a dispute is determined without an oral hearing. Written representations are a combination of submissions and evidence, and as we saw in Chapter 1, may be used in Lands Tribunal proceedings (p. 17 above) and for planning appeals (p. 32 above). They are also much used in rent review disputes, whether settled by an arbitrator or independent expert. This procedure has the advantages of greater speed at lower cost, provided it is properly used.

The two most common faults in written representations are excessive length and poor drafting. The former is caused by the duplication of material which should appear in a statement of agreed facts, the inclusion of irrelevant matter, the incorporation in the main text of material which should be in an appendix, and excessive and repeated comment and exchange of representations. Poor drafting is due to the writer's inability to marshall facts and arguments into a logical order and to write clear English.

Written representations should be accompanied by a statement of agreed facts. The material in this statement should not be reproduced again in the parties' representations, except where this is necessary for comment and argument. Cross reference to the agreed statement is more satisfactory than duplication. This practice has two advantages: first, it reduces the length of each party's statement and thus the time spent by the tribunal and the other party in reading them; secondly, it enables the tribunal to see more clearly the facts agreed and in dispute and the issues between the parties.

Many written representations contain irrelevant material which could be omitted without detriment to the party's case. For example, it would not be uncommon for representations for a rent review of a shop in (say) Oxford to include a short history of the city, its importance as a place of learning, communications and industries, all written in the style of a guidebook; some derogatory remarks about the opposing party's conduct of negotiations; and a description of the property written in the style of an estate agent's letting brochure. This should all be left out. (A description of the property should be put in the statement of agreed facts). Circular 38/81 (Appendix C p. 561 below), which gives guidance on the content of written representations in planning appeals (see Chapter 1 p. 32 above), mentions two items which should be omitted from written statements in planning appeals: a description of those characteristics of the site which are readily apparent from the plan and a detailed history of the planning applications where this is not relevant to the appeal (paragraph 11). A person drafting written representations should always ask himself: is the material relevant? does it help my client's case?

Written representations should not incorporate in the main text lengthy tables of figures or long extracts from other documents. These should be in an appendix. This is particularly relevant to planning appeals. Circular 38/81 (paragraph 11) recommends that the following should be set out in an annex to, or attached to, the text of the statement: lengthy rehearsals or interpretations of general planning policies, comments of persons (other than the appellant and the local planning authority) adduced in support of the case and relevant planning decisions.

A common fault of the written representations procedure is the repeated exchange of statements by the parties. Circular 38/81 comments on this in relation to planning appeals (paragraph 13):

> "Whether intended to reinforce points by repetition, to have the last word or to save the best arguments to the end, such tactics are not helpful. They confer no advantage, encourage responses in kind, and serve only to prolong the appeal process."

The written representations procedure should be limited to an initial statement by each party, containing the main points of their case, and a second statement restricted to arguments and evidence in rebuttal only of points made in the other party's initial statement.

In addition to their excessive length many written representations are badly drafted. The writer should ensure that his representations are concise, logical and clearly expressed in plain English, which is easy to read and understand. The phraseology of the guidebook, the extravagances of the estate agent's brochure and the meaningless jargon of the modern development plan should be omitted (except, of course, in the latter case when it is necessary to comment on such a plan in a planning appeal).

Finally, the participants in an exchange of written representations must kept to the timetable laid down by the arbitrator, independent expert, Department of the Environment or the Lands Tribunal. One of the advantages of this procedure is speed, which will be lost if there is delay in the submission of statements.

(c) *Relationship with client and other advisers.* In a simple case before an inferior tribunal the expert witness may work alone, combining the roles of advocate and expert, but he usually works in a team comprising all or most of the following: client, solicitor, counsel, other expert witnesses and witnesses of fact. It is important that this team should get to know each other as well as possible before the hearing to gain confidence in each other's abilities.

The *client* may take either an active or passive role in the dispute. If he is active the expert may receive his instructions from him and may report to him. If he is passive the expert will have little contact with him and will usually receive instructions and report to another person, usually the solicitor. The client may be a witness of fact, e.g. in a claim for disturbance compensation where he may explain the action he took to mitigate his loss.

The expert will probably have most contact with his client's *solicitor*, although his closest working relationship will be with counsel. The solicitor usually performs a two-fold role in a dispute: as lawyer and administrator. If counsel is not retained, the solicitor will be the only lawyer in the team. His duties will include the conduct of the proceedings, the drafting of documents, advising on law and evidence, arguing the case at the hearing and advising on an appeal. This role will be reduced where counsel is instructed. The solicitor will then be the main channel of communication with counsel and the opposing party. All communications to counsel should pass through him and, although experts for opposing parties often communicate direct (e.g. to agree facts), this should only be done with the consent of their respective solicitors. Formal contact with the opposite party should always be through solicitors.

The day to day conduct of a case will be the responsibility of the solicitor and he will, therefore, also act as an administrator. He will instruct counsel and the expert witnesses, receive and circulate counsel's opinions and expert reports, organise evidence, arrange hearing dates (ensuring that counsel and the experts will be available) and arrange conferences with counsel.

Where *counsel* is briefed he is in charge of the case. Where two counsel are instructed the senior counsel, usually a QC, will be in charge. He will advise on law and evidence and the conduct of the case. He will carry out most of the advocacy at the hearing. Junior counsel will be responsible for the paperwork, drafting opinions, settling pleadings, making interlocutory applications and some advocacy. The preparation of a case for hearing will usually progress by a series of conferences (called consultations where leading counsel is instructed). These will be attended by all the parties, although where a case is complex and involves issues of fact and law, the witnesses may not attend those parts of conferences concerned solely with questions of law. It is important that the matters to be considered at each conference should be known in advance by the expert witness and that he should be prepared to discuss them when he attends. As a general rule there should be no direct contact between counsel and witnesses: all communications should pass through the solicitor and he should attend all meetings between counsel and witnesses. This rule is often relaxed in practice on the initiative of counsel, who will suggest that an expert witness should send documents direct to him or telephone him on matters of difficulty, particularly where the matter is urgent or, as is often the case, counsel and expert are known to each other from past cases.

The relationship between counsel and expert witness is important and both must have confidence in the other's abilities. Counsel must be confident that the expert has prepared his evidence competently (without disguising the weaknesses and without exaggeration), that he will keep to his proof of evidence in examination-in-chief and that he will not falter under cross-examination. The expert must be confident that counsel has understood his evidence, that he will ask the right questions in examination-in-chief and that he will note any unsatisfactory answers in cross-examination and rectify the position in re-examination. Before the hearing counsel and expert should rehearse the latter's evidence and discuss the approach to be adopted by counsel at the hearing. It must be remembered, however, that the evidence is that of the expert and, although he will carefully consider any suggestions counsel may make to assist a better presentation, he should not alter it against his will. It is not the province of counsel to settle an expert's report or proof of evidence.

In a case with several technical issues there may be *several expert witnesses*. It is important that each expert should establish as early as possible the relationship of his evidence with that of the other experts. There should be no inconsistencies. Where common facts form the underlying basis of several expert opinions the experts should ensure that they all use the same facts. Where the opinion of one expert is dependent on the opinion of another (e.g. a planning expert providing planning assumptions for a valuer's opinion of value), there should be a clear understanding of the relationship between the two fields of evidence and a full exchange of information. It is the task of the solicitor to co-ordinate the work of the various experts.

The order in which experts are to present their evidence at the hearing should be established as early as possible. This will affect the content of each expert's evidence: those called later in the hearing should avoid repetition and bear in mind what has been proved and what has to be proved. This is particularly important at planning inquiries where part of the task of the appellant's first expert witness is to provide the essential background to enable the inspector to understand the issues and subsequent evidence.

Where a case involves issues of fact, *witnesses of fact* will also be called. Where an expert is basing his opinion on facts to be proved by such a witness, he should ensure that the facts to be proved and the factual basis of his opinion coincide. He should be told immediately if a witness of fact alters his evidence.

An expert witness should have contact with an *opposing expert* only with the consent of his client's solicitor. He may, of course, have had much contact with him in the past when attempting to negotiate a settlement of the dispute. Opposing experts will meet or correspond to agree facts (or ideally an agreed expert report) and to continue negotiations towards a settlement.

(d) *Negotiation, settlement and sealed offer.* During the period before a hearing an expert witness should be alert to the possibilities of a settlement. He may be asked to advise regarding an offer to settle, received or to be made, including a sealed offer.

Where a dispute is solely one of fact (e.g. compensation for compulsory purchase), counsel with his experience of judicial decision-making and the strengths and weaknesses of a case, will be able to express an opinion on the likely decision, but the expert witness is best qualified to advise on the question of amount. The size of an offer to settle should be decided having regard to the expert's objective opinion, the strength of the respective cases and the cost of a hearing. Where the dispute involves issues of law and fact, liability and amount (e.g. a claim for damages), counsel should advise on a settlement with the advice of the expert as to quantum.

Where a client wishes to make a payment into court or submit a sealed offer the expert should advise on the amount. Such a payment or offer is an attempt to settle the dispute and is also relevant as to costs. For example, in a compensation dispute before the Lands Tribunal the award of costs incurred before a sealed offer is at the discretion of the tribunal, but the award of costs after a sealed offer is governed by section 4(1)-(3) of the Land Compensation Act 1961, which deal with awards in excess of or below such an offer or the failure of the claimant to deliver a claim in sufficient time for an offer to be made. Where an expert is advising an acquiring authority, should he advise that a sealed offer be submitted in excess of his valuation? The argument in support of such an offer is that the Lands Tribunal rarely award the figure suggested by the acquiring authority but usually an amount between the two party's figures: a sealed offer is an attempt to forecast that amount and so avoid the payment of costs. This practice may be open to criticism when the offer is considerably more than the authority's valuation. In *Fawcett v Newcastle upon Tyne Metropolitan District Council* [1980] RVR 300, the President said he was "not a little disturbed" to find that the acquiring authority had made a sealed offer in excess of the figure put forward by their valuer at the hearing. "It seems to me", he said, "that in the absence of any explanation either (the council's) valuation is unfair or the amount of the unconditional offer was excessive". Where the value is very much a matter of opinion or the dispute is mainly one of law, then a sealed offer above the value submitted may be made without criticism provided it is not far above that value.

Where an amount of compensation is dependent upon a point of law or a particular view of the facts (e.g. the effective cause of a loss), an acquiring authority should try to agree figures on the two parties' alternative bases and then make a sealed offer at their figure. The tribunal will not be able to make an award between the alternative figures and so penalise the authority in costs. It must award the authority's figure (claimant pays the costs) or the claimant's figure (the authority pays the costs). The tribunal may, however, refuse to accept agreements in the alternative because this deprives them of expert evidence and prevents them awarding an intermediate figure should they wish to do so.

(2) At the hearing

The hearing is the performance for which the expert has been rehearsing for weeks, months—even years. He has two roles: to assist the tribunal by giving evidence and to assist counsel in dealing with opposing evidence.

(a) *Assisting the tribunal (evidence)*. The giving of evidence is divided into four parts: examination-in-chief, cross-examination, re-examination and questions from the tribunal. In examination-in-chief the expert is taken through his evidence by counsel, usually by question and answer, although at administrative inquiries (e.g. planning inquiries) he usually reads his proof of evidence with occasional questions from counsel. In an arbitration where proofs of evidence have been exchanged before the hearing, the expert's proof may be tabled as read and constitute his examination-in-chief. In cross-examination opposing counsel tests the evidence, seeking to reveal mistakes and inconsistencies. He must put his own expert's evidence to the witness under cross-examination to enable him to comment on it, although an expert's own counsel will usually put his opponent's valuation to him for comment in examination-in-chief. Re-examination is usually short and may be unnecessary. The witness's counsel asks questions designed to correct any ambiguities or apparent errors and allow the witness to expand on any matters mentioned only briefly in cross-examination. Finally, the tribunal may ask the witness questions.

An expert witness should ensure that his files, plans and documents are complete and in order before he enters the witness box. Although oral evidence is usually given with little or no reference to working papers, the expert may be required to look at his files. He will give a poor impression if he spends an excessive amount of time searching through them and they look dog-eared and untidy. He should take into the witness box all the papers he is likely to need.

Where the oath is taken this is usually administered standing and, if the witness is provided with a chair, he should not sit down until invited to do so by the judge or tribunal. He should then arrange his papers, taking his time in doing so, take a deep breath and is ready to begin. If his examination-in-chief takes the form of a reading of his proof, he should ensure that copies have been distributed before he starts to read. First, counsel usually asks him questions about his qualifications and experience and then invites him to read his proof, possibly stopping him from time to time to emphasise an important point.

In judicial proceedings evidence is given by question and answer. Leading questions may not be asked in examination-in-chief. A leading question is one which suggests the answer. Counsel will usually follow the expert's proof, commencing with his qualifications and experience and proceeding from fact to opinion. Concentration by the witness is important. He should think out his answer before he speaks and then give it slowly and clearly, not dropping his voice at the end of his reply. Fingers and spectacles should be kept away from his mouth so that his words are not muffled and the witness should avoid mannerisms. His answers should be addressed to the judge and not to his counsel. This is not always easy as it often requires the witness to receive questions from one direction and give his answers in another, but it is vital if the tribunal is to hear and understand all his evidence. He should watch the judge and not race ahead of his pen.

In examination-in-chief answers should be full and to the point, but without padding, repetition or irrelevances. A bad impression is given if answers are given hesitantly or reluctantly, as if the expert is unsure of his evidence or has something to hide. The question should never be repeated in the answer. An expert should watch the judge's expression and tailor his answer accordingly: if the judge is clearly satisfied no more need be said; if he looks puzzled further explanation may be necessary; if he looks annoyed or impatient the point should be dropped. A witness should remember that he has lived with the case for months, but the judge is new to it and must have the facts explained to him. Furthermore, an expert should not assume that because expert witness documents have been submitted (e.g. rule 42 documents to the Lands Tribunal), they have been read before the hearing. They are not before the tribunal until they have been given in evidence by the witness. An expert witness should not appear to read from his proof. If he needs to refer to it (or any other document not submitted in evidence) to verify figures or other information, he should always ask permission to do so.

After the witness has given his evidence-in-chief he will be cross-examined by opposing counsel. This can be an ordeal, even for the expert who has prepared his evidence thoroughly. He is unlikely, however, to echo the words of an unfortunate witness, reduced to a state of fear and trembling by the notorious Judge Jeffreys, who cried out:

> "My Lord, I am so baulked, I do not know what to say myself. I am cluttered out of my senses; tell me what you would have me say."

Under cross-examination the expert should stay calm and courteous. He should never be provoked to rudeness or indulge in an acrimonious debate with his cross-examiner. He should not make jokes or exercise his wit at the expense of opposing counsel.

He may find that his questioner is better at this than he is, and it also lays him open to the criticism that he is not treating the case seriously enough.

Answers should be brief: "yes", "no", "I do not agree" are the best answers. Short answers give the cross-examiner less time to prepare the next question. If an explanation can be given it should be offered after a short answer. Opposing counsel will probably not wish to hear it because he knows it will not assist him; if he declines the invitation the judge may ask for it, also the expert's counsel will have been alerted to deal with the point on re-examination. If hypothetical questions are asked, on an assumption unacceptable to the witness, he should usually answer the question but reject the assumption. There is no reason, however, why he should not refuse to make the assumption.

If an expert realises that he has made a mistake he should immediately admit it and state the effect upon his evidence. His credibility will not suffer if the error is a minor one and does not fundamentally affect his opinion. Any attempt to hide or reject it will, however, inflate it, possibly turning it into a significant matter and destroying his credibility in the eyes of the court. An expert witness should resist giving impromptu answers to difficult technical questions which require thought or investigation. This is particularly so where the question is on a matter on the fringe of or outside his expertise. In this latter case he should decline to give an answer, explaining his lack of knowledge or experience, and in the former case he should offer an answer only after full consideration during a lunch or overnight adjournment. A witness is incommunicado during cross-examination and should not have any contact with his own side, except with the consent of opposing counsel or the court.

After cross-examination a witness is usually re-examined by his own counsel. The introduction of new matters is not permitted. If cross-examination has not shaken the witness's evidence then re-examination will be short. But if his evidence has been badly shaken then his counsel will have a difficult and perhaps lengthy task to restore his credibility.

Finally, the tribunal may ask questions on any matter which is still unclear. The witness's own counsel may have the right to re-examine on any of the matters raised by the tribunal. The witness should not leave the witness box until told he may do so.

(b) *Assisting counsel.* The second task of an expert witness at the hearing is to assist counsel to deal with other evidence, particularly that of the opposing expert. Where the hearing is short or is wholly or mainly concerned with an expert matter then the witness should attend throughout the hearing. Where the hearing is lengthy and concerned with issues outside the expert's province, he should attend to give his evidence and to hear that of every witness of fact or opinion which has a bearing on it, particularly the opposing expert. If an expert witness wishes to leave permission can always be asked for him to be released.

The presence of the expert witness is particularly important when the opposing expert is giving evidence. He should listen carefully to his evidence-in-chief, take notes and tell counsel of any points not covered in his proof which counsel may wish to use in cross-examination. It is probably better to advise counsel by notes rather than by whispering to him, particularly when he is conducting a cross-examination.

Where the parties arrange for a transcript of the evidence to be prepared, it is usually the task of junior counsel and the expert witness to check each day's transcript after the court has risen. The court is then told next day of any agreed amendments. Also at the end of each day's hearing counsel will probably wish to have a conference to discuss progress and to plan the strategy for the following day. It may be necessary for an expert witness to prepare further valuations, calculations or opinions overnight, to assist counsel or the court. He may find it advisable, therefore, not to plan any social engagements in the evenings during a hearing.

(3) After the hearing

When the hearing has finished there will be little for the expert witness to do except await the decision. But first he may be required to attend a view. For example, a site inspection is usually held by an inspector immediately after a planning or compulsory purchase order inquiry. This is usually attended by expert witnesses from both sides. Where an attended view takes place, this is not an opportunity for the experts to give additional evidence. If the expert is asked questions he should answer them but should not voluntarily add to his evidence while walking round the property.

After a decision has been given, the question of an appeal may arise. In most cases an appeal may only be made on a point of law and it is the task of the client's counsel or solicitor to advise on an appeal. There may be occasions, however, where the expert witness has a contribution to make. For example, an appeal to the Lands Tribunal from a decision of a local valuation court in a rating dispute may be made on an issue of fact, namely the amount of the assessment. No point of law need be involved. The form of appeal should be drafted by the client's lawyers but an expert witness may advise on the question of value. Similarly, a refusal of planning permission by the Secretary of State for the Environment may be accompanied by a statement indicating that planning permission would be granted for a modified form of development. The expert planning witness may be required to advise on this and submit a revised planning application.

At the end of the case the expert witness will have the pleasant task of submitting his final fee account. Where there is an interval between the hearing and the decision, an account is usually submitted immediately after the hearing since it will not be related to the decision.

CHAPTER FIVE

Expert Witness Documents

INTRODUCTION

As stated in the previous chapter, an expert witness will spend much of his time preparing documents, particularly proofs of evidence, reports, valuations, maps and plans. These are briefly described in Chapter 4 (pp. 106 to 114 above) and five examples are given below.

We find these examples by going to the west of England, to the fictitious cathedral city of Melchester in the county of Loamshire. Here are the offices of Messrs Wilberforce and Dodgson, chartered surveyors, established 1874. James Oliver Dodgson FRICS FCIArb, the senior partner, specialises in valuations, rating, compensation and town planning. He is the archetypal surveyor in court and will make several appearances in this book. In Chapter 6 he appears in the dual role of an expert witness – advocate, pursuing a rating appeal before a local valuation court; in Chapter 7 he is an independent expert determining a dispute of value on written representations; in Chapter 13 we find him acting as an arbitrator in a rent review arbitration, giving a reasoned award after an oral hearing. First, however, we look through his files and extract some of the documents prepared by him as an expert witness. These are an initial report (Example 1); valuation and schedule of comparables, in a compensation dispute heard before the Lands Tribunal (Example 2); an expert report for exchange prior to a hearing in the High Court on an application for the renewal of a business tenancy (Example 3); a proof of evidence for a local inquiry in respect of an appeal against refusal of planning permission (Example 4); and written representations in a rent review arbitration (Example 5).

EXAMPLE 1 (INITIAL REPORT)

(See Chapter 4 p. 107 above)
The property boom of 1972–73 did not pass by the quiet city of Melchester. In 1973 Mr Dodgson found himself advising on the compensation payable for the compulsory purchase of a house close to the city centre, in an area where developers were buying properties at high and increasing prices.

In October 1973 Mr Dodgson was approached by Mr B Sykes, managing director of T. A. Sykes & Co Ltd. This company owned 22 Fisher Street, Melchester, a terraced house close to the city

centre, which was being compulsorily acquired by Melchester City
Council as part of the site of a new museum. Mr Sykes decided to
negotiate the compensation himself, but was unable to reach agreement with the City Valuer. Mr Sykes claimed £50,000 on the
grounds that planning permission would be granted for an office
development on his company's land and other land. The City
Valuer offered £7,500 on the basis that the property had no permission or potential for office development and should be valued as a
vacant house in poor repair.

   Mr Sykes decided to refer the dispute to the Lands Tribunal and
asked Mr Dodgson to appear as an expert witness in support of his
claim for £50,000. Mr Dodgson would not commit himself to this
role without further investigation. He agreed to prepare an initial
report. This is his report.

Dear Mr Sykes,

CITY OF MELCHESTER (CENTRAL MUSEUM) CPO 1970
22 FISHER STREET, MELCHESTER, LOAMSHIRE

In accordance with the instructions contained in your letter dated
10th October last, I have now inspected 22 Fisher Street and given
consideration to the amount of compensation which should be paid
to your company for the compulsory purchase of the freehold interest in this property. My report is as follows.

1. As you know the above property is a two-storey terraced house
   built about 90 years ago. It is situated on the edge of the city
   centre. The property is in poor condition and has been vacant
   since January 1972.
2. Your company's freehold interest in this property is being
   compulsorily acquired by Melchester City Council for part of the
   site of a new central museum. The council took possession on
   29th May 1973; this is the date of valuation.
3. You have claimed compensation of £50,000 on the basis that, if
   the compulsory acquisition had not taken place, planning permission would have been granted for office development on your
   property and the adjoining land. I am of the opinion that, in the
   absence of the compulsory purchase, it cannot reasonably be
   assumed that planning permission would have been granted for
   office development on 22 Fisher Street and the adjoining land.
   My reasons are as follows:
   (a) The property is allocated in the City of Melchester Town
       Map for business purposes, a land use allocation which
       specifically excludes office use.
   (b) The office development policies of Loamshire County

Council and Melchester City Council are restrictive. Melchester is not an approved major office centre in the County of Loamshire Development Plan.

(c) An area of land bounded by Paternoster Street, South Walls and Landgate Street has been allocated for office development in Melchester and new offices will not normally be permitted outside this area.

(d) Planning permission for office development was refused on appeal in January 1973 for an adjoining site (79/81 High Street and 2/10 Arnold Street); the Secretary of State's decision letter specifically upheld the office policy referred to above.

On this point, therefore, I agree with the City Valuer.

4. I do not agree, however, with his opinion that the market value of 22 Fisher Street on the valuation date was only £7,500. This is the value of the property as a terraced house in poor condition. Since the beginning of the year two London-based property companies have shown considerable interest in the Fisher Street – Arnold Street area and have been purchasing properties at prices above existing use value. I believe that these companies are speculating on a change of planning policy and hope eventually to obtain planning permission for offices, although, for the reasons set out above, this is unlikely to be granted. I believe that their interest in the area would have included the properties on the site of the proposed museum (including 22 Fisher Street) if this proposal had not been in existence. I am of the opinion, therefore, that your company's property had a "hope value", above existing use value but below office development value, at the date of valuation.

5. On the basis of transactions known to me I am of the opinion that the open market value for compulsory purchase purposes of your company's freehold interest with vacant possession in 22 Fisher Street as at 29th May 1973 was about £24,000 (twenty four thousand pounds). This amount is considerably more than the final offer made by the City Valuer. Accordingly, I recommend that, if agreement cannot be reached with the City Valuer at or near £24,000, you should instruct your solicitor to refer the matter to the Lands Tribunal. I would be pleased to give evidence in support of this amount. I have first hand knowledge of the transactions referred to above and would, therefore, be able to give direct evidence of these comparables to support my opinion of value. I regret that I could not support a claim for £50,000 based on an assumed office planning permission, for the reasons set out above.

I shall be pleased to discuss this report with you and wait to hear from you.

Yours sincerely,

J. O. Dodgson

NOTES:

(a) This report is brief and informal. It contains the basic facts, Mr Dodgson's opinion and recommendation, and the minimum of reasons.

(b) Following a meeting Mr Sykes decided to accept Mr Dodgson's opinion of value and, after further lengthy but abortive negotiations, his solicitors referred the matter to the Lands Tribunal for determination. Mr Dodgson declined to make the reference himself on the grounds that this is a task for his client's solicitors who should become involved in the matter at an early stage in the proceedings.

EXAMPLE 2 (DOCUMENTS SUBMITTED UNDER RULE 42(4) OF THE LANDS TRIBUNAL RULES 1975)

(See Chapter 1 p. 15 and Chapter 3 p. 87 above)

Following the reference to the Lands Tribunal of the disputed compensation for the acquisition of 22 Fisher Street, the registrar requested the parties to submit to him within 28 days their expert witness documents under rule 42(4) of the Lands Tribunal Rules 1975 (Appendix C p. 537 below) Mr Dodgson sent three documents to his client's solicitors for transmission to the registrar. These were:

(1) a valuation of the subject-property (document *JOD/1*);
(2) a schedule of comparables (document *JOD/2*);
(3) a map showing the subject-property and the comparable properties (document *JOD/3*).

The three documents were placed in a folder clearly labelled with the name of the case, the reference no, the address and a description of the contents, namely "Documents submitted under rule 42(4) of the Lands Tribunal Rules 1975 in respect of the expert evidence of J. O. Dodgson FRICS FCIArb, for the claimants".

The valuation and schedule of comparables are reproduced below:

IN THE MATTER OF A REFERENCE BETWEEN:

T. A. SYKES AND CO LTD (Claimants)

and

MELCHESTER CITY COUNCIL (Acquiring Authority)

IN RESPECT OF 22 FISHER STREET, MELCHESTER, LOAMSHIRE
(ref 120/1974)

DOCUMENTS SUBMITTED IN ACCORDANCE WITH RULE 42(4) OF THE LANDS TRIBUNAL RULES 1975

DOCUMENT JOD/1

VALUATION OF THE SUBJECT-PROPERTY BY JAMES OLIVER DODGSON FRICS FCIARB OF WILBERFORCE AND DODGSON, FOR THE CLAIMANTS

Date of valuation: 29th May 1973 (date of possession).

Interest: Freehold with vacant possession of 22 Fisher Street, Melchester, Loamshire (edged red on Map JOD/3).

Valuation: Open market value under sections 5(2) and 14(3) of the Land Compensation Act 1961:
site area 1,200 sq ft @ £20 per sq ft = £24,000
(twenty four thousand pounds)

DOCUMENT JOD/2
SCHEDULE OF PRICES IN SUPPORT OF VALUATION IN DOCUMENT JOD/1

Ref no. on Map JOD/3	Address	Transaction	Date of exchange of contracts	Price	Site area (sq ft)	Price per sq ft of site area	Remarks
1.	8 Fisher Street	Sale of freehold with vacant possession	4th May 1973	£30,000	1,000	£30	House
2.	10 Fisher Street	Sale by auction of freehold with vacant possession	9th January 1973	£27,500	1,100	£25	Vacant site
3.	39 Fisher Street	Sale of freehold with vacant possession. Vendor remained in possession as licensee paying £4 pw inclusive.	2nd June 1973	£37,500	1,250	£30	House Listed building (grade II).
4.	11 Fisher Street	Sale of freehold with vacant possession	10th December 1973	£39,500	875	£45	Shop and flat
5.	5 Arnold Street	Sale of freehold with vacant possession	22nd July 1973	£14,500	1,200	£12	House
6.	25 Arnold Street	Sale of freehold with vacant possession	10th September 1973	£27,250	1,150	£15	House
7.	54 Arnold Street	Sale of freehold subject to weekly tenancy of shop at rent of £6 pw inclusive	19th June 1973	£10,000	1,000	£10	Shop and flat

NOTES:
(a) These rule 42 documents are brief. They contain only sufficient information about Mr Dodgson's valuation and comparables to enable the City Valuer to prepare his answer and to avoid surprise at the hearing.
(b) The comparable transactions in Document JOD/2 are listed in descending order of importance. They were subsequently agreed; if they had not been agreed it would have been necessary to prove them by evidence at the hearing.
(c) The extract from the 1/1250 Ordnance Survey Map (Map JOD/3) is not reproduced in this chapter. The subject-property was edged red on this map and the properties in Schedule JOD/2 were edged blue and numbered to correspond with the Schedule. The map was folded with the title clearly visible, and contained a north point, scale and key.

EXAMPLE 3 (EXPERT REPORT FOR EXCHANGE)

(See Chapter 3 p. 86 above and Chapter 4 p. 107 above).

In December 1980 Mr Dodgson was instructed by Morton House Investments Ltd, landlords of an office block, Dunbar House, Melchester, to negotiate terms for a renewal of the lease to the existing tenants, Superbuild Limited. These negotiations produced agreement on all the terms of a new tenancy except the initial rent. The tenants applied to the High Court for a new business tenancy under Part II of the Landlord & Tenant Act 1954 and, at the first hearing of the tenants' originating summons, the master ordered exchange of expert reports under RSC Order 38 rules 36 and 38 (Appendix C p. 531 below). This is Mr Dodgson's report.

IN THE MATTER OF DUNBAR HOUSE, MEADOW LANE, MELCHESTER, LOAMSHIRE AND IN THE MATTER OF THE LANDLORD AND TENANT ACT 1954 BETWEEN:

SUPERBUILD LTD   Plaintiffs
and
MORTON HOUSE INVESTMENTS LTD   Defendants

REPORT OF JAMES OLIVER DODGSON FRICS FCIArb OF WILBERFORCE AND DODGSON (FOR THE DEFENDANTS)

THE PREMISES

Situation

1. I attach to this report an extract from the 1/1250 Ordnance Survey Map (Map JOD/1) on which Dunbar House is edged red

and the comparable properties listed in Appendix A to this report are edged blue and numbered 1 to 6.

2. Dunbar House is situated on the north side of Meadow Lane, about ½ mile east of the city centre of Melchester. The surrounding area is predominantly commercial and industrial. At the rear of the premises is John Smith House, a modern two-storey building used as a printing school by the John Smith Home for Boys. On the west side of Dunbar House is an area of derelict land, formerly Melchester gas works, and to the east are three office buildings fronting Meadow Lane and the Meadowlands Trading Estate, comprising factories, warehouses and offices.

3. Opposite Dunbar House, on the south side of Meadow Lane, is the railway line from Melchester East to Bristol. The area immediately to the south of the railway is predominantly residential. Meadow Lane is a public highway. It is a narrow road with a 15 ft (4.5 m) carriageway and a 6 ft (1.8 m) footpath on the north side only. It joins the ring road round Melchester city centre (A371) about 300 yards (273 m) to the west of Dunbar House.

Description

4. I attach to this report 1/50 floor plans, sections and elevations of Dunbar House, numbered JOD/2-6. I also attach six photographs of the exterior of the premises, labelled JOD/7-12. The position from which each photograph was taken and the direction of the camera are shown on Map JOD/1.

5. Dunbar House is a three storey office building with car parking. It was built in 1967. It is of brick and pre-cast concrete frame construction with a dormer-type roof covered with "Eternite" Duchess slates. The building has concrete floors, plastered and painted walls, metal casement windows and suspended ceilings with concealed fluorescent lighting. There is a central staircase but no lift. There is toilet accommodation on each floor. The building has central heating provided by a Potterton Diplomat gas boiler. It has a fire alarm system and external fire escapes on the east and west flank walls. Dunbar House is supplied with gas, electricity and water and has main drainage.

6. The site of Dunbar House has a frontage to Meadow Lane of 35 ft (10.67 m), a depth of 120 ft (36.58 m) and a site area of 4,200 sq ft or 0.06 acre (390 sq m or 0.0024 ha). There is a car park at the rear of the building with 40 parking spaces.

7. Dunbar House is wholly occupied by Superbuild Ltd (the plaintiffs). The accommodation, uses and net internal floor areas are as follows:

Floor	Use	Net internal floor areas sq ft		sq m	
Ground	Reception and offices		3,100		288
First	Drawing offices	2,790		259	
	Stores	300	3,090	28	287
Second	Offices	1,750		163	
	Canteen	1,000	2,750	93	256
	TOTAL		8,940		831

The above floor areas have been measured in accordance with the Code of Measuring Practice issued by The Royal Institution of Chartered Surveyors and the Incorporated Society of Valuers and Auctioneers.

8. Although I did not carry out a full structural survey of the premises, I am of the opinion that they are in good repair and decorative condition and that the tenants have complied with the repairing and decorating covenants in their existing lease. I was unable to find any serious defects. I have been informed by Messrs O. S. Johnson and Partners, the architects who designed and supervised the building of Dunbar House, that no high alumina cement concrete, calcium chloride additive or other deleterious materials were used as structural materials in the original construction of the building.

9. No improvements have been carried out to the premises by either the landlords or the tenants.

TOWN PLANNING

10. In the old-style development plan, the City of Melchester Town Map, Dunbar House is in an area allocated for office use.

11. The Loamshire Structure Plan was approved on 22nd September 1979. A Local Plan has not been prepared for Melchester. Melchester is one of five "Restraint Areas" in the Loamshire Structure Plan. In these areas "planning permission for office development will generally be refused unless the County Planning Authority is satisfied that there is a special employment or economic justification" for such development (Policy OD/1). A justification will exist "when the office development is needed for firms providing a local service, provided that such development is acceptable in traffic and environmental terms" (paragraph 7.6).

12. Outline planning permission was granted on 10th June 1966 (ref. no. 12/66) for the construction of Dunbar House. It was for "the erection of an office building containing 10,500 sq ft (gross) with associated parking for 40 cars at Meadow Lane, Melchester". Approval of reserved matters was given on 24th September 1966 (ref. no. 70/66). Copies of this permission and approval are attached to this report (Appendix C). I was informed by the City Planning Officer of Melchester that there are no planning or highway schemes likely to affect the premises.

RATING

13. The current entry in the valuation list is:

	Gross value	Rateable value
Offices and premises	£7,500	£6,222

TERMS OF NEW LEASE

14. All the terms and conditions of a new lease of Dunbar House have been agreed, except the initial rent. I attach to this report a copy of the agreed draft lease (Appendix D). Briefly, the main terms are as follows:

(a) Term—10 years from 24th June 1981.

(b) Rent review—the initial rent shall be reviewed at the end of the fifth year of the term and for the remainder of the term shall be either the initial rent or the then current open market rental value, whichever shall be the higher.

(c) Outgoings—the tenants shall be responsible for general and water rates and all other outgoings.

(d) Repairs, decorations and insurance—the tenants shall be responsible for all repairs and decorations and to insure the premises in the full reinstatement cost against fire, storm, tempest and other specified perils, plus fees and two years loss of rent.

(e) Assignment and sub-letting—with the landlords' prior written consent, the tenants may assign or sub-let the whole of the premises, or sub-let part or parts (not being less than a whole floor or floors).

(f) Permitted use—offices.

RENTAL VALUATION

15. I am of the opinion that, having regard to the comparable trans-
    actions set out in Appendix A and the agreed terms of the new
    lease, the open market rent of the subject-property under section
    34 of the Landlord and Tenant Act 1954 (as amended) as at
    24th June 1981 was £29,000 per annum (twenty nine thousand
    pounds per annum).

16. I arrived at this opinion of open market rent as follows:

Ground floor	Reception and Offices	3,100 sq ft @ £3.50 = £10,850
First floor	Drawing offices and stores	3,090 sq ft @ £3.25 = £10,042
Second floor	Offices and canteen	2,750 sq ft @ £3.00 = £ 8,250
	Total	8,940 sq ft @ £3.25 = £29,142

Say   £29,000

17. This report has been prepared solely as an expert report for
    exchange under RSC Order 38 rules 36 and 38, following an
    application by the plaintiffs for a renewal of their business
    tenancy of Dunbar House, Meadow Lane, Melchester. It may
    only be used for this purpose and may not otherwise be
    disclosed to any third party or used in any other way without
    my prior written approval. No liability to any third party can be
    accepted for this report or any part thereof.

....

J. O. Dodgson FRICS FCIArb
Wilberforce and Dodgson

Date ....

APPENDIX A

SCHEDULE OF COMPARABLE TRANSACTIONS

Ref no on Map JOD/1	Address	Description & floor areas	Rent £ pa (exclusive)	Transaction	Remarks
1.	Conway House, Meadow Lane	Modern office building on north side of Meadow Lane about 200 yards east of Dunbar House. Central heating, lift, car parking. Ground floor— 4,250 ft² First floor — 4,000 ft² Second floor — 3,500 ft² Third floor — 3,250 ft² Total 15,000 ft²	£47,500	Lease for 10 years from 25th December 1980. Rent review to "fair open market rental value" at 25th December 1985. Tenants responsible for all repairs, decorations and insurance.	I negotiated this letting on behalf of the tenants. Landlords' surveyors— Muddle & Co of Melchester. New letting.
2.	Cumberland House, Station Road	Modern office building on outskirts of city centre about ¼ mile from Dunbar House. Central heating, car parking, no lift. Ground floor— 2,250 ft² First floor — 2,100 ft² Second floor — 2,000 ft² Total 6,350 ft²	£24,000	Rent review at 25th March 1981 to "fair rack rental value" in lease with 5 years unexpired at review date. Tenants responsible for all repairs, decorations and insurance.	Neither party represented by surveyors.

Four other comparable transactions were dealt with in the same way.

NOTES:
(a) The above report contains only the "substance" of Mr Dodgson's evidence-in-chief, i.e. his opinion of rental value and the relevant facts on which that opinion is based. It does not include the reasons for his opinion, e.g. the weight given to the comparable transactions.
(b) Following exchange of expert reports Mr Dodgson prepared a proof of evidence, based on his report but expanded to include the reasoning behind his opinion, the strengths and weaknesses of his evidence and a discussion of the opposing expert's report. The two expert witnesses subsequently agreed a statement of agreed facts, a town map showing the subject-property and the comparable properties, plans and elevations of the subject-property and photographs (with an associated plan showing the position from which each photograph was taken and the direction of the camera).
(c) The facts contained in the above report must be agreed or proved by evidence. Problems may arise in connection with proof of comparables. If any are hearsay and not agreed, Mr Dodgson must tell his client's solicitor so that the necessary notices under the Civil Evidence Act 1968 may be served on the tenants (see Chapter 2 p. 48 above). But Woodfall *Landlord and Tenant* (28th edition) expresses the view that the problem of hearsay evidence of comparables "... will in practice be resolved, without such notice being given, by a report under Order 38 rule 38, which refers to the transactions in question" (para 2–0695). Mr Dodgson should, therefore, look carefully at the transactions in his opponent's report and, in respect of hearsay comparables, where he is not satisfied as to the accuracy of the information or knows of any other reason why a witness of fact should be available for cross-examination, he should advise his client's solicitor to serve a counternotice requiring them to be proved by direct evidence.
(d) An expert report is usually put in evidence at the commencement of the witness's evidence-in-chief. The rule is that it may be put in evidence at that time or at such other time as the court may direct.
(e) Map JOD/1, drawings of Dunbar House, photographs, outline planning permission, approval of details and the agreed lease, all referred to in this report, are not reproduced in this chapter.

EXAMPLE 4 (PROOF OF EVIDENCE)

(See Chapter 4 p. 108 above)
In September 1981 Mr Dodgson was instructed by Mr B. Sykes

136   *The Surveyor in Court*

(of Example 1) in a planning matter. Mr Sykes was the owner of a house, Juniper Cottage, in the village of Stanton Episcopi. He had a swimming pool in his garden and wished to fix and inflate a transparent polythene dome (a Polydome) over it to enable the pool to be used in all weathers. He asked Mr Dodgson whether he needed planning permission.

Mr Dodgson advised that there is doubt as to whether the proposed work is development. If it is not development then planning permission is not required. If it is development, planning permission must be obtained because the pool is sited in front of the house (see General Development Order 1977 (Class I.3 in Schedule 1 as amended)). He therefore submitted two alternative applications. The first was for a determination under section 53 of the Town and Country Planning Act 1971 that the proposed work is not development requiring planning permission; the second was an application for planning permission. On the first application it was determined by the local authority that the proposed work is development requiring planning permission and permission was refused on the second application.

Mr Sykes was very annoyed because he alleged that these decisions were made by the local authority at the instigation of his councillor neighbour, with whom he has a boundary dispute. He instructed Mr Dodgson to appeal against both decisions. He did so and agreed to act as expert witness at the local inquiry. Mr Sykes also instructed his solicitor to present his case. This is the proof of evidence prepared by Mr Dodgson (omitting the title page).

JAMES OLIVER DODGSON

will say

Qualifications and experience

1. I am a Fellow of The Royal Institution of Chartered Surveyors. I am also a Fellow of the Chartered Institute of Arbitrators. I have been in private practice for the past 24 years and, apart from 5 years spent in London, all my professional life has been spent in Melchester. I am now senior partner of Wilberforce and Dodgson, chartered surveyors, of Melchester and I specialise in town planning, valuation, rating and compensation. I have had a wide and long experience in town planning. I am planning adviser to the Retail Shops Federation and the National Association of Small Businesses and visiting lecturer in Applied Town Planning at the University of Melchester. I am author of "Town Planning for Students".

Outline of evidence

2. I will give my evidence under the following headings:
   (a) The appeal property.
   (b) Town planning: policies, applications and appeals.
   (c) The proposed operations.
   (d) Planning considerations.
   (e) Summary.
3. I will produce the following exhibits:
   (i)   A map showing the appeal property and surrounding area (Map JOD/1).
   (ii)   The Written Statement to the Loamshire Structure Plan (JOD/2).
   (iii) A brochure describing Polydomes (JOD/3).
   (iv)   Photographs of the appeal property (JOD/4–8).

The appeal property

4. I produce Map JOD/1 which shows the appellant's house, Juniper Cottage (the appeal property) edged red, and the existing swimming pool, edged blue. The appeal property is on the eastern side of the A371 road on the northern outskirts of the small village of Stanton Episcopi about 10 miles north of Melchester.
5. Juniper Cottage stands on a rectangular plot with a frontage of about 38.1 m (125 ft) to the road, a depth of about 60.96 m (200 ft) and a site area of about 1.23 ha (0.57 ac).
6. Juniper Cottage was built at the beginning of the nineteenth century. It is an attractive two and three storey detached house built of brick with a pitched tiled roof. It is sited east to west close to the southern boundary of the site. It has 7 rooms, a kitchen and 2 bathrooms. To the north-east of the house is a double garage with a gravel drive leading from the road to the garage. To the north of this is the garden comprising lawn, fruit trees, flower beds, rockery, swimming pool, changing room and fuel tank. The swimming pool is in the north-west corner of the garden. It is edged blue on Map JOD/1. It is proposed to cover this pool with an inflatable Polydome.
7. The swimming pool measures 4.88 m (16 ft) east to west and 9.14 km (30 ft) north to south. It has a maximum depth of 2.29 m (7 ft 6 ins) and a minimum depth of 0.91 m (3 ft). It is heated; the heating equipment being housed in a wooden hut 1.83 m by 3.05 m (6 ft by 10 ft) sited to the south of the pool; this hut is also used as a changing room. A fuel tank adjoins the hut. The pool is surrounded by a paved area which varies in width from 0.91 m to 3.66 m (3 ft to 12 ft). Immediately to the west of the pool and the paved surround is a screen of about 30 mature Cupresses trees planted at 0.91 m (3 ft) intervals and varying in

height from 2.9 m to 3.35 m (9 ft 6 ins to 11 ft). Along the road frontage, which is the western boundary of the appeal site, is a woven panel fence (1.22 m (4 ft) in height). The southern boundary of the site is a brick wall (0.91 m (3 ft) high) and the flank wall of the adjoining house, High Trees. The northern boundary is a thick hedge about 1.83 m (6 ft) high.

8. To the north and east of the appeal property is open pasture land, and to the south and west are the scattered houses, war memorial, church, vicarage and public house which form the small village of Stanton Episcopi. This village is generally on a level site but to the north, past Juniper Cottage, the land slopes down to a stream and then rises gently on the northern side. Views of Juniper Cottage from the north (looking south) are obscured by a large tree in the field to the north of the garden and also by a belt of trees and bushes lining the road. The road changes direction in the village to the south of the house and this results in the appeal property being obscured from the south by buildings and trees.

9. I inspected the appeal property and surrounding area on 10th October 1981 and 2nd June 1982.

Town planning: policies, application and appeals

10. The appeal property is in the County of Loamshire. The Loamshire Structure Plan was approved on 22nd September 1979. I produce a copy of the Written Statement to this Plan (JOD/2). In strategic terms the operations which are the subject of this appeal are of minor importance and only one of the Structure Plan Policies is relevant. This is Policy VE 1 (p. 89):

> "*VE 1.* In rural settlements the primary planning policy will be the conservation and enhancement of special character; development in or adjoining a rural settlement will be required to comply with paragraphs 8.10 to 8.15, as appropriate."

The appropriate paragraph is 8.12 (p. 90):

> "8.12. In considering any application for new development in or adjoining a rural settlement the objectives will seek to ensure:
>
> (i)   a land use compatible with the character, appearance and well-being of the settlement;
> (ii)   sympathetic siting and design in relation to adjoining development and existing spaces;
> (iii) a high standard of intrinsic visual design, both of buildings and other features."

A local plan has not been prepared for Stanton Episcopi.

11. On 15th October 1981 I submitted two applications in respect of

the fixing and inflation of a semi-circular transparent polythene dome (a Polydome) over the swimming pool at the appeal property. These applications were, first, for a determination under section 53 of the Town and Country Planning Act 1971 that the siting, fixing and inflation of a Polydome over the swimming pool is not development requiring planning permission; and secondly, if such a determination is not given, an application for planning permission for those operations.

12. A decision on the section 53 application was given on 20th January 1982. It was determined that "the proposed operations would effect a change in the physical character of the land and are, therefore, development under section 22 of the 1971 Act for which planning permission is required."

13. A decision was also given on the same date on the alternative application. Planning permission was refused in the following terms:

> "The erection of an inflated Polydome in this prominent location would be highly detrimental to the considerable visual and environmental amenities of the area in general and the immediate street scene in particular."

14. On 14th February 1982 I submitted an appeal against the section 53 determination on the grounds "that having regard to all the relevant circumstances, the placing, fixing and inflation of a Polydome over the existing swimming pool at Juniper Cottage would not alter the physical character of the land and would not, therefore, constitute development requiring planning permission under section 22 of the Town & Country Planning Act 1971."

15. On the same date I also submitted an appeal under section 36 of the 1971 Act against the above refusal of planning permission on the following grounds:

> "(i) Having regard to Circular 22/80, Development Control Policy Note No 2 and Class I of Schedule 1 to the General Development Order 1977 (as amended), there is a presumption in favour of the grant of planning permission for the proposed development unless there are substantial planning objections.
>
> (ii) The only planning objection raised by the local planning authority relates to the appearance of the proposed development; this is of little weight due to the excellent screening of the site of the Polydome.
>
> (iii) The proposed operations are not contrary to the policy regarding development in rural settlements in the Loamshire Structure Plan."

16. It is agreed that both appeals should be dealt with at this inquiry.

The proposed operations.

17. I now describe the operations which are the subject-matter of these two applications and then give my opinion that they do not constitute development requiring planning permission. The operations are the placing, fixing and inflation of a Polydome over the existing swimming pool at the appeal property. A Polydome is a semi-circular dome made of tough transparent polythene. After it is fixed to the ground it is inflated with air from a fan unit which keeps it rigid. This air can be heated. Polydomes are manufactured and installed by Poly International Ltd of Currock Street, Carlisle. I produce a brochure "Polydomes for an Improved Life-style" (JOD/3) containing general information.

18. The dimensions of the proposed Polydome are 7.31 m long by 11.58 m wide (24 ft by 38 ft) with a maximum height of 2.44 m (8 ft). The Polydome will be secured to the surround of the swimming pool by securing the D shackles and ropes attached to the circumference of the Polydome to 25 mm (1 inch) eyebolts inserted in the paved surround at 0.61 m (2 ft) intervals and at each corner (see page 4 of the above brochure (JOD/3). The initial installation of the Polydome (including the insertion of the eyebolts in the paved surround) will take less than 1 day. Thereafter, it can be deflated, removed and stored in a small space, all in about 1 hour. Subsequent fixing and inflation would take about 1 hour. A Polydome has, therefore, little permanent attachment to the ground and is as portable as a large tent.

19. I now consider whether the above operations are development within section 22 (1) of the Town and Country Planning Act 1971. I am of the opinion that they do not constitute development. The question whether or not operations on land constitute development is one of fact and degree, decided within the framework of law provided by the relevant statutory provisions and case law. The appellant's solicitor will address you on the law and I will confine my evidence to matters of fact.

20. I do not regard a Polydome as a building (as defined in section 290 of the 1971 Act), nor do I regard the operations to secure and inflate the Polydome as a "building, engineering, mining or other operations in, on, over or under land". In my opinion they are operations which do not fall within the scope of development. They are not really operations at all but a use of land

which, being a domestic use, does not require planning permission. I accept, however, that this may be a border-line case and it is helpful, therefore, to ask whether the proposed operations change the physical character of the land in the way that the erection of a building or structure does. There is no single test to be applied, one must look at all the surrounding circumstances, but three factors are particularly relevant. These are the <u>size</u> of the Polydome, its degree of <u>permanence</u> and method of <u>attachment</u> to the ground.

21. First, the question of size. The Polydome will be of a small size and will be brought to the site ready-made. This may be contrasted with a building or structure which is normally too large for this to be feasible: it must be built on site. Secondly, permanence. A building or structure is permanent. When built it remains, and can normally be removed only by demolition or removal in pieces. It cannot normally be removed intact. This may be contrasted with a Polydome which can be deflated, unfixed and stored away intact in less than an hour. Conversely, it can be re-fixed, inflated and ready for use again in the same time. It is no more permanent than a tent. The third factor is attachment to the ground. Does the degree of attachment of a Polydome make it part of the realty? This is allied to the question of permanency. I do not think that the insertion of an eye-bolt in the paved surround of the swimming pool is a building, engineering or other operation. Further, I do not think that the fixing of the Polydome to the eye-bolts forms a sufficient degree of attachment to the ground to make the Polydome part of the realty. It is analogous to a tent or a cover over a swimming pool to keep out falling leaves. If the appellant moves from Juniper Cottage he can take his Polydome with him.

22. I am, therefore, of the opinion that the fixing and inflation of a Polydome over the swimming pool at the appeal property is not development requiring planning permission. If, however, the Secretary of State decides that it is and the planning merits fall to be considered, then I am of the opinion that planning permission should be granted for the following reasons.

Planning considerations

23. First, I refer to the basic principle which applies to all planning applications. This is that a person should be allowed to develop his land as he wishes unless there are good planning reasons why he should be prevented or restricted from so doing in the public interest. The spirit of this principle was found in Circular 69 of 1949 and more specifically in Circular 61/53 (now withdrawn). It is now in Circular 22/80:

"2. ... This circular is concerned with planning applications. It has two aims .... The second is to ensure that development is only prevented or restricted when this serves a clear planning purpose and the economic effects have been taken into account ....
3. ... Development control must avoid placing unjustified obstacles in the way of any development. ... Local planning authorities are asked ... always to grant planning permission, having regard to all material considerations, unless there are sound and clear-cut reasons for refusal ...."

24. Secondly, the general principle to which I have just referred is further extended in an applicant's favour in the case of development within the curtilage of a dwelling house. Thus, in Development Control Policy Note No. 2 (Development in Residential Areas), paragraph 12 states:

> "*Garages and other outbuildings* ... In general it is considered that householders should be free to carry out development of this kind as they wish, and permission is likely to be refused only if there is some substantial objection to the particular proposal. This may be a matter of amenity, for example, if it is a question of preventing the appearance of well-designed houses or a pleasant street scene being spoilt by the addition of incongruous buildings. In that case the solution might be to redesign or resite the building ...."

I will deal with the question of appearance when I consider the planning objections to the proposed development raised by the local planning authority.

25. Thirdly, I refer to the permitted development within the curtilage of a dwelling house in Class I of Schedule 1 to the General Development Order 1977 (as amended by the General Development (Amendment) Order 1981) which reinforces still further the general principle that domestic development should normally be permitted.

26. The general principle to be applied in this appeal is, therefore, that there is a strong presumption in favour of granting planning permission for the proposed development unless there are substantial planning objections to such development. I disagree, therefore, with paragraph 14 of the local authority's Rule 6 Statement which states that "due to the attractive environment within the village envelope of Stanton Episcopi, the presumption must be against any further development unless the applicant can demonstrate an overriding local need".

27. The only planning objection raised in this case is the effect of the

Polydome on the character and appearance of the village. In my opinion this objection carries little weight due to the excellent natural and artificial screening of the site of the Polydome. It is not sufficient to displace the clear presumption in favour of allowing the development. To illustrate this point I produce photographs numbered JOD/4–8. They are described and numbered on their face and the positions from which they were taken and the directions of the camera are shown in red on Map JOD/1.

28. The site of the Polydome is screened by a fence 1.22 m (4 ft) high along the western boundary, behind which is a line of mature evergreen trees, varying in height from 2.9 m to 3.35 m (9 ft 6 ins to 11 ft) and by a hedge 1.83 m (6 ft) high along the northern boundary. The highest part of the Polydome would be 2.44 m (8 ft) high and, therefore, wholly screened by these trees (see photograph JOD/4). In addition to the fence, hedge and tree screens, there is a large tree in the field immediately to the north of the northern boundary of Juniper Cottage and also a north/south belt of trees and bushes along the eastern edge of the A371 road. Thus, the Polydome would be completely screened from public view when the village is approached from the north (see photographs JOD/4–6). The site of the proposed Polydome is equally well screened from the south by Juniper Cottage, the adjoining house (High Trees) and a large tree at the front of Juniper Cottage (see photograph JOD/7). The Polydome would also not be seen from the higher ground across the road to the west of Juniper Cottage. It would be screened by the fence and trees referred to above and the public hall fronting the road opposite the appeal property (see photograph JOD/8). The Polydome would only be seen to a material extent from the private land to the east of Juniper Cottage. It might glisten in the sunlight but would not be any more obtrusive than a greenhouse or large tent in a garden.

29. I think it is relevant that, in the absence of a direction under article 4 of the General Development Order 1977, and if the swimming pool were not in front of Juniper Cottage, planning permission for a Polydome over it would be granted by article 3 and Class I.3 of Schedule 1 to that Order (as amended).

30. I am of the opinion that the proposed operations would not be contrary to the general policy for development in rural areas set out in the Loamshire Structure Plan, Policy VE1 and paragraph 8.12 (see paragraph 10 above). First, it is a domestic land use "compatible with the character, appearance and well-being of the settlement" of Stanton Episcopi. Secondly, owing to the excellent screening of the site of the Polydome and its appearance which resembles a domestic greenhouse, it achieves the objective of "sympathetic siting and design in relation to adjoining

development and existing spaces." Thirdly, although it cannot
be said that the Polydome has a "high standard of intrinsic visual
design" it would not be obtrusive when seen from the public
areas outside the appeal property.

Summary

31. I now summarise my evidence. First, I am of the opinion, that as
a matter of fact and degree, the siting, fixing and inflation of the
proposed Polydome would not be development requiring planning permission. My reason for this opinion is the lack of any
change in the physical character of the land having regard to the
size of the Polydome, its permanence and method of attachment
to the ground.
32. Secondly, I am of the opinion that, if planning permission is
required for the proposed operations, it should be granted for the
following reasons:

(a) In accordance with Circulars 69/49 and 22/80, paragraph
12 of Development Control Policy Note No. 2 and Class I of
Schedule 1 to the General Development Order 1977 (as
amended), there is a presumption in favour of the grant of
planning permission for domestic development within the
curtilage of a dwelling house unless a substantial planning
objection can be shown.
(b) The only planning objection raised by the local authority
relates to the appearance of the Polydome; it has excellent
screening and, therefore, this objection is of insufficient
weight to displace the clear presumption in favour of the
grant of planning permission.
(c) The proposed operations do not conflict with the policy relating to development in rural settlements in the Loamshire
Structure Plan.

NOTES:

(a) Mr Dodgson was the first witness at this inquiry. It was his
function, therefore, to "set the scene" by stating all the relevant
facts necessary to an understanding of his opinion and the subsequent evidence.
(b) Mr Dodgson resisted Mr Sykes's request to include in his proof
reference to his neighbour's alleged part in the local authority's
decision.
(c) The question whether or not the operations to fix and inflate the
Polydome constitute development presented a problem in Mr
Dodgson's evidence. This question is essentially one of fact and

degree answered within a framework of law. Mr Dodgson restricted his evidence to matters of fact leaving his client's solicitor to explain and apply the law.

(d) This proof was read out at the inquiry and was written with this in mind. In more complicated planning appeals Mr Dodgson would usually prepare a supplementary proof for use by his client's solicitor and/or counsel.

EXAMPLE 5 (WRITTEN REPRESENTATIONS)

(See Chapter 4 p. 112 above)

Abbots Meadow is a quiet street of Georgian houses close to Melchester Cathedral. No. 27 is occupied as offices by Thompson, Smith & Partners, consulting engineers, on a lease for 20 years from 25th December 1978 at a rent of £4,750 per annum with five yearly rent reviews.

In October 1983 Mr Dodgson was instructed by the tenants to negotiate the review rent from 25th December 1983. Negotiations with the landlords' surveyor took place but agreement could not be reached. In April 1984 an arbitrator was appointed to determine the review rent and the parties agreed to the use of the written representations procedure. They were directed by the arbitrator to produce a statement of agreed facts and an agreed map, and, with co-operation on both sides, were able to do so before the submission of representations. This statement is not reproduced here but it included a description of the subject-property (including agreed floor areas) and its location, a summary of the town planning position, a schedule of agreed comparables (related to the agreed map) and an appendix containing extracts from the development plans and copies of relevant planning permissions and refusals.

The following initial written representations were submitted by Mr Dodgson on behalf of the tenants (respondents).

IN THE MATTER OF THE ARBITRATION ACTS 1950 AND 1979 AND IN THE MATTER OF AN ARBITRATION BETWEEN:

MELCHESTER DEVELOPMENT GROUP (Claimants)
and
THOMPSON, SMITH & PARTNERS (Respondents)

RELATING TO 27 ABBOTS MEADOW, MELCHESTER, LOAMSHIRE

REPRESENTATIONS OF JAMES OLIVER DODGSON

FRICS FCIArb OF WILBERFORCE AND DODGSON ON

BEHALF OF THE RESPONDENTS

Qualifications and experience

1. I am a Fellow of The Royal Institution of Chartered Surveyors and of the Chartered Institute of Arbitrators. I have been in private practice for the past 28 years and, apart from five years spent in London, I have spent all my professional life in Melchester. I am senior partner of Wilberforce and Dodgson, chartered surveyors, of Melchester. I specialise in valuation, rating, compensation and town planning. I have had considerable experience in the valuation, sale and letting of commercial property in Melchester. I am frequently appointed as an arbitrator or independent expert in rent reviews. I am the author of "The Law and Practice of Rent Reviews."

Basis of rental valuation

2. Clause 5(1) of the lease of the subject-property dated 4th January 1979 provides that the rent shall be reviewed at five yearly intervals, the reviewed rent to be either (a) the rent payable immediately preceding the relevant review date, or (b) the market rent at that date, whichever is the greater. We are concerned with the rent review at 25th December 1983.

3. The term "market rent" is defined in clause 5(2) as:
   "... the yearly rental value of the property let by a willing landlord to a willing tenant for a term of 20 years with vacant possession without a premium on the terms of this lease (other than as to rent) and on the assumption (whether or not the same may be the case) that the tenant has fully performed all his obligations thereunder but disregarding
   (a) any effect on rent of the fact that the tenant may have been in occupation of the property
   (b) any goodwill attributable to the property by reason of the tenant's trade or business
   (c) any effect on rent of any improvements to the property carried out by the tenant otherwise than in pursuance of an obligation to the landlord"

4. Two of the terms of the lease particularly relevant to the assessment of the market rent on review are the tenant's covenants relating to user (clause 4(17)) and town planning (clause 4(22)).

5. The effect of the user clause is that the subject-property may only be used as "professional offices" (the actual use) or such

other use as may be permitted by the landlord, such permission not to be unreasonably withheld.

6. The clause relating to town planning is lengthy and detailed; sub-clauses (a) and (b) are particularly relevant. Sub-clause (a) requires the tenant to comply with the provisions and requirements of the Planning Acts and all permissions or consents granted therunder. Sub-clause (b) prohibits the tenant from developing or using the premises in breach of planning control and requires him to obtain all necessary consents or permissions for the carrying out of any operations or continuance of any use which may constitute development.

7. The combined effect of the user and town planning clauses at the date of review was that the tenant could not, without permission from the landlord, use the demised premises for any use other than as professional offices and was required to comply with the provisions of any planning permission granted for that use or to obtain such permission if that use were in breach of planning control. Furthermore, the definition of market rent requires the assumption to be made that the tenant has fully performed all his obligations under the lease: this would include the obligation not to use the premises in breach of planning control.

8. The planning position in respect of the subject-property, relevant to the assessment of the market rent, is summarised in paragraphs 7 to 10 of the statement of agreed facts. I refer first to paragraph 7 which sets out the relevant planning history of the subject-property. It will be seen that planning permission has not been granted for use as offices and that this use commenced after 31st December 1963. It is not, therefore, authorised by planning permission nor is it an established use under section 94 of the Town and Country Planning Act 1971. It is in breach of planning control and there is a conflict between the permitted office use under the user clause in the lease and the tenant's obligations under the town planning clause. How is this conflict to be resolved when assessing the review rent? Is the rent to be determined having regard only to the permitted office use even though this is in breach of planning control? Or in accordance with some other use, permitted under planning law but in contravention of the use clause? Or in accordance with the user clause but recognising the need to obtain planning permission for such use in order to reconcile the user and planning clauses? In my view this last basis is the correct basis of valuation: the user clause prevails, subject to the need to obtain planning permission.

9. There is no direct authority on this point but the two cases

discussed in paragraph 10 below indicate that this view is correct. A recent decision which appears to indicate that the user clause prevails, whatever the planning position, can be distinguished as explained in paragraphs 11–13 below. Copies of these three decisions are attached to these representations with the relevant passages marked in red.

10. In <u>Compton Group Ltd v Estates Gazette Ltd</u> (1977) 244 EG 799, one of the questions put to the Court of Appeal was whether the surveyor determining the review rent "ought to exclude from consideration the possibility of any future use of the premises in breach of planning control?" The Court unanimously held that a possible future use in breach of planning control should not be taken into consideration when assessing the review rent. In <u>Molton Builders Ltd v Westminster City Council</u> (1975) 30 P & CR 182, the Court of Appeal affirmed the principle that a landlord who lets property for a purpose which is unlawful is not derogating from his grant and that the permitted use under the lease is always subject to the proviso that such use is lawful.

11. The recent decision of the Court of Appeal in <u>Bovis Group Pension Fund Ltd v G. C. Flooring and Furnishing Ltd</u> (1984) 269 EG 1252, appears to indicate at first glance that the permitted office use of the subject-property should prevail, coupled with the assumption that this use has planning permission. In this case the permitted use under the user clause in the lease was as "professional offices", and the review rent was defined as ". . . the rent at which having regard to the terms hereof (other than as to rent and user) the demised premises might reasonably be expected to be let for office purposes . . .". Planning permission had not been granted for the use of the whole building as offices and it was only partly used for this use. It was held by a majority that the review rent must be assessed on the assumption that the premises could lawfully be used as offices and that planning permission had been granted for such use.

12. In my view, the facts of the <u>Bovis</u> case are materially different from those relating to the subject-property. In <u>Bovis</u> there was a clear direction in the definition of the review rent requiring an office use. to be assumed; this was the basis of the majority decision. Eveleigh LJ said (p. 1253):

> "The clause indicates to me that the valuer has to assume that there are these premises in use as offices. The clause uses the phrase 'let for office purposes'. That to my mind, is another way of describing the premises as office premises. The object is to value the premises on the basis that you are

able to let them for office purposes. It seems to me that that is saying that we are concerned to determine the value of these premises as office premises . . ..

We are not seeking here to value a lease with a user clause permitting office use when in fact it may or may not have real office value, and the fact that a property can be let with a permitted purpose that requires planning permission does not, to my mind, show it is being let as such premises. It is a different case."

A similar view was expressed by Griffiths LJ (p. 1253):

"I read the clause as indicating an intention to use the going rate for office space in the Berners Street area at the time of the rent review as the yardstick by which the rent is to be fixed."

13. The rent review clause in the lease of the subject-property does not contain a direction that the premises are to be valued as offices (as in Bovis). It should be construed as requiring the market rent to be assessed on the basis that the permitted use under the lease is as professional offices, but that the tenant is required to obtain planning permission for that use. An assumption is not to be made that the office use is authorised by planning permission. He may or may not receive such permission, depending upon the planning position at the review date (discussed below), and this uncertainty will be reflected in the rental bid of the hypothetical willing tenant.

Rental valuation

14. Having regard to the above basis of rental valuation, my approach to the assessment of the market rent as at 25th December 1983 is in two parts.

First, I assess the rent on the assumption that the permitted office use under the lease is not in breach of planning control. Secondly, I make a deduction from that market rent to reflect the actual position, namely that the permitted office use is not authorised by planning permission and that an application must be made for such permission. There is uncertainty as to whether it will be granted.

15. Paragraph 11 of the statement of agreed facts sets out details of five agreed comparable rental transactions. I have relied on the lettings of nos 17 and 42 Abbots Meadow and the renewal of the lease of 19 Priors Mead in the first part of my rental valuation of the subject-property. These properties are terraced Georgian houses used as offices, close to the subject-property and similar

in size, construction and accommodation. Each property has planning permission for office use.

16. My analysis of these transaction is as follows:

17 Abbots Meadow

Let for a term of 15 years from 25th December 1983 at a rent of £6,325 per annum exclusive; five yearly rent reviews; full repairing and insuring lease.

					£ pa
Basement	Store	120 sq ft	@	£1.25	150
Ground floor	Offices	575 sq ft	@	£4.00	2,300
First floor	Offices	547 sq ft	@	£3.50	1,914
Second floor	Offices	520 sq ft	@	£3.00	1,560
		1,762 sq ft	@	£3.36	£5,924
2 car spaces @ £200					400
					£6,324

Overall rent per sq ft, ground to second floors
= £3.52

say £6,325 pa

42 Abbots Meadow

Let for a term of 20 years from 29th September 1983 at a rent of £7,900 per annum exclusive; five yearly rent reviews; full repairing and insuring lease.

					£ pa
Basement	Store	150 sq ft	@	£1.50	225
Ground floor	Offices	650 sq ft	@	£4.00	2,600
First floor	Offices	645 sq ft	@	£3.50	2,257
Second floor	Offices	600 sq ft	@	£3.00	1,800
Third floor	Offices	500 sq ft	@	£2.00	1,000
		2,545 sq ft	@	£3.10	£7,882

Overall rent per sq ft, ground to second floors
= £3.51

say £7,900 pa

19 Priors Mead

Renewal of a tenancy for a term of 10 years from 25th March 1984 at a rent of £7,000 per annum exclusive; five yearly rent reviews; full repairing and insuring lease.

				£ pa	
Ground floor	Offices	725 sq ft	@	£4.25	3,081
First floor	Offices	712 sq ft	@	£3.75	2,670
Second floor	Offices	410 sq ft	@	£3.25	1,332
		1,847 sq ft	@	£3.83	£7,083
				say	£7,000 pa

17. Having regard to the above rental analysis and the differences between the subject-property and the comparable properties, I am of the opinion that the market rent of the subject-property as at 25th December 1983, on the assumption that planning permission had been granted for the use of the property as offices, was £7,142 per annum, calculated as follows:

				£ pa	
Basement	Store	250 sq ft	@	£1.25	312
Ground floor	Offices	725 sq ft	@	£4.00	2,900
First floor	Offices	730 sq ft	@	£3.50	2,555
Second floor	Offices	550 sq ft	@	£2.50	1,375
		2,255 sq ft	@	£3.17	£7,142

Overall rent per sq ft, ground to second floors
= £3.40

18. The next step in my rental valuation is to make a deduction from the above rent to reflect the fact that the permitted and actual office use is in breach of planning control and must be authorised by the grant of planning permission. This deduction will be assessed by reference to the office policies current at the date of review and my analysis of the review rents of two other agreed comparable properties where office uses exist without planning permission or an established use certificate. These properties are 37 Abbots Meadow and 21 Priors Mead. The same planning policies apply to these two properties as to the subject-property.

19. A tenant taking a lease of the subject-property for offices would take into account the likelihood of the grant of planning permission for that use. The more likely the grant of office planning permission then the higher the bid and the smaller the deduction from the above rental value. It is, therefore, necessary to look at the planning policies relating to offices in Melchester. These are set out in paragraphs 8 to 10 and the appendix to the statement of agreed facts. I draw attention to the following

matters which indicate uncertainty as to the grant of planning permission for the use of the subject-property as offices:

(a) Melchester is one of five "Restraint Areas" in the Loamshire Structure Plan. In these areas planning permission for offices will generally be refused except where there is a special employment or economic justification for such use or development.

(b) The subject-property is shown in the City of Melchester District Plan as part of the Cathedral Precinct Area where the policy is to preserve and encourage residential uses; offices and other commercial uses will only be permitted where the particular property is unlikely to be used for residential purposes and the prospective occupiers can show that they have a local connection with the centre of Melchester.

(c) Over the past two years planning permission for office use has been refused in respect of 45 and 54 Abbots Meadow, but granted conditionally in respect of 12 and 26 Abbots Meadow (copies of these decisions are included in the appendix to the statement of agreed facts).

(d) I believe that Melchester City Council are aware of the office use of the subject-property but have not taken enforcement action to stop it.

20. The effect of these policies and decisions would be to produce in the mind of a prospective tenant uncertainty as to whether he could bring himself within their scope and obtain an office planning permission for the subject-property. This would result in a reduction in the amount of rent he would pay.

21. An indication of the amount of this reduction can be found by comparing the rents of comparable properties which have an authorised office use with those without such authorisation. The remaining agreed comparable properties, 37 Abbots Meadow and 21 Priors Mead, do not have an authorised office use and can, therefore, be compared with the three comparables analysed in paragraph 16 above. Any reduction in the rent per square foot is likely to be wholly or partly due to the lack of planning permission for office use.

22. My analysis of the rents of the above two properties is as follows:

37 Abbots Meadow

Rent review at 24th June 1983 in a full repairing and insuring lease for a term of 15 years from 24th June 1978 with five yearly rent reviews. The agreed review rent (the rack rental value) was £5,000 per annum exclusive.

					£ pa
Ground floor	Offices	450 sq ft	@	£3.75	1,687
First floor	Offices	432 sq ft	@	£3.25	1,404
Second floor	Offices	400 sq ft	@	£2.75	1,100
		1,282 sq ft	@	£3.27	£4,191
4 car spaces @ £225					· 900
					£5,091
					say £5,000 pa

The overall rents per square foot (ground to second floors) for nos 17 and 42 Abbots Meadow (with planning permission for offices) are £3.52 and £3.51 respectively (paragraph 16 above), compared with £3.27 per square foot for no 37 (without planning permission for offices). This represents a reduction of 7.1% in the latter rent.

21 Priors Mead

Rent review at 25th December 1983 in a full repairing and insuring lease for a term of 20 years from 25th December 1978; five yearly rent reviews. The agreed review rent (the market rental value) was £7,500 per annum exclusive.

					£ pa
Basement	Store	225 sq ft	@	£1.50	337
Ground floor	Offices	625 sq ft	@	£4.00	2,500
First floor	Offices	620 sq ft	@	£3.50	2,170
Second floor	Offices	600 sq ft	@	£3.00	1,800
		2,070 sq ft	@	£3.29	£6,807
3 car spaces @ £250					750
					£7,557

Overall rent per sq ft, ground to second floors
= £3.51

say £7,500 pa

The overall rent per square foot for 19 Priors Mead (with planning permission for offices) is £3.83 (paragraph 16 above), compared to £3.51 per square foot on the ground to second floors of 21 Priors Mead (without planning permission for offices). This is a reduction of 8.35% in the latter rent.

23. On the above evidence of reductions of 7.1% and 8.35%, I have formed the opinion that a reduction of 7.5% should be made to the market rent for the subject-property of £7,142 per annum

(paragraph 17 above). This reduces the rent to £6,500 per
annum and I ask you to make your award at this figure.

....
J. O. Dodgson FRICS FCIArb
Wilberforce and Dodgson
Date ....

NOTES:

(a) If a statement of agreed facts and map had not been prepared when Mr Dodgson made the above representations it
would have been necessary for him to include those facts,
etc in his representations. The order of contents would then
have been as follows: qualifications and experience; situation and description of the subject-property; town planning;
basis of rental valuation; rental valuation; Appendix A—a
schedule of comparable transactions; Appendix B—relevant extracts from Loamshire Structure Plan and the City of
Melchester District Plan and copies of relevant planning
permissions and refusals; a map showing the subject-
property edged red and the comparables edged blue and
related to Appendix A; floor plans, elevations and photographs of the subject-property (related to a plan showing
the position of each photograph and the direction of the
camera).

(b) Initial representations may contain specific criticisms of the
opposing case where this has been established in sufficient
detail in prior negotiation. Mr Dodgson was uncertain as to
the exact nature of his opponent's case, which had changed
during negotiations, and therefore he decided to defer his
rebuttal of his opponent's case until the subsequent exchange of cross-representations.

(c) In the above initial representations Mr Dodgson did not
conclude with a summary of his submissions and evidence,
but he put this at the end of his cross-representations.

(d) It was agreed between the parties that the arbitrator would
prepare an interim award determining the amount of the
market rent. He would then make a final award dealing
with costs, following further representations from the
parties in the light of his award on rent. Accordingly, Mr
Dodgson did not include any submissions on costs in his
initial representations.

CHAPTER SIX

The Advocate-Expert Witness: Combining the Roles

INTRODUCTION

On 9th November 1868 John Clutton gave the first Presidential Address to the newly formed Institution of Surveyors. In it he criticised the surveyor who acted as an advocate:

> "The business of a surveyor, I hold to be is to give an unbiased opinion on the subject placed before him and not to become in any way an advocate."

Clearly he held the view that the functions of advocate and expert witnes were incompatible. The difference between these two roles may be clearly seen. An advocate speaks for his client. In Dr Johnson's words he "... is to do for his client all that his client might fairly do for himself if he could." His task is to present his client's case: to persuade the court that he is right and his opponent is wrong. He can, quite properly, change his submissions according to the party he represents. An expert witness, on the other hand, speaks for himself. His task is to inform the court, to assist it with fact and opinion on a technical matter. Unlike the advocate he does not make submissions but expresses opinions, which should remain constant whichever party employs him. The common ground is that both advocate and expert have a duty to assist the court.

Can these different roles be combined in the same person? In some circumstances they cannot: rules of procedure or of a professional body do not allow it. A surveyor cannot appear as an advocate in the High Court or a county court (except as a litigant in person) and only with leave, which is rarely given, before the Lands Tribunal. Before July 1982 a member of the Royal Town Planning Institute was prohibited from acting as an advocate before any tribunal, unless he was also a barrister or solicitor. Now he may act as an advocate at a planning inquiry, where this is appropriate, but he may not become an all purpose advocate. A surveyor may appear as an advocate before an arbitrator, a local valuation court, a rent assessment committee, a rent tribunal, a leasehold valuation tribunal or at a planning inquiry.

Combining the two roles in one person can be unsatisfactory and lead to criticism. For example, in a compensation case before the Lands Tribunal, the expert witness for the claimants was allowed to "manage" their cases because they were not legally represented.

The tribunal said, after giving a list of his errors (both as advocate and expert), that "this is a classic example, if ever one was needed, of the undesirability of having a valuer attempting to double his role of expert witness with that of advocate." In rating appeals before the Lands Tribunal the valuation officer frequently appears on behalf of himself, as a litigant in person. This has sometimes produced unfavourable comment from the tribunal. In *W. & R. R. Adam Ltd v Hockin (VO)* (1966) 13 RRC 1, the member said (p. 4):

> "I mean no disrespect to Mr Hockin ... when I remind him that the position of an expert witness is quite distinct from and not always compatible with that of an advocate. It goes without saying that the duty of the advocate is to present his client's case as best he may on the evidence available whereas the expert witness is there to give the court the benefit of his special training and/or experience in order to help the court come to the right decision. It is important, therefore, that the expert witness should be consistent in his opinions and should not be, nor appear to be, partisan, for his opinions then become of less weight.
>
> It is because the functions of an advocate and of an expert witness are different though complementary that this tribunal normally refuses to permit the expert witness to act also as a party's advocate".

But, despite these criticisms and the difficulties inherent in combining these two roles, surveyors frequently appear in a dual capacity before the more informal tribunals. Where the circumstances are right and the surveyor is competent, advocate and expert can exist in the same person without detriment to his client's case or inconvenience to the tribunal. A surveyor should, of course, only act as an advocate-expert witness where his evidence in the latter capacity supports his client's case. Moreover, his objective evidence should never be altered by his other, and more subjective role, as an advocate.

Not every case before an informal tribunal is suitable for such composite representation. I suggest that if one or more of the following factors are present then the client should seek legal representation, allowing the surveyor to restrict his role to that of an expert witness. These factors are:

(1) the case includes a difficult point of law which is material to the decision;
(2) one or both of the parties regard the initial hearing as the first step to a decision by a higher tribunal;
(3) the other party will be legally represented;

(4) the issues of fact and/or opinion are numerous, requiring evidence from several witnesses on each side;

(5) the amount at stake is high.

The ideal case for an advocate-expert is one where the issues are simple questions of fact or opinion and there is similar advocate-expert representation on each side.

One practical difficulty in combining the two roles should be mentioned: how is the court to know which role the representative is playing at any particular time? Is he an advocate making a submission, or an expert expressing an opinion? There are two approaches to this problem which may be termed the formal and informal approaches. The formal approach makes it clear to the court, by words and actions, which role is being played. For example, the opening address as an advocate will be made standing; he will then sit in the witness box, remind the court that he is now an expert witness, give his evidence, submit to cross-examination and then re-examine himself; he will then go back to his former seat transformed again into an advocate, and so on. The informal approach ignores such distinctions: the opening address and examination-in-chief merge into one statement and no clear distinction is made, either by words or actions, between the advocate's submissions and the expert's evidence. The formal approach is probably the better one and should avoid confusion as to the role being played at any particular time.

DUTIES OF AN ADVOCATE

An advocate has a three-fold duty: to the court, to his client and to his opponent. His *duty to the court* is paramount. It is to assist the court to reach a correct and just decision. Thus, an advocate should not knowingly mislead the court about the law. He should cite *all* relevant cases and statutory provisions even though some may be detrimental to his client's case. His skill as an advocate will lie in his ability to distinguish or criticise the unhelpful cases and to show that the statutory provisions do not apply. An advocate's duty on matters of fact is different. He must not deliberately mislead the court on the facts, but, in the words of Lord Denning, "short of that, he may put such matters in evidence or omit such others as in his discretion he thinks will be most to the advantage of his client". An advocate must present his case with integrity.

As we saw in Chapter 4, however, an expert witness has a duty to put before the court *all* relevant facts and his true opinion. It is here in the realm of fact that, when advocate and expert are the same person, conflict may arise between their respective duties. When this occurs I suggest that the duty of the expert must prevail: all relevant facts must be brought to the attention of the court. It is also in pursuance of his duty to the court that an advocate should not make allegations or criticisms of his opponent, witnesses or third parties solely on his client's instructions. He should only do so (as part of his duty to his client) if he is satisfied that his client has reasonable grounds for such allegations or criticisms and they are relevant to the case. It is not unknown for a client to allege, for example, that for improper reasons a planning officer has recommended refusal of a planning permission or a valuation officer has increased his rating assessment, without any evidence to support such statements.

An advocate's *duty to his client* is to prepare and present his case in a competent manner making (again in the words of Lord Denning) "every honest endeavour to succeed". He must remember that he is the spokesman for his client and, subject to any restrictions imposed by his overriding duty to the court, must "do for his client all that his client might fairly do for himself if he could."

An advocate's *duty to his opponent* is to act fairly and openly, to be trustworthy and not betray a confidence. To what extent should an advocate inform his opponent in advance of the law and evidence in his case? He should, of course, comply with any rules of procedure requiring the prior exchange of documents and he should seek the agreement of as many facts as possible. He need not reveal the evidence he will adduce to prove disputed facts. He should inform his opponent of the cases and statutory provisions on which he intends to rely. This is not always the practice in the county courts but it is generally done in criminal cases and in the High Court, Court of Appeal and House of Lords. I suggest that it should also be done in the informal courts and tribunals before which a surveyor may appear. Here we see all three duties operating in different directions. The advocate's duty to the court and to his opponent indicate that there should be prior disclosure, to allow full discussion for the assistance of the court and fair and open dealing between the parties. His duty to his client implies secrecy to preserve an element of surprise to the detriment of his opponent. I suggest that the advocate's duty to the court should prevail.

ADVOCACY: STYLE AND QUALITIES

Style and method in advocacy may take many forms. They are the product of the personality and temperament of the advocate, the age in which he practises, the nature of the dispute and the tribunal before which he appears. At the end of the last century and during the early part of this one public attention was often focussed on the dramatic murder trial, fashionable divorce suit or sensational libel action. Two of the great advocates of this age, with different styles, were Marshall Hall and Patrick Hastings.

Sir Edward Marshall Hall was an actor, a master of rhetoric, frequently quoting poetry and forever making dramatic gestures. In court in a murder trial he would surround himself with revolvers or other lethal weapons and sometimes bottles of poison, all of which he would use to dramatic effect during the trial. In one case, while cross-examining a witness on his plan of the scene of the crime, he asked him whether he had ever seen a more misleading plan in his life, crumpled it in his hands and threw it aside—an example not, perhaps, to be followed at a planning inquiry but typical of Marshall Hall's flamboyant style of advocacy.

Sir Patrick Hastings was altogether different. His skill lay in his powers of cross-examination, his ability to summarise a case in a few sentences and his use of brief, simple, unadorned speech. His style of advocacy is more suited to the advocate-expert appearing at an arbitration, planning inquiry or local valuation court, where clarity is more important than the dramatic gesture or rhetorical address.

We can look at other great forensic advocates of the past. Sir Edward Clarke had the gift needed by all successful advocates: the gift of persuasion. He presented his cases clearly, directly and with indisputable logic. He took great pains to prepare himself, particularly in technical matters. For example, when briefed in 1886 to defend Adelaide Bartlett on a charge of murdering her husband with liquid chloroform, he later wrote:

> "I shut myself off entirely from Parliament, the Law Courts and social engagements, and devoted myself to studying at the British Museum, or in my own library, the chief medical authorities upon the action and administration of chloroform".
> (*Cornhill Magazine*, December 1920)

The result was that, when he rose to cross-examine the expert witnesses for the prosecution, he had a complete grasp of the medical questions in the case. He did not call expert medical evidence in rebuttal, but relied on his own knowledge and skill in cross-examination.

Sir Rufus Isaacs was versatile; a master of detail, particularly in financial cases; brilliant in cross-examination, which he conducted calmly, courteously, subtly and analytically but with devastating effect. Finally, Sir Charles Russell, who achieved a reputation as a great advocate by his vigour, passion and force of personality.

All these famous advocates exercised their profession in a different time and in different courts to the modern advocate. But we can deduce from this brief survey of their style and methods the qualities needed for successful advocacy to-day. An advocate should possess at least four qualities. First, a logical mind; secondly, a clear presentation; thirdly, a good memory; and fourthly, a calm temperament.

(1) A logical mind

An advocate, like an expert witness, should have a logical mind. He should adopt an analytical approach to every case. He must be able to distinguish between law, fact and opinion; between relevant and irrelevant facts, assembling the former into a logical order within the relevant framework of law. He should be able to isolate the facts in issue, which must be proved by evidence, from agreed facts. He must be able to see the strong and weak points in his case and the issues on which he should concentrate. He must impose order on his submissions and evidence so that he may present them clearly and persuasively.

(2) A clear presentation

An advocate must have complete mastery of his case. Only slightly less important is presentation. The three essentials of successful presentation are order, clarity and coherence.

As we have seen, an advocate must arrange his case into a logical order for clear, persuasive and interesting presentation. This is most important. In his book, *Six Great Advocates*, the late Lord Birkett tells a story of Mr Justice Maule, who once said to a barrister who was presenting his case in a most confusing manner:

> "Mr Smith, do you think by introducing a little order into your narrative you might possibly render it a trifle more intelligible? It may be my fault that I cannot follow you—I know my brain is getting a little dilapidated; but I should like to stipulate for some sort of order. There are plenty of them. There is the chronological, the botanical, the metaphysical, the geographical, why even the alphabetical order would be better than no order at all".

Having imposed order on his facts, the advocate must present them clearly, coherently, and in an interesting manner, using the main tool of his trade, words. He must strive for a mastery of the English Language, remembering the three basic rules in Sir Ernest Gowers' *The Complete Plain Words*—be brief, use familiar words, use precise words.

The third essential of presentation is coherence: the advocate should develop his case step by step to form a coherent whole, leading to a logical conclusion in his client's favour. He should ensure, when acting as both advocate and expert, that the submissions in his former capacity are proved by and agree with his evidence in his latter capacity. It may be useful to remember

Aristotle's order for speeches, which can still be used even at the mundane level of a planning inquiry or local valuation court. First, an introduction; secondly, a statement of the issues; thirdly, proof; finally, a peroration or summing up.

An advocate should be brief. He should be courteous to the tribunal, his opponent and witnesses. Mannerisms and irritating habits, such as the constant jingling of money in his pocket, should be avoided: they divert attention from his words.

(3) A good memory

A good memory is a desirable quality in an advocate. Sir Patrick Hastings relied mainly on memory and little on notes. He gave the reason in his *Autobiography*:

> "I wrote little or nothing, and my case was carried in my head. In my early days it became apparent to me that no human intellect can foretell how a case may ultimately develop; one incautious question, one unexpected answer may well alter the whole atmosphere, and the advocate who is bound too closely by his written instructions may find himself floundering, hopelessly bogged in the totally unexpected developments with which he is faced."

Mastery of the facts and law, a good memory and a facility with words will leave the advocate free to judge their effect on the tribunal. He can think ahead, planning and shaping his arguments outside the confines of a written statement or copious notes.

An advocate has a greater need for a good memory than an expert witness; one who combines the two roles has an even greater need. An expert witness answers questions or reads his proof (at a planning inquiry), but an advocate-expert must give an opening address, his evidence (as a single statement, without the benefit of questions), withstand a cross-examination, re-examine himself, note his opponent's opening address and evidence, conduct a cross-examination and make a final speech. Only his opening address and evidence can be planned in advance, the remainder must be largely improvised relying largely on memory with little time to make notes or search for facts.

(4) A calm temperament

The obituary of the late Lord Widgery LCJ in *The Times* stated that "he possessed nearly all the essential weapons in the armoury of a successful advocate" including "a temperament which ensured that he was never panicked or ruffled, whatever changes and chances might arise in the forensic battles in which he was engaged." As we have seen, Sir Patrick Hastings carried his case in

his head so that he could meet unexpected developments in the
course of the trial. Flexibility allied to a calm temperament are
essential qualities for a successful advocate. He will be helped by an
orderly approach, sound preparation, mastery of the facts and a
good memory. These should give him the necessary confidence and
ability to shift his position to meet new and unexpected directions
during a hearing. He should be calm and unruffled in temperament
when those unexpected changes of direction are suddenly thrust
upon him.

The qualities discussed above are not exhaustive. Others are also
desirable: honesty, e.g. admitting a mistake or refusing to use improper arguments; courage and the tenacity to pursue a course he
thinks is right; sincerity, easier for an advocate-expert who should at
least believe in the opinion he puts forward as an expert witness; wit,
industry. It should, of course, be realised that a surveyor who performs the dual roles of advocate and expert should possess the qualities and has the duties of both. Unlike other advocates, particularly
barristers who must, as a general rule, accept any brief which is
offered, an advocate-expert should only act where his role as expert
witness allows him to give an objective opinion in support of his
client's case. When performing this role he is not the mouthpiece of
his client and must give a truthful and honest opinion. But this is not
so when he changes into an advocate: he must be honest but there is
nothing improper in his putting forward a submission in which he
does not wholly believe, provided it is consistent with and does not
cast doubt on the truth of his expert evidence.

THE ADVOCATE-EXPERT WITNESS IN PRACTICE

We now look at the advocate-expert witness in practice. In June
1980 Mr J. O. Dodgson of Melchester, our typical surveyor in court,
who we met in the last chapter, took a rating appeal to the local
valuation court appearing as an advocate-expert on behalf of the
appellant ratepayers. We look at his files to see how he dealt with
this matter.

In November 1979 Mr Dodgson was instructed by Dombey &
Son Ltd to advise on the rating assessment of their new shop at 10
Wellington Arcade, Melchester. This arcade was opened for trading
in March 1979. The valuation officer made a proposal to include
number 10 in the list at GV £2,600 RV £2,138. The ratepayers did
not object at the time, but, after discussions with other traders, they
formed the opinion that their assessment was too high. They sought
Mr Dodgson's advice. Mr Dodgson formed the same opinion and on
10th November 1979 he served a proposal to reduce the assessment
to GV £2,250 RV £1,847. The valuation officer objected; there was a

deemed appeal to the local valuation court; negotiations failed to produce a settlement and the appeal was eventually heard on 16th June 1980.

(1) Preparation

The onus of proof is on the party making a proposal (the appellant): he must prove to the satisfaction of the local valuation court that his contention is well-founded. It was Mr Dodgson's task, therefore, to prove that the existing assessment was excessive *and* that it should be reduced to GV £2,250 RV £2,138.

The preparation of Mr Dodgson's submissions and evidence may be summarised as follows:

(a) *The law.* Mr Dodgson first established the framework of law for his submissions and evidence.

(b) *The facts.* Mr Dodgson's next task was to ascertain the facts relevant to his opinion of value and to agree as many of these as possible with the valuation officer and rating authority (if necessary).

(c) *Agreed documents.* The agreed facts were incorporated in a statement of agreed facts (p. 165 below) and an agreed map.

(d) *Evidence.* Mr Dodgson now considered the evidence necessary to prove the facts in issue. He wished to show that the rent of the appeal hereditament was a full market rent and that the letting was an arm's length transaction. He decided to call evidence from Mr Dombey on this point and to produce as an exhibit the landlord's letting brochure. Mr Dodgson would give expert evidence on value and prove certain High Street shop rents by giving direct evidence himself of those rents.

Details of lettings may be proved in local valuation court and Lands Tribunal proceedings by rent returns (see Chapter 1 p. 20 above). In this case the valuation officer served notice regarding returns for nos. 7, 8, 9, 17, 18 and 19 Wellington Arcade and Mr Dodgson's counternotice specified nos. 5, 6, 10, 11, 12 and 16 Wellington Arcade. Details of these lettings (including an analysis) were subsequently agreed and included in the statement of agreed facts (Table 8.1) (p. 165 below).

(e) *Documents to be submitted in evidence.* Mr Dodgson was aware of the need to assist the court (and his own case) by producing documents summarising the main points of his evidence. The documents he prepared were: a table and plan showing the results of a pedestrian count in Wellington Arcade (JOD/1 & 1A) (p. 172 below), valuations (JOD/2) (p. 173 below) and an analysis of rents of three High Street shops to show the growth in shop rents in Melchester (JOD/3) (p. 175 below).

Documents not prepared specifically for litigation, but which are to be submitted in evidence, should be kept to a minimum and restricted to those documents (or pages) which are essential to a proper understanding of the issues. In a town planning case in the High Court, *Edwin H. Bradley & Sons Ltd v Secretary of State for the Environment* (1982) 264 EG 926, Glidewell J, after referring to the fact that he had been supplied with documents totalling 1,198 pages, only one in ten of which had been referred to at the hearing, made the following comments (p. 932):

> "I do realise that copying machines gather a momentum of their own and that in some respects it may be easier to have large quantities of material copied than to spend time deciding what ought to be weeded out. I do urge that in future cases of this nature the material should be examined and time taken to examine it so as to provide a much more selective bundle of documents and to exhibit, as far as possible, erring no doubt on the side of liberality, only those pages that are going to be necessary for understanding the matters in issue. If that proves to be impossible, or very difficult, then at least may I please request that if I or one of my brothers are going to be treated in future to a group of documents such as this counsel should supply beforehand an indication as to what the judge's advance reading might conveniently be."

(f) *Preparation of submissions and evidence.* Mr Dodgson's final task was to prepare his submissions and evidence for orderly and clear presentation at the hearing. As the representative of the appellants he opened the proceedings. He was able, therefore, to decide in advance the form of his opening address without fear that it would need to be changed to meet subsequent and perhaps unexpected developments at the hearing. Mr Dodgson made notes for this address.

Before the hearing he prepared, with Mr Dombey, a short proof of the latter's evidence to be used in his examination-in-chief of this witness. Mr Dodgson built his own evidence round the three documents for submission referred to in (e) above. It was not necessary for him to prepare a proof of evidence. Such a proof would, of course, have been required if his role had been restricted to that of an expert witness. A good memory and full documentation were important in this case because Mr Dodgson could not give his evidence by reading it from a proof, or from his notes or by question and answer. He considered the aims of his cross-examination of the valuation officer and prepared the first few questions and the last one. Finally, Mr Dodgson prepared the outline of his final address.

(2) Statement of agreed facts

The following is the statement of agreed facts prepared by Mr Dodgson and the valuation officer:

IN THE MATTER OF AN APPEAL BEFORE MELCHESTER LOCAL VALUATION COURT ON 16TH JUNE 1980

RE: 10 WELLINGTON ARCADE, MELCHESTER
Dombey & Son Ltd (Appellants) v. Crabtree
(Valuation Officer) (Objector)
(Appeal No. 5/22061)

STATEMENT OF AGREED FACTS

The appeal hereditament

1. The appeal hereditament is a ground floor shop in the north east corner of a small square which forms part of Wellington Arcade, Melchester. Wellington Arcade is edged red on the agreed map and the appeal hereditament is hatched red. Wellington Arcade is a pedestrian shopping arcade which links High Street and St Thomas's Street. It consists of 26 shops on the ground floor with 50 flats on the first and second floors. It opened for trading in March 1979.
2. The appeal hereditament has a frontage of 4.88 m (16 ft), a depth of 5.90 m (19 ft 4 ins), a gross internal floor area of 28.8 sq m (310 sq ft) and a net internal floor area (all zone A) of 26 sq m (280 sq ft). The front part of the shop is used for retail sales with a window display; a removable partition has been erected across the shop at a depth of 3.05 m (10 ft) and the area to the rear of this is used as a store and staffroom. There is a toilet (2.8 sq m (30 sq ft)) with wc, basin and electric water heater. Double doors in the rear wall lead to a service corridor which leads to a loading yard with access from St Thomas's Street. At the date of the proposal the hereditament had plastered walls and ceiling, fluorescent lighting, a plastic tile floor and an aluminium shop front.
3. Attached to this statement are 10 photographs of the appeal hereditament and Wellington Arcade, labelled A to J. The position from which each photograph was taken and the direction of the camera are shown on the agreed map.

Tenure

4. Dombey & Son Ltd occupy the appeal hereditament under a lease
   dated 1st July 1979. It is for a term of 15 years from 24th June 1979
   at an initial rent of £1,925 per annum exclusive. This rent is
   subject to review at the end of the fifth and tenth years of the term.
   The rent from each review date will be (a) the open market rental
   value, or (b) the rent payable immediately before the review date,
   whichever shall be the greater amount. The tenants are responsible for internal repairs and decorations to the hereditament, for
   the payment of a service charge and for the reimbursement of 1%
   of the insurance premiums paid by the landlords in respect of
   Wellington Arcade. The landlords are responsible for external repairs and decorations, the repair, maintenance, decoration and
   supervision of the common parts and for insurance.
5. The service charge is a fair and just proportion of the cost of the
   repair, maintenance, decoration and supervision of the common
   parts of Wellington Arcade.
6. The permitted (and actual) use of the appeal hereditament is as a
   retail shop for the sale of sweets, chocolates, confectionery and allied food products.
7. The appeal hereditament was let as a "shell" and the tenant incurred shopfitting costs of £7,500.

Analysis of rents and assessments of comparable hereditaments

8. An agreed analysis of rents and assessments of comparable shops
   in Wellington Arcade is set out in Table 8.1 (p. 167).
   The comparable shops in the Table are edged blue and numbered
   on the agreed map. (*Note:* this map is not reproduced in this
   chapter).

(3) Hearing

The parties assembled for the local valuation court hearing at the
Moot Hall, Melchester at 10.00 am on 16th June 1980. The clerk to
the court announced the details of the case, the reduction requested
and ascertained that only the appellant ratepayers and the valuation officer were represented.

The order of appearance at this hearing was as follows:

(a) opening address by Mr J. O. Dodgson (for the appellants);
(b) evidence of fact by Mr J. G. Dombey (for the appellants);
(c) expert evidence by Mr J. O. Dodgson (for the appellants);
(d) opening address by Mr P. J. Crabtree (valuation officer)
    (objector);
(e) expert evidence by Mr P. J. Crabtree (valuation officer)
    (objector);

TABLE 8.1

No. in Wellington Arcade and occupier	Date of commencement of rent	Area ITZA m²	Rent in terms of gross value		Gross value		GV as a % of rent in terms of GV
			Rent	per m² zone A	GV	per m² zone A	
5 Roper Bros	March 1979	41	£5800	£141.5	£4300	£105	74.1%
6 Hi-Fi Centre	March 1979	41	£5625	£137.2	£4300	£105	76.4%
7 Diamond (Jewellers) Ltd	June 1979	41	£7000	£169.5	£4300	£105	61.4%
8 The Hot Bread Oven	April 1979	41	£5750	£140.2	£4300	£105	74.8%
9 Blue Jeans	June 1979	26	£3175	£122.1	£2600	£100	81.2%
APPEAL HEREDITAMENT 10 Dombey & Son Ltd	June 1979	26	£3000	£115.4	£2600	£100	86.7%
11 J. Jones Ltd	May 1979	30	£3700	£123.3	£2850	£ 95	77.0%
12 Oriel Records	May 1979	30	£3750	£125.0	£2850	£ 95	76.0%
16 Lights & Things	June 1979	27	£3600	£133.3	£2600	£ 95	72.2%
17 Heel Bar	Sept 1979	26	£3350	£128.8	£2600	£100	77.6%
18 A. J. Smith Ltd	Sept 1979	26	£3200	£123.1	£2600	£100	81.2%
19 The Toy Shop	October 1979	41	£6150	£150.0	£4300	£105	69.9%

(f)   final address by Mr P. J. Crabtree (valuation officer) (objector);

(g)   final address by Mr J. O. Dodgson (for the appellants).

(a)   *Opening address of Mr J. O. Dodgson (for the appellants).* Mr Dodgson opened his case as follows:

"Gentlemen, my name is James Oliver Dodgson. I am a Fellow of The Royal Institution of Chartered Surveyors and of the Chartered Institute of Arbitrators. I am senior partner of Wilberforce and Dodgson, chartered surveyors of Melchester, and I represent the appellants in this appeal.

I propose to proceed as follows. First, I shall open my case briefly; secondly, I will call a witness, Mr J. G. Dombey; thirdly, I will give expert evidence myself, submit myself to cross-examination and, if necessary, re-examine myself; lastly, I will make a final address at the conclusion of the valuation officer's case.

This appeal concerns number 10 Wellington Arcade, a ground floor shop in a new shopping arcade in the centre of Melchester. The appeal arises out of a proposal made on behalf of the ratepayers on 10th November 1979. The issue between the parties is a simple one: the valuation officer has entered this hereditament in the valuation list at gross value £2,600 rateable value £2,138; the appellants contend that this assessment is excessive and seek a reduction to gross value £2,250 rateable value £1,847, the figures in the proposal.

The parties have prepared a statement of agreed facts and an agreed map, copies of which I now distribute. I would ask you to look first at the map. This shows the layout of Wellington Arcade (edged red) and its location at the eastern end of High Street, Melchester. This arcade consists of 26 shops on the ground floor with flats on the upper floors. The ground floor may briefly be described as a pedestrian mall, 13 shops on either side, with a small square about two thirds of the way along its length. The appeal hereditament (hatched red on this map) forms one of the four corners of this square. It is next to a staircase leading to the flats on the upper floors and to the blank wall of shop unit 11. Immediately in front of it is an area of landscaping. These are some of the disabilities which affect the rental value of this unit.

I would ask you to turn now to the statement of agreed facts."

Mr Dodgson then read paragraphs 1 to 7 of this statement, that is to say the description and tenure of the appeal hereditament, and continued:

"I refer now to two statutory provisions: sections 19 and 20 of the General Rate Act 1967. Section 19 requires the appeal hereditament to be valued to gross value. This must be assessed as at the date of the proposal, 10th November 1979. Section 20, however, sets a limit to the gross value which would otherwise be found under section 19, by requiring the hereditament to be valued as if it had existed throughout the year immediately before the current valuation list came into force on 1st April 1973 but on the assumption that the hereditament and the locality were the same as at 10th November 1979.

The object of section 20 was clearly stated by the Lands Tribunal in *Hiltons Footwear Ltd v Leicester City Council & Culverwell (VO)* (1977) 242 EG 213 at p. 216:

> "The object of these provisions appears to be to ensure that when a proposal is made at some later date after the date on which a valuation list has come into force ... the value to be determined shall not reflect any increase in values due to general factors such as inflation but shall properly reflect an increase in value due to particular factors affecting the hereditament in question or the locality in which it is situated."

In effect we are required to value a November 1979 hereditament and locality at April 1973 values. It is clear from *R v Paddington VO & Another ex. p. Peachey Property Corporation Ltd* [1964] 1 WLR 1186, that a valuation list should reflect the values prevailing when it took effect, i.e. 1st April 1973.

Would you please look now at Table 8.1 which forms part of the statement of agreed facts. This is an analysis of rents and assessments in Wellington Arcade. I will refer to this Table in detail in my evidence but I now make some general comments.

If you look at the entry for the appeal hereditament (which is about half way down the Table) you will see that the rent in terms of gross value has been devalued to produce a price of £115.40 per square metre zone A. This is lower than all the other devalued rents in the Table. In particular, it is lower than the rents for the units which form the other three sides of the square, namely units 9, 17 and 18. It might be argued that because the rent of my client's shop is particularly low, it is not a true open market rent and is unreliable as evidence of value compared with the rents of the other shops. This is not correct. You will hear evidence from Mr Dombey of the negotiations which led to agreement of this rent. You will hear that it was the asking rent; that the landlords are an experienced property company, unlikely to make a mistake by assessing the rent at less than full market value. You will hear the reasons for this low rent, namely the disabilities suffered by this shop: poor pedestrian flow due to dead frontage on either side and obstructive landscaping in front and poor access for servicing. I will then give evidence that the gross value in the list of £2,600 is excessive; I will put before you three valuations each producing the same lower gross value of £2,250.

The first valuation is based on the rent adjusted to terms of gross value and reduced to April 1973 levels by reference to the rise in rents of comparable shops in High Street, Melchester between 1970 and 1980.

The second valuation is based on the ratio of gross value to rent in terms of gross value for shops in Wellington Arcade. This ratio represents the tone of the list and I refer you to the decision of the Lands Tribunal in *W. H. Smith & Son Ltd v Clee (VO)* (1977) 243 EG 667, where this method of measuring the tone of the list was approved. My valuation on this basis will show that the appellant's shop has been assessed at a figure above the tone of the list.

Valuation 3 is based on assessments of other shops in Wellington Arcade. It will be shown that the price per square metre used by the valuation officer for the appeal hereditament is excessive when compared with the prices used for other shops in the arcade, having regard to the rents of those shops.

My valuations show that the gross value per square metre on zone A should be reduced from £100 to £87. A reduction to this latter figure will be in accordance with the rent in terms of gross value, it will bring the assessment into line with the tone of the list for Wellington Arcade and it will be in the correct relationship with other assessments in the arcade. Thus, the valuation officer's gross value is too high on three counts, by reference to rent, tone of the list and comparable assessments. It should be reduced to £2,250.

I now call my witness, Mr John George Dombey."

Comment. The right to begin and end a hearing is a great asset but carries with it the burden of proof. An opening address should include the advocate's name, the party he represents, the decision he is seeking, the way in which he will present his case and a brief summary of the facts and issues to be raised at the hearing. If the case contains several issues or a single but divisible issue, then they can be expressed at the end of the opening address as a series of questions for the court to answer, the questions formulated as far as possible to the advantage of the advocate's case. This will give him the initiative in assisting the court and in shaping the arguments to be used at the hearing. Where the case contains a novel point, or interesting or unusual facts or has an importance which extends beyond the parties (e.g. a test case), then this should be mentioned in the opening address. It is usually inadvisable to include a lengthy attack on an opponent's case in an opening address. This should be left to the final address.

An opening address should be short and simple. This is particularly important where advocate and expert witness are the same person: it would be tiresome for the court to listen to the advocate explaining the evidence he will give and then listen to him giving it in his other role. The members of the court do not know the facts and they must be explained in sufficient detail to enable them to understand the evidence. This should be done with a minimum of comment, except where this is necessary to explain the significance of a particular fact. Only facts which are agreed or will be proved by evidence can be mentioned in opening. Weak points in a case should be brought out in the opening address: this will make them seem less of a weakness than if they are first revealed in evidence, or, even worse, in cross-examination. Where an agreed map and statement of agreed facts have been prepared these should be introduced by the advocate giving the opening address. Copies of all cases cited (with important passages marked) should be distributed to the court and the other parties. An opening address may finish with either a short summary of the facts and arguments or with a single important point.

Note: it was subsequently confirmed by the House of Lords in *K Shoe Shops Ltd v Hardy (VO)* (1983) 269 EG 37, that assessments in the 1973 valuation list should be based on values prevailing at 1st April 1973 (see above).

(b) *Evidence of Mr J. G. Dombey (for the appellants)*. Mr Dombey gave the evidence summarised below in answers to questions put to him by Mr Dodgson.

He said that his name is John George Dombey and he is Managing Director of Dombey & Son Ltd (the appellants). He conducted the negotiations which preceded the grant of the lease of 10 Wellington Arcade. He produced a copy of the landlords' letting brochure for Wellington Arcade (marked JGD/1), sent to him at the start of the negotiations. This brochure contains a list of asking rents. The asking rent for unit 10 was £1,925 per annum, the rent subsequently agreed. He opened negotiations by offering a rent of £1,800 per annum: this was refused. He then offered a rent of £1,825 per annum for the first three years of the term rising to £1,925 per annum. This offer was also refused and he finally accepted the asking rent of £1,925 per annum. The only concession he could obtain from the landlords was a 6 months rent-free period for shopfitting.

The valuations officer did not cross-examine this witness and the court did not ask any questions. No re-examination was, therefore, necessary.

Comment. Mr Dodgson was careful to avoid three pitfalls in his questions to Mr Dombey. First, he did not asking leading questions, i.e. questions which suggest the answer required. Secondly, he did not ask Mr Dombey whether he thought the agreed rent was an open market rent: this would have been opinion evidence admissible only from an expert witness. Mr Dombey was a witness of fact. Thirdly, he did to not ask the witness to give evidence about the landlord's attitude to the rental negotiations. This would have been inadmissible hearsay.

(c) *Expert evidence of Mr J. O. Dodgson (for the appellants).* Mr Dodgson now changed his role to that of expert witness for the appellants. Before he gave his evidence he handed to the members of the court, the clerk and the valuation officer a labelled folder containing three documents and a plan.

(i) *Documents*
The three documents were as follows:

DOCUMENT JOD/1
Pedestrian Count taken in Wellington Arcade,
Melchester on Friday 23rd November 1979
between 9.00 am and 5.00 pm.

Plan ref.	Survey point	Average hourly flow (adults, each direction)	% of maximum flow
1.	Entrance to Arcade from High Street	420	100%
2.	In mall between units 8 and 19	315	75%
3.	Outside unit 10	168	40%
4.	In mall between units 17 and 18	231	55%
5.	In mall between units 11 and 26	252	60%
6.	Entrance to Arcade from St Thomas's Street	169	40%

(*Note:* a plan of Wellington Arcade (JOD/1A) was attached to this document showing the positions of the six survey points. It is not reproduced in this chapter).

DOCUMENT JOD/2

<u>Valuations of appeal hereditament by James Oliver Dodgson</u>
<u>FRICS FCIArb for the appellants</u>

All valuations are in accordance with sections 19 and 20 of the General Rate Act 1967.

<u>Valuation 1</u>
Valuation by reference to lease rent.

Lease rent	£1,925
<u>Add:</u> for tenants' improvements £7,500 amortised over 15 years at 7 and 3% (8.1)	£ 926
	£2,851
<u>Add:</u> for landlords' repairs and insurance, 5%	£ 143
Rent in terms of GV as at date of proposal	£2,994
(10th November 1979) say	£3,000

Reduce to equivalent rent at 1st April 1973
by reference to rise in shop rents in High
Street, Melchester from 1st April 1973 to
10th November 1979 (see <u>Document JOD/3</u>)

$6\frac{1}{2}$ years (approx) @ $4\frac{1}{2}$% per annum		
PV of £1 in $6\frac{1}{2}$ years @ $4\frac{1}{2}$%		0.751
	Gross value	£2,253
	Gross value say	£2,250

<u>Valuation 2</u>
Valuation by reference to the tone of the list in Wellington Arcade, as evidenced by the ratio of gross value to rent in terms of gross value (see column 8 in Table 8.1 in the statement of agreed facts).

Rent in terms of GV as at date of proposal (see Valuation 1)	£3,000

Apply tone of the list in Wellington Arcade

No. in Wellington Arcade	GV as a % of the rent ITGV
5	74.1%
6	76.4%
7	61.4%
8	74.8%
9	81.2%
11	77.0%
12	76.0%
16	72.2%
17	77.6%
18	81.2%
19	69.9%
average	74.71%

	@74.71%
Gross value	£2,241
Gross value say	£2,250

Valuation 3

Valuation by reference to assessments of comparable shops, having regard to the relationship between GV per square metre zone A and the rent in terms of GV per square metre zone A (see Table 8.1 in the statement of agreed facts).

(a) Shops in Wellington Arcade assessed at £105 per square metre zone A:

No.	Rent ITGV per sq m zone A
5	£141.5
6	£137.2
7	£169.5
8	£140.2
19	£150.0
average	£147.7

Equivalent GV per square metre zone A for appeal hereditament = rent of appeal hereditament in terms of GV per square metre zone A (115.4) ÷ by above average rent in terms of GV per square metre zone A (147.7) × £105 GV per square metre zone A = £82.0 per square metre zone A.

(b) Shops in Wellington Arcade assessed at £95 per square metre zone A:

No.	Rent ITGV per sq m zone A
11	£123.3
12	£125.0
16	£133.3
average	£127.2

Equivalent GV per square metre zone A for appeal hereditament = rent of appeal hereditament in terms of GV per square metre zone A (115.4) ÷ by above average rent in terms of GV per square metre zone A (127.2) × £95 GV per square metre zone A = £86.2 per square metre zone A.

(c) Shops in Wellington Arcade assessed at £100 per square metre zone A:

No.	Rent ITGV per sq m zone A
9	£122.1
17	£128.8
18	£123.1
average	£124.7

Equivalent GV per square metre zone A for appeal hereditament = rent of appeal hereditament in terms of GV per square metre zone A (115.4) ÷ by above average rent in terms of GV per square metre zone A (124.7) × £100 GV per square metre zone A = £92.5 per square metre zone A.

(d) Gross value of appeal hereditament:
take average of £82.0 + £86.2 + £92.5 = £86.9 say £87 per square metre zone A.

26 square metres @ £87 = £2,262

Gross value say £2,250

DOCUMENT JOD/3

Analysis of rents of 120, 157 and 175 High Street, Melchester to show increase in shop rents 1970–1980

120 High Street

(a) Ground floor shop and store with staffroom on first floor.
(b) Let to Timpson Toys Ltd for 14 years from 29th September 1972 at initial rent of £5,000 per annum exclusive with rent review to open market rental value at end of 7th year of term. Tenants responsible for all repairs, decorations and insurance. Rent reviewed at 29th September 1979 to £6,750 per annum.

(c) Increase in rent September 1972–79 = about 4½% pa compound.

(d) Relationship of GV to review rent in terms of GV:

Review rent at 29th September 1979	£6,750
Add: for landlord's repairs, decorations and insurance, 10%	£ 675
Rent in terms of GV	£7,425

GV £5,300 = 71.38% of rent in terms of GV

157 High Street

(a) Ground floor shop and store.

(b) Let to Pringle & Sons for 5 years from 25th March 1974 at £4,000 per annum exclusive. Tenants responsible for all repairs, decorations and insurance. Lease renewed for 5 years from 25th March 1979 at a rent of £5,100 per annum exclusive.

(c) Increase in rent March 1974–79 = about 5% pa compound.

(d) Relationship of GV to rent on renewal in terms of GV:

Rent at 25th March 1979	£5,100
Add: for landlord's repairs, decorations and insurance, 10%	£ 510
Rent in terms of GV	£5,610

GV £3,925 = 70% of rent in terms of GV

175 High Street

(a) Ground floor shop with stores, staffroom and ancillary accommodation on first and second floors.

(b) Let to Lawrence Bros. for a term of 15 years from the 25th March 1970 at a rent of £4,500 per annum exclusive with rent reviews to the rack rental value at the end of the 5th and 10th years. Tenants responsible for internal repairs and decorations only. The rent was reviewed to £5,750 per annum from 25th March 1975 and to £6,750 per annum from 25th March 1980.

(c) Increases in rent:

March 1970–80 = about 4% pa compound

or

March 1970–75 = about 5% pa compound

March 1975–80 = about 3¼% pa compound.

(d) Relationship of GV to review rent in March 1980 in terms of GV:

Review rent at 25th March 1980	£6,750
Add: for landlord's repairs, 5%	£ 337
Rent in terms of GV	£7,087

GV £4,750 = 67% of rent in terms of GV

Summary

	No. 120	No. 157	No. 175	or	No. 175
March 1970					
Sept 1972					5% pa
March 1974	4½% pa				
March 1975		5% pa	4% pa		
March 1979					
Sept 1979					3¼%
March 1980					

Assume 4½% pa increase in rental value of appeal hereditament from 1st April 1973 to 10th November 1979.

(ii) *Oral evidence*

Mr Dodgson began his evidence by referring to the disabilities suffered by the appeal hereditament, namely poor pedestrian flow, due to the blank frontages on two adjoining sides and obstructive landscaping, and poor servicing arrangements. In support of the first disability he produced a pedestrian count carried out in Wellington Arcade under Mr Dodgson's supervision (*Documents JOD/1* and *1A*).

Mr Dodgson then turned to the rent of the appeal hereditament. He referred to Mr Dombey's evidence of the negotiations which led to its agreement, the disabilities of the appellants' shop (which are peculiar to this shop) and then expressed the opinion, based on this evidence and his knowledge of the landlords, that the rent of £1,925 was a full market rent.

He asked the court to look at the three valuations in *Document JOD/2* and continued:

> "Valuation 1 is my primary valuation. For the reasons I have given I regard the rent of the appeal hereditament as the best evidence of value and, although I do not disregard other evidence (as will be seen from Valuations 2 and 3), I place greater weight on this rental evidence.
>
> Valuation 1 starts with the lease rent. This was for the "shell" only and my clients carried out shopfitting works at an agreed cost of £7,500. This work was completed before the date of the relevant proposal (10th November 1979) and the shop must therefore be valued in its improved state. I have amortised the improvements over the term of the lease at 7 and 3%. An addition of 5% is then made for landlord's repairs. This produces a total rent in terms of gross value, as at the date of proposal, of £3,000. This figure has been agreed. It is the gross value under section 19 of the General Rate Act 1967.

Section 20 of the 1967 Act, however, sets a limit to the gross value under section 19. The section 19 gross value is not to exceed the value which would have been given to the hereditament if it and the locality had been in existence during the year 1st April 1972 to 1st April 1973. The hereditament is to be valued by reference to values current at 1st April 1973.

How are we to find this upper limit? In the absence of rents in Wellington Arcade for earlier than 1979 I decided to use the rent of the appeal hereditament projected back to the rental level which would have prevailed at 1st April 1973, checked by reference to both the tone of the list for the Arcade, measured by the ratio of gross value to rent in terms of gross value (Valuation 2) and comparable assessments (Valuation 3). I projected the rent of the appeal property back to 1st April 1973 on the evidence of rental increases for three shops in the High Street, close to Wellington Arcade and in a similar location. I would ask you to turn now to *Document JOD/3* where the rents of these shops are analysed to show rental growth between 1970 and 1980".

At this point, the valuation officer objected to the admissibility of this evidence. His objection was that these shops were not included on Mr Dodgson's counternotice requiring the production of rent returns under section 83(5) of the General Rate Act 1967 and, therefore, evidence of their rents would be inadmissible hearsay only. Mr Dodgson temporarily assumed the role of advocate and made the following statement in support of this evidence:

"In support of the admissibility of this evidence I refer to two cases. In *Wilks v Cawley* [1965] RA 632, a rating case decided by the Lands Tribunal in 1965, it was held that if an appellant is able to produce satisfactory evidence of rents from other sources he does not need to ask the valuation officer to produce rent returns. I negotiated all the rents referred to in *Document JOD/3* and can, therefore, give direct evidence of them. I refer to *English Exporters (London) Ltd v Eldonwall Ltd* (1973) 25 P & CR 379, where Megarry J said (pp. 383–4):

". . . the expert is often able to give factual evidence as well. If he has first-hand knowledge of a transaction he can speak of that . . . So far as the expert gives factual evidence, he is doing what any other witness of fact may do, namely, speaking of that which he has perceived for himself."

The court, after hearing the valuation officer in reply to Mr Dodgson, ruled that this evidence was admissible and Mr Dodgson continued:

"We were looking at *Document JOD/3* before Mr Crabtree's

objection. This document contains details of seven rents agreed between 1970 and 1980, for three shops in High Street, Melchester, all situated close to Wellington Arcade. These shops are numbered and edged green on the agreed map. They are typical of the shops in High Street, Melchester. I am of the opinion that, if Wellington Arcade had been in existence throughout the period 1970 to 1980, there would have been increases in rents similar to those shown by the three shops, which show a remarkably consistent pattern of rental growth.

I look first at 120 High Street, which is next to the entrance to Wellington Arcade. This is a ground floor shop with a store and staffroom on the first floor. In 1972, on behalf of the landlords, I negotiated a letting for 14 years from 29th September 1972 at an initial rent of £5,000 pa. In September 1979 I negotiated a rent of £6,750 pa on a rent review. The increase in rent is equivalent to an average annual increase of about $4\frac{1}{2}$% per annum compound over the period September 1972 to 1979. I have also converted the September 1979 rent into terms of gross value (£7,425) and it is interesting to note that the gross value of £5,300 is 71.38% of rent in terms of gross value, a percentage similar to the percentages in Wellington Arcade (see column 8 of Table 8.1 in the statement of agreed facts)''.

Mr Dodgson then explained his analysis of the rents and assessments of 157 and 175 High Street and continued:

"At the end of *Document JOD/3* I have summarised the results of my analysis of the seven rents of these three High Street shops. Rental growth is within a narrow range of $3\frac{1}{4}$% to 5% pa. From this evidence and my experience of values in Melchester, I have formed the opinion that, if Wellington Arcade had been in existence on 1st April 1973, the rental value of the appeal hereditament would have increased at an average rate of $4\frac{1}{2}$% per annum compound from that date to 10th November 1979. I applied this percentage growth rate to reduce the rent in terms of gross value at the date of proposal to an equivalent rent as at 1st April 1973, i.e. the section 20 gross value or gross value in accordance with the tone of the list. This is £2,250.

I then prepared alternative valuations by reference to the tone of the list in Wellington Arcade (Valuation 2) and by reference to assessments of adjoining shops, having regard to the relationship between gross value per square metre zone A and the rent in terms of gross value per square metre zone A (Valuation 3)."

Mr Dodgson explained Valuations 2 and 3 in greater detail and concluded his evidence with a brief summary.

He was then cross-examined by the valuation officer, who was careful to challenge him on any point with which he disagreed and to put to him the evidence he will give later in order that Mr Dodgson could deal with it. This cross-examination did not reveal any serious weaknesses in Mr Dodgson's evidence and he only made a brief statement by way of re-examination. He was careful not to introduce any material in his re-examination which did not arise from the questions put in cross-examination. The court did not ask any questions. Mr Dodgson announced that the evidence for the appellants was now concluded and left the witness box.

(d) *Opening address of the valuation officer (objector).* Mr P. J. Crabtree opened his case by giving his name and qualifications and said that he has been valuation officer for Melchester for the past 7 years. He objected to the proposal to reduce the assessment. He said that he will give a short opening address and then give evidence in support of the assessment in the list of gross value £2,600 rateable value £2,138.

The valuation officer said that Mr Dodgson placed too much reliance on the lease rent. This was only part of the relevant evidence: he should have looked more closely at the rents and assessments of other shops in the arcade. Mr Crabtree handed to the court and Mr Dodgson copies of selected dicta from the following three cases and the whole of the decision in the *Lotus and Delta* case referred to below. He referred to *Garton v Hunter (VO)* [1969] 2 QB 37, *R v Paddington VO ex p. Peachey Property Corporation Ltd* [1966] 1 QB 380 and *Baker Britt & Co Ltd v Hampsher (VO)* (1976) 239 EG 971. These cases established certain propositions, later summarised by the Lands Tribunal in *Lotus & Delta Ltd v Culverwell (VO) & Leicester City Council* (1976) 239 EG 287, as follows (p. 289):

> "(i) Where the hereditament which is the subject of consideration is actually let, that rent should be taken as a starting point;
> (ii) the more closely the circumstances under which the rent is agreed, both as to time, subject-matter and conditions, relate to the statutory requirements contained in the definition of gross value ..., the more weight should be attached to it;
> (iii) where rents of similar properties are available they, too, are properly to be looked at through the eye of the valuer in order to confirm or otherwise the level of value indicated by the actual rent of the subject hereditament;
> (iv) assessments of other comparable properties are also relevant ...;
> (v) in the light of all the evidence an opinion can then be formed of the value of the subject hereditament, the weight to be attributed to the different types of evidence depending on the one hand on the nature of the actual rent and, on the

other hand, on the degree of comparability found in other properties;"

He continued by saying that the rent of the appeal hereditament is out of line with all other rents in the arcade and should be rejected as evidence of gross value. Preference should be given to comparable rents and assessments.

The valuation officer then considered the question of tone of the list under section 20 of the General Rate Act 1967. He read the section and said that it is not solely concerned with changing the date of valuation from the date of proposal (10th November 1979) to 1st April 1973, as maintained by Mr Dodgson, but with ensuring uniformity of valuation by assuming that the hereditament was valued when the list was prepared. Assessments may be above or (more usually) below the level of values at 1st April 1973, but this is not important provided there is uniformity throughout the list. It is wrong, therefore, to discount the 1979 rent to April 1973 levels by reference to the rental growth for similar properties in the locality, or to treat the proportion which an assessment bears to a later adjusted rent as representing the tone of the list.

Tone of the list means the levels of value appearing in a valuation list. Rental levels are subsumed into assessments. As the Lands Tribunal said in *Burroughs Machines Ltd v Mooney (VO)* (1976) 241 EG 845:

> "(The ratepayer's valuer) made the comment that 'by 1976 rating surveyors tend to pay little attention to rents and considerable attention to assessments,' and this seems to me right and proper with a list that has settled."

We should, therefore, reject the rent of the appeal hereditament, because it stood out like "a sore thumb" compared to the other rents in Wellington Arcade (particularly the other shops in the square, numbers 9, 17 and 18). The assessment of the appeal hereditament should be found by reference to other assessments (in Wellington Arcade, High Street and St Thomas's Street) as related to rents in the arcade.

Mr Crabtree said he would now give evidence himself in support of his gross value of £2,600.

(e) *Expert evidence of the valuation officer.* Mr Crabtree went into the witness box and gave his evidence. He said that he saw Wellington Arcade as the missing piece of a jig-saw puzzle, to be fitted into the space left in the existing pattern of values in central Melchester. It had frontages to the High Street and St Thomas's Street and, therefore, provided a link between the established shopping values in these primary and secondary locations. The High Street shops on either side of the entrance to Wellington Arcade, numbers 110 to 130, now had an established basis for zone A of £120 per square metre. The stretch of St Thomas's Street on either side of the other entrance to the arcade, numbers 47 to 55, had an established basis of £90 per square metre zone A. He took the view, therefore, that to relate to this pattern of values, the gross values of the shops in the arcade should range from £120 per square metre zone A at the High Street end to £90 per square metre at the St Thomas's Street end.

First, Mr Crabtree said, he looked at the position of the shops in the arcade relative to High Street and St Thomas's Street and, using the yardsticks of £120 and £90 for these two streets, he drew up the following table of relative values (which he handed in as *Document VO/1*):

DOCUMENT VO/1

Table of Relative Values in Wellington Arcade

No. in Wellington Arcade	Location	GV per sq m zone A
1, 26	Frontage to High Street	£120
2 to 8 19 to 25	Frontage to mall from High Street to square	£105
9, 10, 17, 18	Frontage to square	£100
11, 12, 15, 16	Frontage to mall from square to St Thomas's Street	£ 95
13 & 14	Frontage to St Thomas's Street	£ 90

Secondly, he checked the relative values of the shops with frontage to the mall against the rents analysed in Table 8.1 in the statement of agreed facts. He did not agree with Mr Dodgson's method of averaging rents to find the relative rental values for different locations, but preferred to select one rent for each location as indicative of rental value.

He dealt first with the mall from High Street to the square, i.e. the rents of shops 5 to 8 and 19. Mr Crabtree rejected the rents of 7 and 19 as too high and, of the three remaining shops, chose number 8 as typical of this position, i.e. £140.2 per square metre zone A. Thus, a rent of £140.2 per square metre is equal to a gross value of £105 per square metre zone A.

Secondly, he dealt with the mall from the square to St Thomas's Street, the rents of shops 11, 12 and 16. He chose shop 12 as providing the most reliable rental evidence for this position, i.e. £125 per square metre zone A. Thus, this figure is equal to a gross value of £95 per square metre zone A. He then checked this arithmetically, by reference to the above figure of £140.2 for the High Street to the square (equal to £105 per square metre zone A), this relationship produced £93.6 gross value per square metre zone A, which he rounded up to £95.

Finally, he considered the square, shops 9, 10, 17 and 18, and chose shop number 17 as providing the most reliable rental evidence for this position, i.e. £128.8 per square metre zone A. This figure is equal to a gross value of £100 per square metre zone A. He then checked this figure arithmetically. By reference to the above figure of £125 for the mall from the square to St Thomas's Street (equal to £95 per square metre zone A), this relationship produced £97.7 gross value per square metre zone A, which he rounded up to £100.

The valuation officer said that he concluded from this analysis of rents and gross values that his relative gross values per square metre zone A of £105, £100 and £95 were correct. The position is summarised in the following table, which he handed in as *Document VO/2*:

DOCUMENT VO/2

Table of Relative Rental Values and Gross Values

Location in Wellington Arcade	Rental value ITGV per sq m	GV per sq m zone A	GV as % of rent ITGV
High Street to the square	£140.2	£105	74.9%
Square	£128.8	£100 (£97.9)	77.6%
Square to St Thomas's Street	£125.0	£ 95 (£93.6)	76.0%

Lastly, Mr Crabtree said that he looked at each shop to see whether it had any particular disabilities not suffered by other shops in the same value band. He considered the alleged disabilities listed by Mr Dodgson but rejected them as reasons for an end deduction, on the grounds that the other shops in the square also suffered from one or more of them to some degree.

The valuation officer said that in his opinion the correct gross value of the appeal hereditament, having regard to tone of the list related to rental evidence, was £100 per square metre zone A. His valuation, which he handed in as *Document VO/3*, was:

DOCUMENT VO/3

Valuation of 10 Wellington Arcade, Melchester

as at 10th November 1979 but having regard to section 20 of

the General Rate Act 1967

Ground floor Shop zone A 26 sq m @ £100   = GV£2,600

This concluded the valuation officer's evidence.

(f) *Cross-examination of the valuation officer.* Mr Dodgson's cross-examination of the valuation officer is not set out here but the following is a summary of the principles which guided him in his task and the techniques he used.

The purpose of cross-examination is to test the accuracy of evidence. The cross-examiner hopes to weaken the opposing case and establish facts which are favourable to his own case. Lord Macmillan said that cross-examination is the finest method of eliciting and establishing the truth. Certainly evidence which sounds wholly convincing in examination-in-chief can become less so when subjected to a penetrating cross-examination.

Mr Dodgson had regard to three general principles when preparing his cross-examination. First, that he must establish the *aims* of his cross-examination and recognise the *weaknesses* in the valuation officer's evidence. These are the *targets* to be attacked. The former should be settled before the hearing commences; the latter can, to a limited extent, be formulated in advance but they will be discovered mainly during the witness's examination-in-chief. The aims of the cross-examination will follow closely the party's case. In the appellant's case they were to establish that the lease rent was an open market rent, that the appeal hereditament suffered from disabilities, that assessments based on the rent, tone of the list and comparable assessments all indicated a gross value of £2,250. The two major weaknesses in the valuation officer's evidence were: his rejection of the lease rent as the best (or any) evidence of value and his use of only three rents to establish a pattern of values within Wellington Arcade. Guided by these aims and weaknesses Mr Dodgson planned the tactics and methods of his cross-examination.

Secondly, it was necessary for Mr Dodgson to remember one of the basic rules of cross-examination, namely that he must put his own case to the valuation officer for comment, if he wished to refer to it in his final address. Mr Dodgson had to structure his cross-examination, therefore, around the main points of his case. These were the same as his aims, namely the open market character of the lease rent, disabilities and his valuations.

Thirdly, and perhaps obviously (but easily overlooked where the roles of advocate and expert are combined), cross-examination may only be directed at evidence and not at the law. The valuation officer could not be questioned, therefore, on the law referred to by him in his opening address; although Mr Dodgson could (and did) comment on this in his final address.

The basic technique of cross-examination is always to prepare the way for a crucial question. The cross-examiner should ask first a series of simple questions, which the witness is likely to answer in the examiner's favour, before asking the important question. The purpose of this is that by securing admissions in the answers to the preliminary questions, he can block all escape routes before the crucial question is asked and make it appear that, as a matter of logic, the answer to the crucial question must be the one required by the questioner. For example, Mr Dodgson did not ask the question: "How can you be sure that the rent of shop 12 is an open market rent?" without first preparing the ground. He proceeded as follows:

Q. Let us look first at the rent of shop 12. You say you regard this rent as an open market rent and the best evidence of value for the shops in the square?

A. Yes.

Q. Did you make any inquiries of the landlords about this rent?

A. No.

Q. Did you make any inquiries of the tenants?

A. No.

Q. Did you make any inquiries of the tenants' agents, Muddle & Co?

A. No.

Q. Have you read the lease?

A. No.

Q. How can you be sure then that this rent is an open market rent?"

This form also allowed Mr Dodgson to shift or abandon a line of questioning if the answers were unhelpful to him. For example, if the answer to his first question had been that the valuation officer had discussed the rent with the landlords and received full information, then Mr Dodgson could quickly move to a different line of questioning with little detriment to his case.

Having established by the line of questioning set out above that the valuation officer had formed an opinion on incomplete information, Mr Dodgson could then use the same form of questioning for the other rents and, most importantly, the rent of the appeal hereditament. The cumulative effect, which Mr Dodgson hoped to achieve, was that the valuation officer had exercised his judgment unwisely in building up a pattern of values in Wellington Arcade and that he should not have rejected the rent of the appeal hereditament as good evidence of value. Within this basic technique of cross-examination Mr Dodgson could use other weapons: probing, undermining a previous answer, repetition of a question which has not been fully answered or which the witness was clearly unhappy in answering, tying the witness down to an answer that he may wish he had not given, concentration on a small item of evidence unfavourable to the witness.

Mr Dodgson was also aware of the need for brevity. Many cross-examinations in inexperienced hands are too long. A witness who will not concede a point is unlikely to do so under prolonged questioning. Also, one question too many may completely spoil an admission made in an earlier answer and perhaps allow the witness to provide a less damaging explanation of this answer.

A cross-examination cannot be wholly planned in advance but the first two or three questions and the last question should be prepared before the hearing. The first questions should lay the foundations for the cross-examination or put the issues before the court in simple terms. An element of surprise is useful at the start of a cross-examination. The first question should be unexpected. The last question should produce an answer in the nature of a grand finale to the detriment of the witness.

Leading questions may be asked in cross-examination. Ideally, the questioner should know the answers to all his questions. A witness should, of course, be treated courteously, fairly and allowed to answer without interruption. He should, however, be treated firmly if he shows a tendency to evade the question or answer with long and discursive speeches. A well prepared, potentially telling cross-examination can be ruined by an evasive or garrulous witness. He must be checked at the start of the examination and made to answer briefly and without qualification.

Finally, Mr Dodgson recalled a passage he had read in Richard du Cann's excellent book, *The Art of the Advocate*:

> "... there is a marked difference in the use of cross-examination in front of different tribunals. Although there may be drama latent in a building dispute over the drains of a bungalow in Palmers Green, and there is at least one case in recent years of an expert being brought to tears by perfectly fair and proper questioning at a planning enquiry, it would be courting disaster for the advocate to conduct all his cross-examinations as if he were attacking a dishonest police officer in front of a jury. The weapons available to him are the same whatever the tribunal. But before expert assessors of fact ... he needs fewer histrionics, much more subtlety and much more speed."

At the end of Mr Dodgson's cross-examination, the valuation officer made a short statement by way of re-examination and answered a few questions from members of the court.

(g) *Final address of the valuation officer.* Mr Crabtree then changed his role from expert witness to advocate and made a short final address summarising his submissions and evidence.

The chairman then called upon Mr Dodgson to make his final address.

(h) *Final address of Mr Dodgson (for the appellants).* This is reproduced in full:

> "Gentlemen, the issue in this appeal is what is the correct gross value of the appeal hereditament: is it £2,600 as contended by the valuation officer? or £2,250 as contended by the appellants? or somewhere between these two figures?
>
> Gross value must be found in accordance with sections 19 and 20 of the General Rate Act 1967. Section 19 defines gross value, which must be assessed as at the date of the proposal, 10th November 1979; section 20 limits the amount of that gross value by requiring the assumption to be made that the hereditament was in existence during the year April 1972 to April 1973, but that the hereditament and locality were in the same state as at the date of the proposal. In other words, we project the shop and the locality backwards in time from November 1979 to the year April 1972 to 1973.
>
> The valuation officer has said that section 20 is not solely concerned with the alteration of the valuation date, but is really concerned with uniformity of valuation – the tone of the list. It is, course, concerned with this concept but it does, in effect, alter the valuation date to 1st April 1973. When the list was in preparation the valuation officer was required to project his values forward to that date; for proposals after that date I submit that we are required to project values back to that date, except where values have fallen and, therefore, the section 20 limit does not apply. In support of this proposition I refer you to *R v Paddington VO & Another ex p. Peachey Property Corporation Ltd* [1964] 1 WLR 1186, where the Divisional Court said (p. 1205):
>
> > "Both parties have assumed that the valuation list should reflect the values prevailing when it takes effect: and though there is no express statutory direction that he should do so, this is highly desirable ..."
>
> We are, therefore, valuing as at 1st April 1973, a property and locality as at 10th November 1979.

My assessment of gross value has been made in three ways: by reference to the rent, by reference to the ratio of gross value to rent in terms of gross value and by reference to assessments of comparable shops.

First, by reference to the rent. You heard evidence from Mr Dombey of the negotiations which led to the agreement of this rent. It was the asking rent not a reduced rent. In my opinion it is the open market rent. The valuation officer did not cross-examine Mr Dombey on his evidence. He did not call evidence in rebuttal. The landlords of Wellington Arcade are an experienced property company, unlikely to let a shop at less than market rent. But, nevertheless, the valuation officer says we must disregard this rent because it is so much lower than other rents in the arcade. It is much lower, but you have heard why this is so, namely the disabilities suffered by this shop. These are the landscaping which forms an obstruction in front of the shop and the blank frontages on either side, both reducing the pedestrian flow (see *Document JOD/1*), and the poor access for servicing. I invite you to view these disabilities for yourselves before making your decision.

The rent should not be rejected in favour of assessments. It is the best evidence and deserves the greatest weight. I refer to the words of Winn LJ in *Garton v Hunter (VO)* [1969] 2 QB 37 at pp. 45–46:

> "Where the particular hereditament is let on what is plainly a rack rent and there are similar hereditaments and similar economic sites which are so let that they are truly comparable, that evidence should be classified in respect of cogency as a category of admissible evidence properly described as superior; in some, but not all cases that category may be exclusive. Any indirect evidence, albeit relevant should be placed in a different category; reference to the latter category may or may not be proper, or indeed necessary, according to the degree of weight of the former kind of evidence."

My first valuation in *Document JOD/2* is based on the rent and deserves the greatest weight. The rent adjusted to terms of gross value and reduced to April 1973 rental levels (as set out in *Document JOD/3*) produces a gross value of £2,250. This valuation does not stand on its own, however, but is supported by two other valuations, also set out in *Document JOD/2*.

The second valuation is based on the ratio of gross value to rent in terms of gross value for other shops in the arcade. This ratio is evidence of the tone of the list. The valuation officer has disputed this. It was not, he said, contrary to section 20 for assessments to bear different relationships to their rents, provided all the zone A prices bear a proper relationship to each other. This argument was rejected by the Lands Tribunal in *W H Smith & Son Ltd v Clee (VO)* (1977) 243 EG 667 at p. 764. It will be remembered that the gross value of the appeal hereditament is 86.7% of the rent in terms of gross value, whereas the average for 11 of the shops in the arcade is 74.71% and most are in the range of 72% to 78%.

When we apply the average percentage of 74.71% to the rent in terms of gross value of the appeal hereditament we arrive again at a gross value of £2,250.

My third valuation in *Document JOD/2* is based on comparable assessments, related to rents to show the relative values of different parts of the arcade, and then applied to the appeal hereditament. The valuation officer's only valuation is also based on comparable assessments, but we part company on methods of analysis. I believe it to be more correct to find the average of the rents for different locations to establish relativities of value. The valuation officer has looked at only three rents, which he has accepted as open market rents, to establish relativities. In my view this is unsafe and can only be accurate if a thorough investigation has been made of all the circumstances of the lettings. He admitted in cross-examination that he did not do this. He did not make inquiries of the landlord or tenant, he did not read the leases, he could be quite unaware of some fact which prevents that rent being an open market rent. I was able to show in cross-examination that, if several different rents are averaged, then a different and lower gross value would be given to the appeal hereditament to reflect the lower rent relative to other rents. Again my valuation on comparables produces a gross value of £2,250.

Three different valuations each producing the same gross value is, I submit, conclusive proof that the existing gross value of £2,600 is excessive and should be reduced to the appellant's figure of £2,250. I ask the court to make this reduction.''

Comment. The points which Mr Dodgson had in mind when he made this final address were as follows. A final address should be brief. It should summarise the submissions. It should review (but not rehearse) the evidence in such a manner that it appears to lead logically to the decision required. It should criticise the valuation officer's case. A final address must not introduce new points of law or fact or new cases not previously cited. When he prepared his case, therefore, Mr Dodgson knew that the whole of it must be contained in his opening address and the evidence of Mr Dombey and himself.

If Mr Dodgson had required the court to give the reasons for its decision he would have included this request in his final address.

Note: As stated above, if this case had been heard after the decision in *K Shoe Shops Ltd v Hardy (VO)* (1983) 269 EG 37, Mr Dodgson would have used this case in place of the *Paddington* case as authority for a valuation date of 1st April 1973 for tone of the list.

(4) Decision

The chairman announced that the court would adjourn while members viewed the appeal hereditament and made their decision. When the court reassembled the chairman thanked the parties for the helpful way in which they had presented their cases and said that the assessment would be reduced to gross value £2,400 rateable value £1,972. Mr Dodgson and the valuation officer thanked the court for a patient and fair hearing.

PART THREE

THE INDEPENDENT EXPERT

CHAPTER SEVEN

The Independent Expert

INTRODUCTION

Where two or more persons are in dispute on a question of fact, or have opposing interests in a matter, such as the amount of a rent or the value of shares, they may agree to refer it to a third party for determination. He will be either an arbitrator or an independent expert. The consequences of this label are important, to the parties and to the appointed person. Thus, an arbitrator is required to act judicially, to hold a hearing (if required) and to make an award on the evidence; but an expert bases his decision on his own investigations, knowledge and experience. An arbitrator probably has immunity from actions for negligence; but an expert has no such immunity. The Arbitration Acts 1950–1979 apply to arbitrations and there is a large body of case law; there is no legislation and little case law regarding independent experts.

This chapter looks first at the criteria for deciding whether an appointed person is an arbitrator or expert, then discusses the consequences of this classification and concludes with a practical example. Chapter 8 discusses the law relating to professional negligence, with particular reference to valuation and the liability of an independent surveyor. The law and practice of arbitration are considered in detail in the last part of this book.

ARBITRATOR OR EXPERT?

Where a lease or other contract provides that a dispute shall be settled by a third party, it is clearly important to decide whether he is an arbitrator or expert. As stated above many consequences flow from this decision.

The question: arbitrator or expert? must be answered by finding the intention of the parties when the contract was made, as evidenced by the words they have used. Words of appointment must be construed in the context of the document as a whole, having regard to the surrounding circumstances (see Appendix A p. 436 below). Several situations can arise when this exercise is carried out. The words of appointment may be clear and unambiguous, or their meaning may become clear when they are construed in the context of the document as a whole or in relation to another clause; or their true meaning may only be found by reference to certain factors in the words used.

(1) Clear words of appointment

Words of appointment may be clear and unambiguous. For example, the appointment of auditors to certify their opinion of the fair selling value of shares, such auditors to act as experts and not as arbitrators, was clearly the appointment of independent experts. The binding force of the valuation might be challenged but the type of appointment was not (see *Baber v Kenwood Manufacturing Co Ltd* [1978] 1 Lloyd's Rep 175, but compare *Leigh v English Property Corporation Ltd* [1976] 2 Lloyd's Rep 298, p. 196 below). Similarly, where there is specific reference to arbitration, arbitrator or the Arbitration Acts, this is the appointment of an arbitrator, even though the words "expert" or "surveyor" may also be used. Thus, the appointment of "an independent expert who shall act as an arbitrator" is the appointment of an arbitrator.

It is not uncommon for a rent review clause in a lease to alter the label attached to the appointed person according to the method of his appointment. For example, the clause may provide that (in the absence of agreement) a review rent shall be determined by an independent surveyor acting as an expert, who shall be appointed jointly by the parties, but if the parties fail to agree on such an appointment, then by an independent surveyor appointed by the President of The Royal Institution of Chartered Surveyors who shall make his determination in accordance with the Arbitration Acts. It is important for the appointed person to relate his appointment to the method of appointment, to ensure that he acts as an expert if appointed by the parties or as an arbitrator if appointed by the President.

(2) Construction in context or by comparison

Where words of appointment are unclear, their meaning may be found by construing them in the context of the document as a whole or by comparing them with another clause with a clear meaning. Thus, in *Langham House Developments Ltd v Brompton Securities Ltd* (1980) 256 EG 719, a rent review clause in a lease provided that, in default of agreement between the parties, the review rent was to be "determined by a chartered surveyor nominated by the President ... of the Royal Institution of Chartered Surveyors." The question inevitably arose: is the surveyor an expert or an arbitrator? The court could see force in both answers when it looked at the clause in isolation, but found the answer by comparing it with another clause which dealt with the abatement of rent following fire damage. That clause, said that judge, "reeks of arbitration", by the use of language such as "in case of difference", "award", "single arbitrator" and "Arbitration Act 1950", whereas the rent review clause uses none of these words. The draftsman of this clause clearly intended the rent to be settled by valuation and not by arbitration. The appointed surveyor was an expert and not an arbitrator.

Similarly, in *Safeway Food Stores Ltd v Banderway Ltd* (1983) 267 EG 850, a comparison between the rent review clause and a tenants' covenant in another part of the lease was one of the four reasons which led the judge to decide that an "umpire" appointed to determine the review rent was an expert and not an arbitrator. The covenant required the tenants to pay a fair proportion of the costs of cleansing, maintaining etc parts used in common and provided that any disputes shall be referred to a single arbitrator under the Arbitration Act 1950. When the draftsman of the lease wanted to provide for arbitration he did so in express terms, which were missing from the rent review clause.

(3) Indicia of appointment

The *Safeway* case also illustrates a third approach to interpretation which seeks in the words used factors indicative of an arbitral or expert appointment. The rent review clause in this case required each party to appoint a valuer "to negotiate and endeavour to reach agreement . . . as to the fair market rack rent of the demised premises . . ." and, in the event of failure to reach agreement, the valuers were to appoint an umpire to settle the question. If either party did not appoint a valuer, or the two valuers did not appoint an umpire, then the President of The Royal Institution of Chartered Surveyors could be requested to appoint a member of that body "to settle the question" with a final and binding decision.

The judge found four reasons (p. 852) which taken together provided a clear pointer that the appointed person (the umpire):

> ". . . was intended to be a valuer who was to use his own knowledge and make such investigations as he, a qualified surveyor, would think fit, not to act as a quasi-judge upon evidence and arguments of the parties or their representatives."

One of those reasons has already been discussed, the other three were as follows. First, the whole question to be settled was one of expertise in arriving at a rent at a particular date: it was in its essential nature one of valuation rather than a question with two clearly defined sides to be argued and decided. Secondly, the umpire was to be appointed and to operate under the same machinery as the valuers appointed by the parties, not only where they disagreed but also where either party had not appointed a valuer within the stipulated time. In this latter case the umpire was intended to supply the place of a valuer who, it was conceded, was not an arbitrator but an expert. Thirdly, the umpire was expressly stated to be a member of The Royal Institution of Chartered Surveyors and it was, therefore, contemplated that he would need expertise in the field of a surveyor.

The principle which may be found in this case is that where the dispute is one of expertise, such as the assessment of a rent, and the appointed person is to be drawn from the membership of an expert body, then there will be a presumption that his role will be as an expert and not as an arbitrator.

We can now look more closely at other factors which indicate whether an appointed person is an arbitrator or expert. These are: whether a dispute has arisen at the time of appointment; the duties of the appointed person; costs.

(a) *Whether a dispute has arisen.* It is often stated as a general rule that an arbitrator determines a dispute which has arisen, but an expert decides a matter in which the parties have opposing interests in order to avoid a dispute. Two cases are authorities for this proposition.

In *Sutcliffe v Thackrah* [1974] AC 747, the issue was whether an architect was liable to the building owner for negligent over-certification under the building contract. It was held by the House of Lords that, although each case depended on its own facts and the relevant contract, an architect or valuer would be immune from actions for negligence if he could show that, by agreement, he had been appointed to act as an arbitrator or quasi-arbitrator, i.e. that he had been appointed to determine a *specific dispute* submitted to him, or *defined differences which might arise in the future*, and there was agreement that his decision would be binding.

Similarly, in *Arenson v Arenson & Casson, Beckman, Rutley & Co* [1976] 1 Lloyd's Rep 179, the issue was whether auditors could be liable for the negligent valuation of shares, where they had been appointed as "experts and not as arbitrators." It was held by the House of Lords that it was an essential prerequisite for a valuer to claim immunity as an arbitrator that, when the matter was submitted to him for decision, there should be a *formulated dispute* between at least two parties which he was required to resolve. It was not enough that the parties who might be affected by his decision had opposing interests in the subject-matter referred to him.

In *Leigh v English Property Corporation Ltd* [1976] 2 Lloyd's Rep 298, Brightman J (whose decision was upheld by the Court of Appeal) found some difficulty in accepting this clear-cut distinction between arbitration and valuation. He said (p. 300):

> "... I will advert shortly to the distinction between an arbitrator, properly so called, and a valuer who is not an arbitrator. An agreement for arbitration is an agreement to settle a difference by recourse to arbitration instead of litigation. An agreement for a valuation is not, *prima facie*, an agreement for an arbitration. The function of the valuer is usually to settle a price so that no difference arises between the parties. His function is not to make an award after a difference has already arisen. But it is easy for the one concept to shade into the other. I confess that I find some difficulty in distinguishing the hall-mark of an arbitrator from the hall-mark of a valuer. To put the matter in another way, in the absence of a formal reference to arbitration proceedings, it may be difficult in a valuation case to tell from the wording of the agreement whether the parties intended the referee to conduct arbitration proceedings in order to determine value or to effect a valuation without conducting any such proceedings."

He found, however, that auditors appointed to certify the fair value of shares, in default of agreement between the parties, had an *arguable* case for claiming that they were selected as arbitrators since it was clearly envisaged that the value was to be certified only in the event of a disagreement between the parties. Unfortunately this case was subsequently settled out of court and the issue as to whether the auditors were arbitrators or experts was never judicially decided.

As a general rule, therefore, *the resolution of a dispute* indicates arbitration, but a decision on a matter of mutual interest *to avoid a dispute* indicates a valuation or some other expert decision.

(b) *Duties of the appointed person.* The true nature of an appointment may be indicated by the duties (express or implied) of the appointed person. If he is required to perform a judicial role, to listen to submissions and evidence before making his decision, then *prima facie* he is an arbitrator. But if his duties are investigatory and a decision may be made on his own inquiries and by his own expertise, then he is an expert. This distinction was explained nearly 100 years ago by Lord Esher in *Re Carus-Wilson* (1886) 18 QBD 7 at p. 9:

> "If it appears from the terms of the agreement by which a matter is submitted to a person's decision, that the intention of the parties was that he should hold an enquiry in the nature of a judicial enquiry, and hear the respective cases of the parties, and decide upon the evidence laid before him, then the case is one of arbitration. . . . On the other hand, there are cases in which a person is appointed to ascertain

some matter for the purpose of preventing differences from arising, not of settling them when they have arisen, and when the case is not one of arbitration but of a mere valuation. There may be cases of intermediate kind where, though a person is appointed to settle disputes that have arisen, still it is not intended that he shall be bound to hear evidence or arguments. In such cases it may often be difficult to say whether he is intended to be an arbitrator or to exercise some other function; such cases must be determined each according to its particular circumstances."

More recently, Lord Salmon in *Sutcliffe* (p. 196 above) stated the position as follows (p. 759).

"Judges and arbitrators have disputes submitted to them for decision. The evidence and the contentions of the parties are put before them for their examination and consideration. They then give their decision. None of this is true about the valuer or architect who were merely carrying out their ordinary business activities. Indeed, their functions do not seem to me even remotely to resemble those of a judge or arbitrator."

Two examples will illustrate this rule. In *Re Hopper* (1867) LR 2 QB 367, a lease of a farm provided that the tenant would quit and deliver up the property if it was sold during the term. Each party would appoint a valuer to assess the compensation payable to the tenant. The property was sold and the question of compensation was referred to two valuers and an umpire, who were given powers to examine the parties and their witnesses. It was held that this was a reference to arbitration. But in *Re Hammond & Waterton* (1890) 62 LT 808, where a reference was made to two arbitrators to determine the amount to be paid to a nurseryman for yielding up his lease, and the arbitrators appointed an umpire who actually made the decision, the court refused to enforce it as an arbitration award because it did not appear that any judicial inquiry was intended (see also the *Safeway* case discussed on p. 195 above).

Unfortunately, on this point also, the distinction between an arbitrator and an independent expert may become blurred. For example, an arbitrator may, with the agreement of both parties, dispense with an oral hearing and decide the dispute on written representations. Similarly, an expert may invite the parties to submit written statements to him, or they may have the right to do so under the terms of his appointment. An arbitrator may be appointed from an expert body in the same way that an expert may be so appointed. Although as a general rule an arbitrator is bound by the rules of evidence, the parties may agree to relax those rules, or this may be implied by a reference to a skilled person in accordance with the practice of a particular trade where those rules are modified or disregarded. Under these circumstances the arbitrator is little different in practice from an expert (see Chapter 10 p. 313 below).

In general terms, however, a requirement that the appointed person shall receive submissions and evidence (i.e. hold a judicial inquiry) and base his decision thereon, indicates the appointment of an arbitrator. But if the appointed person is free to carry out his own investigations and may use his own expertise in reaching his decision, then this indicates an expert appointment. It follows, therefore, that although the words "final and binding" are often used to describe both an arbitrator's award and an expert's determination, words which state that the decision is to be "in the absolute discretion" of the appointed person indicate an expert appointment.

(c) *Costs.* Words of appointment may provide that the appointed person shall determine the liability for the costs of his decision. If they provide that the parties shall bear their own costs then this is an indication that the appointment is as an independent expert. Under section 18 of the Arbitration Act 1950 a provision that the parties shall bear their own costs is void in an arbitration agreement and this points, therefore, to the likelihood that the appointed person is an independent expert.

ARBITRATOR AND EXPERT COMPARED

The consequences to the parties and the appointed person, of the label attached to that person may be discussed under two general headings. First, the Arbitration Acts, because those Acts only apply to an arbitrator not to an expert. Secondly, negligence, because an arbitrator probably has immunity from actions for negligence in the performance of his duties, but an independent expert does not have such immunity.

(1) Arbitration Acts

The Arbitration Acts 1950–1979 apply to an "arbitration agreement", which is defined as a "written agreement to submit present or future differences to arbitration, whether an arbitrator is named therein or not." They apply to all arbitrations where the arbitration agreement is in writing and, in respect of many of the provisions, provided the parties have not expressly excluded those provisions.

They do not apply to independent expert appointments. This produces important differences between the two types of appointment which may be considered under the headings: appointment, procedure, judicial control, award or determination and costs. (The Arbitration Acts are discussed in detail in the last part of this book and their provisions will, therefore, only be sufficiently outlined here to illustrate the differences between arbitrators and independent experts).

(a) *Appointment.* Where an arbitration agreement is silent on some procedural matter concerning appointment, or one of the parties fails to proceed in accordance with that agreement, then the resultant vacuum may be filled by the Arbitration Acts. For example, where the mode of reference is not specified in the agreement, it will be deemed to be to a single arbitrator. Where the agreement provides for a reference to two arbitrators, one to be appointed by each party and one party fails to appoint, then the arbitrator appointed by the other party becomes the sole arbitrator. The High Court has power to appoint an arbitrator in certain circumstances (see Chapter 9 p. 278 below).

These provisions do not apply to the appointment of an independent expert. The parties must ensure that their agreement has adequate machinery for appointment and determination, which cannot be unilaterally frustrated by one of the parties. If the machinery breaks down then the Arbitration Acts cannot be used to repair the defect but the courts may assist. For example, in *Sudbrook Trading Estate Ltd v Eggleton* (1982) 265 EG 215, four leases of adjoining property each contained a tenants' option "to purchase the reversion ... at such price ... as may be agreed upon by two valuers one to be nominated by the lessor and the other by the lessee and in default of such agreement by an umpire appointed by the ... valuers." The tenants exercised their options and nominated their valuer but the landlords refused to do so. It was held by the House of Lords that the options had been validly exercised, that specific performance of the contract of sale would be ordered and, because the machinery for the ascertainment of price constituted a subsidiary and non-essential part of the contract, the court would, the machinery having broken down, substitute its own machinery for determining a fair and reasonable price upon the expert evidence of valuers. This decision was based upon an implied waiver by the landlords of their right to have the price fixed under the terms of the contract and a resultant corresponding waiver by the tenants, leaving it to the court to fix the price.

The question whether the court could compel the landlords to appoint their valuer was discussed but not decided. Lord Diplock expressly left the point open; Lord Fraser of Tullybelton stated that this would not be a suitable alternative because, if the order were not obeyed, the only sanction would be imprisonment for contempt of court, which would clearly be inappropriate. Lord Russell of Killowen (in a dissenting judgment) said that he did not understand it to be suggested that the court can nominate a party's valuer nor order nomination on pain of contempt of court for disobedience.

It is interesting to note that, if the agreements had provided for the appointment of arbitrators and not valuers, the tenants could have relied on section 7(b) of the Arbitration Act 1950 to convert their nominee into a sole arbitrator whose award would have been binding on both parties (see Chapter 9 p. 276 below).

(b) *Procedure.* As stated above, an arbitrator performs a judicial function but an expert does not. Thus, an arbitrator must observe the rules of natural justice; he must hold a hearing, unless the parties agree otherwise; he must base his award on the submissions and evidence of the parties (or one of them where he is proceeding *ex parte*), unless they have agreed to waive the strict rules of evidence or this is implied in a particular type of trade or commodity arbitration.

An arbitrator is assisted in his judicial role by the Arbitration Acts. He is given powers to examine the parties and witnesses and to require the production of documents. He may take evidence on oath or affirmation. Any party to the reference may apply to the High Court for the issue of *subpoenas* compelling witnesses to give evidence or produce documents. The court may make orders for discovery of documents or interrogatories (see Chapter 10 p. 301 below).

Except in certain trade or commodity arbitrations, where the arbitrator may make full use of his expertise, an arbitrator has limitations on the use of his own expert knowledge. He may use it to evaluate the evidence. He must not use his own special knowledge to form a different view of the facts from that given to him by expert witnesses without putting that view to the parties and giving them an opportunity of dealing with it (see Chapter 10 p. 320 below).

The position of an independent expert is quite different. His role is investigatory: he will usually assemble his own information and apply his own expertise to reach his decision. He may receive written representations from the parties, but he is not bound to do so (unless expressly required under the terms of his appointment) and he need not take them into account in his decision. The parties cannot insist on a hearing, the rules of evidence do not

The Surveyor in Court

apply, evidence is not given on oath, the parties cannot seek orders for discovery nor administer interrogatories. In short, an expert proceeds with his task in essentially the same way as any other professional man performing a similar task unconnected with a dispute.

Some of the differences between the procedures in an arbitration and an independent expert appointment can be seen by comparing two cases decided in 1981. In *Fox v P. G. Wellfair Ltd* [1981] 2 Lloyd's Rep 514, the Court of Appeal removed an arbitrator and set aside his award on two main grounds. First, that he gave himself evidence or acted on his own private opinion without disclosing it to the parties. Secondly, that although as an expert arbitrator he could use his own expert knowledge, there is a distinction between general and special knowledge and, in this case, the awards could only have been made by the arbitrator, in effect, giving himself evidence in flat contradiction to that given to him by the expert witnesses called by the parties.

In *Belvedere Motors Ltd v King* (1981) 260 EG 813, however, in an unsuccessful action for negligence against an independent valuer appointed to determine a review rent under a lease, among the steps taken by the defendant before making his decision, and either accepted by the parties as correct or given judicial approval, were: the obtaining of particulars of neighbouring premises noticed by him during an earlier rent review on other premises; the obtaining of rateable values of comparable premises and the adjustment of agreed floor areas of the subject-premises.

The defaulting arbitrator in the first case would have acted quite properly if he had been appointed as an expert, and the blameless expert in the second case would have been guilty of misconduct if he had been appointed as an arbitrator.

(c) *Judicial control.* In addition to the powers given to the courts to appoint arbitrators (p. 200 above) and to remit or set aside awards (p. 203 below), the courts have a wide supervisory jurisdiction over arbitration proceedings. For example, the High Court has a general power to grant leave to a party to revoke an arbitrator's appointment, coupled with a specific power to remove an arbitrator who has misconducted himself or the proceedings (see Chapter 9 p. 282 below). The court may remit any of the matters referred to the arbitrator to his reconsideration (see Chapter 12 p. 372 below). The court may, with the consent of the arbitrator or the parties, determine a preliminary point of law arising during the reference (see Chapter 10 p. 304 below). These powers can be invoked on the application of one or more of the parties. Similar powers do not exist, however, in relation to an independent expert, except in the unlikely event that the parties have written them into the instrument of appointment. For example, the authority of an independent expert cannot be revoked except with the consent of both parties (*Northampton Gaslight Co v Parnell* (1855) 15 CB 630).

(d) *Award or determination.* An arbitrator's award and an expert's determination are both subject to limited but different rights of challenge.

As a general rule, an award is final and binding, but there are several ways in which it may be challenged by a dissastisfied party (see Chapter 12 p. 359 below). Under the Arbitration Acts, application may be made to the court to remit or set aside an award or, with the consent of all parties or leave of the court, to appeal on any question of law arising out of the award. If the appeal proceeds the court may confirm, vary or set aside the award or remit it to the reconsideration of the arbitrator.

These provisions do not apply to a valuation or other expert determination. The agreement to refer usually provides that the expert's decision shall be final and binding upon the parties, but the courts have recognised certain grounds on which a decision may be challenged by one of the parties. These may be found in four recent cases.

In *Campbell v Edwards* (1975) 237 EG 647, a lease of a flat contained a provision that, if the tenant wished to assign the premises, she must first offer to surrender them to the landlord at a price to be fixed by an independent valuer. The tenant wished to assign, the surrender provisions were brought into operation, the price was fixed and the surrender took place. The landlord later disputed the price and claimed that he was not bound by the valuation. It was held by the Court of Appeal that he was bound by it on two grounds. First, both parties were contractually bound by the valuation in the absence of fraud or collusion. Secondly, the transaction based on the valuation had been completed and restitution was now impossible. Lord Denning MR said (pp. 647 and 649):

> "It is simply the law of contract. If two persons agree that the price of property should be fixed by a valuer on whom they agree, and he gives that valuation honestly and in good faith, they are bound by it. Even if he has made a mistake they are still bound by it. The reason is because they have agreed to be bound by it. If there were fraud or collusion, of course, it would be very different. Fraud or collusion unravels everything. It may be that if a valuer gives a speaking valuation— if he gives his reasons or his calculations—and you can show on the face of them that they are wrong, it might be upset.

But this is not such a case. Chestertons simply gave the figure. Having given it honestly, it is binding on the parties. It is no good for either party to say that it is incorrect. But even if the valuation could be upset for mistake, there is no room for it in this case. The premises have been surrendered to the landlord. He has entered into occupation of them. Months have passed. There cannot be *restitutio in integrum*."

This decision was followed in *Baber v Kenwood Manufacturing Co Ltd* [1978] 1 Lloyd's Rep 175, a case which concerned the value of shares certified by the company's auditors acting as experts and not as arbitrators. As in *Campbell* the auditors' certificate gave no reasons for the valuation (a non-speaking valuation) and the Court of Appeal refused to set it aside on grounds of mistake. It was held that a non-speaking valuation cannot be impugned for a negligent mistake but it may cease to be binding if it contains a fundamental error, e.g. if the auditors had valued the shares of some different company, or the wrong number of shares or if the valuation had not been made in accordance with the express terms of the contract.

The third decision, *Burgess v Purchase & Sons (Farms) Ltd* [1983] 2 All ER 4, also concerned a valuation by auditors of shares in a company but they gave a speaking valuation. The articles of association of the company gave members a right of pre-emption at a fair value over the issued shares, that value to be fixed by the company's auditors whose decision shall be final, binding and conclusive. On the death of one of the shareholders, his executors, the plaintiffs, gave the company notice of sale in respect of the deceased's shareholding and the company then became the plaintiffs' agents for the sale of those shares to a member of the company. The company's auditors provided a certificate of value and explained how they had arrived at their valuation. The valuation was not accepted by the plaintiffs and litigation ensued. The plaintiffs' statement of claim was not, however, struck out on this occasion (as it had been in *Campbell* and *Baber*) because the valuation, being a speaking one, might be impugned on the grounds alleged in the plaintiffs' claim. Nourse J said (p. 11):

"In my judgment the present state of the law can be summarised as follows. The question whether a valuation made by an expert on a fundamentally erroneous basis can be impugned or not depends on the terms expressed or to be implied in the contract pursuant to which it is made. A non-speaking valuation made of the right property by the right man and in good faith cannot be impugned, although it may still be possible, in the case of an uncompleted transaction, for equitable relief (as opposed to damages) to be refused to the party who wishes to sustain the valuation. On the other hand, there are at least three decisions at first instance to the effect that a speaking valuation which demonstrates that it has been made on a fundamentally erroneous basis can be impugned. In such a case the completion of the transaction does not necessarily defeat the party who wishes to impugn the valuation."

This decision was subsequently followed by the Court of Appeal in *Heyes v Earl of Derby* (1984) 272 EG 935.

There is no duty on either an arbitrator or an expert to state the reasons for his decision, unless he is required to do so under the arbitration agreement or contract of appointment. In the absence of such a requirement an expert can never be compelled to give the reasons for his decision, but an arbitrator can be compelled to do so under section 1 of the Arbitration Act 1979 (see Chapter 11 p. 332 below). Any party to the reference may, with the consent of all other parties or with leave of the court, apply to the court for an order requiring the arbitrator to state his reasons in sufficient detail to enable the court to consider any question of law arising out of the award in the event of an appeal. Where an award does not contain *any* reasons, the court will only order them to be given if the arbitrator was asked to give them before he made his award or there was some special reason why such a request was not made.

In the absence of a contrary intention in the arbitration agreement, an arbitrator may correct his award in respect of any clerical mistake or error arising from any accidental slip or omission. It is unlikely that an expert has power to alter or correct his determination after it has been made, except where he is allowed to do so under his terms of appointment or with the consent of all parties.

An award may be enforced either summarily as a judgment of the court or by an action on the award (see Chapter 12 p. 383 below). An expert's determination forms part of the contract between the parties and can only be enforced by action.

(e) *Costs.* An arbitrator derives his power to deal with the costs of the reference from the arbitration agreement and, except where a contrary intention is expressed in that agreement, from the Arbitration Acts (see Chapter 11 p. 344 below). An independent expert derives his power to award costs (if any) solely from the terms of his appointment.

Thus, an arbitrator will look first to the arbitration agreement to see whether it gives specific directions as to costs or otherwise removes his power to deal with them under the Arbitration Acts. Unless the arbitration agreement contains a contrary intention, section 18(1) of the Arbitration Act 1950 gives the arbitrator a discretion as to the award, payment and taxation of costs. No such general power is available to an expert who can look only to the specific provisions, if any, in his contract of appointment.

Where an arbitration agreement relating to a future dispute contains a provision requiring a party or the parties to pay his or their own costs, this provision is void and the arbitrator's discretion as to costs is restored. This rule does not apply to experts and, as stated above, one of the factors which is indicative of an expert appointment is the existence of such a provision in the agreement.

It is usual practice for an arbitrator or expert to deliver his award or determination after his fees and costs have been paid. Where an arbitrator follows this practice any party to the reference who has not agreed his fees may require the court to order the arbitrator to release the award upon payment of his fees into court. These will then be taxed by the court, a reasonable sum being allowed to the arbitrator and any balance repaid to the applicant. These provisions do not apply to an expert. His fees cannot be taxed by the court; they form part of his contract with the parties and are payable by one or all of them in the same manner as other fees for professional services (see also p. 210 below regarding an implied term regarding fees under the Supply of Goods and Services Act 1982).

(2) Liability for negligence

Liability for professional negligence arises out of an express or implied term in a contract or in tort and is discussed in Chapter 8.

(a) *Position at common law.* As a general rule an independent expert is liable for negligence in the performance of his duties, but an arbitrator is immune from such an action. Unfortunately, the law is not as certain regarding the immunity of arbitrators as this clear statement suggests: certain *obiter dicta* in the *Arenson* case (p. 196 above) have cast doubts on the immunity of arbitrators. Furthermore, the central question discussed above still remains: when is an appointed person an arbitrator and when is he an expert? It will be necessary, therefore, to examine the *Sutcliffe* and *Arenson* decisions and then Part II of the Supply of Goods and Services Act 1982. It will be convenient for the purposes of comparison to consider the liability of an arbitrator for negligence in this chapter rather than in the last part of this book.

In *Sutcliffe v Thackrah* [1974] AC 747, the issue between the parties was whether architects appointed to design and supervise the construction of a house were liable to the building owner for the negligent certification of work on interim certificates. The architects claimed, and this was upheld by the Court of Appeal, that when issuing certificates they were acting in an arbitral capacity and, provided they acted honestly, they were not under any duty to exercise care or professional skill.

The House of Lords, however, held that architects have no such immunity for the issue of certificates. The giving of an interim certificate was not a decision in respect of a dispute between the building owner and the contractor. There was no agreement to abide by the decision of the architects as to the value of work carried out (the building contract, in fact, contained arbitration clauses for disputes including those relating to interim certificates) and the defendant architects owed a duty to the plaintiff building owner to exercise care and skill in the issue of certificates. Furthermore, the architects were not placed in the position of arbitrators by the fact that the building owner was compelled to pay the amount certified, nor because the architects could only properly perform their duties if they acted fairly between the parties.

All five law lords accepted that an arbitrator had immunity from actions for negligence and all drew a distinction between the functions of an arbitrator and those of an architect issuing certificates under a building contract.

Lord Reid (with whom Lord Hodson agreed) referred to the judicial character of an arbitrator's duties, namely the reference of a dispute to him for decision, his receipt of submissions and evidence from the parties and the absence of investigation by him. He then referred to the absence of any judicial character in an architect's function when determining whether work is defective. Lord Morris of Borth-y-Gest also saw a dispute as a necessary preliminary to arbitration and said that an architect, surveyor or valuer must be appointed as an arbitrator before a claim for immunity for negligence could be sustained. Both Viscount Dilhorne and Lord Salmon drew distinctions between the judicial functions of an arbitrator and the functions of an architect or valuer, who merely carry out their ordinary business activities.

In the later case of *Arenson v Arenson & Casson, Beckman Rutley & Co* [1976] 1 Lloyd's Rep 179, the House of Lords gave consideration to the distinction between an arbitrator and a valuer and to the immunity of arbitrators from actions for negligence. Unfortunately, although their Lordships were unanimous in their decision, they differed on the question of the immunity of arbitrators.

In this case the issue between the parties was whether auditors instructed to value shares for the purposes of a sale from one shareholder to another, and who were to act as experts and not as arbitrators and give a final and binding decision, could be sued for negligence in respect of that valuation. The matter came before the courts on an application by the defendants to have the claim struck out as disclosing no cause of action. The House of Lords allowed the plaintiff's appeal from a decision of the Court of Appeal striking out the claim and held that the statement of claim was not misconceived because it had not been shown that the auditors were acting in a judicial capacity when carrying out their valuation. Thus, the auditors could be liable for negligence.

Lord Simon of Glaisdale appeared to accept that an arbitrator has immunity from actions for negligence but considered that a valuer could only claim such immunity if he could show that he was performing a judicial role. He said (p. 188):

> "There may well be other indicia that a valuer is acting in a judicial role, such as the reception of rival contentions or of evidence, or the giving of a reasoned judgment. But in my view the essential prerequisite for him to claim immunity as an arbitrator is that, by the time the matter is submitted to him for decision, there should be a formulated dispute between at least two parties which his decision is required to resolve. It is not enough that parties who may be affected by the decision have opposed interests—still less that the decision is on a matter which is not agreed between them."

Lord Wheatley referred to the immunity doctrine, which gives immunity to persons in certain positions from the consequences of negligence in their duties, and which has been extended to arbitrators and, it would appear, also to "quasi-arbitrators." A valuer does not possess this immunity but he may be clothed with it if he can show that by the terms of his appointment he has been constituted as an arbitrator or quasi-arbitrator. Each case must be decided on its own facts, said Lord Wheatley, but the following were indicia of an arbitral or quasi-arbitral appointment (p. 191):

> "(a) there is a dispute or a difference between the parties which has been formulated in some way or another;
> (b) the dispute or difference has been remitted by the parties to the person to resolve in such a manner that he is called upon to exercise a judicial function;
> (c) where appropriate, the parties must have been provided with an opportunity to present evidence and/or submissions in support of their respective claims in the dispute;
> (d) the parties have agreed to accept his decision."

Lord Kilbrandon questioned whether an arbitrator is immune
from actions for negligence, particularly where he uses his expertise to decide a dispute, as by inspecting a sample of merchandise
to give his opinion on quality or value.

Lord Salmon, while accepting that arbitrators have immunity
when carrying out much the same functions as judges, also
expressed the view that an arbitrator with a limited and non-
judicial role of investigating goods and making a decision without
receiving submissions and evidence, should not enjoy judicial
immunity. This was a matter which may have to be examined in
the future. Similarly, a valuer does not have immunity when
acting in an expert and investigatory capacity but may have when
he acts judicially. He said (p. 198):

> "I would sum it up by stating that it was long ago rightly
> decided in *In Re Hopper* that a valuer enjoys the immunity of
> a judge or arbitrator only if what he does assumes the
> character of a judicial inquiry, e.g. by the parties submitting
> their dispute to the valuer for adjudication and the valuer
> listening to or reading the contentions made by or on behalf
> of the parties and to any evidence which they may put before
> him and then publishing a decision which is final and
> binding save for any appeal which the law allows."

Finally, Lord Fraser of Tullybelton shared the difficulty experienced by Lord Kilbrandon in understanding why arbitrators
should have immunity if mutual valuers do not, and agreed with
Lord Salmon that it may be that all arbitrators should not have
this privilege. Both parties in *Arenson*, however, accepted the
immunity of arbitrators and he, therefore, expressed no opinion
on the matter. He agreed that no sufficient reason could be shown
for treating a mutual valuer as an exception to the general rule of
liability for negligence.

The position at common law which arises from the above two
decisions is, therefore, as follows. It is clear that an independent
expert, who is required to act in an investigatory capacity and rely
on his specialised knowledge and experience to reach a decision,
will be liable for any negligence in the performance of his duties.
In the absence of a term in his contract of appointment excluding
such liability (see Chapter 8 p. 249 below), he will only have
immunity from actions for negligence if he can show that he acted
judicially, e.g. by deciding a formulated dispute on the basis of
submissions and evidence. An arbitrator who is required to act in
a judicial capacity probably has immunity from actions for negligence, but his immunity is in doubt if he is appointed to make a
decision on the basis of his own investigations and expertise

without conducting judicial proceedings, e.g. in a commodity arbitration.

Although the judgments in *Arenson* leave some doubt as to the true position of an arbitrator, Lord Denning MR in the later case of *Campbell v Edwards* (p. 203 above) was certain as to the state of the law. He said (p. 649):

> "The position of a valuer is very different from an arbitrator. If a valuer is negligent in making a valuation, he may be sued by the party—vendor or purchaser—who is injured by his wrong valuation. But an arbitrator is different. In my opinion he cannot be sued by either party to the dispute, even if he is negligent. The only remedy of the party is to set aside the award, and then only if it comes within the accepted grounds for setting it aside. If an arbitrator is guilty of misconduct, his award can be set aside. If he has gone wrong on a point of law which appears on the face of it, it can be corrected by a court. But the arbitrator himself is not liable to be sued. I say this because I should be sorry if any doubt should be felt about it. This case is just a postscript to *Arenson*."

It is open to an independent expert or arbitrator to exclude liability for negligence by incorporating into his terms of appointment a clause excluding such liability. This exclusion clause must satisfy the requirement of "reasonableness" under the Unfair Contract Terms Act 1977 (see Chapter 8 p. 251 below).

(b) *Position under Supply of Goods and Services Act 1982*. The effect of Part II of the Supply of Goods and Services Act 1982 is usually to include in a contract for the supply of a service implied terms relating to care and skill (negligence), time for performance and consideration. There was originally some doubt as to whether the Act imposed liability for negligence on arbitrators but this uncertainty has now been resolved by their exclusion from the operation of the Act (see below).

Part II of the 1982 Act came into force on 4th July 1983. It applies to a "contract for the supply of a service", which is defined as a contract under which a person (the supplier) agrees to carry out a service, irrespective of whether or not goods are transferred or hired under the contract and whatever is the value of the consideration. Contracts of service or apprenticeship are excluded (section 12(1)–(4)).

The general rule is that three terms are implied in every contract for the supply of a service. These are: first, that the supplier will exercise reasonable care and skill (i.e. he will not be negligent) (section 13); secondly, where the time for the performance of the service is not fixed or left to be fixed in an agreed manner or by a course of dealing between the parties, that the supplier will carry out the service within a reasonable time (section 14); and thirdly, where the consideration is not determined by the contract or left to be determined in an agreed manner or by a course of dealing between the parties, that the supplier will be paid a reasonable charge (section 15). The terms relating to care and skill and time apply only where the supplier is acting in the course of a business.

One or more of the above terms may be excluded or become inapplicable in the following ways:

(i) by order made by the Secretary of State that one or more of those terms shall not apply to certain specified services (orders have been made covering advocates, company and building society directors and arbitrators) (section 12(4) and (5) and, in respect of arbitrators, the Supply of Services (Exclusion of Implied Terms) Order 1985 operative from 1st March 1985);

(ii) by express agreement between the parties, i.e. by the incorporation of an exclusion clause, which must satisfy the test of "reasonableness" under the Unfair Contract Terms Act 1977 (section 16(1) and (2));

(iii) by the course of dealing between the parties (section 16(1));

(iv) by such usage as binds both parties to the contract (section 16(1)).

Section 16(3) provides that nothing in this Part of the Act shall prejudice, first, any rule of law which imposes on the supplier stricter duties relating to care and skill and time for performance than those in the Act; or secondly, and subject to the above, any rule of law whereby any term not inconsistent with the above provisions is to be implied in a contract for the supply of a service.

Section 16(4) states that all the above provisions shall have effect subject to any other enactment which defines or restricts the rights, duties or liabilities arising in connection with a service of any description.

The appointment of an independent expert to determine a matter in which the parties have opposing interests is a contract for the supply of a service. It will, therefore, usually include implied terms relating to care and skill, time for performance and consideration. These terms will not be included in an agreement for the appointment of an arbitrator, at least not from 1st March 1985.

PRACTICE AND PROCEDURE

The remainder of this chapter comprises a practical example of the work of an independent expert. We look again at the files of Mr J. O. Dodgson of Melchester, who we first met in Chapter 5, and follow a case where he was appointed to determine the price to be paid by a tenant on her exercise of an option to purchase the landlord's interest.

(1) Appointment

In April 1984 Mr Dodgson received a letter from Messrs Grimes & Co, solicitors for Mrs N. A. Sedley, tenant of The Priory School for Girls in Melchester. The letter stated that their client's lease of the school contained a tenant's option to purchase the landlord's interest in the property, that Mrs Sedley had exercised that option, but the parties had failed to agree the price and had agreed to appoint Mr Dodgson as the independent surveyor to determine that price. Would Mr Dodgson accept this appointment? A copy of the lease of the school was enclosed with the letter, clause 5(2) of which contained the tenant's option to purchase the freehold in the following terms:

> "If the tenant shall at any time during the said term desire to purchase the reversion in fee simple in the demised premises and shall give to the landlord three months' notice in writing of such desire then the landlord will upon the expiration of such notice and on payment of such sum as may be agreed between the landlord and the tenant or in the absence of such agreement as may be determined by an independent surveyor (who shall be a chartered surveyor and shall act as an expert and not as an arbitrator) to be appointed jointly by the parties or in default of such appointment to be nominated by the President of The Royal Institution of Chartered Surveyors on the application of either party and so that the amount to be determined by the independent surveyor shall be such amount as shall in his absolute discretion represent the fair market price for the demised premises on the date of such determination having regard to values of property then current for comparable properties in comparable areas to the demised premises (the costs of such determination to be borne by the landlord and the tenant in equal shares) convey the demised premises to the tenant in fee simple free from encumbrances"

Mr Dodgson read the lease and checked on three matters before agreeing to accept this appointment. First, he satisfied himself that he was expert in the type of property to be valued and that he fulfilled the only specific requirement as to qualifications and experience, namely that he was a chartered surveyor. Secondly, Mr Dodgson satisfied himself that he could complete the work within a reasonable time. Thirdly, he checked that he had no present or recently past relationship with the parties or the property and that there were no other reasons which would prevent him acting fairly between them, e.g. a strong bias against one of the parties or their agents. He also made inquiries within his firm to ensure that no other partner or member of staff had such a relationship or reason for possible bias. When Mr Dodgson had satisfied himself on these three matters he wrote to Messrs Grimes & Co stating that he would be willing to accept this appointment and setting out the basis of his fee. His fee quotation included provision for an abortive fee in the event of a settlement before he made his determination, the reservation of the right to take legal advice and to include the cost as part of his fee and the addition of value added tax and expenses. Mr Dodgson requested the parties to state their agreement to this fee basis in the letter of appointment. Mr Dodgson did not seek to include in his terms of appointment a clause excluding the implied terms relating to care and skill and time for completion.

On 3rd May 1984 the solicitors for both parties wrote a joint letter of appointment to Mr Dodgson and requested him to correspond with the surveyors to the parties as to the procedure to be followed in reaching his determination. Mr Dodgson read again the relevant parts of the lease to satisfy himself on three preliminary matters. First, that he had been validly appointed as an independent surveyor, and not as an arbitrator. Secondly, that his only task is to determine the fair market price of the landlord's interest in the demised premises at the date of his determination. Thirdly, that he was not required to follow any special procedure. Mr Dodgson was aware that an appointment as an independent expert is a personal appointment. It cannot be delegated to another person although some of the duties may be delegated, such as the collection and analysis of information and the measurement of buildings.

(2) Initial letter
Mr Dodgson commenced his task by writing the following joint letter to the surveyors to the parties:

Dear Sirs,
The Priory School for Girls, Priory Lane, Melchester, Loamshire
(1) On 3rd May 1984 I was appointed by the parties to a lease of the above property dated 14th March 1980 to act as the independent surveyor under clause 5(2) of that lease to determine the fair market price for the purposes of a conveyance of the freehold

interest following the exercise by the tenant of an option to purchase that interest.

(2) If the parties require more time to reach an agreement on the price I will defer proceeding with this matter, provided I am requested in writing to do so by *both* parties. Until I receive such a request I will proceed towards a determination.

(3) I am prepared to receive written representations from the parties in accordance with the following procedure. The parties shall submit to me their written representations in duplicate on or before 28th May 1984. When I have received representations from both parties I will send one copy of each to the other party. The parties may then submit to me cross-representations in duplicate within 14 days of receipt of the opposing party's initial representations. The cross-representations shall not contain any new material but shall be restricted to a rebuttal of the opposing party's initial representations. When I have received cross-representations from both parties I will send one copy of each to the other party. No further representations will be allowed unless I give consent.

(4) The source of all facts in the parties' representations (other than those agreed) shall be stated, together with supporting letters or other documents in order that I may decide what weight to give to them.

(5) If either party wishes to raise an issue of law affecting my determination he shall include it in his representations together with his contentions thereon.

(6) I am prepared to receive from the parties a statement of agreed facts, containing agreed floor areas, accommodation, facilities, plans and other relevant facts relating to the above property and any comparable properties and transactions referred to by the parties in their written representations. The statement of agreed facts shall be submitted to me not later than the last date for the submission of cross-representations under paragraph (3) above.

(7) No "without prejudice" correspondence or statements shall be disclosed to me nor included in the written representations unless agreed by *both* parties.

(8) A copy of every letter or other document sent to me shall be sent to the other party.

Yours faithfully,

J. O. Dodgson

The above letter may be compared with the initial letter and order for directions for written representations in the arbitration discussed in Chapter 13 (pp. 389 and 396 below).

(3) Procedure before determination

No request was received from either party for a deferment of proceedings and Mr Dodgson received the parties' representations and a statement of agreed facts in accordance with the prescribed timetable.

When Mr Dodgson received initial representations from both parties he sent one copy of each to the other party's surveyor with the following joint letter:

Dear Sirs,
The Priory School for Girls, Priory Lane, Melchester, Loamshire
I have now received initial representations from both parties and I enclose a copy of those submitted by the other party. If you wish to submit cross-representations please send them to me within 14 days of receipt of this letter. These cross-representations shall not contain any new material but shall be restricted to a rebuttal of the enclosed representations.

Yours faithfully,

J. O. Dodgson

When Mr Dodgson received cross-representations from both surveyors he sent one copy of each to the other surveyor with the following joint letter:

Dear Sirs,
The Priory School for Girls, Priory Lane, Melchester, Loamshire
I have now received cross-representations from both parties and enclose one copy of those submitted by the other party. The exchange of representations is now complete and no further representations are to be made.

I confirm that I will inspect the above property at 2.30 p.m. on Monday 18th June 1984.

I will notify both parties when I have made my determination.

Yours faithfully,

J. O. Dodgson

Both parties submitted written representations in this matter. But, if one party had declined to do so, Mr Dodgson would still have accepted them from the other party and would have sent them to the reluctant party for comment. The first party would then have been given an opportunity to reply to any comments made. If one party only had submitted representations Mr Dodgson would have been careful to check the accuracy of any facts before relying on them.

It should be noted that facts contained in representations submitted to an expert do not need to be strictly proved. The rules of evidence do not apply: "hearsay evidence" of comparables may be put before an expert, although, for reasons of public policy, he should not receive "without prejudice" statements. In paragraph (4) of his initial letter Mr Dodgson asked the parties to state the source of their facts, together with supporting letters etc so that he may decide the reliability of this information. An expert has a duty to verify the accuracy of all facts put to him.

Mr Dodgson was not, of course, bound to accept agreed facts but could disregard them and substitute his own if he wished. Thus, he could substitute his own measured floor area for an agreed floor area, something he could not do if he had been appointed as an arbitrator (see Chapter 10 p. 317 below).

When Mr Dodgson read the written representations he saw that a fundamental question of law was in issue, namely the basis of valuation. The landlord argued that the "fair market price" of his freehold interest should be the value with vacant possession, whereas the tenant contended that the freehold should be valued subject to the existing lease. This was a dispute on the interpretation of the tenant's option to purchase. How did Mr Dodgson deal with it?

There are three ways in which a question of law may be resolved in a reference to an independent expert. First, the expert may (and must if so required by the parties) make his own decision. He is, however, free to do his own research and make his own inquiries, provided he does not actually delegate the responsibility for his decision to a third person without the consent of the parties. Secondly, if the question of law can be dealt with separately from issues of fact, then either party may seek a declaration in the High Court by an originating summons (see Chapter 1 p. 5 above). The expert should not proceed to his determination until this question has been settled by the court. It should be noted that the procedure under section 2 of the Arbitration Act 1979, whereby the High Court may be asked to determine any question of law arising during a reference to arbitration cannot be used where a matter has been referred to an independent expert. Thirdly, and again if the question of law can be decided independently of the facts, the parties may agree that it shall be referred to a legal expert or arbitrator, e.g. solicitor or counsel. This course of action requires the agreement of both parties. The independent surveyor should defer his determination until the legal expert or arbitrator has made his decision on the preliminary point of law.

Mr Dodgson drew the parties' attention to the issue of law which had arisen. He said that he would be able to decide it himself but inquired whether the parties wished to seek a declaration in the High Court or refer it for decision to a legal expert or arbitrator. The parties asked Mr Dodgson to deal with it.

Mr Dodgson noticed that the wording of the option in the lease of The Priory School for Girls was substantially the same as the tenant's option to purchase which came before the High Court for interpretation in the case of *Re Nagel's Lease* (1974) 232 EG 455. Accordingly, he followed that decision and took as his basis of valuation the value of the freehold interest with vacant possession. Neither of the parties referred to this case in their written representations. If Mr Dodgson had been an arbitrator it would have been necessary for him to bring it to their attention for comment before taking it into account in his decision (see Chapter 10 p. 323 below). As an expert, however, this was not necessary: he could base his decision on it without reference to the parties.

Following receipt of the parties' written submissions, Mr Dodgson inspected The Priory School for Girls and the comparable properties referred to by the parties. The tenant was in occupation of the school and, therefore, to avoid any possible allegation of bias, Mr Dodgson invited the landlord's representative to attend this inspection. He inspected the comparable properties unaccompanied. Mr Dodgson also inspected two other schools, not referred to by the parties, recently sold by Mr Dodgson's firm in their capacity as surveyors to the Bishop Tanner Educational Trust. He took these sale prices into consideration when making his determination, as he was entitled to do as an expert, although if he had been an arbitrator he could not have done so, at least not without informing the parties of this additional evidence and giving them an opportunity of dealing with it (see Chapter 10 p. 317 below).

Throughout the period before he made his determination Mr Dodgson ensured that he was seen to be acting fairly between the parties. Correspondence was either sent as a joint letter to both parties or, if sent to one party only, a copy was sent to the other. If he received a letter from one party, a copy of which had not been sent to the other, he then sent a copy of that letter to that party. He tried to avoid telephone conversations and meetings with one party and, if this were not possible, he immediately told the other party what had happened.

Mr Dodgson was aware that there is always a possibility, however small, that his decision would result in an action for negligence by one of the parties. He ensured, therefore, that his conduct before he reached his decision was well documented by file notes and letters and, although he did not give a reasoned decision, he made a detailed note setting out the reasons for his determination.

(4) Determination

When Mr Dodgson had completed his inspections and investigations and read the parties' representations, he prepared his valuation and then set it out in the following formal and traditional form:

IN THE MATTER OF THE PRIORY SCHOOL FOR GIRLS, PRIORY LANE, MELCHESTER, LOAMSHIRE AND IN THE MATTER OF THE APPOINTMENT OF AN INDEPENDENT SURVEYOR TO DETERMINE THE FAIR MARKET PRICE UNDER A TENANT'S OPTION TO PURCHASE IN A LEASE DATED 14TH MARCH 1980

DETERMINATION OF JAMES OLIVER DODGSON FRICS FCIArb

WHEREAS:

(1) By a lease dated 14th March 1980 between (i) Captain Horace Balstrode R. N. (landlord) and (ii) Natasha Adelaide Sedley (tenant), premises known as The Priory School for Girls, Priory Lane, Melchester, Loamshire (the demised premises) were leased for a term of 25 years from 25th December 1979.

(2) The above lease provides (inter alia) that the tenant may purchase the landlord's freehold interest in the demised premises at the fair market price, such price to be agreed between the parties or, in the absence of such agreement, determined by an independent surveyor appointed jointly by the parties, or in default of such appointment, nominated by the President of The Royal Institution of Chartered Surveyors.

(3) The parties having failed to agree the amount of the fair market price I was appointed by the parties on 3rd May 1984 as the independent surveyor to determine the fair market price at the date of determination.

Now I, James Oliver Dodgson, having accepted the said appointment, inspected the demised premises and considered the written representations submitted to me, do hereby determine that the fair market price of the demised premises in accordance with clause 5(2) of the lease dated 14th March 1980 as at the date hereof is £125,000 (one hundred and twenty five thousand pounds).

Dated this .... day of 1984

Signed ....
James Oliver Dodgson FRICS FCIArb

If Mr Dodgson had used an informal determination it would have been as follows:

LEASE DATED 14TH MARCH 1980 OF THE PRIORY SCHOOL FOR GIRLS, PRIORY LANE, MELCHESTER, LOAMSHIRE BETWEEN CAPTAIN HORACE BALSTRODE R. N. (LANDLORD) AND NATASHA ADELAIDE SEDLEY (TENANT)

On 3rd May 1984 I, James Oliver Dodgson FRICS FCIArb, was appointed by the parties to the above lease to be the independent surveyor to determine the fair market price of the demised premises pursuant to a tenant's option to purchase the landlord's freehold interest contained in clause 5(2) of that lease.

I determine that the fair market price of the demised premises under clause 5(2) of the above lease as at the date hereof is £125,000 (one hundred and twenty five thousand pounds).

....1984

....
James Oliver Dodgson FRICS FCIArb

When Mr Dodgson had made his determination he wrote the following joint letter to the surveyors to the parties:

Dear Sirs,
The Priory School for Girls, Priory Lane, Melchester, Loamshire
I have now made my determination of the fair market price of the above property under the tenant's option to purchase contained in clause 5(2) of the lease dated 14th March 1980. I will send a copy of my determination to each party upon payment of my total fee of £——, inclusive of value added tax and expenses. If you wish to collect the determination from this office please inform my secretary

and arrangements will be made for it to be left at our reception desk, to be released on receipt of a cheque for the above amount.

Yours faithfully,

J. O. Dodgson

An expert is *functus officio* when he has made his determination and should take no further part in the matter. In particular, he should not give reasons for his decision nor discuss it with the parties. As stated above, an arbitrator generally has the power to correct any clerical mistake or error in his award due to an accidental slip or omission, but it is doubtful whether an expert can subsequently alter his determination without the consent of both parties.

In this case no complications arose: the parties jointly sent a cheque for the whole of Mr Dodgson's fee and he released his determination to both parties who accepted it.

CHAPTER EIGHT

Professional Negligence

INTRODUCTION

An independent expert does not have the immunity from actions for negligence enjoyed by an advocate and probably also by an arbitrator and an expert witness. He is in the same position as other professional men and may be sued for negligence in the performance of his duties. Negligence is a wide and rapidly developing branch of the law: it cannot be dealt with comprehensively in this chapter. I shall concentrate on those matters of particular reference to an expert appointed to decide a dispute of value, although I hope that it will also serve as a useful summary of the law of negligence in valuation.

A person who wishes to bring a successful action for professional negligence must prove the following. First, that the defendant owed him a duty of care in contract or tort, which was not excluded or modified by a contract term or a notice in tort. Secondly, that the defendant was in breach of that duty by failing to exercise the standard of care required of him. Thirdly, where the action is brought in tort, that the plaintiff has suffered loss as a result of the negligence. Fourthly, that the action was commenced within the period prescribed by the Limitation Act 1980.

The burden of proof in an action for professional negligence is the same as in other actions, namely on the balance of probabilities. But the burden of achieving something more than the mere balance of probabilities is greater when dealing with the complicated and sophisticated actions of professional men than when inquiring into other allegations of negligence, such as the momentary inattention of the driver of a car (*Dwyer v Rodrick* (1983) *Law Society's Gazette*, 23rd November 1983 p. 3003).

DUTY OF CARE

A professional man owes to his client concurrent duties of care in contract and tort. He may also owe a duty of care in tort to certain third parties. He may be able to exclude these duties by a contract term or a notice in tort provided certain requirements are satisfied (see p. 249 below).

(1) Duty to client

A duty of care to a client or other contractual party arises under an

221

express or implied term in a contract or in tort. For example, in *Batty v Metropolitan Property Realisations Ltd* (1978) 246 EG 43, a development company which built and sold a house on an unstable hillside was held liable in damages to the purchasers for breach of an express warranty in the contract of sale that the house had been built in an efficient and workmanlike manner, of proper materials and fit for habitation. In *Perry v Sidney Phillips & Son* (1982) 263 EG 888, a chartered surveyor who negligently carried out a structural survey was found to be in breach of an implied contract term that he would exercise that degree of care expected of a reasonably competent chartered surveyor. A valuer appointed by two parties to fix a price or rent between them owes a duty to both parties. In *Campbell v Edwards* (1975) 237 EG 647, Lord Denning MR said (p. 647).

> "It is now clear that he owes a duty to both parties to act with reasonable care and skill in making his valuation. If he makes a mistake owing to want of care and skill he may be liable to damages."

The implied contract term at common law is now given statutory force by section 13 of the Supply of Goods and Services Act 1982 (see Chapter 7 p. 210 above).

An express term regarding the duty of care will always displace the implied term (at common law and under statute) where they are inconsistent. It may impose a higher standard of care. Furthermore, an implied contract term may, in certain circumstances, impose a higher standard of care than that imposed in tort (see p. 225 below).

A professional man's concurrent but independent liability to his client in tort is a recent development in the law. Before the decisions in *Esso Petroleum Co Ltd v Mardon* [1976] 2 WLR 583 and *Midland Bank Trust Co Ltd v Hett, Stubbs & Kemp* [1978] 3 WLR 167, it was generally thought that a professional man could be sued *by his client* only in contract, although it was already established that he was also liable in tort *to third parties* to whom he owed a duty of care. It is now clear that a client may sue his professional adviser for negligence in contract or tort. Where a plaintiff proceeds in tort the contract is only relevant to the action if it excludes or restricts the claim in tort (*Coupland v Arabian Gulf Petroleum Co* [1983] 3 All ER 226).

Allied to the imposition of concurrent liabilities in contract and tort, the courts have shown a tendency to merge the law relating to negligence in these two branches. There are, however, still differences which are of practical importance. First, under certain circumstances, an implied duty of care in a contract for professional services may impose a higher standard of care and skill than the corresponding standard in tort (see p. 225 below). Secondly, the date when a cause of action arises (which determines the start of the limitation period after which an action will become statute-barred) may be different in contract and tort (see p. 247 below). Thirdly, the measure of damages may be different (see p. 232 below). Fourthly, a writ for breach of contract may be served out of the jurisdiction.

(2) Duty to third parties

A professional man may, under certain circumstances, owe a duty of care in tort to a third party. The rules for deciding whether a person is a third party to whom this duty of care is owed were explained by Lord Wilberforce in *Anns v Merton London Borough Council* (1977) 243 EG 523 at p. 525:

> "Through the trilogy of cases in this House—*Donoghue v Stevenson* [1932] AC 562, *Hedley Byrne & Co Ltd v Heller & Partners Ltd* [1964] AC 465, and *Dorset Yacht Co Ltd v Home Office* [1970] AC 1004, the position has now been reached that in order to establish that a duty of care arises in a particular situation, it is not necessary to bring the facts of the situation within those of previous situations in which a duty of care has been held to exist. Rather the question has to be approached in two stages. First, one has to ask whether, as between the alleged wrongdoer and the person who has suffered the damage, there is a sufficient relationship of proximity or neighbourhood such that, in the reasonable contemplation of the former, carelessness on his part may be likely to cause damage to the latter—in which case a *prima facie* duty of care arises. Secondly, if the first question is answered affirmatively, it is necessary to consider whether there are any considerations which ought to negative or reduce or limit the scope of the duty or the class of person to whom it is owed or the damages to which a breach of it may give rise (see *Dorset Yacht* case, *loc cit*, p. 1027 per Lord Reid). Examples of this are *Hedley Byrne* where the class of potential plaintiffs was reduced to those shown to have relied upon the correctness of statements made, and *Weller & Co v Foot & Mouth Disease Research Institute* [1966] 1 QB 569; . . . . . ."

For example, solicitors instructed to prepare a will owed a duty of care to a beneficiary, who was a third party within their direct contemplation as likely to suffer loss as a result of their negligence (*Ross v Caunters* [1979] 3 WLR 605). Surveyors instructed by a building society to value a house for mortgage purposes owed a duty of care to the borrowers (the purchasers), despite the usual statutory notice given by the society to the borrowers disclaiming on its own behalf any implied warranty that the price was reasonable and the society's literature which disclaimed responsibility for the condition of the house and advised the purchaser to commission an independent survey (*Yianni v Edwin Evans & Sons* (1981) 259 EG 969). Auditors who produced and certified a company's accounts owed a duty of care to subsequent purchasers of that company (*JEB Fasteners Ltd v Marks Bloom & Co* [1983] 1 All ER 583).

STANDARD OF CARE

(1) General rule

As a general rule, the standard of care required of a professional man is that he should exercise the skill and competence of an ordinarily competent practitioner in that profession. A professional man may be liable for negligence either because he did not possess the requisite skill, or, where he did have it, that he did not exercise it in the particular case.

The starting point is the test laid down by McNair J in *Bolam v Friern Barnet Hospital Management Committee* [1957] 1 WLR 582 at p. 586:

> "... where you get a situation which involves the use of some special skill or competence, then the test as to whether there has been negligence or not is not the test of the man on the top of a Clapham omnibus, because he has not got this special skill. The test is the standard of the ordinary skilled man exercising and professing to have that special skill .... A man need not possess the highest expert skill; it is a well established law that it is sufficient if he exercises the ordinary skill of an ordinary competent man exercising that particular art."

More recently in the *Hett Stubbs* case (p. 222 above) Oliver J said (p. 180): "The test is what the reasonably competent practitioner would do having regard to the standards normally adopted by his profession, ...". This standard is not normally, therefore, that of the highest in the profession but of the average practitioner. Furthermore, a professional man does not usually warrant that he will produce the result required by his client and will not necessarily be negligent if he fails to do so. A doctor does not undertake that he will cure his patient, a solicitor that he will win his client's case or a valuer that he will produce a "correct" valuation:

> "The valuer does not warrant the accuracy or sufficiency of his valuation; he fulfils his part of the bargain if in making his valuation he exercises the care and skill reasonably to be expected from a member of his profession."
>
> (per O'Connor LJ in *London & South of England Building Society v Stone* (1983) 267 EG 69 at p. 70).

In the *Esso* case (p. 222 above), Lord Denning MR referred to the same duty to use reasonable care in both contract and tort. There are indications, however, that in certain circumstances, the courts may impose a higher standard of care under an implied term in a contract than in tort. For example, in *Duchess of Argyll v Beuselinck* [1972] 2 Lloyd's Rep 172, Megarry J said *obiter* at p. 183:

> "In actions in tort, the standard or care to be applied will normally be that of the reasonable man .... But to say that in tort the standard of care is uniform does not necessarily carry the point in circumstances where the action is for breach of an implied duty of care in a contract whereby a client employs a solicitor ... if the client employs a solicitor of high standing and great experience, will an action for negligence fail if it appears that the solicitor did not exercise the care and skill to be expected of him, though he did not fall below the standard of the reasonably competent solicitor? If the client engages an expert, and doubtless expects to pay commensurate fees, is he not entitled to expect something more than the standard of the reasonably competent?"

In *Maynard v West Midlands Regional Health Authority* [1984] 1 WLR 634, it was held by the House of Lords in a medical case that what had to be proved to show negligence was a failure to exercise the skill of a reasonably competent doctor (in the appropriate speciality if he professes a specialism) and that in the realm of diagnosis and treatment negligence is not established simply by preferring one body of professional opinion to another.

A man who accepts instructions in a professional matter holds himself out as possessing the necessary skill and experience to carry out these instructions in a competent manner. Thus, it was no defence for an unqualified "estate agent, valuer and surveyor," who negligently failed to recognise rising damp, dry rot and wet rot, to argue that he only had a working knowledge of structures from the point of view of buying and selling property. If he held himself out in practice as a surveyor he must be deemed to have the skills of a surveyor and be adjudged upon them (*Freeman v Marshall & Co.* (1966) 200 EG 777).

The standard of care of the hypothetical ordinary practitioner, against which the actual conduct of the defendant must be measured, is that which prevailed when he was alleged to have been negligent. Subsequent knowledge or later events, which might have caused him to act differently, are to be disregarded. For example, when considering whether a structure had been negligently designed, it was necessary to apply the professional standards of that time and not any later standards (*Wimpey Construction UK Ltd v Poole* [1984] 2 Lloyd's Rep. 499).

It would appear that the standard of care to be exercised by a professional man is now a question of law, to be decided by the court having regard to the evidence (if any) of accepted standards of conduct or usage in the particular profession. Thus, in the *Hett Stubbs* case (p. 222 above) Oliver J, after referring to evidence of what an "average" solicitor would have done in the circumstances of the defendant, said (pp. 179–180):

> "I must say that I doubt the value, or even the admissibility of this sort of evidence, which seems to be coming customary in cases of this type. The extent of the legal duty in any given situation must, I think, be a question of law for the court. Clearly, if there is some practice in a particular profession, some accepted standard of conduct which is laid down by a professional institute or sanctioned by common usage, evidence of that can and ought to be received. But the evidence which really amounts to no more than an expression of opinion by a particular practitioner of what he thinks he would have done had he been placed, hypothetically and without the benefit of hindsight, in the position of the defendants, is of little assistance to the court; whilst evidence of the witnesses' view of what, as a matter of law, the solicitor's duty was in the particular circumstances of the case is, I should have thought inadmissible, for that is the very question which it is the court's function to decide."

In *Singer & Friedlander Ltd v John D. Wood & Co* (1977) 243 EG 212 (a case of negligent valuation), Watkins J said (p. 217) that the expert evidence he heard on standards of professional practice in valuation was invaluable to him when deciding whether the valuer employed by the defendants had been negligent.

(2) Standard of care in valuation

A valuer is not necessarily negligent because his valuation is wrong. In *Sutcliffe v Thackrah* [1974] AC 747, Lord Salmon said (p. 760): "it by no means follows that a professional valuation or opinion was negligently given because it turns out to have been wholly wrong." Watkins J expressed a similar view in *Singer & Friedlander* (above) and then went on to say (p. 213) that a valuation which falls outside a "bracket", which on the evidence was 10 to 15% either side of the figure which a competent, careful and experienced valuer would have produced at the time of valuation, after making all necessary inquiries and paying proper regard to the state of the market, brings into question the competence of the valuer and the care he exercised when making his valuation.

Negligence in valuation, therefore, arises where a valuer gives an opinion of value outside a permissible bracket *and* can be shown to have acted otherwise than as a reasonably competent valuer. For example, in *Belvedere Motors Ltd v King* (1981) 260 EG 813, an unsuccessful action against an independent expert, Kenneth Jones J referred to the "bracket" of values and said (p. 814):

> "In this case the defendant can only be found guilty of negligence if it can be shown that he has omitted to consider some matter which he ought to have considered, or that he has taken into account some matter which he ought not to have taken into account, or in some way has failed to adopt the procedure and practices accepted as standard in his profession and has so failed to exercise the care and skill which he, on accepting the appointment, held himself out as possessing."

We can extract from cases on negligent valuation the following matters, procedures and practices which determine whether or not a valuer has failed to exercise the requisite standard of care.

(a) *Instructions*. A surveyor may be negligent if he fails to carry out the particular instructions given to him. For example, in *Buckland v Watts* (1968) 208 EG 969, the Court of Appeal held that a surveyor instructed to prepare a survey of a house being purchased by the plaintiff was negligent in preparing only measured drawings and in not carrying out a structural survey and bringing the defective condition of the premises to the plaintiff's attention. An independent expert, should, therefore, ensure that this instructions are clear, and that he carries them out precisely.

(b) *Knowledge of the law*. A valuer must have a *general* knowledge of the law relating to his valuation, but "minute and accurate knowledge" is not required (*Jenkins v Betham* (1855) 15 CB 168). For example, in *BL Holdings Ltd v Robert J Wood & Partners* (1979) 12 BLR 883, an architect who relied on the local authority's policy regarding the calculation of floor space for office development permit purposes and a planning permission granted in accordance therewith, was held by the Court of Appeal not to have been negligent, even though the policy was wrong in law and the permission of no effect. There were two reasons for this decision. First, the complexity of the question of law made it reasonable for the architect to rely on the local authority's policy and the planning permission subsequently granted. Secondly, the architect's clients were experienced property developers who knew that it was common practice for developers to calculate office floor space in the manner proposed by the local authority.

A valuer's legal knowledge must be kept up-to-date, at least in respect of significant changes which are well-publicised. Thus, in *Weedon v Hindwood Clarke & Esplin* (1974) 234 EG 121, a surveyor instructed to negotiate compensation for compulsory purchase was held to have been negligent in failing to reflect in his valuation the important decision in *West Midland Baptist (Trust) Association (Incorporated) v Birmingham Corporation* (1969) 20 P & CR 1052, which altered the date of valuation to the advantage of the claimant.

An independent valuer must, therefore, have a general but up-to-date knowledge of the legal framework of his valuation, usually found in the document governing his valuation (e.g. a rent review clause) and relevant case law.

(c) *Current defects and future expenditure.* This topic has limited application to rent reviews, where the independent valuer is usually required to assume that the tenant has carried out his repairing obligations, but it is relevant where an independent capital valuation is required by two parties. A failure to recognise serious defects in a property being valued, with consequent overvaluation is evidence of negligence. *Corisand Investments Ltd v Druce & Co* (1978) 248 EG 315, is an example of failure to deduct or comment on the cost of necessary works. The valuer of a hotel for mortgage purposes was held to have been under a duty either to make an allowance in his valuation for the cost of works necessary for the grant of a fire certificate under the Fire Precautions Act 1971, or to inform the intending lender that he had not done so because, in his view, the market for the property was such that purchasers would disregard it.

There is, of course, a difference between a valuation and a structural survey. A surveyor carrying out the latter must inspect the property more thoroughly than would be necessary for a valuation. He may be liable in negligence for missing a hidden defect which would be outside the scope of a valuation inspection. But in *Stevenson v Nationwide Building Society* (1984) 272 EG 663, it was held that, even though the surveyor was carrying out a building society valuation and not a structural survey, he was negligent in not inspecting the underside of a building built over a river or arranging for some other competent person to do so.

(d) *Collection of information.* A valuer whose opinion of value is outside the permissible bracket and who failed to collect all relevant information or carry out all necessary investigations is likely to be found negligent.

In *Corisand*, Gibson J listed the matters to which an ordinarily competent valuer must have regard to in order to discharge the duty of care. First of these was that he must by inspection of the property and inquiry, learn enough about it to be able to start upon the basic method of valuation. In *Singer & Friedlander Ltd v John D. Wood & Co* (1977) 243 EG 212, part of the valuer's negligence when preparing a valuation of building land for the purposes of loan, was his failure to collect sufficient information himself to enable him to prepare a soundly based valuation. He did not inspect the site but sent his assistant to the area "for a time insufficient for that young man to become acquainted with the journey there and back," he relied on information given by his client (not the plaintiffs) without checking it, he failed to make inquiries of the local planning authority about the future development of the land he was valuing and he ignored, without justification, a colleague's earlier and thorough appraisal of the development potential of the land.

In *Baxter v F. W. Gapp & Co Ltd* [1939] 2 All ER 752, the valuer's negligence included a failure to inquire about local prices when valuing a house in an unfamiliar area, and a failure to inquire what price the house he was valuing realised on recent sales.

One of the duties of the independent expert (unlike an arbitrator) is to collect all the information necessary for his decision (see Chapter 7 p. 201 above); he may be negligent if he fails to do so.

(e) *Inexperience.* A man who undertakes professional work holds himself out as possessing the necessary skill and experience to carry it out in a reasonably competent manner. Inexperience is not, therefore, a defence to negligence; on the contrary, coupled with substantial under or overvaluation, it may be evidence of negligence. For example, in *Kenney v Hall Pain & Foster* (1976) 239 EG 355, Goff J concluded, on the evidence, that the valuation was so wide of the mark that it was erroneous and it was also negligent having regard to the valuer's inexperience. When he carried out the valuation his property experience consisted of only six months in New Zealand and three months in his present locality. He lacked the skill which could reasonably be expected of him and failed to exercise reasonable care by not referring his valuation back to his office (although instructed to do so) for an opinion by a more experienced colleague. In the *Gapp* case the valuer lacked experience of the locality of his valuation and failed to make good this deficiency by making proper inquiries as to local values.

(f) *Errors of judgment.* An error of judgment in the performance of a professional service may be a breach of the requisite standard of care. But, like all aspects of professional work, it must be measured against the general standard of care of the ordinary skilled practitioner as laid down in the *Bolam* case (p. 224 above). The question to be asked is would such a practitioner have made such an error of judgment? If he would not have done so then the defendant has failed to achieve the requisite standard of care (*Whitehouse v Jordan* [1981] 1 All ER 267.)

Failure to judge the property market correctly has been held to be a breach of the standard of care. In *Bell Hotels (1935) Ltd v Motion* (1952) 159 EG 496, the defendants were instructed to value a hotel for the purposes of sale and advised that, although a brewery could not be completely ruled out as a prospective purchaser, such a sale was unlikely. Accordingly, they advised a sale at £20,000 or at a price close to this figure. The plaintiffs sold it to a private buyer for £17,750 plus £3,980 for contents. Within a week it was re-sold to a brewer for £25,000. The defendants were held to have been negligent in not recognising this particular market. In *Corisand*, the valuer of a hotel for mortgage purposes in September 1973, near the end of the property boom, was negligent in failing to recognise the speculative element in market prices and not excluding it from his valuation or identifying it for the guidance of the lenders.

(g) *Method.* As we have seen, the standard of care necessary to avoid liability for negligence is that of the reasonably competent practitioner acting in a manner commonly found in his profession. It follows, therefore, that a professional man whose method of carrying out a particular task follows that generally adopted by his profession is unlikely to be found negligent on this ground. Where there is more than one method in use, a defendant will not be liable for negligence because he follows one method, acceptable to a responsible body of opinion, in preference to another, also supported by professional opinion (see *Bolam* (p. 224 above) and *Maynard* (p. 225 above)). The position was summarised by Kekewich J in *Love v Mack* (1905) 92 LT 345:

> "The law does not say that in any branch of intelligent operation, intelligent skill, there is necessarily one defined path which must be strictly followed, and that if one departs by an inch from that defined path one were necessarily at fault .... There is no absolute rule as regards the proper method of ascertaining the value in this case, and (the defendants) adopted methods, which, if they are not perfect, if they are not the best, if they might have been improved upon, still are methods which a man of position, endeavouring to do his duty might fairly adopt without it being said he was wanting in reasonable care and skill."

DAMAGES

Breach of an express or implied *contractual* duty of care is actionable without loss, but the plaintiff will obtain only nominal damages (see *Carreras Ltd v D. E. & J. Levy* (1970) 215 EG 707 p. 245 below). Loss or damage is an essential ingredient in a successful action for negligence in *tort*. For example, in *Garland v Ralph Pay & Ransom* (1984) 271 EG 106, a merchant bank lent the plaintiff £230,000 on a 12 monthly loan on the security of commercial property which he intended to redevelop. He was unable to obtain finance for such redevelopment. The bank eventually decided to exercise their power of sale and instructed Douglas Young & Co (the third and only defendants by the time the hearing was completed) to sell the property. The bank also entered into an agreement with the plaintiff that his debt would be reduced to £250,000, the property would be sold at whatever price the bank wished and the proceeds of sale, if less than £250,000, would belong absolutely to the bank. The property was sold for £75,000, a figure stated by the defendants to be the current market value. The plaintiff claimed that the property was worth £461,000 and brought an action in tort for negligence against them.

It was held that the defendants were negligent in both their opinion of value and their marketing of the property, but were not liable to the plaintiff because he had not suffered any loss. The judge found that the property was worth between £38,000 and £125,000 at the date of sale; this was below £250,000 and, therefore, the whole of the proceeds of sale went to the bank. No loss was suffered by the plaintiff as a result of the negligent valuation and sale.

The consequences of professional negligence can be far-reaching, both as regards the persons affected and the amount of loss. For reasons of expediency and public policy, the courts have placed limits on the persons who may sue and the losses they may recover. The persons who may sue are those who have privity of contract with the negligent person or who are owed a duty of care in tort. These are questions of liability which are discussed under duty of care (p. 221 above). The amount of recoverable loss is kept within reasonable bounds in three ways: first, by an underlying principle that damages are compensatory and not punitive; secondly, by restricting the measure of damages to contemplated or foreseeable loss; and thirdly, by invoking the doctrine of remoteness of loss. These topics are now considered followed by a brief discussion of contributory negligence, the liability of joint defendants and some examples of the assessment of damages for professional negligence.

(1) Measure of damages

It will be convenient to deal with the compensatory nature of damages and their restriction to contemplated or foreseeable loss under one heading of measure of damages. Remoteness of loss will then be dealt with separately, although it will be seen that there is a close relationship between contemplated or foreseeable loss and remoteness. The basic principle underlying the law of damages is restitution in money terms (*restitutio in integrum*):

> "The general object underlying the rules for the assessment of damages is, so far as is possible by means of a monetary award, to place the plaintiff in the position which he would have occupied if he had not suffered the wrong complained of, be that wrong a tort or a breach of contract."
>
> (per Donaldson LJ in *Dodd Properties (Kent) Ltd v Canterbury City Council* (1979) 253 EG 1335 at p. 1341).

In *contract*, the starting point for any discussion of damages is the decision in *Hadley v Baxendale* (1854) 9 Exch 341. Damages for breach of contract must fall within the two rules laid down in that case. First, they must be fairly and reasonably considered to arise naturally from the breach, sometimes referred to as general or normal damages. Secondly, they must be reasonably supposed to have been in the contemplation of the parties at the time the contract was made, as the probable result of the breach, called special or abnormal damages. These two rules were restated in *Victoria Laundry (Windsor) Ltd v Newman Industries Ltd* [1949] 2 KB 528 and *Czarnikow Ltd v Koufos (The Heron II)* [1969] 1 AC 350, and may now be stated as a single rule. The measure of damages recoverable by a plaintiff for breach of contract is that part of his loss resulting from the breach as was at the time of the contract reasonably contemplated by the parties as liable to result from the breach. The extent of the loss contemplated by the parties, or at least by the defendant, is governed by his imputed everyday knowledge of the ordinary consequences of his breach, and his actual knowledge of any special circumstances likely to cause additional loss.

In *tort*, the rule relating to the measure of damages is found in two cases known as *The Wagon Mound* and *The Wagon Mound (No 2)* (*Overseas Tankers (UK) Ltd v Morts Dock and Engineering Co Ltd* [1961] 2 WLR 126 and *Overseas Tankers (UK) Ltd v The Miller Steamship Co Pty* [1967] AC 617). A person who is negligent in tort will be liable in damages for all those losses which a reasonable man should have foreseen at the time of the negligent act might have resulted from his negligence.

It would appear that the measure of damages in contract and tort differs, at least semantically if not in practice. In contract, a defendant is liable for those losses which he should reasonably have *contemplated* would flow from his breach; in tort, he is liable for those losses which he should reasonably have *foreseen* might result from his tortious act. Is there is difference between "contemplated" loss and "foreseeable" loss?

The position is unfortunately not clear. In *The Heron II* (p. 232 above) Lord Reid said *obiter* (p. 385) that the modern rule in tort is quite different from contract and imposes a much wider liability. This must be balanced against *dicta* in other cases to the effect that damages which relate to the same facts should be the same, whether the action is in contract or tort (e.g. *Perry v Sidney Phillips & Son* (1982) 263 EG 888). The difference may be theoretical and not real. In practice the position may be as stated by Scarman LJ in *H. Parsons (Livestock) Ltd v Uttley Ingham & Co Ltd* [1978] QB 791 at p. 807:

> "... the law must be such that ... the amount of damages recoverable does not depend on whether as a matter of legal classification, the plaintiff's cause of action is breach of contract or tort. It may be that the necessary reconciliation is to be found ... in holding that the difference between 'reasonably forseeable' (the test in tort) and 'reasonably contemplated' (the test in contract) is semantic, not substantial."

(2) Remoteness of loss

As outlined above, the courts have placed limits on the losses for which a negligent person will be liable. The doctrine of remoteness of loss is one means of limitation. The question is asked: is the loss suffered too remote from the negligent act to be recoverable as damages?

Traditionally, remoteness is concerned with the *items* of loss for which damages may be recovered; it is distinguished from the prior question of liability (discussed above under duty of care) and the later question of amount of loss (discussed below), although in practice these distinctions are often blurred. It is a subject of considerable difficulty: its boundaries are undefined; it serves as an umbrella doctrine to limit recoverable loss where commonsense, policy, impression or fairness are often the real determining factors. For example, the question of damages for economic loss is usually treated as a question of remoteness. There was a distinction in *tort* (which may now have been removed) between physical loss or injury and pure economic or financial loss. Damages have always been recoverable for the physical loss or injury caused by a defendant's negligence, whatever form that negligence took. Damages for pure economic or financial loss, however, were only recoverable where the negligence took the form of an incorrect statement, made to a person who was owed a duty of care by the maker of that statement and who acted in reliance on it to his detriment (*Hedley*

Byrne & Co Ltd v Heller & Partners Ltd [1964] AC 465). This is, of
course, the typical situation in professional negligence in tort, e.g.
where the plaintiff suffers financial loss from his reliance on the
defendant's valuation, advice or other statement.

   This distinction between a negligent *act*, which does not produce
liability for economic loss, and a negligent *statement* which does, may
now have been removed by the recent decision in *Junior Books Ltd v
Veitchi Co Ltd* [1982] 3 WLR 477. In this Scottish case the pursuers
(plaintiffs), owners of a recently constructed factory, sued the
specialist flooring sub-contractors in tort for negligently laying a
defective floor. They claimed damages for the estimated cost of
relaying the floor and for consequential financial loss, such as the
cost of removing machinery and loss of profits while the floor was
being relaid. It was held by a majority of the House of Lords that, if
the defenders (defendants) had been negligent, there was a sufficient
degree of proximity between the parties to give rise to a duty of care
and the defenders would be liable for this financial loss even though
it resulted from a negligent *act*. This decision, important though it is
in the development of the law of tort, does not extend a valuer's
liability, which, at least since the *Hedley Byrne* decision, always
included economic loss suffered as a result of a negligent statement.

   Remoteness of loss is usually associated with two topics. First,
causation: is there a direct link between negligence and loss, usually
given the existence of a third factor, such as the conduct of the
plaintiff? Secondly, certainty of loss: is the loss too speculative, contingent or incapable of assessment? Despite its abstract nature, the
doctrine of remoteness is relevant to professional negligence and
occurs in several cases of negligence in valuation.

   (a) *Causation.* Remoteness of loss is usually treated as a question of
   causation: is the loss a *direct* consequence of the professional negligence? In contract the defendant will be liable for damages for
   those consequences of his breach as were in his contemplation at
   the time of the contract. In tort he will be liable for those losses
   which he could reasonably have foreseen would flow from his
   wrongful act. Professional negligence frequently produces direct
   economic loss and problems of remoteness do not always arise,
   e.g. where a negligent valuation results in the plaintiff paying
   more for a property than its true value. But a third factor, a *novus
   actus interveniens*, may intervene and break the chain of causation
   between the negligence and the loss. This factor may take many
   forms but four broad categories can be seen: (i) the conduct of the
   plaintiff, or (ii) a third party, (iii) the personal circumstances of
   the plaintiff and (iv) an external condition or event.
      (i) *Conduct of the plaintiff.* Clearly, the *conduct* of the plaintiff can

affect the amount of his loss after the negligent act. For example, in *Kenney v Hall Pain & Foster* (1976) 239 EG 355, the plaintiff, in reliance on a negligent overvaluation of his present house, purchased another and committed himself to substantial expenditure on it before he had sold his existing house. As a result he suffered financial loss. It was argued by the defendants that these actions were unreasonable and amounted to a *novus actus interveniens* causing loss for which they should not be liable. This argument was rejected, on the grounds that the plaintiff's actions were not unreasonable in the circumstances, but his damages were reduced because his expenditure on the new house was excessive. It was not within the reasonable contemplation of the defendants that Mr Kenney would commit himself to such substantial expenditure before he had sold his other house.

In *JEB Fasteners Ltd v Marks Bloom & Co* [1983] 1 All ER 583, the defendant auditors, who negligently prepared accounts of a company, were not liable for the losses suffered by the plaintiffs (purchasers of the company) because the plaintiffs, although aware of the accounts, had not been materially influenced by them in making their decision to purchase. Their main reason for the takeover was their wish to secure the services of the company's two directors and there was no direct causal connection between the incorrect accounts and the takeover decision.

A plaintiff has a duty to minimise his loss and reasonable conduct by him in so doing will not break the chain of causation. The authorities establish four general propositions regarding mitigation of loss.

First, the plaintiff must take all reasonable steps to mitigate his loss: he cannot recover for avoidable loss or unreasonable expenditure. In *London & South of England Building Society v Stone* (1983) 267 EG 69, the defendant valuer failed to notice settlement cracks when valuing a house for the purposes of loan by the plaintiffs. The house deteriorated, the plaintiffs decided to spend a considerable sum on repairs and underpinning, but relieved the owners, their mortgagors, from any liability for those costs. They claimed them from the defendant as damages. They failed to recover this measure of damages. In the High Court ((1981) 261 EG 463) it was held that the Society had not acted reasonably to mitigate their loss, having regard to their limited interest in the property. They were awarded as damages the much lower amount of their loan less a deduction for the continuing benefit of the mortgagors' personal covenants plus their reasonable costs of investigating the matter.

The case then proceeded to the Court of Appeal on the

narrow issue of whether the trial judge had been right to make a
deduction from the damages for the benefit of the mortgagors'
personal covenants. In other words, was it encumbent upon the
plaintiffs to enforce those covenants for repayment in mitigation
of the defendant's damages? The court held by a majority, but
for different reasons, that such a deduction should not have
been made. O'Connor LJ said that the plaintiffs were under
no duty to the defendant to mitigate their loss by trying to
extract money from the mortgagors, whereas Stephenson LJ
based his decision to allow the appeal on the fact that it was not
unreasonable on the evidence and in the circumstances for the
plaintiffs to waive their contractual right to recover their loss
from the borrowers.

The second general proposition is that the financial circumstances of the plaintiff are relevant when judging the reasonableness of his conduct in mitigation. For example, in *Dodd
Properties (Kent) Ltd v Canterbury City Council* (1979) 253 EG
1335, the plaintiffs' premises were damaged by building operations on adjoining land carried out by the defendants. The
main issue before the Court of Appeal was the correct date for
the assessment of damages. Was it when the necessary repairs
could reasonably have been started (1970) or the date of the
High Court hearing or judgment (1978)? The start of the repairs was deferred because the provision of money for this work
would have caused the plaintiffs a measure of "financial strin-
gency". Furthermore, the defendants denied liability until
shortly before the hearing. It was held that the correct date for
the assessment of damages (cost of repairs) was 1978 and that it
was reasonable to defer those repairs until the liability of the
defendants had been established. Megaw LJ said (p. 1339):

> "A plaintiff who is under a duty to mitigate is not obliged,
> in order to reduce the damages, to do that which he cannot
> afford to do: particularly where, as here, the plaintiffs'
> 'financial stringency', so far as it was relevant at all, arose
> as a matter of commonsense, if not as a matter of law,
> solely as a consequence of the defendants' wrongdoing."

The situation described above, where the financial circumstances of the plaintiff may be taken into account when judging
the reasonableness of his conduct in mitigation, must be distinguished from the similar situation discussed on p. 238 below,
where the financial circumstances of the plaintiff may form a
separate cause of loss breaking the chain of causation and
making this loss irrecoverable on grounds of remoteness.

Thirdly, a plaintiff who takes reasonable steps to mitigate his

loss can recover the reasonable expense of so doing. Thus, in
Baxter v F. W. Gapp & Co Ltd [1939] 2 All ER 752, the plaintiff
was induced by a negligent valuation to make an excessive loan
on a house. The mortgagor defaulted and the plaintiff mitigated
his loss by selling the house, although at a loss. It was held that
the measure of damages was the total loss sustained by the
plaintiff, including the costs of mitigation comprising expenses
of abortive sales, insurance premiums, repairs, mortgagee's
expenses and disbursements and agent's commission on the
ultimate sale.

Fourthly, any benefit arising out of mitigating conduct must
be set off against the loss caused by the wrongful act. This can
be achieved by taking as the time for the assessment of damages
the date when the plaintiff completed his mitigating action.
Thus, in *Techno Land Improvements Ltd v British Leyland (UK) Ltd*
(1979) 252 EG 805, the defendants were found to be in breach
of an agreement to take a lease of two factory units. The plaintiffs mitigated their loss by allowing licensees into occupation
and then reletting the premises, which took about 21 months to
complete. It was held that damages should be assessed as at the
date of the completion of the lettings, and not the earlier date
when the first licensee went into occupation, so that the benefits
of reletting could be taken into account in the computation of
the actual loss.

Throughout the duty to mitigate runs the standard of reasonableness. The plaintiff's conduct must be measured against that
of the reasonable man. What is reasonable is a question of fact
having regard to the circumstances of each particular case, and,
when deciding that question, the court will not weigh the plaintiff's conduct in not taking steps to mitigate his loss in nice
scales at the instance of the party who caused the loss. In the
Stone decision (above), Stephenson LJ said that the authorities
relating to reasonableness in mitigation establish the following
principles. First, a plaintiff need not take the risk of starting
uncertain litigation against a third party, including litigation
which may be reasonably certain of success but where there is
no certainty that the judgment will be satisfied. Secondly, a
plaintiff need not take steps to recover compensation for his loss
from parties who, in addition to the defendant, are liable to
him. Thirdly, a plaintiff need not act so as to injure innocent
persons nor to the prejudice of its commercial reputation.

(ii) *Conduct of a third party.* The actual loss suffered by the plaintiff as the result of negligence may be wholly or partly due to an
intervening act by a third party. Generally, such an act will
snap the chain of causation if it is independent of the original

wrong (i.e. not voluntarily prompted or inspired by it), performed by a responsible person and not performed under a legal
or moral obligation arising out of the original wrong. Thus, in
Weld-Blundell v Stephens [1920] AC 956, an accountant (the
defendant) was instructed by the plaintiff to investigate the
affairs of a company and his letter of instruction contained
libellous statements relating to two officials of that company. It
was accidently left at the company's office and shown to the
officials by a third party. They recovered damages from the
plaintiff for libel, and he was unable to recover an indemnity
from the defendant for breach of his duty to keep the letter secret
because it had been brought to the officials' attention by the intervening act of a third party.

(iii) *Personal circumstances of the plaintiff.* A defendant in tort must
take his victim as he finds him (*talem qualem*) and will be liable for
any exceptional loss or injury due to the latter's personal circumstances. This rule applies to *mitigation* of loss (p. 236 above) and
the *measure* of loss of an admissible item of claim but not to
remoteness of loss, where a particular *item* of loss caused by the
plaintiff's personal circumstances may be too remote to be recoverable in damages. The plaintiff's health, age or financial position may each form a separate cause of loss which may be too
remote to be recoverable. Two examples may make the position
clearer.

In *Bailey v Derby Corporation* (1965) 16 P & CR 192, in the analogous field of compensation for compulsory purchase, the personal circumstances were the claimant's ill-health. Mr Bailey's
business premises were compulsorily acquired. He found an
alternative property but, because of ill-health (not caused by the
acquisition but coincidental with it), he decided not to continue
in business on his own account but to let the other property to
business associates and take employment with them. It was held
by the Court of Appeal that the correct basis of compensation
was the cost of transferring the business to the new premises and
not total extinguishment. The extinguishment of the claimant's
business was not the natural and reasonable consequence of the
acquisition: it was due to his ill-health, an independent and extraneous cause of loss which broke the chain of causation
between acquisition and loss.

The second example is the leading case of *The Liesbosch* (*Liesbosch Dredger v SS Edison* [1933] AC 449). Here the appellants'
financial position was the extraneous factor rendering an item of
loss irrecoverable on grounds of remoteness. Their dredger was
negligently sunk by the SS Edison when it was in use under a
constructional contract which imposed penalties or cancellation

for delays in the completion of the work. Owing to lack of capital and credit the appellants were unable to purchase a replacement dredger and hired one to complete their contract. The House of Lords held that the measure of damages was the value of the dredger to her owners as a profit-earning dredger; they rejected a claim for the cost of hire of a replacement on the grounds that any special loss or extra expense due to the financial position of the parties is to be ignored.

This decision has been much criticised and is now often distinguished by treating the current case as one of mitigation, where the plaintiff's financial circumstances are a relevant consideration (see p. 236 above). The distinction between the relevance of financial circumstances in mitigation on the one hand and remoteness of loss on the other is difficult to grasp but it is concisely set out in the well-known passage from Lord Collins' judgment in *Clippens Oil Co Ltd v Edinburgh & District Water Trustees* [1907] AC 291 at pp. 303–304:

> "... the wrongdoer must take his victim *talem qualem* and if the position of the latter is aggravated because he is without the means of mitigating it, so much the worse for the wrongdoer, who has got to be answerable for the consequences flowing from his tortious act. On the other hand, the victim being in fact a poor man is not entitled to claim damages in respect of lost opportunities which he could not have utilised unless he had been rich."

(iv) *An external condition or event.* Finally, under the heading of causation, loss caused by an external condition or event will be too remote and not a proper subject for damages. For example, in *Singer & Friedlander Ltd v John D. Wood & Co* (1977) 243 EG 212, the plaintiffs made a loan of £1,500,000 to a development company during the 1972 property boom in reliance on the defendants' negligent valuation. The borrowers defaulted and went into liquidation. The plaintiffs received agreed damages of £491,250, although their total loss was about £900,000 (the amount loaned less the later value of the land). The loss in excess of that for which damages were awarded was due to a sudden fall in property values and could not be said to be a consequence of the defendants' negligence (see also *Corisand Investments Ltd v Druce & Co*, p. 246 below).

(b) *Certainty of loss.* The second aspect of remoteness arises in the context of certainty of loss. A loss may be beyond the limits of recoverable damages because it is too speculative, too contingent or incapable of assessment.

It is a fundamental principle of the law of damages that all loss resulting from one and the same cause of action must be recovered once for all in a lump sum award. If the plaintiff later discovers that his loss is greater than he thought, he cannot recover further damages, unless he can show that the subsequent loss arises out of a separate cause of action. This principle imports into an award future loss which may be speculative, contingent or difficult to assess. The problem faced by the courts when assessing damages for future loss is essentially one of degree: where to draw the line between recoverable loss and loss which is too remote. The trend has been from a reluctance to award damages for future pecuniary loss to a recognition that difficulties in assessment should not relieve the wrongdoer, and that uncertainty and contingency can be reflected by a reduction in the award. For example, in *Nash v Phillips* (1974) 232 EG 1219, the plaintiffs were unable to purchase the house of their choice due to the negligence of their solicitor. The damages awarded were, however, reduced by 10 per cent to reflect the possibility that they may not in fact have gone ahead with this purchase.

Modest damages may be awarded for the anxiety, distress and inconvenience suffered by a plaintiff as a result of the defendant's professional negligence. These "vexation" damages are not now too remote and their award represents a significant development in the law of damages (see e.g. *Fryer v Bunney* (1981) 263 EG 158, *Perry v Sidney Phillips & Son* (1982) 263 EG 888, *Bolton v Puley* (1982) 267 EG 1160 and *Treml v Ernest W. Gibson & Partners* (1984) 272 EG 68).

(3) Contributory negligence and joint defendants

It may be necessary in the circumstances of a particular case to reduce or apportion the total amount of damages. Damages are reduced where the plaintiff contributed to his own loss (contributory negligence) and apportioned where the loss was caused by two or more defendants (joint defendants or tortfeasors).

(a) *Contributory negligence.* The loss or damage suffered by a person may be due partly to his own fault and partly to the fault of another person. Section 1(1) of the Law Reform (Contributory Negligence) Act 1945 provides that, where this occurs, the damages recoverable "shall be reduced to such extent as the court thinks just and equitable having regard to the claimant's share in the responsibility for the damage." The "fault" referred to here means "negligence, breach of statutory duty or other act or omission which gives rise to a liability in tort or would, apart from this Act, give rise to the defence of contributory negligence" (section 4). This defence does not apply where the plaintiff brings his action or claim in contract (*Basildon District Council v J. E. Lesser (Properties) Ltd* [1985] 1 All ER 20, *AB Marintrans v Comet Shipping Co Ltd* (1985) *The Times* 19th March 1985).

Contributory negligence is uncommon in cases of professional negligence, probably due to the fact that the two parties are not on an equal footing.

(b) *Joint defendants.* Where a client's loss is caused by the negligence of two or more of his professional advisers then the total damages will be apportioned between them. Where the loss occurred and the defendant's obligations were assumed on or after 1st January 1979, then the position is governed by the Civil Liability (Contribution) Act 1978 (otherwise the Law Reform (Married Women and Tortfeasors) Act 1935 applies (not discussed here)). Where the 1978 Act applies "any person liable in respect of any damage suffered by another person may recover contribution from any other person liable in respect of the same damage (whether jointly with him or otherwise)" (section 1). The amount of the contribution recoverable will be that found by the court to be just and equitable having regard to the other person's responsibility for the damage. When apportioning the damage, the court will have regard to culpability and the extent to which each party's conduct caused the loss.

An apportionment of liability will often occur in a case concerning the construction of a defective building, e.g. the *Batty* case discussed on p. 222 above, where the developers and the builders were each held 50 per cent liable for the construction of a house on an unstable hillside.

(4) Assessment of damages

We have considered the basic principle underlying the assessment of damages (namely compensation to the injured party for the loss he has suffered), the limitations imposed by the doctrine of remoteness of loss and the reduction and apportionment of damages. It remains to consider some examples of the assessment of damages for professional negligence in valuation.

(a) *Purchase of defective property.* Where a person buys a property in reliance on a negligent structural survey report or a negligent overvaluation due to a failure to take into account defects in the property, so that he pays more than the property is worth, the question arises as to whether his damages should be the loss of value or the cost of repairs. Before 1956 the measure of damages was the cost of repairing the defects negligently omitted in the survey or valuation. This was changed by the leading case of *Philips v Ward* [1956] 1 WLR 471. The plaintiff purchased a house for £25,000 in reliance on a survey and valuation report. This report had been negligently prepared: the house was found to contain defects which would have cost £7,000 to eradicate, but which reduced the value by only £4,000. The Court of Appeal held that the measure of damages was the difference between the value of the house in the condition as described in the surveyor's report (£25,000) and its value as it should have been described (£21,000). The amount awarded was, therefore, the loss in value at the date of purchase (£4,000) and not the cost of repairs (£7,000).

This measure of damages was later modified in *Ford v White & Co* [1964] 1 WLR 885, to the difference between the price paid and the market value at the date of purchase. But where professional negligence deprives a person of the chance of purchasing a property, which he subsequently buys at an inflated price, the measure of damages is the difference between the *market value* at the date of subsequent purchase and the price he originally agreed to pay. Thus, in *Simpson v Grove Tompkins & Co* (1982) *The Times* 17th May 1982, the plaintiff was prevented by his solicitor's negligence from purchasing a property at an agreed price of £53,750. He was subsequently able to buy it for £92,500 when the market value was only £75,000. The Court of Appeal altered the amount of damages to £20,542, the difference between the market value at the date of subsequent purchase (£75,000) and the original price (£53,750).

The value approach to the assessment of damages for financial loss in relation to property was generally followed after *Philips v Ward* (e.g. *Lees v English & Partners* (1977) 242 EG 293, *Daisley v B. S. Hall & Co* (1973) 225 EG 1553, *Morgan v Perry* (1973) 229 EG 1937), although in at least one case (*Freeman v Marshall & Co* (1966) 200 EG 777) the loss of value was measured by the cost of repairs.

In 1979 the Court of Appeal delivered judgment in *Dodd Properties (Kent) Ltd v Canterbury City Council* (1979) 253 EG 1335. This was not a case of professional negligence but concerned physical damage to a property due to building operations on adjoining land (nuisance). The measure of damages was agreed to be the cost of repairs and the only outstanding issue was the date of assessment.

Donaldson LJ, after referring to the compensatory nature of damages, said that the measure of damages for tort causing damage to real property was the reduction in value of the property, or the cost of repairs, or occasionally a combination of these two bases. The appropriate measure depended on a number of factors, such as the plaintiff's future intentions regarding the property (e.g. whether he intended to sell or retain it) and their reasonableness.

In *Perry v Sidney Phillips & Son* at first instance ((1981) 260 EG 389), the judge referred to *Dodd* (and in particular to the judgment of Donaldson LJ) and concluded that the correct measure of damages to compensate Mr Perry for purchasing a defective cottage in reliance on the defendants' report, was the cost at the date of the hearing of the repair of those defects which would have been revealed by a proper inspection by a reasonably competent surveyor. He rejected the value approach which he said was not a universal rule, and appeared to take the view that *Dodd* had altered the law. Damages were also awarded for the estimated expense of living out of the cottage while the repairs were in progress and for distress and discomfort (vexation damages).

An appeal was made against this decision ((1982) 263 EG 888) but, before it was heard, the plaintiff sold the cottage in its unrepaired condition at a price considerably more than he paid for it. The cost of repair basis for the assessment of damages was, therefore, no longer appropriate. The issues before the Court of Appeal were the measure of damages on the value basis, the date of assessment and the recoverability of vexation damages.

Lord Denning MR was in no doubt regarding the assessment of damages. Where there is a contract to do works or repairs and the work is badly done, or a neighbouring house is damaged by negligence or nuisance, then the plaintiff is entitled to recover as damages the reasonable cost of works to make good the breach or to repair the damage. They are to be assessed at the time when it would be reasonable for the works to be carried out. But where a survey for a prospective purchaser is negligently carried out, then the damages are the difference between the price paid and the price which would have been paid if the report had been carefully prepared (i.e. market value). Thus, the damages in *Perry* were to be assessed on the latter basis as at the time of the breach. Both Oliver and Kerr LJJ agreed that the cost of repairs basis of damages did not now arise due to the sale. The judge's award of vexation damages was upheld.

It may be, of course, that the difference in value is measured by the cost of repairs. Thus, in *Fryer v Bunney* (1981) 263 EG 158, a decision in the Official Referees Court before the appeal decision in *Perry*, damages for a negligent structural survey were awarded at a figure equal to the cost of repairing the omitted defects "either as damages for diminution in the value of the property or as the cost of repairs and redecoration". The judge concluded that if the plaintiff continued to live in the house, repairs would have been necessary and, if he sold it, a purchaser would deduct the cost of repairs from the price, so the cost of repair in both cases would be the true measure of loss. But in another case concerning a negligent structural survey, *Bolton v Puley* (1982) 267 EG 1160, Talbot J, while accepting the loss of value measure of damages, found that loss by taking 75% of the cost of repairs on the grounds that a purchaser of the defective property might well accept 25% of the risk of expenditure upon the property (a figure put to him in expert evidence).

Where damages for the purchase of a defective house following a negligent report were assessed on a loss of value basis and the plaintiff received a discretionary grant towards repairs from the local authority, it was held that the amount of this grant should not be deducted from the damages recoverable. It was irrelevant to a claim where the difference in value was the measure of damages and it was a collateral benefit (similar to a charitable donation or private benevolence) which did not have to be taken into account (*Treml v Ernest W. Gibson & Partners* (1984) 272 EG 68). This decision is also interesting as an illustration of other heads of damages in such a case. These included: interest on the amount awarded for loss of value, cost of emergency repairs (including fees), interest on a mortgage raised by the plaintiff to pay for emergency repairs, hire of props to prop up the defective house while the plaintiff was living there, cost of temporary accommodation for the plaintiff and her family while repairs were carried out, removal costs and a sum for vexation and inconvenience.

Where an independent expert is required to fix a price on purchase between two persons and negligently omits to take into account defects in the property, he will be liable to the purchaser for damages equal to the amount of the overvaluation plus any consequential loss. The former amount may be found solely by reference to value or by reference to the whole or part of the cost of repairing the defects negligently omitted from the valuation by the expert. The date of assessment is when the breach occurred, i.e. the date of the expert's determination.

(b) *Negligent valuation for sale, purchase or rental.* Where a valuation for sale or purchase is negligently made for reasons other than a failure to take account of defects, then damages can only be assessed on a loss of value basis. For example, in *Bell Hotels (1935) Ltd v Motion* (1952) 159 EG 496 (p. 230 above), the defendants valued a hotel for the purposes of sale at about £20,000. It was sold for £17,750 plus £3,980 for contents but resold within a week for £25,000. The plaintiff vendors were awarded £5,000 as damages for this negligent valuation, namely the difference between the resale price (i.e. the correct value) of £25,000 and the incorrect value of £20,000.

Where there is a negligent overvaluation for the vendor then the amount of damages may depend on the action which he took in reliance on that valuation. Thus, in *Kenney v Hall Pain & Foster* (1976) 239 EG 355 (p. 235 above), the plaintiff vendor, in reliance on a negligent overvaluation, purchased another house and committed himself to considerable expenditure on it before he had sold his existing house. It was agreed between the parties that, if he had been properly advised, the plaintiff would have bought another house at a lower price and, therefore, the damages were found by comparing this hypothetical situation with the actual situation, subject to deductions for excessive expenditure on the other house and expenditure on carpets, curtains etc which would still have been necessary on the purchase of the other house.

An independent surveyor who is appointed to fix the purchase price between two parties will be liable in damages to the party suffering loss as a result of his under or overvaluation. In both cases damages will usually be equal to the difference between the correct value (e.g. market value) and the value determined by the independent surveyor.

Where a surveyor is negligent in agreeing or assessing a rent on review or at the commencement of a lease, the damages will be the difference between the true rental value and the rent agreed or assessed, capitalised for the residue of the lease or to the next review date. (If the rent is so excessive that it is still likely to be so after the next review date, assuming an upwards only review, then presumably the capitalisation period should be longer unless this additional loss is considered to be too remote).

But, in order to prove loss in the above two cases, it must be shown that the rent or price agreed or assessed is outside a permissible bracket of rental or capital value established by the evidence. Thus, in *Carreras Ltd v D. E. & J. Levy* (1970) 215 EG 707, the defendants, who were retained by the plaintiffs to find them office accommodation, incorrectly calculated the floor area of certain premises, in reliance on which the plaintiffs took a lease. When the correct (and smaller) area was discovered the plaintiffs claimed damages equal to the difference between the actual rent and the rental value calculated on the correct area, capitalised for the residue of the lease. The defendants were held to have been negligent but, although *prima facie* the measure of damages was as claimed, it was held on the evidence to be only possible to assess rental value within a bracket, the actual rent was in that bracket and, therefore, no loss could be proved. Nominal damages only were awarded (this was an action for breach of contract).

(c) *Negligent valuation for a loan.* Where the plaintiff is a mortgagee suing in respect of a negligent valuation, the measure of damages will normally be the loss suffered as a result of a loan based on that valuation. Thus, in *Baxter v F. W. Gapp & Co Ltd* [1939] 2 All ER 752, the plaintiff lost the whole of his loan when the mortgagor defaulted and recovered damages for his total loss, consisting of the difference between the amount loaned on the negligent valuation and the amount received on a subsequent sale, plus consequential losses such as the expenses of abortive sales, cost of repairs, insurance premiums, etc. But in *Corisand Investments Ltd v Druce & Co* (1978) 248 EG 315, the mortgagees were awarded damages equal to the difference between (i) the amount they lent in reliance on the negligent valuation (£60,000), and (ii) the amount they would have lent if the valuation had been correct (£16,300) plus the mortgage interest they received (£9,075), but with interest on the damages from the date of the loan. The plaintiffs recovered damages of £34,625 plus interest. As second mortgagees they recovered nothing from the sale of the property. They were not, therefore, compensated for the whole of their loss: part was due to a fall in values after the date of valuation and not to the valuation itself (see also *Singer & Friedlander Ltd v John D. Wood & Co* on p. 239 above where this point is considered in the context of remoteness).

In *Eagle Star Insurance Co Ltd v Gale & Power* (1955) 166 EG 37, the plaintiffs lent £3,015 on mortgage on the strength of the defendants' valuation of £3,350. The defendants had failed to notice defects in the house which the plaintiffs asserted was not worth more than £1,500. It was agreed that the necessary repairs would have cost £950 at the date of valuation. If the plaintiffs had realised the security for their loan they would have obtained £3,100 comprising £1,600 for the house and £1,500 on the mortgagor's personal covenant to repay this amount out of his retirement gratuity in the year following the hearing. The plaintiffs would not, therefore, have suffered any loss. The judge awarded them £100 to indemnify them against the possibility that they would not have been able to recover their money from the mortgagor, plus £52.10s. for the cost of surveys and reports.

This decision was not followed in *London & South of England Building Society v Stone* (1983) 267 EG 69, where the Court of Appeal held (by a majority) that a deduction should not be made for the value to the lenders of the borrowers' personal covenants to repay the loan. O'Connor LJ said that the *Gapp* case above was not cited in the *Eagle Star* case which was, as a result, wrongly decided. In *Stone* the lenders were not under any duty to the defendant valuer to mitigate their loss by trying to extract money from the borrowers. Stephenson LJ thought that in some circumstances it might be reasonable for a lender to enforce the borrower's personal covenant but, on the evidence, it was not shown to be reasonable in this case.

(d) *Date of assessment.* The general rule of law is that damages are to be assessed as at the date of the breach of contract or the tort (the cause of action), so as to put the plaintiff in the same position as he would have been in if the contract had been properly performed or the tort had not occurred. This is a general but not a universal rule and there are exceptions. In every case regard should be had to the underlying principle that damages are compensation for loss.

Where the wrong suffered is damage to a building, the damages are the cost of the necessary works assessed at the date when it would be reasonable for them to be carried out, not the date when the cause of action arose (see *Dodd* discussed on p. 236 above). But where the breach of contract or tort is a negligent survey or valuation, and damages are assessed by reference to the resultant diminution in value, then they are normally assessed as at the date when the cause of action arose, e.g. the date of the report in contract or the purchase in tort (see *Perry* per Lord Denning MR at p. 888 and *Dodd* per Donaldson LJ at p. 1343).

Where damages are claimed for the negligent assessment or agreement of a review rent in a lease, then it may be that they should be fixed as at the date of judgment (and not breach) and comprise the actual amounts under or overpaid to that date (with interest) plus a capital sum representing discounted future loss (see *Techno Land Improvements Limited v British Leyland (UK) Limited*, p. 237 above).

Perhaps the position regarding the date of assessment of damages is best summarised as follows:

> "It is for the courts or for arbitrators to work out a solution in each case best adapted to giving the injured plaintiff that amount of damages which will most fairly compensate him for the wrong which he has suffered).
> (per Lord Wilberforce in *Miliangos v George Frank (Textiles) Ltd* [1976] AC 443 at p. 468).

The court may award interest on damages for loss up to the date of judgment but not on damages for future loss. Interest may also be subsequently claimed for late payment of a judgment debt (see Chapter 11 p. 342 below for the award of interest in arbitrations).

LIMITATION OF ACTIONS

The Limitation Act 1980 provides that, subject to certain exceptions (e.g. personal injuries and fraud), actions founded on a simple contract (section 5) or on tort (section 2) cannot be brought after the expiration of six years from the date on which the cause of action accrued.

A cause of action in contract normally accrues when the breach occurs, irrespective of the time when the loss flowing from the breach is actually suffered.

A cause of action in tort accrues when damage is suffered by the injured party. This simple rule has within it the difficult problem of deciding in practice exactly when the damage was suffered. Where damage is caused to a building by negligent design or construction, the date of accrual of the cause of action is the date when the damage came into existence and not when it was discovered or should with reasonable diligence have been discovered. The duty of builders and local authorities in respect of defective property is owed to the owners of that property as a class: when time begins to run against one owner it also runs against all future owners (*Pirelli General Cable Works Ltd v Oscar Faber & Partners* (1982) 262 EG 879). Where further defendants are properly joined as parties to an action, the proceedings against them are deemed to have started when the writ was issued against the original defendants (*Ketteman v Hansel Properties Ltd & Others* (1984) 271 EG 1099).

A similar problem of deciding when damage occurred arises where economic loss (as opposed to physical damage) is caused by negligence. For example, in *Forster v Outred & Co* [1982] 1 WLR 86, Mrs Forster signed a mortgage deed in the defendant solicitors' office mortgaging her farm to a finance company as security for a loan to her son. Later, he was unable to repay the loan and the company wrote to her requiring her to repay it or they would exercise their power of sale. This was followed by a formal demand to repay and a few months later she did so. She sued her solicitors for negligently failing to explain to her the effect of the mortgage arrangements. It was agreed that the plaintiff's cause of action on the contract accrued when she signed the mortgage deed. But the important question in the circumstances of the case was: when did her cause of action arise in tort? When did she suffer loss? When she signed the mortgage deed? When the company wrote to her requiring her to repay the loan? When it served a formal demand? Or when Mrs Forster repaid the loan? It was held by the Court of Appeal that she suffered loss on the day she signed the mortgage deed and thereby encumbered her farm and diminished its value. The court found the recent cases on defective buildings unhelpful when considering the date of the accrual of a cause of action resulting in economic loss (see also *Costa v Georghio* (1984) 8 CSW 322).

But in *Mathew v Maughold Life Assurance Co Ltd* (1985) *The Times* 23rd January 1985, where accountants negligently failed to warn the plaintiff before she entered into an estate duty avoidance scheme that she would suffer financial loss if she failed to exercise an option before her husband had survived seven years, it was held that the cause of action against them did not accrue until the failure to exercise the option, which caused monetary loss capable of assessment The *Forster* decision was distinguished on the grounds that, in that case, the creation of the mortgage caused the plaintiff's loss by a diminution in value of her property, whereas in *Mathew* the plaintiff could safely have entered into the scheme provided she was properly advised about the exercise of the option.

It would appear, therefore, that a cause of action in contract or tort for the negligent determination of a review rent by an independent expert will arise on the date that he issues his determination.

It should be noted that the date when a cause of action accrues is not necessarily the same as the date for the assessment of damages.

EXCLUSION OF LIABILITY

Liability for negligence may be excluded by operation of law, or under the terms of a contract or by a notice in tort.

(1) Exclusion by operation of law

For reasons of public policy, certain persons are given immunity from negligence in the performance of their duties. Thus, it is well-established that a barrister cannot be sued for negligence arising out of his conduct of litigation and this immunity has now been extended to all advocates, in court or before any tribunal, inquiry or arbitrator and in carrying out preliminary work affecting the conduct of the hearing (see Chapter 7 p. 211 above). An arbitrator who is required to act in a judicial capacity probably has immunity from actions for negligence at common law and is not now liable under the Supply of Goods and Services Act 1982 (see Chapter 7 p. 211 above). An independent expert has no such immunity unless perhaps he is acting in a judicial capacity (see Chapter 7 p. 206 above). An expert witness probably has immunity from actions for negligence in respect of evidence given in judicial proceedings, including work done before the issue of a writ or commencement of a prosecution (see Chapter 3 p. 64 above).

(2) Exclusion under the terms of a contract

(a) *Position at common law.* At common law it is possible to exclude or restrict liability for negligence by an appropriate contract term. Suppliers of goods frequently exclude or restrict liability for defective goods. A valuer can exclude liability for a negligent valuation and an independent expert for his determination. But it is unusual for a professional man to exclude liability to his client for negligence, although it is common for reports to include a term excluding liability to third parties. These exclusion clauses often worked harshly against injured parties and the courts sought ways to avoid or restrict their operation. The position is now largely governed by the Unfair Contract Terms Act 1977, but two common law rules still apply. First, the clause must be incorporated into the contract when it is made: it will not be effective if it is brought to the other party's notice after the contract has been concluded. Secondly, an exclusion clause will be construed against the party seeking to rely on it: it must expressly exclude liability for negligence if it is to have that effect, although a clause *limiting* liability is not to be construed as strictly as one *excluding* all liability (*Ailsa Craig Fishing Co Ltd v Malvern Fishing Co Ltd* [1983] 1 All ER 101, see Appendix A p. 439 below). If an exclusion clause satisfics thcsc two common law rulcs thcn it must also satisfy the requirements of the Unfair Contract Terms Act 1977 if it is to be effective. The following summary of this Act is not comprehensive but is restricted to those provisions likely to affect a surveyor in his practice.

(b) *Application of 1977 Act.* Sections 2 to 7 of the Unfair Contract Terms Act 1977 deal with the avoidance of liability for negligence and breach of contract and liability arising from the sale or supply of goods. They apply only to business contracts, namely those entered into in the course of business (which includes a profession, a government department, local or public authority) or for the occupation of business premises, other than the classes of contract listed in Schedule 1 to the Act, e.g. certain contracts of insurance, contracts relating to the creation or transfer of an interest in land or securities.

A person cannot exclude or restrict his liability for negligence causing death or personal injury (section 2 (1)). In the case of other loss or damage, a person can only exclude or restrict his liability for negligence by a contract term to the extent that the term satisfies the requirement of "reasonableness" under the Act (section 2 (2)). This rule also applies to contract terms which make liability or enforcement subject to restrictive or onerous conditions, or exclude or restrict any right or remedy in respect of liability, or subject a person to any prejudice in consequence of his pursuit of such right or remedy or exclude or restrict rules of evidence or procedure (section 13). (An agreement to submit differences to arbitration is not within this rule). Section 10 prevents the use of an exclusion cause in a second contract to exclude liability.

Negligence is defined in relation to an express or implied duty of care, as any obligation to take reasonable care or exercise reasonable skill in the performance of the contract (section 1 (1) (a)). This includes the implied term that a professional man will use reasonable care and skill when performing his services under the contract.

Special provisions apply to contracts where one party "deals as consumer" (as defined) or the contract is on the other's written standard terms of business (not defined). In the case of such contracts, the non-consumer (or business party) can only exclude or restrict his liability for breach by a contract term, or claim to be entitled to render a substantially different contractual performance or no performance at all, if that term satisfies the requirement of reasonableness (section 3). It is important, therefore, that in a contract for professional services with a consumer the scope of those services should be made clear at the outset. Failure to do so may be viewed as an attempt to render a substantially different contractual performance. Broadly, a party "deals as consumer" where he does not make the contract in the course of a business nor does he hold himself out as so doing and the other party does (sections 12 (1) and 14). A buyer in a sale by auction or competitive tender is not treated as dealing as consumer. The restrictive provisions of section 3 above, therefore, do not apply to auctions and competitive tenders (section 12 (2)).

(c) *Reasonableness.* The requirement of reasonableness is that the contract term which seeks to exclude or restrict liability shall have been a fair and reasonable one to be included in the contract having regard to the circumstances which were, or ought reasonably to have been, known to or in the contemplation of the parties when the contract was made (section 11 (1)). The onus of proof is on the party seeking to rely on the exclusion clause (section 11 (5)). Where the requirement of reasonableness is considered in relation to a contract term which restricts liability to a specified sum of money, regard shall be had to the resources available to meet the liability and the availability of insurance cover (section 11 (4)).

The 1977 Act does not define further the requirement of reasonableness in relation to contract terms which seek to exclude or limit liability for negligence, although Schedule 2 to the Act provides guidelines for the application of the reasonableness test in relation to contracts for sale, hire purchase and other transfers of goods (sections 6 and 7). Two recent cases give some guidance as to the attitudes of the courts to reasonableness but neither of them relate to professional negligence.

In *George Mitchell (Chesterhall) Ltd v Finney Lock Seeds Ltd* [1983] 2 All ER 737, farmers bought Dutch winter white cabbage seeds for £201.60 from seed merchants. The contract of sale included a standard term limiting the merchants' liability for defective seed to replacement or a refund of the purchase price. The seed was defective, the crop it produced was commercially worthless and the farmers claimed damages of £61,500. The seed merchants relied on the contract term to limit their liability to £201.60.

The House of Lords held that the term applied to this transaction, but then went on to consider whether it would be fair and reasonable to allow the seed merchants to rely upon it. (This case was decided under section 55 of the Sale of Goods Act 1979 which provides as the test of an enforceable exclusion or limitation clause whether it would be fair and reasonable to allow reliance on it, applying the test at the time of the breach).

It was then further held that it would not be fair and reasonable to allow the seed merchants to rely on this term to limit their liability. The reasons for this decision included: the fact that the seed merchants regularly waived reliance on the limitation clause and negotiated on claims due to seed failure; the supply of defective seed was due to the merchants' negligence; and they could have insured against claims for damages arising from the supply of defective seed. The farmers succeeded in their claim for £61,500 damages.

The decision of the High Court in *South Western General Property Co Ltd v Marton* (1982) 263 EG 1090, concerned the reasonableness of disclaimer clauses in an auction catalogue relating to the sale of a plot of land. These clauses were: first, that incorrect statements, errors or omissions shall not annul the sale nor discharge the purchaser; secondly, that no objection or requisition shall be raised as to the permitted user of the property for town planning purposes and that the purchaser shall take the property as it is under the planning legislation; thirdly, statements in the particulars are to be taken as statements of opinion and not of fact, to be checked by the purchaser, and no representations or warranties are given in relation to the property.

The judge held that the vendors, by the omission of material facts in the description of the property in the catalogue, falsely represented that the land could be used for building; the purchaser relied on these representations; and, if the disclaimer clauses were included in the contract of sale, they did not in the circumstances satisfy the test of reasonableness under section 11(1) of the 1977 Act. These clauses would have excluded liability for a failure to tell all the facts about the possible development of the property, the omitted facts being amongst those most material to the whole contract of sale. The plaintiff vendors were, therefore, unable to rely upon the disclaimer clauses in the auctioneer's catalogue.

(3) Exclusion under a notice in tort

This heading deals with the situation where a person who could become liable in tort for negligence seeks to exclude or restrict that liability by notice given to those persons to whom he owes a duty of care. In the leading case of *Hedley Byrne & Co Ltd v Heller & Partners Ltd* [1964] AC 465, the defendant bankers escaped any possible liability for negligence in connection with the references they gave concerning the financial standing of a customer, who later went into liquidation causing loss to the plaintiffs, because they were given "without responsibility". Lord Reid explained the courses of action open to a person who knew that his skill and judgment were being relied on by a third party, one of which was that (p. 486):

> ". . . he could give an answer with a clear qualification that he accepted no responsibility for it or that it was given without that reflection and enquiry which a careful answer would require; . . ."

Such a qualification would now need to satisfy the requirements of the Unfair Contract Terms Act 1977.

Negligence in relation to tort is defined in section 1(1)(b) of the Act as the breach "of any common law duty to take reasonable care or exercise reasonable skill (but not any stricter duty)." As in contract, the Act only applies to business liability, that is to say liability for duties arising in the course of business or from the occupation of business premises (section 1(3)). The position regarding the effectiveness of an exclusion notice in tort is similar to an exclusion clause in contract. A person cannot exclude or restrict his liability for death or personal injury resulting from negligence (section 2(1)). In the case of other loss or damage a person can only exclude or restrict his liability for negligence in tort by notice given generally or to particular persons to the extent that this notice satisfies the requirement of reasonableness (section 2(2)). This requirement in respect of a notice in tort differs from an exclusion clause in contract. It is that it "should be fair and reasonable to allow reliance on it, having regard to all the circumstances obtaining when the liability arose or (but for the notice) would have arisen" (section 11(3). For example, in *Stevenson v Nationwide Building Society* (1984) 272 EG 663, the plaintiff applied for a loan from the defendants to purchase a commercial property. The application form contained a clause stating that the inspection by the society's valuer was not a structural survey (it also asked whether the applicant required such a survey at an additional cost) and a disclaimer of liability by the society to the purchaser for the value or condition of the property. This latter was as follows:

> "I/We understand that the report and valuation on the property made by the society's valuer is confidential and is intended solely for the consideration of the society in determining what advance (if any) may be made on the security, and that no responsibility is implied or accepted by the society or its valuer for either the value or condition of the property by reason of such inspection and report."

The report from the society's valuer recommended the property as suitable for the advance required, subject to a retainer for certain specified repairs. The property was purchased but was later found to contain serious structural defects not mentioned in the building society report. The plaintiff brought an action for damages in tort against the society on the grounds of a negligent report, a copy of which had been given to him and on which he had relied in purchasing the property.

It was held that the society's report had been negligently prepared and that the defective condition of the property should have been noted, even though the inspection was for a valuation report and not for a structural survey. The defendants were vicariously liable for the negligence of their employee (the valuer who prepared the report), unless it could be shown that the above disclaimer satisfied the requirement of reasonableness under section 11(3) of the Unfair Contract Terms Act 1977.

It was held that under the circumstances, and looking at the matter subjectively, it was fair and reasonable for the defendants to rely upon the disclaimer. J. Wilmers QC, sitting as a deputy judge, said (p. 671):

> "Here we have, on the one hand, a building society which follows what is accepted to be fairly standard practice in importing this term or notice or disclaimer. It does so with a full warning, and it offers the applicant a way of circumventing the refusal to accept responsibility by its offer to arrange for a full survey, provided the applicant will pay the extra cost. Since such a survey would involve extra cost, I can see nothing unfair in this. Moreover, when I bear in mind that the person affected by the disclaimer is someone well familiar with such disclaimers and with the possibility of obtaining a survey, and also familiar with the difference between a building society valuation and a survey and their different costs, it seems to me perfectly reasonable to allow the building society, in effect, to say to him that if he chooses the cheaper alternative he must accept that the society will not be responsible for the content to him."

Thus, it would appear that the factors which influenced the judge in reaching his decision were: the alternative course of action which could have been taken by the applicant at additional cost (i.e. a full structural survey) and the fact that the applicant was an estate agent and insurance broker who admitted that he was familiar with both disclaimers and the difference between a valuation and a structural survey.

PART FOUR

ARBITRATION

CHAPTER NINE

Law of Arbitration – I

Nature of arbitration; how arbitrations arise; the arbitration agreement; limitation; appointment and removal of arbitrators; stay of court proceedings

INTRODUCTION

Arbitration is a private procedure for settling disputes, whereby a difference between two or more parties is referred not to the courts, but to the determination of one or more persons, usually chosen for their expertise in the subject-matter of the dispute.

Arbitration usually derives from an agreement between the parties, referred to as arbitration by agreement or by consent, but it may also arise under the provisions of a statute or by order of court. The subject-matter of the disputes usually submitted to arbitration is varied, and most matters affecting the civil interests of the parties may be so referred. Arbitration is normally used, however, for disputes of fact, usually of a technical or commercial nature. Common examples are disputes arising under a charterparty (shipping), or under contracts of insurance, or for the provision of a holiday, under building and civil engineering contracts, commodity contracts and rent review clauses in leases. The person or persons appointed to determine a dispute by arbitration (the arbitrators or umpires) may be appointed by the parties, or by a third party chosen by them or by the court. Arbitrators and umpires are usually required to act in a judicial capacity and are, therefore, to be distinguished from independent experts who are not so constrained in their duties (see Chapter 7 p. 201 above). An arbitrator's decision (his award) is normally final and binding on the parties, but in exceptional circumstances it may be subject to an appeal to the court on a point of law or it may be set aside or remitted to the arbitrator for reconsideration.

This chapter deals with the nature of arbitration, how arbitrations arise and other preliminary matters leading to the commencement of arbitration proceedings, namely the arbitration agreement, limitation, appointment and removal of arbitrators and the stay of concurrent proceedings in court. In the following chapters I discuss the duties of an arbitrator, procedure and evidence (Chapter 10); the award, including costs (Chapter 11) and the position after the award (Chapter 12). Chapter 13 contains a practical example of an arbitration under a rent review clause in a lease.

ARBITRATION AND THE COURTS

The courts originally saw arbitration as a rival jurisdiction and treated it with a suspicion and hostility which persisted until the latter part of the nineteenth century. This is seen in the old rule that an arbitration agreement which excludes the jurisdiction of the courts is contrary to public policy and, therefore, void. Following the Arbitration Act 1698, however, various statutes were passed to cure the defects of arbitration, e.g. by making an arbitration agreement a "rule of court" and, therefore, enforceable in the courts. The effect was that the courts and arbitration met at various points and their relationship changed, particularly after the establishment in 1895 of the Commercial Court of the Queens Bench Division of the High Court, now the main point of contact between the courts and arbitration.

Today, the relationship of the court to arbitration is one of support and supervision. The court has no inherent jurisdiction to intervene in an arbitration: its powers derive from statute (now the Arbitration Acts 1950 to 1979) and it can only act at the request of the arbitrator or one or more of the parties. The court's current concern with arbitration may be considered under three broad headings.

First, the court will uphold an arbitration agreement and help the arbitrator in his task. For example, the commencement of an action in the courts in a dispute covered by an arbitration agreement will not terminate that arbitration; the court may order a stay of the court proceedings and give its assistance to the arbitrator (see p. 285 below). Where an arbitrator does not have power under the arbitration agreement to make interlocutory orders in respect of such matters as security for costs, discovery, interrogatories, etc, the court may make such orders to assist him (see Chapter 10 p. 301 below).

Secondly, the court may intervene where an arbitration has been improperly conducted. Thus, where an arbitrator has misconducted himself or the proceedings, the court may remove him and set aside his award (see Chapter 12 p. 377 below). Where an arbitator is dilatory he may be removed by the court and lose his remuneration (see p. 283 below).

Thirdly, the court will ensure that arbitrators apply the general law correctly and do not build up their own independent body of case law. It has, therefore, a supervisory jurisdiction over questions of law. This is now exercised mainly by an appeal on a point of law under the Arbitration Act 1979. An arbitrator may also be required by the court to state the reasons for his award in sufficient detail to enable the court to consider any question of law arising out of it (Chapter 12 p. 332 below). The court has jurisdiction to determine a preliminary point of law, with the consent of the arbitrator or the parties (see Chapter 10 p. 304 below).

It is in these (and other) ways that the High Court concerns itself with arbitration. These points of contact have produced a body of case law which, with the Arbitration Acts 1950–1979, comprise the law of arbitration. The Arbitration Act 1950 is a consolidation of earlier legislation and has been amended by the Arbitration Acts 1975 and 1979. The 1975 Act deals with foreign arbitral awards and will not be considered further. The 1950 Act is still the principal Act and, with the 1979 Act, provides a general code of law and procedure governing arbitrations, although many provisions may be excluded by agreement between the parties. Part I of the 1950 Act and the 1979 Act apply to arbitrations to which the Crown is a party (section 30 of the 1950 Act and section 7(1)(e) of the 1979 Act, Appendix C pp. 476 and 509 below). Throughout the remainder of this part of the book the Arbitration Acts 1950 and 1979 will be referred to as the 1950 Act and 1979 Act respectively.

HOW ARBITRATIONS ARISE

An arbitration may arise by agreement between the parties, under statute or by order of court.

(1) Arbitration by agreement
This is the most common form of arbitration and is also known as a reference by consent. The parties to a present, or possible future, dispute agree to submit that dispute to arbitration. It is the subject-matter of the remaining chapters of this book (other than the following summary of arbitration under statute and by order of court).

(2) Arbitration under statute
Certain statutes provide that disputes arising under their provisions shall (or sometimes may) be determined by arbitration. A submission to arbitration will be obligatory where the statute clearly states that this particular tribunal shall be used. A statute may specify the form of arbitration.

The 1950 and 1979 Acts (other than those provisions relating to foreign awards) apply to a statutory arbitration as if it had arisen out of an arbitration agreement and as if the particular statute were such an agreement (sections 31(1) and (2) of the 1950 Act and 7(1) of the 1979 Act, Appendix C pp. 476 and 509 below). This general rule is subject to three exceptions:

(a) The 1950 and 1979 Acts do not apply where they are inconsistent with the Act governing the statutory arbitration or with any rules or procedure authorised or recognised thereby.

(b) The following provisions of the 1950 Act are expressly stated not to apply: sections 2(1) and (3) (effect of death or bankruptcy), 5 (reference of interpleader issues to arbitration), 18(3) (costs), 24 (relief for bias of arbitrator and issues of fraud), 25 (appointment of arbitrators after removal by court), 27 (extension of time for commencement of proceedings) and 29 (Merchant Shipping Act 1894).

(c) Certain other sections of the 1950 Act may be excluded by implication because they could frustrate the intention of the statute to make arbitration the sole tribunal with jurisdiction in the dispute. These are sections 1 (power of court to revoke arbitrators' appointment), 4 (1) (power of court to refuse to stay proceedings) and 23(1) (removal of arbitrator for misconduct).

The parties to an arbitration by agreement may enter into an exclusion agreement removing their rights of appeal on a question of law, or to ask for reasons for an award or for the determination of a preliminary point of law (sections 1 and 2 of the 1979 Act, see Chapter 12 p. 366 below). An exclusion agreement is of no effect in a statutory arbitration (section 3(5) of the 1979 Act, Appendix C p. 507 below).

An award under an arbitration by agreement may be enforced as a judgment or order of the High Court (section 26 of the 1950 Act, see Chapter 12 p. 383 below). An award under a statutory arbitration may not be enforced in this manner where the statute prescribes the method of enforcement (*Re Willesden Local Board & Wright* [1896] 2 QB 412).

The following are some examples of property statutes which provide for arbitration.

Agricultural Holdings Act 1948. This Act (as amended) provides for arbitration on various matters between landlords and tenants of agricultural holdings. A summary of these provisions is contained in Appendix B.

Public Health Act 1936. Certain disputes arising under this Act may or must be referred to arbitration. For example, where a local authority requires the drains of a new building to be connected to a sewer more than 100 feet away it must bear the cost in excess of a 100 foot connection, and any dispute as to this amount shall be determined by a court of summary jurisdiction or, at the request of the owner, by arbitration (section 37). The reference shall be to a single arbitrator appointed by agreement between the parties or, in default of agreement, by the Secretary of State for the Environment (section 303). The Arbitration Acts 1950 and 1979 apply to arbitrations under this Act.

Housing Act 1957. A local authority has power to remove or alter apparatus belonging to a statutory undertaker and any dispute in connection therewith (other than as to compensation) shall be determined by an arbitrator appointed, in default of agreement, by the Secretary of State for the Environment (section 65). The Arbitration Acts apply.

General Rate Act 1967. As we saw in Chapter 1, a rating appeal is normally heard at first instance by a local valuation court. The parties may, however, agree in writing to refer the matter to arbitration (section 78). The Arbitration Acts apply.

Proceedings before the Lands Tribunal (e.g. in respect of disputed compensation or a rating appeal from a local valuation court) do not constitute a statutory arbitration. The tribunal may, however, act as an arbitrator on a reference by consent (e.g. under a rent review clause in a lease) (section 1(5) Lands Tribunal Act 1949) or in a direct rating appeal by arbitration under section 78 of the General Rate Act 1967 (above).

(3) Arbitration by order of court

An arbitration by order of court arises where proceedings are commenced in court but are then referred to arbitration.

(a) *High Court.* The High Court has an inherent jurisdiction to refer "the cause and all matters in difference" to arbitration, but only with the consent of the parties. The resultant arbitration will be conducted in the same way as a reference by consent.

The reference of a matter by a judge to an official referee or, with the consent of the parties, to a special referee, either for full trial or for inquiry and report, is not a reference to arbitration. It is part of High Court proceedings. Under section 11 of the 1950 Act, however, an official referee is bound to act as an arbitrator where he is required to do so under an arbitration agreement or by order of the court (Appendix C p. 469 below). But he has the wider powers of an official referee and his award will be a judgment of the court.

(b) *County court.* Under section 64 of the County Courts Act 1984 and Order 19 of The County Court Rules 1981 a claim not exceeding £500 *must* be referred to arbitration. But, on the application of any party, such a reference may be rescinded for certain reasons, e.g. the agreement of the parties to a trial or where the dispute involves a difficult question of law. Where a claim exceeds £500 it *may* be referred to arbitration on the application of any party.

A county court arbitration is normally conducted by the registrar, with special rules regarding procedure and evidence, unless the court directs otherwise. For example, an informal hearing will be held where the strict rules of evidence do not apply; the arbitrator has the power, with the consent of the parties, to consult any expert, call for an expert report or sit with an expert assessor; there is no recovery of solicitor's costs where the amount of the claim does not exceed £500 (subject to certain exceptions); and the award is entered as a judgment of the court. The judge may set aside an award on the application of any party or he may, with the consent of the parties, revoke the reference or order another reference to be made. The Arbitration Acts do not apply to a county court arbitration (section 7(3) of the 1979 Act, Appendix C p. 510 below).

ARBITRATION AGREEMENT

An arbitration agreement is a document which provides that present or future disputes between the parties shall be sumitted to arbitration. It is the foundation of every arbitration by agreement. An arbitration agreement may form part of a wider contract and is then often referred to as an arbitration clause.

(1) Form and effect

(a) *Form.* An arbitration agreement is, or forms part of, a contract; it is, therefore, governed by the law of contract in addition to the law of arbitration. Thus, the ability of a person to enter into an enforceable arbitration agreement will depend upon his capacity to enter into a binding contract relating to the same subject-matter. For example, an infant may only enter into a binding arbitration agreement relating to a contract for the supply of necessities, or to a reasonable contract of service or which is or forms part of a contract for his benefit. Any other agreement, like any other contract by an infant, is not binding but is voidable at his option.

An arbitration agreement may be written, oral or under seal. An oral agreement, however, will only be enforceable at common law and is not within the Arbitration Acts. These only apply to an "arbitration agreement" as defined in section 32 of the 1950 Act, namely a *"written* agreement to submit present or future differences to arbitration, whether an arbitrator is named therein or not." This definition is satisfied provided there is a document or documents, in writing, which recognise, incorporate or confirm the existence of an agreement to submit to arbitration (*Excomm Ltd v Bamaodah* (1984) *The Times* 17th January 1985). It follows, therefore, that the Arbitration Acts cannot be used to rectify omissions in an oral arbitration agreement as they can in one which is in writing or by deed.

An arbitration agreement need not be in any particular form, but it must clearly indicate that the dispute is to be determined by arbitration and not by other means, e.g. by an independent expert (see Chapter 7 p. 193 above). An agreement to refer disputes to arbitration may encompass more than one document. Thus, in *Wade-Gery v Morrison* (1878) 37 LT 270, a lease containing a clause which required the reference of all disputes to arbitration was later varied by a supplemental deed, which did not contain such a clause. It was held that a dispute on the supplemental deed must be referred to arbitration: the two documents should be read together and the supplemental deed did not vary the arbitration provisions in the original lease.

The above definition of an arbitration agreement covers both an agreement to refer possible future disputes to arbitration (sometimes called an "agreement to refer") and an agreement to submit an actual dispute to arbitration (sometimes called a "submission").

(b) *Effect.* An arbitration agreement will bind the parties to it, their assignees and, generally, persons claiming under them (*Shaylor v Woolf* [1946] Ch 320). It will not bind strangers. Thus, where an arbitrator, appointed under an arbitration clause in a charterparty between Garward Shipping Corporation Ltd and Phoenician Express SARL, stated in his award that the latter had changed their name to Phoenician Lines SARL, he thereby exceeded his jurisdiction by making an award against a party who were strangers to the arbitration agreement (*Phoenician Express SARL v Garward Shipping Corporation Ltd* (1983) *The Times* 23rd November 1983).

Sections 2 and 3 of the Arbitration Act 1950 contain provisions relating to the death or bankruptcy of a party to an arbitration agreement (Appendix C p. 466 below). Except where a right of action is extinguished by death, an arbitration agreement is not discharged by the death of any party to it but will be enforceable by or against the personal representative of the deceased (section 2(1) and (3)). Where a contract to which a bankrupt is a party contains an arbitration clause, his trustee in bankruptcy will, if he adopts the contract, be bound by and have the benefit of that clause (section 3(1)). Where a bankrupt entered into an arbitration agreement before his bankruptcy and any matter in that agreement requires to be determined in connection with the bankruptcy proceedings, then, provided section 3(1) above does not apply, the trustee in bankruptcy (with the consent of the committee of inspection) or any other party to the agreement may apply to the court to have that matter determined by arbitration (section 3(2)).

It is not clear whether a binding arbitration agreement must give every party the right to refer a dispute to arbitration, or whether such right may be given to one party only. The former view was expressed in *Baron v Sunderland Corporation* [1966] 2 QB 56. Mr Baron was a teacher employed by the defendants who were required to pay him a salary in accordance with the Burnham Report. Section V of that Report established a joint committee of reference to determine questions of interpretation brought to them by certain bodies and persons, which did not include the plaintiff. A dispute arose regarding the plaintiff's remuneration and he sued the defendants for additional salary. The Court of Appeal refused to stay the plaintiff's action under section 4 of the 1950 Act (see below). It held that it was an essential ingredient of an arbitration clause that it must give bilateral rights of reference, so that either party may refer the dispute to arbitration and that, since the plaintiff had no right to refer his claim to the committee, but had to depend on some other body or person to do so, Section V of the Burnham Report did not constitute a valid submission to arbitration. This decision was recently applied to a rent review clause in a lease in *Tote Bookmakers Ltd v Development & Property Holding Co Ltd* (1984) 129 SJ 153, discussed on p. 270 below. &ᴺᵒᵗ ⃰follow⃰ed ⃰in ⃰Pitta⃰s ⃰vSharp⃰thᴬᴺ ⃰ ⃰/ ⃰/⃰9⃰5⃰4⃰)

This interpretation of the position is disputed in *Russell on Arbitration* (20th edition) at p. 39 and Halsbury *Laws of England* (4th Edition) (Vol 2 para 528), both expressing the opinion that a valid arbitration clause may allow a submission at the suit of one party only.

(2) Content

In addition to the express terms contained in an arbitration agreement, other terms may be deemed to be included by the Arbitration Acts or by the courts.

Under the 1950 Act certain terms will be deemed to be included in a written arbitration agreement unless a contrary intention is expressed therein. For example, if the agreement is silent as to the mode of reference, it will be deemed to be to a single arbitrator. Other implied terms relate to the appointment of umpires, the conduct of the arbitration, interim awards, specific performance of certain contracts, the finality of an award and costs. These topics are discussed under the appropriate headings in this and the following chapters.

In addition to the above terms certain terms will be implied by the court, e.g. that an arbitrator has a duty to decide a dispute according to the ordinary law of the land (*Chandris v Isbrandtsen Moller Co Inc* [1951] 1 KB 240).

An arbitration agreement may restrict the reference of a dispute to arbitration. For example, in *A. E. Farr Ltd v Ministry of Transport* [1960] 1 WLR 956, a contract for the construction of an underpass incorporated the appointment of an engineer to certify certain matters, with provision for arbitration in the event of a dispute. It further provided that a reference to arbitration shall not be made until after completion of the works, except where the dispute concerned the withholding of any certificate. A dispute arose during the contract regarding a claim by the contractor for payment for additional work. The engineer rejected the claim and the question arose as to whether this was a difference which could be submitted to arbitration. It was held that, on the true construction of the contract, this was a dispute regarding the withholding of a certificate and could, therefore, be referred to arbitration before completion of the works.

This point is similar to the question of limitation, where a time limit specifically imposed in the arbitration agreement or generally imposed under the Limitation Act, may bar a submission to arbitration (see below).

An arbitration agreement should clearly state the subject-matter of the dispute: what the arbitrator is to decide. An arbitrator's jurisdiction arises out of the agreement and he must determine the dispute within the boundaries set out therein. For example, in *National Westminster Bank Ltd v BSC Footwear Ltd* (1980) 257 EG 277, a lease contained a tenant's option to renew "at the then prevailing market rent", such rent to be determined by arbitration in default of agreement. The new lease was otherwise to be subject to the same covenants, provisos and conditions as the original lease, which did not contain rent reviews. The question arose as to whether the arbitrator had power to determine a rent for the new lease which would be subject to periodic review. It was held by the Court of Appeal that the task of the arbitrator was to determine a single rent for the whole of the term of the new lease and he had no power to introduce periodic rent reviews. Similarly, in *Clarke v Findon Developments Ltd* (1983) 270 EG 426, an arbitrator appointed to determine a review rent in a lease, which required the assumption to be made that the tenant had complied with his repairing obligations, had no jurisdiction to fix a rent which varied according to the state of repair of the premises.

These decisions also illustrate the rule that an arbitration clause can only be altered by agreement between the parties. It cannot be altered by the arbitrator, as would in effect have happened if he had introduced rent reviews into the new lease in the *National Westminster Bank* case and variable rents in the *Clarke* case.

The signatures of the parties or their agents are not necessary to a binding arbitration agreement (*Excomm Ltd v Bamaodah* (1984) *The Times* 17th January 1985). Although it would appear that they may be necessary where it is sought to enforce the agreement against a party to a contract under the Statute of Frauds or under section 40 of the Law of Property Act 1925.

LIMITATION

An arbitration agreement may provide that particular steps in the arbitration must be taken within specified times, failure to do so resulting in loss of the right to pursue or defend a claim, unless relief is given by the court. Furthermore, the Limitation Act 1980 imposes general time limits in litigation and applies to arbitrations in the same way as it applies to High Court actions.

(1) Time limits imposed by arbitration agreement

(a) *Procedure before arbitration.* An arbitration agreement may set out the procedure (with time limits) for preliminary steps leading to the commencement of an arbitration. Thus, it is common for a rent review clause in a lease to provide for the service of a land-lord's "trigger" notice, setting the review in motion, with a period for negotiation and then (if agreement cannot be reached) a tenant's counternotice expressing disagreement with the land-lord's proposed rent and requiring it to be determined by arbitra-tion. Time may be of the essence of the contract in connection with the service with one or more of these notices. For example, time may not be of the essence in connection with the landlord's notice, but it may be in connection with the tenant's counternotice, failure to serve such a notice within the specified time resulting in acceptance of the landlord's rent and loss of the right to refer the matter to arbitration (unless relief is given by the courts as discussed below).

A distinction must be drawn between the preliminary steps and the last step before commencement of arbitration proceedings. Relief may be given by the courts under section 27 of the 1950 Act in respect of this last step, even though time is of the essence of the contract, but not usually in respect of the preliminary steps. The following examples illustrate the position.

In *Shirlcar Properties Ltd v Heinitz* (1983) 268 EG 362, a rent review clause in a lease provided that the rent shall be reviewed every five years to the higher of the rent passing at the review date and the open market rental value. This rental value was to be the amount: (a) specified in a written notice served by the landlords, or (b) agreed between the parties within three months of such notice, or (c) determined by an arbitrator at the election of the tenant by counternotice within three months of the landlords' notice. It was expressly stated that time is of the essence of the contract. The landlords served a notice stating the amount of the proposed rent but also containing the words "subject to contract". It was held by the Court of Appeal that this was not a valid notice because, by the addition of these words, the tenant was left in doubt as to whether the proposed rent was a firm figure intended to set in motion the rent review procedure or a provisional figure put forward as a basis for negotiation.

In *Amalgamated Estates Ltd v Joystretch Ltd* (1980) 257 EG 489, a lease contained a rent review clause with the same procedure as in the *Shirlcar* case. The landlords served notice specifying the amount of the proposed rent. By letter the tenants objected to that rent but did not indicate that they wished to go to arbitration. It was held by the Court of Appeal that this was not a counternotice which referred the dispute to arbitration and, in the absence of an application for an extension of time under section 27 of the Arbitration Act 1950 (see below), the tenants were barred from arbitration and bound to accept the landlords' proposed rent. Templeman LJ referred to the form of a counternotice as follows (p. 493):

> "It is true that no magic formula is required but, in my judgment the tenant must make it clear to the landlord that he proposed to have the rent decided by arbitration in accordance with the provisions of the lease."

Thus, it is not enough merely to object to the proposed rent.

In a similar case, *Edlingham Ltd v MFI Furniture Centres Ltd* (1981) 259 EG 421, the court arrived at a similar decision but granted a stay for a limited period to allow the tenants to pursue an application under section 27 of the 1950 Act for an extension of time in which to elect for arbitration.

(b) *Relief under section 27 of the 1950 Act (Appendix C p. 475 below).* This section provides that where an arbitration agreement states that any claims to which the agreement applies shall be barred, unless within a specified period:

(i) notice to appoint an arbitrator is given, or

(ii) an arbitrator is appointed, or

(iii) some other step to commence arbitration proceedings is taken,

and a dispute arises to which the agreement applies, the High Court may (on such terms as the justice of the case may require) extend that period:

(i) if it is of the opinion that in the circumstances undue hardship would otherwise be caused, and

(ii) notwithstanding that the time so fixed for the specific action has expired.

This section is without prejudice to any enactment limiting the time for the commencement of arbitration proceedings, i.c. now the Limitation Act 1980 which is discussed below.

Thus, section 27 applies to an arbitration agreement which expressly or impliedly bars a claim if the arbitration is not commenced within a prescribed period. If the agreement has this effect then it must be read as if it were subject to the court's power to extend that period. Lord Denning MR referred to section 27 as being in effect, "... an additional statutory term written into the arbitration clause" (*International Tank & Pipe SAK v Kuwait Aviation Fuelling Co KSC* [1975] QB 224 at p. 233).

As stated above, section 27 does not usually apply to time limits in a contract which relate to preliminary steps not directly concerned with the commencement of an arbitration. For example, it does not give the court power to extend a time limit for making a claim under a contract, even though this might be a condition precedent to the commencement of arbitration proceedings, on the grounds that the claim does not of itself commence the proceedings nor necessarily lead to their commencement. The claim might be conceded, discontinued or settled by agreement (*Babanaft International Co SA v Avant Petroleum Inc* [1982] 1 WLR 871). But where the terms of an arbitration agreement link the claim with the commencement of the arbitration, so that the two go hand in hand and are inextricably bound up together, then the discretion of the court under section 27 could apply to the time limit for making the claim (*Jedranska Slobodna Plovidba v Oleagine SA* [1983] 3 All ER 602).

Section 27 does not usually apply to the preliminary steps leading to a rent review arbitration (e.g. the service of a landlord's trigger notice), but it applies to the last step before the reference even though time is expressly made of the essence in relation to that step. Although it would appear from the recent decision in *Tote Bookmakers Ltd v Development & Property Holding Co Ltd* (1984) 129 SJ 153, that relief under section 27 is only available where the rent review clause gives *both* parties the right to refer the disputed rent to arbitration. In this case the rent review clause provided that the review rent is to be determined by the landlord serving on the tenant a notice specifying the proposed rent or, in default of agreement, by arbitration "at the election of the lessee by counternotice ... to the lessor not later than three months after the lessor's said notice (time to be of the essence thereof) ..."

The tenant failed to serve a counternotice and applied under section 27 for an extension of time to do so. This was refused on the grounds that the decision in *Baron v Sunderland Corporation* (p. 266 above) stated that it is an essential ingredient of an arbitration clause that *either* party should have the right of reference to arbitration (bilateral rights) and that this particular clause gave only a unilateral right to the tenant to do so. It was not, therefore, an arbitration agreement enabling the tenant to apply for relief under section 27 of the 1950 Act.

The doubts as to the correctness of the decision in *Baron* are referred to above (p. 266) and the *Tote Bookmakers* decision appears to be in conflict with the other rent review cases on section 27 discussed here. Unfortunately, only a short report of this decision was available at the time of writing and it was not possible to assess fully its significance.

The court may only grant relief under section 27 if it is of the opinion that "undue hardship" would otherwise be caused. In *Liberian Shipping Corporation "Pegasus" Ltd v A. King & Sons Ltd* [1967] 2 QB 86, the Court of Appeal considered the meaning of "undue hardship" and their conclusions were later summarised by Brandon J in *Moscow V/O Exportkhleb v Helmville Ltd (The Jocelyne)* [1977] 2 Lloyd's Rep 121 at p. 129:

> "The guidelines laid down in the majority judgments in *The Pegasus* case can, in my view, be summarised as follows: (1) The words "undue hardship" in section 27 should not be construed too narrowly. (2) Undue hardship means excessive hardship and, where the hardship is due to the fault of the claimant, it means hardship, the consequences of which are put out of proportion to such a fault. (3) In deciding whether to extend time or not, the Court should look at all the relevant circumstances of the particular case. (4) In particular, the following matters should be considered: (a) the length of the delay; (b) the amount at stake; (c) whether the delay was due to the fault of the claimant or to circumstances outside his control; (d) if it was due to the fault of the claimant, the degree of such fault; (e) whether the claimant was misled by the other party; (f) whether the other party has been prejudiced by the delay and, if so, the degree of such prejudice."

In *The Pegasus* Lord Denning MR put the matter shortly by saying that "undue" simply means excessive: undue hardship "means greater hardship than the circumstances warrant" (p. 98).

The operation of section 27 in relation to a rent review clause was recently considered in *Chartered Trust PLC v Maylands Green Estate Co Ltd* (1984) 270 EG 845. In this case the rent review clause contained the usual machinery for review comprising a landlords' "trigger" notice stating the proposed rent (to be served before the expiry of the first $4\frac{1}{2}$ years of the term), a period of three months for the parties to agree a rent and, in the event of failure to agree, a tenants' counternotice to be served not later than three months after the landlords' notice. Time was of the essence of the contract in respect of the tenants' counternotice, but not in respect of the previous steps.

The landlords served a notice, the tenants failed to serve a counternotice and then brought an action for negligence against their surveyors, who denied this allegation, and, as part of their defence, alleged that the landlords' notice was defective and of no effect. The landlords then served two fresh notices (relating to the two separate leases held by the tenants) but the tenants again failed to serve counternotices within the specified period. The tenants sought relief under section 27 of the 1950 Act in respect of the first and second set of counternotices.

Counsel for the landlords accepted, in the light of earlier authorities, that section 27 applies to the appointment of an arbitrator to fix a review rent, even though time is made of the essence of the contract. The judge considered it relevant in deciding whether a refusal to extend the time for service of counternotices would result in hardship to the tenants that they may have claims for negligence against their professional advisers in respect of both notices.

When he considered the first notice, the judge stated that there were powerful arguments for granting the tenants' application but finally came to the conclusion that, by commencing proceedings against their surveyors (and joining their landlords as defendants) and by waiting 18 months before commencing the current proceedings for relief, the tenants must be taken to have waived their right to seek relief under section 27.

He then considered the application in respect of the second notices and formed the view that there was only a possibility that the tenants would succeed in actions for negligence against their advisers. The two factors weighed by him in reaching his decision were: the likelihood of prejudice to the landlords and any delay by the tenants in seeking relief. It was not established that the landlords would suffer hardship if the period for serving counternotices were extended (except by delay in the receipt of increased rents), and the tenants had not been guilty of unreasonable delay in seeking relief under section 27, having regard to the negotiations between surveyors and then solicitors which followed the failure to serve the counternotices. Accordingly, he granted an extension of time for the service of counternotices by the tenants, subject to a condition that interest shall be added to any arrears of rent payable when arbitration is concluded.

(2) Time limits imposed by Limitation Act 1980

The Limitation Act 1980 lays down various time limits for the commencement of actions in the courts (see Chapter 8 p. 247). For example, subject to certain exceptions (e.g. personal injuries or fraud), an action in respect of a tort or a simple contract must be brought within six years of the date on which the cause of action accrued; an action upon a deed or to recover land must be brought within twelve years of that date. Failure to commence an action within the relevant period (e.g. by the issue of a writ) will normally result in the notional plaintiff losing his right of action: his claim will be statute-barred.

The Limitation Act and others relating to limitation of actions, apply to arbitrations as they apply to actions in the High Court (section 34(1) Limitation Act 1980, Appendix C p. 510 below). Thus, the time limit for the commencement of a High Court action will apply to the settlement of that dispute by arbitration, unless the arbitration agreement specifies a shorter period (see p. 268 above).

The period of limitation for a High Court action commences with the date when the cause of action accrues, e.g. when a breach of contract occurs. The corresponding period in arbitration commences with the "cause of arbitration", that is to say the date when the claimant first acquired a right to proceed to arbitration in respect of the dispute (*Pegler v Railway Executive* [1948] AC 332 and section 34(2) Limitation Act 1980). Thus, for the purposes of limitation, a cause of arbitration is to be treated in the same way as a cause of action would be treated if the proceedings were in a court of law.

An arbitration is commenced:

(a) when one party serves on the other a notice requiring him to appoint an arbitrator or to agree to such an appointment; or
(b) when one party serves notice on the other requiring him to submit the dispute to the arbitrator named or designated in the arbitration agreement (section 34(3) and (4) Limitation Act 1980).

Where the High Court intervenes in an arbitration, either by ordering an award to be set aside or (after the commencement of an arbitration) that the arbitration agreement shall cease to have effect with respect to that dispute, the court may further order that the period between the commencement of the arbitration and the order shall be excluded when computing the limitation period for that dispute (section 34(5) Limitation Act 1980). Thus, the time occupied by an abortive arbitration may be ignored for the purposes of limitation.

The above provisions apply to arbitrations by agreement and statutory arbitrations (section 34(6) Limitation Act 1980). The provisions of the Limitation Act 1980 relating to the enforcement of an award are considered in Chapter 12 pp. 385 and 386 below.

APPOINTMENT OF ARBITRATORS

(1) Who may be appointed?

A person may be disqualified from acting as arbitrator in a particular dispute for one or more of the following reasons.

First, he may lack the special qualifications or experience required by the arbitration agreement. For example, a rent review clause in a lease may stipulate that, if the parties cannot agree, the rent shall be determined by an arbitrator who shall be "a practising chartered surveyor having not less than five years valuation experience in Melchester and recent substantial experience in the valuation of premises of a kind and character similar to those of the demised premises and who is a partner in a leading firm of surveyors practising in the locality". This clause requires a prospective arbitrator to satisfy four conditions relating to qualifications, experience and position before he can accept such an appointment.

Secondly, a person may be disqualified from accepting an arbitral appointment due to a physical or mental disability, e.g. deafness, blindness or mental illness.

Thirdly, the holding of a particular office or position may prevent a person from accepting an appointment as arbitrator. For example, before the repeal of section 6(b) of the County Courts Act 1959 a circuit judge was not allowed to act as an arbitrator for remuneration; but a judge of the Commercial Court of the High Court may, where the dispute appears to be of a commercial character and with the consent of the Lord Chief Justice, accept an appointment as sole arbitrator or umpire under a written arbitration agreement. (Where a judge-arbitrator is appointed, the Administration of Justice Act 1970 Schedule 3 contains special provisions modifying the operation of the 1950 Act in relation to that appointment). A person who is a necessary witness in a dispute cannot act as arbitrator in that dispute (*Hogg v Belfast Corporation* [1919] 2 Ir Rep 305).

Fourthly, a person may be disqualified on the grounds of dishonesty, bias or an interest in the dispute. For example, in *Sellar v*

Highland Railway 1919 56 Sc LR 216, a railway company, party to an arbitration, nominated a shareholder as its arbitrator, but it was held that he was disqualified and his award was set aside. In *Blanchard v Sun Fire Office* (1890) 6 TLR 365, an action on a fire policy between the assured and the insurance company was referred to arbitration. Each party appointed an arbitrator and the arbitrators appointed an umpire. The arbitrators and umpire sat together, but differed and the umpire made the award. It subsequently appeared that, after appointment and before the meeting, the assured had assigned his claim under the policy to his arbitrator. The court set aside the award on the application of the insurance company.

The court will uphold the general rule that persons appointed to settle disputes should be honest and impartial, and even where the parties have chosen an arbitrator with actual or presumed knowledge of his disabilities the court will not decline to intervene on this ground (see section 24(1) of the 1950 Act discussed on p. 283 below).

The question of partiality due to a business connection between the arbitrator and one of the parties was considered in a recent Scottish case, *Johnson v Lamb* 1981 SLT 300. A dispute arose out of a building contract and it was agreed that it should be submitted to the first defender as arbiter. Later the pursuer (plaintiff) alleged that the arbiter was disqualified from acting because, at the time he was appointed, he had a regular business contact with the other party to the dispute, the contractors (the second defenders), namely he was architect for a local authority which had a school building contract with them as main contractors. This argument was rejected by the court: this particular business contact was insufficient to disqualify the arbiter from acting. Lord Maxwell said (p. 303):

> "It is to be noted first, that the alleged relationship between the first and second defenders had nothing to do with the subject-matter of the arbitration. Second, it is not suggested that the first defender had any interest whatever in the outcome of the arbitration and, third, the relationship founded on was not one in which the first and second defenders had a common interest. They were not, as it were, on the same side. An architect is employed by the building owner not the builder and, in so far as his duty is not owed to the building owner his function is quasi-judicial."

(2) Methods of appointment

An arbitrator is usually appointed by the parties to the arbitration agreement, either directly or indirectly by an agreed third party to whom they have given powers of appointment. The court has statutory powers to appoint in certain circumstances and may do so at other times by agreement with the parties.

(a) *Appointment by the parties.* An arbitration agreement will usually specify the mode of reference (e.g. to a single arbitrator) and either name him or provide for his appointment by agreement between the parties or, in default of agreement, by a third party. No special form of appointment is needed, unless required by the arbitration agreement. Where a reference is to be made to a single arbitrator his appointment is complete when it has been agreed by the parties and notified to and accepted by him. Where a reference is to two arbitrators, one to be appointed by each party, the appointments will be complete when each party has communicated his appointment to the other and the arbitrators have accepted them (*Tew v Harris* (1848) 11 QB 7; *Tradax Export SA v Volkswagenwerk AG* [1970] 1 QB 537).

Sections 6–8 of the 1950 Act (Appendix C pp. 467 to 468 below) contain the following provisions regarding the appointment of arbitrators and umpires. These will be deemed to apply where the arbitration agreement is in writing and there is no contrary intention therein.

Where an arbitration agreement does not provide for the mode of reference it is deemed to be to a single arbitrator (section 6).

Where an agreement provides for a reference to two arbitrators, one to be appointed by each party, four provisions are deemed to apply:

(i) If either of the appointed arbitrators refuses to act, or is incapable of so doing, or dies, the party who appointed him may appoint a new arbitrator in his place (section 7(a)). The court has power to set aside such an appointment (see p. 283 below).

(ii) If one party fails to appoint an arbitrator (either originally or in substitution) for seven clear days after the other party (who has so appointed) has served on him notice to appoint, then the party who has made his appointment may appoint his arbitrator as sole arbitrator. His award will be binding on both parties (section 7(b)). The court has power to set aside any appointment made (see p. 283 below).

(iii) Where a reference is to two arbitrators, the arbitration agreement is deemed to include a provision that they may appoint an umpire at any time after their appointment, and shall do so forthwith if they cannot agree (section 8(1) as amended by section 6(1) of the 1979 Act).

(iv) A provision is also deemed to be included that, if the two arbitrators have delivered to any party to the agreement or to the umpire written notice that they cannot agree, then the umpire may forthwith enter on the reference in lieu of the arbitrators (section 8(2)). At any time after the appointment of an umpire (however appointed) the court may, on the application of any party, order that the umpire shall enter on the reference and act as sole arbitrator in place of the two appointed arbitrators (section 8(3)). (Where two arbitrators disagree and the umpire therefore assumes responsibility for the decision, the arbitrators become *functus officio* as arbitrators and each becomes the advocate of his appointor).

(b) *Appointment by a third party*. It is common for an arbitration agreement to provide that, if the parties are unable to agree on an appointment, an arbitrator shall be appointed by a named third party, e.g. the President of a professional body. The phrases "in default of agreement" and "failing to reach agreement", which make appointment by a third party necessary, have been interpreted by the courts to mean the factual situation that the parties have not reached agreement, irrespective of whether they have tried to do so. A positive attempt to reach agreement is not therefore a condition precedent to a request for the appointment of an arbitrator, lack of agreement is sufficient. If the parties wish to make an attempt to agree a necessary step in the procedure, a condition precedent to the appointment of an arbitrator, then they must do so in clear terms or by necessary implication (*Re Essoldo (Bingo) Ltd's Underlease* (1971) 220 EG 1437; *Wrenbridge Ltd v Harries (Southern Properties) Ltd* (1981) 260 EG 1195).

The appointment of an arbitrator by a third party is valid when it is made by him and accepted by the arbitrator. Notification to the parties is not essential to the validity of such an appointment. Thus, in *University College, Oxford v Durdy* (1982) 262 EG 338, it was held by the Court of Appeal that the date of appointment by the Minister of an arbitrator under the Agricultural Holdings Act 1948 was when he performed the official act of appointment by signing and sealing the document: it was not the date when notification of that appointment was received by the tenant. Griffiths LJ said (p. 343):

> "... I can see no reason why, in the case of the appointment of an arbitrator by the Minister under this Act, the appointment should not be complete once the appointment has been made in writing and the arbitrator has agreed to act. As a matter of practice, I will expect the Minister to communicate with the arbitrator and ask whether he is willing to act before he makes the appointment."

A third party is *functus officio* when he has made his appointment and cannot make a second appointment, unless the parties agree that he may do so.

Where a third party refuses to make an appointment, or fails to make it within the time specified in the agreement or, if no time is specified, within a reasonable time, then any party to the agreement may serve notice on him to appoint and, if he still fails to do so within seven clear days, that party may apply to the court to appoint an arbitrator. He will then have the same powers as if he had been appointed under the arbitration agreement (section 10 (2) of the 1950 Act inserted by section 6(4) of the 1979 Act).

(c) *Appointment by the court.* The High Court may appoint an arbitrator or umpire under the following three powers.

First, section 10(1) and (2) of the 1950 Act (as amended by section 6 of the 1979 Act) (Appendix C p. 468 below) give the court power to appoint an arbitrator or umpire in any of the following cases:

(i) Where an arbitration agreement provides for a reference to a single arbitrator and, after differences have arisen, the parties cannot concur in the appointment of an arbitrator (section 10 (1)(a)). This is the situation where the agreement does *not* provide for appointment by a third party in default of agreement by the parties.

(ii) Where an appointed arbitrator refuses to act, is incapable of acting or dies, and the arbitration agreement does not indicate that it was intended that the vacancy should not be filled, and the parties do not fill the vacancy (section 10(1)(b)).

(iii) Where the parties or two arbitrators may or must appoint an umpire or third arbitrator and do not do so (section 10(1) (c)).

(iv) Where an appointed umpire or third arbitrator refuses to act, or is incapable of acting or dies, and the arbitration agreement does not indicate that it was intended that the vacancy should not be filled, and the parties or arbitrator do not fill the vacancy (section 10(1)(d)).

(v) Where a third party refuses or fails to make an appointment (section 10(2) inserted by section 6(4) of the 1979 Act) (see above).

The procedure to be followed in the above cases is that any party to the arbitration agreement may serve written notice on the other parties, third party or arbitrators to appoint an arbitrator, umpire or third arbitrator (or concur in an appointment) and, if the appointment is not made within seven clear days, the court may then appoint on the application of that party. An arbitrator, umpire or third arbitrator appointed by the court has the same powers as if he had been appointed by the parties.

The court cannot impose conditions on the appointment of an arbitrator; but the powers of appointment under section 10(1) of the 1950 Act allow the court to appoint a single arbitrator to hear two separate but related disputes, e.g. in two separate arbitrations under contracts for the erection of a building between employer and main contractor and main contractor and sub-contractor respectively. It is highly desirable that the same arbitrator should be appointed in each arbitration in order to avoid inconsistent findings, but it is equally desirable that neither party should feel that any issue had been decided against them beforehand or without an opportunity of their being heard on that matter. The arbitrator should, therefore, at an early stage in the proceedings, hold a pre-trial conference (or preliminary meeting) with all the parties in the arbitrations, at which the issues should be divided into those that could be separated and decided by the arbitrator at that stage and those that could not be so separated, e.g. issues of causation. If, during or on the completion of the first arbitration, the arbitrator felt that there was a possibility of prejudice, then he could himself seek release from the second arbitration. Also, the parties, by consent, could apply to the court for the appointment of a new arbitrator for the second arbitration if, at any stage before the completion of the first arbitration, they felt that there was a risk of some prejudice arising in the second by reason of what had occurred in the first (*Abu Dhabi Gas Liquefaction Co Ltd v Eastern Bechtel Corporation* [1982] 2 Lloyd's Rep 425). (See Chapter 10 p. 297 below for the consolidation of arbitrations).

The same principles of appointment would apply where an arbitrator is appointed for two rent review arbitrations on adjoining shops with the same landlord but different tenants.

The second power possessed by the court to appoint an arbitrator or umpire arises where the court revokes an arbitrator's authority or removes him (see below). Section 25 of the 1950 Act (Appendix C p. 474 below) empowers the court to appoint a replacement arbitrator or umpire. Where it removes an arbitrator (who is not a sole arbitrator), or two or more arbitrators (being *all* the arbitrators), or an umpire who has *not* entered on the reference, the court may, on the application of any party to the arbitration agreement, appoint a replacement arbitrator or umpire (section 25(1)). Where the court revokes the authority of an arbitrator, or arbitrators or umpire, or removes a sole arbitrator, or *all* the arbitrators or an umpire who *has* entered on the reference, it may, on the application of any party to the arbitration agreement, either appoint a sole arbitrator to decide the dispute or order that the arbitration agreement shall cease to have effect with respect to that dispute (section 25(2)). A person appointed by the court under the above provisions has the same powers as if he had been appointed in accordance with the arbitration agreement (section 25(3)). Where the court orders that an arbitration agreement shall cease to have effect and it is provided (whether in the agreement or otherwise) that an award shall be a condition precedent to the bringing of an action in the courts, the court may further order that this particular provision shall cease to have effect as regards that dispute (section 25(4)).

Thirdly, where the court does not otherwise have power to appoint, it may appoint an arbitrator with the consent of *all* the parties to the arbitration agreement.

(3) Revocation of appointment and removal

An arbitrator's appointment may be revoked (a) by agreement between the parties, or (b) by order of the court. In addition, his authority will cease when he has completed his duties, e.g. by the making of an award.

(a) *Revocation by agreement.* An arbitrator's authority derives from the arbitration agreement; it follows, therefore, that this authority may be expressly revoked with the agreement of *all* parties. Alternatively, the parties may impliedly revoke his authority by agreeing not to submit the dispute to arbitration at all but to resolve it by other means, e.g. by an action in the courts. The parties may settle their dispute by agreement with the following consequential effects on the arbitrator's authority.

Where the parties settle the dispute by agreement after the arbitrator has made his award, he will not be involved: at this stage in the proceedings he is *functus officio*. He will, however, be concerned if the parties reach agreement before he makes his award. Two alternative situations will arise.

First, he may be actively involved by the parties in their settlement. Where a settlement is reached and the parties agree to an award being made in the terms of that settlement (a consent award), the arbitrator retains his authority but it is varied from authority to decide the dispute to authority to make an award in the agreed terms. The arbitrator should satisfy himself that he can lawfully make such an award. Secondly, the arbitrator may not be involved by the parties in their settlement. In this case, they settle their differences by agreement but do not require him to issue a consent award. His authority ceases when this settlement is made and he becomes *functus officio*, but still has a right to his remuneration up to the date of settlement.

(b) *Revocation by order of court.* Part of the supervisory jurisdiction over arbitrations possessed by the court lies in its power to revoke an arbitrator's authority, to remove him (with resultant powers of re-appointment as discussed above) and, in certain circumstances, to order that the arbitration agreement shall cease to have effect in relation to that dispute. These powers are exercised on the application of one or more of the parties by the issue of an injunction, or a declaration, or by an order under the general or specific provisions for revocation in the 1950 Act.

In general, one or other of the following situations will arise where the court exercises the above powers: either the arbitration will cease, e.g. by the issue of an injunction or the revocation of the arbitrator's appointment coupled with an order that the arbitration agreement shall cease to have effect, or the arbitration will continue with a new arbitrator appointed by the court.

(i) *Injunction and declaration.* The court has an inherent jurisdiction to issue an injunction to restrain the arbitration proceedings at the request of one of the parties.

An injunction may be granted where the arbitrator is corrupt (*Malmesbury Ry v Budd* (1876) 2 Ch D 113), unfit to act or incompetent (*Kitts v Moore & Co* [1895] 1 QB 253), or where there is a dispute in the courts as to the validity of the arbitration agreement (*Beddow v Beddow* (1878) 9 Ch D 89). An injunction will not usually be issued on the grounds of excessive delay in the prosecution of a claim. Thus, in *Bremer Vulcan Schiffbau Und Maschinenfabrik v South India Shipping Corporation Ltd* [1981] AC 909, the House of Lords held that where there has been a repudiatory breach of an arbitration agreement by one of the parties and the other has treated the agreement as at an end, he could obtain an injunction to stop the arbitration. But (by a majority) that in this case both parties were under an obligation to keep the arbitration proceedings moving and one party, in the absence of an application to the arbitrator to prevent inordinate delay, could not rely on the other's inaction to treat the agreement as at an end.

This decision was quickly distinguished by the Court of Appeal but then reaffirmed by the House of Lords in *Paal Wilson & Co A/S v Partenreederei Hannah Blumenthal* [1982] 3 WLR 1149, where it was held that an arbitration agreement could not be repudiated due to excessive delay by one of the parties, even though such delay would justify the dismissal of an action in the courts for want of prosecution. If there was inordinate delay by the claimant, the respondent could and should request the arbitrator to issue peremptory directions to end the delay and, if the claimant failed to do so, the arbitrator could apply to the court for power to dismiss the claim under section 5 of the Arbitration Act 1979 (see Chapter 10 p. 296

below). Frustration and abandonment were two other concepts advocated in this case to justify the application for a declaration that the arbitration agreement had been discharged and for an injunction restraining further proceedings.

It was held in respect of frustration, that an arbitration agreement could not be frustrated by excessive delay by one or both of the parties, because both parties were under an obligation to apply to the arbitrator to prevent such delay and failure to do so thereby excluded the operation of the doctrine of frustration. The fact that delay would prevent a satisfactory hearing by the arbitrator was not a good reason in law for holding that an arbitration had been frustrated.

Where a party claims that an arbitration has been abandoned by mutual agreement, be must prove: first, that the conduct relied on as constituting abandonment was such as to induce a reasonable belief that abandonment was intended, and, secondly, that he did in fact believe such intention and acted on it to his detriment.

Where the court is unable to grant an injunction it may issue a declaration stating that the arbitrator is unfit or incompetent or that the reference is outside his jurisdiction (*The Phonizien* [1966] 1 Lloyd's Rep 150). Section 24(1) of the 1950 Act provides that an injunction to restrain arbitration proceedings on the grounds that the arbitrator might not be impartial shall not be refused because the applicant knew or ought to have known when he made the agreement that the arbitrator might not be capable of acting impartially (see p. 283 below).

(ii) *Revocation and removal under the Arbitration Act 1950.* The 1950 Act contains a general power of revocation by the court (section 1) and several specific powers of revocation (sections 7, 13(3), 23(1) and 24(2)). As explained above (p. 279), section 25 of the 1950 Act gives the court power to appoint a new arbitrator to replace one or more arbitrators or umpires which it has removed.

General power of revocation (section 1) (Appendix C p. 466 below). This section provides that "the authority of an arbitrator or umpire appointed by virtue of an arbitration agreement shall, unless a contrary intention is expressed in the agreement, be irrevocable except by leave of the High Court or a judge thereof". Thus, the court has a general power to consider applications for the revocation of an arbitrator's appointment and to grant leave to revoke it where it thinks fit. The removal of an arbitrator is a serious matter, for him and for the parties, who must begin the whole proceedings again. It is, therefore, a remedy of last resort and the court should not intervene in this way with an established reference unless it is convinced that this is the only right course to take (*Succula Ltd v Harland & Wolff Ltd* [1980] 2 Lloyd's Rep 381 at p. 388).

The grounds on which the court may exercise this discretion to revoke include: excess or refusal of jurisdiction (e.g. where an arbitrator admits evidence of a claim which is outside his jurisdiction (*Re Gerard (Lord) & London & North Western Ry* [1895] 1 QB 459) or, conversely, where he refuses to hear evidence on a valid claim); misconduct by the arbitrator (see below) (*European & American SS Co v Croskey & Co* (1860) 8 CB (NS) 397); the disqualification of the arbitrator from acting in that dispute (see p. 274 above). The court may also exercise its discretion to grant leave to revoke where injustice would be done and the applicant has no other remedy available to him (*Cooper v Shuttleworth* (1856) 25 LJ Ex 114).

Section 24(1) of the 1950 Act (Appendix C p. 473 below) states that, where an arbitration agreement provides for possible future disputes to be referred to a named or designated arbitrator and, after a dispute has arisen, application is made to the court for the revocation of that appointment (or for an injunction) for reasons of partiality, it shall not be a ground for refusing such application that the applicant knew or ought to have known when he made the agreement that the arbitrator might not be impartial because of his relation towards any party or his connection with the subject-matter of the dispute.

As stated above (p. 265), the authority of an arbitrator is not revoked by the death of the party who appointed him (section 2(2)), nor is an arbitration agreement discharged by the death of any party to it (section 2(1)). These provisions do not affect any enactment or rule of law under which a right of action is extinguished by the death of a person (section 2(3)).

The general power to grant leave to revoke contained in section 1, overlaps with the specific powers given by later sections of the Act, and discussed below, e.g. an application to remove an arbitrator on grounds of misconduct may be brought under section 1 or section 23(1).

Revocation of a replacement appointment (section 7) (Appendix C p. 467 below). As discussed above (p. 276), section 7 is concerned with an arbitration agreement that requires the appointment of two arbitrators, one by each party. It deals with two situations: first, where a party's arbitrator refuses to act or cannot do so, and the appointing party appoints a replacement; secondly, where one party fails to appoint, and the appointed person becomes the sole arbitrator. In both cases, the court may set aside the appointment and then has power, on the application

of any party to the arbitration agreement, to appoint another
person to act as sole arbitrator in the dispute (section 25(1)).

*Revocation due to delay (section 13(3)) (Appendix C p. 470
below).* Where an arbitrator or umpire "fails to use all reasonable dispatch in entering on and proceeding with the reference
and making an award" he may be removed by 'the court on the
application of any party to the reference. An arbitrator or
umpire removed under this sub-section loses his right to
remuneration.

Delay under section 13(3) means delay by the arbitrator
and not by the parties. It means serious delay sufficient to
amount to misconduct. An arbitrator will not be guilty of
delay where he has not been required to take any action by the
parties (*Succula Ltd v Harland & Wolff Ltd* [1980] 2 Lloyd's Rep
381).

It would appear that a dilatory arbitrator should be called
upon to proceed with the reference before application is made
to the court to remove him (*Drummond v Hamer* [1942] 1 All ER
398 at p. 401). An award made after a summons to remove the
arbitrator has been issued may still be valid (*Lewis Emanuel &
Son Ltd v Sammut* [1959] 2 Lloyd's Rep 629). Where delay is
caused by the arbitrator's misconduct, this is not necessarily a
failure to use "reasonable dispatch" and the arbitrator ought
not to be removed for delay under section 13(3) but for misconduct under section 23(1) (see below) (*Pratt v Swanmore
Builders Ltd* [1980] 2 Lloyd's Rep 504).

*Revocation due to misconduct (section 23(1)) (Appendix C p. 473
below).* Under this sub-section the court may remove an arbitrator or umpire who has misconducted himself or the proceedings. The term "misconduct" is used here in a legal or
technical sense. It means irregularity and not moral turpitude
(*London Export Corporation Ltd v Jubilee Coffee Roasting Co Ltd*
[1958] 1 WLR 661 at p. 665).

Misconduct by an arbitrator which leads to his removal by
the court will be of the more serious kind. In *Modern Engineering
(Bristol) Ltd v C. Miskin & Son Ltd* [1981] 1 Lloyd's Rep 135,
Lord Denning MR stated that the test of removal for misconduct was (p. 138):

> "... whether his conduct was such as to destroy the confidence
> of the parties, or either of them, in his ability to come to a fair
> and just conclusion."

Misconduct is discussed in detail in Chapter 12 pp. 374 and
377 below but it will be briefly described here under three
broad headings.

First, it may be misconduct outside the arbitration proceedings, e.g. where the arbitrator takes a bribe from one of the parties. Secondly, an arbitrator will be guilty of misconduct where he fails to act judicially in his conduct of the proceedings, e.g. where he gives himself evidence without giving the parties an opportunity of dealing with it (*Fox v P. G. Wellfair Ltd* [1981] 2 Lloyd's Rep 514). Thirdly, the misconduct may be of a technical nature, e.g. where the arbitrator makes an excessive charge for his services (*Appleton v Norwich Union Fire Insurance Society Ltd* (1922) 13 Ll L Rep 345).

Not all mistakes or misbehaviour amount to misconduct, e.g. it is not misconduct in itself for an arbitrator to make an error of fact or law (*Schofield v Allen* (1904) 116 LTJ 239), although where he makes numerous mistakes in his conduct of the proceedings these may be evidence of incompetence amounting to misconduct (*Pratt v Swanmore Builders Ltd* [1980] 2 Lloyd's Rep 504).

Revocation where dispute relates to fraud (section 24(2)) (Appendix C p.473 below). Where an agreement provides that future disputes shall be referred to arbitration, and a dispute which so arises involves the question whether any party has been guilty of fraud, the court shall, so far as may be necessary to enable that question to be determined by the court, have power to order that this agreement shall cease to have effect and to give leave to revoke the arbitrator's authority.

STAY OF CONCURRENT PROCEEDINGS IN COURT

(1) Arbitration not terminated by action

An agreement to refer present or future differences to arbitration does not prevent a party from commencing an action in the courts in respect of a dispute covered by that agreement. An arbitration clause which seeks to prohibit access to the courts is an ouster of the court's jurisdiction and void on grounds of public policy. Furthermore, the parties cannot remove their rights under the 1979 Act to appeal to the courts on a question of law, or to ask for an order for reasons in an award or to ask the court to determine a preliminary point of law, except by an "exclusion agreement" under section 3 of the 1979 Act (see Chapter 12 p.366 below). An arbitration agreement specifies the tribunal chosen by the parties to determine their dispute, but it is for the court to decide whether it will assume jurisdiction over that dispute or whether, on the application of a party to the agreement, it will stay court proceedings and thus force the notional plaintiff back to arbitration.

An arbitration is not brought to an end by the commencement of an action by one of the parties relating to a matter covered by the arbitration agreement. Thus, in *Lloyd v Wright* [1983] 3 WLR 223, a dispute was referred to arbitration and the plaintiffs subsequently issued a writ with a statement of claim which substantially repeated the points of claim in the arbitration. The arbitrator made an order for discovery and inspection of documents and for the service of further and better particulars of defence. The defendant issued a summons to stay the court proceedings, but then withdrew it and was given an extension of time to serve a defence. The following day the parties appeared before a master on the plaintiffs' summons for an order requiring the defendant to comply with the arbitrator's above order. The master dismissed the summons on the grounds that the commencement of an action in the courts rendered the arbitrator *functus officio*.

It was held on appeal by the Court of Appeal that an arbitration is not terminated by one party issuing a writ in respect of the same dispute. Unless that party consented to discontinue his action or the court ordered a stay of proceedings, the court will grant its assistance and, if necessary, retain control of the matter. The arbitration could continue concurrently with the action in the courts although the arbitrator could not make an effective award while the action subsisted, without the agreement of the parties. In this case, therefore, the Court of Appeal restored the order made on an appeal from the master to a judge in chambers, requiring the defendant to comply with the arbitrator's order.

(2) Statutory provisions

The statutory provisions which give the court discretion to accept or reject jurisdiction over a dispute covered by an arbitration agreement are sections 4, 5 and 24(3) of the 1950 Act.

Section 4 provides that, if any party to an arbitration agreement commences legal proceedings in any court against another party to that agreement, in respect of any matter agreed to be referred to arbitration, any other party to those proceedings may apply to that court to stay them (Appendix C p. 466 below). The court *may* make an order staying the proceedings provided it is satisfied on two matters. First, that there is no sufficient reason why the matter should not be referred to arbitration under the agreement; secondly, that the applicant is, and was at the commencement of the proceedings, ready and willing to do all things necessary to the proper conduct of the arbitration. An application to stay court proceedings may be made at any time after the applicant has entered an appearance but before the delivery of pleadings or the taking of any other steps in the proceedings (see Chapter 1 p. 5 above for appearance and pleadings).

Where a person under a liability for a debt or any money, goods or chattels is, or expects to be, sued by two or more persons, he may seek relief against these conflicting claims by an interpleader summons. Where such relief is granted by the High Court and it appears that the claims in question are matters to which an arbitration agreement, to which the claimants are parties, applies then the court may direct the issue between the claimants to be determined under that agreement (section 5 of the 1950 Act, Appendix C p. 467 below). The discretion of the court under section 5 is to be exercised on similar grounds to the exercise of the discretion under section 4 (see below) (*Re Phoenix Timber Co Ltd's Application* [1958] 2 QB 1 at p. 7).

Section 24(3) of the 1950 Act provides that, where the court has power to order that an arbitration agreement shall cease to have effect or to revoke an arbitrator's authority under section 24 (partiality or fraud), then it *may* refuse to stay any action brought in breach of the arbitration agreement (Appendix C p. 473 below).

The above provisions give the court a *discretion* to stay proceedings, and this must be exercised "judicially". The court must not act capriciously but must show a proper reason connected with the case for the exercise of its discretion. In particular, the exercise of a discretion must not produce a manifest injustice (for further discussion of discretion see Chapter 11 p. 345 below).

The following examples illustrate the exercise of the court's discretion to stay proceedings:

(a) Where the dispute involves questions of fraud, dishonesty, incompetence or other personal charges, the court will usually refuse a stay and allow the action to continue (*Turner v Fenton* [1982] 1 All ER 8).

(b) Normally, the plaintiff's poverty, which would render it financially impossible or additionally expensive for him to go to arbitration, will not in itself be a sufficient ground for the court to refuse to order a stay. Thus, the court will not allow an action in court to continue merely because the plaintiff is poor (*Smith v Pearl Assurance Co* [1939] 1 All ER 95, *Ford v Clarksons Holidays* [1971] 1 WLR 1412). But where the plaintiff is able to bring an action in the courts due to legal aid, which would not be available for arbitration, *and* his poverty is due to the defendant's own conduct, the court will refuse to order a stay of proceedings (*Fakes v Taylor Woodrow Construction Ltd* [1973] 1 QB 436).

(c) The court will be reluctant to grant a stay where the principal issue in the dispute is a point of law or a question of the construction of documents (see *Turner* above). Where, however, the question of law relates to technical matters connected with questions of fact, the court may order a stay to allow these matters to be decided by the arbitration (*Metropolitan Tunnel etc Ltd v London Electric Ry* [1926] 1 Ch 371).

(d) A stay may be refused where the arbitrator has misconducted himself, is disqualified from acting, has an interest in the subject-matter of the dispute or is otherwise biased (*Blackwell v Derby Corporation* (1911) 75 JP 129).

(e) Where a contract contains a clause making an arbitration award a condition precedent to an action in the courts (a "*Scott v Avery* clause"), the court will stay proceedings commenced before an award has been made (*Scott v Avery* (1851) 5 HLC 811).

CHAPTER TEN

Law of Arbitration—II

Duties of an arbitrator; procedure; evidence.

INTRODUCTION

In Chapter 9 I discuss matters leading to the commencement of a reference to arbitration (e.g. the appointment of an arbitrator) and other matters outside usual arbitration procedure (e.g. the stay of concurrent proceedings in court). I now turn to a detailed consideration of the law relating to procedure after the appointment of an arbitrator. This chapter deals with his powers and duties before and at a hearing and the law of evidence applicable to arbitration. Chapter 11 takes the arbitration process one step further by considering the arbitrator's award and Chapter 12 completes the process by looking at the position after the award. These chapters deal mainly with the law; Chapter 13 is a practical example of a rent review arbitration.

DUTIES OF AN ARBITRATOR

The acceptance by a person of an arbitral appointment gives him certain powers and imposes on him certain duties. These are now discussed, commencing with his duties. They arise out of the arbitrator's judicial role and may be found in the arbitration agreement, the Arbitration Acts and the rules of natural justice.

(1) Duties imposed by the arbitration agreement
In arbitration by consent, the arbitrator derives his authority from the arbitration agreement. This also imposes on him certain duties.

An arbitrator's first duty is to check that his appointment is in order and in accordance with the agreement. For example, he must ask himself whether the agreement requires him to have specified qualifications, skills or experience and, if so, whether he satisfies those requirements. Is the appointment immediately effective, allowing him to proceed with the reference, or must further steps be taken before it becomes effective? Is the appointment really that of an arbitrator or is he an independent expert (see Chapter 7 p. 193 above)? These, and possibly other questions according to the circumstances of each case, must be answered before the arbitrator can be satisfied that his appointment is valid and effective.

Where an arbitrator is appointed by the parties, he should ask to
see the arbitration agreement and satisfy on the above matters *before*
accepting the appointment. But, where an appointment is made by a
third party, the arbitrator does not usually see the agreement until
after he has been appointed. He must rely on the appointor to satisfy
himself on these matters although he should check them all on
appointment. If he subsequently discovers that his appointment is
not valid, he may decide that he cannot proceed with the arbitration,
but his authority can only be revoked with the agreement of all parties
or by order of the court. Moreover, the appointing third party will
have become *functus officio* and, in the absence of specific power to do
so in the agreement, has no power to make a second appointment. In
practice it is open to the parties to ratify the arbitrator's appointment,
thus waiving the invalidity, or to revoke it and either appoint a replacement arbitrator or request the appointing third party to do so.
But where agreement cannot be reached application must be made to
the court under section 1 of the 1950 Act for leave to revoke the arbitrator's authority.

An arbitrator's second duty under the agreement is to ascertain the
extent of his jurisdiction. He may only decide the dispute submitted
to him and may not go outside his jurisdiction when making his
award, however fair and just that may appear to him to be (see
Chapter 9 p. 267 above). As stated below (p. 302), an arbitrator has
no power to determine his own jurisdiction.

Finally, the arbitrator must consider whether the arbitration
agreement requires him to follow a particular procedure. Thus, in
Spence v Eastern Counties Ry (1839) 7 Dowl 697, the arbitrator was
required to view the property, the subject-matter of the dispute,
within a stated time before proceeding with the reference. Failure to
do so would be a reason for questioning the validity of his award on
the ground that he had not acted in accordance with the powers given
to him.

Where an arbitration agreement is silent as to the procedure to be
followed the arbitrator has a discretion in the matter, subject to his
overriding duty to act impartially and fairly. This normally requires
him to observe the ordinary basic rules of procedure adopted by arbitrators, the courts and other judicial tribunals. The parties may, however, agree that these ordinary rules shall not apply. The arbitrator
will be bound to give effect to such an agreement, unless it "is so contrary to fundamental principles that it is treated as contrary to public
policy" and, therefore, unenforceable (per Scrutton LJ in *Nauman v
Nathan* (1930) 37 Ll L Rep 249). For example, in *E. E. & Brian
Smith (1928) Ltd v Wheatsheaf Mills Ltd* [1939] 2 KB 302, the question
arose as to whether two claims could be brought in respect of one
cause of arbitration. It was held that the arbitration agreement was

subject to the rules of a trade association, a custom of which was that disputes might be settled in stages. This custom was not illegal, it was convenient and, therefore, the general rule of law that a person could only claim relief once in respect of one cause of action did not apply to this matter.

The fact that an arbitration is a commercial arbitration is not in itself a reason for departing from the ordinary rules of procedure. Where, however, the parties clearly intend the arbitration to be conducted in accordance with the established procedures of a particular trade (which may not follow the ordinary rules), the arbitrator will be bound to do so and the court will not set aside his award on this ground. For example, disputes relating to quality (e.g. of goods, materials or crops) are frequently referred, by the practice of a particular trade, to an expert arbitrator who bases his decision solely on his own inspection:

> "... a trade tribunal is entitled to make use of its own know-ledge and indeed in a quality dispute it is often wholly appropriate that the tribunal should itself 'look and sniff' if this is the best way of determining the issue between the parties. Indeed this is much better than evidence of others as to what they saw and smelt, ie 'hear-sniff' evidence."
> (per Donaldson J in *Faure, Fairclough Ltd v Premier Oil & Cake Mills Ltd* [1968] 1 Lloyd's Rep 237 at p. 240).

These arbitrations are distinguishable from those with more formal proceedings where the arbitrator bases his award on submissions and evidence, and it is this latter type of arbitration which is used for disputed rent reviews in leases and disputes under building and civil engineering contracts (see p. 314 below).

An arbitrator has a duty to apply a fixed and recognisable system of law to the facts of the dispute before him. This will primarily and normally be English Law. He must not decide the matter according to his own views of abstract justice or equitable principles (*Orion Compania Espanola de Seguros v Belfort Maatschappij Voor Algemene Verzekgringun* [1962] 2 Lloyd's Rep 257).

It is not wholly clear whether an arbitrator owes a duty of care to the parties to the arbitration agreement. This matter is discussed in Chapter 7 p. 206 above.

(2) Duties imposed by Arbitration Acts

The Arbitration Acts are mainly permissive, that is to say that, in the absence of a contrary intention in the arbitration agreement, they give an arbitrator powers which he may use if he so wishes. The Acts also impose duties on an arbitrator. For example, in the absence of a contrary intention in the arbitration agreement, section

8(1) of the 1950 Act states that when a reference is made to two arbitrators, the agreement shall be deemed to include a provision that the arbitrators shall have *power* to appoint an umpire at any time, but, if they cannot agree, then they have a *duty* to appoint one forthwith (see Chapter 9 p. 276 above). Section 1(2) of the 1979 Act imposes a duty on an arbitrator, whose award is remitted to him by the High Court for reconsideration following an appeal on a point of law, to make his award within three months, unless directed otherwise (see Chapter 12 p. 360 below).

(3) Duties imposed by the rules of natural justice

Arbitration is a judicial process and is, therefore, subject to the rules of natural justice:

> "Arbitrators are not merely valuers; they have judicial functions to perform. Though intending no injustice they must observe the fundamental rules which govern judicial proceedings."
>
> (per Mathew J in *Re Gregson and Armstrong* (1894) 70 LT 106).

There are two basic rules of natural justice. First, a man may not be judge in his own cause, i.e. he must not be biased (see Chapter 9 p. 274 above). He must act fairly and impartially and treat both parties equally. Secondly, each party must have notice of the case against him and be given a reasonable opportunity to reply to it and to state his own case. This is known as the *audi alteram partem* rule. For example, an arbitrator must not hear one party in the absence of the other, unless he is forced to proceed *ex parte* due to the obstructive conduct of one of the parties (*Harvey v Shelton* (1844) 7 Beav 455). He must not receive secret information from one party which he does not disclose to the other (*Re Camillo Eitzen & Jewson & Sons* (1896) 40 SJ 438). He should not give himself evidence without giving the parties an opportunity to reply to it (see p. 317 below). He should not determine a dispute (including issuing an interim award) without hearing both parties (see p. 324 below), but there is no rule of natural justice which entitles a litigant to put his case in any form he pleases, e.g. by film, tape recording, writing or any other method, nor to conduct his case in writing without attending a hearing (*Banin v MacKinlay* [1984] 1 All ER 1116). The two rules of natural justice are separate concepts governed by separate considerations.

A breach of the rules of natural justice occurs where a person has or *might have* suffered injustice by what has been done or failed to be done. Natural justice is concerned with matters of substance and not with the observance of mere technicalities. There cannot, therefore, be a technical breach of the rules of natural justice (*George v Secretary of State for the Environment* (1979) 250 EG 339).

ARBITRATION PROCEDURE

An arbitrator should be guided by his duty to act fairly and impartially between the parties so that he may achieve a fair, just and efficient procedure.

The conduct of an arbitration is a matter wholly within the discretion of the arbitrator, but he should keep control over the proceedings. He should make firm decisions after listening to the arguments addressed to him, leaving it to the parties to take action, by appeal or otherwise, if they are dissatisfied. An arbitrator will not be criticised for taking a wrong decision, provided it is not unfair or contrary to the rules of natural justice, but he would be open to criticism by the courts if he did not exercise firm control over the proceedings (see the remarks of Donaldson LJ in *F. G. Whitley & Sons Co Ltd v Clwyd County Council* (1982) 22 BLR 48).

A summary of arbitration procedure from the initial letter to the parties to the conclusion of the hearing is set out below. It is necessarily a mixture of law and practice, and the latter is considered further in Chapter 13.

(1) Procedure: before the hearing

(a) *Initial letter to the parties.* After an arbitrator has carried out his three initial duties, namely checking the validity of his appointment, determining the extent of his jurisdiction and ascertaining the procedure to be followed, he should write an initial letter to the parties. This will contain some or all of the following matters: notification of his appointment (particularly when made by a third party), an inquiry as to whether the parties require further time for negotiations towards a settlement, the form of arbitration (oral hearing or written representations), an inquiry as to whether there appears to be an issue of law in the dispute, directions that no "without prejudice" or other privileged matter be put before the arbitrator and that copies of the letters, etc sent to the arbitrator be sent to the other party, fees and a time limit for reply. An example of an initial letter is contained in Chapter 13 p. 390 below.

(b) *Preliminary meeting.* Where *all* parties agree to written representations, the arbitrator will probably be able to issue his directions for the submission and content of those representations without the need for a preliminary meeting. Where, however, a hearing is to be held, or the dispute is not a simple one, then a preliminary meeting should be arranged. This is similar to a pre-trial review in Lands Tribunal proceedings (see Chapter 1 p. 16 above). The purpose of such a meeting is to inform the arbitrator of the general nature of the dispute so that he can issue directions for the future conduct of the arbitration. In complicated cases several preliminary meetings may be necessary. Before the preliminary meeting the arbitrator should send the parties a letter stating the date and time with a request that they notify him and each other of the names and positions of those attending. Where a party intends to be represented at the hearing by a solicitor or counsel, the solicitor should be urged to attend the preliminary meeting and, if counsel is also to be instructed, that he should have discussed the likely or required directions with him. The arbitrator may enclose with his letter his draft directions for comment and agreement at the preliminary meeting. Suggested wording for such a letter is set out in Chapter 13 p. 391 below.

The arbitrator should not receive evidence at a preliminary meeting nor deal with the substantive issues in the dispute: the subject-matter of such a meeting is procedure. Before the meeting he should prepare a check-list of points which he thinks should be considered. He should open by giving his name, details of his appointment and the nature of the dispute. The parties should then identify themselves and their representatives. The arbitrator will question the parties on the points on his list, allowing each party to make a statement in turn. The arbitrator may receive submissions and applications from the parties on procedural matters.

The matters to be considered at a preliminary meeting will include the following:

(i) who is to be the claimant and who the respondent (in a rent review arbitration the party who initiated the reference, e.g. by application for the appointment of an arbitrator, is designated the claimant and the other party is the respondent);

(ii) representation at the hearing, in particular, whether counsel are to be briefed (all parties should be given the opportunity to brief counsel and one party should not be taken by surprise at the hearing);

(iii) the general nature of the dispute and whether the respondent intends to make a counterclaim;

(iv) the possibility of a settlement and whether the proceedings should be deferred to allow further negotiations;

(v) whether the arbitration agreement contains any impediment to the continuation of the arbitration or whether any special procedure is to be followed;

(vi) the nature and timetable for the exchange of pleadings;

(vii) the preparation of a statement of agreed facts, agreed maps, plans and other exhibits;

(viii) the maximum number of expert witnesses to be called by the parties and the prior exchange of their reports or proofs;

(ix) whether the dispute contains an issue of law (including a preliminary point of law) and how it is to be dealt with;

(x) whether the parties intend to enter into an exclusion agreement under section 3 of the 1979 Act (see Chapter 12 p. 366 below);

(xi) the venue for the hearing, the estimated length and possible dates (it is likely that the date of the hearing can only be fixed after the arbitrator has issued his directions following the preliminary meeting);

(xii) whether a shorthand transcript of the hearing will be required and who will bear the cost;

(xiii) whether one or both of the parties require a reasoned award (see Chapter 11 p. 332 below);

(xiv) whether it is desirable for the arbitrator to make a preliminary inspection before the hearing;

(xv) security for costs (see p. 298 below).

The above list is not exhaustive but contains most of the points likely to arise in an arbitration.

(c) *Order for directions.* After the preliminary meeting, the arbitrator will issue his order for directions, which may or may not have been agreed by the parties at that meeting. These directions require the parties to take certain action and follow certain procedures before the hearing. They are normally drafted in imperative terms and typical items in such an order are:

(i) the name of the claimant and respondent respectively;

(ii) the timetable for the submission and exchange of pleadings;

(iii) the preparation of a statement of agreed facts, agreed maps, plans and other exhibits.

(iv) any restrictions on the number of expert witnesses to be called by the parties and a timetable for the exchange of their valuations, reports or proofs;

(v) the dates and times of any inspections of the property by the arbitrator;

(vi) the date, time and venue of the hearing;

(vii) a warning that "without prejudice" statements or other privileged matter must not be disclosed to the arbitrator;

(viii) a reminder that facts to be adduced in evidence at the hearing must be agreed or proved by admissible evidence;

(ix) the form of the award: with or without reasons;

(x) where applicable, that lists of documents relevant to the dispute which are or have been in the possession, custody or power of the respective parties shall be exchanged within a stated time after the close of the pleadings (discovery of documents);

(xi) costs of the directions are to be costs in the arbitration;

(xii) the parties are to identify any issues of law in the dispute and are each to submit a brief summary of their arguments thereon with a list of supporting cases and statutory provisions;

(xiii) the parties "shall be at liberty to apply", that is to say any party may apply to the arbitrator for the cancellation or amendment of the order for directions.

An example of an order for directions in a rent review arbitration is included in Chapter 13 p. 393 below.

In a simple arbitration only one order for directions will be necessary. But where the issues are complicated or one of the parties is unco-operative, the arbitrator may need to issue several orders for directions, particularly "peremptory" orders requiring the reluctant party to take certain action or suffer the consequence of the arbitration proceeding in his absence.

Where a party fails to comply with an arbitrator's directions within the time specified or within a reasonable time, then the arbitrator or another party may apply to the High Court under section 5 of the 1979 Act (Appendix C p. 508 below) for an order extending the arbitrator's powers to enable him to deal effectively with the situation. The arbitrator should first give the parties (or one of them) notice that unless his directions are complied with within a stated time, he intends to make such an application.

An order made by the court under section 5 may, subject to any conditions attached to it, allow the arbitrator to continue with the reference in default of appearance or of any other act by the unco-operative party, in the same manner as a judge might continue with proceedings where a litigant fails to comply with an order of court or a requirement of rules of court. For example, the arbitrator may prevent the respondent from defending where he has failed to supply particulars, or refuse to allow certain evidence to be given where the party seeking to adduce it has failed to comply with directions in respect of such evidence, e.g. exchange of an expert witness proof. In particular, an order under this section may give the arbitrator power to proceed *ex parte*, (which he already has by virtue of his judicial office but which is of uncertain extent) or to dismiss a claim for want of prosecution.

Section 5(5) of the 1979 Act provides that the powers given to an arbitrator by an order under this section cannot be excluded or over-ridden by the arbitration agreement. Conversely, similar powers given by that agreement or otherwise are not reduced by the new powers under section 5. This section should be- distinguished from section 12(6) of the 1950 Act which allows the High Court to assist the arbitrator by making orders for certain interlocutory matters such as security for costs and discovery of documents (see pp. 298 and 301 below).

Where the parties have agreed to written representations, an order for directions will be shorter and simpler. It will usually include the following matters:

(i) the preparation of a statement of agreed facts, agreed maps, plans and other exhibits;

(ii) the dates for the submission to the arbitrator of representations and cross-representations in duplicate, one copy of each then to be sent by him to the other party;

(iii) a reminder that cross-representations are to be restricted to comment on the other party's representations and are not to contain new matter;

(iv) a reminder that facts contained in written representations must be proved or agreed;

(v) a warning that "without prejudice" or other privileged statements are not to be disclosed to the arbitrator;

(vi) the date and time of the arbitrator's view of the property (frequently reserved for later notification);

(vii) a reservation by the arbitrator of his right to direct a hearing if he considers this necessary following his reading of the representations.

(d) *Consolidation.* Unlike the High Court, an arbitrator has no general power to consolidate separate references to arbitration or to join third parties to the proceedings. He may only do so under express powers in the arbitration agreement or with the consent of all parties. Thus, where A is the landlord of two adjoining shops let to B and C respectively and rent reviews on both shops are submitted to the same arbitrator under separate references, he cannot consolidate them unless both leases give him power to do so or he has the agreement of A, B and C. Where X has a claim against Y, which is referred to arbitration, and Y has an indemnity from Z, the arbitrator cannot join Z in the arbitration unless there is express provision for this in the arbitration agreement or he obtains the agreement of all three parties.

The position was recently summarised by Legatt J in *Oxford Shipping Co Ltd v Nippon Yusen Kaisha* [1984] 2 Lloyd's Rep 373 at p. 379:

"... arbitrators enjoy no power to order concurrent hearings, or anything of that nature, without the consent of the parties. The concept of private arbitrations derives simply from the fact that the parties have agreed to submit to arbitration particular disputes arising between them and only between them. It is implicit in this that strangers shall be excluded from the hearing and conduct of the arbitration and that neither the tribunal nor any of the parties can insist that the dispute shall be heard or determined concurrently with or even in consonance with another dispute, however convenient that course may be to the parties seeking it and however closely associated with each other the disputes in question may be. The only powers which an arbitrator enjoys relate to the reference in which he has been appointed. They cannot be extended merely because a similar dispute exists which is capable of being and is referred separately to arbitration under a different agreement."

The High Court may be able to achieve some degree of rationalisation of separate references by the exercise of its powers to remove and replace arbitrators, particularly by the appointment of a single arbitrator to hear separate references arising out of the same facts (see Chapter 9 p. 279 above).

(e) *Security for costs.* An arbitrator has no general power to order the parties to give security for costs. He may only do so if there is an express provision to that effect in the arbitration agreement (*Re Unione Stearinerie Lanza & Wiener* [1917] 2 KB 558).

The court may make an order for security for costs under either section 12(6)(a) of the 1950 Act or section 28 of that Act. Section 12(6)(a) of the 1950 Act (Appendix C p. 470 below) gives the High Court the same power to make orders for security for costs in relation to a reference to arbitration as it has in relation to its own proceedings. This power cannot be removed by agreement between the parties because section 12(6) of the 1950 Act is not qualified by the words "unless a contrary intention is expressed" in the arbitration agreement (unlike most other sections of the Act). Section 28 of the 1950 Act (Appendix C p. 475 below) provides that any order made by the court may be made on such terms as to costs or otherwise as the court thinks just. Thus, the court may include provisions relating to security for costs in any order it makes under the Act, if it considers that it is just to do so.

(f) *Pleadings.* Where an arbitration is to proceed to an oral hearing, the arbitrator will usually order an exchange of pleadings, even in a simple case. Their purpose is to isolate the matters in dispute, and to let each party know the case he will have to meet, and, therefore, the evidence he must adduce at the hearing. Pleadings in arbitration are frequently modelled on those in a High Court action commenced by writ (see Chapter 1 p. 5 above). They are as follows:

   (i) points of claim submitted by claimant;
   (ii) points of defence and any counterclaim submitted by respondent;

(iii) points of reply and any defence to counterclaim submitted by claimant;

(iv) points of reply to the defence to counterclaim submitted by respondent.

Four general points regarding pleadings should be noted. First, the order for directions will prescribe the timetable for their exchange, which should be kept by the parties unless delay is unavoidable. An arbitrator may be asked for an extension of time to deliver pleadings and he will give his decision in the form of a revised order for directions. Secondly, pleadings should contain facts and not evidence. Thirdly, pleadings deal with facts and not law, although the arbitrator may require the parties to notify him separately of any issues of law in the dispute (see p. 295 above). Fourthly, the pleadings mark out the boundaries of each party's case and they should keep within them unless leave to amend has been given.

During or after the exchange of pleadings one party may require more information about the facts in his opponent's pleadings. He will apply for "further and better particulars" of the facts in question. If he is unsuccessful he can apply to the arbitrator who has an implied power to order further particulars. Where the arbitrator is satisfied that the request is reasonable and that the applicant is not seeking delay nor "fishing" for information, he should order further and better particulars:

> "What particulars are to be stated must depend on the facts of each case. But in my opinion it is absolutely essential that the pleading, not to be embarrassing to the defendants, should state those facts which will put the defendants on their guard and tell them what they will have to meet when the case comes on for trial."
>
> (per Cotton LJ in *Philipps v Philipps* (1878) 4 QBD 127 at p. 139).

An arbitrator has no statutory powers relating expressly to the exchange of pleadings, although section 12(1) of the 1950 Act (Appendix C p. 469 below) states that, unless a contrary intention is stated therein, every arbitration agreement shall, where such a provision is applicable to the reference, be deemed to contain a provision that the parties shall, subject to any legal objection, do all things which the arbitrator may require during the proceedings. An arbitrator has the right to order pleadings under his inherent powers as a judicial officer and under the above section (*Re Crighton & The Law Car & General Insurance Corporation Ltd* [1910] 2 KB 738 at p. 745). As stated above (p. 296), the arbitrator (or any party to the reference) may apply to the High Court under section 5 of the 1979 Act for an order authorising the arbitrator to proceed *ex parte* where a party fails to comply within a stated or reasonable time with an order made by him in the course of the reference. This power could be used, for example, where one party refuses to deliver pleadings ordered by the arbitrator or is guilty of excessive delay in so doing.

An arbitrator has a discretion to allow an amendment of pleadings (see *Re Crighton* above), but he has no power to allow an amendment which introduces a new dispute or takes the existing dispute outside the scope of the arbitration agreement. An arbitrator should normally allow an amendment which can be effected without manifest injustice to the other party. An amendment may be allowed on terms that the amending party shall bear the resultant costs caused to the other party.

An arbitrator has no power to strike out a party's pleadings on the grounds of want of prosecution. Also, as discussed in Chapter 9 p. 281 above, the courts will not restrain an arbitration by injunction for inordinate and inexcusable delay. Where one party is guilty of excessive delay in pursuing his case, the other party could and should apply to the arbitrator for the issue of peremptory directions to the offending party to end that delay. If there is still failure to comply, then the arbitrator can apply to the High Court for power to dismiss the claim or to proceed *ex parte* under section 5 of the 1979 Act (*Paal Wilson & Co A/S v Partenreederei Hannah Blumenthal* [1982] 3 WLR 1149).

It should be noted that the courts have no *inherent* power to supervise arbitrations (including preliminary matters) and can only act where they have statutory powers to do so. Thus, where an arbitrator refused leave to a party to amend his pleadings, it was held that the court had no jurisdiction to order him to do so (*Exormisis Shipping SA v Oonsoo* [1975] 1 Lloyd's Rep 432). The remedy of the aggrieved party is to challenge the award, e.g. under section 23(2) of the 1950 Act on the grounds of misconduct by the arbitrator.

The pleadings described above are designed to isolate issues of fact. A different form is required where the dispute is essentially one of expert opinion, e.g. a rent review arbitration. Here, each party requires to know the opposing party's opinion of value, and the facts on which it is based. The pleadings are, therefore, a mixture of fact and opinion. Thus, in a rent review arbitration the arbitrator may order the following pleadings:

(i) where tenant's improvements are to be disregarded when assessing the review rent, the tenant is to submit to the landlord and arbitrator a list of such improvements;

(ii) the landlord is to indicate which are agreed as improvements to be disregarded and which, if any, are in dispute (these are pleadings of fact designed to isolate the improvements agreed and in dispute, the latter to be proved by evidence);

(iii) both parties are to serve on each other and the arbitrator a statement showing the rental value proposed (including all supporting calculations), any valuation assumptions (whether of fact or law) and a schedule of comparable transactions.

The arbitrator may also order the preparation of a statement of agreed facts (particularly with regard to each party's comparables), agreed maps, plans and other exhibits and may order the prior exchange of proofs of evidence or reports of expert witnesses to be called at the hearing. The above procedure may be compared with that of the Lands Tribunal and the High Court for the prior exchange of the substance of expert evidence (see Chapter 3 pp. 84 and 87 respectively).

(g) *Discovery of documents.* An order for directions may require the parties to exchange lists of *all* relevant documents after the close of pleadings. This is the first stage of discovery of documents (see Chapter 1 p. 6 above). The second stage is the inspection and copying of those documents, except where a valid objection is raised, e.g. on the grounds of privilege. Where one party is obstructive, application may be made to the arbitrator for an order for discovery. Unfortunately, the arbitrator has no power to enforce such an order but application may be made to the High Court under section 12(6)(b) of the 1950 Act (Appendix C p. 470 below) and the court has the same power to make orders for discovery of documents in an arbitration as it has in relation to its own proceedings. Also, any party to an arbitration may apply under section 12(4) of the 1950 Act (Appendix C p. 469 below) for a writ of *subpoena duces tecum* to compel a person to produce a document in his possession (see Chapter 2 p. 43 above). In addition, section 12(1) of the 1950 Act states that, unless a contrary intention is expressed therein, every arbitration agreement shall, where such a provision is applicable to the reference, be deemed to contain a provision that every party to the reference shall produce before the arbitrator all documents within their possession or power which may be required or called for, unless legal objection is raised thereto.

(h) *Interrogatories.* In an exceptional case one party may wish to administer interrogatories to another party. These are questions which must be answered on oath. Their purpose is to obtain further information about the other party's case, including admissions, and they are particularly useful where the facts sought to be revealed are solely within the knowledge of the other party. Interrogatories should not be used to "fish" for information which *might* be useful to the administering party. In the High Court leave to administer interrogatories is obtained from a master (see Chapter 1 p. 7 above). In an arbitration, an application to administer interrogatories must be made to the arbitrator, and, if satisfied, he may so order. Again, however, the arbitrator cannot himself enforce this order against a reluctant party. If persuasion is unsuccessful application may be made to the High Court, which has the same power to make orders for interrogatories in an arbitration as it has in its own proceedings (section 12(6)(b) of the 1950 Act).

(i) *Denial of jurisdiction.* The jurisdiction of an arbitrator may be questioned by one or more of the parties before or during a hearing. For example, where a rent review clause in a lease provides that the review rent shall be determined by an arbitrator, in default of agreement between the parties, one of the parties may challenge the arbitrator's jurisdiction on the grounds that no attempt has been made to agree the rent and that this was a condition precedent to his appointment (e.g. *Wrenbridge Ltd v Harries (Southern) Properties Ltd* (1981) 260 EG 1195, Chapter 9 p. 277 above).

What is an arbitrator's position when faced with a denial of his authority? He has no power to decide whether or not he has jurisdiction over the dispute submitted to him, unless he is expressly given such power by the parties (see below). He cannot make a *determination* as to existence of facts which, if they *do* exist, give him jurisdiction, but if they *do not* exist, remove that jurisdiction. For example, he cannot make a determination as to the existence or validity of a contract containing an arbitration clause under which he was appointed, nor whether he is qualified to accept the appointment nor the validity of his appointment. These are all conditions precedent to the reference which he must accept. Disputes on these matters are for the courts to decide.

An arbitrator is, however, always entitled to *inquire* whether or not he has jurisdiction (*Christopher Brown Ltd v Oesterreichischer Waldbesitzer R Gmbh* [1954] 1 QB 8). This is not a determination of the matter but an inquiry as to the position in order that he may decide what course of action to take.

Where objection is made to an arbitrator's jurisdiction he should listen to the arguments of both parties, adjourn the hearing (if necessary), perhaps seek legal advice and then make a decision as to how he should proceed. There are several courses of action open to him. He may decide that he has no jurisdiction in the matter and refuse to continue with the reference, leaving it to the parties to go to court.

He may suggest that the parties give him authority to decide the preliminary issue as to whether or not he has jurisdiction (see below). He may adjourn the proceedings to allow an application to be made to the court for a declaration or for a determination of the matter as a preliminary question of law under section 2 of the 1979 Act. In this respect he may be asked by the parties to make preliminary findings of fact to support such an application. He may be satisfied that the objection to his jurisdiction is wholly unfounded and may decide to proceed with the reference, putting the onus on the dissatisfied party to take action, e.g. by an application to the court for an injunction, or for a declaration as to the correct position or for the revocation of the arbitrator's authority under section 1 of the 1950 Act.

Whatever action the arbitrator takes, it should be noted that, unless his jurisdiction has been enlarged by the parties, he is not determining the preliminary matter of his authority but is simply making a decision as to the course of action he should take under the circumstances revealed by his inquiry.

It is, of course, open to the parties to enlarge the arbitrator's authority to include the preliminary issue as to the extent of his jurisdiction. For example, where a dispute arose as to an arbitrator's jurisdiction and he was not restricted in his preliminary inquiries to finding facts which would found an application to the court, but was asked to decide after a full hearing with evidence, documents and argument whether or not he had jurisdiction, it was held that this was an *ad hoc* submission and the arbitrator's decision was binding on the parties (*Higgs & Hill Building Ltd v Campbell Denis Ltd* [1983] Com LR 34).

(2) Issues of law

Arbitration is essentially a procedure for settling disputes of fact. Issues of law, however, frequently arise on either procedural or on substantive matters. It will be convenient to consider here the procedures available for settling those questions of law.

An issue of law in an arbitration may be dealt with in three ways. First, it may be determined by the courts. Secondly, it may be decided by the arbitrator, either alone or with expert legal assistance. Thirdly, it may be referred for decision to a third party or tribunal.

It is important that any issues of law arising in the proceedings should be identified and understood by the arbitrator at the start of the arbitration. As we saw above (p. 295), this is a matter for consideration at the preliminary meeting and should be included in an order for directions (p. 296 above). If the parties or the arbitrator wish to have the issue settled otherwise than by the arbitrator, then this should be agreed at an early stage.

(a) *Determination by the courts.* Under section 21 of the 1950 Act an arbitrator could state any question of law arising during the reference, or his award, in the form of a special case for the decision of the High Court. A distinction arose in practice, therefore, between issues of fact, which were decided by the arbitrator, and issues of law, which were decided by the courts. The special case procedure was, however, a fertile source of delay for the party who wished to postpone the final day of decision. It was abolished by section 1 of the 1979 Act and replaced by two provisions. First, a limited right of appeal on a question of law arising out of an award (section 1(2) of the 1979 Act). This is dealt with in Chapter 12 p. 360 below. Secondly, a right to apply to the High Court for the determination of a preliminary question of law (section 2 of the 1979 Act). This is now considered.

Section 2 of the 1979 Act (Appendix C p. 505 below) provides that any party to an arbitration may apply to the High Court to determine any question of law arising in the course of the reference. Such an application may only be made with the consent of an arbitrator (or umpire) who has entered on the reference or with the consent of all other parties (section 2(1)). Where application is made with the consent of the arbitrator the court will not consider it where the parties have entered into an exclusion agreement under section 3 of the 1979 Act; otherwise the court must be satisfied that the determination might produce substantial savings in costs to the parties, *and* that the question of law is one in respect of which leave to appeal would be likely to be given under section 1, that is to say the question could substantially affect the rights of one or more of the parties (section 2(2), see Chapter 12 p. 361 below). These conditions do not have to be satisfied where the application is made with the consent of all other parties (*Gebr Broere BV v Saras Chimica SpA* [1983] 2 Lloyd's Rep 436).

There is, therefore, an important distinction between applications made with the consent of the arbitrator and those made with the consent of all other parties. In the former application, the court must first decide whether or not to entertain the application at all and, in reaching that decision, it will apply the above criteria, namely whether the determination of the question of law is likely to result in substantial savings in costs and have a possible substantial effect on the rights of the parties. Secondly, if the court grants leave for the application, it will then make a substantive decision on the question of law raised. But where an application is made with the consent of all other parties, the first stage is omitted and the court will proceed directly to a determination of the question of law.

This distinction between applications made with the consent of the arbitrator and those made with the consent of all other parties also affects the rights of appeal against the decision of the court on the application. Where application is made with the consent of the arbitrator, an appeal against the court's initial decision whether or not to entertain the application may only be made with leave of the High Court (section 2(2A) inserted by section 148(3) of the Supreme Court Act 1981). Where the High Court makes a determination on the question of law put to it, either after grant of leave or where this is unnecessary because the application is made with the consent of all parties, then an appeal against this determination may only be made with leave of the High Court or Court of Appeal, and provided it is certified by the former that the question of law either is one of general public importance or there is some other special reason why the application should be considered by the Court of Appeal (section 2(3)). The Court of Appeal has indicated that leave to appeal against such a determination will be less readily given than on an appeal under section 1 of the 1979 Act in respect of a question of law arising out of an award (*Babanaft International Co SA v Avant Petroleum Inc* [1982] 1 WLR 871).

The rights of the parties to apply to the High Court under section 2 of the 1979 Act for the determination of a preliminary question of law have effect notwithstanding anything in any agreement purporting to prohibit or restrict access to the court or to restrict its jurisdiction (section 3(4) of the 1979 Act, Appendix C p. 507 below). The parties may, however, enter into an exclusion agreement under section 3 of the 1979 Act. The effect of such an agreement in relation to section 2 is to remove the parties' rights to seek a determination on a question of law, but only where the application is made with the consent of the arbitrator. Where the application is made with the consent of all other parties then an exclusion agreement will not prevent an application to the court to determine the question of law. Exclusion agreements are discussed in more detail in Chapter 12 p. 366 below.

The operation of section 2 of the 1979 Act may be illustrated by reference to two recent rent review cases. In *Chapman v Charlwood Alliance Properties Ltd* (1981) 260 EG 1041, two applications were made seeking determinations on preliminary points of law. They were made with the consent of the arbitrator and it was necessary, therefore, for the judge to make an initial decision whether or not to entertain the applications.

The two questions of law were as follows. First, a declaration was sought that on the true construction of the lease, and in the events which had happened, the review rent was to be the best rent at which the premises could be let for a term of 108 years without review, but otherwise upon the terms of the current lease. The judge agreed that this was a point of construction of the lease and, therefore, a question of law, but held that it ought not to be considered in the abstract but only in relation to the matrix of surrounding facts. It should not be decided, therefore, until the arbitrator had made his findings of fact. Furthermore, the point raised might prove to be academic. This question of law was one in respect of which leave to appeal could be given but the judge was not satisfied that a preliminary determination might produce substantial savings in costs to the parties.

Secondly, a declaration was sought that, on the true construction of the lease, the review rent was to be the best rent for a letting of the premises as a whole or the best aggregate rents for letting in parts, whichever is the higher. The judge held that this was a pure question of valuation (that is to say of fact) which the parties had specifically agreed should be decided by an arbitrator. This application, therefore, failed completely.

Finally, the judge held that, even if he were wrong in his decisions on both points, he would still refuse leave because there would be dangers in the court deciding these preliminary points of construction without having the full findings of fact before it. In this case the applications for leave were refused and the judge did not proceed to the second stage of determining the questions of law put to him.

In *Bovis Group Pension Fund Ltd v GC Flooring & Furnishing Ltd* (1984) 269 EG 1252, an application was made with the consent of all parties and, therefore, it was not necessary for the court to decide the preliminary question whether or not to entertain it. In this case, the permitted use of commercial premises under a lease was as "professional offices" and the review rent was defined as "... the rent at which having regard to the terms hereof (other than as to rent and user) the demised premises might reasonably be expected to be let for office purposes...". Planning permission had not been granted for the use of the whole building as offices and it was only partly used for this purpose. It was held by a majority of the Court of Appeal that, on a true construction of the rent review clause, the rent must be assessed on the assumption that the premises could lawfully be used as offices and that planning permission had been granted for such use.

The parties had agreed alternative rental figures corresponding to the two alternative meanings put forward respectively by them and it was, therefore, a simple matter for the arbitrator to issue his award in the appropriate figure according to the decision of the court. The problems of the inter-relationship of fact and law which existed in the *Chapman* case did not arise in *Bovis* to prevent a determination of the question of law.

(b) *Determination by the arbitrator.* The effect of the Arbitration Act 1979 and the guidelines for judicial review of awards laid down by the House of Lords in *The Nema* [1981] 3 WLR 292 (see Chapter 12 p. 361 below) has been to give greater finality to arbitration awards. Recourse to the courts for guidance as to the law should be less frequent. Furthermore, as stated above, the parties to a reference may enter into an agreement under section 3 of the 1979 Act to exclude their rights of appeal under section 1 or to seek a determination on a preliminary point of law under section 2. A lay arbitrator may now have no alternative but to make his own decision on any points of law arising during the proceedings. It should be particularly noted that, except to the limited extent discussed below, he cannot seek outside assistance, from the courts or otherwise, in answering questions of law arising out of the reference.

To what extent can an arbitrator properly seek assistance in matters of law? It is settled law that an arbitrator may seek legal advice from a third party, but the extent to which he may do so without the agreement of the parties is unclear. It would appear that he may seek advice regarding the drawing up of his award, the conduct of the reference and the *general* principles of law governing that class of case, but he may not seek advice relating to the *actual* questions of law in dispute in the arbitration. In all cases, however, he may only seek advice to assist him in making his decision: he cannot delegate the making of that decision to his adviser (*Ellison v Bray* (1864) 9 LT 730) unless, of course, the parties agree that he may do so. (This is then the situation under (c) below).

An arbitrator may agree with the parties the extent to which he may seek legal advice. For example, he may stipulate that he will only accept the appointment provided he is able to seek such advice as in his absolute discretion he thinks desirable and that the cost thereof will be included in his fee. His agreement with the parties may allow him to delegate part of his duties to a third party. Thus, where a submission to arbitration allowed the arbitrator to be attended by his attorney, who prepared the award, it was held that this was not an improper delegation of his authority (*Baker v Cotterill* (1849) 18 LJQB 345).

Where the issues in a reference are complex, comprising mixed issues of fact and law, the parties may agree that the arbitrator shall be assisted by a legal assessor. He will sit with the arbitrator, hear evidence and argument and advise him as to the law. He cannot make the decision, however, which must still be made by the arbitrator.

(c) *Determination by a third party or tribunal.* As a general rule an arbitrator may not delegate his judicial duties without the consent of the parties. Where complicated issues of law arise they may agree that he may delegate his duties wholly or partly to a third party or tribunal.

Where a clear cut issue of law arises during the proceedings the parties may agree to submit it for decision to counsel or a solicitor. The agreement to take this course of action should be in writing, it should include an agreement to pay his fees and be bound by his decision. A submission to a legal arbitrator should be in the form of a joint case containing the facts and the contentions of each party.

A similar situation may arise where it becomes apparent during the proceedings that the only or main issue in the arbitration is one of law. The parties may agree that the reference shall be wholly dealt with by a legal arbitrator in place of the appointed lay arbitrator. Alternatively, it may be agreed to refer the dispute to an official referee or to the Lands Tribunal.

Section 11 of the Arbitration Act 1950 (Appendix C p. 469 below) provides that, where an arbitration agreement states that the reference shall be to an official referee, any such referee to whom application is made shall hear and determine the matters referred to him. He has all the powers of a judge and his award will be a judgment of the High Court. Unless the arbitration agreement provides for a reference to an official referee it will be necessary for the parties to enter into a further agreement to make such a reference.

Similarly, the parties may agree to submit their dispute to the Lands Tribunal. Section 1(5) of the Lands Tribunal Act 1949 allows the tribunal to act as an arbitrator on a reference by consent. The procedure is contained in Part IV of the Lands Tribunal Rules 1975 (as amended).

(3) Procedure: at the hearing

(a) *Need for a hearing.* It is usually necessary for an arbitrator to hold a hearing before he makes his award although this may be dispensed with under certain circumstances, e.g. where there is a contrary intention in the arbitration agreement, or under a special procedure of a particular trade or by agreement between the parties (*The Myron* [1970] 1 QB 527). The parties must be given adequate notice of the date, time and place of a hearing. It may be possible to do this in the order for directions following the preliminary meeting, otherwise a separate direction must be issued.

(b) *Adjournments.* After the date of the hearing has been fixed by the arbitrator he may receive an application for an adjournment. He has a discretion in this matter, which must be exercised in good faith and in accordance with the rules of natural justice, e.g. before making his decision he must give all parties an opportunity to make representations to him on the matter (*R. v Secretary of State for the Environment ex p Mistral Investments Ltd* [1984] JPL 516). The courts will not readily interfere with the exercise by an arbitrator of this discretion provided he acts in good faith. His award will not be impeached even though the court thinks he acted wrongly (*Larchin v Ellis* (1862) 11 WR 281), but an arbitrator must consider any application for an adjournment on its merits and his award may be set aside where he exercises his discretion on the basis of an irrelevant consideration (*Thomas v Official Solicitor* (1983) 265 EG 601).

When considering an application for an adjournment, the arbitrator should weigh in the balance the need to be fair and just to both parties with the desirability of proceeding expeditiously with the arbitration. He must consider whether an adjournment is reasonably necessary to enable the applicant to prepare and present his case, or whether it has been requested unreasonably in order to delay the proceedings. Thus, an adjournment should be granted to enable one party to investigate an unexpected case raised by the other party (*Solomon v Solomon* (1859) 28 LJ Ex 129), or to deal with evidence given by a witness improperly called by the arbitrator himself (*Re Enoch & Zaretzky Bock & Co* [1910] 1 KB 327) or to instruct counsel where one party attends the hearing with counsel without having given prior notice to the other party that he intended to do so (*Whatley v Morland* (1833) 2 Dowl 249). It would be unreasonable for an arbitrator to refuse an adjournment where this would leave the applicant with insufficient time to prepare and present his case (*R v A Rent Assessment Committee for London, ex p Ellis-Rees & Others* (1982) 262 EG 1298).

(c) *Attendance and representation.* Arbitration is a private method of settling disputes and the public may not attend a hearing unless allowed to do so by the parties and the arbitrator. The persons who may attend as of right are the parties, persons claiming through them and persons interested for or attending on behalf of them, e.g. solicitors, counsel and witnesses. A party is allowed to have another person present to assist him in presenting his case. In *Haigh v Haigh* (1861) 3 De G F & J 157, an award was set aside where the arbitrator refused to allow the attendance of the son of one of the parties, who assisted his father in the business and was familiar with the accounts. He also refused to permit the attendance of a shorthand writer to take notes for the same party. But in *Tillam v Copp* (1847) 5 CB 211, the court refused to set aside an award, where the arbitrator excluded from the hearing a skilled person who intended to be present to assist the defendant's attorney, on the grounds that an arbitrator has a general discretion as to the conduct of the proceedings.

A party to an arbitration may be represented by counsel or a solicitor, unless such representation is expressly or impliedly prohibited by the arbitration agreement (*Henry Bath & Son Ltd v Birgby Products* [1962] 1 Lloyd's Rep 389), or any other person. A party who intends to be represented by counsel has a duty to notify the other party in sufficient time to allow that party to instruct counsel (*Whatley v Morland* (1833) 2 Dowl 249).

(d) *Ex parte proceedings*. Where one party fails to attend a hearing after proper notice has been given to him, the arbitrator may proceed *ex parte*. His power to do so is a general one arising out of his judicial office, and is not dependent on any express power in the arbitration agreement. He may now proceed *ex parte* pursuant to an order of the High Court made under section 5 of the 1979 Act (see p. 296 above). An arbitrator who finds that one of the parties is a "reluctant litigant", necessitating the issue to him of "peremptory" directions, should ensure that they are clear and reasonable. An arbitrator should not proceed *ex parte* without giving the absent party clear warning of his intention to do so. If a party fails to attend a hearing without reasonable cause the arbitrator should not immediately proceed but should adjourn it to another date and time. He should then notify the absent party of the new hearing by a peremptory notice, informing him of his intention to proceed with the hearing if he fails to appear a second time.

Where an arbitrator proceeds *ex parte* he should still act fairly towards the absent party:

> "... the claim was undefended at the hearing. That did not mean that the arbitrator was obliged to accept the claim without question. Nor did it mean that he was under an obligation to protect the party who was not present. His function was to hold the scales as evenly as he could and to act fairly and judicially in the conduct of the hearing".

(per Dunn LJ in *Fox v P. G. Wellfair Ltd* [1981] 2 Lloyd's Rep 514 at p. 528).

(e) *Order of appearance*. The arbitrator has a discretion regarding the form of hearing but, where both parties attend, the order of appearance normally follows that of a civil action in the High Court (see Chapter 1 p. 7 above). This is as follows:

(i) The arbitrator opens the proceedings by stating who he is, what the arbitration is about, how he was appointed, what pleadings have been exchanged, how many days and hours per day have been reserved for the hearing and the procedure to be adopted; he will then ask for any comments and, finally, invite the parties to introduce themselves.

(ii) The claimant introduces himself and his witnesses (and sometimes his opponent) and then opens his case, including any reply to a counterclaim by the respondent.

(iii) The claimant calls his witnesses, who are subjected to examination-in-chief, cross-examination, re-examination and possibly to questions by the arbitrator.

(iv) The respondent opens his case, comprising his defence and possibly a counterclaim.

(v) The respondent calls his witnesses, who are also subjected to examination-in-chief, cross-examination, re-examination and to questions by the arbitrator.

(vi) The respondent gives his final address.

(vii) The claimant gives his final address (if the respondent does not call any evidence then the order of final addresses is reversed).

(viii) The arbitrator closes the hearing and usually announces arrangements for a view and the publication of his award; it should be noted that an arbitrator is not *functus officio* until he has made his award and, until that time, he may receive and deal with applications by the parties and receive new evidence at a re-opened hearing or by written submissions.

(f) *Notes of hearing.* It is the duty of the arbitrator to make his own notes of the hearing: he cannot employ a shorthand writer at the parties' expense (unless they consent). The parties may, however, agree to pay for the preparation of a verbatim record of the proceedings by such a writer, and this is often done when the sums at stake are large or where an appeal is contemplated. The costs of a shorthand writer may not be recovered in a taxation without a specific direction; the arbitrator, should, therefore, be requested to include in his award a direction regarding the payment of these costs.

(g) *Witnesses and evidence.* The responsibility for presenting evidence at an arbitration rests with the parties. The arbitrator has no power to call a witness, certainly not one of fact, although he may recall a witness for further questioning (*Re Enoch & Zaretzky Bock & Co* [1910] 1 KB 327 at p. 333). Section 12 of the 1950 Act (Appendix C p. 469 below) contains the rights, powers and duties of the parties, the High Court and the arbitrator in relation to witnesses and evidence.

Where a party requires a person to attend a hearing to give oral evidence or to produce a document, he may apply to the High Court for the writs of *subpoena ad testificandum* or *subpoena duces tecum* respectively (section 12(4)). The court or a judge thereof may issue these writs to compel the attendance of a witness who is within the United Kingdom, but that witness can still resist the production of a document on grounds of public policy or privilege (see Chapter 2 p. 56 above). In the unlikely event that the required witness is in prison, the appropriate writ is *habeas corpus ad testificandum*, which will issue from the High Court to compel the attendance of the prisoner for examination before the arbitrator (section 12(5)).

The High Court has power to order that evidence be given on affidavit (section 12(6)(c)), to make orders in respect of the examination on oath of any witness before an officer of the Court or any other person, and to issue a commission or request for the examination of a witness out of the jurisdiction (section 12(6)(d)). The power of the High Court to issue the above writs and orders is without prejudice to any similar power vested in the arbitrator.

Section 12(1) of the 1950 Act sets out the powers of the arbitrator in relation to the parties to the dispute. It provides, that unless a contrary intention is expressed therein, every arbitration agreement shall be deemed (where applicable) to contain a provision that the parties to the reference (and all persons claiming through them) shall, subject to any legal objection:

(i) submit to examination by the arbitrator on oath or affirmation in relation to the matters in dispute;

(ii) produce before the arbitrator all documents within their possession or power which may be called for;

(iii) do all other things which the arbitrator may require during the proceedings on the reference.

Section 12(2) and (3) contain the arbitrator's powers regarding the examination of witnesses. Unless a contrary intention is expressed therein, and where such a provision is applicable, every arbitration agreement shall be deemed to contain a provision that witnesses shall be examined on oath or affirmation, at the arbitrator's discretion (section 12(2)). The arbitrator has power to administer oaths and take affirmations of the parties and their witnesses, provided that no contrary intention is expressed in the arbitration agreement (section 12(3)). These provisions do not compel the arbitrator to hear evidence on oath and affirmation but allow him to do so.

EVIDENCE AND SUBMISSIONS

Chapter 2 contains an outline of the law of evidence and expert evidence is discussed in Chapter 3. I now consider the applicability of these rules of evidence to arbitration and the powers and duties of an arbitrator in relation thereto.

(1) General rule

The general rule is that an arbitrator is bound by the same rules of evidence as a court of law, unless the parties agree otherwise:

> "It is plain that the courts do allow considerable latitude, in practice at any rate, to the reception of evidence by umpires, but to say as a general proposition that they are not bound by the rules of evidence appears to me to be entirely misleading and likely to produce very great injustice."
>
> (per Farwell J in *Re Enoch & Zaretzky Bock & Co* [1910] 1 KB 327 at p. 336)

(2) Relaxation of general rule

The parties may expressly agree to the relaxation of the strict rules of evidence, or this may be implied by a reference to a skilled person for decision in accordance with the practice of a particular trade where those rules are modified or disregarded:

> "There are some arbitrations in which the arbitrator is expected to form his own opinion and act on his own knowledge without recourse to evidence given by witnesses on either side; such as an arbitrator who is to decide as to whether goods are up to sample, see *Mediterranean & Eastern Export Co Ltd v Fortress Fabrics (Manchester) Ltd* [1948] 2 All ER 186.
>
> But there are other arbitrations in which the arbitrator is expected to receive the evidence of witnesses and the submissions of advocates and to be guided by them in reaching his conclusions; such as arbitrations on shipping contracts or on building contracts."
>
> (per Lord Denning MR in *Fox v P. G. Wellfair Ltd* [1981] 2 Lloyd's Rep 514 at pp. 521–522).

In the *Mediterranean & Eastern Export* case, a dispute regarding the quality of goods was referred to arbitration in accordance with the rules of a chamber of commerce. These provided for the determination of such disputes "by commercial men of experience and special knowledge of the subject-matter". Written statements were submitted to the arbitrator in accordance with the rules, but neither party called expert evidence nor had professional representation at the hearing. The arbitrator found for the sellers and awarded damages. It was held that he was entitled to do so without hearing expert evidence. Lord Goddard CJ said (pp. 187–8):

"There can be no doubt that with regard to questions of quality and matters of that description an arbitrator of this character can always act on his own knowledge."

The extent to which the rules of evidence may be relaxed must, however, be clearly ascertained and not stretched further than the agreement allows. For example, in *Finney Lock Seeds Ltd v George Mitchell (Chesterhall) Ltd* [1979] 2 Lloyd's Rep 301, a dispute regarding the quality of seeds was submitted to arbitration under trade rules which provided that "the arbitrators ... are at liberty to act upon evidence and/or information as they may think fit and to call for such documents in the possession of the parties to the dispute as they deem necessary...." It was held that this rule did not (in the absence of consent) allow the arbitrators to have regard to evidence of "without prejudice" negotiations, although it might enable them in a proper case to disregard the hearsay rule.

There is no direct authority as to whether a rent review arbitration falls within the first of Lord Denning's categories, that is to say arbitrations (usually of a trade or commercial character) which may be determined by the expertise of the arbitrator without recourse to evidence. It is certainly current practice in rent review disputes for evidence to be adduced by the parties, either at an oral hearing or in written representations, notwithstanding the arbitrator's skill and experience in valuation. Recent cases on the admissibility of evidence in rent review arbitrations appear to have proceeded on the basis that the strict rules of evidence apply (see e.g. *Segama NV v Penny Le Roy Ltd* (1983) 269 EG 322, Chapter 3 p. 71 above and *Town Centre Securities Ltd v Wm Morrison Supermarkets Ltd* (1981) 263 EG 435, Chapter 2 p. 46 above). Moreover, in *Amherst v James Walker Goldsmith & Silversmith Ltd (No. 1)* (1980) 254 EG 123, Megaw LJ drew a distinction between leases and commercial contracts and it is usually in relation to commercial contracts that the rules of evidence are waived in arbitration.

Some nineteenth century cases, however, suggest that a surveyor appointed as arbitrator may make an award without receiving evidence. For example, in *Eads v Williams* (1854) 4 De GM & G 674, surveyors were appointed as arbitrators to settle the rent and other terms of a lease of a coal mine. The court refused to set aside their award even though they did not examine witnesses:

"I do not think, when a matter is referred to surveyors or other persons of skill to fix the value of property to be bought or let, that the meaning is that they are necessarily to examine witnesses; they are instructed from their experience and observation to form a judgment which the parties referring to them agree shall be considered satisfactory".

(per Lord Cranworth LC in *Eads* (above) at p. 687).

Similarly, in *Oswald v Earl Grey* (1855) 24 LJQB 69, a usage, under which arbitrators made their award between outgoing and incoming tenants of a farm solely on their inspection and without evidence, was held to be good. But the award of an arbitrator, appointed to determine a dispute regarding the obligation to repair a house, was set aside because it was based solely on his inspection of the premises and there may have been other relevant facts on which he should have received evidence, such as payments or excuses for non-repair (*Anon* (1814) 2 Chit 44).

It might appear, therefore, that a skilled arbitrator appointed to determine a review rent, could do so solely on the basis of his skill and experience and an inspection, without the taking of evidence, provided he could be sure that the parties could not put before him any additional facts necessary to a proper decision. In practice, however, he would be unwise to do so, particularly in view of the distinction which now exists between an arbitrator and an independent expert (see Chapter 7 p. 199 above).

As explained in Chapters 2 and 3 above, the Civil Evidence Acts 1968 and 1972 and the rules of court made thereunder, contain procedures for the admission of hearsay and expert evidence in civil proceedings. The procedure for hearsay is contained in RSC Order 38 rules 20–34 and for expert evidence in RSC Order 38 rules 35–44. These provisions apply to arbitrations where the strict rules of evidence apply, but they may be modified "as may be appropriate" by the arbitrator (sections 10(3) and (4) and 18(1)(b) of the 1968 Act and section 5 of the 1972 Act). Thus, an arbitrator may modify the rules relating to the admission of hearsay evidence. He also has a discretion to admit such evidence under sections 2, 4 or 5 of the 1968 Act even though the prior notice procedure for the admission of such evidence has not been followed (see RSC Order 38 rule 29(1) and *Gredley (Investment Developments) Co Ltd v London Borough of Newham* (1973) 26 P & CR 400). Hearsay evidence may also be received by agreement between the parties and will also be admissible where one party waives his right to object to it (*Town Centre Securities Ltd v Wm Morrison Supermarkets Ltd* (1981) 263 EG 435, Chapter 2 p. 46 above).

An arbitrator may (and usually does) prescribe his own procedure for the prior exchange and admission of expert evidence. This is usually modelled on the procedures for such evidence in the High Court or the Lands Tribunal (see Chapter 3 pp. 84 and 87 above). The arbitrator's chosen procedure for expert evidence will be set out in his order for directions (see p. 295 above and Chapter 13 p. 393 below).

(3) Admissibility of evidence

The admissibility of evidence is a question of law, but the weight to be given to admissible evidence is a question of fact solely within the province of the arbitrator. Disputes about the admissibility of evidence can usually be resolved into one or other of two basic questions: did the arbitrator admit evidence which should not have been admitted? Or did he refuse to admit evidence which should have been admitted?

Where an arbitrator, acting honestly and judicially, erroneously admits inadmissible evidence that is not *in itself* misconduct on his part. His award will not necessarily be set aside because he has not strictly complied with the rules of evidence. But the receipt of inadmissible evidence which goes to the root of the issue submitted to the arbitrator will be misconduct and the award may be set aside. For example, in *Walford Baker & Co v Macfie & Sons* (1915) 84 LJKB 2221, a dispute arising out of a contract for the sale of sugar was submitted to arbitration and, on an appeal against the award, the court was satisfied that the arbitrator was influenced in making his award by evidence of a *former* contract between the same parties. The award was set aside on the grounds of misconduct by the arbitrator. Lush J said (p. 2223):

> "There is another way in which this conclusion might be justified. It may be that the rules of evidence which are acted on in these courts may not be strictly enforced in proceedings before a lay arbitrator. It is unnecessary to express an opinion whether that is so or not. But when it appears that an umpire allows to be given, and acts upon, evidence which is absolutely inadmissible, and which goes to the very root of the question before him, this court has ample jurisdiction to set the award aside on the ground of legal misconduct on the part of the umpire."

Similarly, in *Finney Lock Seeds Ltd v George Mitchell (Chesterhall) Ltd* [1979] 2 Lloyd's Rep 301 (p. 314 above), the judge rejected a submission that the reception by an arbitrator of evidence of "without prejudice" negotiations was not misconduct. It was, he said, evidence which goes to the root of the case and the award should be set aside.

A distinction is made, therefore, between evidence which goes to the root of the dispute and evidence of collateral matters. Where an objection relates to the reception by an arbitrator of inadmissible evidence of a collateral matter, then the court will not set aside the award, because he has authority to inquire into such matters where this is necessary to enable him to come to a right decision on the question referred to him. Thus, in *Falkingham v Victorian Railways Commissioner* [1900] AC 452, an award was not set aside where arbitrators admitted evidence on matters outside their jurisdiction but which was not shown to be irrelevant to the inquiry nor taken into account in the lump sum award. For example, it might be necessary for arbitrators to take evidence in order to ascertain whether the subject-matter of that evidence was within their jurisdiction or, as in this case, where the claims referred were mixed up together.

Although the wrongful admission of evidence by an arbitrator is an error of law, an applicant who appeals against an award under section 1 of the 1979 Act on this ground must show that, having regard to all circumstances, the error is one which could substantially affect the rights of one or more of the parties (see Chapter 12 p. 361 below).

A party cannot challenge an award on the grounds of exclusion of admissible evidence unless that evidence was actually tendered to the arbitrator. A party could not, therefore, question an award where he put an abstract proposition to the arbitrator and, after receiving his decision, then declined to give evidence or prefer a claim. He should have put a specific case and specific evidence to the arbitrator (*Craven v Craven* (1817) Moore CP 403).

An award cannot be challenged on the grounds that the arbitrator received inadmissible evidence unless the party making the application objected to the admission of the evidence during the arbitration proceedings. Such objections can be waived in the same way as other procedural matters (*Town Centre Securities Ltd v Wm Morrison Supermarkets Ltd* (1981) 263 EG 435, discussed in Chapter 2 p. 46 above (hearsay evidence) and *Shield Properties & Investments Ltd v Anglo-Overseas Transport Co Ltd* (1984) 273 EG 69 (evidence of "without prejudice" discussions)).

(4) Arbitrator receiving secret evidence

An arbitrator should not receive evidence without the knowledge of all the parties. Such evidence is not inherently inadmissible but its receipt by the arbitrator without giving the parties an opportunity of dealing with it is a breach of the *audi alteram partem* rule of natural justice (see p. 292 above). An arbitrator receives secret evidence where he gives himself evidence, or obtains it from a third party or from one of the parties without the knowledge of the other party.

It is normal practice for an arbitrator to view the property (real or personal) involved in the dispute after the hearing. Where he is unfamiliar with the property and the locality, he may find it helpful to make an unaccompanied inspection before the hearing. An arbitrator has the right to inspect either under express powers in the arbitration agreement or, more usually, under section 12(1) of the

1950 Act which gives him deemed powers to order a party to allow such an inspection (*The Vasso* [1983] 2 Lloyd's Rep 346). Furthermore, the High Court has power under section 12(6)(g) of the 1950 Act to make orders in an arbitration in respect of the detention, preservation or inspection of any property or thing which is the subject of the reference, or as to which any question may arise, and for authorising any persons to enter land or buildings in the possession of any party to the reference, or to take samples, or make observations or experiments. It is entirely within the discretion of the arbitrator whether or not he inspects (*Munday v Bluck* (1861) 9 CB (NS) 557) and how he does so (*Johnson v Lamb* 1981 SLT 300).

It would appear that a view constitutes real evidence. In *Goold v Evans & Co* [1951] 2 TLR 1189, Lord Denning said (p. 1191):

> "Speaking for myself, I think that a view is part of the evidence, just as much as an exhibit. It is real evidence. The tribunal sees the real thing instead of having a drawing or a photo of it."

The arbitrator should give adequate notice to the parties of the date and time of his inspection in order that they may be present if they so wish. In practice, in rent review arbitrations, it is common for one or both of the parties to waive their right to attend the arbitrator's inspection. He should still ensure, however, that he does not take further oral evidence at such a view or give himself evidence in the absence of the parties.

The former situation occurred in *Hibernian Property Co Ltd v Secretary of State for the Environment* (1973) 27 P & CR 197. Following a public local inquiry into a compulsory purchase order in respect of unfit houses, the inspector visited the order land unaccompanied by any representatives of Hibernian, owners of the land and objectors to the order. During this inspection occupiers of many of the houses affected were asked whether they wished to go or stay if the houses were improved. They expressed views which were considered by the Secretary of State as a relevant factor in his decision to confirm the order. It was held that the receipt of this additional information by the inspector was a failure to observe the rules of natural justice, which might have prejudiced the owners. The compulsory purchase order was quashed.

The decision in *Hickmott v Dorset County Council* (1977) 35 P & CR 195, is an example of a tribunal giving itself evidence in the absence of the parties. This case concerned injurious affection under Part I of the Land Compensation Act 1973, where the claimant sought compensation for the depreciation in value of his house due to noise and vibration following the re-alignment of a sharp bend in an adjoining road. After the hearing the member inspected the house and road and carried out his own test of speed by driving round the bend in question. He incorporated the results of this test in his decision and rejected the claim for compensation. The claimant appealed on the grounds that the member had erred in law in substituting for the evidence given his own observations regarding traffic, and gave evidence to himself after the hearing. The Court of Appeal reluctantly agreed, but dismissed the appeal because there was ample other evidence to support the tribunal's decision and no miscarriage of justice had occurred. Lord Denning MR said (p. 198):

"Although I can sympathise entirely with the member of the Lands Tribunal, we have to remember that this is a judicial inquiry. It is a judicial inquiry in which the general rule is that a tribunal should act on all appropriate evidence. There are no strict rules. The member can act on his own view, but he should not himself be a witness—giving evidence to himself—which the parties concerned have not heard and have not had an opportunity of challenging."

Stephenson LJ was more specific regarding the scope of a view (p. 199):

"I think it would be most undesirable to try to restrict a member of the Lands Tribunal seeking to assess compensation under this statute too narrowly. It may be that a more generous use of ears and eyes in matters outside his particular field of expertise should be permitted to a member of the Lands Tribunal in viewing premises—seeing, hearing and feeling, if need be, the volume of traffic and at what speed it is going past premises which are alleged to be depreciated by it. But his observations did go beyond that, and he did create evidence, as it seems to me, by making an experiment or test of his own. If he were going to make such an experiment or test, he ought to have made it with the knowledge or agreement of the parties."

Similarly, an arbitrator should not make use of knowledge acquired by him in a different capacity and should not introduce into the proceedings evidence which has not been adduced by the parties. Thus, in *Owen v Nicholl* [1948] 1 All ER 707, an award made by a county court registrar acting as an arbitrator, was set aside for misconduct because he introduced into the arbitration evidence obtained by him in earlier proceedings in which neither of the parties to the arbitration were concerned (see also *Top Shop Estates Ltd v Danino and Another*, p. 322 below).

(5) Arbitrator's use of own expert knowledge
To what extent can an arbitrator use his own expert knowledge and experience in an arbitration to which the rules of evidence apply?

The leading case is *Fox v P. G. Wellfair Ltd* [1981] 2 Lloyd's Rep 514, which concerned two arbitrations under the NHBC scheme for the protection of house purchasers. The proceedings were conducted by the arbitrator with the utmost diligence and good faith; evidence was formally given on oath by six witnesses including two expert witnesses; the claimant flat owners were represented by leading counsel but the respondent builder and NHBC were not represented. In the main arbitration the claim was for £93,000 plus damages for loss of amenity and inconvenience during the remedial works; in the second arbitration the claim was for £3,817 plus similar damages. The arbitrator awarded only £12,471 in the main arbitration and £1,213 in the second arbitration. He rejected the claims for damages.

The claimants applied to the court for the removal of the arbitrator for misconduct and for the awards to be set aside on the grounds (*inter alia*) that he took into account facts and matters which tended to contradict the unchallenged evidence without giving the claimants an opportunity of dealing with it, and that he failed to conduct the arbitration in accordance with the rules of natural justice.

The Court of Appeal removed the arbitrator for misconduct and set aside his awards. It held that an expert arbitrator should not give evidence to himself without disclosing it to the parties (or one of them where the other parties are not represented). He should not act on his private opinion without disclosing it. Although an expert arbitrator could use his own expert knowledge, there is a distinction between general expert knowledge and knowledge of special facts relevant to the particular case. The awards made by the arbitrator could only have been made by, in effect, giving evidence to himself in flat contradiction to that given by the expert witnesses, without giving them an opportunity of dealing with it. This was a breach of the rules of natural justice and technical or legal misconduct.

All three judgments of the court were founded on a breach of the rules of natural justice by the arbitrator. Lord Denning MR said (p. 522):

> "He can and should use his special knowledge so as to understand the evidence that is given—the letters that have passed—the usage of the trade—the dealings in the market—and to appreciate the worth of all that he sees upon a view. But he cannot use his special knowledge—or at any rate, he should not use it—so as to provide evidence on behalf of the defendants which they have not chosen to provide for themselves.... At any rate he should not use his own knowledge to derogate from the evidence of the plaintiff's experts—without putting his own

knowledge to them and giving them a chance of answering it and showing that his own view is wrong."

Dunn LJ expressed similar opinions but drew a distinction between general expert knowledge, which may be used by an arbitrator without disclosure, and special knowledge of relevant *facts*, which should be disclosed. He said (pp. 528–9):

"... it seems to me that an expert arbitrator should not in effect give evidence to himself without disclosing the evidence on which he relies to the parties, or if only one to that party. He should not act on his private opinion without disclosing it. It is undoubtedly true that an expert arbitrator can use his own expert knowledge. But a distinction is made in the cases between general expert knowledge and knowledge of special facts relevant to the particular case.
... So if the arbitrator is relying upon general expert knowledge, there is no need to disclose it."

He then gave some examples of the use of special knowledge (p. 529):

"An arbitrator is required to value a bull killed by the negligence of one of the parties. If the expert arbitrator relies on his general knowledge of the value of bulls, including fluctuations in the market known to anyone who studies the market, there is no need to disclose it. But if he has recently sold an identical bull for a certain sum, it is necesary to disclose that to the parties. Or if the dead bull is found by the arbitrator, unknown to the parties, to be suffering from some disease or injury which reduces its value, it is necessary to disclose the fact to the parties. So in assessing rents, an expert arbitrator can rely on his general knowledge of comparable rents in the district. But if he knows of a particular comparable case, then he should disclose details of it before relying on it for his award."

Dunn LJ then explained the position where an arbitrator takes a different view of the facts to that put to him by the parties. He said (pp. 529–30):

"If the expert arbitrator, as he may be entitled to do, forms a view of the facts different from that given in the evidence which might produce a contrary result to that which emerges from the evidence, then he should bring that view to the attention of the parties. This is especially so where there is only one party and the arbitrator is in effect putting the alternative case for the party not present at the arbitration.
Similarly, if an arbitrator as a result of a view of the premises

reaches a conclusion contrary to or inconsistent with the evidence given at the hearing, then before incorporating that conclusion in his award he should bring it to the attention of the parties so that they may have an opportunity of dealing with it."

O'Connor LJ saw the facts of the *Wellfair* case as special and outside the usual run of building contract arbitrations. He specifically confirmed the power of an arbitrator to use his expert knowledge in reaching a decision (p. 533):

"Nothing that I say in this case must impugn the right of arbitrators to use their own knowledge in appropriate cases; that is essential to arbitration in very many cases. It will be right in most cases where the NHBC arbitration clause is involved that the arbitrator from the skilled panel will use without fear his own ability. That is the ordinary building contract dispute. That freedom of decision which arbitration submissions have always given to arbitrators does not go to support the award in this case."

The use of technical knowledge by a trade tribunal was also considered recently in *F. R. Waring (UK) Ltd v Administracao Geral Do Acucar E Do Alcool EP* [1983] 1 Lloyd's Rep 45. It was held that a trade tribunal was entitled to take into account its own experience of the trade when considering the evidence presented to it. But if the tribunal possessed some *particular* knowledge about the events in question, independently of the evidence, and they intended to rely upon it, they should draw the parties' attention to that knowledge to enable them to comment upon it. *General* knowledge of a trade was, however, something which it was understood that a trade tribunal might apply when evaluating the evidence and it was not necessary for that knowledge to be canvassed before the parties at the hearing.

In *Top Shop Estates Ltd v Danino & Another* (1984) 273 EG 197, awards in two rent review arbitrations were set aside where the arbitrator organised (and took into account in his awards) pedestrian counts carried out by a qualified assistant, made use of studies of pedestrian flow at busy periods, made use of his own knowledge (part of which was obtained from other arbitrations) and inspected the comparable properties without expressly stating in his directions that he would do so, all without the consent of the parties and without disclosing this additional information to them and giving them an opportunity to adduce evidence or make submissions in relation to it. The judge said that it is not the function of the arbitrator to play the part of Perry Mason when he feels that the submissions or evidence of the parties might usefully be supplemented.

The position regarding the use by an arbitrator of his expert knowledge (fact or opinion) may, therefore, be summarised as follows:

(a) He may use his *general* expert knowledge to understand and evaluate the evidence without disclosing it to the parties.

(b) An arbitrator must not give himself evidence of fact without disclosing it to the parties and giving them an opportunity of commenting upon it.

(c) Where an arbitrator, applying his expert knowledge to the evidence, forms a view of the facts different from that given in evidence and which might produce a contrary result to that which arises from that evidence, he should bring this view to the attention of the parties.

(d) An arbitrator is not bound to accept expert evidence put to him: it may be rejected even though the experts are of the highest standing or the evidence in uncontradicted (*Kentucky Fried Chicken (GB) Ltd v Secretary of State for the Environment* (1977) 245 EG 839). An expert arbitrator may decline to hear evidence on a matter within his expertise (*Winchester City Council v Secretary of State for the Environment* (1980) 39 P & CR 1), but, as stated below, he should be cautious in excluding relevant evidence.

(6) Arbitrator's view of the law

Analogous to the situation discussed above, where an arbitrator forms a different view of the facts to that put to him by the parties, is that which arises where he takes a materially different view of the law, or wishes to rely on a point not argued before him. In both cases he should put his view to the parties for comment. Thus, in *Societe Franco-Tunisienne D'Armement-Tunis v Government of Ceylon* [1959] 1 WLR 787, it was held that an umpire had misconducted himself because his view of the law as applied to the facts involved a radical departure from the cases as presented by the parties, and raised complicated issues of law on which further evidence might be required. On the evidence before the court it did not appear either that that change was made sufficiently clear to one of the parties or that they were given a sufficient opportunity to reframe their case in the light of this unexpected development. The proceedings were, therefore, unsatisfactory and contrary to natural justice.

In a more recent case, *Pancommerce SA v Veecheema BV* [1982] 1 Lloyd's Rep 645, Bingham J said that where arbitrators had it in mind to rely on a point not argued they should always put it to the parties for their comments.

(7) Arbitrator's failure to hear evidence or submissions

An arbitrator should listen to all relevant and admissible evidence put before him by the parties. He may indicate to them (or to one of them) that he has heard enough on a particular point and, although he probably has a discretion regarding the *quantity* of evidence he will hear, he should only exclude relevant evidence after full consideration of the position. Failure to hear all relevant evidence submitted to him and to which objection has not been made, may be misconduct resulting in his award being set aside.

Similarly, where an arbitrator makes an award without hearing submissions of law by the parties, he may be removed for misconduct and his award set aside. In *Modern Engineering (Bristol) Ltd v C. Miskin & Son Ltd* [1981] 1 Lloyd's Rep 135, an arbitrator appointed to determine a dispute under a building contract was advised by counsel for Miskin that a point of law was in issue, namely whether an architect's certificate was conclusive or whether it could be re-opened. This point was not argued at that time but, after confirmation by counsel for the other party that he would be taking it, it was left to be dealt with later in the proceedings. The arbitrator, however, proceeded to issue an interim award holding that the architect's certificate was not conclusive and could be re-opened. It was held by the Court of Appeal that he had misconducted the proceedings because he had decided a case against a party without hearing all the submissions and this was a breach of the rules of natural justice. He was removed and his interim award set aside.

CHAPTER ELEVEN

Law of Arbitration—III

The Award

INTRODUCTION

The purpose of arbitration is to obtain a decision (an award) on the matters in dispute. It is important, therefore, that the arbitrator should know his powers and duties in respect of the award. In particular, he should know the essentials of a valid award and the nature of a reasoned award. The whole of this chapter is devoted to the making and contents of an award, including the giving of reasons and the award of interest and costs. The effect of an award, rights of challenge and enforcement are discussed in Chapter 12. Examples of awards in a rent review arbitration are included in Chapter 13.

MAKING THE AWARD

(1) Time for making the award

The general rule is that an arbitrator may make his award at any time (section 13(1) of the 1950 Act, Appendix C p. 470 below). This is subject to two exceptions. First, the arbitration agreement may specify a time limit for the making of an award: this must be complied with unless subsequently extended by agreement or enlarged by order of the court. Under section 13(2) of the 1950 Act the High Court, or a judge thereof, may enlarge the time limited for the making of an award, whether that time has expired or not. Secondly, where an award is ordered to be remitted to the arbitrator by the court he shall make his award within three months or such other time as may be directed by that order (section 22(2) of the 1950 Act, see Chapter 12 p. 381 below).

Although an award may be made at any time, the parties may agree to revoke the authority of an arbitrator who is dilatory and he may also be removed for this reason by the court under section 13(3) of the 1950 Act (see Chapter 9 p. 283 above).

(2) Delegation

As a general rule an arbitrator may not delegate the making of his award to a third party. There are three exceptions to this rule. First, an arbitrator may seek legal assistance in the drawing up of his award, provided his adviser is disinterested and unconnected with the parties to the dispute (*Re Underwood & Bedford Ry* (1861) 11 CB (NS) 442). Secondly, he may delegate the performance of a ministerial act in connection with his award, but not a judicial act; a distinction which may not always be clear in practice. For example, the *award* of costs between the parties is a judicial act, which cannot be delegated, but the *taxation* of costs is a ministerial act which may be (and usually is) delegated to the court (*H. G. Perkins Ltd v Best-Shaw* [1973] 1 WLR 975, and see now section 18(2) of the 1950 Act, discussed below). The measurement of land is a ministerial act and it would appear that an arbitrator may properly award a rate per acre and direct that the number of acres be ascertained by measurement (*Thorp v Cole* (1836) 1 M & W 531). Thirdly, the parties may agree that the arbitrator may delegate his duties to a third party. Any delegation under this power must be in accordance with the terms of that agreement.

(3) The award of several arbitrators

Where a reference is made to three arbitrators the award of any two of them shall be binding, unless a contrary intention is expressed in the arbitration agreement (section 9 of the 1950 Act as substituted by section 6(2) of the 1979 Act, Appendix C p. 468 below). Where a reference is made to two arbitrators and they fail to agree, the duty of making the award passes to an umpire (section 8(2) of the 1950 Act, Appendix C p. 468 below). (For the signing of an award by three arbitrators see p. 331 below).

(4) Final and interim awards

An arbitrator may only make one *final* award, unless the arbitration agreement provides otherwise. Normally, however, he may make an *interim* award. Section 14 of the 1950 Act provides that "unless a contrary intention is expressed therein, every arbitration agreement shall, where such provision is applicable to the reference, be deemed to contain a provision that the arbitrator or umpire may, if he thinks fit, make an interim award" (Appendix C p. 471 below). This section does not require that the power to make an interim award must be included in the arbitration agreement: it is implied in the absence of a contrary intention.

The agreement should be construed as a whole and, if it leads to the conclusion that it does not allow the arbitrator to make an interim award, then he has no such power. Thus, in *Town Centre Securities Ltd v Wm Morrison Supermarkets Ltd* (1981) 263 EG 435, it was held that an arbitrator assessing a rent under a rent review clause in a lease did not, under that particular clause, have the power to make the interim award in question (believed to have been for an interim rent). Notwithstanding this decision, however, an arbitrator in such an arbitration probably does have the power to make an interim award, provided it is within the jurisdiction given to him by the particular rent review clause, e.g. he may make an interim award determining the review rent but omitting an award of costs, such costs to be included in a final award.

In *Fidelitas Shipping Co Ltd v V/O Exportchleb* [1966] 1 QB 630, Lord Denning MR defined an interim award as follows (p. 638):

> "Nowhere is an interim award defined. But it seems to me that an interim award may be of two kinds. It may be an interim order made pending the final determination of the case; such as an award that an instalment under a building contract be paid pending final determination of the amount due. Or it may be an interim decision, given on a particular issue or issues between the parties, pending final determination of the whole case; such as a decision that a contract was concluded, but leaving over the question of damages. Such an award is not a final award because the arbitrator has not exhausted his duties. It is, however, an award because it is an order or decision on an issue calling for determination. It is, therefore, an interim award; ..."

The making of an interim award is a judicial act and it must, therefore, be done in accordance with the principles of law applicable to the dispute. For example, an arbitrator may make an interim award requiring A to pay B a certain sum, because he determines that at least that sum is payable. But he cannot generally order such a payment on the grounds that on a rough look at the case it would appear that A will owe B at least that sum, but without also deciding the issue of liability (*SL Sethia Lines Ltd v Naviagro Maritime Corporation* [1981] 1 Lloyd's Rep 18 at p. 25).

An interim award which is final in respect of all matters other than costs should expressly state that this is the position. This will allow the award to be implemented even though the question of costs is still outstanding. For example, the following words may be used in a rent review arbitration: "This is an interim award and I reserve my award as to the costs of the reference. Otherwise, it is my final award as to the market rent of the subject-premises."

FORM AND CONTENT OF THE AWARD

(1) Writing or parol

A written award is not essential unless the arbitration agreement specifically so provides; otherwise a parol award is good, but it is only effective where it is irrevocably communicated to the parties by some external act by the arbitrator.

(2) Form to comply with submission

The form of an award must comply with any directions in the submission, except where such directions are immaterial in character. Thus, in *Gatliffe v Dunn* (1738) Barnes 55, the submission required the award to be in writing indented. It was not indented but an objection on this ground was held to be immaterial.

(3) Award must be final and complete

An award (other than an interim award) must be final and complete. It must be final in the sense that all matters referred must have been decided, without the reservation of any further judicial act and with all necessary directions to give effect to it. An award must be complete in the sense that it deals with *all* matters properly referred for decision. It should not deal with matters not so referred.

An award which is an alternative award may still be final, e.g. an award which directs the losing party to do one of two things in the alternative. Thus, in *Simmons v Swaine* (1809) 1 Taunt 549, an award that directed that money shall be paid *or* be secured to be paid was held to be good. An alternative award will still be final where only one of the two alternatives is capable of performance. An alternative award may also be used where the determination is dependent on an issue of law. Such an award should contain a final determination, based on the view of the law accepted by the arbitrator, but with an alternative award based on an alternative view (see the alternative award in Chapter 13 p. 416 below).

(4) Award must be certain

An award must be certain: no doubt should exist as to its meaning. Where there is doubt as to whether the arbitrator has decided the matter submitted to him, or how he has decided it, then the award may be set aside for uncertainty. In particular, an award must be certain in its directions.

Where an award orders the payment of an unquantified sum and sets out the rules for its calculation, it will not be bad for uncertainty provided the calculation is only a matter of "mere arithmetic" (*Higgins v Willes* (1828) 3 Man & Ry KB 382).

The need for certainty in an award does not require any special form of words. Technical expressions are not necessary. All that is required is that the operative part of the award should state clearly and precisely the arbitrator's decision.

(5) Award must be consistent

The various parts of an award must be consistent. In *Ames v Milward* (1818) 8 Taunt 637, in a reference to arbitration of an action for fraudulent representation of a person's circumstances, the award acquitted the defendant of fraud but concluded with a finding in favour of the plaintiff. It was set aside. Park J said (p. 642): "The conclusion to which the arbitrator has come in this case is quite absurd. He says, I think he is innocent, and then awards against him."

(6) Award must be possible

An award must be possible of performance at the time it was made, it must not be immoral, contrary to public policy or offend the rules of natural justice. Thus, a direction in an award requiring a party to commit a trespass was void (*Turner v Swainson* (1836) 1 M & W 572). An award based on a misconstruction of certain trade rules so that an innocent party was required to pay damages to a party guilty of a breach of contract was held to be bad, the court refusing to support a construction at variance with the principles of natural justice (*Cassir, Moore & Co Ltd v Eastcheap Dried Fruit Co* [1962] 1 Lloyd's Rep 400). A party to an award will not be freed from an obligation imposed on him which was possible at the time of the award but which subsequently becomes impossible of performance due to his act or that of a third party.

(7) Recitals

An award usually commences with introductory recitals explaining how the arbitrator came to make it. In a formal award they are usually preceded by the word "whereas". They usually contain such matters as the arbitration agreement, appointment, the procedure adopted and the subject-matter of the dispute (see Chapter 13 p. 403 below).

Although recitals are desirable to explain how an award came to be made, they are not essential to the validity of the award. An award was held to be good although the arbitrator failed to state his authority. A false recital will not invalidate an award (*Baker v Hunter* (1847) 16 M & W 672), and it will not give the arbitrator a jurisdiction in excess of that conferred on him by the arbitration agreement (*Price v Popkin* (1839) 10 A & E 139).

(8) Determination and directions

The operative part of an award, that is to say the arbitrator's determination, will usually take one or more of the following forms. It may state an amount in dispute, e.g. a rent or purchase price; it may declare the rights of the parties; or it may direct the performance of an act or acts by one or both of the parties. As we have seen, directions must be clear, certain, complete and lawful.

The arbitrator's power to give directions is governed by the arbitration agreement and the nature of the dispute. Clearly, he cannot give a direction which is outside his jurisdiction. For example, in *Price v Popkin* (above), one of the questions referred to the arbitrator was whether some fixtures removed by the landlord were part of the demised premises. His jurisdiction was declaratory only and it was held that he had no power to order the replacement of the fixtures by the tenant at the cost of the landlord.

An arbitrator may only give directions where he is given power to do so by the arbitration agreement, or they are required by the particular nature of the dispute, or under section 15 of the 1950 Act (Appendix C p. 471 below). This section provides that:

> "Unless a contrary intention is expressed therein, every arbitration agreement shall, where such provision is applicable to the reference, be deemed to contain a provision that the arbitrator or umpire shall have the same power as the High Court to order specific performance of any contract other than a contract relating to land or an interest in land."

An arbitrator has no *implied* power to give directions which would have the effect of making a fresh contract between the parties. This would clearly be an excess of jurisdiction. For example, in *National Westminster Bank Ltd v BSC Footwear Ltd* (1980) 259 EG 277, the issue was whether an arbitrator appointed to determine the rent on the renewal of a lease could introduce periodic rent reviews in the new lease. Templeman LJ said (p. 278):

> "All that the arbitrator is empowered to determine, and is bound to determine, is rent. He is not empowered to impose any formula and redraft the lease by virtue of his award. The arbitrator is concerned with an amount and not with a formula."

The parties can, of course, give the arbitrator express powers to settle the terms of the agreement between them.

A common direction in an award is an order for the payment of money. In making such an order the arbitrator may fix the time for payment, direct payment by instalments and impose a penalty for non-payment by the due date. A direction that payment shall be made by one of the parties to a stranger is void, unless it can be shown by the party seeking to enforce the award that the payment is for his benefit. For example, an award directing a party to pay a sum to the arbitrator, such sum to be immediately paid by him to another party to the reference, was held to be good (*Wood v Adcock* (1852) 7 Ex 468).

The issue of a certificate may, under the terms of an arbitration clause, be a condition precedent to payment, e.g. in a building or civil engineering contract. Where the question referred to arbitration is the failure to issue such a certificate and the arbitrator finds that it should have been issued, he will usually have power to direct that payment shall be made in respect of that certificate.

It should be emphasised that the provisions described above relating to an arbitrator's power to issue directions relate to his *implied* power to do so. It is open to the parties to give him *express* powers of direction and a common provision in an arbitration agreement is that he shall be authorised "to determine what he shall think fit to be done by the parties respecting the matters in dispute."

Directions relating to interest and costs are considered under these headings below.

(9) Declaratory awards

As stated above, an award may consist of or include a declaration as to the rights of the parties. Where a dispute concerns their rights in the subject-matter of the dispute, then the arbitrator must necessarily give a declaratory award. Where the dispute is specific such as a money claim requiring the arbitrator to award a particular sum, then it may be necessary for him to decide the rights of the parties in respect of that claim as a preliminary to his decision. He may include in the award his decision on that preliminary question and will almost certainly need to do so if he gives a reasoned award (see p. 332 below). This is not, however, a decision as to the *general rights* of the parties, but is limited to the particular claim. If the parties want a decision for the future, as to their *general rights* in a particular dispute, then the submission must specifically include both the claim and the general question.

Interim awards are often declaratory and decide the rights and liabilities of the parties, leaving the question of amount to be settled by agreement or determined by a final award.

(10) Signature and stamping

It is usual for an arbitrator to sign his award and he may have his signature attested by a witness. Where three arbitrators are appointed to resolve a dispute, they must communicate together, by telephone, correspondence or in person, to decide the issues, but, having done so, they could each sign the award separately provided it was in the proper form. It was misconduct for one of the arbitrators to sign a blank award before final agreement had been reached (*European Grain & Shipping Ltd v Johnston* [1982] 3 All ER 989). An award no longer requires to be stamped (section 35 and Schedule to Finance Act 1949).

REASONS

(1) Duty to give reasons

Before the Arbitration Act 1979 came into operation on 1st August 1979, an arbitrator would only have been under a duty to give a reasoned award where this was required by the arbitration agreement. "Non-speaking" awards were the rule, reasoned awards the exception. This position has been altered by the 1979 Act, but an arbitrator still has no *general* duty to give a reasoned award. He will be compelled to do so only where this is required by the arbitration agreement or under section 1(5) and (6) of the 1979 Act (Appendix C p. 504 below). Non-speaking awards will continue to be issued, particularly in commodity, quality and other arbitrations where the issues are wholly of fact.

Section 1 of the 1979 Act abolished the case stated procedure and removed the court's jurisdiction to set aside or remit an award for error of fact or law on the face of the award. These methods of challenge have been replaced by an appeal on a question of law (see Chapter 12 p. 360 below). To enable the court to consider such an appeal an arbitrator can now be compelled to state the reasons for his award, unless the parties have entered into an exclusion agreement under section 3 of the 1979 Act.

Section 1(5) of the 1979 Act provides that any party to a reference may (i) with the consent of all other parties, or (ii) except where the parties have entered into an exclusion agreement, with leave of the court, apply to the High Court for an order for reasons. If it appears to the court that the award does not or does not sufficiently set out the reasons for the award, it may order the arbitrator to state them in sufficient detail to enable the court to consider any question of law arising out of the award in the event of an appeal under section 1 of the Act, provided that when the award does not contain any reasons the court shall not make an order unless it is satisfied on either of the following matters. First, that *before* the award was made one of the parties gave notice to the arbitrator that a reasoned award would be required; or secondly, that there is some special reason why such a notice was not given (section 1(6)).

An application to the court for an order for reasons must be made within 21 days after the award has been made and published to the parties.

The question as to what constitutes a "special reason" why a notice requiring reasons was not given was considered in *Hayn Roman & Co SA v Cominter (UK) Ltd* [1981] Com LR 239. This case concerned a misunderstanding as to whether a notice requiring a reasoned award had been given. One party to the reference was under the impression that it had; the secretary to the arbitral tribunal thought that it had not. Robert Goff J held that a notice had not been given, but that the circumstances of the case constituted a special reason for allowing the court to exercise its discretion to order a statement of reasons. He said (p. 240):

"In my judgment the sub-section must be construed sensibly in its intent. The purpose of the prior notice to the arbitrator, as it seems to me, is to prevent arbitrators from being required to give reasons after the award, by which time their memories may have become dimmed and it may become difficult for them to recall the case in sufficient detail to give a reasoned award. For my part, I can see no reason why an error which does not derive from any misleading of the party who should have given notice, should not constitute a special reason within section 1(6)(b). For example, if the notice went astray by accident, that could well be a special reason why the notice was not given. Similarly, I can see no good reason why a *bona fide* misunderstanding between a solicitor acting for one of the parties, and the secretary of the trade federation as a result of which the solicitor mistakenly believed in all good faith that a request for a reasoned award had been made before the end, should not constitute a special reason why a notice was not given."

Where application is made under section 1(5) of the 1979 Act in respect of an award which contains some, but insufficient reasons, the court will take into account two matters when considering whether to exercise its discretion to order further reasons. First, the prospect of leave being granted for an appeal against the award on a question of law. Secondly, whether there was anything in the applicant's conduct which should lead to the discretion being exercised against him. Thus, the court may take into account as a ground for refusing to order further reasons the fact that the applicant did not ask the arbitrator for such reasons before he made his award. Although, where an arbitration was conducted under a code of practice which stated that awards shall contain full reasons, the applicant could not be criticised for failing to ask for them and the court exercised its discretion in his favour and made an order for further reasons (*Warde v Feedex International Inc* [1984] 1 Lloyd's Rep 310).

The court has power to impose conditions on an order for reasons, e.g. requiring a payment into court (section 28 of the 1950 Act as applied by section 7(1) of the 1979 Act, see *Warde* above).

It should be noted that, where an application for reasons is made with the consent of all other parties, it is a one-stage process. The court may deal with the application for an order straight away without considering the preliminary matter of leave. But where application is *not* made with the consent of all other parties, it is a two-stage process. The court initially considers whether leave should be given and then, if given, proceeds to consider whether to grant an order for reasons. In practice, however, applications for leave and for reasons are treated as one and the same application and dealt with together (see *Warde* at p. 311).

An appeal to the Court of Appeal from a decision of the High Court in respect of leave or the making of an order for reasons (after leave or where this is not required) may only be made with leave of the High Court (section 1(6A) of the 1979 Act inserted by section 148(2) Supreme Court Act 1981, Appendix C p. 505 below).

(2) When should a reasoned award be given?

Although the court may order an arbitrator to give reasons or further reasons for his award, the initial decision whether or not to give a reasoned award rests with him. This point should be considered at the preliminary meeting and dealt with in the arbitrator's order for directions (see Chapter 10 p. 295).

The following judicial guidance has been given to arbitrators as to when a reasoned award should be made:

> "... I would respectfully agree with the proposition, ... that parties to an arbitration other than one which raises only a simple question of fact are entitled, if they wish, to be told the reasons for the arbitrator's conclusion.
>
> I would suggest that the practice should be as follows: (a) If one party requests a reasoned award, the arbitrator should make a reasoned award, save in very exceptional cases. (b) If both parties ask that there should not be a reasoned award, the arbitrator should respect their wish; but he should also, if asked, provide reasons in a separate document which is not incorporated in the award and does not form part of it. (c) If one party asks that there should not be a reasoned award and the other says nothing, the arbitrator should not make a reasoned award. But if he is doubtful whether the other party is aware of his rights, the arbitrator should consider whether it would be right for ask him. (d) The difficult case is where nothing is said by either party. In those circumstances the arbitrator should again consider whether it would be right to ask the parties what form of award they want. But there will be some arbitrations where the parties are represented by sophisticated advocates who are as familiar with arbitral law as the arbitrator. It would be impertinence to ask them if they were aware of their rights. In such a case the arbitrator would be justified in assuming that both parties wanted an award that would be final."

(per Staughton J in *Warde* above pp. 315–316).

(3) Judicial guidance as to reasons

Guidance as to the form and content of a reasoned award under the 1979 Act was given by Donaldson LJ in *Bremer Handelsgesellschaft mbH v Westzucker GmbH* [1981] 2 Lloyd's Rep 130. He said (pp. 132–3):

> "No particular form of award is required. Certainly no one wants a formal 'Special Case'. All that is necessary is that the arbitrators should set out what, on their view of the evidence did or did not happen and should explain succinctly why, in the light of what happened, they have reached their decision and what that decision is. This is all that is meant by a 'reasoned award'.
>
> For example, it might be convenient to begin by explaining briefly how the arbitration came about.... The award could then briefly tell the factual story as the arbitrators saw it. Much would be common ground and would need no elaboration. But when the award comes to matters in controversy, it would be helpful if the arbitrators not only gave their view of what occurred, but also made it clear that they have considered any alternative version and had rejected it,... The arbitrators should end with their conclusion as to the resulting rights and liabilities of the parties. There is nothing about this which is remotely technical, difficult or time consuming.
>
> It is sometimes said that this involves arbitrators in delivering judgments and that this is something which requires legal skills. This is something of a half truth. Much of the art of giving a judgment lies in telling a story logically, coherently and accurately. This is something which requires skill, but it is not a legal skill and it is not necessarily advanced by legal training. It is certainly a judicial skill, but arbitrators for this purpose are Judges and will have no difficulty in acquiring it. Where a 1979 Act award differs from a judgment is in the fact that the arbitrators will not be expected to analyse the law and the authorities. It will be quite sufficient that they should explain how they reached their conclusion,... It can be left to others to argue that this is wrong in law and to a professional Judge, if leave to appeal is given, to analyse the authorities. This is not to say that where the arbitrators are content to set out their reasoning on questions of law in the same way as Judges, this will be unwelcome to the Courts. Far from it. The point which I am seeking to make is that a reasoned award, in accordance with the 1979 Act is wholly different from an award in the form of a special case. It is not technical, it is not difficult to draw and above all it is something which can and should be

produced promptly at the conclusion of the hearing. That is the time when it is easiest to produce an award with all the issues in mind."

The above guidance is particularly directed to disputes of fact. Arbitrators in value disputes are mainly concerned with conflicts of opinion. Moreover, valuation is an abstract process, frequently an intuitive one, and it is often difficult to give reasons for a value award. I am not aware of any reported case which deals with the content of a reasoned award in a rent review or other value arbitration, but in *Re Poyser & Mills Arbitration* [1964] 2 QB 467, Megaw J made the following comments regarding the statutory duty to give reasons under the Tribunals and Inquiries Act 1958 (p. 479):

"Parliament provided that reasons shall be given, and in my view, that must be read as meaning that proper, adequate reasons must be given. The reasons that are set out must be reasons which will not only be intelligible, but which deal with the substantial points that have been raised...."

This case concerned a statutory arbitration under the Agricultural Holdings Act 1948. We can also find guidance in cases where a decision of a rent assessment committee or the Secretary of State for the Environment in a planning appeal has been challenged in the courts on grounds of inadequacy of reasons and in the reasoned decisions of the Lands Tribunal in a variety of valuation disputes. These decisions form a useful guide to the preparation of reasoned awards in value arbitrations (see *Guppys Properties Ltd v Knott (No. 2)* (1979) 253 EG 907 at p. 909).

The adequacy or otherwise of reasons depends upon the facts of the case and the problem before the tribunal:

"... it is, I think, obvious that the character of the reasons given, the nature of the reasons, the extent of the reasons, must in some measure be governed by the nature of the problem which the particular tribunal has been set to resolve."
(per Lord Widgery CJ in *Metropolitan Property Holdings Ltd v Laufer* (1974) 29 P & CR 172 at p. 176).

Reasons should not be too lengthy, detailed or elaborate:

"In general, business men are interested in the decision, not in its underlying legal philosophy, however much lawyers may have that wider interest."
(per Lord Roskill in *Antaios Compania Naviera SA v Salen Rederierna AB* [1984] 2 Lloyd's Rep 235 at p. 243).

The application of these general principles will be seen in the cases discussed below, particularly in connection with the use of expert knowledge and the nature of the valuation process.

(a) *Three rules for reasoned decisions.* In *Guppys Properties Ltd v Knott (No. 3)* (1981) 258 EG 1083, Sir Douglas Frank QC (sitting as a deputy judge) analysed the earlier authorities and formulated three rules regarding reasoned decisions by rent assessment committees. These rules will apply to any expert tribunal required to give a reasoned decision, including an arbitrator giving a reasoned award. Furthermore, they apply to disputes dealt with either by an oral hearing or written representations: the use of the latter procedure is not a reason for relaxing the standards laid down by the courts for reasoned decisions (*Westminster City Council v Secretary of State for the Environment & City Commercial Real Estates Investments Ltd* [1984] JPL 27 at p. 30). The three rules as are follows:

(i) *Reasons must be intelligible.* The first rule is that reasons must be intelligible. For example, in a planning case, *Givauden & Co Ltd v Minister of Housing & Local Government* [1967] 1 WLR 250, the Minister's decision letter incorporated by reference the inspector's conclusions, summarised certain statements in the report, referred to an irrelevant statute without stating whether or not it had been taken into account and omitted part of the inspector's words which showed his conclusion on a point. It was held that this letter was so obscure that it would leave in the mind of an informed reader a real and substantial doubt as to the reasons for the decision and the matters taken into account in making it. But decision letters and planning inspector's reports must not be construed too strictly. It is sufficient if the reasons can be generally ascertained, notwithstanding certain grammatical or logical ambiguities in the wording used (*William Boyer & Sons v Minister of Housing & Local Government* (1968) 20 P & CR 176).

Factual mistakes in the giving of reasons, such as a glaring inaccuracy or a clerical error, do not necessarily make those reasons unintelligible. For example, in *Elmbridge Borough Council v Secretary of State for the Environment & Baptist* (1980) 39 P & CR 543, a planning inspector put an incorrect measurement in his decision letter, but his reasons were otherwise clear and both parties recognised that a mistake had been made. It was held on appeal that this was an obvious mistake which did no harm and produced no doubt as to the reasons for the decision and as to whether or not it had been reached according to law.

(ii) *Reasons must deal with substantial points made.* The second rule is that, although a tribunal does not have to deal with every point, it must deal with the substantial points raised, showing what matters were taken into consideration and what view was reached on them. It is not necessary, however, for a tribunal to follow the Scottish practice of stating the method or methods of valuation used and applying them to the facts found.

In *Mountview Court Properties Ltd v Devlin* (1970) 21 P & CR 689, Lord Parker CJ said (p. 692):

> "... reasons are not deficient merely because every process of reasoning is not set out. I further think that reasons are not insufficient merely because they fail to deal with every point raised before the committee at the hearing."

Although a tribunal does not have to refer to every matter raised, and, as will be explained under rule 3 below, can use its own expert knowledge, it should not reject evidence without saying why it has done so (*Metropolitan Properties Co (FGC) Ltd v Lannon* [1969] 1 QB 577 at p. 597 and *Metropolitan Properties Co (FGC) Ltd v Good* (1981) 260 EG 67 at p. 72). Nor should a tribunal ignore in its decision a major point raised in the evidence (*London Borough of Camden v Secretary of State for the Environment & Herweld* [1980] JPL 31).

In *Waddington v Surrey & Sussex Rent Assessment Committee* (1982) 264 EG 717, Stephen Brown J dealt with the rejection of evidence of comparables by a rent assessment committee. He said (p. 718):

> "I am bound to say that, while one does not expect a rent assessment committee to give very detailed reasons, it is incumbent upon them to deal with the hard evidence which is before them; if they are going to reject it or disregard it as being irrelevant, then they ought to specify that fact, and in the event of finding that the alleged comparables are not in fact comparable there should be some indication as to the reason for that. I think this is particularly relevant where one has a next-door property which one would expect should carry considerable weight."

Although reasons should be given for the rejection of evidence of fact it would appear that, where conflicting evidence of opinion is before a tribunal, it is not required to explain why it accepts or rejects that evidence (see *Metropolitan Property Holdings Ltd v Laufer* (1974) 29 P & CR 172 and *R v London Rent Assessment Panel ex p. Cliftvylle Properties Ltd* (1982)

266 EG 44). In *Guppys (Bridport) Ltd v Sandoe* (1975) 235 EG 689, Lord Widgery CJ said (p. 693):

> "There are plenty of judicial offices, not the least a High Court judge, where reasons undoubtedly have to be given for every decision, but that does not mean that if the judge has two conflicting opinions put before him in evidence, he has to explain why he chooses one in preference to the other. Such explanations are not possible. They are matters of judgment, impression and sometimes even instinct, and it is impossible to give detailed reasons to explain how the system of decision has worked."

The second part of rule 2 is that the English authorities do not support the rule, which applies in Scotland, that a rent assessment committee (or other valuation tribunal) should state the method of valuation used and its application to the facts of the case.

In *Guppys Properties Ltd v Knott* (1977) 245 EG 1023 at pp. 1023–4, Lord Widgery CJ observed that valuation is not a science but an art, and there will be many cases where all that an assessment committee can do is to say that, on the basis of the information provided, the rent should be £X. In *Midanbury Properties (Southampton) Ltd v Houghton T. Clark & Son Ltd* (1981) 259 EG 565, Sir Douglas Frank QC (sitting as a deputy judge) rejected a submission that a rent assessment committee are required to identify in their reasoned decision the principal yardstick on which they relied in fixing a fair rent. He said (p. 567):

> "I do not think the committee are bound, at the end of the day to say what was their principal yardstick or even whether there was a principal yardstick. I think they are quite entitled to say 'These various points were raised: this is what we thought about them, or these were the comments on them.' Then at the end of the day they are entitled to put everything in the pot and stir it all together, and what comes out as the cooked dish is the fair rent as they find it.
>
> I will stress again that unlike the Scottish committees, the English committees are not required to regard valuation as an exact science, as a mathematical calculation, which it is not."

In the above extract Sir Douglas Frank was apparently correcting part of his earlier judgment in *Guppys Properties Ltd v Knott (No. 2)* (1979) 253 EG 907, where he approved the Scottish

doctrine regarding reasons which require a committee to state
the method of valuation used and its application to the facts.

(iii) *Reasons may take into account tribunal's knowledge and experience.*
The use which a tribunal may make of its expert knowledge and
experience is discussed in Chapter 10 (p. 319 above). Briefly, a
tribunal may use its own general expertise to understand and
evaluate the evidence without disclosing it to the parties, but
may not give itself evidence nor take a different view of the facts
to that put in evidence and submissions without disclosing it to
the parties for comment. An expert tribunal may reject or decline to hear expert evidence. These principles are reflected in
the third of Sir Douglas Frank's rules which states that a committee (or other expert tribunal) which has dealt with the substantial points raised by the parties may rely on their own
knowledge and experience in reaching a decision and are not
required to explain further how their figures are determined
(see also *Metropolitan Property Holdings Ltd v Laufer* (1974) 29 P
& CR 172 at pp. 176–177).

(b) *Reasons for findings of fact.* One of the tasks of a tribunal of fact
is to make essential findings of fact after listening to the
evidence. It is not strictly necessary for the tribunal to state the
reasons for those findings. For example, in a compensation case,
J. Bibby & Sons Ltd v Merseyside County Council (1979) 39 P & CR
53, a claim was made for increased operating costs at new
premises taken by the claimants following compulsory purchase.
The Lands Tribunal found as a fact that the claimants received
a benefit from those costs and, therefore, suffered no loss ranking
for compensation. On appeal the claimants contended, *inter alia*,
that the tribunal's decision did not contain sufficiently clear or
detailed reasons for this finding: the tribunal should have quantified the expenditure and benefit respectively, seen whether
they were equal and, if not, should have allowed part of the
extra operating costs as compensation. These contentions
were rejected by the Court of Appeal. Brandon LJ said
(pp. 63–64):

> "It would, no doubt, have been helpful if the member had
> stated more fully and in greater detail the basis on which
> he came to the conclusion that there was no loss, but I do
> not know of any principle that requires a tribunal charged
> with finding essential facts to do more than make the
> essential findings. It is not necessary for such a tribunal to
> give the basis of its findings or the reasons for its findings,
> although it is often very helpful and convenient if it does
> so. The member who gave the decision was an experienced

surveyor. Questions of valuation and assessment come naturally to a person who is experienced in that way. I can only conclude that, having looked at the matter from a practical surveyor's point of view, he came to the conclusion that Bibby had had value for the extra expenditure. That was a conclusion to which an experienced tribunal of that kind was entitled to come, and I do not see how this court can do other than accept that finding as an unassailable finding of fact.''

(c) *Summary.* The guidance given above may be adapted to a reasoned award and summarised as follows:

(i) An award should begin by explaining briefly how the arbitration came about. This will usually be in the form of recitals.

(ii) Agreed facts should either be set out in the award or in a statement of agreed facts attached to it.

(iii) An arbitrator should make any findings of fact which are necessary to his decision and set these out in his award. Although it might be helpful and convenient if the reasons for these findings were given, this is not essential.

(iv) The reasons given by an arbitrator for his award will depend upon the facts of the case and the problem before him, but they must always be intelligible.

(v) Where an arbitrator receives conflicting evidence of fact he should state which evidence he prefers and why. But where conflicting evidence of opinion is put before him he need not give reasons for the acceptance or rejection of this evidence.

(vi) Submissions of law should be set out in the award with the arbitrator's decision thereon. An arbitrator is not required to analyse the law and the authorities (although this would not be unwelcome to the courts), but he should explain how he has reached his conclusions. His reasons should not be too lengthy, detailed or elaborate and should avoid discussing the underlying legal philosophy.

(vii) Where different methods of valuation are put to an arbitrator he should summarise them and, although this is not strictly necessary, he should state which he prefers. He need not explain the method of valuation used in reaching his determination.

(viii) A reasoned award need not deal with every point raised but it should deal with the substantial points, showing what matters have been taken into consideration and what views have been reached on them.

(ix) An arbitrator may use his own expert knowledge and

experience and, provided he deals in his award with the substantial points raised by the parties, he need not explain further how his figures were determined.

(x) The above rules apply to all reasoned awards irrespective of whether they follow an oral hearing or the exchange of written representations.

The giving of reasons for an award of costs is discussed on p. 351 below.

INTEREST

Where an arbitration contains a dispute concerning the payment of money, the question arises as to whether the arbitrator can award interest to compensate the successful creditor for the time he has been kept out of his money. There are three situations, relating respectively to the payment of interest for the period before the commencement of proceedings, after such commencement but before the date of the award and after the award.

(1) Interest for the period before the commencement of proceedings

A debtor may make a payment after the due date but *before* the commencement of proceedings by his creditor. Where those proceedings take place the arbitrator has no common law power to award interest on the sums paid late but *before* the start of proceedings (*President of India v La Pintada Compania Navigacion SA* [1984] 3 WLR 10). The arbitration agreement may, of course, give the arbitrator power to award interest under these circumstances.

(2) Interest for the period after commencement of proceedings and before the award

This situation is now governed, in the absence of a contrary intention in the arbitration agreement, by section 19A of the 1950 Act (Appendix C p. 472 below). This was inserted by section 15(6) and Part IV of Schedule 1 to the Administration of Justice Act 1982, with effect from 1st January 1983. Section 19A(1) provides that:

> "Unless a contrary intention is expressed therein, every arbitration agreement shall, where such provision is applicable to the reference, be deemed to contain a provision that the arbitrator or umpire may, if he thinks fit, award simple interest at such rate as he thinks fit—
>
> (a) on any sum which is the subject of the reference but which is paid before the award, for such period ending not later than the date of the payment as he thinks fit; and

(b) on any sum which he awards, for such period ending not later than the date of the award as he thinks fit."

Sub-section (1)(a) above allows an arbitrator to award interest where a party to the dispute, having failed to make payment on the due date, makes payment after the commencement of the proceedings but *before* the award. The creditor receives his money but has suffered financial loss by being denied the use of it for a period of time. The arbitrator may now award interest, usually from the date when the sum became due (although he has a discretion), to a date not later than the date of payment.

Sub-section (1)(b) deals with the situation where no payment has been made but is directed to be made in the award. The arbitrator may direct that interest shall be paid on that sum for a period ending not later than the date of his award. Again, the date for the start of the period of interest is in the arbitrator's discretion but it usually runs from the date when payment should have been made.

Section 19A(2) provides that the statutory power to award interest is without prejudice to any other power to do so possessed by the arbitrator. Thus, the power to award interest under the arbitration agreement or under section 20 of the 1950 Act in respect of the period *after* the award (see below) is unaffected by the above provisions.

It should be noted that, in the absence of a contrary intention in the arbitration agreement, an arbitrator has discretion whether or not to award interest, what rate per cent to adopt and the commencement date, but he cannot award compound interest. Although an arbitrator has a discretion regarding the commencement date for interest, the *general* rule (which is subject to exceptions) is that interest should run from the date of loss (*BP Exploration Co (Libya) Ltd v Hunt (No. 2)* [1982] 1 All ER 925 at pp. 974–5). Thus, in *Allied London Investments Ltd v Hambro Life Assurance Ltd* (1985) 274 EG 148, it was held in an action for arrears of rent against original tenants, that interest on those arrears should be calculated from the date when each payment of rent became due and not from the date of a subsequent letter informing the original tenants (the defendants) of the default by their assignee.

(3) Interest for the period after the award

Section 20 of the 1950 Act (Appendix C p. 473 below) provides that

"A sum directed to be paid by an award shall, unless the award otherwise directs, carry interest from the date of the award at the same rate as a judgment debt."

It is not necessary for the award to direct in express terms that the

sum awarded shall carry interest from the date of the award: the
provisions of section 20 automatically apply unless the award
directs that no interest is payable. In *Timber Shipping Co SA v London
& Overseas Freighters Ltd* [1972] AC 1, it was held that section 20 gave
an arbitrator discretion to decide whether or not an award should
carry interest, but not to determine the rate at which it should do so.
This can only be that applicable to a judgment debt, sometimes
called "statutory interest". The rate of interest is that in force at the
date of the award and does not vary according to changes in the
prescribed rate after that date (*Rocco Guiseppe & Figli v Tradax Export
SA* [1983] 3 All ER 598). The period of interest runs from the date of
the award to the date of payment.

(4) Interest in rent review arbitrations

The question of interest only arises where an arbitrator has power to
direct the payment of money. In a rent review arbitration he is
normally required only to determine the *amount* of the review rent.
In the absence of a specific power to order *payment* of that rent he
cannot award interest. It is open to the parties to give the arbitrator
power to direct the payment of arrears of rent: interest may then
become payable thereon. In the absence of an express term in a lease
requiring the payment of interest on unpaid rent, the court will not
imply such a term. It is not necessary to do so in order to give
business efficacy to the contract (*Trust House Forte Albany Hotels Ltd v
Daejan Investments Ltd* (1980) 256 EG 915 and see Appendix A p. 431
below).

COSTS

Costs in litigation are discussed in Chapter 1; I now consider an
arbitrator's powers and duties relating thereto. A final award must
deal with costs otherwise it will not be complete.

(1) Arbitrator's power regarding costs

An arbitrator's power to award costs arises out of the arbitration
agreement or under section 18(1) of the 1950 Act, which gives him a
wide discretion to order the payment and taxation of costs.

(a) *The arbitration agreement.* An arbitrator should look first at the
arbitration agreement to see whether it gives specific directions as
to costs or otherwise removes his power to deal with them under
section 18(1) of the 1950 Act. Where an arbitration agreement contains an express provision allocating liability for costs, the arbitrator generally has no discretion in this matter except where such
provision is rendered void under section 18(3) of the 1950 Act (see

below). Thus, in *Fitzsimmons v Lord Mostyn* [1904] AC 46, a lease contained a covenant for renewal "at the costs of the lessee" and on payment of a fine, to be determined by arbitration if not agreed. It was held that the costs of the reference and award were costs of the renewal of the lease payable by the lessee, and the arbitrator had no discretion to deal with them.

Where an arbitration agreement contains a provision that the parties or any party shall in any event pay their or his own costs, and the agreement relates to the submission of possible *future* disputes to arbitration, this provision is void (section 18(3) of the 1950 Act, Appendix C p. 471 below, *Windvale Ltd v Darlington Insulation Co Ltd* (1983) *The Times* 22nd December 1983). The arbitration agreement will have effect as if this provision regarding costs were not contained in it: the arbitrator then has a discretion regarding the award of costs. Section 18(3) does not, however, render void an agreement as to costs where the dispute was in existence when it was made.

An arbitrator has no general power to order the parties to give security for costs and may only do so if there is an express provision to that effect in the arbitration agreement (see Chapter 10 p. 298 above).

(b) *Section 18(1) of the 1950 Act (Appendix C p. 471 below)*. This sub-section provides that, unless a contrary intention is expressed therein, every arbitration agreement shall be deemed to include a provision that:

(i) the costs of the reference and award shall be in the discretion of the arbitrator or umpire;

(ii) he may direct to and by whom the costs (or part thereof) shall be paid;

(iii) he may direct in what manner those costs shall be paid;

(iv) he may tax or settle the amount of costs;

(v) he may award costs on a solicitor and client basis (see Chapter 1 p. 10 above).

The "costs of the reference" include all costs properly incurred by the parties in the course of the arbitration. The "costs of the award" are the remuneration and expenses of the arbitrator; they are part of the costs of the reference.

(2) Arbitrator's discretion regarding costs

The discretion of an arbitrator regarding costs is the same as that of a High Court judge (*Stotesbury v Turner* [1943] 1 KB 370). It must be "judicially exercised":

"Those words 'judicially exercised' are always difficult to apply, but they mean that the arbitrator must not act capri-

ciously and must if he is going to exercise his discretion (to the detriment of the successful party) show a reason connected with the case and one which the court can see is a proper reason."
(per Lord Goddard CJ in *Lewis v Haverfordwest RDC* [1953] 1 WLR 1487).

An award of costs by an arbitrator cannot be reviewed by the court solely on the grounds that the court disagrees with it. The court can only intervene where the arbitrator has exercised his discretion in an arbitrary manner or taken into account an irrelevant consideration or otherwise made an error of law:

"In reviewing an arbitrator's decision on costs, it is of the greatest importance to remember that the decision is within his discretion and not that of the courts. It is nothing to the point that I might have reached a different decision and that some other judge or arbitrator might have differed from both of is. I would neither wish, nor be entitled, to intervene, unless I was satisfied that the arbitrator had misdirected himself."
(per Donaldson J in *Tramountana Armadora SA v Atlantic Shipping Co SA* [1978] 2 All ER 870).

The general rule for an award of costs is that "costs follow the event", that is to say they are awarded to the successful party. This is the "primary principle" governing costs and, although an arbitrator may quite properly depart from it in appropriate circumstances, he may only do so where there is a good reason connected with the case.

Costs may be awarded to a party who recovers less than his claim, if he has been forced to resort to litigation or arbitration in order to recover the amount to which he is entitled. For example, in *Nicholson v Little* [1956] 1 WLR 829, a surveyor acting on behalf of a houseowner in respect of war damage claims retained £84 of the money paid to him on account of his claim for fees of £105. He refused to pay over the retained amount following repeated requests to do so and the owner sued him in the county court. The surveyor counterclaimed for £105 fees. The judge found that £61 was due to him, dismissed the counterclaim and awarded the balance of £23 to the plaintiff houseowner with costs. The surveyor appealed against the order of costs. It was dismissed. Denning LJ said (pp. 831–2):

"I can see no fault of principle in what (the judge) has done. It is to be remembered that this really was the houseowner's money, and the surveyor was clinging on to it and claiming it as being his, the surveyor's money; he wishes to put it in his own pocket for his fees and did put it in his own pocket for his fees, and it would have remained in there but for the fact that the houseowner brought this action. The houseowner had to bring this action to recover his money. He succeeded in getting it, and he did so by greatly reducing this surveyor's claim for fees. The judge probably said to himself 'It would be unjust for this house-owner, having had to bring this action to recover money due to him, to find himself, by reason of costs, with nothing in hand at all and rather out of pocket.' That is the consideration which I think the judge was well entitled to take into account in exercising his discretion, it seems to me that there is no ground on which we can interfere with his discretion."

It may arise, however, that one party recovers only slightly less than his claim but does not recover all his costs due to other considerations. For example, in *P. Rosen & Co Ltd v Dowley & Selby* [1943] 2 All ER 172, a claimant for compensation before an official arbitrator recovered only slightly less than his claim but was awarded only part of his costs. The court refused to interfere with the award of costs since the arbitrator may have taken the view that more evidence was called than was necessary, or that more costs were incurred than was reasonable, and it was impossible for the court to say that there was no material on which he could exercise his discretion.

In a rent review arbitration the rent determined usually lies somewhere between the figures contended for by the landlord and tenant respectively. How are the costs to be awarded? If the result can truly be said to be a "draw", in that the rent determined is mid-way between reasonable figures submitted by the parties, then the proper award would be for each party to bear his own costs and to pay half the costs of the award. But where the result is much closer to one party's figure than the other's, then the arbitrator may properly require the "losing party" to bear all or part of the other party's costs, particularly where the rent advocated by the former was unreasonably high or low.

Where an arbitrator wishes to divide the liability for costs equally between the parties the proper order is for each party to bear his own costs of the reference and half the costs of the award. He should not order each party to pay half the costs of the reference and award, because this will require a taxation of each party's costs, something which will be avoided if the former order is made.

Sealed offers. A sealed offer is an unconditional offer usually marked "without prejudice save as to costs" or containing some other statement which indicates that it is intended to perform the function of a sealed offer. The amount of a sealed offer is not known to the tribunal until after he has made his decision: it is in a sealed envelope which is then opened and may be taken into account when exercising his discretion as to costs. The sealed offer procedure plays an important part in determining liability for costs in compensation disputes before the Lands Tribunal (see Chapter 1 p. 18 above). In arbitration, an apportionment of costs between the parties may properly be made by reference to the amount and date of a sealed offer. A sealed offer is the equivalent in arbitration of a payment into court (see Chapter 1 p. 8 above). Although it is not exactly the same because the Rules of the Supreme Court do not apply to arbitrations, the sealed offer procedure should be considered against the background of the law relating to payments into court.

In *Tramountana Armadora SA v Atlantic Shipping Co SA* [1978] 2 All ER 870, Donaldson J gave valuable guidance to arbitrators on the effect of a sealed offer on costs. He said (p. 877):

> "How should an arbitrator deal with costs where there has been a 'sealed offer'? I think he should ask himself the question: 'Has the claimant achieved more by rejecting the offer and going on with the arbitration than he would have achieved if he had accepted the offer?' This is a simple question to answer, whether the offer does or does not include interest. The arbitrator knows what the claimant would have received if he had accepted the offer. He would have received that sum and could not have asked the arbitrator to award any interest. In order that like should be compared with like, the interest element must be recalculated as if the award had been made on the same date as the offer. Alternatively, interest from the period between offer and award must notionally be added to the amount of the sealed offer. But, subject to that, the question is easily answered.
>
> If the claimant in the end has achieved no more than he would have achieved by accepting the offer, the continuance of the arbitration after that date has been a waste of time and money. *Prima facie*, the claimant should be ordered to pay the respondent's costs after that date. If he has achieved more by going on, the respondent should pay the costs throughout."

Although liability for costs may be determined by reference to the amount and date of a "sealed offer", costs should not be awarded by reference to some arbitrary date which has no significance either with reference to the comparable success of the parties or their relevant conduct. Thus, the commencement of the hearing would not be a relevant date in respect of an award of costs (*Archital Luxfer Ltd v Henry Boot Construction Ltd* [1981] 1 Lloyd's Rep 642).

Without prejudice statements. The law relating to "without prejudice" statements is discussed in Chapter 3 p. 78 above. When awarding costs an arbitrator should not have regard to correspondence or statements made "without prejudice", except with the consent of both parties (*Walker v Wilsher* (1889) 23 QBD 335). For example, in *Stotesbury v Turner* [1943] 1 KB 370, it was held that an arbitrator, when dealing with the question of costs, was wrong to take into consideration statements made "without prejudice" at the preliminary meeting before him and a letter marked "without prejudice" containing a rejection of the respondent's offer to settle.

But a "without prejudice" offer to settle, which is also subject to the right to refer to it on the question of costs (very similar to a sealed offer and sometimes called a Calderbank letter), is admissible for that purpose in all cases where the issue between the parties is more than a simple money claim and, therefore, payment into court would not be appropriate. Thus, where the plaintiff in an action relating to access over the defendant's land made an offer to settle, marked "without prejudice" but expressly subject to a reservation that it may be referred to on the question of costs, and the action proceeded to a decision less beneficial to the defendant than the plaintiff's offer, it was held that the offer could be taken into consideration on the question of costs: the right order would be to award the plaintiff all his costs from the date when his offer ought reasonably to have been accepted (*Cutts v Head* [1984] 2 WLR 349).

An arbitrator cannot force the parties to disclose "without prejudice" material, and one party cannot unilaterally waive the privilege he enjoys by reason of that label. It is, however, open to *both* parties to agree on disclosure and the arbitrator may then properly look at the privileged material when making his order of costs.

(3) Payment and taxation of costs

As stated above an arbitrator has power to direct the payment and taxation of costs, either under the arbitration agreement or under the wide discretion as to costs given to him by section 18 of the 1950 Act. He may order the payment and taxation of costs in one of three ways.

First, he may order one party to pay a lump sum of costs to the other party. This direction is only suitable for simple cases. In effect, the arbitrator taxes the costs himself in a lump sum when making his award.

Although a lump sum award of costs is not common practice, it is usual for an arbitrator to tax and settle his own fees and costs (i.e. the costs of the award as opposed to the costs of the reference) in a lump sum, to be paid by one or both of the parties as he directs (see Chapter 13 p. 416 below). Where a lump sum for arbitrator's fees and costs has been paid, that amount cannot later be taxed, except where it was paid following an order of court under section 19 of the 1950 Act (see below) or the arbitrator's award is subsequently set aside on the grounds that his fees are so excessive as to amount to misconduct (see Chapter 12 p. 379 below).

Secondly, an arbitrator may direct the payment of costs between the parties, such costs to be agreed or taxed by the arbitrator in the absence of agreement. It is unusual for an arbitrator to tax the costs of the reference himself, except in simple cases where lawyers are not involved.

Thirdly, the arbitrator may direct the payment of costs between the parties, such costs to be agreed or taxed by the court in default of agreement. Thus, the arbitrator performs the judicial task of awarding costs but delegates the ministerial task of taxing those costs to the taxing officer of the court. This is the usual way for an arbitrator to direct the payment and taxation of costs (see Chapter 13 p. 416 below). An arbitrator may provide for taxation in either the county court or the High Court, but he cannot delegate it to some other third party (*Knott v Long* (1735) 3 Stra 1025). Where the arbitrator does not state which court is to carry out the taxation, it will be the High Court (section 18(2) of the 1950 Act, Appendix C p. 471 below) and where he directs that costs shall be taxed in the High Court, they will be taxed on the High Court scale even though the amount involved in the arbitration is small (*H. G. Perkins Ltd v Best-Shaw* [1973] 1 WLR 975). An arbitrator may state which basis of taxation is to be used, e.g. party and party, and in particular, he has power under section 18(1) of the 1950 Act to award costs on the solicitor and client basis. If the award is silent as to the basis of taxation, as is frequently the case, the party and party basis will be used (see Chapter 1 p. 9 above).

An arbitrator has a lien on his award for his fees and will not usually release it until they have been paid. In practice, one or both of the parties will usually pay the arbitrator's fees to obtain the award. But a party to the arbitration who thinks that the arbitrator's fees are excessive may use the procedure under section 19 of the 1950 Act to obtain the award (Appendix C p. 472 below). This provides that if an arbitrator refuses to deliver his award except on payment of the fees demanded by him, any party to the arbitration (other than one who has entered into a written agreement with the arbitrator fixing his fees) may apply to the High Court and the court may order the arbitrator to deliver his award to the applicant on payment into court of the fees demanded. These are then taxed by the taxing officer: the arbitrator is paid a reasonable sum and the balance, if any, is repaid to the applicant (section 19(1) and (2)). Taxation of an arbitrator's fees is subject to review in the same manner as a taxation of costs, and the arbitrator is entitled to appear on such taxation or review (section 19(3) and (4)).

A party who has paid the arbitrator's fees, and who subsequently finds that the other party is directed to pay the whole or part thereof, may recover the overpayment from that party (*Hicks v Richardson* (1797) 1 B & P 93).

(4) Reasons for an award of costs

An arbitrator's *reasoned award* should, where he departs from the general rule that "costs follow the event", include reasons for his order of costs. For example, in *Pepys v London Transport Executive* (1975) 29 P & CR 248, the Lands Tribunal considered a claim for compensation for injurious affection due to the construction of an underground railway. The claimant was unable to produce evidence to substantiate her claim and the tribunal rejected it. London Transport Executive had made a sealed offer of £500 compensation. The tribunal ordered the claimant to pay the Executive's costs from the date of this offer, and, following their usual procedure, ordered the Executive to pay her costs up to that date. The Executive appealed against the latter part of this order. The Court of Appeal held that, although the tribunal had a discretion regarding costs before the date of a sealed offer, that discretion must be judicially exercised. Good reasons must be shown for ordering a successful party to pay the costs of an unsuccessful party and no such reasons had been given or existed in this case. Lord Denning MR, referring to the exercise of the discretion regarding costs, said (pp. 251–252):

> "The cases show that the discretion is to be judicially exercised, and that it is usually exercised in this way; that if the plaintiff fails he has normally to bear his own costs and often pay the costs of the other side. Sometimes each side is left to bear its own costs. But it is exceedingly rare for a successful defendant to pay the costs of a plaintiff who has failed. This should never be done except for very special reasons, and in that case the tribunal ought to state its reasons for so exceptional a course....
>
> ... It seems to me that if a tribunal is departing from the ordinary exercise of discretion—in so exceptional a way—it ought to give its reasons. The same would apply to an arbitrator."

Where an arbitrator gives a *non-speaking award* it is not necessary for him to give reasons for the exercise of his discretion as to costs, although it would be helpful if he did so where he departs from the general rule that costs follow the event. In *The Erich Schroeder* [1974] 1 Lloyd's Rep 192, Mocatta J said (p. 193):

"... there is no need for an arbitrator or umpire, if he so exercises his discretion as to depart from the general rule, to state
the reason why he does so in his award. On the other hand, in
all probability, in most cases where an umpire/arbitrator does
so act, it would save costs if he were to state his reasons in his
award. In that event the parties would not be put to the
expense of trying to ascertain what his reasons were and
possibly moving the court to set aside the award."

This decision was given before the Arbitration Act 1979 and an
arbitrator can now, of course, be required by the court to state his
reasons (see p. 332 above).

(5) Costs and the completeness of awards

As stated above, a valid award must be final and complete: this
includes an order for costs where these are within the arbitrator's
jurisdiction. Where an award is incomplete because it is silent as to
costs, three courses of action are available to rectify this omission.

First, application may be made to the arbitrator under section
18(4) of the 1950 Act for an order of costs (Appendix C p. 471
below). This is the simplest procedure to deal with an award which
is incomplete in this respect. Where an award is silent as to costs,
any party to the reference may within 14 days of the publication of
the award apply to the arbitrator for an order directing payment of
the costs of the reference. The arbitrator shall, after hearing any
party who desires to be heard, amend his award by the addition of
such directions as he thinks proper with respect to the payment of
costs. The 14 day period for application to the arbitrator may be
extended by the High Court. It would appear that an arbitrator may
deal with costs under this provision even though he had no power to
do so when making his award.

Secondly, application may be made to the High Court under
section 22 of the 1950 Act for an order remitting the award to the
arbitrator for him to consider the question of costs. The arbitrator
shall make his award within three months unless the order directs
otherwise (see Chapter 12 p. 381 below).

Thirdly, application may be made to the High Court under
sections 22 and 23 of the 1950 Act to remit or set aside the award
where the arbitrator has misconducted himself or the proceedings (see
Chapter 12 p. 370 below). Misconduct includes a failure by the
arbitrator to deal with the question of costs or the making of an error
of law in the exercise of his discretion as to costs. For example, in *The
Erich Schroeder* (above), the umpire ordered the successful party to
pay their own costs of the reference and half the costs of the award.
The court held that there were no grounds to justify his departure

from the general principle that costs follow the event; the umpire was guilty of misconduct and that part of his award was set aside. Normally, remission of the award is a more suitable remedy than setting aside.

Where an award is set aside on grounds of excess of jurisdiction by the arbitrator, the party to whom he awarded costs cannot recover them (*Davis v Witney UDC* (1899) 15 TLR 275).

PUBLICATION, DELIVERY AND CORRECTION OF AWARD

(1) Publication

There is no distinction in practice between the making and publication of an award: an award is generally regarded as published as soon as it has been made. There is, however, a distinction between "publication" and "publication to the parties". The latter has practical importance because that is the date from which time starts to run for certain purposes, e.g. an application to the court to set aside an award. An award will be published to the parties when it is complete *and* notice has been served on the parties that it is made and ready for delivery. Time begins to run from the date of publication to the parties and it is immaterial that the parties have not received copies of the award and are unaware of the contents (*South Tottenham Land Securities v R & A Millett (Shops) Ltd* (1983) 269 EG 630; *Bulk Transport Corporation v Sissy Steamship Co Ltd* [1979] 2 Lloyds's Rep 289).

(2) Delivery

A submission to arbitration may require an award to be "ready to be delivered" or "delivered" by a certain date. An award is ready to be delivered when it has been made and the parties have been informed that it is ready for delivery. Actual delivery is not essential (*Brown v Vawser* (1804) 4 East 584). An award can only be said to be delivered when it has actually been delivered to one or all of the parties.

(3) Correction

The limited powers of an arbitrator to correct an award after publication are discussed in Chapter 12 p. 359 below. A form of words for such a correction is set out in Chapter 13 p. 423 below.

CHAPTER TWELVE

Law of Arbitration—IV

After the Award

INTRODUCTION

The majority of arbitrations end with the publication of the award. The unsuccessful party complies with it; enforcement is not necessary; the award is not challenged. In a minority of cases, however, the arbitration does not end with the award. Questions may arise as to the effect on the parties, strangers or the arbitrator. It may be challenged by one of the parties: by an apeal on a point of law or by an application to remit or set aside the award. The unsuccessful party may fail to comply with it necessitating enforcement by the other party. These are the subjects considered in this chapter.

EFFECT OF AN AWARD

The effect of an award on a person will depend upon whether that person is a party to the arbitration agreement, a stranger or the arbitrator.

(1) Effect on the parties

The general rule is that an award is final and binding on the parties and those claiming under them. Section 16 of the 1950 Act states that a provision to this effect shall be deemed to be included in every arbitration agreement, in the absence of a contrary intention therein and where such provision is applicable to the reference (Appendix C p. 471 below). An award is final in two ways. First, there is only a limited right of appeal. The ways of challenging an award are discussed later in this chapter (p. 359 below). Secondly, an award is a final judgment between the parties and cannot be re-opened in subsequent proceedings. This is now discussed.

It is the *making* of an award, not its performance, which produces its final effect. Performance is only relevant to enforcement (see p. 387 below). This is illustrated by an old case with rather unusual facts. In *Purslow v Bailey* (1705) 2 Ld Raym 1039, an action was brought for trespass and the defendant pleaded that the dispute had already been settled by arbitration. The award in this arbitration directed the defendant to provide a couple of pullets to be eaten by the plaintiff at the defendant's house in settlement of the trespass. The defendant provided the pullets but the plaintiff did not come to eat them. In the subsequent action the plaintiff argued that the award was no defence because it had not been performed. It was held that the award was a good defence without performance.

In this case the defendant put forward the defence of judgment estoppel, that is to say he pleaded that the plaintiff was estopped from pursuing his action for trespass because it had already been dealt with by a previous judgment, namely the arbitration award. Judgment estoppel also arises where there is subsequent litigation between the parties, in which the cause of action is different but one or more issues are the same. This is "issue estoppel". The parties will be estopped from raising again issues which were decided, or which they failed to bring forward or admitted, in the earlier litigation (see Chapter 2 p. 55 above).

The doctrine of judgment estoppel applies to arbitration. Thus, subject to the limited rights of challenge discussed below (p. 359) and provided the arbitration agreement does not give the award only a temporary effect, an award, other than an interim award, is a final and conclusive judgment between the parties on all matters referred to arbitration. For example, in *Willday v Taylor* (1976) 241 EG 835, the claimants entered into a contract and a supplemental contract for the construction of a bungalow, both containing an arbitration clause. A claim brought under one of the contracts for certain defects, including dampness, was settled by arbitration. The award gave the claimants a small sum in respect of this dampness. They then brought an action in the courts under the other contract for the same defect. It was held by the Court of Appeal that the two contracts were so related that the award made under one was final in respect of both claims relating to the same defect, the claimants having expressly agreed that the award would be in complete satisfaction of their claim.

An award is only conclusive, however, in respect of the questions actually referred to arbitration. For example, in *H. E. Daniels Ltd v Carmel Exporters & Importers Ltd* [1953] 2 QB 242, the parties agreed to refer to arbitration all disputes arising out of a contract and a dispute regarding the quality of the goods was settled in this manner. A second dispute, regarding misdescription, was then referred by one of the parties but the other objected on the grounds of judgment estoppel. The court held that there were two separate disputes between the parties and only the first had been in dispute when the first arbitration took place. This was the only matter dealt with at that arbitration. The second dispute clearly arose out of the contract, it related to a different matter and the award made under this reference should stand, although had the defendants taken steps in the second arbitration to have the award stated in the form of a special case alleging judgment estoppel, they might well have been entitled to succeed under the rule that all damages resulting from the same cause of action must be assessed and recovered at one time.

Where an award is made upon a reference of "all matters in difference" then the doctrine of judgment estoppel will apply both to the matters *actually* brought before the arbitrator and those which *could* have been referred to him. In *Fidelitas Shipping Co Ltd v V/O Exportchleb* [1966] 1 QB 630, the doctrine of judgment estoppel in arbitration was discussed and Lord Denning MR said (p. 640):

> "The law, as I understand it, is this: if one party brings an action against another for a particular cause and the judgment is given upon it, there is a strict rule of law that he cannot bring another action against the same party for the same cause .... But within one cause of action, there may be several issues raised which are necessary for the determination of the whole case. The rule then is that, once an issue has been raised and distinctly determined between the parties, then, as a general rule, neither can be allowed to fight that issue all over again .... And within one issue, there may be several points available which go to aid one party or the other in his efforts to secure a determination of the issue in his favour. The rule then is that each party must use reasonable diligence to bring forward every point which he thinks would help him. If he omits to raise any particular point, from negligence, inadvertence, or even accident (which would or might have decided this issue in his favour), he might find himself shut out from raising that point again, at any rate in any case where the self-same issue arises in the same or subsequent proceedings."

An award on a reference of "all matters in difference" is not conclusive in respect of a matter which existed as a claim at the time of the reference, but was not then in dispute and was not, therefore, referred to arbitration (*Ravee v Farmer* (1791) 4 TR 146).

An award is generally conclusive evidence between the parties as to the facts stated in it. For example, in *Whitehead v Tattersall* (1834) 1 Ad & El 491, a landlord and tenant submitted to arbitration the question of the amount of damages for breach of covenant to repair. The arbitrator made an award of £55.5s. In an action on the covenant it was held that the award was conclusive as to the amount of damages, unless it could be impeached.

An award cannot have the effect of transferring property, real or personal, but where appropriate it can (and should) contain directions for effecting such a conveyance or transfer (see Chapter 11 p. 329 above).

Where one party tenders an award in evidence it is open to the other party to give evidence to destroy its effect, e.g. by showing that the arbitrator did not deal with all of the matters referred to him.

(2) Effect on strangers

Strangers to an arbitration agreement are not as a general rule bound by an award arising out of that agreement. They will only be bound if they so agree. Thus, an award is not admissible in evidence *against* a stranger to the arbitration. For example, in *Evans v Rees* (1839) 10 Ad & El 151, at the trial of an issue in respect of a parish boundary, an award setting out the boundary in an arbitration between other parties was held to be inadmissible in evidence. Lord Denman CJ said (p. 155):

> "The authority of an arbitrator is entirely derived from the consent of the parties to the reference; his award has no force except by reason of that consent, and no instance can be proved in which strangers have been held to be in any way affected in their rights by an award either as evidence of right or of reputation."

But under certain circumstances an award may be put in evidence in other proceedings *for* a stranger to the arbitration. Thus, in *Shelling v Farmer* (1725) 1 Stra 646, in an action for damages between S and F, F produced an award of compensation and subsequent release under an arbitration between S and F's employers, which included the same matters as those upon which the present action was founded. It was held that the award and release were good evidence in favour of F even though he was a stanger to the award.

The original tenant under a lease containing a rent review clause who assigns his interest is liable to pay the revised rent agreed or otherwise determined upon review, even though he may not have been a party to such agreement or determination. Where the revised rent is determined by arbitration between the landlord and an assignee of the term, the original tenant will not usually be a party to that reference, but he will not be a stranger to the arbitration clause in the lease and will be bound by privity of contract to pay the new rent if the assignee defaults (*Centrovincial Estates PLC v Bulk Storage Ltd* (1983) 268 EG 59).

(3) Effect on the arbitrator

An award (other than an interim award) is final in the sense that the arbitrator becomes *functus officio* when it is made, and, subject to the three exceptions listed below, he cannot alter it nor make a second award. Thus, in *Re Stringer & Riley Bros* [1901] 1 QB 105, an arbitrator made an award which did not deal with the disputes specified in the arbitration agreement. When this was pointed out to him he destroyed the award and made a second award. It was held that when he made his first award he became *functus officio* but nevertheless the award would be remitted to him and his powers would revive as a result of the remission. There are three exceptions to the general rule that an arbitrator may not subsequently alter his award.

First, he may correct accidental mistakes. Unless a contrary intention is expressed in the arbitration agreement, section 17 of the 1950 Act gives an arbitrator power to correct any clerical mistake or error in his award arising from any accidental slip or omission (Appendix C p. 471 below). (For the form in which a correction to an award may be made see Chapter 13 p. 423 below.)

It should be noted that the scope of this power is strictly limited. There is a distinction between the arbitrator having second thoughts on his decision and the arbitrator correcting his award to give effect to his initial thoughts. Only the latter is permissible under section 17. Thus, in *Sutherland & Co v Hannevig Bros Ltd* [1921] 1 KB 336, the arbitrator altered his award in respect of costs, but the court held that his original award must stand. It came to the conclusion that the arbitrator made his award as he intended to make it and, therefore, he had not made an error arising out of an accidental slip or omission. But in a recent case, *Mutual Shipping Corporation of New York v Bayshore Shipping Co of Monrovia* [1985] 1 Lloyd's Rep 189, the Court of Appeal remitted an award for correction by the arbitrator, who had correctly recorded the evidence but had accidentally attributed it to the wrong parties and thereby made an incorrect award. Sir John Donaldson MR said this was a classic case of error arising from an accidental slip which the arbitrator had power to correct himself. He also said that, where an arbitrator intends to exercise the power of correction under section 17, he should notify the parties and give them an opportunity of challenging in the courts the applicability of this power to the facts of the particular case.

Secondly, an arbitrator may add to his award directions as to the payment of costs where these have been omitted. This power is given by section 18(4) of the 1950 Act on the application of any party to the reference (see Chapter 11 p. 352 above).

Thirdly, an arbitrator may make an amended award where it is remitted to him by the court under section 22 of the 1950 Act (see p. 381 below) or section 1 of the 1979 Act (see p. 360 below).

CHALLENGING AN AWARD

As a general rule an award is final and binding, but there are nevertheless several ways in which it may be challenged by a dissatisfied party. He may seek leave to appeal to the High Court on a question of law; or he may apply to the court to remit or set aside the award. He may challenge the award when the successful party brings an action to enforce it. He may seek a declaration relating to the award. The arbitration agreement may give the parties rights of appeal to an umpire or other appeal tribunal. These rights of challenge are now discussed.

(1) Appeal on a question of law

(a) *The new right of appeal.* Section 1(1) of the 1979 Act abolished the special case procedure under section 21 of the 1950 Act, whereby an arbitrator could, or could be directed to, state any question of law or his award in the form of a special case for the decision of the High Court. It also removed the court's jurisdiction to set aside or remit an award on the ground of errors of fact or law on the face of the award (Appendix C p. 504 below). These lost rights are replaced by a limited right of appeal on any question of law arising out of an award and the right to apply to the court for the determination of a preliminary point of law (see Chapter 10 p. 304 above).

Section 1(2) and (3) of the 1979 Act provide that an appeal shall lie to the High Court by any of the parties to a reference on any question of law arising out of the award:

(i) with the consent of all other parties to the reference; or

(ii) with the leave of the court and provided that the parties have not entered into an exclusion agreement under section 3 of the Act (see p. 366 below) (Appendix C p. 506 below).

An appeal must be made within 21 days after the award has been made and published to the parties, or, where reasons are given after the publication of the award, within 21 days from the date of reasons (RSC Order 73 rule 5(2)).

It should be noted that a party who wishes to appeal under section 1 must first obtain the consent of all other parties or leave of the court before he can pursue his appeal on its merits. The court may grant leave to appeal subject to conditions, e.g. by requiring a payment into court or the giving of security for costs (section 1(4)).

Where consent or leave is given, then on the determination of the appeal, the court may:

(i) confirm, vary or set aside the award; or

(ii) remit the award to the reconsideration of the arbitrator together with the court's opinion on the question of law which was the subject of the appeal (section 1(2)).

Where an award is remitted the arbitrator shall, unless otherwise directed, make his award within three months of the order of the court. The power of the court is not limited to the confirmation, setting aside or remission of an award but it may, by varying it, effectively re-write it. An award which is so varied shall have effect as if it were the award of the arbitrator except, of course, for the purposes of a further appeal under this section (section 1(8) of the 1979 Act, Appendix C p. 505 below).

As discussed in the previous chapter (p. 332 above), the court may order an arbitrator to state the reasons for his award in sufficient detail to enable the court to consider any question of law arising out of the award should an appeal be brought under section 1 (section 1(5) and (6) of the 1979 Act).

An appeal under section 1 is limited to "any question of law arising out of an award", but it is not always easy to draw a distinction between questions of fact and questions of law (see Chapter 2 p. 38 above). For example, in a rent review, the *subject-matter* of the rental valuation is a question of law, necessitating interpretation of the relevant clauses in the lease; but the *value* of that subject-matter is a question of fact, dependent upon valuation technique. The admissibility of evidence is a question of law; the weight to be given to admissible evidence is a question of fact. In *Edwards v Bairstow* [1956] AC 14, Lord Radcliffe explained the scope of a point of law as follows (p. 36):

> "If the case contains anything *ex facie* which is bad law and which bears upon the determination, it is, obviously, erroneous in point of law, but, without such misconception appearing *ex facie*, it may be that facts found are such that no person acting judicially and properly instructed as to the relevant law could come to the determination under appeal. In these circumstances, too, the court must intervene. It has no option but to assume that there has been some misconception of the law and that this has been responsible for the determination. So there, too, there has been an error in point of law."

Thus, reduced to simple terms, a question of law may arise out of a "pure" determination of law, such as the construction of a document or statute, or it may also arise where a decision of fact is so clearly incorrect that the court can assume that it is based on an error of law, e.g. where it is unsupported by the evidence or is consistent with or contradictory of it (see also *Bracegirdle v Oxley* [1946] 1 KB 349 at p. 353 and *Ashbridge Investments Ltd v Minister of Housing & Local Government* [1965] 1 WLR 1320 at p. 1326).

(b) *Guidelines for the grant of leave to appeal.* As we have seen a party who wishes to appeal on a question of law must first obtain the consent of the parties or leave of the court before he may proceed with his appeal. In the latter case section 1(4) of the 1979 Act provides that the court shall not grant leave to appeal against an award on a question of law "unless it considers that, having regard to all the circumstances, the determination of the question of law concerned could substantially affect the rights of one or more of the parties to the arbitration agreement" (Appendix C p. 504 below). For example, in *Duvan Estates Ltd v Rossette Sunshine Savouries Ltd* (1981) 261 EG 364, the court refused leave to appeal because the question of law, on the admissibility of evidence of trading accounts in a rent review arbitration, was in the context of the case, a marginal point which could not substantially affect the rights of the parties.

Section 1(4) of the 1979 Act contains the only specific fetter on the discretion of the court to grant or refuse leave to appeal on a point of law. The courts have, however, formulated their own guidelines governing the exercise of this discretion.

The leading case is the decision of the House of Lords in *Pioneer Shipping Ltd v BTP Tioxide Ltd (The Nema)* [1981] 3 WLR 292. The facts, which concern a charterparty, are unimportant, but Lord Diplock devoted his judgment to a consideration of the judicial review of arbitrator's awards under the 1979 Act and laid down guidelines for the assistance of the High Court in dealing with applications for leave to appeal.

He said that the exercise of the court's judicial discretion involved deciding between the rival merits of finality on the one hand and legal correctness on the other, having regard to the nature and circumstances of the particular dispute. The 1979 Act, however, contained several indications that the intention of the Act was in favour of finality in awards, at any rate where this did not expose arbitrators to a temptation to depart from settled principles of law.

Lord Diplock's guidelines for the giving or withholding of leave to appeal depend upon the nature of the clause producing the question of law under consideration. If it is a "one-off" clause, peculiar to that contract and unlikely to be found elsewhere, then the presumption is for finality and against the giving of leave to appeal. Lord Diplock said (p. 303):

> "Where, as in the instant case, a question of law involved is the construction of a 'one-off' clause the application of which to the particular facts of the case is an issue in the arbitration, leave should not normally be given unless it is apparent to the judge upon a mere perusal of the reasoned award itself without the benefit of adversarial argument, that the meaning ascribed to the clause by the arbitrator is obviously wrong. But if on such perusal it appears to the judge that it is possible that argument might persuade him, despite first impression to the contrary, that the arbitrator might be right, he should not grant leave; the parties should be left to accept, for better or for worse, the decision of the tribunal that they have chosen to decide the matter in the first instance."

The position is different, however, where the question of law arises out of a "standard" clause, commonly found in contracts in that particular trade. Standard clauses should be construed uniformly to produce similar legal rights and obligations in all arbitrations with similar relevant facts. An authoritative ruling of the court as to the construction of a standard clause, binding upon all arbitrators, performs a useful function that would be lacking in the substitution by the court of its own opinion for that of a commercial arbitrator in respect of a "one-off" clause.

The appropriate guidelines for standard clauses are, therefore, as follows (p. 304):

> "For reasons already sufficiently discussed, rather less strict criteria are in my view appropriate where questions of construction of contracts in standard terms are concerned. That there should be as high a degree of legal certainty as it is practicable to obtain as to how such terms apply upon the occurrence of events of a kind that it is not unlikely may reproduce themselves in similar transactions between other parties engaged in the same trade, is a public interest that is recognised by the Act particularly in section 4. So, if the decision of the question of construction in the circumstances of the particular case would add significantly to the clarity and certainty of English commercial law it would be proper to give leave in a case sufficiently substantial to escape the ban imposed by the first part of section 1(4) bearing in mind always that a superabundance of citable judicial decisions arising out of slightly different facts is calculated to hinder rather than to promote clarity in settled principles of commercial law. But leave should not be given even in such a case, unless the judge considered that a strong *prima-facie* case had been made out that the arbitrator had been wrong in his construction: and when the events to which the standard clause fell to be applied in the particular arbitration were themselves 'one-off' events, stricter criteria should be applied on the same lines as those I have suggested as appropriate to 'one-off' clauses."

Shortly after the decision in *The Nema*, however, there were indications that these guidelines might not be wholly acceptable to the lower courts. Thus, in *Italmare Shipping Co v Ocean Tanker Co Inc (The Rio Sun)* [1982] 1 WLR 158, Lord Denning MR emphasised the restrictive nature of *The Nema* guidelines and the complete discretion of the court to give or refuse leave to appeal. They are, he said, only guidelines and not barriers: you can step over them without causing them any harm and you can move them if necessary. Each case must depend on its own circumstances. The only fetter on the judge's discretion is the statutory provision that leave is not to be given *unless* the question of law is one which substantially affects the rights of the parties. Griffiths LJ, however, felt that guidance given by a unanimous decision of the House of Lords should be followed and that it would be an act of judicial anarchy for the Court of Appeal to refuse to do so.

In *BVS SA & Another v Kerman Shipping Co SA* [1982] 1 WLR 166, Parker J, in a detailed analysis of the position considered *The Nema* guidelines, as incorporated in *The Rio Sun* (above), and referred to two difficulties of application. First, a judge could rarely, if ever, exclude the possibility that he might be persuaded that an arbitrator might be right. It would follow, therefore, that under the guidelines leave could *never* be granted in a "one-off" case and this could not have been the intention of the House of Lords. Secondly, Lord Diplock appeared to envisage that the judge would make his decision on the papers alone whereas applications for leave are dealt with in open court with argument. (Subsequently in *The Antaois* (see below) Lord Diplock recognised that, although the perusal of an award and the application would play the major part in the judge's decision-making process, this would not preclude brief oral argument. Furthermore, applications for leave to appeal are now heard in chambers, and not in open court.)

The judge concluded that the combined effect of *The Nema* and *The Rio Sun* was:

(i) that in a "one-off" case, in the absence of special circumstances, leave should not be given unless at the conclusion of argument on the application for leave the court had formed the provisional view that the arbitrator was wrong and considered that it would need a great deal of convincing that he was right; and

(ii) that if the court did form such a view then, in the absence of special circumstances, leave should be granted.

Where a case did not fall within the guidelines more was required than the old criteria under the special case procedure before leave to appeal would be given. The more far-reaching the effects of the determination of the point of law would be, the less strict the criteria should be. Furthermore, if, in addition, the point of law is an entirely new one not covered by authority, that is a special circumstance making it proper for the court to grant leave on no more than the old criteria which applied to the special case procedure. These criteria required the point of law to be: (i) a real and substantial one, open to serious argument and suitable for the court; (ii) clear-cut, so that it could be accurately stated as a point of law; and (iii) necessary for the proper determination of the case.

In the middle of 1984 the House of Lords found it necessary to reaffirm and extend *The Nema* guidelines in *Antaios Compania Naviera*

SA v Salen Rederiena AB [1984] 2 Lloyd's Rep 235. Lord Diplock said (p. 237):

> "From the general guidelines stated in *The Nema* I see, as yet no reason for departing. Like all guidelines as to how judicial discretion should be exercised they are not intended to be all-embracing or immutable, but subject to adaptation to match changes in practices when these occur or to refinement to meet problems of kinds that were not foreseen, and are not covered by, what was said by this House in *The Nema*. The instant case, too, in the view of an Appeal Committee of this House, disclosed a need for some addition to *The Nema* guidelines particularly in relation to the practices to be followed upon the refusal by a commercial Judge of leave to appeal to the High Court from an arbitral award."

As we have seen, the guidelines relating to standard terms in a contract state that, where the case turns on the construction of such a term, the judge should not give leave to appeal against an award unless a strong *prima facie* case has been made out that the arbitrator is wrong. Lord Diplock said that this rule applied even though there may be *dicta* in other reported cases at first instance which suggest that there might be two schools of thought among commercial judges on the point. But where there are conflicting *decisions* (as opposed to *dicta*) on the matter, then the judge should give leave to appeal to the High Court followed by leave to appeal to the Court of Appeal against the judge's decision, with a certificate that the question of law is one of general public importance (see p. 368 below). It is only in this way that a desirable degree of certainty in English commercial law can be attained.

On an application for leave to appeal to the High Court against an arbitral award, the judge should listen to brief oral argument from both sides. This should be directed, not to the substance of the appeal for which leave is sought, but to the matters which must be proved if leave to appeal is to be given. Reasons for the grant or refusal of leave should not normally be given; they should only be given in the exceptional case where leave to appeal to the Court of Appeal against the judge's decision is granted because the particular case called for some amplification, elucidation or adaptation of existing guidelines laid down by the appellate courts (see p. 368 below).

The decision in *The Antaios* strongly supports the principle of finality in arbitration awards established in *The Nema*. Both Lord Diplock and Lord Roskill, with whom the other Law Lords agreed, expressed their concern that the purpose of the 1979 Act to achieve such finality was in danger of being thwarted by making appeals to the High Court and beyond too readily available.

The position relating to the grant or refusal of leave to appeal against an aribtrator's award may be summarised as follows:

(i) The applicant must show that, having regard to all the circumstances, the determination of the question of law could substantially affect the rights of one or more of the parties.

(ii) If this hurdle is overcome, the judge must then decide whether the dispute relates to a one-off clause or event or a standard clause or an event which is a common occurrence in the trade or commercial activity concerned.

(iii) If it is a one-off clause or event, the judge should only grant leave to appeal against the arbitrator's award if he is satisfied that the arbitrator was so obviously wrong as to preclude the possibility that he might be right.

(iv) If it is a standard clause or common event, the judge should grant leave to appeal where a strong *prima facie* case has been made out that the arbitrator is wrong.

(v) The guideline in (iv) above applies even though there may be conflicting *dicta* in reported cases at first instance on the point in issue; but where there are conflicting decisions the judge should grant leave to appeal with further leave to appeal from his decision to the Court of Appeal.

(vi) Reasons should not normally be given for the grant or refusal of leave to appeal to the High Court against an arbitrator's decision; they should only be given in the exceptional case where leave to appeal to the Court of Appeal is granted because the case calls for some amplification, elucidation or adaptation of existing guidelines.

(vii) A perusal of the award and application should play the major part in the judge's decision on an application for leave to appeal, but with brief oral argument directed, not to the substance of the appeal for which leave is sought, but to the matters which must be proved if leave to appeal is to be given.

(viii) Guidelines for leave to appeal are not intended to be all-embracing or immutable, but subject to adaptation to match changes in practice or to refinement to meet unforseen problems.

(c) *Exclusion agreements.* The limited rights of appeal on a question of law in section 1 of the 1979 Act can only be excluded by an "exclusion agreement" under sections 3 and 4 of the Act (Appendix C p. 506 below). Section 3(4) provides that the rights of appeal shall have effect notwithstanding anything in any agreement (other than an exclusion agreement) purporting to prohibit or restrict access to, or the jurisdiction of, the court, or to prohibit or restrict the making of a reasoned award. Parties to an arbitration who wish to make the award truly final and binding, with *no* possibility of judicial review, may only accomplish this by entering into a binding exclusion agreement under section 3 of the 1979 Act.

Section 3(1) provides that the High Court shall not grant leave to appeal with respect to a question of law arising out of an award if the parties to the reference have entered into a written agreement which excludes their rights of appeal under section 1 in relation to that award. (This sub-section also allows an exclusion agreement to exclude the right to apply for an order for reasons or for the determination of a preliminary point of law.) Where the reference to arbitration arises out of a "domestic arbitration agreement" (see below), an Admiralty claim, or an insurance or commodity contract, then the exclusion agreement shall not have effect unless it was entered into *after* the commencement of the arbitration (see below), or in the case of a marine, insurance or commodity contract, the award relates to a contract which is expressed to be governed by a law other than that of England and Wales (sections 3(6) and 4(1) of the 1979 Act). The Secretary of State for Trade may by order provide that provisions relating to marine, insurance or commodity contracts shall cease to have effect or (subject to conditions) shall not apply, to any specified exclusion agreement (section 4(3) and (4) of the 1979 Act, Appendix C p. 508 below).

An arbitration is "commenced" when one party serves on the other a notice requiring him to appoint or concur in the appointment of an arbitrator, or to submit the dispute to the arbitrator named or designated in the arbitration agreement (section 29(2) and (3) of the 1950 Act as applied by section 7(2) of the 1979 Act, Appendix C p. 475 below and p. 510 below).

A "domestic arbitration agreement" means an agreement which does not provide, expressly or by implication, for arbitration in a State other than the United Kingdom, and to which the parties at the time it was entered into were neither an individual who was a national of, or habitually resident in, any State other than the United Kingdom, nor a corporate body incorporated in, or whose central management and control were exercised in, any State other than the United Kingdom (section 3(7) of the 1979 Act).

An exclusion agreement may relate to a particular award, to awards under a particular reference or to any description of awards, whether arising out of the same reference or not. It may be entered into before or after the passing of the 1979 Act (on 4th April 1979) and it need not form part of an arbitration agreement (section 3(2) of the 1979 Act). An exclusion agreement has no effect in relation to a statutory arbitration under section 31(1) of the 1950 Act (section 3(5) of the 1979 Act).

(d) *Appeal to Court of Appeal.* There are two appeal provisions relating to the judicial review of awards dealing respectively with (i) the initial decision to grant or refuse leave to appeal, and (ii) the decision on the appeal.

(i) *Appeal against grant or refusal of leave.* No appeal shall lie to the Court of Appeal from a decision of the High Court granting or refusing leave to appeal against an award, except with leave of the High Court (section 1(6A) of the 1979 Act inserted by section 148(2) of the Supreme Court Act 1981, Appendix C p. 505 below).

Leave to appeal to the Court of Appeal under section 1(6A) should be granted only in cases where a decision to grant or refuse leave to appeal against an award calls for some amplification, elucidation or adaptation to changing practices of existing guidelines laid down by appellate courts. Leave should not be granted in any other type of case (*The Antaios* above).

(ii) *Appeal against decision.* The second appeal provision relates to the decision of the High Court on an appeal after leave to appeal has been given or the consent of all other parties has been obtained. No appeal shall lie to the Court of Appeal from such a decision, unless the High Court or Court of Appeal gives leave *and* it is certified by the High Court that the question of law to which its decision relates is either one of general public importance or there is some other special reason why it should be considered by the Court of Appeal (section 1(7) of the 1979 Act, Appendix C p. 505 below).

Where leave to appeal to the High Court has been granted in a standard term case because there are conflicting reported decisions on a matter at first instance, then the judge should give leave to appeal to the Court of Appeal with a certificate under section 1(7) certifying the point as one of general public importance (*The Antaois* above).

Where all parties agree to an appeal to the High Court against an award (and therefore leave of the court is unnecessary) this agreement is not to be extended to a further appeal to the Court of Appeal. The strict conditions of section 1(7) of the 1979 Act apply to an appeal to the Court of Appeal and, although the wishes of the parties would no doubt be a powerful factor, *The Nema* guidelines indicate (p. 301) that it is, and should be, more difficult to appeal to the Court of Appeal than to the High Court (*Babanaft International Co SA v Avant Petroleum Inc* [1982] 1 WLR 871.

(e) *Rent review arbitrations.* How are rent review arbitrations affected by section 1 of the 1979 Act and *The Nema* guidelines? At the time of writing I am aware of only two reported decisions on applications for leave to appeal against a rent review award.

In *Duvan Estates Ltd v Rossette Sunshine Savouries Ltd* (1981) 261

EG 364, leave was sought to appeal against a rent review award and the point of law was that the arbitrator had incorrectly had regard to rents and trading accounts relating to the period after the rent review date. The judge found that the arbitrator had not based his award on post-review date rents, but had used them merely as confirmation of his determination on other evidence. The arbitrator had considered the trading accounts and thus erred in law by so doing, but this particular point was found to be a marginal one and failed to satisfy the prior test under section 1(4) of the 1979 Act, namely that the determination of the question of law could substantially affect the rights of one or more of the parties. Leave to appeal was refused and *The Nema* guidelines were not considered.

In *Segama NV v Penny Le Roy Ltd* (1983) 269 EG 322, application was made for leave to appeal against an award on two questions of law, relating to the admissibility of post-review date rental evidence and evidence of rents agreed between existing landlords and existing tenants. The judge stated that, having regard to the wording of the rent review clause, this was not a one-off case, both questions of law were of general importance to landlords and tenants, and the second question (the admissibility of rents agreed between existing landlords and existing tenants) could substantially affect the rights of the parties. He was not, however, satisfied that a *prima facie* case had been made out that the arbitrator was wrong to admit this evidence: on the contrary, the judge thought that he was right on both points. Applying *The Nema* guidelines on standard clauses, therefore, the judge refused leave to appeal.

It is difficult to draw any firm conclusions from the above two cases as to the effect of the appeal provisions in section 1 of the 1979 Act on rent review arbitrations. Clearly, from the *Segama* decision, a rent review clause is capable of being a standard clause where it is expressed in terms to be found in many leases or the problem raised is a common one. Leave to appeal may be given where a strong *prima facie* case has been made out that the arbitrator was wrong. Where the wording of the clause or the question of law is, however, uncommon it may be placed in the category of a one-off clause. Leave to appeal will only be given where the judge is satisfied that the arbitrator was so obviously wrong as to preclude the possibility that he might be right. In both cases the prior test that the determination of the question of law could substantially affect the rights of one or more of the parties must also be satisfied before leave to appeal is given.

Leave to appeal is not, of course, necessary where both parties to the rent review arbitration consent to the appeal; the judge will then deal directly with the point of law in issue (e.g. *99 Bishopsgate Ltd v Prudential Assurance Co Ltd* (1985) 273 EG 984).

The parties to a lease containing an arbitration clause can, of course, expressly exclude judicial review by entering into an exclusion agreement under section 3 of the 1979 Act. This agreement must be entered into *after* the commencement of the arbitration and cannot be contained in the lease, except where one of the parties is an individual who is a national of, or habitually resident in, a State outside the United Kingdom, or a body corporate incorporated or managed and controlled from outside the United Kingdom.

(2) Application to remit or set aside an award

(a) *Introduction*. An award may be challenged by application to the court under section 22 of the 1950 Act to remit it to the arbitrator for reconsideration, or to have it set aside under section 23 of that Act or under the court's inherent jurisdiction (Appendix C p. 473 below). Either application must be made within 21 days after the award has been made and published to the parties (RSC Order 73 rules 5(1) (a) and (b)).

Both rights of challenge have survived the introduction of the new appeal provisions in section 1 of the 1979 Act, subject to one or perhaps two changes. First, the jurisdiction of the court to remit or set aside an award for error of fact or law on the face has been abolished. Secondly, it would appear that the power of the court to set aside (but not remit) an award on the grounds of admitted mistake by the arbitrator has been removed.

An application to remit or set aside an award is not to be used as an alternative method of bringing the award before the court, thus avoiding the restrictions placed on the power of the court to intervene under section 1 of the 1979 Act. In *Moran v Lloyd's* [1983] 2 All ER 200, the applicant sought leave to appeal against an award and to have it set aside or remitted to the arbitrator. These applications were refused in the High Court and leave to appeal against these decisions was also refused. The applicant, nevertheless, brought his case before the Court of Appeal on the grounds that leave to appeal was not required in respect of the application to remit or set aside the award (see p. 382 below), but he could not pursue further the matter of leave to appeal against the award on a point of law due to the clear prohibition in section 1 (6A) of the 1979 Act (see p. 368 above). The reason he put forward for the application to remit or set aside the award was misconduct by the arbitrator, namely an inconsistency between different parts of his award and a failure to allow the applicant a reasonable and proper opportunity to present his case. The Court of Appeal found the second allegation unfounded, and stated that it is doubtful whether an inconsistency in an award could constitute misconduct but it could be an error of fact or law (not amounting to misconduct). The power of the court to intervene for errors of fact or law had been abrogated by section 1(1) of the 1979 Act and replaced with new rights of appeal. Sir John Donaldson MR said (p. 204):

> "We stress this aspect in order to make it clear to all who are concerned in and with arbitration that neither section 22 nor section 23 of the 1950 Act is available as a back-door method of circumventing the restrictions on the court's power to intervene in arbitral proceedings which had been created by the 1979 Act."

Where application is made to remit or set aside an award, the court has a discretion whether or not to make an order and, if so, what order to make. It will have regard to the particular circumstances of the case as a whole. In the exercise of its discretion the court may refuse to make an order even though there are grounds for so doing, e.g. where the award is in respect of a very small claim (*Hellaby v Brown* (1875) 1 H & N 729) or the applicant has not suffered loss as a result of the erroneous award (*Re Bradshaw's Arbitration* (1848) 12 QB 562).

It is difficult to lay down rules for the exercise of a discretion but the following general points may be made. Remission of an award is more appropriate where the arbitrator is guilty of an omission. An award will be set aside where it would be pointless to remit it, e.g. where an award arose out of an illegal contract and the only conclusion which the arbitrator could reach on remission was that the contract was illegal (*David Taylor & Son Ltd v Barnett Trading Co* [1953] 1 WLR 562 at p. 570). Misconduct by the arbitrator is common to both remedies. Where the misconduct is such that justice demands that the award be set aside then this is the appropriate remedy, e.g. where the arbitrator might be prejudiced against one of the parties or could not approach the issue with a fresh mind. But where the misconduct is less serious so that the court would not wish to remove the arbitrator and would still trust him, then remission is more appropriate.

The setting aside of an award is a serious matter for the parties. Where it is ordered the current arbitration is at an end but the parties have achieved nothing. They must start again, usually with a new arbitrator, or bring an action in the courts. The costs of the first arbitration will be lost. Where remission is ordered the arbitrator retains his jurisdiction and is merely required to amend his award in accordance with the order of the court.

Under certain circumstances a party may be prevented from challenging an award. There may be an express agreement between the parties restricting this right. Thus, in a building contract the parties agreed to refer disputes to an arbitrator, whose decision shall be final and binding and shall not be set aside on any ground, or for any reason, or for any pretence, suggestion, charge or insinuation of fraud, collusion or confederacy. It was held that this agreement was not against public policy and was effective in the absence of fraud by either of the parties (*Tullis v Jacson* [1892] 3 Ch 441).

A party may be estopped by his conduct from challenging an award, e.g. where he did not object to an excess of authority by the arbitrator at an early stage in the proceedings (*Macaura v Northern Assurance Co Ltd* [1925] AC 619), or where they agreed to the appointment of an interested party as arbitrator, knowing that he could not come to the dispute with an open judgment, they could not subsequently challenge his award on that ground unless it could be shown that he had so made up his mind that he would be unable to change it after argument (*Jackson v Barry Ry* [1893] 1 Ch 238). (For the position under section 24(1) of the 1950 Act where application for the revocation of an arbitrator's appointment is made on grounds of paratiality see Chapter 9 p. 283 above.)

A party may also lose his right of challenge by his acquiescence, e.g. where he knowingly accepts a benefit under the award (*Kennard v Harris* (1824) 2 B & C 801). It is probably not acquiescence, however, for a party to perform an award (*Bartle v Musgrave* (1841) 1 Dowl (NS) 325) nor to permit the other party to perform it, without some positive act of acquiescence (*Hayward v Phillips* (1837) 6 A & E 119).

(b) *Remission of an award.* Section 22(1) of the 1950 Act provides that:

> "In all cases of reference to arbitration the High Court or a judge thereof may from time to time remit the matters referred, or any of them, to the reconsideration of the arbitrator or umpire."

Two general points may be noted. First, this sub-section refers not to the award but to "the matters referred, or any of them". Thus, such matters may be remitted to the arbitrator for reconsideration before or after the award, in addition to the remission of the award itself (including an interim award). Secondly, the court has a wide discretion to remit which is unfettered by reference to specific grounds, unlike the power to set aside under section 23 which is concerned with misconduct and the improper procuring of the arbitration or award (although the court also has an inherent jurisdiction to set aside on other grounds). Part only of an award may be remitted, e.g. as to costs, leaving the remainder unaffected.

As a general rule an arbitrator is *functus officio* when he has made his award and he cannot make a second award. This does not affect the discretion of the court to remit the award to him: his powers are revived by the remission (*Re Stringer & Riley Bros* [1901] 1 KB 105).

In *Montgomery, Jones & Co v Liebenthal & Co* (1898) 78 LT 406, Chitty LJ stated that the grounds for remission of an award were as follows:

> "(1) where the award is bad on the face of it;
> (2) where there has been an admitted mistake and the arbitrator himself asks that the matter may be remitted;
> (3) where there has been misconduct on the part of the arbitrator;
> (4) where additional evidence has been discovered after the making of the award."

These grounds are not exhaustive and the court can remit an award for other reasons where this is necessary to avoid injustice. The many reported decisions on remission give guidance only as to the exercise by the court of its discretion and do not increase or restrict the jurisdiction of the court in this respect (*Re Baxters & Midland Ry* (1906) 95 LT 20 at p. 23).

(i) *Award bad on the face.* As discussed in Chapter 11 above, a valid award must comply with certain requirements, e.g. it must be final, complete, certain, consistent, etc. Where an award lacks one or more of these essentials it may be remitted to the arbitrator. For example, in *Montrose Canned Foods Ltd v Eric Wells (Merchants) Ltd* [1965] 1 Lloyd's Rep 597, an award arising out of a dispute on a contract for the sale of Chilean prunes determined that:

> "... the Buyers pay the Sellers for all the losses arising from non-payment of documents on presentation ...."

It was remitted because, although the award was not a nullity, it was defective and could not be enforced in any practical way because it merely provided for liability and did not make provision for quantification or payment.

(ii) *Admitted mistake.* If an arbitrator admits to a mistake in his award the court will usually remit it to him for correction, where, due to the error, the award fails to state the arbitrator's true intention. The position is similar to the rectification of a written document which does not correctly express the prior agreement between the parties (see Appendix A p. 428 below). Examples of mistaken awards remitted for correction are: where the arbitrator referred to one of the parties by an incorrect name (*Davies v Pratt* (1855) 16 CB 586); where the arbitrator intended to award £X but by mistake awarded £Y (*Mutual Shipping Corporation of New York v Bayshore Shipping Co of Monrovia*, discussed on p. 359 above), and where he intended to make an award covering all matters referred to him but by mistake failed to do so.

Where, however, an arbitrator makes a mistake, of fact or law, in reaching his decision, but his award correctly states that decision, then the court will not usually remit it for correction (*Allen v Greenslade* (1875) 33 LT 567). But where a mistake is an inadvertent slip, such as an arithmetical error, then the court may remit the award to the arbitrator for reconsideration. For example, in *Fuga AG v Bunge AG* [1975] 2 Lloyd's Rep 192, a dispute arising out of a contract for the sale of 120,266 metric tons of soya bean meal was referred to arbitration and, by mistake, the arbitrators based their award on 20,266 metric tons. They asked to be allowed to correct the error and the award was remitted to them for reconsideration, otherwise the gravest injustice would have been caused to the buyers through no fault of their own.

A mistake which is a clerical mistake or error arising from an accidental slip or omission may, unless the arbitration agreement states otherwise, be corrected by the arbitrator under section 17 of the 1950 Act without the need for remission (see p. 359 above).

(iii) *Misconduct*. An award may be remitted on the grounds of misconduct by the arbitrator, which may occur at any time between appointment and award. The special nature of misconduct in arbitration is discussed later in this chapter in the context of the setting aside of an award (see p. 377 below). It is sufficient to state here that the term refers to a wide variety of matters ranging from gross, wilful or corrupt conduct to mere procedural irregularities, and misconduct leading to remission is usually of the less serious kind such as mistaken conduct, irregular behaviour or breaches of the rules of natural justice. As a general rule, misbehaviour for which other remedies are available cannot be the basis of an application to remit or set aside an award.

The following examples of misconduct by the arbitrator all

resulted in remission of the award: refusing to receive relevant evidence, which should then have been open to question by both parties (*Faure, Fairclough Ltd v Premier Oil & Cake Mills Ltd* [1968] 1 Lloyd's Rep 237); refusing to postpone a hearing to allow a party to instruct counsel where the other party unexpectedly appeared by counsel (*Whatley v Morland* (1834) 2 C & M 347); deciding a dispute on a view of the law which did not agree with the views of either party, without making this clear to the parties at the hearing and giving them an opportunity of presenting arguments to him (*Societe Franco-Tunisienne D'Armement-Tunis v Government of Ceylon* [1959] 1 WLR 787); failing to state his award in a form which could be enforced as a judgment (*Margulies Bros Ltd v Dafnis Thomaides & Co (UK) Ltd* [1958] 1 WLR 398); failing to make it sufficiently clear to a party that he will proceed *ex parte* in the absence of pleadings from that party (*The Myron v Tradax Export SA* [1969] 1 Lloyd's Rep 411). Examples of behaviour which do not amount to misconduct can be more conveniently discussed under the setting aside of an award (p. 379 below).

(iv) *Discovery of additional evidence.* The discovery of additional evidence after an award has been made may be a ground for remission, provided that the evidence satisfies three conditions. First, it must be material to some point in issue in the dispute. Secondly, it would probably have a substantial effect or an important influence on the arbitrator's decision having regard, *inter alia*, to the apparent credibility of the evidence (*Aiden Shipping Co Ltd v Interbulk Ltd* (1984) *The Times* 5th December 1984). Thirdly, it was not known to be available and could not reasonably have been discovered at the date of the hearing (*Eardley v Otley* (1818) 2 Chit 42). An award was not remitted where a party was surprised at the hearing by an unexpected case, because the arbitrator has power to postpone the proceedings upon any reasonable application for that purpose (*Solomon v Solomon* (1859) 28 LJ Ex 129). An award will not be remitted (or set aside) where fresh evidence is discovered which tends to throw doubt upon the veracity of a witness who gave evidence before the arbitrator (*Re Glasgow etc Ry & London & North Western Ry* (1888) 52 JP 215.

(v) *Want of justice.* The court may remit an award "if justice cannot otherwise be done" (*Universal Cargo Carriers Corporation v Citati* [1957] 3 All ER 234 at p. 240), but the court cannot send an award back to the arbitrator to ensure "that justice which may possibly not have been done is done" (*GKN Centrax Gears Ltd v Matbro Ltd* [1976] 2 Lloyd's Rep 555 at p. 576). Remission under the head of want of justice allows the court to remedy injustice resulting from "procedural mishaps" in the arbitration. For example, in *Shield Properties & Investments Ltd v Anglo-Overseas Transport Co Ltd* (1984) 273 EG 69, the arbitrator in a rent review arbitration conducted by written representations directed that details of comparable transactions should be agreed by the parties, whenever possible, and those in which the parties were not personally involved should be supported by written evidence from agents who were concerned. The landlords sent a list of comparables, without substantiation, but with a covering letter stating that written confirmation had been obtained and copies of this correspondence could be made available to the arbitrator if required. A copy of this letter was not sent to the tenants. The arbitrator did not ask to see the supporting correspondence. The tenants objected to the failure by the landlords to comply with the arbitrator's directions regarding the substantiation of comparables but, nevertheless, commented on them in their counter-submissions.

The tenants later applied to have the award remitted or set aside on the grounds of misconduct, namely the improper admission of hearsay evidence of comparables from the landlords and the failure by the arbitrator to disclose to the tenants the landlords' covering letter offering substantiation of those transactions.

It was held that there was no misconduct by the arbitrator. He did not receive evidence, but received an offer from one party of evidence which he did not take up and did not communicate to the other party. His conduct did, however, produce a procedural mishap which could, or might, lead to an unjust result. The matter was remitted to the arbitrator for his further consideration on the basis that it was a matter for his own judgment, in the light of representations from the parties, whether he requires the production of the landlords' correspondence in verification of his comparables (with copies to the tenants) or whether he ignores completely the comparables for which no adequate verification has been produced.

(vi) *Award in excess of jurisdiction.* An award may be remitted where the arbitrator has exceeded his authority. For example, in an arbitration under the Lands Clauses Act 1845 relating to compensation for compulsory purchase, the matter submitted was the damage suffered by the claimants on the assumption that they had an absolute right in a term of years. The award, however, was made on the basis that the term was subject to the lessor's right to take away part of the land. It exceeded the arbitrator's jurisdiction and was remitted to him for reconsideration (*Re Dare Valley Ry* (1868) LR 6 Eq 429).

An award will not be in excess of jurisdiction where there is only a possibility that the arbitrator may have taken into account matters outside his authority. It must be shown that he did in fact do so (*Falkingham v Victorian Railways Commissioner* [1900] AC 452).

It is the submission to arbitration which determines the arbitrator's jurisdiction and not the way in which the parties present their cases (*Mediterranean & Eastern Export Co v Fortress Fabrics (Manchester) Ltd* [1948] 2 All ER 186). If both parties go outside the submission, however, it may be inferred that they have agreed to enlarge the arbitrator's jurisdiction. Under these circumstances it would be prudent for him to have this confirmed in writing by the parties.

(c) *Setting aside an award.* Section 23(2) of the 1950 Act provides:

"Where an arbitrator or umpire has misconducted himself or the proceedings, or an arbitration or award has been improperly procured, the High Court may set the award aside."

This sub-section specifies two grounds for the setting aside of an award: misconduct and the improper procuring of the arbitration or award, but the court also has an inherent jurisdiction to set aside on other grounds e.g. where additional evidence is discovered, where the award is invalid or where it exceeds the arbitrator's jurisdiction. As stated above, the power of the court to set aside for error of fact or law on the face of the award has been removed by section 1(1) of the 1979 Act and this would also appear to be the case with regard to admitted mistake by the arbitrator.

Where an application is made to set aside an award, the court may order that any money made payable by the award shall be brought into court or otherwise secured pending the determination of the application (section 23 (3) of the 1950 Act).

(i) *Misconduct.* The first of the grounds for setting aside an award under section 23(2) of the 1950 Act is that the arbitrator has misconducted himself or the proceedings. The court also has power to remove him for this reason under section 23(1) (see Chapter 9 p. 284 above).

The term "misconduct" is not used in arbitration in the ordinary sense of that word, to mean improper conduct such as dishonesty or a breach of business morality, but it has a special and wider meaning which can give a wholly misleading impression of the complaint against the arbitrator. Misconduct in arbitration means irregularity in the conduct of the proceedings rather than improper conduct. It includes, for example, procedural errors or omissions by arbitrators who are doing their best to uphold the highest standards of their profession (*Moran v Lloyd's* [1983] 2 All ER 200 at p. 203). But great care should be taken when reading the decisions of a century or half a century ago as to the powers of arbitrators to-day. The courts will now only interfere where it has been shown that some real impropriety has been committed (*Henry Bath & Son Ltd v Birgby Products* [1962] 1 Lloyd's Rep 389 at p. 399). Furthermore, an application to remit or set aside an award is not to be used to circumvent the restrictions on the powers of the court to intervene in arbitration proceedings imposed by the 1979 Act (see *Moran* above). Misconduct in its milder form, leading only to remission and not to the setting aside of an award, is discussed earlier in this chapter (p. 374 above). Misconduct which justifies the setting aside of an award is of the more serious kind and may be divided into three broad categories.

First, there is misconduct which occurs outside the arbitration proceedings. For example, where an arbitrator accepts a bribe, or even where he accepts payment of his charges from one party *before* making his award (*Shephard v Brand* (1734) 2 Barnard 463), but not where one party gives an undertaking to take up the award in any event (*Re Kenworthy & The Queen Assurance Co* (1893) 9 TLR 181). The acceptance by the arbitrator of hospitality from one of the parties, although improper, will not usually constitute misconduct unless there was an intention to corrupt or influence him and he was in fact corrupted or influenced (*Re Hopper* (1867) LR 2 QB 367). There may be misconduct where an arbitrator is employed or instructed in another capacity by one of the parties, provided it can be shown that, having regard to his standing and position, he is likely to have been influenced by the party employing him. Thus, in *Re Haigh & London & North Western & Great Western Railways* [1896] 1 QB 649, an award was *not* set aside where an umpire, appointed to assess compensation for the compulsory acquisition of land for a railway, was later retained by the respondents as a witness in another inquiry as to the value of land taken for the same line under the same Act. It could not be supposed that in these circumstances the mind of the umpire was substantially affected in favour of the respondents.

The second category of misconduct arises where the arbitrator fails to act judicially in his conduct of the proceedings. For example, where he holds a hearing in the absence of the parties (*London Export Corporation Ltd v Jubilee Coffee Roasting Co Ltd* [1958] 1 WLR 661), or receives further evidence after the close of the hearing (unless it can be shown that it could not have affected the award) (*Eastcheap Dried Fruit Co v NV*

Gebroeders Catz Handelsvereeniging [1962] 1 Lloyd's Rep 283), or gives himself evidence without giving the parties an opportunity of dealing with it (*Fox v P. G. Wellfair Ltd* [1981] 2 Lloyd's Rep 514, see Chapter 10 p. 317 above), or makes an award without hearing the parties' submissions (*Modern Engineering (Bristol) Ltd v C. Miskin & Son Ltd* [1981] 1 Lloyd's Rep 135). In *Micklewright v Mullock* (1974) 232 EG 337, the arbitrator appointed under a building contract announced his intention of viewing the premises before the hearing (but did not do so) and then failed to inspect at all, but without stating his changed intention. One of the parties conducted his case on the basis that the arbitrator would inspect and suffered injustice by his failure to do so. It was held that the arbitrator misconducted himself and the award was set aside.

The third category of misconduct comprises errors of a technical nature. For example, an award may be set aside where the arbitrator makes an excessive charge for his services (*Appleton v Norwich Union Fire Insurance Society Ltd* (1922) 13 Ll L Rep 345).

Not all mistakes and misbehaviour by an arbitrator constitute misconduct. As a general rule, an error or other act by an arbitrator will not be misconduct where other remedies are available, e.g. it is not misconduct for an arbitrator to come to an incorrect decision (*Gillespie Bros & Co v Thompson Bros & Co* (1922) 13 Ll L Rep 519 at p. 524). Furthermore, as we have seen (p. 370 above), the limited powers of the courts to intervene in arbitral proceedings on questions of law are not to be circumvented by sections 22 and 23 of the 1950 Act. An arbitrator does not misconduct himself or the proceedings merely because he makes an error of fact or law:

> "... there is a distinction between error and misconduct. To err in fact or law is not only human but an occupational hazard. Unless it is so often repeated as to give rise to some suggestion of incompetence it happily involves absolutely no reflection upon the person concerned, whether judge, umpire or arbitrator."
> (per Donaldson J in *Port Sudan Cotton Co v Govindaswamy Chettiar & Sons* [1977] 1 Lloyd's Rep 166 at p. 178).

But where an arbitrator made so many mistakes that he failed to show the elementary skill of his office and reduced the proceedings to such confusion that there was no reasonable prospect of justice being done, this was held to be misconduct justifying his removal and, presumably, if he had made an award it would have been set aside (*Pratt v Swanmore Builders*

Ltd [1980] 2 Lloyd's Rep 504, Chapter 9 p. 285 above).

(ii) *Arbitration or award improperly procured*. The second of the statutory grounds under which the court may set aside an award, is that the arbitration or award has been improperly procured (section 23(2) of the 1950 Act). Here the emphasis is on the behaviour of the parties; misconduct is concerned with the behaviour of the arbitrator, although there may be some overlap, e.g. the acceptance of a bribe by the arbitrator will constitute both misconduct and the improper procuring of the award.

Section 23(2) operates where an *arbitration* or *award* has been improperly procured. The circumstances under which an arbitration has been improperly procured are unclear. It would appear that this will occur where one party is persuaded to enter into an arbitration agreement by fraud or misrepresentation by the other party. An award will be improperly procured where one of the parties fraudently conceals matters which ought to have been disclosed to the arbitrator, or has wilfully misled or deceived him (*South Sea Co v Bumstead* (1734) 2 Eq Cas Ab 80). This is not the same as the discovery of additional evidence (see below).

(iii) *Discovery of additional evidence*. The court has an inherent power to set aside an award where new and material evidence is discovered after the making of the award. This is discussed under remission (p. 375 above) and this remedy would normally be more appropriate than setting aside.

(iv) *Award in excess of jurisdiction*. As stated above (p. 376), an award may be remitted to the arbitrator where he has exceeded his authority. The court may also set aside an award on this ground. For example, in *Price v Popkin* (1839) 10 A & E 139, one of the questions submitted to arbitration was whether some fixtures removed by a landlord were part of the demised premises. An award ordering the tenant to replace the fixtures at the expense of the landlord was set aside on the grounds of excess of jurisdiction. The arbitrator's authority was declaratory only, he had no power to give directions.

(v) *Award bad on the face*. The power of the court to remit an award which is invalid because it lacks one or more of the essentials of a valid award, is discussed under remission (p. 373 above). The court may also order such an award to be set aside. Thus, in *Re Tribe & Upperton* (1835) 3 A & E 295, an award was set aside for uncertainty where the main question referred to the arbitrator was whether an agreement should be rescinded and his award was unclear whether it should be at an end or not.

(d) *Effect of remission or setting aside*. The remission or setting aside of an award will affect the arbitrator and the parties. Remission affects mainly the arbitrator; setting aside is of major concern to the parties.

(i) *Remission.* An arbitrator is *functus officio* when he has made a final award, but his powers revive when the award is remitted to him by order of the court. He is no longer *functus officio* in respect of those parts of the award which are remitted. Where an award is bad in parts, and these are severable from the good parts, then the former only may be remitted and the arbitrator's powers revive in relation to those parts only. He remains *functus officio* in relation to the good parts of the award. An award can only be remitted or set aside in part where the good and bad parts are clearly severable.

Where an award is remitted, the extent to which the arbitrator may hear fresh evidence will depend upon the order of remission. For example, in *Re Huntley* (1853) 1 E & B 787, the court ordered an award to be remitted to enable the arbitrator to ascertain the costs payable by one party to the other. One of the parties claimed to be allowed to give fresh evidence and to be heard in further proceedings. The arbitrator's rejection of those claims was upheld by the court; the award was remitted for a specific purpose and he had the right to refuse to hear additional evidence. An arbitrator has a duty to receive fresh evidence on remission in three cases. First, where he has omitted to decide some matter referred to him. Secondly, where fresh evidence has been discovered after the making of his award. Thirdly, where he refused to hear evidence which he should have heard. Where an award is remitted upon a question of law the arbitrator's duty to hear fresh evidence is limited to such further evidence as is necessary to enable him to come to a correct decision on the question of law.

A fresh award made after remission should not be restricted in content to those matters remitted, but should cover all matters originally referred to the arbitrator for decision. Thus, his new award should contain the unremitted, or good parts of the first award, plus his revised decision on the matters remitted. The new award must not, however, have the effect of altering the good parts of the first award; the arbitrator can only deal afresh with the remitted parts. It is not necessary for the revised award to contain a recital referring to the order for remission (*Baker v Hunter* (1847) 16 M & W 672), although this would be desirable.

After remission a fresh award must be made within three months of the order, or such other time as may be directed (section 22(2) of the 1950 Act). This time may be enlarged by the court under section 13(2) of the 1950 Act, whether or not it has expired (Appendix C pp. 473 and 470 below). It will be remembered that section 22(1) of the 1950 Act allows the court to remit any of the *matters* referred to arbitration, as distinct from the award. There is no time limit in respect of such matters: the arbitrator is not required to deal with them within a stated time, although he must not be dilatory or he may be removed by the court under section 13(3) of the 1950 Act (see Chapter 9 p. 283 above).

Where an order remitting an award is silent as to costs and the arbitrator had jurisdiction to deal with them under the original reference, then he may deal with costs in the fresh award (*M'Rae v M'Lean* (1853) 2 E & B 946).

(ii) *Setting aside.* Where an award is set aside by the court the parties must commence the arbitration again, or settle the dispute by agreement or in some other way. When setting aside an award the court may order that the period between the commencement of the arbitration and the order shall be exluded when computing the limitation period for that dispute (section 34(5) Limitation Act 1980, Appendix C, p. 511 below). Thus, the time occupied by the arbitration which is rendered abortive by the setting aside of the award is ignored for the purposes of limitation.

(e) *Appeals.* An appeal lies to the Court of Appeal from a decision of the High Court on a motion to remit or set aside an award, but leave to appeal is required (*Moran v Lloyd's* [1983] 2 All ER 200). An appeal must be made within four weeks from the date on which the judgment or order of court below was signed, entered or otherwise perfected (RSC Order 59 rule 4).

(3) Defence to an action on the award

The defendant in an action to enforce an award may challenge the award, e.g. on the grounds of excess of jurisdiction by the arbitrator. The various defences to an action on the award are discussed on p. 386 below.

(4) Declaration

As we saw in Chapter 9 (p. 282 above), the court may issue a declaration that an arbitrator is unfit or incompetent or that the reference is outside his jurisdiction. A declaration may also be granted concerning an award. For example, an award may be declared null and void because the whole arbitration is a nullity due to the absence of a valid submission (*Oil Products Trading Co Ltd v Societe de Gestion d'Enterprises Coloniales* (1934) 150 LT 475); or where the arbitrator exceeded his jurisdiction when making his award; or where he is disqualified or was improperly appointed (*Burkett Sharp & Co v*

Eastcheap Dried Fruit & Perara [1962] 1 Lloyd's Rep 267). Conversely, a declaration may be sought that an award is binding (*Birtley Co-operative Society Ltd v Windy Nook & District Industrial Co-operative Society Ltd (No. 2)* [1960] 2 QB 1).

(5) Appeal by agreement

An arbitration agreement may expressly provide for an appeal to an umpire or appeal committee, e.g. by incorporating into the contract between the parties the rules of a trade association. Thus, in the *Faure, Fairclough* (pp. 291 and 375 above), the rules of the London Oil & Tallow Association, which governed the arbitration, provided for an initial hearing before two arbitrators and, if necessary, an umpire, with a right of appeal to the Board of Appeal of the Association, consisting of four members of the Committee of Appeal. This appeal was a re-hearing, but the original award would stand unless three members of the Board decide to vary it.

Rules relating to an appeal may prescribe time limits or contain other procedural requirements and as a general rule time will be of the essence and the time limits must be strictly observed. They may be waived by agreement between the parties but not by the appellate tribunal unless they have been given powers to do so (*Amalgamated Metal Corporation Ltd v Khoon Seng Co* [1977] 2 Lloyd's Rep 310). For the purposes of challenge in the courts the award of an appeal committee or umpire will be treated as the award of an ordinary arbitrator. A party to arbitration who wishes to challenge an award in the courts, need not exhaust all his rights of appeal under the arbitration agreement before so doing.

ENFORCING AN AWARD

An award may be enforced in two ways: as a judgment under section 26 of the 1950 Act or by an action on the award. A third method of enforcement, by attachment, is now obsolete and will not be considered further.

(1) Enforcement as a judgment

This is also known as "summary enforcement". The award is enforced as if it were a judgment of the court. Section 26(1) of the 1950 Act provides that:

> "An award on an arbitration agreement may, by leave of the High Court or a judge thereof, be enforced in the same manner as a judgment or order to the same effect, and where leave is so given, judgment may be entered in terms of the award."

New sub-sections (2) and (3) to section 26 have been added by section 17(2) of the Administration of Justice Act 1977 (Appendix C p. 474 below). Their effect is that, if the amount sought to be

recovered under the award does not exceed the current county court
limit, and a county court so orders, then it shall be recoverable as if
payable under an order of that court and not through the High Court
under sub-section (1) above. An application to the High Court to
enforce an award precludes a similar application to a county court,
and conversely an application to the latter prevents an application to
the High Court.

Summary enforcement under section 26 of the 1950 Act is the usual
and most convenient method of enforcing an award, but it cannot
always be used. There are five situations where an English award in
an arbitration by agreement cannot be summarily enforced under
section 26. In these cases the successful party must bring an action on
the award. These five situations are as follows:

(a) *Parol agreement.* The Arbitration Acts apply only to written arbitration agreements (section 32 of the 1950 Act). An arbitration
arising out of a parol agreement is not, therefore, within the Acts
and the award cannot be summarily enforced under section 26.

(b) *Declaratory award.* An award which is declaratory only cannot be
enforced as a judgment (*Re Willesden Local Board & Wright* [1896] 2
QB 412). A common example of a declaratory award is an award in
a rent review arbitration. Normally, the arbitrator determines the
amount of the review rent (and costs); his award is declaratory and
can only be enforced by an action on the award. It would be
unusual for an arbitrator to be given powers to order the payment
of the review rent, although it is open to the parties to agree to this
extension of his jurisdiction and he may then include in his award
directions as to payment or he may make a supplementary award
to that effect. The award or supplementary award may then be enforced as a judgment under section 26.

(c) *Doubt as to validity of award.* As a general rule, and in the absence
of a contrary intention in the arbitration agreement, an award
(other than an interim award) is conclusive and leave should be
given to enforce it as a judgment unless there is real ground for
doubting the validity of the award (*Middlemiss & Gould v Hartlepool
Corporation* [1972] 1 WLR 1643). For example, in *Smith v Martin*
[1925] 1 KB 745, a clause in a building contract provided that a
reference to arbitration shall not be opened until after completion
of the works, but an arbitration was commenced before the works
were completed. The Court of Appeal held that the validity of the
award was sufficiently doubtful to render it improper to enforce it
summarily as a judgment.

(d) *Lack of clarity in award.* An award which is lacking in clarity
cannot be summarily enforced; an action must be brought to
enforce it.

(e) *No judgment "to the same effect" possible.* Section 26(1) of the 1950 Act provides that an award may be enforced in the same manner as a judgment or order "to the same effect". It follows, therefore, that where it is not possible for the court to give a judgment or order "to the same effect" as the award, it will not grant leave for the award to be enforced as a judgment. For example, in *Dalmia Cement Ltd v National Bank of Pakistan* [1974] 2 Lloyd's Rep 98, an award directed that a certain sum of money be paid in India. It was held that this award could not be enforced under section 26 for two reasons. First, an English court would not ordinarily order a defendant to make a payment outside the jurisdiction, even in the face of an express contractual obligation to do so. Secondly, a judgment to pay a certain sum in this country was not "to the same effect" as the payment of that sum in India.

For reasons of completeness, it should be mentioned that the summary procedure under section 26 cannot generally be used to enforce a foreign award, nor an award arising out of a statutory arbitration where express provisions for enforcement are contained in the statute.

An application to enforce an award is made to a master in chambers with a right of appeal to a judge in chambers and then to the Court of Appeal. The application must be made within six years (or twelve years if the submission to arbitration is under seal) from the date when the cause of action accrued, that is to say when the party against whom the award has been made fails to honour it (sections 7 and 8(1) Limitation Act 1980 and *Agromet Motoimport v Maulden Engineering Co (Beds) Ltd* [1985] 2 All ER 436).

Where leave is given for the enforcement of an award, the applicant will be in the same position as if he had obtained a judgment or order in the terms of the award. He may enforce it by any of the methods available for enforcing a judgment of the court. An order for the enforcement of an award may be made on such terms as to costs as the authority making the order thinks just (section 28 of the 1950 Act, Appendix C p. 475 below).

(2) Action on the award

An agreement to refer a dispute to arbitration will contain an implied term that the parties agree to comply with the arbitrator's award. Failure to do so by one of the parties will be a breach of that term giving the other party the right to enforce it by an action on the award. The original rights of the parties disappear and their place is taken by their rights under the award (see *Agromet* case above).

A party seeking to enforce an award must prove certain facts and may be met with one or more defences. He must prove: a submission to arbitration or an arbitration clause or agreement followed by a dispute within that clause or agreement, the appointment of an arbitrator, the making of an award, and a failure to comply with that award (*Christopher Brown Ltd v Oesterreichischer Waldbesitzer R GmbH* [1954] 1 QB 8 at p. 9). The defences available to an action on the award are as follows:

(a) *Limitation.* The position regarding limitation is the same as for the summary enforcement of an award, namely an action on the award must be brought within six (or twelve) years from the date when the party against whom the award has been made fails to honour it (see *Agromet* case p. 385 above).

(b) *Revocation of arbitrator's authority.* Where the authority of an arbitrator can be revoked it will be a good defence to an action on the award that his authority was revoked before the award was made (*Marsh v Bulteel* (1822) 5 B & Ald 507).

(c) *Excess of jurisdiction.* An action on the award may be defended on the grounds that the arbitrator has exceeded his jurisdiction, e.g. by including in his award matters not referred to him for determination (*Davies v Price* (1864) 11 LT 203). Where an arbitrator is disqualified from accepting an appointment (see Chapter 9 p. 274 above), this constitutes an excess of jurisdiction and the whole arbitration will be a nullity.

(d) *Attachment.* Where an action for debt is brought to enforce a sum payable under an award, the defence may be raised that the money has already been attached by a person other than the plaintiff.

(e) *Award has ceased to be binding.* Under certain circumstances an award may cease to be binding on the parties. An arbitration clause or agreement is subordinate to the primary contract to which it is connected, and an award made in pursuance of that agreement will cease to be binding if the clause or agreement ceases to be binding. For example, in *Bellshill & Mossend Co-operative Society Ltd v Dalziel Co-operative Society Ltd* [1960] AC 832, an award was made against a member society of a co-operative union in respect of trading rights in a certain area. The society then withdrew from the union, as allowed by the rules. It was held that the award ceased to be binding when they withdrew.

An award will continue to be binding, however, where the contract to which it is related continues to exist, or because the obligation survives the termination of the contract. In *Torminster Properties Ltd v Green* (1983) 256 EG 267, it was held that an award determining a review rent under a lease made after the surrender of that lease, but in respect of a rent review date before the surrender, was binding on sureties who were liable for the rent determined from the review date to the date of surrender.

An award ceases to be binding when it has been performed or otherwise complied with.

Accord and satisfaction is a good defence to an action on the award. For example, in *Smith v Trowsdale* (1854) 3 E & B 83, partners in dispute with each other agreed that one of them would retire and receive a payment to be determined by an arbitrator. His award directed payment of a certain sum by instalments, but only part was paid and the parties made a parol agreement that a lesser sum should be paid. In an action on the award it was held that the parol agreement could be pleaded as a defence of accord and satisfaction. Since the later case of *Foakes v Beer* (1884) 9 App Cas 605, however, there must be proper consideration for the subsequent agreement or the accord and satisfaction will not be binding.

The bankruptcy of a party between the submission to arbitration and the execution of the award does not affect the enforceability of the award (section 3 of the 1950 Act, Appendix C p. 466 below; *Re Smith ex p Edwards* (1886) 3 Morrell's Bank Rep 179). But where the only matter referred to arbitration is the liability for, or the amount of, a debt, and after the reference but before the award, one of the parties becomes bankrupt, an award against him does not stop him from claiming relief under bankruptcy law from liability for all debts from which he would have been discharged in the absence of the reference. In these circumstances the award will be set aside (*R v Bingham* (1831) 2 C & J 130).

(f) *Specific performance.* The court has power to enforce an award by an order for specific performance (although in practice it is usually more convenient to enforce the award as a judgment under section 26). The defendant in an action for the specific performance of an award may have several defences available to him. For example, he may be able to argue that the plaintiff has delayed for an unreasonable period of time before seeking to enforce the award (laches) (*Eads v Williams* (1854) 4 De GM & G 674); or that the submission and the award constitute an unreasonable agreement; or that the terms of the award are mutual and it is not possible to give full relief to both parties by specific performance (*Blackett v Bates* (1865) LR 1 Ch 117).

(g) *Merger of award in judgment.* The principle of judgment estoppel (see p. 356 above) prevents the enforcement of an award in respect of a matter which has already been settled by the judgment of an English civil court.

It will be noted that the above defences do not include misconduct by the arbitrator, nor can the defendant counterclaim that the award be remitted or set aside. The defendant cannot plead that the award was not made within a reasonable time where the arbitration agreement does not state a time limit for the making of an award (*Curtis v Potts* (1814) 3 M & S 145).

CHAPTER THIRTEEN

Arbitration in Practice

INTRODUCTION

The previous four chapters deal with the law of arbitration; this chapter describes arbitration in practice, seen mainly from the viewpoint of the arbitrator. Once again I look at the files of Mr J. O. Dodgson of Melchester and examine a rent review dispute where he was nominated arbitrator by the President of The Royal Institution of Chartered Surveyors. He gave a reasoned award following an oral hearing.

APPOINTMENT

In February 1983 Mr Dodgson received a letter from the arbitrations officer of The Royal Institution of Chartered Surveyors. It was headed 10 South Street, Melchester, Loamshire and told him that application had been made to the President for the appointment of an arbitrator to determine a review rent for this property. Brief details of the lease and the parties were enclosed. Mr Dodgson was asked whether he would allow his name to be submitted to the President for consideration for this appointment. He first checked that neither he nor any of his partners or staff had any connection with the parties or the property and that his work over the next few months would allow him to carry out the duties of an arbitrator without delay. He then wrote to the arbitrations officer stating that he would accept this appointment.

Ten days laters he received a letter enclosing his nomination as arbitrator and a copy of the lease of 10 South Street, Melchester. Mr Dodgson immediately carried out his three initial duties. First, he read the lease and the nomination to satisfy himself that he had been validly appointed arbitrator under the terms of the lease. Secondly, he checked the extent of his jurisdiction, namely to determine the "market rent" of the demised premises as at the review date and the liability for costs. Thirdly, he checked that he was not required to follow any special procedure.

Initial letter

On 9th March 1983 Mr Dodgson wrote the following letter to the surveyors to the parties:

Dear Sirs,

Rent review arbitration—10 South Street, Melchester, Loamshire

(1) On 4th March 1983 I was nominated by the President of The Royal Institution of Chartered Surveyors to be the arbitrator in this reference. A copy of my nomination is enclosed.

(2) If the parties require more time to reach a settlement I will defer proceeding with this reference, provided I am requested in writing to do so by both parties.

(3) Will each party please tell me whether he requires an oral hearing or whether he wishes the matter to be dealt with by written representations.

(4) If one or both of the parties requires an oral hearing I will arrange a preliminary meeting to consider the conduct of this arbitration. Following the meeting I will issue my order for directions setting out the procedure to be followed. If both parties agree to the use of the written representations procedure I will normally agree to this procedure and, without holding a preliminary meeting (unless I am expressly requested to do so or it appears to me to be expedient to hold such a meeting), I will issue my directions for the submission and exchange of such representations. I will reserve the right, however, to call an oral hearing if I consider this is necessary.

(5) Will each party please tell me whether there appears to be an issue of law in this dispute.

(6) I direct that no "without prejudice" or other privileged correspondence, documents or statements shall be disclosed to me except with the agreement of both parties.

(7) I direct that a copy of every letter sent to me shall be sent to the other party.

(8) My fee for acting as arbitrator in this reference will be at the rate of £— per hour plus value added tax and reasonable out-of-pocket expenses, subject to a minimum fee of £— plus value added tax. Will each party please confirm to me that this fee basis is accepted.

(9) Will each party please reply to this letter on or before 31st March 1983.

Yours faithfully,

J. O. Dodgson

Mr Dodgson soon received replies from both parties. Mr Jones, for the landlords, requested an oral hearing and stated that he did not require more time for negotiation. Mr Stewart, for the tenants, requested that the matter be dealt with by written representations and asked for a stay of proceedings to allow more time for negotiation. Both parties stated that an issue of law had arisen in the dispute, namely whether the tenants' occupation of an adjoining shop could be taken into consideration when assessing the review rent. Both parties agreed to the basis of Mr Dodgson's fees.

PRELIMINARY MEETING

In the absence of the agreement of *both* parties to a stay of proceedings and to the use of the written representations procedure it was necessary for Mr Dodgson to proceed towards an oral hearing. The next procedural step was a preliminary meeting (see Chapter 10 p. 293 above). This was arranged by his secretary by telephone.

(1) Notification to the parties

Mr Dodgson then wrote the following joint letter to the parties:

Dear Sirs,
Rent review arbitration—10 South Street, Melchester, Loamshire
I have now received replies from both parties to my letter dated 9th March last. One of the parties has requested an oral hearing and I will adopt this procedure for this reference. It will be necessary for a preliminary meeting to be held to decide the future conduct of the arbitration. This will be held at my office at 10.00 am on Friday 15th April 1983. Following this meeting I will issue my order for directions and I enclose a draft order for your consideration. At the preliminary meeting I will hear comments on this order and receive applications and submissions (if any) from the parties on procedural matters.

If it is the intention of either party to be represented at the hearing by counsel or a solicitor I would ask that the solicitor be present at the preliminary meeting. Where counsel is to be instructed I would further ask that he be consulted regarding the directions he may require and as to any other matters relating to procedure and evidence.

Will each party please inform the other party and me of the names of those persons who will be attending the preliminary meeting.

Yours faithfully,

J. O. Dodgson

The draft order for directions referred to above, formed the basis of Mr Dodgson's check-list of subjects for consideration at the preliminary meeting. (The draft order corresponded very closely to the order issued after the preliminary meeting and reproduced on p. 393 below). Other items on Mr Dodgson's check-list were:

(a) representation at the hearing and, in particular, whether either or both of the parties intend to be represented by counsel;

(b) agreement that the only matter in dispute is the amount of the "market rent" of the demised premises as at 25th December 1982;

(c) the possibility of a settlement and whether the parties require time for further negotiation;

(d) the way in which the issue of law is to be dealt with: by the arbitrator alone, by the arbitrator and a legal assessor, by reference to a third party (e.g. counsel) or other tribunal, or by a stay of proceedings to enable application to be made to the court under section 2 of the 1979 Act for a determination of the point of law (see Chapter 10 p. 303 above);

(e) whether the parties intend to enter into an exclusion agreement under section 3 of the 1979 Act (see Chapter 12 p. 366 above);

(f) whether a shorthand writer is to be engaged for the hearing and, if so, who will arrange it and who will bear the cost.

(2) Preliminary meeting

Mr Dodgson opened the meeting by giving his name, details of his appointment and the nature of the dispute. He then noted the names and status of the persons attending on behalf of the parties. Procedure was informal. Mr Dodgson went through the draft order for directions, listening to each party in turn and seeking agreement on each item. He sought the parties' views on the six additional topics listed above. He asked whether there were any applications or submissions relating to procedure or evidence. The preliminary meeting was solely concerned with procedure and evidence. Mr Dodgson did not allow discussion on the substantive issue in the arbitration.

The contents of the order for directions were agreed (see below) and the position on the additional topics referred to above was as follows:

(a) both parties would be instructing counsel;

(b) the only matter in dispute was the amount of the "market rent" of the demised premises as at 25th December 1982;

(c) there was no possibility of a negotiated settlement of the dispute and, therefore, no stay of proceedings was required;

(d) the arbitrator was requested to decide the issue of law;

(e) the parties did not wish to enter into an exclusion agreement;

(f) a shorthand writer would not be engaged.

Neither party made any additional applications or submissions.

ORDER FOR DIRECTIONS

Immediately after the preliminary meeting Mr Dodgson issued the following order for directions:

ORDER FOR DIRECTIONS
IN THE MATTER OF THE ARBITRATION ACTS
1950 AND 1979
AND IN THE MATTER OF AN ARBITRATION BETWEEN
SUPERBUILD LIMITED (LANDLORDS) AND GREYFRIARS
LIMITED (TENANTS) ARISING OUT OF A RENT REVIEW
CLAUSE IN A LEASE DATED 29TH DECEMBER 1977 OF 10
SOUTH STREET, MELCHESTER, LOAMSHIRE.

Claimants and respondents

(1)   The landlords (Superbuild Limited) shall be the claimants and the tenants (Greyfriars Limited) shall be the respondents.

Schedule of works

(2) (a) If the respondents intend to claim that certain works carried out to the subject-premises are tenants' improvements to be disregarded in assessing the market rent under clause 6(3)(c) of the above lease, they shall prepare a schedule of such works. This schedule shall contain a brief description of each item of work, the date of execution and the cost as at that date. If possible, the respondents shall produce drawings showing the works. Copies of this schedule and any drawings shall be sent to the claimants and to me on or before 29th April 1983.

(b) Within 14 days of receipt of the above schedule, the claimants shall serve on the respondents and on me a copy thereof, annotated to show those works that are agreed as tenants' improvements and those that are not so agreed. In respect of the latter the claimants shall state their contrary contentions in respect thereof, whether that the works have not been carried out or that they are not tenants' improvements or any other contention.

(c) If the respondents should decide that they do not intend to claim that tenants' improvements have been carried out to the subject-premises they shall serve notice to this effect on the claimants and on me on or before 29th April 1983.

Statement of agreed facts

(3)   The parties shall prepare a statement of agreed facts, which shall include agreed floor areas, dimensions, plans

and other relevant facts relating to the subject-premises and the comparable properties referred to in paragraph (6)(b) below. Any correspondence and other documents to be submitted in evidence are to be agreed (where possible) and included in an agreed bundle. The statement of agreed facts and the agreed bundle shall be delivered to me on or before 14th July 1983. Both the statement of agreed facts and the agreed bundle shall be signed as agreed by both parties.

Issue of law

(4)   The parties shall prepare a statement setting out the issue of law between them. This shall contain a brief summary of each party's contentions thereon with a list of supporting cases or statutory provisions (if any). A copy of this statement signed as agreed by both parties shall be sent to me on or before 13th May 1983.

Expert evidence

(5)   Each party shall be limited to one expert witness only.

(6)   Each party who intends to call an expert witness shall submit to me on or before 1st June 1983 two copies of a document summarising the following evidence to be given by that witness:

(a) his rental valuation of the subject-premises (including any plans, calculations and assumptions in support thereof);

(b) a schedule of rents, prices and other particulars relating to the comparable properties to be referred to in support of his rental valuation.

The above documents shall be limited to facts, assumptions and valuations only and shall not contain any arguments, reasons or other explanatory material to be included in the witness's proof of evidence referred to in paragraph (7) below. When I have received documents from both parties I will send one copy of each to the other party.

(7)   Each expert witness shall submit to me on or before 20th June 1983 two copies of his written proof of evidence. When I have received proofs from both witnesses I will send one copy of each to the other party. The witnesses may supplement their proofs at the hearing by oral evidence, including evidence dealing with matters contained in the other expert's proof.

(8)   All facts, including facts relating to comparable

properties, shall be proved by evidence unless agreed by both parties. No hearsay, privileged or other inadmissible evidence (including statements made "without pre-judice") shall be contained in the documents specified in paragraphs (2), (6) and (7) above or otherwise put before me, unless agreed by both parties.

Inspections

(9) I shall make an unaccompanied preliminary inspection of the subject-premises at 10.00 a.m. on Thursday 14th July 1983. I shall make a further inspection of the subject-premises and the comparable properties referred to by the parties after the hearing. I shall invite the parties to attend that inspection.

Hearing

(10) A hearing will be held at 22 High Street, Melchester, Loamshire, commencing at 10.00 a.m. on Wednesday 20th July 1983.

Costs

(11) Costs of these directions shall be costs in the arbitration.

Award

(12) I shall issue an award with reasons in sufficient detail to enable the High Court to consider any question of law arising out of the award in the event of an appeal under section 1 of the Arbitration Act 1979.

Liberty to apply

(13) Each party shall be at liberty to apply.

DATED this .... day of 1983

SIGNED ....
J. O. Dodgson FRICS FCIArb

If both parties had agreed to the use of written representations and the dispute had been suitable for this procedure, then Mr Dodgson would have issued the following order for directions:

<u>ORDER FOR DIRECTIONS</u>
<u>IN THE MATTER OF THE ARBITRATION ACTS</u>
<u>1950 AND 1979</u>
AND IN THE MATTER OF AN ARBITRATION BETWEEN
SUPERBUILD LIMITED (LANDLORDS) AND GREYFRIARS
LIMITED (TENANTS) ARISING OUT OF A RENT REVIEW
CLAUSE IN A LEASE DATED 29TH DECEMBER 1977 OF 10
SOUTH STREET, MELCHESTER, LOAMSHIRE.

Claimants and respondents

1. The landlords (Superbuild Limited) shall be the claimants and the tenants (Greyfriars Limited) shall be the respondents.

Statement of agreed facts

2. The parties shall prepare a statement of agreed facts, which shall include agreed floor areas, dimensions, plans and other relevant facts relating to the subject-premises and the comparable properties and transactions referred to by the parties in their written representations. Any correspondence and other documents to be submitted in evidence are to be agreed (where possible) and attached to the statement. The statement and any agreed correspondence and documents shall be submitted to me during the exchange of written representations but not later than the last date for the submission of cross-representations under paragraph 4 below. The statement of agreed facts and any agreed correspondence and documents shall be signed as agreed by both parties.

Written representations

3. The parties shall submit to me their initial representations in duplicate on or before 9th May 1983. When I have received representations from both parties I will send one copy of each to the other party.

4. The parties may submit to me cross-representations in duplicate within 14 days of receipt of the opposing party's initial representations. These cross-representations shall not include any new matter, but shall be restricted to submissions and evidence in rebuttal of the opposing party's initial representations. When I have received cross-representations from both parties I will send one copy of each to the other party.

5. No further representations shall be submitted to me unless I give leave.

6. Facts included in the written representations shall be agreed between the parties or, where not agreed, shall be proved by the party relying on them. Facts relating to comparable properties and transactions may be proved by a letter or other written

statement from a person with direct knowledge of those facts. No hearsay, privileged or other inadmissible evidence (including statements made "without prejudice") shall be included in the representations or otherwise put before me unless agreed by both parties.

Inspection

7. When I have received initial and. cross-representations from both parties I shall notify each party of the date and time when I shall inspect the subject-premises and the comparable properties referred to by the parties. I shall invite the parties to attend that inspection.

Costs

8. Costs of these directions shall be costs in the arbitration.
9. The parties shall include in their representations their submissions as to costs.

Hearing

10. I reserve the right to call an oral hearing at any time if I consider this necessary after considering the parties' representations.

Award

11. I shall issue an award with reasons in sufficient detail to enable the High Court to consider any question of law arising out of the award in the event of an appeal under section 1 of the Arbitration Act 1979.

Liberty to apply

12. Each party shall be at liberty to apply.

DATED this .... day of 1983
SIGNED ....
      J. O. Dodgson FRICS FCIArb

BEFORE THE HEARING

(1) Arbitrator's functions

During the period between the order for directions and the hearing, Mr Dodgson had two main functions. First, to supervise the exchange of documents between the parties; secondly, to rule on any procedural applications by the parties.

Mr Dodgson's main task was to supervise the submission, exchange and content of the pre-hearing documents, to ensure that they were prepared and submitted in accordance with the instructions and timetable laid down in his order for directions.

There are three main reasons for the exchange of pre-hearing documents. First, each party will become aware of his opponent's case so that neither party is taken by surprise at the hearing. Secondly, the issues between the parties will be defined and some perhaps agreed. Facts in issue and agreed will be identified. Thirdly, the length of the hearing should be reduced.

The documents referred to in the order for directions before an oral hearing should contain facts and opinions but not evidence. For example, the respondent's schedule of works in paragraph (2)(a) should be limited to a brief statement of facts, and should not contain the evidence to prove those facts, such as specifications, bills of quantities, builder's estimates or final accounts. The expert witness documents in paragraph (6) should not contain reasons or excessive descriptive material, which should be reserved for the proof of evidence.

Mr Dodgson's second function during the period before the hearing was to deal with any procedural applications by the parties. These may take many forms, e.g. an application for a stay of proceedings pending further negotiations, requests for the discovery of documents, to administer interrogatories, to amend a submitted document or for an extension of time to deliver documents. The arbitrator's powers in this respect are discussed in Chapter 10 pp. 296 to 302 above.

(2) Reading the documents

There are two schools of thought as to whether an arbitrator should read documents submitted by the parties before a hearing. The argument that an arbitrator should not read those documents usually rests on the following grounds.

First, the documents are not evidence and, therefore, are not properly before the arbitrator until their contents have been given in evidence at the hearing. Secondly, they may contain inadmissible evidence, to which objection may be made and upheld at the hearing. This evidence may influence the arbitrator, however much he tries to dismiss it from his mind. (This objection may be overcome by requiring the parties to exchange documents before submission to the arbitrator and for each party to say whether or not he objects to the admissibility of any part of the document). Thirdly, the arbitrator may form a preliminary view of the merits of a case from a reading of the documents, thus perhaps relegating the hearing to a subordinate place in the decision-making process. In particular, the arbitrator may be influenced by evidence which appears to be strong when read, but which is subsequently shown to be unreliable under cross-examination. Fourthly, a party may not subsequently rely on the whole of the material included in his submitted documents. The arbitrator may be influenced, or perhaps confused, by points raised in the documents which are not taken at the hearing.

The case for the prior reading of documents by the arbitrator is suggested for the following reasons. First, where the arbitrator reads the documents he should be able to start the hearing with a clear understanding of the facts and issues. This will enable him to follow the submissions and evidence more easily and should reduce the length of the hearing. Secondly, proofs of evidence can be "tabled as read" thus removing the need for them to be read out in examination-in-chief or their contents disclosed by question and answer. Thirdly, by reading the documents in advance the arbitrator can decide on the issues which he thinks are important and on which he wishes to hear submissions and evidence. He is able to play a more active role at the hearing by asking questions on these points, provided, of course, that he does not adopt too inquisitorial a role, thus departing from his position as an "umpire" between the parties. Fourthly, as stated above, one of the arbitrator's functions before the hearing is to supervise the exchange and content of documents. This necessitates the reading of those documents to ensure that their contents are in accordance with his order for directions. He should check the arithmetic in all calculations and advise the parties of any errors he may find.

On balance, the most satisfactory procedure would appear to be that an arbitrator should read the documents before the hearing, not in order to form a view of the merits of the respective parties' cases, but to understand the facts and issues, to decide what points he thinks are important, to check all calculations and to ensure that the contents of documents are in accordance with his order for directions.

HEARING

(1) Arrangements

In Mr Dodgson's arbitration the documents were submitted and exchanged in accordance with his order for directions and the day of the hearing arrived. It was held in the conference room at the offices of Wilberforce and Dodgson, 22 High Street, Melchester. Before the parties arrived Mr Dodgson checked that the room had been arranged in accordance with his instructions. It was laid out as follows:

(a) Several tables and chairs were arranged in a U-shape with an additional small table and chair in the middle of the U. The table which formed the short side of the U was for Mr Dodgson, the tables which formed the two long arms of the U were for each of the parties respectively and the table in the middle was the witness box.

(b) Mr Dodgson's table had a comfortable chair. On the table were his files, the documents submitted by the parties under the order for directions, two blank spiral bound notebooks with margins (one for each day), coloured pens, scales for all plans submitted, copies of the Arbitration Acts 1950 and 1979, several textbooks on arbitration and evidence, a carafe of water and a glass.

(c) On each of the long tables was a card marked "Claimants" or "Respondents", several carafes of water and glasses.

(d) On the small table in the middle of the U-shaped arrangement of tables (facing the arbitrator's table) was a card marked "Witness Box", copies of the Old and New Testaments, two cards containing the words of the oath and affirmation respectively (see Chapter 3 p. 90 above), a carafe of water and two glasses.

(e) At the far end of the room were several spare chairs.

If a shorthand writer had been engaged it would have been necessary to provide an additional small table and chair.

Mr Dodgson was aware that last minute preparations are a fact of litigation and arranged for rooms to be available for each of the parties before the hearing. The parties' representatives were met by Mr Dodgson's secretary on arrival, shown the location of the conference room for the hearing and then given the use of another room for their last minute discussions.

(2) Procedure

At the appointed time for the commencement of the hearing Mr Dodgson's secretary checked with both parties that they were ready to begin, and then told Mr Dodgson, who took his place and opened the proceedings. The procedure at the hearing was as follows:

(a) Mr Dodgson opened the hearing by making the following statement:

> "Good morning, ladies and gentlemen, my name is James Oliver Dodgson and I am the arbitrator in this reference. This is a hearing in a reference to arbitration arising out of a rent review clause in a lease dated 29th December 1977 of 10 South Street, Melchester, Loamshire. The parties are Superbuild Limited (landlords and claimants) and Greyfriars Limited (tenants and respondents).
>
> On 6th January 1983 the landlords' surveyor applied to the President of The Royal Institution of Chartered Surveyors for the appointment of an arbitrator to determine the market rent

of the subject-premises as at 25th December 1982. I was nominated as that arbitrator on 4th March 1983.

I held a preliminary meeting and issued an order for directions dated 18th April 1983. Statements, proofs of evidence and other documents have been submitted or exchanged in accordance with my directions. I made an unaccompanied preliminary inspection of the subject-premises on 14th July 1983.

I propose to adopt the following procedure for this hearing. In accordance with the indication given to me by the parties at the preliminary meeting I have reserved to-day and to-morrow. If the hearing is not completed to-morrow I will not be available on the following day and it will be necessary to adjourn the hearing to a later date. I propose to adjourn for lunch each day for one hour at about 1.00 pm. I shall adjourn this afternoon at about 4.30 pm but I am able to continue after that time to-morrow afternoon if this is necessary to complete the hearing. I propose to commence at 10.00 am tomorrow morning.

Unless I am requested otherwise by the parties, I propose to follow the normal procedure for a High Court hearing and to take evidence on oath or affirmation. I suggest that counsel remain seated when addressing me. Following this hearing I shall make another inspection of the subject-premises and the comparable properties referred to by the parties. I shall make a reasoned award, but I would ask counsel to let me know before the close of the hearing whether they wish me to make a final award, dealing with both the market rent and costs, or an interim award, determining the market rent only, to be followed by a final award in respect of costs after further submissions in the light of my award on rent.

Before we begin does either party wish to make any representations regarding procedure?''

(b) There were no representations regarding procedure and Mr Dodgson called upon counsel for the claimants to begin.

(c) Mr B. Kenyon, counsel for the claimants, introduced himself and his opponent, Mr H. Lawrence of counsel. Mr Kenyon then made his opening address.

(d) Mr Kenyon called his expert witness, Mr J. Jones FRICS, who was sworn by Mr Dodgson. It was agreed that Mr Jones's proof of evidence should be tabled as read. He was asked a few additional questions by Mr Kenyon to complete his examination-in-chief. He was cross-examined by Mr Lawrence; re-examined by Mr Kenyon and answered some questions put to him by Mr Dodgson.

(e) Mr Lawrence made a short opening address on behalf of the respondents.

(f) Mr Lawrence called his expert witness, Mr J. Stewart ARICS, who was sworn by Mr Dodgson. It was agreed that Mr Stewart's proof of evidence should also be tabled as read. He was asked further questions in examination-in-chief, cross-examined by Mr Kenyon, re-examined by Mr Lawrence and answered a few questions put to him by Mr Dodgson.

(g) Mr Dodgson then adjourned the hearing until 10.00 am on the following day. During this adjournment he read his notes of the day's hearing, which were written on the right hand pages of his notebook with bold headings for each stage of the proceedings. He amplified his notes from memory where the speed of the proceedings had forced him to take only a brief note, and he used the blank left hand pages for his comments on the submissions and evidence and for sub-headings.

(h) When the hearing reopened the following morning Mr Lawrence, for the respondents, said that both counsel had taken instructions on the question of the award and both parties required a final award dealing with rent and costs.

(i) Mr Lawrence then made his final address which was in three parts: the issue of law, the market rent and costs.

(j) Mr Kenyon, for the claimants, made his final address under the same three general headings.

(k) Mr Dodgson made arrangements for his inspection of the subject-premises and the comparable properties.

(l) Mr Dodgson thanked the parties for their co-operation in the speedy completion of the proceedings and stated that he would notify the parties when his award had been made. He then closed the hearing.

AWARD

The essentials of a valid award are discussed in Chapter 11 p. 327 above. There is no definitive form for an award, either with or without reasons. The reasoned award set out below is formal, detailed and lengthy. It is followed by an example of a short form of award without reasons.

(1) Award with reasons

IN THE MATTER OF THE ARBITRATION ACTS
1950 AND 1979 AND IN THE MATTER OF AN
ARBITRATION BETWEEN:

SUPERBUILD LIMITED   (Claimants)

and

GREYFRIARS LIMITED   (Respondents)

RELATING TO 10 SOUTH STREET, MELCHESTER,
LOAMSHIRE

FINAL AWARD OF JAMES OLIVER DODGSON FRICS FCIArb

WHEREAS:

(1) By a lease dated 29th December 1977 between (a) Superbuild Limited (landlords), (b) Turner Fabrics Limited (tenants) and (c) John Edward Turner (surety) ("the lease of the subject-premises") premises described as shop and premises situate at 10 South Street, Melchester, Loamshire ("the subject-premises") were demised for a term of 10 years from 25th December 1977 at a rent of £4,000 per annum.

(2) By an assignment dated 2nd May 1981 the tenants' interest in the subject-premises became vested in the respondents.

(3) By a lease dated 28th June 1976 between (a) Superbuild Limited (landlords) and (b) Greyfriars Limited (tenants) ("the lease of the adjoining premises") premises described as ground floor shop situate at 8 South Street, Melchester, Loamshire ("the adjoining premises") were demised for a term of 15 years from 24th June 1976.

(4) By a licence dated 10th October 1981 between (a) Superbuild Limited and (b) Greyfriars Limited, consent was given to Greyfriars Limited for the removal of part of the party wall at ground floor level between the subject-premises and the adjoining premises.

(5) The lease of the subject-premises provides (<u>inter alia</u>) for a revision of the rent at the expiration of the fifth year of the term, that is to say on 25th December 1982, in the manner set out in clause 6 of that lease.

(6) Clause 6(2) of the lease of the subject-premises provides that the revised rent shall be the greater of (a) the rent payable of £4,000 per annum and (b) the market rent (as defined) of the demised premises at the review date.

(7) Clause 6(4) of the lease of the subject-premises provides that the market rent shall be agreed between the landlords and the

tenants, and if they are unable to agree on the amount of such rent, it shall be determined by an arbitrator appointed by the President of The Royal Institution of Chartered Surveyors on the application of either party.

(8) No agreement on the amount of the market rent having been reached between the parties, the landlords made application on 6th January 1983 to the said President for the appointment of an arbitrator.

(9) On 4th March 1983 I, James Oliver Dodgson FRICS FCIArb, was nominated by the President as that arbitrator. I informed the parties of this nomination by letter dated 9th March 1983.

(10) The landlords and the tenants, represented by their surveyors, attended a preliminary meeting with me on 15th April 1983 and I issued an order for directions dated 18th April 1983.

(11) This order for directions provided (<u>inter alia</u>) that the landlords shall be the claimants in this reference and the tenants shall be the respondents.

(12) In accordance with my order for directions the following documents were submitted to me:

   (a) a schedule of works prepared by the respondents containing details of works claimed to be tenants' improvements;

   (b) a copy of the above schedule annotated by the claimants to show those works that are agreed to be tenants' improvements and those that are not so agreed; (a list of tenants' improvements to be disregarded when assessing the market rent was subsequently agreed between the parties and is incorporated in the statement of agreed facts attached as an appendix to this award);

   (c) a rental valuation of the subject-premises and a schedule of rents of comparable properties prepared by Mr J. Jones FRICS, for the claimants;

   (d) a rental valuation of the subject-premises and a schedule of rents of comparable properties prepared by Mr J. Stewart ARICS, for the respondents;

   (e) a proof of evidence of Mr J. Jones FRICS, for the claimants;

   (f) a proof of evidence of Mr J. Stewart ARICS, for the respondents;

   (g) a statement of agreed facts (attached as an Appendix to this award);

   (h) a statement setting out the issue of law between the parties;

   (i) a certified copy of the lease of the adjoining premises;

   (j) a certified copy of a licence dated 10th October 1981 relating to the removal of part of the party wall between the subject-premises and the adjoining premises.

(13) I made an unaccompanied inspection of the subject-premises on 14th July 1983.

(14) I held a hearing at 22 High Street, Melchester, Loamshire, on 20th and 21st July 1983. Mr B. Kenyon of counsel (instructed by Messrs Medwin and Co) appeared for the claimants and called one expert witness, Mr J. Jones FRICS; Mr H. Lawrence of counsel (instructed by Messrs Muir and Locke) appeared for the respondents and called one expert witness, Mr J. Stewart ARICS.

(15) At the hearing I was given a folder containing copies of the following documents:

    (a) a lease dated 1st October 1977 of 2 South Street, Melchester;

    (b) an underlease dated 1st July 1982 of 16 South Street, Melchester;

    (c) an underlease dated 2nd February 1978 of 22 South Street, Melchester.

(16) On 25th July 1983 I made an inspection of the subject-premises, the adjoining premises and the comparable properties referred to by the parties accompanied by both expert witnesses.

(17) I have agreed to make a final award determining the amount of the market rent of the subject-premises and the liability for the costs of this reference, and to state my reasons in sufficient detail to enable the High Court to consider any question of law arising out of this award in the event of an appeal under section 1 of the Arbitration Act 1979.

NOW I, JAMES OLIVER DODGSON FRICS FCIArb,
DO HEREBY MAKE AND PUBLISH THIS MY FINAL
AWARD AS FOLLOWS:

ISSUE OF LAW

1. The issue of law in this reference is whether the respondents' occupation of the adjoining premises under a separate lease may be taken into consideration when assessing the market rent of the subject-premises. The claimants contend that this occupation may be taken into account and has the effect of increasing the market rent of the subject-premises. The respondents contend that it may not be taken into account, and, therefore, has no effect on that rent.

2. The definition of "market rent" in clause 6(3) of the lease of the subject-premises is relevant to this issue. It is as follows:

    "The market rent for the purposes of this lease shall mean the rent at which the demised premises might reasonably

be expected to be let by a willing lessor to a willing lessee in
the open market with vacant possession without a premium
and in all respects on the same terms and conditions as are
herein contained (save as to rent) there being disregarded
(a) any effect on rent of the fact that the lessee has or his
predecessors in title have been in occupation of the demised
premises (b) any goodwill attached to the demised
premises by reason of any trade or business carried on
therein (c) any effect on rent of any improvements carried
out by the lessee or a predecessor in title of his otherwise
than in pursuance of an obligation under this lease"

Claimants' submissions

3. Mr Kenyon, for the claimants, submitted that, as a matter of
law, the respondents' occupation of the adjoining premises may
be taken into consideration when assessing the market rent of
the subject-premises. He looked first at the above definition of
the market rent and, in particular, at the words "the rent at
which the demised premises might reasonably be expected to be
let ... in the open market. ..." Clearly, he said, "market rent"
means open market rent.

4. He then referred me to IRC v Clay & Buchanan [1914] 3 KB
466, where the Court of Appeal considered open market value in
the context of a valuation for the purposes of taxation. It was
held that on a sale in an open market it must be assumed that
intending purchasers are aware that an adjoining owner might
be interested in purchasing and would be prepared to give a
high price for the property and that its value would thereby be
increased. Swinfen Eady LJ said (p. 474):

"A value ascertained by reference to the amount obtain-
able in an open market shows an intention to include every
possible purchaser. The market is to be an open market, as
distinct from an offer to a limited class only, ..."

Mr Kenyon submitted that, having regard to this decision, the
market rent of the subject-premises must be determined on the
assumption that all other prospective tenants are aware that the
respondents, as adjoining occupiers, would be interested in
renting the subject-premises for an extension of their business
and would make a higher rental bid than any other prospective
tenant. It was recognised that an open market rent could be
exceptionally high. In Ponsford v HMS Aerosols Ltd [1978] 3
WLR 241, Lord Fraser drew a distinction between a "reasonable rent" and an "open market rent" and said (p. 253):

"I think that the effect of the word 'reasonable' is to

exclude any exceptional or freak rent that might have had to be taken into account if the clause had referred to the open market rent."

5. Furthermore, the respondents' occupation of the adjoining premises is not to be disregarded under clause 6(3) of the lease of the subject-premises. The first matter to be disregarded relates to the tenants' occupation of the demised premises, which are defined in Schedule 1 to the lease as "all that shop and premises situate at 10 South Street...". The lease of the subject-premises was granted after the commencement of the respondents' occupation of the adjoining premises and, if the intention of the parties had been to exclude that occupation from consideration at the rent review, this would have been expressly stated in the lease of the subject-premises. In the absence of express words it cannot now be added by implication.

6. The decision in F. R. Evans (Leeds) Ltd v English Electric Co Ltd (1977) 36 P & CR 185, that both the landlord and the tenant in a rent review are to be assumed to be hypothetical persons and not the actual parties, does not extend to the occupation of adjoining premises. Adjoining occupiers are actual and not hypothetical persons, although an actual adjoining tenant can become the hypothetical tenant of the subject-premises.

7. Finally, Mr Kenyon submitted that as a matter of law the additional price or rent offered by a special purchaser or tenant would not be restricted to one bid more than the highest "general" market bid. In support of this contention he cited Clay (above) and Raja Vyricherla Narayana Gajapatiragu v The Revenue Divisional Officer, Vizagapatam [1939] AC 304.

Respondents' submissions

8. Mr Lawrence, for the respondents, submitted that as a matter of law the respondents' occupation of the adjoining premises should be disregarded. He gave three reasons for this submission.

9. First, it was held in the Evans case (above) that the actual parties to a rent review negotiation are to be disregarded: both landlord and tenant must be assumed to be hypothetical persons. He referred me to the following passage from the judgment of Donaldson J (p. 189):

"In a sense the willing lessor must be the landlords because only they can dispose of the premises, but for the purposes of the clause the landlord is an abstraction—a hypothetical person ...

Similarly, in my judgment, the willing lessee is an abstraction—a hypothetical person actively taking premises to fulfil needs which these premises could fulfil . . .

In a word, his profile may or may not fit that of the (actual tenant), but he is not that (tenant)."

Mr Lawrence drew my attention to the last sentence in the above quotation. He submitted that, because it has to be assumed that the tenant of the subject-premises is a purely hypothetical person, then he cannot be the occupier of adjoining premises. The hypothetical tenant of the subject-premises is not necessarily the actual tenant, and cannot be assumed to be in occupation of the shop next door.

10. Secondly, Mr Lawrence submitted that the same result will arise due to the direction in clause 6(3) of the lease of the subject-premises that the effect on rent of the tenants' occupation of those premises is to be disregarded. This clause requires the premises to be valued with vacant possession. The effect is that, although the adjoining premises are occupied by the respondents, the subject-premises are assumed to be vacant and will be let to hypothetical willing lessees who are not the respondents. The respondents are assumed never to have been in occupation of the subject-premises and, therefore, there is no indication whatsoever that they would be interested in extending their business into those premises. Furthermore, it has been agreed that the removal of part of the party wall between the two properties is a tenants' improvement to be disregarded when assessing the market rent. This supports the respondents' contention that their occupation of the adjoining premises is assumed not to have extended to the subject-premises and does not, therefore, increase the market rent of those premises.

11. Thirdly, Mr Lawrence said that an exceptionally high rental bid (such as might be made by an adjoining occupier) cannot be included in a market rent. In support of this proposition he referred me to part of the speech of Lord Keith in Ponsford (above). Lord Keith, when considering the expressions "reasonable rent" and "open market rent", said (p. 255):

"I am not impressed by the suggestion that the expression 'a reasonable rent' might have been used merely in order to exclude any freak or special rent that a prospective tenant might be prepared to pay, because I think that in estimating the market rent, a valuer would proceed on the general level of rents for comparable premises without reference to any such freak or special rent."

12. Finally, Mr Lawrence submitted that, if I should decide that

the respondents' occupation of the adjoining premises may be taken into consideration, then the effect of this on the market rent of the subject-premises is a question of fact. It does not automatically follow as a matter of law that the additional rental bid <u>must</u> be more than one bid above the "general" market level of rental bids. The respondents will call expert evidence that the additional rental bid of an adjoining occupier would not increase the rent by more than £250 per annum.

My decision

13. I accept the contention of the claimants that, as a matter of law, I may take into consideration the respondents' occupation of the adjoining premises when determining the market rent of the subject-premises. Authority for this proposition is <u>IRC v Clay & Buchanan</u> (above) and, in my view, it is not affected by the <u>Evans</u> decision (above) nor by the direction in clause 6(3) of the lease of the subject-premises which requires the tenants' occupation of those premises to be disregarded. The <u>Evans</u> decision requires me to ignore the characteristics of the actual tenant of the subject-premises (e.g. liquidity problems), but it does not require me to ignore the fact that the hypothetical tenant of the subject-premises may also be the actual tenant of the adjoining premises. Similarly, although clause 6(3)(a) of the lease of the subject-premises states that the tenants' occupation of the <u>demised premises</u> is to be disregarded, this does not extend to the tenants' occupation of the adjoining premises. There is no justification for implying additional words to this effect in this part of the clause.

14. In my view, the true position is that the subject-premises are to be valued as vacant and to let, by a willing lessor to a willing lessee, who are both hypothetical persons. The respondents are assumed not to have been in occupation of the subject-premises, but the fact that they are in occupation of the adjoining premises may be taken into consideration. This occupation may lead them to make a higher rental bid for the subject-premises than other prospective tenants in order to secure them for the expansion of their business. This additional rent is not, as a matter of law, excluded nor is it necessarily restricted to one bid more than the "general" level of rental bids. The amount of this additional bid is a question of fact to be decided on the expert evidence submitted to me.

THE MARKET RENT

15. Mr Kenyon, for the claimants, called one expert witness, Mr J. Jones FRICS, who spoke to a market rent of £10,250 per

annum. Mr Lawrence, for the respondents, also called one expert witness, Mr J. Stewart ARICS, who spoke to a market rent of £7,300 per annum. Both witnesses referred me to the same five comparable transactions. The agreed facts relating to these transactions are set out in the statement of agreed facts, which is attached as an appendix to this award.

16. The witnesses' respective analyses of these transactions were as follows:

Address Transaction Accommodation	J. Jones FRICS for claimants	J. Stewart ARICS for respondents
	£ per sq ft pa	£ per sq ft pa
2 South Street Letting from 29th September 1982 at a rent of £5,725 pa		
Basement —cellar	£ 0.50	£ 0.50
Ground floor—shop zone A	15.15	14.55
shop zone B	7.57	7.27
store	2.00	2.75
First floor —store	1.00	1.50
6 South Street Rent review 29th September 1982, review rent £3,350 pa		
Basement —store	£ 0.50	£ 0.75
Ground floor—shop zone A	12.00	11.80
shop zone B	6.00	5.90
16 South Street Letting from 24th June 1982 at a rent of £7,825 pa		
Ground floor—shop zone A	£25.00	£24.54
shop zone B	12.50	12.27
First floor —store	1.25	1.75
Second floor —vacant	0.50	0.75
18 South Street Renewal of lease from 29th September 1982 at a rent of £2,775 pa		
Basement —store	£ 0.50	£ 0.75
Ground floor—shop zone A	18.17	18.00

Address Transaction Accommodation	J. Jones FRICS for claimants	J. Stewart ARICS for respondents
22 South Street Letting from 25th December 1982 at a rent of £12,000 pa		
Basement —store	£ 0.75	£ 1.00
Ground floor—shop zone A	27.00	26.87
shop zone B	13.50	13.43
shop remainder	6.75	6.71
First floor —sales	4.25	4.00
store	1.25	1.50

17. It will be seen from the above table that the two expert witnesses differed little from each other in their analyses of the comparable transactions. They differed greatly, however, in their interpretation of this rental evidence. Their respective assessments of the market rent of the subject-premises were as follows:

	J. Jones FRICS for claimants		J. Stewart ARICS for respondents	
		£ pa		£ pa
Basement —store 150 sq ft	@ £ 0.75 =	112	@ £ 0.50 =	75
Ground floor—shop zone A				
300 sq ft	@ £22.50 =	6,750	@ £17.50 =	5,250
shop zone B				
200 sq ft	@ £11.25 =	2,250	@ £ 8.75 =	1,750
First floor —store 175 sq ft	@ £ 1.25 =	219	@ £ 1.25 =	219
		£ 9,331		£7,294
add: for additional bid of				
tenants of adjoining premises	say 10%	933		nil
		£10,264		£7,294
Market rent	say	£10,250 pa	say	£7,300 pa

Expert evidence for the claimants

18. Mr Jones FRICS, for the claimants, assessed the market rent of the subject-premises at £10,250 per annum. This directly disregards tenants' improvements. He said that the rental evidence

set out above included shops along the whole length of one side of South Street, from no. 2, situated at the point where the street bends and becomes Lower South Street, to no. 22 where South Street joins the High Street, the main shopping street of Melchester. Rental values increase from £15.00 per square foot zone A for no. 2 to £27.00 per square foot zone A for no. 22. The subject-premises are about halfway along South Street. The rise in rental values, from no. 2 to no. 22, is not, however, constant. There is a pedestrian crossing immediately outside the subject-premises which leads to the main entrance of the Market Hall, which is on the opposite side of the road and slightly to the north of the crossing. A thriving indoor market is held in this Hall and it is open 6 days a week. Thus, said Mr Jones, the pedestrian flow is from High Street along South Street to the subject-premises and across to the Market Hall. This has affected rental values in South Street: they are relatively low for nos. 2 to 8, where the pedestrian flow is light, with a sudden increase at the subject-premises and then a more gradual rise to no. 22 close to the High Street. The properties most comparable to the subject-premises are, therefore, nos. 16, 18 and 22 South Street.

19. Mr Jones drew my attention to the fact that the three comparables which are open market lettings (nos. 2, 16 and 22 South Street) show comparatively higher rents than the rent review or renewal evidence. For example, no. 2 (a letting) has a zone A rent of £15.15 per square foot but no. 6 (a rent review) has a zone A rent of only £12.00 per square foot, although in a better position. No. 16 (a letting) has a zone A rent of £25 per square foot but no. 18 (a renewal) has a lower zone A rent of £18.17 per square foot. This evidence confirmed Mr Jones's general opinion that a two-tier rental market existed: rents on new lettings were at a relatively higher level than rents on the renewal of leases and rent reviews. In his closing address Mr Kenyon referred me to the open market character of the market rent of the subject-premises and urged me to give greater weight to the comparable rents for new lettings.

20. For the reasons set out above, Mr Jones formed the opinion that the best comparables were nos. 16 and 22 South Street (£25 and £27 per square foot zone A respectively). The subject-premises are slightly inferior in location to no. 16 and he therefore used £22.50 per square foot zone A and, following his devaluation of other rents, 75p per square foot for the basement and £1.25 per square foot for the first floor. He took the view that the respondents, as adjoining tenants, would wish to expand their business into the subject-premises and would make an

additional rental bid. The effect of this would be that either the respondents would bid more than anyone else to secure the subject-premises or their interest would force up the rental bids of other hypothetical tenants. Based on his experience his estimate of the amount of the addition was 10% of the rent. Mr Jones said in examination-in-chief that if he had been advised that, as a matter of law, the respondents' occupation of the adjoining premises was to be ignored, he would have assessed the market rent of the subject-premises at £9,300 per annum.

Expert evidence for the respondents

21. Mr Stewart ARICS, for the respondents, assessed the market rent of the subject-premises at £7,300 per annum. This also directly disregards tenants' improvements. The inferences he drew from the rental evidence and his knowledge of the locality differed from those drawn by Mr Jones. Mr Stewart thought that Mr Jones had exaggerated the effect of the pedestrian crossing outside the subject-premises. He could accept a sudden drop in rental values but not immediately to the south of the subject-premises, i.e. affecting nos. 2 to 8 South Street. He saw the drop in rental values occurring at about 16 South Street. The reason he gave was that barriers existed along the pavement edges of South Street from the High Street to no. 16. Mr Stewart's observations showed that shoppers walked along the west side of South Street, from the High Street to the end of the barriers, and then dodged across the road to the entrance to the Market Hall which is situated at about the end of the barriers. Shoppers did not walk to the pedestrian crossing, cross and then walk back to the Market Hall.

22. For the above reasons, Mr Stewart derived little assistance from the rents of nos. 16, 18 and 22 South Street, which are all in better trading positions. He derived most assistance from the rents of nos. 2 and 6 South Street. He agreed that the rent of no. 6 was unduly low and relied mainly on the rent of no. 2 (£14.55 per square foot zone A). The subject-premises are in a better trading position than no. 2 and Mr Stewart, therefore, chose £17.50 per square foot zone A. He said that this was also consistent with £25 per square foot zone A for 16 South Street, a more modern shop in a better trading position. From his analysis of the comparables Mr Stewart put 50p per square foot on the basement and £1.25 per square foot on the first floor. He was advised that, as a matter of law, the respondents' occupation of the adjoining premises was to be disregarded and, therefore, he did not make an addition to the rent on this account. In examination-in-chief he was asked what addition (if any) he would

have made if the respondents' occupation of the adjoining premises could be taken into consideration. He said only £250 per annum. He did not share Mr Jones's optimism about the amount of the additional rent in these times of recession.

My determination of the market rent

23. I now set out my determination of the market rent of the subject-premises, having regard to my decision that, as a matter of law, the respondents' occupation of the adjoining premises may be taken into consideration. My determination is made in the light of the evidence summarised above and my inspection of the subject-premises and the five comparable properties.

24. I prefer Mr Stewart's interpretation of the rental evidence, but I am of the opinion that he has made insufficient allowance for the better trading position of the subject-premises relative to 2 South Street. I put £18.00 per square foot on zone A in place of his £17.50. This is also more consistent with £25 per square foot on zone A for 16 South Street, a modern shop in a better trading position. I prefer Mr Stewart's figure of 50p per square foot for the basement store and both witnesses are agreed on £1.25 per square foot for the first floor store. I have already decided that the respondents' occupation of the adjoining premises may be taken into consideration. This increases the market rent of the subject-premises but I think that Mr Jones is too optimistic about the size of this additional bid and Mr Stewart's figure of £250 is too low. I put this additional bid at £500. My determination of the market rent of the subject-premises as at 25th December 1982 is, therefore, £8,000 per annum calculated as follows:

Basement	—store 150 sq ft	@ 50p	£ 75
Ground floor	—shop zone A 300 sq ft	@ £18	£5,400
	shop zone B 200 sq ft	@ £ 9	£1,800
First floor	—store 175 sq ft	@ £1.25	£ 219
			£7,494
add: for additional bid of tenants of adjoining premises, say			£ 500
			£7,994

say £8,000 per annum

25. In reaching the above determination I followed the approach adopted by both expert witnesses and proceeded directly to an estimate of the market rent which disregards the works agreed by the parties to be tenants' improvements.

My alternative determination of the market rent

26. The above determination is on the basis that, as a matter of law, the respondents' occupation of the adjoining premises may be taken into consideration when assessing the market rent of the subject-premises. I now make an alternative award on the assumption that, as a matter of law, the respondents' occupation of the adjoining premises must be disregarded. On this assumption I would not have included in my rental calculation the £500 for the additional bid of the tenants of the adjoining premises. My calculation would have produced, therefore, a market rent of £7,494 per annum which I would have rounded up to £7,500 per annum.

COSTS

27. I was requested by the parties to make a final award and I must, therefore, deal with the question of costs. Clause 6(4) of the lease of the subject-premises states (inter alia) that the costs of the reference shall be in the discretion of the arbitrator.

Claimants' submissions

28. Mr Kenyon, for the claimants, urged me to award costs to the claimants if I determine a market rent above the figure of £7,300 per annum put forward by the respondents. This would show, he said, that the claimants had to resort to arbitration to obtain the correct market rent as determined by me. They had, therefore, succeeded in the reference and should be awarded their costs in accordance with the general rule that "costs follow the event".

Respondents' submissions

29. Mr Lawrence, for the respondents, made a similar submission. He urged me to award costs to the respondents if I determine a market rent below the rent of £10,250 per annum put forward by the claimants. This would show, he said, that the respondents were justified in refusing to agree to the claimants' estimate of the market rent, thus forcing them to refer the matter to arbitration. If they achieve less than the figure they contended for they had lost the reference, and, under the general rule of costs, should pay all the costs.

My award of costs

30. Neither party submitted a sealed offer and the parties did not put before me by agreement any evidence of offers and counter-offers made during negotiations.
31. The claimants submitted that, as a matter of law, the respondents' occupation of the adjoining premises could be taken

into consideration in determining the market rent and, on this basis, contended for a figure of £10,250 per annum. This would have been £9,300 per annum if the respondents' occupation of the adjoining premises must be disregarded. The respondents submitted that, as a matter of law, their occupation of the adjoining premises should be disregarded in determining the market rent of the subject-premises and, on this basis, contended for a figure of £7,300 per annum. This would have been increased to £7,550 per annum if the respondents' occupation of the adjoining premises could be taken into consideration.

32. I have found for the claimants on the issue of law but have determined a market rent of £8,000 per annum which is much closer to the respondent's figure than the claimants' figure of £10,250 per annum. Accordingly, I think it right to reflect the fact that I have substantially found in favour of the respondents by directing the claimants to bear all the costs.

My alternative award of costs

33. If my decision on the issue of law had been to the effect that the respondents' occupation of the adjoining premises should be disregarded, my determination of the market rent would have been £7,500 per annum, even closer to the respondents' figure of market rent and I would again have directed the claimants to bear all the costs.

AWARD

34. I HEREBY AWARD AND DETERMINE that the market rent under clause 6(4) of the lease of the subject-premises as at 25th December 1982 was £8,000 per annum (eight thousand pounds per annum).

35. I HEREBY FURTHER AWARD AND DIRECT that the claimants shall pay the respondents' costs of the reference, such costs to be taxed by the High Court (if not agreed), and shall also pay and bear the costs of this my final award which I hereby tax and settle in the sum of £—— (including value added tax). If the respondents shall have paid all or part of the costs of my award those costs shall be reimbursed by the claimants within 14 days.

Alternative award

36. If I had accepted the contention of the respondents that their occupation of the adjoining premises is, as a matter of law, to be disregarded in assessing the market rent of the subject-premises, I would have awarded and determined that the market rent under clause 6(4) of the lease of the subject-premises as at 25th

December 1982 was £7,500 per annum (seven thousand five
hundred pounds per annum).

37. I would have further awarded and directed that the claimants
shall pay the respondents' costs of the reference, such costs to be
taxed by the High Court (if not agreed), and shall also pay and
bear the costs of this my award which I hereby tax and settle in
the sum of £— (including value added tax). If the respondents
shall have paid all or part of the costs of my award, those costs
shall be reimbursed by the claimants within 14 days.

DATED this .... day of 1983
SIGNED ....
JAMES OLIVER DODGSON FRICS FCIArb

APPENDIX

STATEMENT OF AGREED FACTS

The subject-premises

(1) The subject-premises comprise a terraced shop constructed of brick with a slate pitched roof. The premises were built in about 1920. Accommodation is on basement, ground and first floors. The net internal floor areas and uses are:

Floor	Use	Sq ft	Sq ft
Basement	store		150
Ground floor	shop zone A	300	
	shop zone B	200	500
Half landing	toilet (wc & lb)		—
First floor	store		175
		Total	825

The frontage to South Street is 16 ft, the internal width of the shop is 14ft 6ins and the shop depth is 34 ft.

(2) The subject-premises are situated on the west side of South Street, about 125 ft from the junction of South Street and High Street. South Street is a secondary shopping street, close to High Street which is the main shopping street of Melchester. Immediately outside the subject-premises is a pedestrian crossing. On the opposite (east) side of South Street, and about 40 ft to the north of the subject-premises, is the main entrance to the Market Hall.

(3) It is agreed that the following works to the subject-premises are tenants' improvements which are to be disregarded when assessing the market rent:

Date of execution	Description	Cost at date of execution
June 1978	Installation of central heating on ground and first floors. Five hot water radiators on ground floor and four on first floor. "Heatwave" gas boiler sited at the rear of the ground floor.	£7,500
February 1982	Removal of part of the party wall on the ground floor between the subject-premises and 8 South Street.	£3,000

(4) Attached to this statement are agreed floor plans of the subject-premises (numbered DWK/1 to 6) and an agreed extract from the 1/1250 Ordnance Survey Map, on which the subject-premises are edged red, 8 South Street is edged green and the comparable properties referred to in the Table of Comparable Properties (below) are edged blue and numbered 1 to 5 respectively. (These plans are not attached to this award).

Comparable properties

The Table on pages 420 and 421 sets out the agreed facts relating to the comparable properties.

Table of Comparable Properties

Ref no on OS Map	Address	Description and floor areas		Rent £ pa (excl)	Rental transaction
1.	2 South Street	End of terrace shop with accommodation on basement ground and first floors. Frontage 15 ft.		£5,725	Lease for 10 years from 29th September 1982; rent review at fifth year to "fair rack rental value".
		Hardware shop			Tenants responsible for all repairs, decorations and insurance.
		Basement —cellar	250 sq ft		
		Ground floor—shop A	300 sq ft		
		shop B	80 sq ft		
		store	100 sq ft		
		First floor —store	250 sq ft		Tenants: The Hardware Shop
2.	6 South Street	Lock-up shop with accommodation on basement and ground floors. Frontage 12 ft.		£3,350	Rent review at 29th September 1982 to the "fair market rent" in a lease with 10 years unexpired at the review date. Tenants responsible for all repairs and decorations; landlords insure and recover premium from tenants.
		Newsagent			
		Basement —store	220 sq ft		
		Ground floor—shop A	215 sq ft		
		shop B	110 sq ft		Tenants: The South Street Library

	Description	Area	Rent	Lease Terms
3.	16 South Street	Partly rebuilt terraced shop with accommodation on ground and two upper floors. Frontage 14 ft. Dress shop Ground floor—shop A 250 sq ft shop B 100 sq ft First floor —store 200 sq ft Second floor —vacant 150 sq ft	£7,825	Lease for 15 years from 24th June 1982; 5 yearly rent reviews to "rack rent"; tenants responsible for all repairs, decorations and insurance. Tenants: Just Dresses
4.	18 South Street	Terraced lock-up shop with accommodation on basement and ground floors. Frontage 12 ft. Tobacconists Basement —store 100 sq ft Ground floor—shop A 150 sq ft	£2,775	Renewal of lease for a term of 5 years from 29th September 1982; tenants responsible for all repairs, decorations and insurance. Tenants: J. H. Smith & Son Ltd
5.	22 South Street	End of terrace shop with accommodation on basement, ground and first floors. Frontage 18 ft. Mens' outfitters Basement —store 250 sq ft Ground floor—shop A 275 sq ft shop B 200 sq ft shop rem 50 sq ft First floor —sales 300 sq ft —store 100 sq ft	£12,000	Lease for 15 years from 25th December 1982; 5 yearly rent reviews to "market rent"; tenants responsible for all repairs, decorations and insurance. Tenants: Browns Clothing Ltd

(2) Award without reasons

If Mr Dodgson had made a short award without reasons it would have been as follows:

IN THE MATTER OF THE ARBITRATION ACTS
1950 AND 1979 AND IN THE MATTER OF AN
ARBITRATION BETWEEN:

SUPERBUILD LIMITED (Claimants)
and
GREYFRIARS LIMITED (Respondents)

RELATING TO 10 SOUTH STREET,
MELCHESTER, LOAMSHIRE

FINAL AWARD OF J. O. DODGSON FRICS FCIArb

WHEREAS:

(1) By a lease dated 29th December 1977 between (a) Superbuild Limited (landlords), (b) Turner Fabrics Limited (tenants) and (c) James Edward Turner (surety), premises at 10 South Street, Melchester, Loamshire were demised for a term of 10 years from 25th December 1977.

(2) By an assignment dated 2nd May 1981 the tenants' interest in the demised premises became vested in the respondents.

(3) The above lease provides (inter alia) for a revision of rent at the expiration of the fifth year of the term (25th December 1982).

(4) The revised rent shall be the greater of (a) the rent payable, and (b) the market rent of the demised premises at the review date, and if the parties are unable to agree the amount of that market rent it shall be determined by an arbitrator appointed by the President of The Royal Institution of Chartered Surveyors on the application of either party.

(5) The parties having failed to reach agreement on the amount of the market rent, application was made by the landlords to the said President for the appointment of an arbitrator and I was nominated as that arbitrator on 4th March 1983.

NOW I, JAMES OLIVER DODGSON FRICS FCIArb, having heard submissions and evidence from the parties and inspected the demised premises, the adjoining premises (8 South Street) and the comparable properties referred to by the parties DO HEREBY MAKE AND PUBLISH THIS MY FINAL AWARD AS FOLLOWS:

1. I HEREBY AWARD AND DETERMINE that the market rent under clause 6(4) of the lease dated 29th December 1977 of 10 South Street, Melchester, Loamshire as at 25th December 1982 was £8,000 per annum (eight thousand pounds per annum).
2. I HEREBY FURTHER AWARD AND DIRECT that the claimants shall pay the respondents' costs of the reference, such costs to be taxed in the High Court (if not agreed) and shall also pay and bear the costs of this my award which I hereby tax and settle in the sum of £— (including value added tax). If the respondents shall have paid all or part of the costs of my award those costs shall be reimbursed by the claimants within 14 days.

DATED this .... day of 1983
SIGNED ....
    J. O. DODGSON FRICS FCIArb

(3) Letter to the parties

Mr Dodgson signed and dated his award on 16th August 1983 and then sent the following joint letter to the solicitors to the parties:

Dear Sirs,
Rent review arbitration—10 South Street, Melchester, Loamshire
I have now made and published my final award in the above. This may be taken up by either party upon payment of my fees and charges of £—, including value added tax. If you wish to have the award sent to you through the post please send me your cheque for this amount and I will send it to you. If you wish to collect the award from this office please inform my secretary and arrangements will be made for it to be left at our reception desk, to be released on receipt of a cheque for the above amount.

Yours faithfully,

J. O. Dodgson

The award was taken up by the claimants who paid Mr Dodgson's fees and charges in full. He then sent the other copy of his award (also signed and dated) to the respondents.

Even though the whole of the costs of the award were paid by the claimants it would have been incorrect for Mr Dodgson to send them both copies. Each party is entitled to receive a copy of the award when it is released upon payment of the total costs. As we have seen (Chapter 12 pp. 360 and 370 above), the time limits for an application for leave to appeal against an award or to have it remitted or set aside start to run from the date of publication and, therefore, it is in the interests of the parties to take up the award as quickly as possible after notification of publication by the arbitrator.

(4) Correction of award

If after publication of his award Mr Dodgson had discovered a clerical error which he wished to correct under section 17 of the Arbitration Act 1950 (see Chapter 12 p. 359 above), he would have issued the following correction to both parties:

IN THE MATTER OF THE ARBITRATION ACTS
1950 AND 1979 AND IN THE MATTER OF AN
ARBITRATION BETWEEN:

SUPERBUILD LIMITED (Claimants)
and
GREYFRIARS LIMITED (Respondents)

RELATING TO 10 SOUTH STREET,
MELCHESTER, LOAMSHIRE

1. I find that in paragraph 24 of my final award dated 16th August 1983 I made a clerical error by stating the floor area of the basement of the subject-premises to be "105 square feet".
2. In the exercise of the power given to me by section 17 of the Arbitration Act 1950 to correct any clerical error arising from an accidental slip, I give notice that I am correcting my award and that the floor area of the basement of the subject-premises in paragraph 24 of my award shall now read "150 square feet". The remainder of my award is unaltered.

DATED this .... day of 1983

SIGNED ....

JAMES OLIVER DODGSON FRICS FCIArb

APPENDIX A

INTERPRETATION OF DOCUMENTS

APPENDIX A

Interpretation of Documents

INTRODUCTION

It will often be necessary for an arbitrator or expert to interpret (construe) a document before he can make his award or determination. This is a question of law. It may be referred to another tribunal for decision, e.g. an application to the High Court under section 2 of the Arbitration Act 1979 or for a declaration as to the true meaning of the words used. A lay arbitrator may sit with a legal assessor. The parties may agree to refer the matter to counsel or a solicitor for a decision (see Chapter 10 p. 303 above). In many cases, however, the arbitrator or expert must decide the point himself, assisted only by the submissions or representations of the parties. He should, therefore, have an understanding of the basic rules of legal interpretation. These are set out briefly in this Appendix.

FUNDAMENTAL QUESTION

The fundamental question to be answered whenever problems of interpretation arise is:

> "... 'What is the meaning of what the parties have said?' not 'What did the parties mean to say?' ... it being a presumption ... that the parties intended to say that which they have said".
> (per Lord Simon of Glaisdale in *Wickman Machine Tool Sales Ltd v L. Schuler AG* [1947] AC 235 at p 263, quoting with approval *Norton on Deeds* (1906) p. 43).

For example, in *Ponsford v HMS Aerosols Ltd* (1978) 247 EG 1171, the question for determination was whether a "reasonable rent" under a rent review clause in a lease should include or exclude the value of tenant's improvements. In the House of Lords Lord Dilhorne, adopting a "literal approach" to the interpretation of the lease (see p. 431 below), said that, although it might be unfair that a tenant should pay a rent which reflected the value of his own improvements, that is not a ground for an interpretation which excludes the benefit of such improvements. It is not for the court to re-write the lease.

Furthermore, the "purposive" approach to interpretation (see p. 433 below), which construes a document by placing it in the surrounding circumstances at the time it was made, also proceeds objectively and should not take into account the subjective intention of the parties. A contract is what the parties have said in the relevant document and it is not for the court (or an arbitrator or independent expert) to make a contract which is different from the words actually used merely because the parties may have intended something different (*Plumb Brothers v Dolmac (Agriculture) Ltd* (1984) 271 EG 373 at p. 374).

The document most likely to require interpretation by a surveyor is a lease. There are no special rules of interpretation. A lease should be interpreted in the same way as any other commercial contract, according to its natural meaning and not by reference "to any of the highly technical points which stem from the intricacies of the ancient law of landlord and tenant" (per Sir Eric Sachs in *C. H. Bailey Ltd v Memorial Enterprises Ltd* (1974) 27 P & CR 188 at p. 195, discussed on p. 438 below). A lease is a commercial document and whenever problems of interpretation arise a commercial solution should be found (*The Law Land Co Ltd v Consumers' Association Ltd* (1980) 255 EG 617 at p. 623, discussed on p. 438 below).

INTERPRETATION, RECTIFICATION AND IMPLICATION

Interpretation should be distinguished from (a) rectification and (b) the implication of a term into a contract. Rectification is the alteration of a document, usually by the court, and is readily distinguishable from interpretation. The implication of a term, however, is more closely allied to interpretation and is the addition of words to those used by the parties as an aid to the proper construction of the contract. The implication of a term does not arise in every exercise in interpretation and should be limited to those circumstances (described below) where it is allowable.

(a) *Rectification.* An application for rectification of a document usually arises where one party to a written contract alleges that it does not set out accurately the prior agreement between the parties, and that the mistake was either mutual or unilateral, that is to say made by one party only but known to the other who, for his own benefit or to the detriment of the other party, did not draw attention to it.

The decision in *Boots The Chemists Ltd v Street* (1983) 268 EG 817, is an example of rectification of a lease due to mutual mistake. The lease in question contained a rent review clause which provided for the service of a landlords' notice to review the rent "during the first six months of every fifth year of the term." The concluding words of the clause, however, provided for the increased rents to be payable "from the end of the seventh and fourteenth years of the Term." There was evidence that the agreement between the parties prior to the execution of the lease was on the basis of five yearly rent reviews. On an application by the landlords for rectification it was held that all the conditions for this relief were satisfied, namely there was clear and unambiguous evidence that a mistake had been made and evidence of the prior intention of the parties (which had continued concurrently in the parties' minds down to the time of execution of the document) but the document did not accurately set out that intention. The lease was rectified by changing the references to the seventh and fourteenth years to references to each fifth year of the term.

In *Thomas Bates & Son Ltd v Wyndhams (Lingerie) Ltd* (1980) 257 EG 381, a lease was rectified for unilateral mistake. It contained five yearly rent reviews, the review rents to be agreed between the parties, but no provision was made for their determination in the event of disagreement. The landlords sought rectification. The Court of Appeal found, on the evidence, that this omission from the rent review clause was a mistake by the landlords, recognised at the time by the tenants but, for their own benefit, not drawn to the landlords' attention. The court rectified the lease by the addition of words defining the review rents and requiring them to be determined, in default of agreement, by a single arbitrator appointed by the President of The Royal Institution of Chartered Surveyors.

Rectification is an equitable remedy and in the discretion of the court. A party against whom rectification of a document is sought may have certain defences available to him, e.g. that he was a *bona fide* purchaser for the value of an interest in land without notice of the right to rectification.

In all cases of rectification the plaintiff must be able to show "exactly and precisely" the amendment required to correct the document. This will be based upon some clear expression of the agreement reached between the parties before the execution of the document now sought to be rectified, e.g. correspondence, travelling drafts of a lease or heads of terms.

An arbitrator or expert may not order rectification of a contract unless he has been given express powers to do so. This rarely occurs in practice. An arbitrator or expert who receives a request for rectification, which is outside his jurisdiction, has three courses of action open to him. First, he may ask the parties to give him jurisdiction to rectify the document and then proceed to do so. This is not recommended: rectification is a matter for the courts. Secondly, he may adjourn the proceedings to allow the party seeking rectification to bring an action in the courts. He will then proceed later on the rectified (or unrectified) document. Thirdly, he may in his discretion proceed on the basis of the document before him, leaving it to the party seeking rectification to make an application for a stay of proceedings while he seeks rectification in the courts.

(b) *Implication of a term.* There are several circumstances where a term will be implied into a contract. In *Liverpool City Council v Irwin* (1976) 32 P & CR 43, Lord Wilberforce summarised the position as follows (pp. 46–47):

> "... there are varieties of implications which the courts think fit to make and they do not necessarily involve the same process. Where there is, on the face of it, a complete, bilateral contract, the courts are sometimes willing to add terms to it, as implied terms: this is very common in mercantile contracts where there is an established usage: in that case the courts are spelling out what both parties know and would, if asked, unhesitatingly agree to be part of the bargain. In other cases, where there is an apparently complete bargain, the courts are willing to add a term on the ground that without it the contract will not work—... the doctrine of *The Moorcock* (1889) 14 PD 64, as usually applied.... There is a third variety of implication, that which I think Lord Denning MR favours, or at least did favour in this case, and that is the implication of reasonable terms. But though I agree with many of his instances, which in fact fall under one or other of the preceding heads, I cannot go so far as to endorse his principle; indeed, it seems to me, with respect, to extend a long, and undesirable, way beyond sound authority.
>
> The present case, in my opinion, represents a fourth category, or I would rather say a fourth shade on a continuous spectrum. The court here is simply concerned to establish what the contract is, the parties not having themselves fully stated the terms. In this sense the court is searching for what must be implied."

In the same decision Lord Cross drew a distinction between those cases where the court lays down a general rule that terms are to be implied into all contracts of a certain type, unless expressly excluded (e.g. landlord and tenant, master and servant), and those cases where the court is asked, in effect, to rectify a particular contract by inserting in it a term which the parties have not expressed, in order to give "business efficacy" to the contract.

The law of landlord and tenant is particularly rich in terms implied by the general law in the absence of a contrary intention by the parties. For example, tenant's implied covenants include the obligations to pay the rent, to use the buildings in a proper and tenant-like manner and not to disclaim the landlord's title; the landlord will also be subject to implied covenants, including the obligations not to derogate from his grant, to give quiet enjoyment and, in the case of a furnished house, to let the premises in a habitable condition.

An arbitrator or independent expert should be cautious about adopting a particular interpretation of a lease which involves implying a term. A term may be implied but the circumstances for implication (as described above) must be present: reasonableness is not enough.

The following cases illustrate the general rules of implication outlined above. In *Liverpool City Council v Irwin* (above), there was implied into a tenancy in a high rise block of council flats, in order to complete it and give it a bilateral character, tenants' easements, or rights in the nature of easements, to use the stairs, lifts and rubbish chutes, with accompanying obligations on the part of the landlord council to carry out reasonable repairs and maintain adequate lighting.

Simlarly, in *Jefferies v O'Neill* (1983) 269 EG 131, the court implied a term into a rent review clause in order to give it practical effect. The lease in this case was of office accommodation on first and second floors with access only at first floor level from adjoining premises owned and occupied by the tenant. The rent review clause provided for the review rent to be on the basis of an open market letting by a willing lessor to a willing lessee, disregarding the lessee's fixtures and fittings, improvements, occupation and goodwill. The court rejected the tenant's argument that the review rent should be assessed on the basis that there is no open market for the demised premises and that the only willing lessee is the tenant or occupier of the adjoining property. It held that a further matter is to be disregarded by implication when assessing the review rent, namely any effect on rental value due to the existing access from the tenant's adjoining premises and the absence of any means of access from the ground floor below the demised premises. (See also *Guys 'N' Dolls Ltd v Sade Bros Catering Ltd*, p. 432 below and *The Law Land Co Ltd v Consumers' Association Ltd* p 438 below).

In *Trust House Forte Albany Hotels Ltd v Daejan Investments Ltd* (1980) 256 EG 915, however, the landlords were unsuccessful in implying into a lease containing rent reviews, a term requiring the tenants to pay interest on the increased revised rent from the review date until the date of determination by the independent expert. The implication of this term was not necessary to give business efficacy to the contract.

LITERAL APPROACH

This approach to interpretation requires words to be interpreted literally, according to their natural and ordinary meaning, where this can be done without producing any apparent or hidden ambiguity in the document or doing violence to the intention of the parties. Where that intention is clear from the words used effect should be given to it, however unfair or unreasonable this may be. The following examples illustrate this approach.

In *Pugh v Smiths Industries Ltd* (1982) 264 EG 823, a clause in a lease required the rent to be reviewed every five years. The review rents were to be assessed under a hypothetical lease, having regard to certain assumptions and disregarding certain matters, including "the provisions of this clause" (i.e. the rent review clause). The exclusion of this clause from the terms of the hypothetical letting would result in a higher rent than if periodic rent reviews were included. The court held that the words used by the parties were clear and must be applied, with the result that the review rents were to be assumed to exist in a lease without periodic reviews.

A similar situation arose in *Safeway Food Stores Ltd v Banderway Ltd* (1983) 267 EG 850, where a rent review clause provided that the revised rent shall be determined under an assumed lease for the unexpired residue of the actual term, disregarding certain matters but "in all other respects on the same terms and conditions as are in these presents contained (save for this proviso)." It was agreed by the parties that "this proviso" referred to the whole of the rent review clause. Goulding J held that the rents under the clause were to be assessed for a fixed term of the remainder of the lease (more than 69 years) even though reviews existed in the actual lease at 21 yearly intervals. Owing to the clear words of the clause under consideration he rejected an approach which required him to look at the spirit of the document and not the letter. He said (p. 852):

> "There is nothing absurd or insensible in the literal construction that required the valuers at the end of the 21st year to consider the proper rent for a lease of approximately 69 years at a single rent throughout. It may not be what one would think most probable, but there is nothing absurd about it, nothing insensible about it. For all that I am entitled to know in a construction case, the matter may have been so arranged as the result of bargaining on various points between the original landlord and the original tenant. If I assume that they had a common intention different from what the words expressed, I think I am merely guessing, . . ."

In *Guys 'N' Dolls Ltd v Sade Bros Catering Ltd* (1983) 269 EG 129, however, a literal approach to the interpretation of a rent review clause was rejected by the Court of Appeal. The lease in question provided for two reviews, the review rent on each occasion to be composed of two elements: the fair rack market rental value and an additional rent of £7,500. The rental value was to be assessed having regard to certain factors "and in all other respects on the terms and conditions of" the existing lease. Slade LJ accepted that a literal reading of that phrase meant that the tenants' obligation to pay the £7,500 additional rent had to be taken into account when assessing the rental value at both reviews, but rejected this approach and implied an exclusion of this obligation in order to give business efficacy and commercial sense to the transaction. The assessment of the fair rack rent must ignore the obligation to pay the additional rent. Robert Goff LJ reached the same conclusion and thought it immaterial whether he did so "as a matter of construction or by way of implication". It would be ridiculous, he said, to add the additional rent on and then immediately take it away again by reducing the market rent by the same sum.

PURPOSIVE APPROACH

As explained above, where the court considers that words are clear and produce a result which is not wholly absurd, it will adopt a literal interpretation even though the result may be surprising or even unfair. It may be questioned whether it was really the intention of the parties in the *Pugh* and *Safeway* cases to have the review rents assessed on a fixed long term basis, or whether the parties in *Ponsford v HMS Aerosols Ltd* (p. 427 above) really intended that the tenants should pay rent on their own improvements, or whether perhaps the parties had simply not addressed their minds to those particular points when the leases were agreed.

An alternative approach to interpretation, sometimes referred to as the "purposive" approach, attempts to overcome the difficulties of literal interpretation by placing the document in its surrounding circumstances in order to find the intention of the parties. In this approach an agreement is not interpreted solely on the internal evidence of the words used but according to the intention of the parties when it was made, having regard to the factual and legal background at that time and the intended commercial purpose of the contract:

> "The time has long passed when agreements, even those under seal, were isolated from the matrix of facts in which they were set and interpreted purely on internal linguistic considerations. There is no need to appeal here to any modern, anti-literal tendencies, for Lord Blackburn's well known judgment in *River Wear Commissioners v Adamson* (1877) 2 App. Cas. 743, 763 provides ample warrant for a liberal approach. We must, as he said, enquire beyond the language and see what the circumstances were with reference to which the words were used, and

the object appearing from those circumstances, which the
person using them had in view."
(per Lord Wilberforce in *Prenn v Simmonds* [1971] 1 WLR 1381
at pp. 1383–4).

In a later case, *Reardon Smith Line Ltd v Yngver Hansen-Tangen* [1976] 1
WLR 989, Lord Wilberforce explained the nature of the surrounding circumstances. He said (pp. 995–6):

"No contracts are made in a vacuum. There is always a setting
in which they have to be placed. The nature of what is
legitimate to have regard to is usually described as 'the surrounding circumstances' but this phrase is imprecise: it can be
illustrated but hardly defined. In a commercial contract it is
certainly right that the court should know the commercial purpose of the contract and this in turn pre-supposes knowledge of
the genesis of the transaction, the background, the context, the
market in which the parties are operating."

It should be noted, however, that the surrounding circumstances do
not include the actions of the parties after the contract (*Wickman
Machine Tool Sales Ltd v L. Schuler AG* [1974] AC 235) nor the negotiations leading up to the finalisation of the agreement. Evidence of
negotiations would not be helpful to interpretation because the
parties' positions would have been changing from day to day and no
consensus, no intention of the parties, could be found.

Evidence of the circumstances surrounding the making of a contract should be limited to the factual background (the factual
matrix) known to the parties at that time, including evidence of the
'genesis' and objectively the 'aim' of the transaction (see *Prenn*
p. 1385). The inquiry as to the intention of the parties must, however, be objective and not subjective. Evidence is not admissible
from the parties as to what their intentions were at the time the
contract was made:

"... in considering what is known as 'the factual matrix'
against which contracts are made, one is entitled to look at the
objective evidence of intention to be derived from such facts,
but one is not entitled to take into account the subjective intentions, however they may be expressed, in carrying out the exercise of construction of the document."
(per Purchas LJ in *Plumb Brothers v Dolmac (Agriculture) Ltd*
(1984) 271 EG 373 at p. 376).

The above principles have been applied to the interpretation of a
rent review clause in a lease. In *Compton Group Ltd v Estates Gazette
Ltd* (1977) 244 EG 799, one of the questions before the Court of

Appeal was whether the Counter Inflation Business Rents Order 1973 (which imposed a temporary "freeze" on business rents) prevented the "fair rack rent" under a rent review clause from being determined at a figure above the current rent. This Order was not in force when the lease was granted but was in operation on the rent review date. It was held that the lease must be construed in the light of the circumstances which existed at the date of grant. At that time there were no statutory restrictions on business rents nor was it reasonable to assume that the parties had such restrictions in comtemplation. Accordingly, the Order did not prevent the review rent from being assessed at a figure above the current "frozen" rent.

The circumstances surrounding the making of an agreement cannot be used to alter the clear meaning of the words in that agreement. Thus, in *Coventry City Council v J. Hepworth & Son Ltd* (1982) 265 EG 608, a long lease was granted in 1953, when the local authority (the landlords) wished to see the premises occupied for a substantial period of time by a reputable trading company. The lease contained a rent review initiated by a landlords' trigger notice with a corresponding tenants' right to determine the lease. The landlords served their notice out of time. They argued, however, that it was still valid because the particular circumstances which existed when the lease was granted should be taken into account when construing the lease. This led to the conclusion that time was not to be of the essence for commencing the rent review, notwithstanding the decision in *United Scientific Holdings Ltd v Burnley Borough Council* [1978] AC 904, that time was deemed to be of the essence where there was a relationship in time between a landlords' trigger notice and a tenants' option to determine. The Court of Appeal rejected this approach. The surrounding circumstances made no difference to the interpretation of the lease, which must be construed according to the factors laid down by the House of Lords in the *United Scientific Holdings* case. Time was of the essence: the landlords' trigger notice was out of time and, therefore, invalid.

Where a contract provides for a valuation, e.g. under a rent review clause in a lease, it will be necessary for an arbitrator (or valuer) to interpret the contract to ensure that he uses the correct method of valuation. Although valuation is a question of fact there will be an error of law if the method adopted does not follow the intention of the parties. For example, in *GREA Real Property Investments Ltd v Williams* (1979) 250 EG 651, a dispute concerning the. correct method for disregarding the value of tenant's improvements when determining a review rent came before the court by way of the old case stated procedure. Such a dispute is, of course, essentially a question of fact and Forbes J declined to decide the correct method of valuation. He stated, however, that such a method must properly reflect the intention of the parties as expressed in the lease, having regard to the factual matrix which existed when the lease was granted. He summarised the intention of the parties in this case under five heads. First, owing to inflation rent reviews are required to do justice between landlord and tenant. Secondly, the sole benefit which the tenant is to receive from his expenditure on improvements is credit for the rental equivalent of the capital cost and this might itself be affected by inflation. Thirdly, the improvements are a wasting asset from the tenant's viewpoint. Fourthly, at each review date the improvements would be no longer new. Fifthly, in making comparisons within the valuation method care must be taken to compare like with like, and it must be borne in mind that, where a method includes both values and costs, inflation may have different effects on these two components.

INTERPRETATION HAVING REGARD TO WHOLE DOCUMENT

Words to be construed should not be considered in isolation, but should be read in the context of the document as whole. In *Beaumont Property Trust v Tai* (1982) 265 EG 872, a clause in a lease provided for the payment of an initial rent of £2,500 per annum "during the first five years (from the date of the lease) of the ... term," with rent reviews at five yearly intervals. The lease was dated 17th December 1979 but the term commenced on 25th March 1976. The question inevitably arose: what is the date of the first rent review? It was held that the intention of the parties when they executed the lease, reading the document as a whole and notwithstanding the words "from the date of the lease", was that the first rent review was to take place five years after the commencement of the *term*. The reference to the date of the lease was to remove the tenant's obligation to pay rent for the period before the execution of the lease. It was clear from the remainder of the lease that the first review was to be five years after the start of the term.

It may be a useful aid to interpretation to compare the clause under consideration with another clause in the document. Thus, in *Langham House Developments Ltd v Brompton Securities Ltd* (1980) 256 EG 719, a rent review clause provided that, if the parties cannot agree the amount of the review rent, it "... shall be determined by a chartered surveyor nominated by the President of the Royal Institution of Chartered Surveyors ...". The landlords sought a declaration that the nominated surveyor is to act as an expert and not as an arbitrator. Megarry VC could see some force in both the landlords' argument that the surveyor is an expert and the tenants' that he is an arbitrator. He decided the question, however, by comparing the words of the rent review clause with the previous clause which dealt with the abatement of rent following fire damage. This clause, he said, "reeks of arbitration", by the use of language such as "in case of difference", "award", "single arbitrator" and "Arbitration Act 1950", whereas the rent review clause uses none of those words. It merely refers to a sum to be determined by a chartered surveyor. The draftsman of this clause clearly intended differences to be settled by valuation and not by arbitration. (See also *Safeway Food Stores Ltd v Banderway Ltd* (1983) 267 EG 850, discussed on p. 432 above). Words may also be interpreted by comparing them with other similar words in the same clause. Thus, in *Cressey v Jacobs* (1977) unreported, Bernstein and Reynolds *Handbook of Rent Review* case 17 p. [DC 97], a rent review clause in a lease with three parties (landlord, tenant and sureties) required "the parties hereto" to agree to the revised rent and, in default of agreement, to agree the appointment of an independent expert, whose fees shall be payable between the landlord and tenant as he may direct. It was held that the words "the parties" included the sureties and, therefore, they were required to agree the revised rent, although they could not be required to pay any part of the independent expert's fees.

Wherever possible, an interpretation should be adopted which gives effect to all relevant words. For example, in *Lewis v Barnett* (1981) 264 EG 1079, paragraphs 2 and 3 of a rent review clause set down time limits for both the landlord's notice requiring a review of rent and, in default of agreement, an application to the President of The Royal Institution of Chartered Surveyors for the appointment of a surveyor to determine the revised rent. Paragraph 6 of the clause further provided that the landlord's notice requiring a review of rent shall be void and of no effect if application is not made to the President within the stated time. The landlord failed to comply with both time limits. It was held by the Court of Appeal that, while the landlord's failure to serve notice of review within the stated time was not fatal (see *United Scientific Holdings Ltd* case p. 435 above), the clause must be read as a whole and effect given to paragraph 6 which, due to the landlord's failure to observe the second time limit, subsequently rendered the initial notice of review void and of no effect.

INTERPRETATION TO PRODUCE A REASONABLE RESULT

Words should be interpreted to produce a result which is reasonable and in accordance with common sense. An absurd or unreasonable result should be avoided:

"The fact that a particular construction leads to a very unreasonable result must be a relevant consideration. The more
unreasonable the result the more unlikely it is that the parties
can have intended it, and if they do intend it the more necessary
it is that they shall make that intention abundantly clear."
(per Lord Reid in *Wickmam Machine Tool Sales Ltd v L. Schuler
AG* [1974] AC 235 at p. 251).

The following decisions illustrate this principle.

In *C. H. Bailey Ltd v Memorial Enterprises Ltd* (1974) 27 P & CR
188, the Court of Appeal were required to construe a rent review
clause, part of which was as follows:

"If on September 21 1969 the market rental value ... shall be
found to exceed the rent of £2,375 hereby reserved there shall
be substituted from such date ... an increased yearly rent equal
to the market rental value so ascertained"

The landlords did not give notice of their intention to increase the
rent as required by the clause until nearly a year after the review
date (September 21 1969). The tenants argued that, unless the
review rent had been ascertained on or before that date, the landlords could not increase the rent at all. Alternatively, if the new rent
were ascertained after that date it could not be back-dated. The
court rejected both contentions. It held that on a true construction
of the clause, according to its natural meaning and as a matter of
commonsense, the revised rent did not have to be ascertained on
September 21 1969 (which was a Sunday) or not at all. The clause
meant that the rent was to be *paid from* that date, whenever agreed
or determined.

A "reasonable" approach to interpretation was also adopted by
the Court of Appeal in *The Law Land Co Ltd v Consumers' Association
Ltd* (1980) 255 EG 617. This case concerned a rent review clause which
required a review to the market rent of the demised premises on
certain assumptions and subject to the provisions of the lease, other
than rent. One of those provisions was a user clause which restricted
the use to offices of the Consumers' Association and its associated
organisations or otherwise only with the prior written consent of the
landlords. The tenants argued that the rent review clause must be
regarded as subject to the strict user clause, so that the market rent
must be ascertained as if the premises were restricted to use only by
the Consumers' Association. This argument was rejected by the
court. It was inconsistent with references in the rent review clause to
"market rent", "open market" and "vacant possession". The true
interpretation of the clause, to give effect to the intention of the
parties, was that it is to be envisaged that the hypothetical tenant
would become entitled to a lease in the form of the existing lease,

except that his name would be substituted for the Consumers' Association in the opening part of the lease and in the user clause. This was a reasonable solution and would avoid the situation where the market rent has to be ascertained on the basis that there is only one possible hypothetical tenant.

The decision in *Guys 'N' Dolls v Sade Bros Catering Ltd*, discussed on p. 432 above, is another example of the reasonable or commonsense approach to interpretation.

CONTRA PROFERENTEM RULE

Where the various principles outlined above fail to resolve an ambiguity in a document then an old rule of interpretation, the *contra proferentem* rule, may be used. This requires the words in question to be interpreted in a manner which is less favourable to the party seeking to rely on them than to the other party. Thus, words of grant are to be resolved against the grantor and in favour of the grantee. Where a clause in a contract seeks to exclude or limit the liability of one of the parties it will be construed against that party. The onus is on him to show that the words of the clause, given their natural, plain meaning, clearly and unambiguously cover the situation which has arisen. It would appear, however, that, although the *contra proferentem* rule is to be applied to a clause *limiting* liability, such a clause is not to be construed as rigidly and as strictly as a clause *excluding* liability, since an agreed *limitation* of liability is more likely to accord with the true intention of the parties than an *exclusion* of *all* liability (*Ailsa Craig Fishing Co Ltd v Malvern Fishing Co Ltd* [1983] 1 All ER 101).

PLANS

A document may contain or refer to a plan or other drawing, e.g. a plan of the demised premises in a lease or a map of the land in a conveyance. To what extent may reference be made to the plan when interpreting the document? There are two situations where such a reference may be made. First, where the plan is expressly referred to in the document. Secondly, where the plan is drawn on or bound up in the document, even though no mention is made of it. For example, in *Leachman v L. & K. Richardson Ltd* [1969] 1 WLR 1129, land was described in a conveyance as known as number 22 Soho Road but there was no reference to any plan. Between two of the pages, however, one was attached showing a plot of land surrounded by a red line and marked "No. 22", with an area of "288 square yards or thereabouts." It was held that this plan was annexed to the conveyance and, although not referred to in it, could be looked at to resolve an ambiguity in the wording.

Where it has been established that a plan may be used to assist in the interpretation of a document, the exact role of that plan will depend upon the words of reference used. A document may refer to land "more particularly delineated" on an annexed plan (or some variation of those words). The plan will then take precedence over the written description if words and plan are inconsistent (*Eastwood v Ashton* [1915] AC 900). Where a document expressly states that the plan shall not control the written description of the land then the words take precedence.

Where plan and words do not conflict, but the words are unclear, the plan may be used to establish the extent of the land even though it is stated to be "for the purposes of identification only". A plan with this label is not now restricted in function to showing only the approximate location of the property, but may be used with the written description to define the extent or boundaries of the land where the description alone is unsufficient for that purpose. For example, in *Wigginton & Milner Ltd v Winster Engineering Ltd* [1978] 3 All ER 436, land conveyed was described in the First Schedule to a conveyance and it was delineated and coloured yellow on an annexed plan, but by way of identification only. It was held by the Court of Appeal that it was clear from the way in which the schedule and plan were linked, that the numbers in the schedule referred to the corresponding numbers on the plan, where they were all to be found and where they served as a key to relate the description in the schedule with the plan. Furthermore, it was clear that the plan was the only means of discovering what the parties intended to be the boundary between certain plots of land. In the circumstances the court could refer to the plan to determine the extent of the land conveyed. Buckley LJ said (p. 445):

> "When a court is required to decide what property passed under a particular conveyance, it must have regard to the conveyance as a whole, including any plan which forms part of it. It is from the conveyance as a whole that that intention must be ascertained. To the extent that the conveyance stipulates that one part of it shall prevail over another part of it in the event of there being any contradiction between them in the ascertainment of the parties' intention, the court must of course give effect to that stipulation. So if the conveyance stipulated that the plan shall not control the description of the parcels, the court must have due regard to that stipulation; but insofar as the plan does not conflict with the parcels, I can see no reason why, because it is described as being 'for identification purposes

only', it should not be looked at to assist in understanding the description of the parcels. The process of identification is in fact the process of discovering what land was intended to pass under the conveyance, and that is the precise purpose which the plan is said to serve. Accordingly, so long as the plan does not come into conflict with anything which is explicit in the description of the parcels, the fact that it is said to be 'for the purposes of identification only' does not appear to me to exclude it from consideration in solving the problems which are left undecided by what is explicit in the description of any parcel."

Where the draftsman of a document has been inconsistent in his words of reference (e.g. by referring to the particular delineation on a plan which is for identification purposes only) then the result is "mutually stultifying". The plan has no predominance over the words and the meaning of those words must be found by reading the document as whole. Thus, in *Neilson v Poole* (1969) 20 P & CR 909, the property conveyed was that "known as Brooklands South ... as the same are for the purposes of identification only more particularly delineated on the plan drawn hereon and thereon coloured blue." Megarry J said (p. 916):

"Where both forms of expression are used together, as in the present case, they may indeed tend to be mutually stultifying. Certainly I do not think that they give the plan any predominance over the parcels. Reading the conveyance as a whole, the most probable meaning, expressed as a paraphrase, seems to be that what is conveyed is whatever is known as Brooklands South, and that in order to discover the identity of Brooklands South (but for no other purpose) there is a more detailed delineation of it on the plan. Such language seems to negative any use of the plan as showing the precise boundaries of the land."

ARBITRATION UNDER THE AGRICULTURAL HOLDINGS ACTS

APPENDIX B

Arbitration under the Agricultural Holdings Acts

INTRODUCTION

As explained in Chapter 9, arbitrations arise by agreement between the parties, by order of court or under statute. Perhaps the best known of the Acts providing for the settlement of disputes by arbitration is the Agricultural Holdings Act 1948, which regulates tenancies of agricultural land. Many disputes arising out of such tenancies are referred to arbitration, using the arbitration code set out in section 77 and the Sixth Schedule to the Act (as amended). The Arbitration Acts 1950 and 1979 do not apply (section 7(1) of the Agricultural Holdings Act 1948, section 31(1) of the 1950 Act and section 7(1) of the 1979 Act). The Agricultural Holdings Act 1948 has been amended, principally by the Agricultural Holdings Act 1984 and these two Acts will be referred to as the 1948 and 1984 Acts respectively. The provisions of the 1948 Act relating to notices to quit and security of tenure have been consolidated in the Agricultural Holdings (Notices to Quit) Act 1977 and the arbitration provisions arising out of this Act are briefly considered at the end of this Appendix.

The parties to an arbitration under the Agricultural Holdings Acts may find it convenient to refer to the arbitrator other disputes which have arisen outside the Acts. Thus, in effect, two arbitrations will be held: one statutory, governed by the arbitration code in the 1948 Act; and one by agreement, governed by the Arbitration Acts 1950 and 1979. Two separate awards should be made.

The arbitration provisions in the 1948 Act (as amended by the 1984 Act) are now summarised. References to the "Minister" are to the Minister of Agriculture, Fisheries and Food; "President" to the President of The Royal Institution of Chartered Surveyors; "landlord", "tenant" and all other tenancy references refer to tenancies of agricultural holdings under section 1 of the 1948 Act (as amended); references to sections are sections of the 1948 Act (except where stated otherwise) and references to paragraphs are to those contained in the Sixth Schedule to that Act, both as amended. Sections 70, 77 and the Sixth Schedule to the 1948 Act (all as amended) and section 8 of the 1984 Act are set out in Appendix C pp. 459 and 512 below).

DISPUTES REFERRED TO ARBITRATION UNDER THE 1948 ACT

The disputes referred to arbitration under this Act may be divided into two categories. First, specific disputes arising out of particular sections of the Act. Secondly, general disputes in respect of claims "of whatever nature" under the Act, custom or agreement at the termination of an agricultural tenancy (section 70 as amended).

(a) *Specific disputes referred to arbitration.* Disputes arising out of the following matters are to be referred to arbitration in the absence of agreement:

(i) the conversion into a yearly tenancy of a tenancy or licence originally granted for less than from year to year (section 2);

(ii) the terms of a written tenancy agreement to be entered into by the parties, where no such agreement is in force or, if in force, is defective in certain respects (section 5 as amended);

(iii) the variation of obligations relating to the maintenance, repair and insurance of fixed equipment, to bring those obligations into conformity with regulations of the Minister (section 6);

(iv) the compensation payable by landlord or tenant due to a failure to repair, maintain and insure fixed equipment before a variation was made in his obligations to do so under (ii) or (iii) above (section 7);

(v) the rent payable for the holding (sections 8 and 8A substituted by section 1 of the 1984 Act);

(vi) the increase in rent due to the execution of certain improvements by the landlord (section 9 as amended);

(vii) the reduction in the amount or proportion of land to be maintained as permanent pasture (section 10 as amended);

(viii) the question as to whether the tenant has disposed of produce or practised a system of cropping which has injured or deteriorated the holding (section 11 as amended);

(ix) the fair value of tenant's fixtures or buildings which the landlord has elected by counternotice to purchase (section 13 as amended);

(x) the compensation payable to the tenant for damage to crops by game and the indemnification of the landlord by a third party (section 14 as amended);

(xi) the apportionment of rent where The Agricultural Land Tribunal directs that part of the land shall be treated as a market garden (section 68 as amended).

(b) *Disputes generally referred to arbitration.* Under section 70 any claim of whatever nature by landlord or tenant, which arises under the Act, custom or agreement *and* on or out of the termination of a tenancy, is to be determined by arbitration if the parties fail to agree.

Section 70 covers a variety of claims which may arise on the termination of a tenancy, e.g. a claim by the tenant for compensation for disturbance (section 34), or a claim by the landlord for compensation due to the tenant's failure to farm in accordance with the rules of good husbandry (section 57).

APPOINTMENT OF ARBITRATOR

Any matter which under the 1948 Act or regulations made thereunder is required to be determined by arbitration under the Act is, notwithstanding any agreement to the contrary, to be determined by a single arbitrator (section 77 (1) as amended).

An arbitrator will be appointed in one of the following ways:

(a) by agreement between the parties (para 1(1));
(b) by the Minister from members of a panel of arbitrators appointed by the Lord Chancellor (paras 1(1) and (3));
(c) by the President of The Royal Institution of Chartered Surveyors where the Minister or the Crown is a party to the arbitration (para 28).

Under section 8(1) of the 1984 Act the Minister may transfer his functions relating to the appointment of arbitrators to the President of The Royal Institution of Chartered Surveyors. This will take effect from the date appointed by the Minister by statutory instrument (section 11(5)(a) of the 1984 Act). The Minister has announced that his powers of appointment will be transferred to the President with effect from 1st January 1986.

All appointments must be in writing (para 4) and an arbitrator shall be taken to have been appointed at the time when the instrument of appointment was executed (para 29 added by para 28(10) of Schedule 3 to the 1984 Act).

An appointment by the Minister or President shall be made by him as soon as possible after receiving the application. Where the application relates to a demand for arbitration under section 8 (rent payable for the holding) the Minister or President may not appoint an arbitrator earlier than four months before the next termination date following the date of such a demand (para 1(1A) inserted by para 28(2) of Schedule 3 to the 1984 Act).

There are also time limits where an arbitrator is to be appointed under section 70. The claimant must serve written notice of his claim within two months of the termination of the tenancy or, where the claimant is a tenant who continues in lawful occupation after such termination, the end of that occupation. The landlord and tenant then have a period of eight months to reach a written agreement on the claim and if it is not settled within that period it is to be determined by arbitration (section 70(2)–(5) as amended)

Where an arbitration relates to land in Wales or Gwent the arbitrator appointed by the Minister or President must possess a knowledge of Welsh agricultural conditions and, if required by either party, a knowledge of the Welsh language (para 1(2)).

If the arbitrator:

(a) dies; or
(b) is incapable of acting; or
(c) fails to act within seven days of notice from either party requiring him to do so;

then a new arbitrator may be appointed as if no arbitrator had been appointed (para 2). Where such a new arbitrator is appointed the date of the reference for the purposes of section 8(2) (the date for the determination of the new rent) is when the original arbitrator was appointed (para 2A inserted by para 28(3) of Schedule 3 to the 1984 Act).

When the functions relating to appointment have been transferred from the Minister to the President (1st January 1986), no application may be made to the President for the appointment of an arbitrator unless it is accompanied by the prescribed fee (prescribed by the Minister by statutory instrument). This fee will also cover any further applications to the President in respect of the same arbitration (e.g. for the appointment of a replacement arbitrator). Any instrument of appointment or other document signed by or on behalf of the President shall be taken to be such an instrument or document unless the contrary is shown (section 8(3)–(5) of the 1984 Act).

REVOCATION OF APPOINTMENT AND REMOVAL

An arbitrator's appointment cannot be unilaterally revoked by either party; it can only be revoked with the consent of the other party. An appointment is not revoked by the death of either party (para 3 as amended). The revocation of an appointment, and the consent to such revocation, must be in writing (para 4). An arbitrator who has misconducted himself may be removed by the county court (para 25(1)).

PROCEDURE

The Lord Chancellor may by order make provision as to the procedure to be followed in, or in connection with, proceedings on arbitrations under the 1948 Act (section 77(2) substituted by para

19(3) of Schedule 3 to the 1984 Act). At the time of writing no order has been made and the procedure for agricultural arbitrations is, therefore, still to be found mainly in the Sixth Schedule to the 1948 Act (as amended). When an order is made the procedure will be contained in this order and those provisions of the Sixth Schedule to the 1948 Act as have remained in force (section 77(1) of the 1948 Act as amended).

Within 35 days of the appointment of the arbitrator each party is required to deliver to him his statement of case with all necessary particulars (para 6 as amended). This 35 day period runs from the time when the Minister or President executes the instrument of appointment (para 29 added by para 28(10) of Schedule 3 to the 1984 Act).

A party cannot, except with the consent of the arbitrator, amend or add to his statement or particulars after the expiration of the period for submission. At the hearing each party must confine his case to the matters alleged in his statement and particulars and any addition or amendment thereto which has been duly made (para 6 as amended).

The principles which should guide an arbitrator when deciding whether to allow an amendment to a statement of case were considered by the Court of Appeal in *E. D. & A. D. Cooke-Bourne (Farms) Ltd v Mellows* (1981) 262 EG 229. In this case, following the surrender of an agricultural tenancy, the tenant indicated that he intended to make a claim under section 70 and an arbitrator was appointed to deal with it. The tenant's statement of claim, however, did not make it clear whether it was made under section 13, in respect of fixtures, or under section 47, in respect of improvements. The landlords contended in their statement that claims under both these sections were not competent. The tenant then submitted a supplemental statement of case and a further amendment. The landlords objected and the arbitrator decided that he could not accept such a fundamental alteration to the tenant's statement of case and refused leave to amend. The Court of Appeal disagreed and held that consent should have been given for the admission of the supplemental case. Templeman L J said (p. 236):

> "Amendments ought to be allowed as of course, unless the landlords have a strong case for saying that because the tenants got it wrong in the first place and because of actions taken thereunder or for various other reasons it would be unfair to allow the amendment; and the test as I have adumbrated it is whether the landlords are any worse off than they would have been if a statement of case had been properly drafted in the first instance."

At the hearing the arbitrator has power to administer oaths and take affirmations of parties and witnesses (para 8), and, subject to any legal objection, the parties and all persons claiming under them shall:

(a) submit to examination by the arbitrator, on oath or affirmation, in relation to all matters in dispute;
(b) produce before the arbitrator all samples and documents within
their possession or power which may be required or called for;
(c) do all other things which during the proceedings the arbitrator
may require (para 7).

The provisions of the county court rules relating to the issue of
witness summonses apply to arbitrations under the 1948 Act
(subject to modifications contained in those rules) as if they are
actions or matters in the county court (para 9). A person summoned
to appear as a witness under the county court rules is entitled to his
expenses on a prescribed scale. These should be paid or tendered to
him at the time of the service of the witness summons. Where such
expenses are paid or tendered, but the person summoned refuses or
neglects, without sufficient cause, to appear at the arbitration or to
produce required documents, or refuses to be sworn or give
evidence, he shall be fined up to £10 as directed by the county court
judge. Any person present at the arbitration who is required to give
evidence, and who refuses to be sworn or give such evidence, shall
also be fined in the same manner. The county court judge has a
discretion to direct that the whole or part of the fine (less costs) shall
be used to indemnify the party injured by a person's failure or
neglect to give evidence, be sworn or produce a document (para 10).

Paragraphs 11 and 12 contain provisions allowing the county
court judge and the High Court to order the attendance as witnesses
of prisoners held for criminal and civil purposes respectively.

At any stage of the proceedings, the arbitrator *may* state in the
form of a special case for the opinion of the county court any question of law arising in the course of the arbitration. The arbitrator
must state a special case where he is directed to do so by the judge of
the county court, following an application by either party (para 24).
These provisions also apply to a question as to the jurisdiction of the
arbitrator (para 21(1) of First Schedule to the Agriculture Act 1958).

The Sixth Schedule does not contain any other provisions relating
to procedure and evidence at a hearing in an arbitration under the
Agricultural Holdings Act 1948. It is, therefore, usual to follow the
procedure in a reference by consent and the same rules of evidence
apply (see Chapter 10 pp. 293 and 312 above).

AWARD

An arbitrator may make an interim award for the payment of a sum
on account of his final award (para 14). An arbitrator shall make
and sign his award within 56 days of his appointment, or within

such further time as may be allowed by the Minister. The Minister may enlarge the time for the making of an award, whether the initial 56 day period has expired or not (para 13 as amended). The Minister may transfer his functions relating to extensions of time to the President to take effect from the date appointed by the Minister (section 8(1) of the 1984 Act). The Minister has announced that these functions will be transferred to the President from 1st January 1986.

The Minister had power to specify by statutory instrument the form of award and it was obligatory for an award to be made in that form (subject to modifications according to the circumstances) (para 15). The Minister made The Agricultural Holdings (England & Wales) Rules 1948, and the prescribed form of award is Form A in the First Schedule. (Other prescribed forms for arbitration proceedings under the 1948 Act are set out in the Second Schedule to these Rules). Paragraph 15 has been repealed by the 1984 Act and the Lord Chancellor now has power to prescribe by statutory instrument the form in which awards are to be made and the forms for proceedings in arbitrations under the 1948 Act (section 77(2)–(6) of the 1948 Act substituted by para 19(3) of Schedule 3 to the 1984 Act). At the time of writing no order has been made.

An arbitrator appointed by the Minister or President is required to give the reasons for his decision if requested to do so on or before the giving of the decision (section 12 and Schedule 1 to the Tribunals and Inquiries Act 1971). A refusal to give reasons when requested, or the giving of inadequate reasons is an error of law on the face of the award (*Re Poyser and Mills Arbitration* [1964] 2 QB 467). These provisions now apply to an arbitrator appointed under the Sixth Schedule to the 1948 Act by agreement between the parties (para 20A inserted by para 28(7) of Schedule 3 to the 1984 Act). (Reasoned awards are discussed in Chapter 11 p. 332 above).

Where several claims are referred to the arbitrator for determination he must state the separate amounts he has awarded for each claim. Also, on the application of either party, he must specify the amount awarded in respect of any particular improvement or matter which is the subject of his award (para 16).

Where the 1948 Act provides that compensation under an agreement is to be substituted for compensation under the Act, for improvements or any of the other matters specified in the Fourth Schedule to the Act, the arbitrator must award such compensation in accordance with the agreement instead of in accordance with the Act (para 17). The Fourth Schedule contains a list of improvements for which compensation is payable without the consent of the landlord to their execution (Part I) and other matters for which compensation is payable (Part II).

The award shall fix a day not later than one month after its delivery for the payment of any money awarded as compensation, costs or otherwise (para 18). Any sum directed to be paid by the award shall, unless it directs otherwise, carry interest from the date of the award at the same rate as a judgment debt (para 20B inserted by para 28(7) of Schedule 3 to the 1984 Act).

The above provisions relate mainly to general matters to be included in a valid award under the 1948 Act. Several sections require specific matters to be included in an award under that section. These are sections 5 (terms to be included in a written tenancy agreement), 6 (prescribed terms deemed to be incorporated in a tenancy agreement for the maintenance, repair and insurance of fixed equipment), 7 (variations in rent in respect of the matters dealt with under section 5 and 6), 10 (variations as to amount of permanent pasture) and 61 (compensation where holding is divided). Reference should be made to these sections to ascertain the specific items which may or must be included in an award under the section.

COSTS AND REMUNERATION

The costs of, and incidental to, an arbitration and award are in the discretion of the arbitrator. He may direct who shall pay and receive costs and in what manner they are to be paid (para 21). The parties may agree how the costs of an arbitration will be borne between themselves (*Mansfield v Robinson* [1928] 2 KB 353). When awarding costs the arbitrator is required to take into consideration:

(a) the reasonableness or unreasonableness of the parties' claims (in respect of amount or otherwise);
(b) any unreasonable demand for particulars or refusal to supply them;
(c) generally all the circumstances of the case.

He may disallow the costs of any witness, if he considers him to have been called unnecessarily, and any other costs which he considers to have been unnecessarily incurred (para 23).

The costs awarded by an arbitrator shall, on the application of either party, be taxable in the county court according to such of the county court scales as may be directed by the arbitrator or, if he does not do so, as directed by the court (para 22 substituted by para 28(8) of Schedule 3 to the 1984 Act).

An arbitrator's remuneration will be fixed in one of the following ways:

(a) Where he is appointed by agreement between the parties, it will be agreed between him and the parties, or, in default of agreement, will be fixed by the registrar of the county court (subject to appeal to the judge of the court) on the application of the arbitrator or either of the parties.

(b) Where he is appointed by the Minister the arbitrator's remuneration will be agreed between the arbitrator and the parties, or in default of agreement, fixed by the Minister. The Minister may transfer his functions in this respect to the President to take effect from the date appointed by the Minister (section 8(1) of the 1984 Act). The Minister has announced that these functions will be transferred to the President from 1st January 1986.

In all cases the arbitrator's remuneration will be recoverable as a debt due from either of the parties (para 5 as amended).

The above provisions regarding costs and remuneration will still apply where the arbitrator has no jurisdiction to decide the question referred to him (para 21(2) of the First Schedule to the Agriculture Act 1958).

Where a party pays an amount in respect of the arbitrator's remuneration, which is in excess of the amount (if any) directed by the award to be paid by him as the costs of the award, the overpayment shall be recoverable from the other party (para 26). The award must fix a day not later than one month after delivery for payment of the amount awarded as costs (para 18).

AFTER THE AWARD

An award is final and binding on the parties and persons claiming under them (para 19), but the arbitrator has power to correct any clerical mistake or error arising from any accidental slip or omission (para 20).

The county court may set aside an award where:

(a) the arbitrator has misconducted himself (he may also be removed on this ground); or
(b) an arbitration or award has been improperly procured; or
(c) there is an error of law on the face of the award (para 25(2) as amended).

The county court may from time to time remit an award (or part) to the reconsideration of the arbitrator. Where remission is ordered the arbitrator shall, unless the order otherwise directs, make and sign his award within 30 days from the date of the order. The county court has power to extend or further extend this period. Where it appears to the court that there is an error of law on the face of the award, it may, instead of remitting it to the arbitrator, vary it by substituting for the parts affected by the error such award as the court considers that it would have been proper for the arbitrator to make in the circumstances. The award shall then have effect as so varied (para 25A inserted by para 28(9) of Schedule 3 to the 1984 Act).

An appeal on a point of law lies to the Court of Appeal from a decision of the county court and it would appear to the House of Lords with leave. It would appear that the High Court does not now have any jurisdiction over awards under the Agricultural Holdings Act 1948.

As stated above, an award must fix a day for payment of compensation, costs or other amount directed to be paid (para 18). Section 71 provides that, where an amount so ordered to be paid is not paid within 14 days of the due date, it shall be recoverable upon a county court order. Sections 72–73 also contain provisions for recovery relating to certain special cases.

AGRICULTURAL HOLDINGS (NOTICES TO QUIT) ACT 1977

A brief summary will be given of the arbitration provisions arising out of the Agricultural Holdings (Notices to Quit) Act 1977 (the 1977 Act). This Act gives security of tenure to tenants of agricultural holdings. The statutory arbitration code contained in the 1948 Act is applied to certain matters arising out of notices to quit.

Arbitrations which arise under the 1977 Act may be divided into three categories. First, where the tenant contests the reasons for a notice to quit served under Cases B, D, E or I; secondly, where the landlord resumes possession of part of a holding and the reduction of rent cannot be agreed; thirdly, where a tenant wishes to contest his liability for works which the landlord requires him to carry out.

The general rule is that a notice to quit is of no effect where the tenant serves a counternotice, unless The Agricultural Land Tribunal consents to its operation. Section 2(2) and (3) of the 1977 Act (as amended), however, provide that in certain Cases a landlord's notice to quit may have effect without the consent of the Tribunal. Section 5 of the 1977 Act gives the Lord Chancellor power to make orders requiring any questions arising under any of those Cases to be determined by arbitration. Two orders have been made: The Agricultural Holdings (Arbitration on Notices) Order 1978 (the 1978 Order) and The Agricultural Holdings (Arbitration on Notices) (Variation) Order 1984 (the 1984 Order) (Appendix C p. 538 below). Their combined effect is that where notice to quit is served under any of the four Cases listed below, a tenant who wishes to contest a reason for the service of such a notice *must* serve a counternotice in writing within one month requiring the matter to be determined by arbitration (art 9 of the 1978 Order). Arbitration is the only remedy available to the tenant; the jurisdiction of the courts is excluded (*Magdalen College, Oxford v Heritage* [1974] 1 All ER 1065).

The Cases to which the above arbitration provisions apply are as follows (section 2(3) of the 1977 Act, as amended):

(i) *Case B*—notice to quit has been given on the grounds that the land is required for a use, except for agriculture, for which planning permission (other than certain permissions granted to the National Coal Board for open cast mining) has been granted, or for which permission is not required.

(ii) *Case D*—at the date of the notice to quit the tenant has failed to comply with a previous notice in writing requiring him either to pay arrears of rent within two months or to remedy within a specified reasonable period any breach of the tenancy that was capable of being remedied and which was not inconsistent with the rules of good husbandry.

(iii) *Case E*—at the date of the notice to quit the landlord's interest had been materially prejudiced by a breach of the tenancy which was not capable of being remedied and which was not inconsistent with the rules of good husbandry.

(iv) *Case I*—notice to quit has been served in respect of a small-holding let by a smallholdings authority or the Minister after 12th September 1984, to a tenant who is aged 65 or over, and suitable alternative living accommodation can be provided for him (where applicable) and the tenancy agreement contained as acknowledgment by the tenant that it is subject to this Case.

A tenant's counternotice requiring arbitration under one of the above Cases ceases to be effective after a period of three months from the date of that notice unless an arbitrator has been appointed by agreement between the parties or (in default of agreement) the tenant has made application for the appointment of an arbitrator (art 9A of the 1978 Order inserted by art 5 of the 1984 Order). The operation of a landlord's notice to quit is suspended until the end of the three months period or until the termination of the arbitration where, within that period, an arbitrator has been appointed or application made for such appointment (art 11 of the 1978 Order, as amended).

Where the landlord of an agricultural holding resumes possession of part of the holding the tenant is entitled to a reduction of rent, which shall be determined by arbitration in default of agreement made after the landlord resumes possession of part of the holding (section 10 of the 1977 Act as amended).

A tenant may require arbitration where the landlord serves on him a notice requiring him to do work (under the second limb of Case D and before notice to quit) and the tenant contests his liability for any work specified in the notice. The tenant's counternotice requiring arbitration must specify the items for which he denies liability and *must* be served within one month of the landlord's notice to do the work (art 3 of the 1978 Order). Again, arbitration is the tenant's only remedy in this matter.

An arbitration under the 1977 Act will be conducted under the provisions of section 77 and the Sixth Schedule to the 1948 Act (as amended) (see above), and the arbitrator is also given certain specific powers to postpone the termination of a tenancy following notice to quit (arts 12 & 13 of the 1978 Order) and in respect of a tenant's liability for work under Case D (arts 5–7 of the 1978 Order).

STATUTES, STATUTORY
INSTRUMENTS AND CIRCULARS

Statutes

	Page
Agricultural Holdings Act 1948, ss. 70 & 77 & 6th Sch.	459
Arbitration Act 1950, ss. 1–34 & 44	466
General Rate Act 1967, ss. 76 & 83 (6)–(9)	477
Civil Evidence Act 1968, ss. 1–10 & 18	478
Town and Country Planning Act 1971, Sch.9	489
Civil Evidence Act 1972, ss. 1–3 & 5	493
Rent Act 1977, ss. 77 & 78, Schs. 11 & 12	495
Arbitration Act 1979	504
Limitation Act 1980, s. 34	510
Agricultural Holdings Act 1984, s. 8	512

Agricultural Holdings Act 1948

Settlement of claims between landlord and tenant on termination of tenancy

70.—(1) Without prejudice to any other provision of this Act, any claim of whatever nature by the tenant or landlord of an agricultural holding against his landlord or tenant, being a claim which arises—

(a) under this Act or any custom or agreement; and

(b) on or out of the termination of the tenancy of the holding or part thereof,

shall, subject to the provisions of this section, be determined by arbitration under this Act.

(2) No such claim as aforesaid shall be enforceable unless before the expiration of two months from the termination of the tenancy the claimant has served notice in writing on his landlord or tenant, as the case may be, of his intention to make the claim.

A notice under this subsection shall specify the nature of the claim, and it shall be a sufficient specification thereof if the notice refers to the statutory provision, custom or term of an agreement under which the claim is made.

*(3) The landlord and tenant may, within the period of eight months from the termination of the tenancy, by agreement in writing settle any such claim as aforesaid.

*(4) Where, by the expiration of the said period any such claim as

aforesaid has not been settled, it shall be determined by arbitration under this Act.

(5) Where a tenant lawfully remains in occupation of part of an agricultural holding after the termination of a tenancy, references in subsections (2) and (3) of this section to the termination thereof shall, in the case of a claim relating to that part of the holding, be construed as references to the termination of the occupation.

(6) This section shall not apply to a claim arising on or out of the termination of a tenancy before the first day of March, nineteenth hundred and fortyeight.

* amended by Agricultural Holdings Act 1984, s.10(1) and Sch. 3 para 18.

Arbitration under this Act

*77.—(1) Any matter which by or by virtue of this Act or regulations made thereunder is required to be determined by arbitration under this Act shall, notwithstanding any agreement, under a contract of tenancy or otherwise, providing for a different method of arbitration, be determined by the arbitration of a single arbitrator in accordance with the provisions of any order under this section, together with the provisions of the Sixth Schedule to this Act (as for the time being in force), and the Arbitration Acts, 1889 to 1934, shall not apply to any such arbitration.

*(2) The Lord Chancellor may by order make provision as to the procedure to be followed in, or in connection with, proceedings on arbitrations under this Act.

*(3) An order under this section may in particular—

    (*a*) provide for the provisions of the Sixth Schedule to this Act, exclusive of those mentioned in subsection (4) of this section, to have effect subject to such modification as may be specified in the order;

    (*b*) prescribe forms for proceedings on arbitrations under this Act which, if used, shall be sufficient;

    (*c*) prescribe the form in which awards in such proceedings are to be made.

*(4) An order under this section shall not make provision inconsistent with the following provisions of the Sixth Schedule, namely paragraphs 1 to 5 and 10 to 12, the proviso to paragraph 13, and paragraphs 17, 19, 20A, 20B and 24 to 28.

*(5) The power to make an order under this section shall be exercisable by statutory instrument which shall be subject to annulment in pursuance of a resolution of either House of Parliament.

*(6) In this section "modifications" includes additions, omissions and amendments.

* amended or substituted by Agricultural Holdings Act 1984, s.10(1) and Sch. 3 para 19.

SIXTH SCHEDULE

Sections 77, 100

PROVISIONS AS TO ARBITRATIONS UNDER THIS ACT

Appointment and Remuneration of Arbitrator

1.—(1) The arbitrator shall be a person appointed by agreement between the parties or, in default of agreement, a person appointed on the application of either of the parties by the Minister from among the members of the panel constituted for the purposes of this paragraph.

*(1A) Any such appointment by the Minister shall be made by him as soon as possible after receiving the application; but where the application is referable to a demand for arbitration made under section 8 of this Act any such appointment shall in any event not be made by him earlier than four months before the next termination date following the date of the demand (as defined by section 8A(20) of this Act).

* inserted by Agricultural Holdings Act 1984, s.10(1) and Sch. 3 para 28.

(2) A person appointed by the Minister as arbitrator shall, where the arbitration relates to an agricultural holding in Wales or Monmouthshire, be a person who possesses a knowledge of Welsh agricultural conditions, and, if either party to the arbitration so requires, a knowledge also of the Welsh language.

*(3) For the purposes of this Schedule there shall be constituted a panel consisting of such number of persons as the Lord Chancellor may determine, to be appointed by him.

* amended by Agriculture Act 1958, s.8(1) and Sch. 1.

2. If the arbitrator dies, or is incapable of acting, or for seven days after notice from either party requiring him to act fails to act, a new arbitrator may be appointed as if no arbitrator had been appointed.

2A. In relation to an arbitrator who is appointed in place of another arbitrator (whether under the foregoing paragraph or otherwise) the reference in section 8(2) of this Act to the date of the reference shall be construed as a reference to the date when the original arbitrator was appointed.

* inserted by Agricultural Holdings Act 1984, s.10(1) and Sch. 3 para 28.

3. Neither party shall have power to revoke the appointment of the arbitrator without the consent of the other party; and his appointment shall not be revoked by the death of either party.

* amended by Agricultural Holdings Act 1984, s.10(1) and Sch. 3 para 28.

4. Every appointment, application, notice, revocation and consent under the foregoing paragraphs must be in writing.

*5. The remuneration of the arbitrator shall be—

    (*a*) where he is appointed by agreement between the parties, such amount as may be agreed upon by him and the parties or, in default

of agreement, fixed by the registrar of the county court (subject to
an appeal to the judge of the court) on an application made by the
arbitrator or either of the parties;

(*b*) where he is appointed by the Minister, such amount as may be
fixed by the Minister,

and shall be recoverable by him as a debt due from either of the parties to
the arbitration.

* amended by Agricultural Holdings Act 1984, s.10(1) and Sch. 3 para 28.

Conduct of Proceedings, Witnesses, etc.

*6. The parties to the arbitration shall, within thirty-five days from the
appointment of the arbitrator, deliver to him a statement of their respective
cases with all necessary particulars and—

(*a*) no amendment or additon to the statement or particulars delivered
shall be allowed after the expiration of the said thirty-five days
except with the consent of the arbitrator;

(*b*) a party to the arbitration shall be confined at the hearing to the
matters alleged in the statement and particulars delivered by him
and any amendment thereof or addition thereto duly made.

* amended by Agriculture (Miscellaneous Provisions) Act 1963, s.20 and Agricultural Holdings
Act 1984, s.10(1) and Sch. 3 para 28.

*7. The parties to the arbitration and all persons claiming through them
respectively shall, subject to any legal objection, submit to be examined by
the arbitrator, on oath or affirmation, in relation to the matters in dispute
and shall, subject as aforesaid, produce before the arbitrator all samples
and documents within their possession or power respectively which may be
required or called for and do all other things which during the proceedings
the arbitrator may require.

8. Witnesses appearing at the arbitration shall, if the arbitrator thinks fit,
be examined on oath or affirmation, and the arbitrator shall have power to
administer oaths to, or to take the affirmation of, the parties and witnesses
appearing.

9. The provisions of county court rules as to the issuing of witness
summonses shall, subject to such modifications as may be prescribed by
such rules, apply for the purposes of the arbitration as if it were an action or
matter in the county court.

10.—(1) Any person summoned in pursuance of county court rules as a
witness in the arbitration who—

(*a*) refuses or neglects, without sufficient cause, to appear or to produce
any documents required by the summons to be produced; or

(*b*) refuses to be sworn or give evidence;

shall forfeit such fine not exceeding ten pounds as the judge of the county
court may direct:

Provided that no person so summoned shall forfeit a fine as aforesaid
unless there has been paid or tendered to him at the time of the service of the
summons such sum in respect of his expenses (including, in such cases as

may be prescribed by county court rules, compensation for loss of time) as may be so prescribed for the purposes of subsection (1) of section eight-one of the County Courts Act, 1934.

(2) Any person present at the arbitration who, being required to give evidence, refuses to be sworn or give evidence shall forfeit such a fine as aforesaid.

(3) The judge of the county court may at his discretion direct that the whole or any part of any such fine, after deducting costs, shall be applicable towards indemnifying the party injured by the refusal or neglect.

11.—(1) The judge of the county court may, if he thinks fit, upon application on affidavit by either party to the arbitration, issue an order under his hand for bringing up before the arbitrator any person (hereafter in this paragraph referred to as a "prisoner") confined in any place under any sentence or under commitment for trial or otherwise, to be examined as a witness in the arbitration:

Provided that no such order shall be made with respect to a person confined under process in any civil action or matter.

(2) The prisoner mentioned in any such order shall be brought before the arbitrator under the same custody, and shall be dealt with in the same manner in all respects, as a prisoner required by writ of habeas corpus to be brought before the High Court and examined therein as a witness:

Provided that the person having the custody of the prisoner shall not be bound to obey the order unless there is tendered to him a reasonable sum for the conveyance and maintenance of a proper officer or officers and of the prisoner in going to, remaining at, and returning from the place where the arbitration is held.

12. The High Court may order that a writ of habeas corpus ad testificandum shall issue to bring up a prisoner for examination before the arbitrator, if the prisoner is confined in any prison under process in any civil action or matter.

Award

*13. The arbitrator shall make and sign his award within fifty-six days of his appointment.

Provided that the Minister may from time to time enlarge the time limited for making the award, whether that time has expired or not.

* amended by Agriculture (Miscellaneous Provisions) Act 1963, s.20.

14. The arbitrator may if he thinks fit make an interim award for the payment of any sum on account of the sum to be finally awarded.

*15. ....

* repealed by Agricultural Holdings Act 1984, s.10(2) and Sch. 4.

16. The arbitrator shall—

    (*a*) state separately in the award the amounts awarded in respect of the several claims referred to him; and

    (*b*) on the application of either party, specify the amount awarded in respect of any particular improvement or any particular matter the subject of the award.

17. Where by vitue of this Act compensation under an agreement is to be substituted for compensation under this Act for improvements or for any such matters as are specified in the Fourth Schedule to this Act, the arbitrator shall award compensation in accordance with the agreement instead of in accordance with this Act.

18. The award shall fix a day not later than one month after the delivery thereof for the payment of the money awarded as compensation, costs or otherwise.

19. The award shall be final and binding on the parties and the persons claiming under them respectively.

20. The arbitrator shall have power to correct in the award any clerical mistake or error arising from any accidental slip or ommission.

Reasons for award

*20A. Section 12 of the Tribunals and Inquiries Act 1971 (reasons to be given for decisions of tribunals etc.) shall apply in relation to the award of an arbitrator appointed under this Schedule by agreement between the parties as it applies in relation to the award of an arbitrator appointed under this Schedule otherwise than by such agreement.

Interest on awards

*20B. Any sum directed to be paid by the award shall, unless the award otherwise directs, carry interest as from the date of the award and at the same rate as a judgment debt.

* inserted by Agricultural Holdings Act 1984, s.10(1) and Sch. 3 para 28.

Costs

21. The costs of, and incidental to, the arbitration and award shall be in the discretion of the arbitrator who may direct to and by whom and in what manner the costs or any part thereof are to be paid.

*22. On the application of either party any such costs shall be taxable in the county court according to such of the scales prescribed by county court rules for proceedings in the county court as may be directed by the arbitrator under the foregoing paragraph or, in the absence of any such direction, by the county court.

* substituted by Agricultural Holdings Act 1984, s.10(1) and Sch. 3 para 28.

23. The arbitrator shall, in awarding costs, take into consideration the reasonableness or unreasonableness of the claim of either party, whether in respect of amount or otherwise, and any unreasonable demand for particulars or refusal to supply particulars, and generally all the circumstances of the case, and may disallow the costs of any witness whom he considers to have been called unnecessary and any other costs which he considers to have been unnecessarily incurred.

Special Case and setting aside Award, etc.

24. The arbitrator may at any stage of the proceedings, and shall, upon a direction in that behalf given by the judge of the county court upon an application made by either party, state in the form of a special case for the opinion of the county court any question of law arising in the course of the arbitration.

25.—(1) Where the arbitrator has misconducted himself the county court may remove him.

*(2) Where the arbitrator has misconducted himself, or an arbitration or award has been improperly procured or there is an error of law on the face of the award, the county court may set the award aside.

* amended by Agriculture (Miscellaneous Provisions) Act 1972, s.15(1).

*25A.—(1) The county court may from time to time remit the award or any part of the award to the reconsideration of the arbitrator.

(2) In any case where it appears to the county court that there is an error of law on the face of the award the court may, instead of exercising its power of remission under the foregoing sub-paragraph, vary the award by substituting for so much of it as is affected by the error such award as the court considers that it would have been proper for the arbitrator to make in the circumstances; and the award shall thereupon have effect as so varied.

(3) Where remission is ordered under that sub-paragraph, the arbitrator shall, unless the order otherwise directs, make and sign his award within thirty days after the date of the order.

(4) If the county court is satisfied that the time limited for making the said award is, for any good reason, insufficient, the court may extend or further extend that time for such period as it thinks proper.

* inserted by Agricultural Holdings Act 1984, s.10(1) and Sch. 3 para 28.

Miscellaneous

26. Any amount paid, in respect of the remuneration of the arbitrator by either party to the arbitration, in excess of the amount, if any, directed by the award to be paid by him in respect of the costs of the award shall be recoverable from the other party.

*27.———

* repealed by Agricultural Holdings Act 1984, s.10(2) and Sch. 4.

*28. Where the Minister or any other person acting on behalf of His Majesty is a party to the arbitration, anything which under this Schedule is to be done by the Minister in relation to the appointment or remuneration of the arbitrator or the extension of time for making and signing his award shall be done instead by the President of the Royal Institution of Chartered Surveyors.

* repealed by Agricultural Holdings Act 1984, s.10(2) and Sch. 4, but this does not come into force until the date appointed by the Minister for the transfer of his functions to the President of the RICS, s.11(5)(b).

*29. For the purposes of this Schedule an arbitrator appointed by the Minister shall be taken to have been so appointed at the time when the Minister executed the instrument of appointment; and in the case of any such arbitrator the periods mentioned in paragraphs 6 and 13 of this Schedule shall accordingly run from that time.

* inserted by Agricultural Holdings Act 1984, s.10(1) and Sch. 3 para 28.

Arbitration Act 1950

Part I

General Provisions as to Arbitration

Effect of Arbitration Agreements, &c.

Authority of arbitrators and umpires to be irrevocable

1. The authority of an arbitrator or umpire appointed by or by virtue of an arbitration agreement shall, unless a contrary intention is expressed in the agreement, be irrevocable except by leave of the High Court or a judge thereof.

Death of party

2.—(1) An arbitration agreement shall not be discharged by the death of any party thereto, either as respects the deceased or any other party, but shall in such event be enforceable by or against the personal representative of the deceased.

(2) The authority of an arbitrator shall not be revoked by the death of any party by whom he was appointed.

(3) Nothing in this section shall be taken to affect the operation of any enactment or rule of law by virtue of which any right of action is extinguished by the death of a person.

Bankruptcy

3.—(1) Where it is provided by a term in a contract to which a bankrupt is a party that any differences arising thereout or in connection therewith shall be referred to arbitration, the said term shall, if the trustee in bankruptcy adopts the contract, be enforceable by or against him so far as relates to any such differences.

(2) Where a person who has been adjudged bankrupt had, before the commencement of the bankruptcy, become a party to an arbitration agreement, and any matter to which the agreement applies requires to be determined in connection with or for the purposes of the bankruptcy proceedings, then, if the case is one to which subsection (1) of this section does not apply, any other party to the agreement or, with the consent of the committee of inspection, the trustee in bankruptcy, may apply to the court having jurisdiction in the bankruptcy proceedings for an order directing that the matter in question shall be referred to arbitration in accordance with the agreement, and that court may, if it is of opinion that, having regard to all the circumstances of the case, the matter ought to be determined by arbitration, make an order accordingly.

Staying court proceedings where there is submission to arbitration

4.—(1) If any party to an arbitration agreement, or any person claiming through or under him, commences any legal proceedings in any court against any other party to the agreement, or any person claiming through or under him, in respect of any matter agreed to be referred, any party to those legal proceedings may at any time after appearance, and before delivering any pleadings or taking any other steps in the proceedings, apply to that court to stay the proceedings, and that court or a judge thereof, if satisfied that there is no sufficient reason why the matter should not be referred in accordance with the agreement, and that the applicant was, at the time when the proceedings were commenced, and still remains, ready and willing to do all things necessary to the proper conduct of the arbitration, may make an order staying the proceedings.

*(2) ....

* repealed by Arbitration Act 1975, s.8(2)(a).

Reference of interpleader issues to arbitration
5. Where relief by way of interpleader is granted and it appears to the High Court that the claims in question are matters to which an arbitration agreement, to which the claimants are parties, applies, the High Court may direct the issue between the claimants to be determined in accordance with the agreement.

Arbitrators and Umpires

When reference is to a single arbitrator
6. Unless a contrary intention is expressed therein, every arbitration agreement shall, if no other mode of reference is provided, be deemed to include a provision that the reference shall be to a single arbitrator.

Power of parties in certain cases to supply vacancy
7. Where an arbitration agreement provides that the reference shall be to two arbitrators, one to be appointed by each party, then, unless a contrary intention is expressed therein—

    (*a*) if either of the appointed arbitrators refuses to act, or is incapable of acting, or dies, the party who appointed him may appoint a new arbitrator in his place;

    (*b*) if, on such a reference, one party fails to appoint an arbitrator, either originally, or by way of substitution as aforesaid, for seven clear days after the other party, having appointed his arbitrator, has served the party making default with notice to make the appointment, the party who has appointed an arbitrator may appoint that arbitrator to act as sole arbitrator in the reference and his award shall be binding on both parties as if he had been appointed by consent:

Provided that the High Court or a judge thereof may set aside any appointment made in pursuance of this section.

Umpires
*8.—(1) Unless a contrary intention is expressed therein, every arbitration agreement shall, where the reference is to two arbitrators, be deemed to include a provision that the two arbitrators may appoint an umpire at any

time after they are themselves appointed and shall do so forthwith if they cannot agree.

(2) Unless a contrary intention is expressed therein, every arbitration agreement shall, where such a provision is applicable to the reference, be deemed to include a provision that if the arbitrators have delivered to any party to the arbitration agreement, or to the umpire, a notice in writing stating that they cannot agree, the umpire may forthwith enter on the reference in lieu of the arbitrators.

(3) At any time after the appointment of an umpire, however appointed, the High Court may, on the application of any party to the reference and notwithstanding anything to the contrary in the arbitration agreement, order that the umpire shall enter upon the reference in lieu of the arbitrators and as if he were a sole arbitrator.

* amended by Arbitration Act 1979, s.6(1).

Majority award of three arbitrators
*9. Unless the contrary intention is expressed in the arbitration agreement, in any case where there is a reference to three arbitrators, the award of any two of the arbitrators shall be binding.

* substituted by Arbitration Act 1979, s.6(2).

Power of court in certain cases to appoint an arbitrator or umpire
*10.—(1) In any of the following cases—

(a) where an arbitration agreement provides that the reference shall be to a single arbitrator, and all the parties do not, after differences have arisen, concur in the appointment of an arbitrator;

(b) if an appointed arbitrator refuses to act, or is incapable of acting, or dies, and the arbitration agreement does not show that it was intended that the vacancy should not be supplied and the parties do not supply the vacancy;

(c) where the parties or two arbitrators are required or are at liberty to appoint an umpire or third arbitrator and do not appoint him;

(d) where an appointed umpire or third arbitrator refuses to act, or is incapable of acting, or dies, and the arbitration agreement does not show that it was intended that the vacancy should not be supplied, and the parties or arbitrators do not supply the vacancy;

any party may serve the other parties or the arbitrators, as the case may be, with a written notice to appoint or, as the case may be, concur in appointing, an arbitrator, umpire or third arbitrator, and if the appointment is not made within seven clear days after the service of the notice, the High Court or a judge thereof may, on application by the party who gave the notice, appoint an arbitrator, umpire or third arbitrator who shall have the like powers to act in the reference and make an award as if he had been appointed by consent of all parties.

*(2) In any case where—

(a) an arbitration agreement provides for the appointment of an arbitrator or umpire by a person who is neither one of the parties nor an existing arbitrator (whether the provision applies directly or in default of agreement by the parties or otherwise), and

(*b*) that person refuses to make the appointment or does not make it within the time specified in the agreement or, if no time is so specified, within a reasonable time,

any party to the agreement may serve the person in question with a written notice to appoint an arbitrator or umpire and, if the appointment is not made within seven clear days after the service of the notice, the High Court or a judge thereof may, on the application of the party who gave the notice, appoint an arbitrator or umpire who shall have the like powers to act in the reference and make an award as if he had been appointed in accordance with the terms of the agreement.

* amended and inserted by Arbitration Act 1979, s.6(3) and (4).

Reference to official referee

11. Where an arbitration agreement provides that the reference shall be to an official referee, any official referee to whom application is made shall, subject to any order of the High Court or a judge thereof as to transfer or otherwise, hear and determine the matters agreed to be referred.

Conduct of Proceedings, Witnesses, &c.

Conduct of proceedings, witnesses, &c.

12.—(1) Unless a contrary intention is expressed therein, every arbitration agreement shall, where such a provision is applicable to the reference, be deemed to contain a provision that the parties to the reference, and all persons claiming through them respectively, shall, subject to any legal objection, submit to be examined by the arbitrator or umpire, on oath or affirmation, in relation to the matters in dispute, and shall, subject as aforesaid, produce before the arbitrator or umpire all documents within their possession or power respectively which may be required or called for, and do all other things which during the proceedings on the reference the arbitrator or umpire may require.

(2) Unless a contrary intention is expressed therein, every arbitration agreement shall, where such a provision is applicable to the reference, be deemed to contain a provision that the witness on the reference shall, if the arbitrator or umpire thinks fit, be examined on oath or affirmation.

(3) An arbitrator or umpire shall, unless a contrary intention is expressed in the arbitration agreement, have power to administer oaths to, or take the affirmations of, the parties to and witnesses on a reference under the agreement.

(4) Any party to a reference under an arbitration agreement may sue out a writ of subpoena ad testificandum or a writ of subpoena duces tecum, but no person shall be compelled under any such writ to produce any document which he could not be compelled to produce on the trial of an action, and the High Court or judge thereof may order that a writ of subpoena ad testificandum or of subpoena duces tecum shall issue to compel the

attendance before an arbitrator or umpire of a witness wherever he may be within the United Kingdom.

(5) The High Court or a judge thereof may also order that a writ of habeas corpus ad testificandum shall issue to bring up a prisoner for examination before an arbitrator or umpire.

(6) The High Court shall have, for the purpose of and in relation to a reference, the same power of making orders in respect of—

(a) security for costs;
(b) discovery of documents and interrogatories;
(c) the giving of evidence by affidavit;
(d) examination on oath of any witness before an officer of the High Court or any other person, and the issue of a commission or request for the examination of a witness out of the jurisdiction;
(e) the preservation, interim custody or sale of any goods which are the subject matter of the reference;
(f) securing the amount in dispute in the reference;
(g) the detention, preservation or inspection of any property or thing which is the subject of the reference or as to which any question may arise therein, and authorising for any of the purposes aforesaid any person to enter upon or into any land or building in the possession of any party to the reference, or authorising any samples to be taken or any observation to be made or experiment to be tried which may be necessary or expedient for the purpose of obtaining full information or evidence; and
(h) interim injunctions or the appointment of a receiver;

as it has for the purpose of and in relation to an action or matter in the High Court:

Provided that nothing in this subsection shall be taken to prejudice any power which may be vested in an arbitrator or umpire of making orders with respect to any of the matters aforesaid.

Provisions as to Awards

Time for making award

13.—(1) Subject to the provisions of subsection (2) of section twenty-two of this Act, and anything to the contrary in the arbitration agreement, an arbitrator or umpire shall have power to make an award at any time.

(2) The time, if any, limited for making an award, whether under this Act or otherwise, may from time to time be enlarged by order of the High Court or a judge thereof, whether that time has expired or not.

(3) The High Court may, on the application of any party to a reference, remove an arbitrator or umpire who fails to use all reasonable dispatch in entering on and proceeding with the reference and making an award, and an arbitrator or umpire who is removed by the High Court under this subsection shall not be entitled to receive any remuneration in respect of his services.

For the purposes of this subsection, the expression "proceeding with a reference" includes, in a case where two arbitrators are unable to agree, giving notice of that fact to the parties and to the umpire.

Interim awards

14. Unless a contrary intention is expressed therein, every arbitration agreement shall, where such a provision is applicable to the reference, be deemed to contain a provision that the arbitrator or umpire may, if he thinks fit, make an interim award, and any reference in this Part of this Act to an award includes a reference to an interim award.

Specific performance

15. Unless a contrary intention is expressed therein, every arbitration agreement shall, where such a provision is applicable to the reference, be deemed to contain a provision that the arbitrator or umpire shall have the same power as the High Court to order specific performance of any contract other than a contract relating to land or any interest in land.

Awards to be final

16. Unless a contrary intention is expressed therein, every arbitration agreement shall, where such a provision is applicable to the reference, be deemed to contain a provision that the award to be made by the arbitrator or umpire shall be final and binding on the parties and the persons claiming under them respectively.

Power to correct slips

17. Unless a contrary intended is expressed in the arbitration agreement, the arbitrator or umpire shall have power to correct in an award any clerical mistake or error arising from any accidental slip or omission.

Costs, Fees and Interest

Costs

18.—(1) Unless a contrary intention is expressed therein, every arbitration agreement shall be deemed to include a provision that the costs of the reference and award shall be in the discretion of the arbitrator or umpire, who may direct to and by whom and in what manner those costs or any part thereof shall be paid, and may tax or settle the amount of costs to be so paid or any part thereof, and may award costs to be paid as between solicitor and client.

(2) Any costs directed by an award to be paid shall, unless the award otherwise directs, be taxable in the High Court.

(3) Any provision in an arbitration agreement to the effect that the parties or any party thereto shall in any event pay their or his own costs of the reference or award or any part thereof shall be void, and this Part of this Act shall, in the case of an arbitration agreement containing any such provision, have effect as if that provision were not contained therein:

Provided that nothing in this subsection shall invalidate such a provision when it is a part of an agreement to submit to arbitration a dispute which has arisen before the making of that agreement.

(4) If no provision is made by an award with respect to the costs of the

reference, any party to the reference may, within fourteen days of the publication of the award or such further time as the High Court or a judge thereof may direct, apply to the arbitrator for an order directing by and to whom those costs shall be paid, and thereupon the arbitrator shall, after hearing any party who may desire to be heard, amend his award by adding thereto such directions as he may think proper with respect to the payment of the costs of the reference.

(5) Section sixty-nine of the Solicitors Act, 1932 (which empowers a court before which any proceeding is being heard or is pending to charge property recovered or preserved in the proceeding with the payment of solicitors' costs) shall apply as if an arbitration were a proceeding in the High Court, and the High Court may make declarations and orders accordingly.

Taxation of arbitrator's or umpire's fees

19.—(1) If in any case an arbitrator or umpire refuses to deliver his award except on payment of the fees demanded by him, the High Court may, on an application for the purpose, order that the arbitrator or umpire shall deliver the award to the applicant on payment into court by the applicant of the fees demanded, and further that the fees demanded shall be taxed by the taxing officer and that out of the money paid into court there shall be paid out to the arbitrator or umpire by way of fees such sum as may be found reasonable on taxation and that the balance of the money, if any, shall be paid out to the applicant.

(2) An application for the purposes of this section may be made by any party to the reference unless the fees demanded have been fixed by a written agreement between him and the arbitrator or umpire.

(3) A taxation of fees under this section may be reviewed in the same manner as a taxation of costs.

(4) The arbitrator or umpire shall be entitled to appear and be heard on any taxation or review of taxation under this section.

Power of arbitrator to award interest

*19A.—(1) Unless a contrary intention is expressed therein, every arbitration agreement shall, where such a provision is applicable to the reference, be deemed to contain a provision that the arbitrator or umpire may, if he thinks fit, award simple interest at such rate as he thinks fit—

(a) on any sum which is the subject of the reference but which is paid before the award, for such period ending not later than the date of the payment as he thinks fit; and

(b) on any sum which he awards, for such period ending not later than the date of the award as he thinks fit.

(2) The power to award interest conferred on an arbitrator or umpire by subsection (1) above is without prejudice to any other power of an arbitrator or umpire to award interest.

* inserted by Administration of Justice Act 1982, s.15(6) and Sch. 1 Pt IV.

Interest on awards

20. A sum directed to be paid by an award shall, unless the award otherwise directs, carry interest as from the date of the award and at the same rate as a judgment debt.

Special Cases, Remission and Setting aside of Awards, &c.

Statement of case
*21. ....

* repealed by Arbitration Act 1979, s.8(3)(b).

Power to remit award
22.—(1) In all cases of reference to arbitration the High Court or a judge thereof may from time to time remit the matters referred, or any of them to the reconsideration of the arbitrator or umpire.

(2) Where an award is remitted, the arbitrator or umpire shall, unless the order otherwise directs, make his award within three months after the date of the order.

Removal of arbitrator and setting aside of award
23.—(1) Where an arbitrator or umpire has misconducted himself or the proceedings, the High Court may remove him.

(2) Where an arbitrator or umpire has misconducted himself or the proceedings, or an arbitration or award has been improperly procured, the High Court may set the award aside.

(3) Where an application is made to set aside an award, the High Court may order that any money made payable by the award shall be brought into court or otherwise secured pending the determination of the application.

Power of court to give relief where arbitrator is not impartial or the dispute involves question of fraud
24.—(1) Where an agreement between any parties provides that disputes which may arise in the future between them shall be referred to an arbitrator named or designated in the agreement, and after a dispute has arisen any party applies, on the ground that the arbitrator so named or designated is not or may not be impartial, for leave to revoke the authority of the arbitrator or for an injunction to restrain any other party or the arbitrator from proceeding with the arbitration, it shall not be a ground for refusing the application that the said party at the time when he made the agreement knew, or ought to have known, that the arbitrator, by reason of his relation towards any other party to the agreement or of his connection with the subject referred, might not be capable of impartiality.

(2) Where an agreement between any parties provides that disputes which may arise in the future between them shall be referred to arbitration, and a dispute which so arises involves the question whether any such party has been guilty of fraud, the High Court shall, so far as may be necessary to enable that question to be determined by the High Court, have power to order that the agreement shall cease to have effect and power to give leave to revoke the authority of any arbitrator or umpire appointed by or by virtue of the agreement.

(3) In any case where by virtue of this section the High Court has power to order that an arbitration agreement shall cease to have effect or to give leave to revoke the authority of an arbitrator or umpire, the High Court may refuse to stay any action brought in breach of the agreement.

Power of court where arbitrator is removed or authority of arbitrator is revoked

*25.—(1) Where an arbitrator (not being a sole arbitrator), or two or more arbitrators (not being all the arbitrators) or an umpire who has not entered on the reference is or are removed by the High Court or the Court of Appeal, the High Court or the Court of Appeal as the case may be, may, on the application of any party to the arbitration agreement, appoint a person or persons to act as arbitrator or arbitrators or umpire in place of the person or persons so removed.

*(2) Where the authority of an arbitrator or arbitrators or umpire is revoked by leave of the High Court or the Court of Appeal, or a sole arbitrator or all the arbitrators or an umpire who has entered on the reference is or are removed by the High Court or the Court of Appeal, the High Court or the Court of Appeal as the case may be, may, on the application of any party to the arbitration agreement, either—

(a) appoint a person to act as sole arbitrator in place of the person or persons removed; or

(b) order that the arbitration agreement shall cease to have effect with respect to the dispute referred.

*(3) A person appointed under this section by the High Court or the Court of Appeal as an arbitrator or umpire shall have the like power to act in the reference and to make an award as if he had been appointed in accordance with the terms of the arbitration agreement.

*(4) Where it is provided (whether by means of a provision in the arbitration agreement or otherwise) that an award under an arbitration agreement shall be a condition precedent to the bringing of an action with respect to any matter to which the agreement applies, the High Court or the Court of Appeal, if it orders (whether under this section or under any other enactment) that the agreement shall cease to have effect as regards any particular dispute, may further order that the provision making an award a condition precedent to the bringing of an action shall also cease to have effect as regards that dispute.

* amended by Administration of Justice Act 1970, Sch. 3 para 11.

Enforcement of Award

Enforcement of award

26.—(1) An award on an arbitration agreement may, by leave of the High Court or a judge thereof, be enforced in the same manner as a judgment or order to the same effect and where leave is so given, judgment may be entered in terms of the award.

*(2) If—

(a) the amount sought to be recovered does not exceed the county court limit, and

(b) a county court so orders,

it shall be recoverable (by execution issued from the county court or otherwise) as if payable under an order of that court and shall not be enforceable under subsection (1) above.

*(3) An application to the High Court under this section shall preclude an application to a county court and an application to a county court under this section shall preclude an application to the High Court.

†(4) In subsection (2)(*a*) above "the county court limit" means the amount which for the time being is the county court limit for the purposes of section 16 of the County Courts Act 1984 (money recoverable by statute).

* inserted by Administration of Justice Act 1977, s.17(2) and amended by County Courts Act 1984, s.148(1) and Sch. 2 para 22(a).
† inserted by County Courts Act 1984, s.148(1) and Sch. 2 para 22(b).

Miscellaneous

Power of court to extend time for commencing arbitration proceedings
27. Where the terms of an agreement to refer future disputes to arbitration provide that any claims to which the agreement applies shall be barred unless notice to appoint an arbitrator is given or an arbitrator is appointed or some other step to commence arbitration proceedings is taken within a time fixed by the agreement, and a dispute arises to which the agreement applies, the High Court, if it is of opinion that in the circumstances of the case undue hardship would otherwise be caused, and notwithstanding that the time so fixed has expired, may, on such terms, if any, as the justice of the case may require, but without prejudice to the provisions of any enactment limiting the time for the commencement of arbitration proceedings, extend the time for such period as it thinks proper.

Terms as to costs &c.
***28.** Any order made under this Part of this Act may be made on such terms as to costs or otherwise as the authority making the order thinks just:

* amended by Arbitration Act 1975, s.8(2)(b).

Extension of s.496 of the Merchant Shipping Act, 1894
29.—(1) In subsection (3) of section four hundred and ninety-six of the Merchant Shipping Act, 1894 (which requires a sum deposited with a wharfinger by an owner of goods to be repaid unless legal proceedings are instituted by the shipowner), the expression "legal proceedings" shall be deemed to include arbitration.

(2) For the purposes of the said section four hundred and ninety-six, as amended by this section, an arbitration shall be deemed to be commenced when one party to the arbitration agreement serves on the other party or parties a notice requiring him or them to appoint or concur in appointing an arbitrator, or, where the arbitration agreement provides that the reference shall be to a person named or designated in the agreement, requiring him or them to submit the dispute to the person so named or designated.

(3) Any such notice as is mentioned in subsection (2) of this section may be served either—

    (*a*) by delivering it to the person on whom it is to be served; or
    (*b*) by leaving it at the usual or last known place of abode in England of that person; or

(*c*) by sending it by post in a registered letter addressed to that person at his usual or last known place of abode in England;

as well as in any other manner provided in the arbitration agreement; and where a notice is sent by post in manner prescribed by paragraph (*c*) of this subsection, service thereof shall, unless the contrary is proved, be deemed to have been effected at the time at which the letter would have been delivered in the ordinary course of post.

Crown to be bound
*30. This Part of this Act shall apply to any arbitration to which His Majesty, either in right of the Crown or of the Duchy of Lancaster or otherwise, or the Duke of Cornwall, is a party.

* amended by Arbitration Act 1975, s.8(2)(c).

Application of Part I to statutory arbitration
31.—(1) Subject to the provisions of section thirty-three of this Act, this Part of this Act, except the provisions thereof specified in subsection (2) of this section, shall apply to every arbitration under any other Act (whether passed before or after the commencement of this Act) as if the arbitration were pursuant to an arbitration agreement and as if that other Act were an arbitration agreement, except in so far as this Act is inconsistent with that other Act or with any rules or procedure authorised or recognised thereby.

*(2) The provisions referred to in subsection (1) of this section are subsection (1) of section two, section three, section five, subsection (3) of section eighteen and sections twenty-four, twenty-five, twenty-seven and twenty-nine.

* amended by Arbitration Act 1975, s.8(2)(d).

Meaning of "arbitration agreement"
32. In this Part of this Act, unless the context otherwise requires, the expression "arbitration agreement" means a written agreement to submit present or future differences to arbitration, whether an arbitrator is named therein or not.

Operation of Part I
33. This Part of this Act shall not affect any arbitration commenced (within the meaning of subsection (2) of section twenty-nine of this Act) before the commencement of this Act, but shall apply to an arbitration so commenced after the commencement of this Act under an agreement made before the commencement of this Act.

Extent of Part I
*34. None of the provisions of this Part of this Act shall extend to Scotland or Northern Ireland.

* amended by Arbitration Act 1975, s.8(2)(e).

Part III

General

Short title, commencement and repeal

44.—(1) This Act may be cited as the Arbitration Act, 1950.

(2) This Act shall come into operation on the first day of September, nineteen hundred and fifty.

(3) The Arbitration Act, 1889, the Arbitration Clauses (Protocol) Act, 1924, and the Arbitration Act, 1934, are hereby repealed except in relation to arbitrations commenced (within the meaning of subsection (2) of section twenty-nine of this Act) before the commencement of this Act, and the Arbitration (Foreign Awards) Act, 1930, is hereby repealed; and any reference in any Act or other document to any enactment hereby repealed shall be construed as including a reference to the corresponding provision of this Act.

General Rate Act 1967

Appeals to local valuation courts against objections to proposals

76.—(1) Where a copy of a proposal is transmitted to the clerk to a local valuation panel and by virtue of section 73(2), 74(3) or 75 of this Act that transmission has effect as an appeal to a local valuation court against an objection to the proposal, it shall be the duty of the chairman or a deputy chairman of that panel to arrange for the convening of such a court.

(2) The procedure of a local valuation court shall, subject to any regulations made in that behalf by the Minister, and subject to subsection (3) of this section, be such as the court may determine; and the court—

   (*a*) shall sit in public, unless the court otherwise order on the application of any party to the appeal and upon being satisfied that the interests of one or more parties to the appeal would be prejudicially affected; and

   (*b*) may take evidence on oath and shall have power for that purpose to administer oaths.

(3) Where, by virtue of section 75 of this Act, the transmission of a copy of a proposal relating to any hereditament has effect as an appeal to a local valuation court, the court may hear and determine the appeal together with any appeal against objections to earlier proposals relating to that hereditament, but except as aforesaid the court shall not hear the first-mentioned appeal until all earlier proposals relating to the hereditament are settled.

(4) On the hearing of an appeal to a local valuation court—

   (*a*) the appellant; and

   (*b*) the valuation officer, when he is not the appellant; and

   (*c*) the owner or occupier of the hereditament to which the appeal relates, when he is not the appellant; and

(*d*) the rating authority for the rating area in which the hereditament in
     question is situated, when that authority are not the appellant; and
(*e*) the objector, where he is not one of the persons aforesaid,

shall be entitled to appear and be heard as parties to the appeal and
examine any witness before the court and to call witnesses.

(5) Subject to the provisions of this Act, after hearing the persons
mentioned in subsection (4) of this section, or such of them as desire to be
heard, the local valuation court shall give such directions with respect to the
manner in which the hereditament in question is to be treated in the valuation list as appear to them to be necessary to give effect to the contention of
the appellant if and so far as that contention appears to the court to be well
founded; and the valuation officer shall cause the valuation list to be altered
accordingly.

Use of returns as evidence
83. ....

(6) Where a notice has been given to the valuation officer under subsection (5) of this section, and the valuation officer refuses or fails to comply
with the notice, the person who gave the notice may apply to the court or
tribunal before which the valuation proceedings in question are to be
brought; and if on any such application the court or tribunal is satisfied that
it is reasonable to do so, the court or tribunal may by order direct the
valuation officer to comply with the notice, either with respect to all the
hereditaments specified therein or with respect to such one or more of those
hereditaments as the court or tribunal may determine.

(7) Subsection (6) of this section shall apply, with the necessary modifications, to proceedings on an arbitration as it applies to proceedings before
a court.

(8) An appeal shall lie from the decision of a local valuation court on an
application under subsection (6) of this section as if it were a decision in the
valuation proceedings to which the application relates.

(9) In this section "valuation proceedings" means any of the following,
that is to say, any proceedings on or in consequence of an appeal to a local
valuation court, and any proceedings on or in consequence of a reference to
arbitration under section 78 of this Act.

Civil Evidence Act 1968

PART I

HEARSAY EVIDENCE

**Hearsay evidence to be admissible only by virtue of this Act and
other statutory provisions, or by agreement**
1.—(1) In any civil proceedings a statement other than one made by a
person while giving oral evidence in those proceedings shall be admissible

as evidence of any fact stated therein to the extent that it is so admissible by virtue of any provision of this Part of this Act or by virtue of any other statutory provision or by agreement of the parties, but not otherwise.

(2) In this section "statutory provision" means any provision contained in, or in an instrument made under, this or any other Act, including any Act passed after this Act.

Admissibility of out-of-court statements as evidence of facts stated

2.—(1) In any civil proceedings a statement made, whether orally or in a document or otherwise, by any person, whether called as a witness in those proceedings or not, shall, subject to this section and to rules of court, be admissible as evidence of any fact stated therein of which direct oral evidence by him would be admissible.

(2) Where in any civil proceedings a party desiring to give a statement in evidence by virtue of this section has called or intends to call as a witness in the proceedings the person by whom the statement was made, the statement—

    (*a*) shall not be given in evidence by virtue of this section on behalf of that party without the leave of the court; and

    (*b*) without prejudice to paragraph (*a*) above, shall not be given in evidence by virtue of this section on behalf of that party before the conclusion of the examination-in-chief of the person by whom it was made, except—

        (i) where before that person is called the court allows evidence of the making of the statement to be given on behalf of that party by some other person; or

        (ii) in so far as the court allows the person by whom the statement was made to narrate it in the course of his examination-in-chief on the ground that to prevent him from doing so would adversely affect the intelligibility of his evidence.

(3) Where in any civil proceedings a statement which was made otherwise than in a document is admissible by virtue of this section, no evidence other than direct oral evidence by the person who made the statement or any person who heard or otherwise perceived it being made shall be admissible for the purpose of proving it:

Provided that if the statement in question was made by a person while giving oral evidence in some other legal proceedings (whether civil or criminal) it may be proved in any manner authorised by the court.

Witness's previous statement, if proved, to be evidence of facts stated

3.—(1) Where in any civil proceedings—

    (*a*) a previous inconsistent or contradictory statement made by a person called as a witness in those proceedings is proved by virtue of section 3, 4 or 5 of the Criminal Procedure Act 1865; or

    (*b*) a previous statement made by a person called as aforesaid is proved for the purpose of rebutting a suggestion that his evidence has been fabricated, that statement shall by virtue of this subsection be admissible as evidence of any fact stated therein of which direct oral evidence by him would be admissible.

(2) Nothing in this Act shall affect any of the rules of law relating to the circumstances in which, where a person called as a witness in any civil proceedings is cross-examined on a document used by him to refresh his memory, that document may be made evidence in those proceedings; and where a document or any part of a document is received in evidence in any such proceedings by virtue of any such rule of law, any statement made in that document or part by the person using the document to refresh his memory shall by virtue of this subsection be admissible as evidence of any fact stated therein of which direct oral evidence by him would be admissible.

Admissibility of certain records as evidence of facts stated

4.—(1) Without prejudice to section 5 of this Act, in any civil proceedings a statement contained in a document shall, subject to this section and to rules of court, be admissible as evidence of any fact stated therein of which direct oral evidence would be admissible, if the document is, or forms part of, a record compiled by a person acting under a duty from information which was supplied by a person (whether acting under a duty or not) who had, or may reasonably be supposed to have had, personal knowledge of the matters dealt with in that information and which, if not supplied by that person to the compiler of the record directly, was supplied by him to the compiler of the record indirectly through one or more intermediaries each acting under a duty.

(2) Where in any civil proceedings a party desiring to give a statement in evidence by virtue of this section has called or intends to call as a witness in the proceedings the person who originally supplied the information from which the record containing the statement was compiled, the statement—

> (a) shall not be given in evidence by virtue of this section on behalf of that party without the leave of the court; and
> (b) without prejudice to paragraph (a) above, shall not without the leave of the court be given in evidence by virtue of this section on behalf of that party before the conclusion of the examination-in-chief of the person who originally supplied the said information.

(3) Any reference in this section to a person acting under a duty includes a reference to a person acting in the course of any trade, business, profession or other occupation in which he is engaged or employed or for the purposes of any paid or unpaid office held by him.

Admissibility of statements produced by computers

5.—(1) In any civil proceedings a statement contained in a document produced by a computer shall, subject to rules of court, be admissible as evidence of any fact stated therein of which direct oral evidence would be admissible, if it is shown that the conditions mentioned in subsection (2) below are satisfied in relation to the statement and computer in question.

(2) The said conditions are—

(a) that the document containing the statement was produced by the computer during a period over which the computer was used regularly to store or process information for the purposes of any activities regularly carried on over that period, whether for profit or not, by any body, whether corporate or not, or by any individual;

(b) that over that period there was regularly supplied to the computer in the ordinary course of those activities information of the kind contained in the statement or of the kind from which the information so contained is derived;

(c) that throughout the material part of that period the computer was operating properly or, if not, that any respect in which it was not operating properly or was out of operation during that part of that period was not such as to affect the production of the document or the accuracy of its contents; and

(d) that the information contained in the statement reproduces or is derived from information supplied to the computer in the ordinary course of those activities.

(3) Where over a period the function of storing or processing information for the purposes of any activities regularly carried on over that period as mentioned in subsection (2)(a) above was regularly performed by computers, whether—

(a) by a combination of computers operating over that period; or

(b) by different computers operating in succession over that period; or

(c) by different combinations of computers operating in succession over that period; or

(d) in any other manner involving the successive operation over that period, in whatever order, of one or more computers and one or more combinations of computers,

all the computers used for that purpose during that period shall be treated for the purposes of this Part of this Act as constituting a single computer, and references in this Part of this Act to a computer shall be construed accordingly.

(4) In any civil proceedings where it is desired to give a statement in evidence by virtue of this section, a certificate doing any of the following things, that is to say—

(a) identifying the document containing the statement and describing the manner in which it was produced;

(b) giving such particulars of any device involved in the production of that document as may be appropriate for the purpose of showing that the document was produced by a computer;

(c) dealing with any of the matters to which the conditions mentioned in subsection (2) above relate,

and purporting to be signed by a person occupying a responsible position in relation to the operation of the relevant device or the management of the relevant activities (whichever is appropriate) shall be evidence of any matter stated in the certificate; and for the purposes of this subsection it shall be sufficient for a matter to be stated to the best of the knowledge and belief of the person stating it.

(5) For the purposes of this Part of this Act—

    (*a*) information shall be taken to be supplied to a computer if it is supplied thereto in any appropriate form and whether it is so supplied directly or (with or without human intervention) by means of any appropriate equipment;

    (*b*) where, in the course of activities carried on by any individual or body, information is supplied with a view to its being stored or processed for the purposes of those activities by a computer operated otherwise than in the course of those activities, that information, if duly supplied to that computer, shall be taken to be supplied to it in the course of those activities;

    (*c*) a document shall be taken to have been produced by a computer whether it was produced by it directly or (with or without human intervention) by means of any appropriate equipment.

(6) Subject to subsection (3) above, in this Part of this Act "computer" means any device for storing and processing information, and any reference to information being derived from other information is a reference to its being derived therefrom by calculation, comparison or any other process.

Provisions supplementary to sections 2 to 5

6.—(1) Where in any civil proceedings a statement contained in a document is proposed to be given in evidence by virtue of section 2, 4 or 5 of this Act it may, subject to any rules of court, be proved by the production of that document or (whether or not that document is still in existence) by the production of a copy of that document, or of the material part thereof, authenticated in such manner as the court may approve.

(2) For the purpose of deciding whether or not a statement is admissible in evidence by virtue of section 2, 4 or 5 of this Act, the court may draw any reasonable inference from the circumstances in which the statement was made or otherwise came into being or from any other circumstances, including, in the case of a statement contained in a document, the form and contents of that document.

(3) In estimating the weight, if any, to be attached to a statement admissible in evidence by virtue of section 2, 3, 4 or 5 of this Act regard shall be had to all the circumstances from which any inference can reasonably be drawn as to the accuracy or otherwise of the statement and, in particular—

    (*a*) in the case of a statement falling within section 2(1) or 3(1) or (2) of this Act, to the question whether or not the statement was made contemporaneously with the occurrence or existence of the facts stated, and to the question whether or not the maker of the statement had any incentive to conceal or misrepresent the facts;

    (*b*) in the case of a statement falling within section 4(1) of this Act to the question whether or not the person who originally supplied the information from which the record containing the statement was compiled did so contemporaneously with the occurrence or existence of the facts dealt with in that information, and to the question whether or not that person, or any person concerned with compiling or keeping the record containing the statement, had any incentive to conceal or misrepresent the facts; and

(c) in the case of a statement falling within section 5(1) of this Act, to the question whether or not the information which the information contained in the statement reproduces or is derived from was supplied to the relevant computer, or recorded for the purpose of being supplied thereto, contemporaneously with the occurrence or existence of the facts dealt with in that information, and to the question whether or not any person concerned with the supply of information to that computer, or with the operation of that computer or any equipment by means of which the document containing the statement was produced by it, had any incentive to conceal or misrepresent the facts.

(4) For the purpose of any enactment or rule of law or practice requiring evidence to be corroborated or regulating the manner in which uncorroborated evidence is to be treated—

(a) a statement which is admissible in evidence by virtue of section 2 or 3 of this Act shall not be capable of corroborating evidence given by the maker of the statement; and

(b) a statement which is admissible in evidence by virtue of section 4 of this Act shall not be capable of corroborating evidence given by the person who originally supplied the information from which the record containing the statement was compiled.

(5) If any person in a certificate tendered in evidence in civil proceedings by virtue of section 5(4) of this Act wilfully makes a statement material in those proceedings which he knows to be false or does not believe to be true, he shall be liable on conviction on indictment to imprisonment for a term not exceeding two years or a fine or both.

Admissibility of evidence as to credibility of maker etc. of statement admitted under section 2 or 4

7.—(1) Subject to rules of court, where in any civil proceedings a statement made by a person who is not called as a witness in those proceedings is given in evidence by virtue of section 2 of this Act—

(a) any evidence which, if that person had been so called, would be admissible for the purpose of destroying or supporting his credibility as a witness shall be admissible for that purpose in those proceedings; and

(b) evidence tending to prove that, whether before or after he made that statement, that person made (whether orally or in a document or otherwise) another statement inconsistent therewith shall be admissible for the purpose of showing that that person has contradicted himself:

Provided that nothing in this subsection shall enable evidence to be given of any matter of which, if the person in question had been called as a witness and had denied that matter in cross-examination, evidence could not have been adduced by the cross-examining party.

(2) Subsection (1) above shall apply in relation to a statement given in evidence by virtue of section 4 of this Act as it applies in relation to a statement given in evidence by virtue of section 2 of this Act, except that references to the person who made the statement and to his making the statement shall be construed respectively as references to the person who originally supplied the information from which the record containing the statement was compiled and to his supplying that information.

(3) Section 3(1) of this Act shall apply to any statement proved by virtue of subsection (1)(*b*) above as it applies to a previous inconsistent or contradictory statement made by a person called as a witness which is proved as mentioned in paragraph (*a*) of the said section 3(1).

Rules of court

8.—(1) Provision shall be made by rules of court as to the procedure which, subject to any exceptions provided for in the rules, must be followed and the other conditions which, subject as aforesaid, must be fulfilled before a statement can be given in evidence in civil proceedings by virtue of section 2, 4 or 5 of this Act.

(2) Rules of court made in pursuance of subsection (1) above shall in particular, subject to such exceptions (if any) as may be provided for in the rules—

(*a*) require a party to any civil proceedings who desires to give in evidence any such statement as is mentioned in that subsection to give to every other party to the proceedings such notice of his desire to do so and such particulars of or relating to the statement as may be specified in the rules, including particulars of such one or more of the persons connected with the making or recording of the statement or, in the case of a statement falling within section 5(1) of this Act, such one or more of the persons concerned as mentioned in section 6(3)(*c*) of this Act as the rules may in any case require; and

(*b*) enable any party who receives such notice as aforesaid by counternotice to require any person of whom particulars were given with the notice to be called as a witness in the proceedings unless that person is dead, or beyond the seas, or unfit by reason of his bodily or mental condition to attend as a witness, or cannot with reasonable diligence be identified or found, or cannot reasonably be expected (having regard to the time which has elapsed since he was connected or concerned as aforesaid and to all the circumstances) to have any recollection of matters relevant to the accuracy or otherwise of the statement.

(3) Rules of court made in pursuance of subsection (1) above—

(*a*) may confer on the court in any civil proceedings a discretion to allow a statement falling within section 2(1), 4(1) or 5(1) of this Act to be given in evidence notwithstanding that any requirement of the rules affecting the admissibility of that statement has not been complied with, but except in pursuance of paragraph (*b*) below shall not confer on the court a discretion to exclude such a statement where the requirements of the rules affecting its admissibility have been complied with;

(*b*) may confer on the court power, where a party to any civil proceedings has given notice that he desires to give in evidence—

(i) a statement falling within section 2(1) of this Act which was made by a person, whether orally or in a document, in the course of giving evidence in some other legal proceedings (whether civil or criminal); or

(ii) a statement falling within section 4(1) of this Act which is contained in a record of any direct oral evidence given in some other legal proceedings (whether civil or criminal),

to give directions on the application of any party to the proceedings as to whether, and if so on what conditions, the party desiring to give the statement in evidence will be permitted to do so and (where applicable) as to the manner in which that statement and any other evidence given in those other proceedings is to be proved; and

(*c*) may make different provision for different circumstances, and in particular may make different provision with respect to statements falling within sections 2(1), 4(1) and 5(1) of this Act respectively;

and any discretion conferred on the court by rules of court made as aforesaid may be either a general discretion or a discretion exercisable only in such circumstances as may be specified in the rules.

(4) Rules of court may make provision for preventing a party to any civil proceedings (subject to any exceptions provided for in the rules) from adducing in relation to a person who is not called as a witness in those proceedings any evidence which could otherwise be adduced by him by virtue of section 7 of this Act unless that party has in pursuance of the rules given in respect of that person such a counter-notice as is mentioned in subsection (2)(*b*) above.

(5) In deciding for the purposes of any rules of court made in pursuance of this section whether or not a person is fit to attend as a witness, a court may act on a certificate purporting to be a certificate of a fully registered medical practitioner.

*(6) Nothing in the foregoing provisions of this section shall prejudice the generally of section 75 of the County Courts Act 1984, section 144 of the Magistrates' Courts Act 1980 or any other enactment conferring power to make rules of court; and nothing in section 75(2) of the County Courts Act 1984 or any other enactment restricting the matters with respect to which rules of court may be made shall prejudice the making of rules of court with respect to any matter mentioned in the foregoing provisions of this section or the operation of any rules of court made with respect to any such matter.

---

* amended by Magistrates' Courts Act 1980, s.154 and Sch. 7; Supreme Court Act 1981, s.152(4) and Sch. 7; and County Courts Act 1984, s.148(1) and Sch. 2 para 33.

Admissibility of certain hearsay evidence formerly admissible at common law

9.—(1) In any civil proceedings a statement which, if this Part of this Act had not been passed, would by virtue of any rule of law mentioned in subsection (2) below have been admissible as evidence of any fact stated therein shall be admissible as evidence of that fact by virtue of this subsection.

(2) The rules of law referred to in subsection (1) above are the following, that is to say any rule of law—

(*a*) whereby in any civil proceedings an admission adverse to a party to the proceedings, whether made by that party or by another person, may be given in evidence against that party for the purpose of proving any fact stated in the admission;

(*b*) whereby in any civil proceedings published works dealing with matters of a public nature (for example, histories, scientific works, dictionaries and maps) are admissible as evidence of facts of a public nature stated therein;

(*c*) whereby in any civil proceedings public documents (for example, public registers, and returns made under public authority with respect to matters of public interest) are admissible as evidence of facts stated therein; or

(*d*) whereby in any civil proceedings records (for example, the records of certain courts, treaties, Crown grants, pardons and commissions) are admissible as evidence of facts stated therein.

In this subsection "admission" includes any representation of fact, whether made in words or otherwise.

(3) In any civil proceedings a statement which tends to establish reputation or family tradition with respect to any matter and which, if this Act had not been passed, would have been admissible in evidence by virtue of any rule of law mentioned in subsection (4) below—

(*a*) shall be admissible in evidence by virtue of this paragraph in so far as it is not capable of being rendered admissible under section 2 or 4 of this Act; and

(*b*) if given in evidence under this Part of this Act (whether by virtue of paragraph (*a*) above or otherwise) shall by virtue of this paragraph be admissible as evidence of the matter reputed or handed down;

and, without prejudice to paragraph (*b*) above, reputation shall for the purposes of this Part of this Act be treated as a fact and not as a statement or multiplicity of statements dealing with the matter reputed.

(4) The rules of law referred to in subsection (3) above are the following, that is to say any rule of law—

(*a*) whereby in any civil proceedings evidence of a person's reputation is admissible for the purpose of establishing his good or bad character;

(*b*) whereby in any civil proceedings involving a question of pedigree or in which the existence of a marriage is in issue evidence of reputation or family tradition is admissible for the purpose of proving or disproving pedigree or the existence of the marriage, as the case may be; or

(*c*) whereby in any civil proceedings evidence of reputation or family tradition is admissible for the purpose of proving or disproving the existence of any public or general right or of identifying any person or thing.

(5) It is hereby declared that in so far as any statement is admissible in any civil proceedings by virtue of subsection (1) or (3)(*a*) above, it may be given in evidence in those proceedings notwithstanding anything in sections 2 to 7 of this Act or in any rules of court made in pursuance of section 8 of this Act.

(6) The words in which any rule of law mentioned in subsection (2) or (4) above is there described are intended only to identify the rule in question and shall not be construed as altering that rule in any way.

Interpretation of Part I, and application to arbitrations, etc.

10.—(1) In this Part of this Act—

"computer" has the meaning assigned by section 5 of this Act;

"document" includes, in addition to a document in writing—

(*a*) any map, plan, graph or drawing;

(*b*) any photograph;

(*c*) any disc, tape, sound track or other device in which sounds or other data (not being visual images) are embodied so as to be capable (with or without the aid of some other equipment) of being reproduced therefrom; and

(*d*) any film, negative, tape or other device in which one or more visual images are embodied so as to be capable (as aforesaid) of being reproduced therefrom;

"film" includes a microfilm;

"statement" includes any representation of fact, whether made in words or otherwise.

(2) In this Part of this Act any reference to a copy of a document includes—

(*a*) in the case of a document falling within paragraph (*c*) but not (*d*) of the definition of "document" in the foregoing subsection, a transcript of the sounds or other data embodied therein;

(*b*) in the case of a document falling within paragraph (*d*) but not (*c*) of that definition, a reproduction or still reproduction of the image or images embodied therein, whether enlarged or not;

(*c*) in the case of a document falling within both those paragraphs, such a transcript together with such a still reproduction; and

(*d*) in the case of a document not falling within the said paragraph (*d*) of which a visual image is embodied in a document falling within that paragraph, a reproduction of that image, whether enlarged or not,

and any reference to a copy of the material part of a document shall be construed accordingly.

*(3) For the purposes of the application of this Part of this Act in relation

to any such civil proceedings as are mentioned in section 18(1)(*a*) and (*b*) of this Act, other than civil proceedings on a reference to arbitration under section 64 of the County Courts Act 1984, any rules of court made for the purposes of this Act under section 99 of the Supreme Court of Judicature (Consolidation) Act 1925 shall (except in so far as their operation is excluded by agreement) apply, subject to such modifications as may be appropriate, in like manner as they apply in relation to civil proceedings in the High Court:

*(3A) For the purposes of the application of this Part of this Act in relation to proceedings on an arbitration under section 64 of the County Courts Act 1984 any rules made for the purposes of this Act under section 75 of that Act shall (except in so far as their operation is excluded by agreement) apply, subject to such modifications as may be appropriate, in like manner as they apply in relation to proceedings in the county court.

(4) If any question arises as to what are, for the purposes of any such civil proceedings as are mentioned in section 18(1)(*a*) or (*b*) of this Act, the appropriate modifications of any such rule of court as is mentioned in subsection (3) above, that question shall, in default of agreement, be determined by the tribunal or the arbitrator or umpire, as the case may be.

* amended and inserted by County Courts Act 1984, s.148(1) and Sch. 2 para 34.

General

General interpretation and savings

18.—(1) In this Act "civil proceedings" includes, in addition to civil proceedings in any of the ordinary courts of law—

(*a*) civil proceedings before any other tribunal, being proceedings in relation to which the strict rules of evidence apply; and

(*b*) an arbitration or reference, whether under an enactment or not,

but does not include civil proceedings in relation to which the strict rules of evidence do not apply.

(2) In this Act—

"court" does not include a court-martial, and, in relation to an arbitration or reference, means the arbitrator or umpire and, in relation to proceedings before a tribunal (not being one of the ordinary courts of law) means the tribunal;

"legal proceedings" includes an arbitration or reference, whether under an enactment or not;

and for the avoidance of doubt it is hereby declared that in this Act, and in any amendment made by this Act in any other enactment, references to a person's husband or wife do not include references to a person who is no longer married to that person.

(3) Any reference in this Act to any other enactment is a reference thereto as amended, and includes a reference thereto as applied, by or under any other enactment.

(4) Nothing in this Act shall prejudice the operation of any enactment which provides (in whatever words) that any answer or evidence given by a person in specified circumstances shall not be admissible in evidence

against him or some other person in any proceedings or class of proceedings (however described).

In this subsection the reference to giving evidence is a reference to giving evidence in any manner, whether by furnishing information, making discovery, producing documents or otherwise.

(5) Nothing in this Act shall prejudice—

(*a*) any power of a court, in any legal proceedings, to exclude evidence (whether by preventing questions from being put or otherwise) at its discretion; or

(*b*) the operation of any agreement (whenever made) between the parties to any legal proceedings as to the evidence which is to be admissible (whether generally or for any particular purpose) in those proceedings.

(6) It is hereby declared that where, by reason of any defect of speech or hearing from which he is suffering, a person called as a witness in any legal proceedings gives his evidence in writing or by signs, that evidence is to be treated for the purposes of this Act as being given orally.

Town and Country Planning Act 1971
SCHEDULE 9

Sections 36, 88, 95, 97 and 103 and paragraph 8 of Schedule 11

DETERMINATION OF CERTAIN APPEALS BY PERSON APPOINTED BY SECRETARY OF STATE

Determination of appeals by appointed person

1.—(1) An appeal to which this Schedule applies, being an appeal of a prescribed class, shall, except in such classes of case as may for the time being be prescribed or as may be specified in directions given by the Secretary of State, be determined by a person appointed by the Secretary of State for the purpose instead of by the Secretary of State.

(2) Regulations made for the purpose of this paragraph may provide for the giving of publicity to any directions given by the Secretary of State under this paragraph.

(3) This paragraph shall not affect any provision contained in this Act or any instrument thereunder that an appeal shall lie to, or a notice of appeal shall be served on, the Secretary of State.

Powers and duties of person determining appeal

2.—(1) A person appointed under this Schedule to determine an appeal shall have the like powers and duties in relation to the appeal as the Secretary of State under whichever are relevant of the following provisions, that is to say—

  (a) in relation to appeals under section 36 subsections (3) and (5) of that section;
  (b) in relation to appeals under section 88 subsections (4) to (6) of that section;
  (c) in relation to appeals under section 95 subsections (2) and (3) of that section;
  (d) in relation to appeals under section 97 subsections (4) and (5) of that section;
  (e) in relation to appeals under section 103 sections 88(4) and (5) of this Act;
  (f) in relation to appeals under paragraph 8 of Schedule 11 of this Act, sub-paragraph (3) of that paragraph.

(2) The provisions of section 36(4), 88(2), 95(4), 97(2) and paragraph 8(4) of Schedule 11 to this Act relating to the affording of an opportunity of appearing before, and being heard by, a person appointed by the Secretary of State, shall not apply to an appeal which falls to be determined by a person appointed under this Schedule but before the determination of any such appeal the Secretary of State shall, unless (in the case of an appeal under section 36) the appeal is referred to a Planning Inquiry Commission under section 48 of this Act, ask the applicant or appellant, as the case may require, and the local planning authority whether they wish to appear before and be heard by the person so appointed, and—

  (a) the appeal may be determined without a hearing of the parties if both of them express a wish not to appear and be heard as aforesaid; and
  (b) the person so appointed shall, if either of the parties expresses a wish to appear and be heard, afford to both of them an opportunity of so doing.

(3) Where an appeal to which this Schedule applies has been determined by a person appointed under this Schedule, his decision shall be treated as that of the Secretary of State and—

  (a) except as provided by Part XII of this Act, the validity of his decision shall not be questioned in any proceedings whatsoever;
  (b) it shall not be a ground of application to the High Court under section 245 of this Act, or of appeal to the High Court under section 246 or 247 thereof, that the appeal ought to have been determined by the Secretary of State and not by that person, unless the challenge to the person's power to determine the appeal was made (either by the appellant or the local planning authority) before his decision on the appeal was given.

(4) Where in any enactment (including this Act) there is a reference to the Secretary of State in a context relating or capable of relating to an appeal to which this Schedule applies, or to any thing done or authorised or

required to be done by, to or before the Secretary of State on or in connection with any such appeal, then so far as the context permits it shall be construed, in relation to an appeal determined or falling to be determined by a person appointed under this Schedule, as a reference to that person.

Determination of appeals by Secretary of State

3.—(1) The Secretary of State may, if he thinks fit, direct that an appeal, which by virtue of paragraph 1 of this Schedule and apart from this sub-paragraph, falls to be determined by a person appointed by the Secretary of State shall instead be determined by the Secretary of State.

(2) A direction under this paragraph shall state the reasons for which it is given and shall be served on the person, if any, so appointed, the applicant or appellant, the local planning authority and any person who has made representations relating to the subject matter of the appeal which the authority are required to take into account under section 29(3)(*a*) of this Act.

(3) Where in consequence of a direction under this paragraph an appeal to which this Schedule applies falls to be determined by the Secretary of State, the provisions of this Act which are relevant to the appeal shall, subject to the following provisions of this paragraph, apply to the appeal as if this Schedule had never applied to it.

(4) Where in consequence of a direction under this paragraph the Secretary of State determines an appeal himself, he shall, unless (in the case of an appeal under section 36) the appeal is referred to a Planning Inquiry Commission under section 48 of this Act, afford to the applicant or appellant, the local planning authority and any person who has made any such representations as aforesaid an opportunity of appearing before and being heard by a person appointed by the Secretary of State for that purpose either—

> (*a*) if the reasons for the direction raise matters with respect to which either the applicant or appellant, or the local planning authority or any such person, have not made representations; or
>
> (*b*) if the applicant or appellant or the local planning authority had not been asked in pursuance of paragraph 2(2) of this Schedule whether they wished to appear before and be heard by a person appointed to hear the appeal, or had been asked that question and had expressed no wish in answer thereto, or had expressed a wish to appear and be heard as aforesaid, but had not been afforded an opportunity of doing so.

(5) Except as provided by sub-paragraph (4) of this paragraph, where the Secretary of State determines an appeal in consequence of a direction under this paragraph he shall not be obliged to afford any person an opportunity of appearing before and being heard by a person appointed for the purpose, or of making fresh representations or making or withdrawing any representations already made; and in determining the appeal the Secretary of State may take into account any report made to him by any person previously appointed to determine it.

Appointment of another person to determine appeal

4.—(1) Where the Secretary of State has appointed a person to determine an appeal under this Schedule the Secretary of State may, at any time before the determination of the appeal, appoint another person to determine it instead of the first-mentioned person.

(2) If before the appointment of a person under this paragraph to determine an appeal, the Secretary of State had with reference to the person previously appointed, asked the question referred to in paragraph 2(2) of this Schedule, the question need not be asked again with reference to the person appointed under this paragraph and any answers to the question shall be treated as given with reference to him, but—

> (*a*) the consideration of the appeal or any inquiry or other hearing in connection therewith, if already begun, shall be begun afresh; and
>
> (*b*) it shall not be necessary to afford any person an opportunity of making fresh representations or modifying or withdrawing any representations already made.

Local inquiries and hearings

5. —(1) A person appointed under this Schedule to determine an appeal may (whether or not the parties have asked for an opportunity to appear and be heard) hold a local inquiry in connection with the appeal and shall hold such an inquiry if the Secretary of State directs him to do so.

(2) Subject to sub-paragraph (3) of this paragraph, the costs—

> (*a*) of any hearing held by virtue of paragraph 2(2)(*b*) of this Schedule; and
>
> (*b*) of any inquiry held by virtue of this paragraph,

shall be defrayed by the Secretary of State.

*(3) Subsections (2) to (5) of section 250 of the Local Government Act 1972 (evidence and costs at local inquiries) shall apply in relation to an inquiry held under this paragraph as they apply in relation to an inquiry caused to be held by a department under subsection (1) of that section, with the substitution for references to a department (other than the first reference in subsection (4)) of references to the Secretary of State.

* amended by Local Government Act 1972, s.272(2).

Stopping of appeals

6. If before or during the determination of an appeal under section 36 of this Act which is to be or is being determined in accordance with paragraph 1 of this Schedule, the Secretary of State forms the opinion mentioned in subsection (7) of that section, he may direct that the determination shall not be begun or proceeded with.

Supplementary provisions

7.—(1) The Tribunals and Inquiries Act 1971 shall apply to a local inquiry or other hearing held in pursuance of this Schedule as it applies to a statutory inquiry held by the Secretary of State, but as if in section 12(1) of that Act (statement of reasons for decisions) the reference to any decision taken by the Secretary of State were a reference to a decision taken by a person appointed to determine the relevant appeal under this Schedule.

(2) The functions of determining an appeal and doing anything in connection therewith conferred by this Schedule on a person appointed to determine an appeal thereunder who is an officer of the Department of the Environment or the Welsh Office shall be treated for the purposes of the Parliamentary Commissioner Act 1967—

  (*a*) if he was appointed by the Secretary of State for the time being having general responsibility in planning matters in relation to England, as functions of that Department; and
  (*b*) if he was appointed by the Secretary of State for the time being having general responsibility in planning matters in relation to Wales, as functions of the Welsh Office.

Civil Evidence Act 1972

Application of Part I of Civil Evidence Act 1968 to statements of opinion

1.—(1) Subject to the provisions of this section, Part I (hearsay evidence) of the Civil Evidence Act 1968, except section 5 (statements produced by computers) shall apply in relation to statements of opinion as it applies in relation to statements of fact, subject to the necessary modifications and in particular the modification that any reference to a fact stated in a statement shall be construed as a reference to a matter dealt with therein.

(2) Section 4 (admissibility of certain records) of the Civil Evidence Act 1968, as applied by subsection (1) above, shall not render admissible in any civil proceedings a statement of opinion contained in a record unless that statement would be admissible in those proceedings if made in the course of giving oral evidence by the person who originally supplied the information from which the record was compiled; but where a statement of opinion contained in a record deals with a matter on which the person who originally supplied the information from which the record was compiled is (or would if living be) qualified to give oral expert evidence, the said section 4, as applied by subsection (1) above, shall have effect in relation to that statement as if so much of subsection (1) of that section as requires personal knowledge on the part of that person were omitted.

Rules of court with respect to expert reports and oral expert evidence

2.—(1) If and so far as rules of court so provide, subsection (2) of section 2 of the Civil Evidence Act 1968 (which imposes restrictions on the giving of a statement in evidence by virtue of that section on behalf of a party who has called or intends to call as a witness the maker of the statement) shall not apply to statements (whether of fact or opinion) contained in expert reports.

(2) In so far as they relate to statements (whether of fact or opinion) contained in expert reports, rules of court made in pursuance of subsection (1) of section 8 of the Civil Evidence Act 1968 as to the procedure to be followed and the other conditions to be fulfilled before a statement can be given in evidence in civil proceedings by virtue of section 2 of that Act (admissibility of out-of-court statements) shall not be subject to the require-

ments of subsection (2) of the said section 8 (which specifies certain matters
of procedure for which provision must ordinarily be made by rules of court
made in pursuance of the said subsection (1)).

(3) Notwithstanding any enactment or rule of law by virtue of which
documents prepared for the purpose of pending or contemplated civil proceedings or in connection with the obtaining or giving of legal advice are in
certain circumstances privileged from disclosure, provision may be made by
rules of court—

> (*a*) for enabling the court in any civil proceedings to direct, with
> respect to medical matters or matters of any other class which may
> be specified in the direction, that the parties or some of them shall
> each by such date as may be so specified (or such later date as may
> be permitted or agreed in accordance with the rules) disclose to the
> other or others in the form of one or more expert reports the expert
> evidence on matters of that class which he proposes to adduce as
> part of his case at the trial; and
>
> (*b*) for prohibiting a party who fails to comply with a direction given in
> any such proceedings under rules of court made by virtue of para-
> graph (*a*) above from adducing in evidence by virtue of section 2 of
> the Civil Evidence Act 1968 (admissibility of out-of-court state-
> ments), except with the leave of the court, any statement (whether
> of fact or opinion) contained in any expert report whatsoever in so
> far as that statement deals with matters of any class specified in the
> direction.

(4) Provision may be made by rules of court as to the conditions subject to
which oral expert evidence may be given in civil proceedings.

(5) Without prejudice to the generality of subsection (4) above, rules of
court made in pursuance of that subsection may make provision for pro-
hibiting a party who fails to comply with a direction given as mentioned in
subsection (3)(*b*) above from adducing, except with the leave of the court,
any oral expert evidence whatsoever with respect to matters of any class
specified in the direction.

(6) Any rules of court made in pursuance of this section may make
different provisions for different classes of cases, for expert reports dealing
with matters of different classes, and for other different circumstances.

(7) References in this section to an expert report are references to a
written report by a person dealing wholly or mainly with matters on which
he is (or would if living be) qualified to give expert evidence.

*(8) Nothing in the foregoing provisions of this section shall prejudice the
generality of section 75 of the County Courts Act 1984, section 144 of the
Magistrates' Courts Act 1980 or any other enactment conferring power to
make rules of court; and nothing in section 75(2) of the County Courts Act
1984 or any other enactment restricting the matters with respect to which
rules of court may be made shall prejudice the making of rules of court in
pursuance of this section or the operation of any rules of court so made.

* amended by Magistrates' Courts Act 1980, s.154 and Sch. 7; Supreme Court Act 1981, s.152(4)
  and Sch. 7 and County Courts Act 1984, s.148(1) and Sch. 2 para 43.

Admissibility of expert opinion and certain expressions of non-expert opinion

3.—(1) Subject to any rules of court made in pursuance of Part I of the Civil Evidence Act 1968 or this Act, where a person is called as a witness in any civil proceedings, his opinion on any relevant matter on which he is qualified to give expert evidence shall be admissible in evidence.

(2) It is hereby declared that where a person is called as a witness in any civil proceedings, a statement of opinion by him on any relevant matter on which he is not qualified to give expert evidence, if made as a way of conveying relevant facts personally perceived by him, is admissible as evidence of what he perceived.

(3) In this section "relevant matter" includes an issue in the proceedings in question.

Interpretation, application to arbitrations, etc., and savings

5.—(1) In this Act "civil proceedings" and "court" have the meanings assigned by section 18(1) and (2) of the Civil Evidence Act 1968.

(2) Subsections (3) and (4) of section 10 of the Civil Evidence Act 1968 shall apply for the purposes of the application of sections 2 and 4 of this Act in relation to any such civil proceedings as are mentioned in section 18(1)(*a*) and (*b*) of that Act (that is to say civil proceedings before a tribunal other than one of the ordinary courts of law, being proceedings in relation to which the strict rules of evidence apply, and an arbitration or reference, whether under an enactment or not) as they apply for the purposes of the application of Part I of that Act in relation to any such civil proceedings.

(3) Nothing in this Act shall prejudice—

    (*a*) any power of a court, in any civil proceedings, to exclude evidence (whether by preventing questions from being put or otherwise) at its discretion; or

    (*b*) the operation of any agreement (whenever made) between the parties to any civil proceedings as to the evidence which is to be admissible (whether generally or for any particular purpose) in those proceedings.

Rent Act 1977

Control of rents

Reference of contracts to rent tribunals and obtaining by them of information

*77.—(1) Either the lessor or the lessee under a restricted contract or the local authority may refer the contract to the rent tribunal.

(2) Where a restricted contract is referred to a rent tribunal under subsection (1) above they may, by notice in writing served on the lessor, require him to give to them, within such period (not less than 7 days from the date

of the service of the notice) as may be specified in the notice, such information as they may reasonably require regarding such of the prescribed particulars relating to the contract as are specified in the notice.

(3) If, within the period specified in a notice under subsection (2) above, the lessor fails without reasonable cause to comply with the provisions of the notice he shall be liable on a first conviction to a fine not exceeding £50 and on a second or subsequent conviction to a fine not exceeding £100.

(4) Proceedings for an offence under this section shall not be instituted otherwise than by the local authority.

* amended by Housing Act 1980, s.152(3) and Sch. 26.

Powers of rent tribunals on reference of contracts

78.—(1) Where a restricted contract is referred to a rent tribunal and the reference is not, before the tribunal have entered upon consideration of it, withdrawn by the party or authority who made it, the tribunal shall consider it.

*(2) After making such inquiry as they think fit and giving to—

(*a*) each party to the contract, and
(*b*) if the general management of the dwelling is vested in and exercisable by a housing authority, that authority,

an opportunity of being heard or, at his or their option, of submitting representations in writing, the tribunal, subject to subsections (3) and (4) below,—

(i) shall approve the rent payable under the contract, or
(ii) shall reduce or increase the rent to such sum as they may, in all the circumstances, think reasonable, or
(iii) may, if they think fit in all the circumstances, dismiss the reference,

and shall notify the parties of their decision.

(3) On the reference of a restricted contract relating to a dwelling for which a rent is registered under Part IV of this Act, the rent tribunal may not reduce the rent payable under the contract below the amount which would be recoverable from the tenant under a regulated tenancy of the dwelling.

(4) An approval, reduction or increase under this section may be limited to rent payable in respect of a particular period.

*(5) In subsection (2) above "housing authority" means a council which is a local authority for the purposes of Part V of the Housing Act 1957.

* amended by Housing Act 1980, s.152(1) and (3), Sch. 26 and Sch. 25 para 42.

SCHEDULE 11

Section 67

APPLICATIONS FOR REGISTRATION OF RENT

PART I

APPLICATION UNSUPPORTED BY CERTIFICATE OF FAIR RENT

Procedure on application to rent officer

1. On receiving any application for the registration of a rent, the rent officer may, by notice in writing served on the landlord or on the tenant (whether or not the applicant or one of the applicants), require him to give to the rent officer, within such period of not less than 7 days from the service of the notice as may be specified in the notice, such information as he may reasonably require regarding such of the particulars contained in the application as may be specified in the notice.

*2.—(1) Where the application is made jointly by the landlord and the tenant and it appears to the rent officer, after making such inquiry, if any, as he thinks fit and considering any information supplied to him in pursuance of paragraph 1 above, that the rent specified in the application is a fair rent, he may register that rent without further proceedings.

(2) Where the rent officer registers a rent under this paragraph he shall notify the landlord and tenant accordingly.

*3.—(1) In the case of an application which does not fall within paragraph 2 above, the rent officer shall serve on the landlord and on the tenant a notice inviting the person on whom the notice is served to state in writing, within a period of not less than seven days after the service of the notice, whether he wishes the rent officer to consider, in consultation with the landlord and the tenant, what rent ought to be registered for the dwelling-house.

(2) A notice served under sub-paragraph (1) above on the person who did not make the application shall be accompanied—

(*a*) by a copy of the application; and

(*b*) where, in pursuance of section 67(2)(*b*), the application was accompanied by details of the landlord's expenditure in connection with the provisions of services, by a copy of those details.

*3A. If, after service of a notice by the rent officer under paragraph 3 (1) above, no request in writing is made within the period specified in the notice for the rent to be considered as mentioned in that paragraph, the rent officer after considering what rent ought to be registered or, as the case may be, whether a different rent ought to be registered, may—

(*a*) determine a fair rent and register it as the rent for the dwelling-house; or

(*b*) confirm the rent for the time being registered and note the confirmation in the register; or

(*c*) serve a notice under paragraph 4 (2) below.

* substituted by Regulated Tenancies (Procedure) Regulations 1980, reg 2 and Sch. 1 para 1.

The Surveyor in Court

*4.—(1) Where, in response to a notice served by the rent officer under paragraph 3(1) above, the landlord or the tenant states in writing that he wishes the rent to be considered as mentioned in that paragraph, the rent officer shall serve a notice under this paragraph.

*(2) A notice under this paragraph shall be served on the landlord and on the tenant informing them that the rent officer proposes, at a time (which shall not be earlier than 7 days after the service of the notice or 14 days in a case falling within paragraph 3(2)(*b*) above) and place specified in the notice, to consider in consultation with the landlord and the tenant, or such of them as may appear at that time and place, what rent ought to be registered for the dwelling-house or, as the case may be, whether a different rent ought to be so registered.

(3) At any such consultation the landlord and the tenant may each be represented by a person authorised by him in that behalf, whether or not that person is of counsel or a solicitor.

*(4) The rent officer may, where he considers it appropriate, arrange for consultations in respect of one dwelling-house to be held together with consultations in respect of one or more other dwelling-houses.

* substituted, amended and inserted by Regulated Tenancies (Procedure) Regulations 1980, reg 2 and Sch. 1 paras 2–4.

5. After considering, in accordance with paragraph 4 above, what rent ought to be registered or, as the case may be, whether a different rent ought to be registered, the rent officer shall, as the case may require,—

> (*a*) determine a fair rent and register it as the rent for the dwelling-house; or
>
> (*b*) confirm the rent for the time being registered and note the confirmation in the register;

and shall notify the landlord and the tenant accordingly by a notice stating that if, within 28 days of the service of the notice or such longer period as he or a rent assessment committee may allow, an objection in writing is received by the rent officer from the landlord or the tenant the matter will be referred to a rent assessment committee.

*5A. Where a rent has been registered or confirmed by the rent officer under paragraph 3A or 5 above, he shall notify the landlord and the tenant accordingly by a notice stating that if, within 28 days of the service of the notice or such longer period as he or a rent assessment committee may allow, an objection in writing is received by the rent officer from the landlord or the tenant the matter will be referred to a rent assessment committee.

* amended by Regulated Tenancies (Procedure) Regulations 1980, reg 2 and Sch. 1 para 5.

*6.—(1) If such an objection as is mentioned in paragraph 5A above is received, then—

> (*a*) if it is received within the period of 28 days specified in that paragraph or a rent assessment committee so direct, the rent officer shall refer the matter to a rent assessment committee;

(*b*) if it is received after the expiry of that period the rent officer may either refer the matter to a rent assessment committee or seek the directions of a rent assessment committee whether so to refer it.

(2) The rent officer shall indicate in the register whether the matter has been referred to a rent assessment committee in pursuance of this paragraph.

* amended by Regulated Tenancies (Procedure) Regulations 1980, reg 2 and Sch. 1 para 6.

Determination of fair rent by rent assessment committee

*7.—(1) The rent assessment committee to whom a matter is referred under paragraph 6 above—

(*a*) may by notice in the prescribed form served on the landlord or the tenant require him to give to the committee, within such period of not less than 14 days from the service of the notice as may be specified in the notice, such further information, in addition to any given to the rent officer in pursuance of paragraph 1 above, as they may reasonably require; and

(*b*) shall serve on the landlord and on the tenant a notice specifying a period of not less than 7 days from the service of the notice during which either representations in writing or a request to make oral representations may be made by him to the committee.

(2) If any person fails without reasonable cause to comply with any notice served on him under sub-paragraph (1)(*a*) above, he shall be liable on a first conviction to a fine not exceeding £50 and, on a second or subsequent conviction, to a fine not exceeding £100.

(3) Where an offence under sub-paragraph (2) above committed by a body corporate is proved to have been committed with the consent or connivance of, or to be attributable to any neglect on the part of, any director, manager or secretary or other similar officer of the body corporate or any person who was purporting to act in any such capacity, he as well as the body corporate shall be guilty of that offence and shall be liable to be proceeded against and punished accordingly.

* amended by Rent Assessment Committees (England and Wales) (Amendment) Regulations 1981, reg 3.

8. Where, within the period specified in paragraph 7(1)(*b*) above, or such further period as the committee may allow, the landlord or the tenant requests to make oral representations the committee shall give him an opportunity to be heard either in person or by a person authorised by him in that behalf, whether or not that person is of counsel or a solicitor.

9.—(1) The committee shall make such inquiry, if any, as they think fit and consider any information supplied or representation made to them in pursuance of paragraph 7 or paragraph 8 above and—

(*a*) if it appears to them that the rent registered or confirmed by the rent officer is a fair rent, they shall confirm that rent;

(*b*) if it does not appear to them that the rent is a fair rent, they shall determine a fair rent for the dwelling house.

*(2) Where the committee confirm or determine a rent under this paragraph they shall notify the landlord, the tenant and the rent officer of their decision and of the date on which it was made.

(3) On receiving the notification, the rent officer shall, as the case may require, either indicate in the register that the rent has been confirmed or register the rent determined by the committee as the rent for the dwelling-house.

* amended by Housing Act 1980, s.61(7).

PART II

APPLICATION SUPPORTED BY CERTIFICATE OF FAIR RENT (EXCEPT WHERE CERTIFICATE ISSUED BY VIRTUE OF PART VIII)

Procedure on application to rent officer

10.—(1) On receiving an application for the registration of a rent which is made as mentioned in section 69 (4) of this Act, the rent officer shall ascertain whether the works specified in the certificate have been carried out in accordance with the plans and specifications which accompanied the application for the certificate or, as the case may be, whether—

(a) the condition of the dwelling-house is the same as at the date of the certificate, and

(b) if any furniture is or is to be provided for use under a regulated tenancy of the dwelling-house, the quantity, quality and condition of the furniture in the dwelling-house accords with the prescribed particulars contained in the application for the certificate.

(2) If the rent officer is satisfied that the works have been so carried out or, as the case may be, that—

(a) the dwelling-house is in the same condition as at the date of the certificate, and

(b) if any furniture is or is to be provided for use under a regulated tenancy of the dwelling-house, the quantity, quality and condition of the furniture in the dwelling-house accords with the prescribed particulars contained in the application for the certificate,

he shall register the rent in accordance with the certificate.

(3) If the rent officer is not satisfied as mentioned in sub-paragraph (2) above, he shall serve on the applicant a notice stating the matters with respect to which he is not so satisfied and informing him that if, within 14 days from the service of the notice or such longer period as the rent officer or a rent assessment committee may allow, the applicant makes a request in writing to that effect, the rent officer will refer the matter to a rent assessment committee.

11. If such a request as is mentioned in paragraph 10 (3) above is made, then—

(a) if it is made within the period of 14 days specified in that paragraph or a rent assessment committee so direct, the rent officer shall refer the matter to a rent assessment committee;

(b) if it is made after the expiry of that period, the rent officer may either refer the matter to a rent assessment committee or seek the directions of a rent assessment committee whether so to refer it.

Procedure on reference to rent assessment committee

12.—(1) The rent assessment committee to whom a matter is referred under paragraph 11 above shall give the applicant an opportunity to make representations in writing or to be heard either in person or by a person authorised by him in that behalf, whether or not that person is of counsel or a solicitor.

(2) After considering any representations made under sub-paragraph (1) above, the rent assessment committee shall notify the rent officer and the applicant whether they are satisfied as mentioned in paragraph 10(2) above and—

(a) if they are so satisfied they shall direct the rent officer to register the rent in accordance with the certificate;

(b) if they are not so satisfied they shall direct the rent officer to refuse the application for registration.

* paras 13–15 repealed by Housing Act 1980, s.152(3) and Sch. 26.

SCHEDULE 12

Section 69 (3)

CERTIFICATE OF FAIR RENT

1. An application for a certificate of fair rent—

(a) must be in the prescribed form;

(b) must state the rent to be specified in the certificate;

(c) in the case mentioned in section 691 (a) of this Act must be accompanied by plans and specifications of the works to be carried out and, if the works to be carried out are works of improvement, must state whether the dwelling-house is for the time being subject to a regulated tenancy; and

(d) if any furniture is to be provided for use under a regulated tenancy of the dwelling-house, must contain the prescribed particulars with regard to any such furniture.

2.—(1) if it appears to the rent officer that the information supplied to him is insufficient to enable him to issue a certificate of fair rent he shall serve on the applicant a notice stating that he will not entertain the application and that, if a request in writing to that effect is made by the applicant within 14 days from the service of the notice or such longer period as a rent officer or a rent assessment committee may allow, the rent officer will refer the application to a rent assessment committee.

*(2) On receiving any application for a certificate of a fair rent, the rent officer may, by notice in writing served on the applicant or on the tenant, (if any), require him to give to the rent officer within such period of not less than seven days from the service of the notice as may be specified in the

notice, such information as he may reasonably require regarding such of the particulars contained in the application as may be specified in the notice.

* substituted by Regulated Tenancies (Procedure) Regulations 1980, reg 3 and Sch. 2 para 1.

*3. If it appears to the rent officer that the information supplied to him is sufficient and that the rent stated in the application would be a fair rent he may, unless the dwelling-house is subject to a regulated tenancy, issue a certificate specifying that rent and the other terms referred to in section 69(2) of this Act.

* amended by Regulated Tenancies (Procedure) Regulations 1980, reg 3 and Sch. 2 para 2.

*4. In the case of an application which does not fall within paragraph 3 above and where the dwelling-house is not subject to a regulated tenancy, the rent officer shall, after consulting the applicant, consider what rent ought to be specified in the certificate, determine a fair rent, and serve notice under paragraph 7 below.

*5.—(1) Where the dwelling-house is subject to a regulated tenancy, the rent officer shall serve on the applicant and on the tenant a notice inviting the person on whom it is served to state in writing, within a period of not less than seven days after the service of the notice, whether he wishes the rent officer in consultation with the applicant and the tenant to consider what rent ought to be specified in the certificate; and the notice served on the tenant shall be accompanied by a copy of the application for the certificate.

(2) If, after service of a notice by the rent officer under sub-paragraph (1) above, no request in writing is made within the period specified in the notice for the rent to be considered as mentioned in that sub-paragraph, the rent officer may—

(a) consider what rent ought to be specified in the certificate, determine a fair rent, and serve a notice under paragraph 7 below, or

(b) serve a notice under paragraph 6(2) below.

*6.—(1) Where, in response to a notice served by a rent officer under paragraph 5(1) above the applicant or the tenant states in writing that he wishes the rent to be considered as mentioned in that paragraph, the rent officer shall serve a notice under this paragraph.

(2) A notice under this paragraph shall state that the rent officer proposes, at a time (which shall not be earlier than seven days after the service of the notice) and place specified in the notice, to consider in consultation with the applicant and with the tenant, or such of them as may appear at that time and place, what rent ought to be specified in the certificate.

(3) At any such consultation the applicant and the tenant may each be represented by a person authorised by him in that behalf, whether or not that person is of counsel or a solicitor.

(4) The rent officer may, where he considers it to be appropriate, arrange for consultations in respect of one dwelling-house to be held together with consultations in respect of one or more other dwelling-houses.

(5) After considering, in accordance with this paragraph, what rent ought

to be specified in the certificate, the rent officer shall determine a fair rent and shall serve a notice under paragraph 7 below.

*7. After determining a fair rent in accordance with paragraphs 4, 5(2) or 6(5) above, the rent officer shall serve on the applicant a notice stating that he proposes to issue a certificate specifying that rent, unless within 14 days from the service of the notice, or such longer period as the rent officer or a rent assessment committee may allow, the applicant requests in writing that the application should be referred to a rent assessment committee.

*8.—(1) If such a request as is referred to in paragraph 7 above is made, then, subject to sub-paragraph (3) below—

(*a*) if it is made within the period of 14 days referred to in that paragraph or a rent assessment committee so direct, the rent officer shall refer the application to a rent assessment committee;

(*b*) if it is made after the expiry of those 14 days, the rent officer may either refer the application to a rent assessment committee or seek the directions of a rent assessment committee whether so to refer to it.

(2) The rent officer shall issue the certificate if—

(*a*) no such request is made, or

(*b*) such a request is made but the application is not referred to a rent assessment committee, or

(*c*) in a case where the dwelling-house is not subject to a regulated tenancy, the applicant informs the rent officer in writing that he does not propose to make such a request.

(3) An application shall not be capable of being referred to a rent assessment committee at any time after the rent officer has issued the certificate in accordance with sub-paragraph (2) above.

*9.—(1) Where an application is referred to a rent assessment committee, they shall serve on the applicant a notice specifying a period of not less than 7 days from the service of the notice during which either representations in writing or a request to make oral representations may be made by him to the committee.

(2) Where, within the period specified under sub-paragraph (1) above or such further period as the committee may allow, the applicant requests to make oral representations, the committee shall give him an opportunity to be heard either in person or by a person authorised by him in that behalf, whether or not that person is of counsel or a solicitor.

*10.—(1) After considering any representation made to them in pursuance of paragraph 9 above, the committee shall determine a fair rent for the dwelling-house and shall notify the applicant and the rent officer accordingly.

(2) On receiving the notification the rent officer shall issue to the applicant a certificate of fair rent specifying the rent determined by the committee.

*11. Where an application under this Schedule is made with respect to a dwelling-house which is subject to a regulated tenancy,—

(*a*) a notice under paragraph 7, 9(1) or 10 above shall be served on the tenant as well as on the applicant and any notice served under paragraph 7 or 9(1) above shall refer to consultation with, or as the case may be, a request or representations by, the tenant as well as the applicant;

(*b*) the tenant may make representations, request reference to a rent assessment committee and be present or represented in like manner as the applicant, and references in this Schedule to the applicant shall be constructed accordingly; and

(*c*) a copy of any certificate of fair rent issued in pursuance of the application shall be sent to the tenant.

* substituted by Regulated Tenancies (Procedure) Regulations 1980, reg 3 and Sch. 2 para 3 and amended by Rent Assessment Committees (England and Wales) (Amendment) Regulations 1981, reg 3.

Arbitration Act 1979

Judicial review of arbitration awards

1.—(1) In the Arbitration Act 1950 (in this Act referred to as "the principal Act") section 21 (statement of case for a decision of the High Court) shall cease to have effect and, without prejudice to the right of appeal conferred by subsection (2) below, the High Court shall not have jurisdiction to set aside or remit an award on an arbitration agreement on the ground of errors of fact or law on the face of the award.

(2) Subject to subsection (3) below, an appeal shall lie to the High Court on any question of law arising out of an award made on an arbitration agreement; and on the determination of such an appeal the High Court may by order—

(*a*) confirm, vary or set aside the award; or

(*b*) remit the award to the reconsideration of the arbitrator or umpire together with the court's opinion on the question of law which was the subject of the appeal;

and where the award is remitted under paragraph (*b*) above the arbitrator or umpire shall, unless the order otherwise directs, make his award within three months after the date of the order.

(3) An appeal under this section may be brought by any of the parties to the reference—

(*a*) with the consent of all the other parties to the reference; or

(*b*) subject to section 3 below, with the leave of the court.

(4) The High Court shall not grant leave under subsection (3)(*b*) above unless it considers that, having regard to all the circumstances, the determination of the question of law concerned could substantially affect the rights of one or more of the parties to the arbitration agreement; and the court may make any leave which it gives conditional upon the applicant complying with such conditions as it considers appropriate.

(5) Subject to subsection (6) below, if an award is made and, on an application made by any of the parties to the reference,—

(a) with the consent of all the other parties to the reference, or

(b) subject to section 3 below, with the leave of the court,

it appears to the High Court that the award does not or does not sufficiently set out the reasons for the award, the court may order the arbitrator or umpire concerned to state the reasons for his award in sufficient detail to enable the court, should an appeal be brought under this section, to consider any question of law arising out of the award.

(6) In any case where an award is made without any reason being given, the High Court shall not make an order under subsection (5) above unless it is satisfied—

(a) that before the award was made one of the parties to the reference gave notice to the arbitrator or umpire concerned that a reasoned award would be required; or

(b) that there is some special reason why such a notice was not given.

*(6A) Unless the High Court gives leave, no appeal shall lie to the Court of Appeal from a decision of the High Court—

(a) to grant or refuse leave under subsection (3)(b) or (5)(b) above; or

(b) to make or not to make an order under subsection (5) above.

(7) No appeal shall lie to the Court of Appeal from a decision of the High Court on an appeal under this section unless—

(a) the High Court or the Court of Appeal gives leave; and

(b) it is certified by the High Court that the question of law to which its decision relates either is one of general public importance or is one which for some other special reason should be considered by the Court of Appeal.

(8) Where the award of an arbitrator or umpire is varied on appeal, the award as varied shall have effect (except for the purposes of this section) as if it were the award of the arbitrator or umpire.

* inserted by Supreme Court Act 1981, s.148(1) and (2).

Determination of preliminary point of law by court

2.—(1) Subject to subsection (2) and section 3 below, on an application to the High Court made by any of the parties to a reference—

(a) with the consent of an arbitrator who has entered on the reference or, if an umpire has entered on the reference, with his consent, or

(b) with the consent of all the other parties,

the High Court shall have jurisdiction to determine any question of law arising in the course of the reference.

(2) The High Court shall not entertain an application under subsection (1)(a) above with respect to any question of law unless it is satisfied that—

(a) the determination of the application might produce substantial savings in costs to the parties; and

(b) the question of law is one in respect of which leave to appeal would be likely to be given under section 1(3)(b) above.

*(2A) Unless the High Court gives leave, no appeal shall lie to the Court of Appeal from a decision of the High Court to entertain or not to entertain an application under subsection (1)(*a*) above.

*(3) A decision of the High Court under subsection (1) above shall be deemed to be a judgment of the court within the meaning of section 16 of the Supreme Court Act 1981 (appeals to the Court of Appeal), but no appeal shall lie from such a decision unless—

(*a*) the High Court or the Court of Appeal gives leave; and

(*b*) it is certified by the High Court that the question of law to which its decision relates either is one of general public importance or is one which for some other special reason should be considered by the Court of Appeal.

* inserted and amended by Supreme Court Act 1981, ss.148(1) and (3) and s.152(1) and Sch. 5.

Exclusion agreements affecting rights under sections 1 and 2

3.—(1) Subject to the following provisions of this section and section 4 below—

(*a*) the High Court shall not, under section 1(3)(*b*) above, grant leave to appeal with respect to a question of law arising out of an award, and

(*b*) the High Court shall not, under section 1(5)(*b*) above, grant leave to make an application with respect to an award, and

(*c*) no application may be made under section 2(1)(*a*) above with respect to a question of law,

if the parties to the reference in question have entered into an agreement in writing (in this section referred to as an "exclusion agreement") which excludes the right of appeal under section 1 above in relation to that award or, in a case falling within paragraph (*c*) above, in relation to an award to which the determination of the question of law is material.

(2) An exclusion agreement may be expressed so as to relate to a particular award, to awards under a particular reference or to any other description of awards, whether arising out of the same reference or not; and an agreement may be an exclusion agreement for the purposes of this section whether it is entered into before or after the passing of this Act and whether or not it forms part of an arbitration agreement.

(3) In any case where—

(*a*) an arbitration agreement, other than a domestic arbitration agreement, provides for disputes between the parties to be referred to arbitration, and

(*b*) a dispute to which the agreement relates involves the question whether a party has been guilty of fraud, and

(*c*) the parties have entered into an exclusion agreement which is applicable to any award made on the reference of that dispute,

then, except in so far as the exclusion agreement otherwise provides, the High Court shall not exercise its powers under section 24 (2) of the principal Act (to take steps necessary to enable the question to be determined by the High Court) in relation to that dispute.

(4) Except as provided by subsection (1) above, sections 1 and 2 above shall have effect notwithstanding anything in any agreement purporting—

(*a*) to prohibit or restrict access to the High Court; or
(*b*) to restrict the jurisdiction of that court; or
(*c*) to prohibit or restrict the making of a reasoned award.

(5) An exclusion agreement shall be of no effect in relation to an award made on, or a question of law arising in the course of a reference under, a statutory arbitration, that is to say, such an arbitration as is referred to in subsection (1) of section 31 of the principal Act.

(6) An exclusion agreement shall be of no effect in relation to an award made on, or a question of law arising in the course of a reference under, an arbitration agreement which is a domestic arbitration agreement unless the exclusion agreement is entered into after the commencement of the arbitration in which the award is made or, as the case may be, in which the question of law arises.

(7) In this section "domestic arbitration agreement" means an arbitration agreement which does not provide, expressly or by implication, for arbitration in a State other than the United Kingdom and to which neither—

(*a*) an individual who is a national of, or habitually resident in, any State other than the United Kingdom, nor
(*b*) a body corporate which is incorporated in, or whose central management and control is exercised in, any State other than the United Kingdom,

is a party at the time the arbitration agreement is entered into.

Exclusion agreements not to apply in certain cases

4.—(1) Subject to subsection (3) below, if an arbitration award or a question of law arising in the course of a reference relates, in whole or in part, to—

(*a*) a question or claim falling within the Admiralty jurisdiction of the High Court, or
(*b*) a dispute arising out of a contract of insurance, or
(*c*) a dispute arising out of a commodity contract,

an exclusion agreement shall have no effect in relation to the award or question unless either—

(i) the exclusion agreement is entered into after the commencement of the arbitration in which the award is made or, as the case may be, in which the question of law arises, or
(ii) the award or question relates to a contract which is expressed to be governed by a law other than the law of England and Wales.

(2) In subsection (1)(*c*) above "commodity contract" means a contract—

(*a*) for the sale of goods regularly dealt with on a commodity market or exchange in England or Wales which is specified for the purposes of this section by an order made by the Secretary of State; and

(*b*) of a description so specified.

(3) The Secretary of State may by order provide that subsection (1) above—

(*a*) shall cease to have effect; or

(*b*) subject to such conditions as may be specified in the order, shall not apply to any exclusion agreement made in relation to an arbitration award of a description so specified;

and an order under this subsection may contain such supplementary, incidental and transitional provisions as appear to the Secretary of State to be necessary or expedient.

(4) The power to make an order under subsection (2) or subsection (3) above shall be exercisable by statutory instrument which shall be subject to annulment in pursuance of a resolution of either House of Parliament.

(5) In this section "exclusion agreement" has the same meaning as in section 3 above.

Interlocutory orders

5.—(1) If any party to a reference under an arbitration agreement fails within the time specified in the order or, if no time is so specified, within a reasonable time to comply with an order made by the arbitrator or umpire in the course of the reference, then, on the application of the arbitrator or umpire or of any party to the reference, the High Court may make an order extending the powers of the arbitrator or umpire as mentioned in subsection (2) below.

(2) If an order is made by the High Court under this section, the arbitrator or umpire shall have power, to the extent and subject to any conditions specified in that order, to continue with the reference in default of appearance or of any other act by one of the parties in like manner as a judge of the High Court might continue with proceedings in that court where a party fails to comply with an order of that court or a requirement of rules of court.

(3) Section 4(5) of the Administration of Justice Act 1970 (jurisdiction of the High Court to be exercisable by the Court of Appeal in relation to judge-arbitrators and judge-umpires) shall not apply in relation to the power of the High Court to make an order under this section, but in the case of a reference to a judge-arbitrator or judge-umpire that power shall be exercisable as in the case of any other reference to arbitration and also by the judge-arbitrator or judge-umpire himself.

(4) Anything done by a judge-arbitrator or judge-umpire in the exercise of the power conferred by subsection (3) above shall be done by him in his capacity as judge of the High Court and have effect as if done by that court.

(5) The preceding provisions of this section have effect notwithstanding anything in any agreement but do not derogate from any powers conferred on an arbitrator or umpire, whether by an arbitration agreement or otherwise.

(6) In this section "judge-arbitrator" and "judge-umpire" have the same meaning as in Schedule 3 to the Administration of Justice Act 1970.

Minor amendments relating to awards and appointment of arbitrators and umpires

6.—(1) In subsection (1) of section 8 of the principal Act (agreements where reference is to two arbitrators deemed to include provision that the arbitrators shall appoint an umpire immediately after their own appointment)—

    (*a*) for the words "shall appoint an umpire immediately" there shall be substituted the words "may appoint an umpire at any time"; and

    (*b*) at the end there shall be added the words "and shall do so forthwith if they cannot agree".

(2) For section 9 of the principal Act (agreements for reference to three arbitrators) there shall be substituted the following section:—

"Majority award of three arbitrators

9. Unless the contrary intention is expressed in the arbitration agreement, in any case where there is a reference to three arbitrators, the award of any two of the arbitrators shall be binding."

(3) In section 10 of the principal Act (power of court in certain cases to appoint an arbitrator or umpire) in paragraph (*c*) after the word "are", in the first place where it occurs, there shall be inserted the words "required or are" and the words from "or where" to the end of the paragraph shall be omitted.

(4) At the end of section 10 of the principal Act there shall be added the following subsection:—

"(2) In any case where—

    (*a*) an arbitration agreement provides for the appointment of an arbitrator or umpire by a person who is neither one of the parties nor an existing arbitrator (whether the provision applies directly or in default of agreement by the parties or otherwise), and

    (*b*) that person refuses to make the appointment or does not make it within the time specified in the agreement or, if no time is so specified, within a reasonable time,

any party to the agreement may serve the person in question with a written notice to appoint an arbitrator or umpire and, if the appointment is not made within seven clear days after the service of the notice, the High Court or a judge thereof may, on the application of the party who gave the notice, appoint an arbitrator or umpire who shall have the like powers to act in the reference and make an award as if he had been appointed in accordance with the terms of the agreement."

Application and interpretation of certain provisions of Part I of principal Act

7.—(1) References in the following provisions of Part I of the principal Act to that Part of that Act shall have effect as if the preceding provisions of this Act were included in that Part, namely,—

(*a*) section 14 (interim awards);
(*b*) section 28 (terms as to costs of orders);
(*c*) section 30 (Crown to be bound);
(*d*) section 31 (application to statutory arbitrations); and
(*e*) section 32 (meaning of "arbitration agreement").

(2) Subsections (2) and (3) of section 29 of the principal Act shall apply to determine when an arbitration is deemed to be commenced for the purposes of this Act.

*(3) For the avoidance of doubt, it is hereby declared that the reference in subsection (1) of section 31 of the principal Act (statutory arbitrations) to arbitration under any other Act does not extend to arbitration under section 64 of the County Courts Act 1984 (cases in which proceedings are to be or may be referred to arbitration) and accordingly nothing in this Act or in Part I of the principal Act applies to arbitration under the said section 92.

* amended by County Courts Act 1984, s.148(1) and Sch. 2 para 70.

Short title, commencement, repeals and extent

8.—(1) This Act may be cited as the Arbitration Act 1979.

(2) This Act shall come into operation on such day as the Secretary of State may appoint by order made by statutory instrument; and such an order—

(*a*) may appoint different days for different provisions of this Act and for the purposes of the operation of the same provision in relation to different descriptions of arbitration agreement; and
(*b*) may contain such supplementary, incidental and transitional provisions as appear to the Secretary of State to be necessary or expedient.

(3) In consequence of the preceding provisions of this Act, the following provisions are hereby repealed, namely—

(*a*) in paragraph (*c*) of section 10 of the principal Act the words from "or where" to the end of the paragraph;
(*b*) section 21 of the principal Act;
(*c*) in paragraph 9 of Schedule 3 to the Administration of Justice Act 1970, in sub-paragraph (1) the words "21(1) and (2)" and sub-paragraph (2).

(4) This Act forms part of the law of England and Wales only.

Limitation Act 1980

Application of Act and other limitation enactments to arbitrations

34.—(1) This Act and any other limitation enactment shall apply to arbitrations as they apply to actions in the High Court.

(2) Notwithstanding any term in an arbitration agreement to the effect

that no cause of action shall accrue in respect of any matter required by the agreement to be referred until an award is made under the agreement, the cause of action shall, for the purposes of this Act and any other limitation enactment (whether in their application to arbitrations or to other proceedings), be deemed to have accrued in respect of any such matter at the time when it would have accrued but for that term in the agreement.

(3) For the purposes of this Act and of any other limitation enactment an arbitration shall be treated as being commenced—

(*a*) when one party to the arbitration serves on the other party or parties a notice requiring him or them to appoint an arbitrator or to agree to the appointment of an arbitrator; or

(*b*) where the arbitration agreement provides that the reference shall be to a person named or designated in the agreement, when one party to the arbitration serves on the other party or parties a notice requiring him or them to submit the dispute to the person so named or designated.

(4) Any such notice may be served either—

(*a*) by delivering it to the person on whom it is to be served; or

(*b*) by leaving it at the usual or last-known place of abode in England and Wales of that person; or

(*c*) by sending it by post in a registered letter addressed to that person at his usual or last-known place of abode in England and Wales;

as well as in any other manner provided in the arbitration agreement.

(5) Where the High Court—

(*a*) orders that an award be set aside; or

(*b*) orders, after the commencement of an arbitration, that the arbitration agreement shall cease to have effect with respect to the dispute referred;

the court may further order that the period between the commencement of the arbitration and the date of the order of the court shall be excluded in computing the time prescribed by this Act or by any other limitation enactment for the commencement of proceedings (including arbitration) with respect to the dispute referred.

(6) This section shall apply to an arbitration under an Act of Parliament as well as to an arbitration pursuant to an arbitration agreement.

Subsections (3) and (4) above shall have effect, in relation to an arbitration under an Act, as if for the references to the arbitration agreement there were substituted references to such of the provisions of the Act or of any order, scheme, rules, regulations or byelaws made under the Act as relate to the arbitration.

(7) In this section—

(*a*) "arbitration", "arbitration agreement" and "award" have the same meanings as in Part I of the Arbitration Act 1950; and

(*b*) references to any other limitation enactment are references to any other enactment relating to the limitation of actions, whether passed before or after the passing of this Act.

Agricultural Holdings Act 1984

Transfer of certain functions of Minister to President of R.I.C.S.

8.—(1) The functions of the Minister under the following provisions of the 1948 Act, namely—

>   section 16(2) (appointment of person to make record of condition of holding);
>
>   paragraph 1 of Schedule 6 (appointment of arbitrator);
>
>   paragraph 5(*b*) of that Schedule (fixing of arbitrator's remuneration); and
>
>   paragraph 13 of that Schedule (extension of time limited for making award);

shall be exercisable instead by the President of the Royal Institution of Chartered Surveyors (referred to in this section as "the President").

(2) Accordingly any reference to the Minister in any of those provisions, or in any other provision of the 1948 Act relating to the appointment of an arbitrator by the Minister or to an arbitrator appointed by him, shall be construed, in relation to any time after the commencement of this section, as a reference to the President.

(3) No application may be made to the President—

>   (*a*) for a person to be appointed by him under section 16(2) of the 1948 Act; or
>
>   (*b*) for an arbitrator to be appointed by him under paragraph 1 of Schedule 6 to that Act;

unless the application is accompanied by the prescribed fee; but once the prescribed fee has been paid in connection with any such application for the appointment of an arbitrator no further fee shall be payable in connection with any subsequent application for the President to exercise any function exercisable by him in relation to the arbitration by virtue of subsection (1) above (including an application for the appointment by him in an appropriate case of a new arbitrator).

(4) In subsection (3) above "the prescribed fee" means in relation to any such application as is mentioned in paragraph (*a*) or (*b*) of that subsection, such fee as the Minister may by regulations made by statutory instrument prescribe as the fee for such an application; but no regulations shall be made under this subsection unless a draft of the regulations has been laid before and approved by a resolution of each House of Parliament.

(5) Any instrument of appointment or other document purporting to be made in the exercise of any function exercisable by the President by virtue of subsection (1) above and to be signed by or on behalf of the President shall be taken to be such an instrument or document unless the contrary is shown.

Statutory Rules, Orders and Instruments

	Page
Rating Appeals (Local Valuation Courts) Regulations 1956	513
Rent Assessment Committees (England and Wales) Regulations 1971	516
Town and Country Planning Appeals (Determination by Appointed Persons) (Inquiries Procedure) Rules 1974	520
Rules of the Supreme Court, Ord. 38 rules 35–44	531
Lands Tribunal Rules 1975, rules 10–14, 33A and 42	533
Agricultural Holdings (Arbitration on Notices) Order 1978	538
Rent Assessment Committees (England and Wales) (Rent Tribunal) Regulations 1980	545
Rent Assessment Committee (England and Wales) (Leasehold Valuation Tribunal) Regulations 1981	547
County Court Rules 1981, Ord. 20 rules 27 and 28	554

Rating Appeals (Local Valuation Courts) Regulations 1956 (SI 1956 No. 632)

Title, commencement and application

1.—(1) These regulations may be cited as the Rating Appeals (Local Valuation Courts) Regulations, 1956, and shall come into operation on the first day of May, 1956.

*(2) Regulations 2 to 11 of these regulations shall apply to appeals arising out of proposals for the alteration of valuation lists made under Part III of the Act of 1948, and regulation 12 to applications made in connection with such appeals.

* the Local Government Act 1948 was repealed by the General Rate Act 1967. These regulations continue in force by virtue of s.117(3) of that Act as if they were made under s.76(2) and, in the case of reg 3, s.88(3).

Interpretation

2.—(1) The Interpretation Act, 1889, applies to the interpretation of these regulations as it applies to the interpretation of an Act of Parliament.

(2) In these regulations, unless the context otherwise requires, the following expressions have the respective meanings hereby assigned to them:—

"the Act of 1948" means the Local Government Act, 1948, as amended by any subsequent enactment;

"court" means a local valuation court convened under subsection (1) of section 48 of the Act of 1948 for the hearing of an appeal;

"chairman" means the person acting as chairman at a meeting of the court;

"the clerk" means the clerk to the local valuation panel from the members of which the court is constituted or other person for the time being authorised by the panel to act as clerk or on his behalf; and

"party" in relation to an appeal means a person entitled to appear who appears at the hearing of the appeal whether in person or in other manner permitted by these regulations.

Jurisdiction as respects extensive undertakings

3. The court to hear and determine any appeal relating to any hereditament or hereditaments the value of which is ascertained by reference to the accounts, receipts or profits of an undertaking carried on thereon, or to hear and determine any appeal in which it is claimed that the value of any hereditament or hereditaments should be so ascertained, shall consist of members of that local valuation panel within whose area are situated hereditaments occupied for the purpose of that undertaking having in the aggregate, and according to the valuation lists for the time being in force, a greater rateable value than have any hereditaments so occupied within the area of any other local valuation panel. In the event of an equality of aggregate rateable values or of none of the hereditaments so occupied being included in any valuation list, the appeal shall be heard and determined by a court consisting of members of such one of the panels within whose area hereditaments so occupied are situated as the Minister of Housing and Local Government may determine.

Date and place of hearing

4.—(1) The clerk shall give not less than 14 days' notice of the date, time and place fixed for the hearing of an appeal to the appellant and to every person who has served, and has not unconditionally withdrawn, a notice of objection to the proposal.

(2) The clerk shall advertise the date, time and place at which a court will sit to hear any appeals by causing a notice of the same to be affixed to the offices of the local valuation panel, and also to be affixed to the offices of the rating authority or posted in some conspicuous place or places within the rating area, and such notice shall name a place where a list of the appeals to be heard may be inspected.

(3) Where, in the scheme for the constitution of the local valuation panel from the members of which the court falls to be constituted, provision is made for the division of the panel area into divisions, every appeal shall, so far as is practicable, be heard within the division of the area of the panel within which the hereditament, or where more than one hereditament is concerned any of those hereditaments, is situated.

Representation

5. On the hearing of an appeal the rating authority may appear by their clerk or other officer duly appointed for the purpose or by counsel or solicitor and any other person entitled to appear may appear in person or by counsel or solicitor or by any other representative.

Provided that no member of the local valuation panel from the members of which the court is constituted shall be entitled to act in relation to the appeal as representative for any person entitled to appear.

Hearing

6. On the hearing of an appeal the appellant shall begin unless the court, having regard to the particular circumstances of the case and with the consent of the appellant, otherwise determine. Subject as aforesaid the parties to the appeal shall be heard in such order as the court may determine.

Non-appearance

7. If any person entitled to appear does not appear at the hearing of an appeal, the court may, upon being satisfied that the requirements of paragraphs (1) and (2) of regulation 4 of these regulations have been duly complied with, proceed with the hearing on the assumption that he does not desire to be heard.

Adjournment and separate hearings

8. The court may postpone or adjourn the hearing of any appeal for such time and to such place and upon such terms, if any, as it thinks fit, or may order that different questions arising in the appeal be heard at such different times or in such order or at such different places as to the court may seem expedient.

Withdrawal of parties, etc.

9. No person, being a party to an appeal or an employee or member of a body which is such a party or a person acting for such a party or a person called as a witness during the hearing, shall be present while the court is considering its decision on the appeal.

Decision

*10.—(1) Except in a case to which the proviso to subsection (3) of section 44 of the Act of 1948 applies, the decision of the majority of the court shall be the decision of the court.

(2) The decision of the court, embodying any directions given under subsection (4) of section 48 of the Act of 1948, shall be in writing and signed by the chairman.

(3) A copy of the decision certified by the clerk shall be sent by him to every party to the appeal and he shall also inform every such party of the right to appeal against the decision of the court. A copy of the decision shall also be sent to the valuation officer where he is not a party to the appeal.

* the reference to the proviso to s.44(3) of the 1948 Act should now be read as a reference to s.88(6) of the General Rate Act 1967.

Non-compliance with regulations

11. Non-compliance with any of these regulations other than regulation 3 thereof shall not render any proceeding in the appeal void unless the court shall so direct, but such proceeding may be set aside either wholly or in part as irregular, or amended, or otherwise dealt with in such manner and upon such terms as the court shall think fit.

Applications in respect of returns

*12.—(1) An application to the court under subsection (6) of section 3 of the Rating and Valuation (Miscellaneous Provisions) Act 1955, shall be made in writing and sent to the clerk and a copy of the application shall forthwith be served by the applicant on the valuation officer.

(2) The clerk shall give not less than 7 days' notice of the date, time and place fixed for the hearing of the application to the applicant and to the valuation officer.

(3) On the hearing of the application the applicant shall be entitled to begin and the valuation officer shall be entitled to appear and be heard.

(4) If any person entitled to appear does not appear at the hearing of the application, the court may, upon being satisfied that the requirements of paragraphs (1) and (2) of this regulation have been duly complied with, proceed with the hearing on the assumption that he does not desire to be heard.

(5) A decision of the court not to make an order shall be in writing and signed by the chairman.

(6) The clerk shall send a copy of the order, or the decision of the court not to make an order, to the applicant and the valuation officer and, if the applicant appeared at the hearing of the application, shall also inform him of the right to appeal against the decision of the court.

(7) Regulation 5 of these regulations shall apply to the applicant and the valuation officer, and regulations 8 and 9, paragraph (1) of regulation 10 and regulation 11 shall apply on the hearing of an application as on the hearing of an appeal.

* the reference to s.3(6) of the 1955 Act should now be read as a reference to s.83(6) of the General Rate Act 1967.

Revocation of existing regulations

13. The Rating Appeals (Local Valuation Courts) Regulations, 1949 are hereby revoked, except in their application to appeals arising out of proposals for the alteration of the valuation lists in force immediately before the first day of April, 1956, and in such application shall be amended by the substitution for the definition of "chairman" contained therein of the definition contained in regulation 2 of these regulations.

Rent Assessment Committees (England and Wales) Regulations 1971 (SI 1971 No. 1065)

Citation and commencement

1. These regulations may be cited as the Rent Assessment Committees (England and Wales) Regulations 1971 and shall come into operation on 2nd August 1971.

Interpretation

2.—(1) The Interpretation Act 1889 shall apply to the interpretation of these regulations as it applies to the interpretation of an Act of Parliament.

*(2) In these regulations, unless the context otherwise requires—

"chairman" means the chairman of a committee;

"committee" means a rent assessment committee constituted under Schedule 10 to the Rent Act 1977, to which a reference is made, but does not include a rent assessment committee carrying out the functions conferred on it by section 72 (Functions of Rent Tribunals) or section 142 (Leasehold Valuation Tribunals) of the Housing Act 1980.

"hearing" means the meeting or meetings of a committee to hear oral representations made in relation to a reference;

"party" means, in the case where a reference is subject to a hearing, any person who is entitled under regulation 3(3) of these regulations to receive notice of the hearing and, in the case where a reference is not to be subject to a hearing, any person who is entitled to make representations in writing to the committee;

"reference" means a matter or an application, as the case may be, which is referred by a rent officer to a rent assessment committee under Schedule 6 or Schedule 7 to the Rent Act 1968, or Part II of Schedule 2 to the Housing Act 1969.

(3) For the purpose of any of these regulations relating to procedure at a hearing, any reference to a party shall be construed as including a reference to a person authorised by a party to make oral representations on his behalf pursuant to paragraph 8, or paragraph 12(1), of Schedule 6, or paragraph 7(3) of Schedule 7, to the Rent Act 1968, or paragraph 13 of Schedule 2 to the Housing Act 1969, as the case may be.

* amended by Rent Assessment Committees (England and Wales) (Amendment) Regulations 1980, reg 2.

Hearings

3.—(1) A hearing by a committee shall be in public unless, for special reasons, the committee decide otherwise; but nothing in these regulations shall prevent a member of the Council on Tribunals in that capacity from attending any hearing.

(2) Such hearing shall be on such date and at such time and place as the committee shall appoint.

*(3) Notices of such date, time and place shall be given by the committee, not less than 10 days before the said date—

(*a*) where the reference is an application for a certificate of fair rent referred pursuant to paragraph 2 or paragraph 6 of Schedule 7 to the Rent Act 1968, to the applicant and, in a case to which paragraph 9 of the said Schedule applies, to the tenant;

(*b*) where the reference is an application supported by a certificate of fair rent referred pursuant to paragraph 11 of Schedule 6 to the Rent Act 1968, to the applicant; and

(*c*) in every other case, to the landlord and the tenant.

518 The Surveyor in Court

†(4) The notice referred to in paragraph (3) above may be given not less than seven days before the date of the hearing if that date has been referred to in the notice given under paragraph 7(1)(b) of Schedule 11 or under paragraph 9(1) of Schedule 12 to the Rent Act 1977 as the date when the hearing would be held if a request to make oral representations were to be made.

* substituted by Rent Assessment Committees (England and Wales) (Amendment) Regulations 1980, reg 3 and amended by Rent Assessment Committees (England and Wales) (Amendment) Regulations 1981, reg. 4(1).

† inserted by Rent Assessment Committees (England and Wales) (Amendment) Regulations 1981, reg 4(2).

4. At the hearing—

    (a) the parties shall be heard in such order, and, subject to the provisions of these regulations, the procedure shall be such as the committee shall determine;

    (b) a party may call witnesses, give evidence on his own behalf and cross-examine any witnesses called by the other party.

Documents, etc.

5.—(1) The committee shall, where the reference is to be subject to a hearing, take all reasonable steps to ensure that there is supplied to each of the parties before the date of the hearing—

    (a) a copy of, or sufficient extracts from or particulars of, any document relevant to the reference which has been received from the rent officer or from a party (other than a document which is in the possession of such party, or of which he has previously been supplied with a copy by the rent officer); and

    (b) a copy of any document which embodies the results of any enquiries made by or from the committee for the purposes of that reference, or which contains relevant information in relation to fair rents previously determined for other dwelling-houses and which has been prepared for the committee for the purposes of that reference.

(2) Where at any hearing—

    (i) any document relevant to the references is not in the possession of a party present at that hearing; and

    (ii) that party has not been supplied with a copy of, or sufficient extracts from or particulars of, that document by the rent officer or by the committee in accordance with the provisions of paragraph (1) of this regulation,

then unless—

    (a) that party consents to the continuation of the hearing; or

    (b) the committee consider that that party has a sufficient opportunity of dealing with that document without an adjournment of the hearing,

the committee shall adjourn the hearing for a period which they consider will afford that party a sufficient opportunity of dealing with that document.

6. Where a reference is not to be subject to a hearing, the committee shall supply to each of the parties a copy of, or sufficient extracts from or particulars of, any such document as is mentioned in paragraph (1)(*a*) of regulation 5 of these regulations (other than a document excepted from that paragraph) and a copy of any such document as is mentioned in paragraph (1)(*b*) of that regulation, and they shall not reach their decision until they are satisfied that each party has been given sufficient opportunity of commenting upon any document of which a copy, or from which extracts or of which particulars, has or have been so supplied, and upon the other's case.

Inspection of dwelling-house

7.—(1) The committee may of their own motion, and shall at the request of one of the parties (subject in either case to any necessary consent being obtained) inspect the dwelling-house which is the subject of the reference.

(2) An inspection may be made before, during or after the close of the hearing, or at such stage in relation to the consideration of the representations in writing, as the committee shall decide, and the committee shall give to the parties and their representatives an opportunity to attend.

(3) Notice of an inspection shall be given as though it were notice of a hearing, save that the requirements for such notice may be dispensed with or relaxed in so far as the committee are satisfied that the parties have received sufficient notice.

(4) Where an inspection is made after the close of a hearing, the committee shall, if they consider that it is expedient to do so on account of any matter arising from the inspection, reopen the hearing; and if the hearing is to be reopened paragraph (3) of regulation 3 of these regulations shall apply as it applied to the original hearing, save in so far as its requirements may be dispensed with or relaxed with the consent of the parties.

Adjournment

8. The committee at their discretion may of their own motion, or at the request of the parties, or one of them, at any time and from time to time postpone or adjourn a hearing; but they shall not do so at the request of one party only unless, having regard to the grounds on which and the time at which such request is made and to the convenience of the parties, they deem it reasonable to do so. Such notice of any postponed or adjourned hearing as is reasonable in the circumstances shall be given to the parties by the committee.

Non-appearance

9. If a party does not appear at a hearing the committee, on being satisfied that the requirements of these regulations regarding the giving of notice of hearings have been duly complied with, may proceed to deal with the reference upon the representations of any party present and upon the documents and information which they may properly consider.

Decisions

*10.—(1) The decision of the committee upon a reference shall be recorded in a document signed by the chairman (or in the event of his absence or incapacity, by another member of the committee) which shall contain no reference to the decision being by a majority (if that be the case) or to any opinion of a minority.

(2) The chairman (or in the event of his absence or incapacity, either of the other members of the committee) shall have power, by certificate under his hand, to correct any clerical or accidental error or omission in the said document.

(3) A copy of the said document and of any such correction shall be sent by the committee to the parties and to the rent officer.

* amended by Rent Assessment Committees (England and Wales) (Amendment) Regulations 1981, reg 4(3).

*10A.—(1) Where the committee are requested, on or before the giving of notification of the decision, to state the reasons for the decision, those reasons shall be recorded in a document.

*(2) Regulation 10 above shall apply to the document recording the reasons as it applies to the document recording the decision.

* inserted by Rent Assessment Committees (England and Wales) (Amendment) Regulations 1981, reg 4(4).

Giving of notices, etc.

11. Where any notice or other written matter is required under the provisions of these regulations to be given or supplied by the committee (including any such matter to be supplied to a party for the purposes of a reference to which regulation 6 of these regulations applies) it shall be sufficient compliance with the regulations if such notice or matter is sent by post in a prepaid letter and addressed to the party for whom it is intended at his usual or last known address, or if that party has appointed an agent to act on his behalf in relation to the reference, to that agent at the address of the agent supplied to the committee.

Town and Country Planning Appeals (Determination by Appointed Persons) (Inquiries Procedure) Rules 1974 (SI 1974 No. 420)

Citation and commencement

1.—(1) These Rules may be cited as the Town and Country Planning Appeals (Determination by Appointed Persons) (Inquiries Procedure) Rules 1974.

(2) These Rules shall come into operation on 1st April 1974 but, save as provided in rule 20, shall not affect any appeal brought before that date.

Application of Rules

2.—(1) These Rules apply—

(a) to local inquiries held by a person appointed by the Secretary of State

for the purpose of appeals to the said Secretary of State under section
36 of the Town and Country Planning Act 1971, where such appeals
fall to be determined by the said person instead of by the said Secretary
of State by virtue of the powers contained in Schedule 9 to that Act and
of regulations made thereunder and (to the extent provided in rule 18)
to hearings before such a person for the purposes of any such appeal;

(*b*) to local inquiries held by a person appointed by the said Secretary of
State for the purpose of appeals to the said Secretary of State under a
tree preservation order, where such appeals fall to be determined as
aforesaid, and (to the extent provided in rule 18) to hearings before
such a person for the purpose of any such appeal, subject to the
following modifications—

> (i) rule 4 shall not apply and the references in these Rules to
> section 29 parties shall be omitted;
> (ii) references to development shall be construed as references to
> the cutting down, topping or lopping of trees;
> (iii) references to permission shall be construed as references to
> consent;

(*c*) to local inquiries held by a person appointed by the said Secretary of
State for the purpose of appeals to the said Secretary of State under
paragraph 8 of Schedule 11 to the Town and Country Planning Act
1971 (including appeals under that paragraph of that Schedule as
applied by section 8 of and Schedule 2 to the Town and Country
Planning (Amendment) Act 1972) where such appeals fall to be
determined as aforesaid, and (to the extent provided in rule 18) to
hearings before such a person for the purpose of any such appeal,
subject to the following modifications—

> (i) references to development shall be construed as references to
> works for the demolition, alteration or extension of a listed
> building or to works for the demolition of a building in a
> conservation area as the case may be;
> (ii) references to permission shall be construed as references to
> listed building consent;

(*d*) to local inquiries held by a person appointed by the said Secretary of
State for the purpose of appeals to the said Secretary of State under the
Town and Country Planning (Control of Advertisements) Regulations 1969 to 1974, where such appeals fall to be determined as
aforesaid, and (to the extent provided in rule 18) to hearings before
such a person for the purpose of any such appeal, subject to the
following modifications—

> (i) rule 4 shall not apply and the references in these Rules to
> section 29 parties shall be omitted;
> (ii) references to development shall be construed as references to
> the display of advertisements;
> (iii) references to permission shall be construed as references to
> consent.

(2) These Rules apply in relation to Greater London, as defined in section 2(1) of the London Government Act 1963, subject to the modifications specified in rule 19.

Interpretation

3.—(1) In these Rules, unless the context otherwise requires—

"the Act" means the Town and Country Planning Act 1971;

"the Act of 1972" means the Local Government Act 1972;

"appointed person" means the person appointed by the Secretary of State to determine the appeal;

"conservation area" means an area designated under section 277 of the Act;

"county planning authority" and "district planning authority" have the meanings assigned to them by section 1 of the Act;

"inquiry" means a local inquiry to which these Rules apply;

"the land" means the land (including trees and buildings) to which the inquiry relates;

"listed building" has the meaning assigned to it by section 54 of the Act;

"listed building consent" means consent required by section 55(2) of the Act in respect of works for the demolition, extension or alteration of a listed building and the consent required by that subsection as applied by section 8 of the Town and Country Planning (Amendment) Act 1972 for works for the demolition of a building in a conservation area;

"local authority" has the meaning assigned to it by section 290(1) of the Act;

"local planning authority" means—

(a) the county planning authority or district planning authority, as the case may be, who were responsible for dealing with the relevant application; or

(b) any local authority or committee (including a National Park Committee) exercising the functions of the said planning authority in relation to the application by virtue of any arrangement under section 101 of the Act of 1972;

"National Park Committee" has the meaning assigned to it by paragraph 5 of Schedule 17 to the Act of 1972;

"section 29 parties" means persons from whom representations are received by the local planning authority in pursuance of section 29(3) of the Act, or by the Secretary of State in pursuance of section 29(3) as applied by section 36(5) of the Act, within the time prescribed and, in relation to appeals brought under paragraph 8 of Schedule 11 to the Act, persons from whom representations are received, in pursuance of regulations made under paragraph 2 of the said Schedule, within the time prescribed;

"tree preservation order" means an order under section 60 of the Act;

"trees" includes groups of trees and woodlands.

(2) References in these Rules to section 29 of the Act shall be construed as

including where appropriate references to regulations made under paragraph 2 of Schedule 11 to the Act.

(3) The Interpretation Act 1889 shall apply to the interpretation of these Rules as it applies to the interpretation of an Act of Parliament.

Preliminary information to be supplied by local planning authority

4.—(1) The local planning authority, on being notified by the Secretary of State of the intention to proceed with the consideration of an appeal to which these Rules apply and of the name and address of any person who, pursuant to the provisions of section 29 of the Act, has made representations to the Secretary of State, shall forthwith inform the appellant in writing of the name and address of every section 29 party and the Secretary of State of all such persons who have made representations to the local planning authority.

(2) Where any local authority has given to the local planning authority a direction restricting the grant of permission for the development for which application was made or a direction as to how an application for planning permission is to be determined and where any government department or local authority has expressed in writing to the local planning authority the view that the application should not be granted either wholly or in part, or should be granted only subject to conditions, or, in the case of an application for consent under a tree preservation order, should be granted together with a direction requiring the replanting of trees, the local planning authority shall inform the government department or authority concerned, as the case may be, that such direction or expression of view is relevant to the application or appeal and the government department or authority, as the case may be, shall (except where such action has already been taken) forthwith furnish to the local planning authority a statement in writing of the reasons for the direction or expression of view.

Notification of inquiry

5.—(1) A date, time and place for the holding of the inquiry shall be fixed and may be varied by the Secretary of State, who shall give not less than 42 days' notice in writing of such date, time and place to the appellant and to the local planning authority and to all section 29 parties at the addresses furnished by them:
Provided that—

(i) with the consent of the appellant and of the local planning authority, the Secretary of State may give such lesser period of notice as shall be agreed with the appellant and the local planning authority and in that event he may specify a date for service of the statements referred to in rule 7(1) later than the date therein prescribed;

(ii) where it becomes necessary or advisable to vary the time or place fixed for the inquiry, the Secretary of State shall give such notice of the variation as may appear to him to be reasonable in the circumstances.

(2) Without prejudice to the foregoing provisions of this rule, the Secretary of

State may require the local planning authority to take one or more of the following steps—

> (*a*) to publish in one or more newspapers circulating in the locality in which the land is situated such notices of the inquiry as he may direct;
>
> (*b*) to serve notice of the inquiry in such form, and on such persons or classes of persons as he may specify;
>
> (*c*) to post such notices of the inquiry as he may direct in a conspicuous place or places near to the land;

but the requirements as to the period of notice contained in paragraph (1) of this rule shall not apply to any such notices.

(3) Where the land is under the control of the appellant he shall, if so required by the Secretary of State, affix firmly to some object on the land, in such a manner as to be readily visible to and legible by the public, such notice of the inquiry as the Secretary of State may specify, and thereafter for such period before the inquiry as the Secretary of State may specify, the appellant shall not remove the notice or cause or permit it to be removed.

Notification of identity of appointed person

6. The Secretary of State shall give to the appellant, to the local planning authority and to all section 29 parties written notice informing them of the name of the appointed person:

Provided that, where, in exercise of his powers under paragraph 4 of Schedule 9 to the Act, the Secretary of State has appointed another person to determine the appeal in the place of a person previously appointed for that purpose and it is not practicable to give written notice of the new appointment before the inquiry is held, in lieu of the Secretary of State's giving such notice the person holding the inquiry shall, at the commencement thereof, announce his own name and the fact of his appointment.

Statements to be served before inquiry

7.—(1) Not later than 28 days before the date of the inquiry (or such later date as the Secretary of State may specify under proviso (i) to paragraph (1) of rule 5), the local planning authority shall—

> (*a*) serve on the appellant and on the section 29 parties a written statement of any submission which the local planning authority propose to put forward at the inquiry, and
>
> (*b*) supply a copy of the statement to the Secretary of State for transmission to the appointed person.

(2) Where a local authority has given a direction restricting the grant of permission for the development for which application was made or a direction as to how the application was to be determined, the local planning authority shall mention this in their statement and shall include in the statement a copy of the direction and the reasons given for it and shall, within the period specified in paragraph (1) above, supply a copy of the statement to the local authority concerned; and where a government department or a local authority has expressed in writing to the local planning authority the view that the application should not be granted, either

wholly or in part, or should be granted only subject to conditions or, in the case of an appeal under a tree preservation order, should be granted together with a direction requiring the replanting of trees and the local planning authority propose to rely on such expression of view in their submission at the inquiry they shall include it in their statement and shall within the period specified in paragraph (1) above, supply a copy of the statement to the government department or local authority concerned.

(3) Where the local planning authority intend to refer to, or put in evidence at the inquiry, documents (including maps and plans), the authority's statement shall be accompanied by a list of such documents, together with a notice stating the times and place at which the documents may be inspected by the appellant and the section 29 parties; and the local planning authority shall afford them a reasonable opportunity to inspect and, where practicable, to take copies of the documents.

(4) The local planning authority shall afford any other person interested a reasonable opportunity to inspect and, where practicable, to take copies of any document referred to in the preceding paragraph of this rule, as well as of any statement served on the authority by the appellant under paragraph (5) of this rule.

(5) The appellant shall, if so required by the Secretary of State, serve on the local planning authority, on the section 29 parties and on the Secretary of State for transmission to the appointed person, within such time before the inquiry as the Secretary of State may specify, a written statement of the submissions which he proposes to put forward at the inquiry; and such statement shall be accompanied by a list of any documents (including maps and plans) which the appellant intends to refer to or put in evidence at the inquiry and he shall, if so required by the Secretary of State, afford the local planning authority and the section 29 parties a reasonable opportunity to inspect and, where practicable, to take copies of such documents.

Appointed person may act in place of the Secretary of State

8. The appointed person may himself in place of the Secretary of State take such steps as the Secretary of State is required or enabled to take under or by virtue of rule 5, rule 7(1) or (5), rule 10(1) or (2), rule 11(1) or (2), or rule 11A(1) or (2) (as provided by rule 19 of these Rules).

Appearances at inquiry

9.—(1) The persons who are entitled to appear at the inquiry shall be—

  (*a*) the appellant;
  (*b*) the local planning authority;
  (*c*) where the land is not in Greater London the council of the administrative county in which the land is situated, if not the local planning authority;
  (*d*) where the land is not in Greater London, the council of the district in which the land is situated (or the Council of the Isles of Scilly, as the case may be) if not the local planning authority;
  (*e*) where the land is in a National Park, the National Park Committee (if any), if not the local planning authority;

    (*f*) any joint planning board constituted under section 1 of the Act (or any
         joint planning board or special planning board reconstituted under
         Part I of Schedule 17 to the Act of 1972), where that board is not the
         local planning authority;
    (*g*) where the land is in an area designated as the site of a new town, the
         development corporation of the new town;
    (*h*) section 29 parties;
    (*i*) the council of the parish or community in which the land is situated if
         that council has made representations to the local planning authority
         in respect of the application in pursuance of a provision of a develop-
         ment order made under section 24 of the Act;
    (*j*) any person on whom the Secretary of State or the appointed person
         has required notice to be served under rule 5(2)(*b*).

(2) Any other person may appear at the inquiry at the discretion of the
appointed person.

(3) A local authority may appear by their clerk or by any other officer
appointed for the purpose by the local authority, or by counsel or solicitor; and
any other person may appear on his own behalf or be represented by counsel,
solicitor or any other person.

(4) Where there are two or more persons having a similar interest in the
matter under inquiry, the appointed person may allow one or more persons to
appear for the benefit of some or all of the persons so interested.

Representatives of government departments at inquiry

10.—(1) Where a government department has expressed in writing the view
that the application should not be granted, either wholly or in part, or should
be granted only subject to conditions or, in the case of an appeal under a tree
preservation order, should be granted together with a direction requiring the
replanting of trees and the local planning authority have included this view in
their statement as required by rule 7(2), the appellant may, not later than 14
days before the date of the inquiry, apply in writing to the Secretary of State for
a representative of the government department concerned to be made available at the inquiry.

(2) The Secretary of State shall transmit any application made to him under
the last foregoing paragraph to the government department concerned, who
shall make a representative of the department available to attend the inquiry.

(3) A representative of a government department who, in pursuance of this
rule, attends an inquiry on an appeal, shall be called as a witness by the local
planning authority and shall state the reasons for the view expressed by his
department and included in the authority's statement under rule 7(2), and
shall give evidence and be subject to cross-examination to the same extent as
any other witness.

(4) Nothing in the last foregoing paragraph shall require a representative of
a government department to answer any question which in the opinion of the
appointed person is directed to the merits of government policy and the
appointed person shall disallow any such question.

Representatives of local authorities at inquiry

11.—(1) Where any local authority has—

(*a*) given to the local planning authority a direction restricting the grant of planning permission or a direction as to how an application for planning permission was to be determined; or

(*b*) expressed in writing the view that an application for planning permission should not be granted wholly or in part or should be granted only subject to conditions, and the local planning authority have included this view in their statement, as required under rule 7(2),

the applicant may, not later than 14 days before the date of the inquiry, apply in writing to the Secretary of State for a representative of the authority concerned to be made available to attend the inquiry.

(2) Where an application is made to the Secretary of State under the last foregoing paragraph he shall transmit the application to the authority concerned, who shall make a representative of the authority available to attend the inquiry.

(3) A representative of a local authority who, in pursuance of this rule, attends an inquiry shall be called as a witness by the local planning authority and shall state the reasons for the authority's direction or, as the case may be, the reasons for the view expressed by them and included in the local planning authority's statement under rule 7(2) and shall give evidence and be subject to cross-examination to the same extent as any other witness.

Procedure at inquiry

12.—(1) Except as otherwise provided in these Rules, the procedure at the inquiry shall be such as the appointed person shall in his discretion determine.

(2) Unless in any particular case the appointed person with the consent of the appellant otherwise determines, the appellant shall begin and shall have the right of final reply; and the other persons entitled or permitted to appear shall be heard in such order as the appointed person may determine.

(3) The appellant, the local planning authority and the section 29 parties shall be entitled to call evidence and cross-examine persons giving evidence, but any other person appearing at the inquiry may do so only to the extent permitted by the appointed person.

(4) The appointed person shall not require or permit the giving or production of any evidence, whether written or oral, which would be contrary to the public interest; but, save as aforesaid and without prejudice to the provisions of rule 10(4), any evidence may be admitted at the discretion of the appointed person, who may direct that documents tendered in evidence may be inspected by any person entitled or permitted to appear at the inquiry and that facilities be afforded him to take or obtain copies thereof.

(5) The appointed person may allow the local planning authority or the appellant, or both of them, to alter or add to the submissions contained in any statement served under paragraph (1) or (5) of rule 7, or to any list of documents which accompanies such statement, so far as may be necessary for the purpose of determining the questions in controversy between the parties, but shall (if necessary by adjourning the inquiry) give the appellant or the local

planning authority, as the case may be, and the section 29 parties an adequate opportunity of considering any such fresh submission or document; and the appointed person may make to the Secretary of State a recommendation as to the payment of any additional costs occasioned by any such adjournment.

(6) If any person entitled to appear at the inquiry fails to do so, the appointed person may proceed with the inquiry at his discretion.

(7) The appointed person shall be entitled (subject to disclosure thereof at the inquiry) to take into account any written representations or statements received by him before the inquiry from any person.

(8) The appointed person may from time to time adjourn the inquiry and, if the date, time and place of the adjourned inquiry are announced before the adjournment, no further notice shall be required.

Site inspections

13.—(1) The appointed person may make an unaccompanied inspection of the land before or during the inquiry without giving notice of his intention to the persons entitled to appear at the inquiry.

(2) The appointed person may, and shall if so requested by the appellant or the local planning authority before or during the inquiry, inspect the land after the close of the inquiry and shall, in all cases where he intends to make such an inspection, announce during the inquiry the date and time at which he proposes to do so.

(3) The appellant, the local planning authority and the section 29 parties shall be entitled to accompany the appointed person on any inspection after the close of the inquiry; but the appointed person shall not be bound to defer his inspection if any person entitled to accompany him is not present at the time appointed.

Procedure after inquiry

14.—(1) If, after the close of the inquiry, the appointed person proposes to take into consideration any new evidence (including expert opinion on a matter of fact) or any new issue of fact (not being a matter of government policy) which was not raised at the inquiry and which he considers to be material to his decision, he shall not come to a decision without first notifying the appellant, the local planning authority and any section 29 party who appeared at the inquiry of the substance of the new evidence or of the new issue of fact and affording them an opportunity of making representations thereon in writing within 21 days or of asking within that time for the re-opening of the inquiry.

(2) The appointed person may, in any case if he thinks fit, cause the inquiry to be re-opened and shall cause it to be re-opened if asked to do so in accordance with the foregoing paragraph; and if the inquiry is reopened, paragraphs (1) and (2) of rule 5 shall apply as they applied to the original inquiry, with the modifications that, for the figure "42" in paragraph (1), there shall be substituted the figure "28" and, for references to the Secretary of State, wherever they occur, there shall be substituted references to the appointed person.

Costs

15. Where any person makes application at the inquiry for an award of costs, the appointed person shall report in writing the proceedings on such application to the Secretary of State, and may in such report draw attention to any considerations which appear to him to be relevant to the Secretary of State's decision on the matter.

Notification of decision

16.—(1) Unless the Secretary of State has, under paragraph 3 of Schedule 9 to the Act, directed that the appeal shall be determined by the Secretary of State, the appointed person shall notify his decision and his reasons therefor in writing to the appellant, the local planning authority and the section 29 parties and to any person who, having appeared at the inquiry, has asked to be notified of the decision.

(2) Any person entitled to be notified of the decision of the appointed person under paragraph (1) of this rule may apply to the Secretary of State in writing within six weeks of the notification to him of the decision for an opportunity of inspecting any documents, photographs or plans listed in the notification and the Secretary of State shall afford him an opportunity accordingly.

Service of notices by post

17. Notices or documents required or authorised to be served or sent under the provisions of any of these Rules may be sent by post.

Hearings

18. These Rules, except paragraphs (2) and (3) of rule 5 and rule 9(1)(*j*), shall apply to any such hearing as is mentioned in rule 2, and for that purpose references in these Rules to an inquiry shall be construed as references to such a hearing.

Application to Greater London

19. In their application to Greater London these Rules shall apply with the following modifications—

(i) In rule 3, after the definition of "the Act", there shall be added—" 'the Act of 1963' means the London Government Act 1963"; and, for the definition of "local planning authority", the following definition shall be substituted:—

" 'local planning authority' means—

(*a*) in relation to the appeals referred to in rule 2(1)(*a*), the authority which, by virtue of section 24 of the Act of 1963 or of regulations made under that section, is the local planning authority in relation to the class of development concerned in the area of Greater London where the land is situated; or

(*b*) in relation to the appeals referred to in rule 2(1)(*b*), (*c*) or (*d*), either the Common Council of the City of London or the council of the London borough in which the land is situated, as the case may be;";

(ii) at the end of rule 4, the following paragraph shall be added:—

"(3) Where either—

(*a*) in pursuance of regulations under section 24(6) of the Act of 1963, the application which is the subject of the appeal was required to be referred to the Greater London Council, or

(*b*) in pursuance of paragraph 6 of Schedule 11 to the Act notification of the application for listed building consent was required to be given to the Greater London Council,

and, in either case, that Council has either—

(i) issued a direction to the local planning authority in whose area the land is situated as to the manner in which the application is to be dealt with or determined, or

(ii) (whether before or after the appeal to the Secretary of State) otherwise expressed an opinion to such local planning authority on any such application,

the Greater London Council shall, at the request of the local planning authority, forthwith furnish to them a statement in writing of their reasons for that direction or opinion.";

(iii) at the end of rule 7, the following paragraph shall be added:—

"(6) In a case falling within rule 4(3) the local planning authority shall include in their statement particulars of the direction or opinion of the Greater London Council and of the reasons given for it.";

(iv) for rule 9(1)(*b*) there shall be substituted the following:—

(*b*) the local planning authority and—

(i) where the application was required to be referred under section 24(6) of the Act of 1963, or required to be notified under paragraph 6 of Schedule 11 to the Act, the Greater London Council, or

(ii) where the Greater London Council is the local planning authority, the Common Council of the City of London or the council of the London borough in which the land is situated as the case may be;";

(v) after rule 11, the following rule shall be inserted:—

"*Representatives of the Greater London Council at inquiry*

11A.—(1) In a case falling within rule 4(3), the appellant or the local planning authority may, not later than 14 days before the date of the inquiry, apply in writing to the Secretary of State for a representative of the Greater London Council to be made available at the inquiry.

(2) The Secretary of State shall transmit any application made to him under the last foregoing paragraph to the Greater London Council who shall make a representative of the Council available to attend the inquiry.

(3) A representative of the Greater London Council who, in pursuance of this rule, attends an inquiry shall be called as a witness by

the local planning authority and shall give evidence and be subject to cross-examination to the same extent as any other witness.".

Revocation of previous Rules

20. The Town and Country Planning Appeals (Determination by Appointed Persons) (Inquiries Procedure) Rules 1968 are hereby revoked, and any appeal to which those Rules applied and which has not been determined when these Rules come into operation shall be continued under these Rules.

Rules of the Supreme Court

Part IV (Expert Evidence) of RSC Order 38 was added by RSC (Amendment 1974), SI 1974 No. 295.

IV. EXPERT EVIDENCE

Interpretation (O.38, r.35)

35. In this Part of this Order a reference to a summons for directions includes a reference to any summons or application to which, under any of these Rules, Order 25, rules 2 to 7, apply and expressions used in this Part of this Order which are used in the Civil Evidence Act 1972 have the same meanings in this Part of this Order as in that Act.

Restrictions on adducing expert evidence (O.38, r.36)

*36.—(1) Except with the leave of the Court or where all parties agree, no expert evidence may be adduced at the trial or hearing of any cause or matter unless the party seeking to adduce the evidence—

    (*a*) has applied to the Court to determine whether a direction should be given under rule 37, 38 or 41 (whichever is appropriate) and has complied with any direction given on the application, or

    (*b*) has complied with automatic directions taking effect under Order 25, rule 8(1)(*b*).

(2) Nothing in paragraph (1) shall apply to evidence which is permitted to be given by affidavit or shall affect the enforcement under any other provision of these Rules (except Order 45, rule 5) of a direction given under this Part of this Order.

* amended by RSC (Amendment No. 2) 1980.

Expert evidence in actions for personal injuries (O.38, r.37)

*37.—(1) This rule applies to any action for personal injuries, except—

    (*a*) any Admiralty action; and

    (*b*) any action where the pleadings contain an allegation of a negligent act or omission in the course of medical treatment.

(2) Where an application is made under rule 36(1) in respect of oral expert evidence, then, unless the Court considers that there is sufficient reason for not doing so, it shall direct that the substance of the evidence be disclosed in the form of a written report or reports to such other parties and within such period as the Court may specify.

(3) Where the expert evidence relates to medical matters the Court may, if it thinks fit, treat the following circumstances as sufficient reason for not giving a direction under paragraph (2) namely that the expert evidence may contain an expression of opinion—

    (i) as to the manner in which the personal injuries were sustained; or
    (ii) as to the genuineness of the symptoms of which complaint is made.

(4) Where the expert evidence does not relate to medical matters, the Court may, if it thinks fit, treat as a sufficient reason for not giving a direction under paragraph (2) any of the circumstances set out in sub-paragraphs (*a*) or (*b*) of rule 38(2).

* substituted by RSC (Amendment No. 2) 1980.

*Expert evidence in other actions (O.38, r.38)

38.—(1) Where an application is made under rule 36(1) in respect of oral expert evidence to which rule 37 does not apply, the Court may, if satisfied that it is desirable to do so, direct that the substance of any expert evidence which is to be adduced by any party be disclosed in the form of a written report or reports to such other parties and within such period as the Court may specify.

(2) In deciding whether to give a direction under paragraph (1) the Court shall have regard to all the circumstances and may, to such extent as it thinks fit, treat any of the following circumstances as affording a sufficient reason for not giving such a direction:—

    (*a*) that the expert evidence is or will be based to any material extent upon a version of the facts in dispute between the parties; or
    (*b*) that the expert evidence is or will be based to any material extent upon facts which are neither—
        (i) ascertainable by the expert by the exercise of his own powers of observation, nor
        (ii) within his general professional knowledge and experience.

* title amended by RSC (Amendment No. 2) 1980.

Disclosure of part of expert evidence (O.38, r.39)

39. Where the Court considers that any circumstances rendering it undesirable to give a direction under rule 37 or 38 relate to part only of the evidence sought to be adduced, the Court may, if it thinks fit, direct disclosure of the remainder.

Expert evidence of engineers in accident cases (O.38, r.40)
*40. ....

* revoked by RSC (Amendment No. 2) 1980.

Expert evidence contained in statement (O.38, r.41)

41. Where an application is made under rule 36 in respect of expert evidence contained in a statement and the applicant alleges that the maker of the statement cannot or should not be called as a witness, the Court may direct that the provisions of rules 20 to 23 and 25 to 33 shall apply with such modifications as the Court thinks fit.

Putting in evidence expert report disclosed by another party (O.38, r.42)

42. A party to any cause or matter may put in evidence any expert report disclosed to him by any other party in accordance with this part of this Order.

Time for putting expert report in evidence (O.38, r.43)

*43. Where a party to any cause or matter calls as a witness the maker of a report which has been disclosed in accordance with a direction given under rule 37 or 38, the report may be put in evidence at the commencement of its maker's examination in chief or at such other time as the Court may direct.

* amended by RSC (Amendment No. 2) 1982.

Revocation and variation of directions (O.38, r.44)

44. Any direction given under this Part of this Order may on sufficient cause being shown be revoked or varied by a subsequent direction given at or before the trial of the cause or matter.

Lands Tribunal Rules 1975
(SI 1975 No. 299)

PART II

APPEALS FROM LOCAL VALUATION COURTS

Notice of intention to appear

10.—(1) Every person upon whom a copy of the notice of appeal is served shall, if he intends to appear on the hearing of the appeal, give written notice of his intention, stating—

(i) whether he intends to appear separately or jointly with some other person;

(ii) the grounds on which he intends to rely;

(iii) whether he does or does not propose to call an expert witness to give evidence;

(iv) an address for service of notices and other documents upon him.

534   *The Surveyor in Court*

(2) The notice of intention to appear shall be given to the registrar and to the appellant within 21 days from the date of service of the copy of the notice of appeal, and the registrar shall serve a copy of the notice of intention on every other party to the appeal.

(3) Nothing in this rule shall entitle the valuation officer to appear on the hearing of an appeal if he was not a party to the valuation proceedings.

Statement of case and exchange of valuations

11. (1) Where notice of intention to appear has been given and the appeal is on a point of law or the net annual value of the hereditament to which the appeal relates exceeds £1,250—

(i) within 28 days after the time limited by rule 10 for giving the notice, the appellant shall send to the registrar and to each party by whom notice has been given a statement of his case, including the facts to be proved and any points of law on which he intends to rely at the hearing;

(ii) within 28 days after receiving the appellant's statement, every party who intends to appear in opposition to the appeal shall send to the registrar, the appellant and every other party to the appeal a reply stating his case, including the facts to be proved and any points of law upon which he intends to rely at at the hearing:

Provided that nothing in this paragraph shall preclude any party from sending a statement of his case to the registrar.

(2) Every statement or reply to the registrar in accordance with paragraph (1) above shall be accompanied by—

(i) every valuation of the hereditament which it is proposed to put in evidence (including particulars and computations in support of the valuation), or a statement of the value or values which the parties have agreed to attribute to the hereditament in the event of the Tribunal allowing or dismissing the appeal, as the case may be, and

(ii) a description of any comparable hereditaments to which the party intends to refer at the hearing in support of his case,

together with sufficient copies of the document for service upon every other party to the appeal; and the registrar shall, within 7 days after receiving all the documents required to be supplied under this paragraph, send to each party a copy of the documents supplied by the other parties.

*(3) If at the hearing of the appeal any party seeks to rely upon any valuation or other document which appears to the Tribunal not to have been sent to the registrar in accordance with this rule the Tribunal may adjourn the hearing on such terms as to costs or otherwise as it thinks fit.

* amended by Lands Tribunal (Amendment) Rules 1981, rule 6.

PART III

OTHER APPEALS

Notice of appeal

*12.—(1) Any appeal to the Lands Tribunal other than one to which Part I or Part II applies may be instituted within 28 days from the date of the decision appealed against by sending to the registrar a written notice of appeal in Form 3 or 3A as may be appropriate together with a copy of the decision. The appellant shall at the same time inform the registrar of the names and addresses of the parties to the dispute in respect of which the decision was given and shall supply the registrar with sufficient copies of the notice of appeal for service upon each of those parties and upon the court, tribunal, authority or person from whose decision the appeal is brought.

(2) Upon receiving a notice of appeal, the registrar shall—

   (i) enter particulars of the appeal in the Register of Appeals;

  (ii) serve a copy of the notice upon every party to the dispute (other than the appellant) and upon the court, authority or person from whose decision the appeal is brought;

 (iii) inform the appellant and every person upon whom a copy of the notice of appeal has been served of the number of the appeal entered in the Register, which shall thereafter constitute the title of the appeal;

 (iv) inform the appellant of the date on which copies of the notice of appeal were served.

* substituted by Lands Tribunal (Amendment No. 2) Rules 1981, rule 4.

Notice of intention to appear

13.—(1) Every party other than the appellant shall, if he intends to appear on the hearing of the appeal, give written notice of his intention, stating—

   (i) whether he intends to appear separately or jointly with some other person;

  (ii) the grounds on which he intends to rely;

 (iii) an address for service of notices and other documents upon him;

*(iv) whether he does or does not propose to call an expert witness to give evidence.

(2) The notice shall be given to the registrar and the appellant within 21 days from the date of service of the copy of the notice of appeal.

* inserted by Lands Tribunal (Amendment No. 2) Rules 1981, rule 5.

Statement of case

14. Where notice of intention to appear has been given, the provisions of sub-paragraph (i) and (ii) of rule 11(1) shall, if the registrar so directs, apply to the appeal.

Part VII

General Procedure

Contested proceedings without hearing

*33A.—(1) Notwithstanding the provisions of rule 39 as to oral evidence and of rule 44, but subject to the provisions of paragraph (2) below, the Tribunal shall have power to determine any appeal, reference or application without an oral hearing and any party to any proceedings instituted under these Rules may apply to the registrar in accordance with the provisions of rule 45 for a direction that the Tribunal shall exercise this power.

(2) An order shall not be made on an application under this rule in respect of any proceedings relating to the amount of compensation—

    (i) which is payable in respect of the compulsory acquisition of land; or

    (ii) which depends directly or indirectly on the value of any land

without the consent signed by or on behalf of the person who is claiming such compensation.

(3) After an order has been made that the Tribunal will determine certain proceedings without an oral hearing, the Tribunal may, of its own motion or on the application of any party to those proceedings, require any party to the proceedings to furnish to the Tribunal such statements of case, or reply thereto, or further and better particulars thereof, as the Tribunal may specify.

(4) After an order has been made that the Tribunal will determine certain proceedings without an oral hearing, any party to those proceedings may submit in writing to the Tribunal any representations which he wishes the Tribunal to take into consideration.

(5) Any statements, replies or particulars required by virtue of paragraph (3) above, and any representations made by any party, and any document or other information required to be delivered by any party to any proceedings to which this rule applies in accordance with the provisions of rule 40, shall be sent to the registrar, together with sufficient copies of the same for all the other parties to the proceedings, within 28 days of the order or requirement (as the case may be).

(6) The registrar shall, within 7 days of receiving by virtue of this rule any statements, replies, particulars, representations, document or other information, send to every other party to the proceedings a copy of the same.

(7) If, after having received a copy of any statements, replies, particulars, representations, document or information under paragraph (6) above, any party to any proceedings wishes to make any representations to the Tribunal he may submit the same in writing to the registrar within 28 days of the receipt by him of the said copy and the provisions of paragraph (5) and (6) above shall apply to such representations; but no party to any proceedings shall make any representations on more than one occasion in those proceedings except by the leave of the Tribunal or the registrar.

(8) If any party to any proceedings to which this rule applies intends to rely upon the evidence of an expert witness, then the provisions of rule 42 shall apply as if references in that rule to the calling of witnesses and the hearing of evidence were references to representations.

(9) The Tribunal may at any time and for any reason order that proceedings

which it was in the process of deciding without an oral hearing shall be heard and may thereupon give directions for the disposal of those proceedings in accordance with these rules.

(10)(*a*)(i) If an application under paragraph (1) above is made in any proceedings before a notice of intention to appear has been given in accordance with rule 6, 10, or 13 or, such notice having been given in accordance with rule 10 before any statement of case or reply has been sent to the registrar in accordance with rule 11, then the time limits specified in rules 10 and 11 respectively shall run from the date upon which an order is made in accordance with this rule that those proceedings shall be heard.

(ii) Where notice of intention to appear is given in accordance with rule 6, 10 or 13 in any proceedings in respect of which an application is made under paragraph (1) above, whether such notice is given before or after such application is made, that notice shall be of no effect as regards appearance unless an order is made in accordance with this rule that the proceedings shall be heard, but the notice shall otherwise be effective according to its tenor subject, however, to the provisions of this rule; and save as aforesaid rule 10 shall not apply to any proceedings to which this rule applies.

(iii) Where any of the provisions of rule 11 have been complied with in proceedings in respect of which an order is made under this rule that those proceedings will be determined without an oral hearing and before that order is made, the statement of case or reply and accompanying documents shall be treated as representations made in accordance with the provisions of this rule; and save as aforesaid rule 11 shall not apply to any proceedings to which this rule applies.

(*b*) Rules 52 and 53 shall not apply to any proceedings to which this rule applies.

* inserted by Lands Tribunal (Amendment) Rules 1977, rule 8.

Expert witnesses

42.—(1) This rule applies to any proceedings except appeals from decisions of local valuation courts under Part II and applications for certificates under Part VI.

(2) Not more than one expert witness on either side shall be heard unless otherwise ordered:

Provided that, where the proceedings include a claim for compensation in respect of minerals or disturbance of business, as well as in respect of land, one additional expert witness on either side on the value of the minerals or, as the case may be, on the damage suffered by reason of the disturbance may be heard.

(3) An application for leave to call more than one, or more than one additional expert witness may be made to the registrar in accordance with the provisions of rule 45 or to the Tribunal at the hearing.

(4) Where more than one party intends to call an expert witness, every such party shall, within 28 days after being so requested by the registrar, send to the registrar a copy of each of the following documents relating to the evidence to be given by the expert witness, together with sufficient copies for service upon the other parties—

    (i) every plan and valuation of the land or hereditament which is the subject of the proceedings (including particulars and computations in support of the valuation) which it is proposed to put in evidence;

   (ii) either a statement of any prices, costs or other particulars and any plans relating to a property or properties other than that land or hereditament which are proposed to be given in evidence in support of the valuation, or a statement that no such prices, costs, particulars or plans will be relied upon.

(5) The registrar shall, within 7 days after receiving all the documents required to be supplied by the parties under paragraph (4) above, send to each party copies of the documents supplied by the other party.

*(6) If an application for leave to call more than one, or more than one additional, expert witness is made at the hearing and is granted by the Tribunal, or if at the hearing any party seeks to rely upon any plans, valuation or particulars which appear to the Tribunal not to have been sent to the registrar in accordance with this rule, the Tribunal may adjourn the hearing on such terms as to costs or otherwise as it thinks fit.

* amended by Lands Tribunal (Amendment) Rules 1981, rule 6.

Agricultural Holdings (Arbitration on Notices) Order 1978 (SI 1978 No. 257)

Part I: PRELIMINARY

Citation and commencement

1. This Order may be cited as the Agricultural Holdings (Arbitration on Notices) Order 1978 and shall come into operation on 7th April 1978.

Interpretation

*2.—(1) In this Order, unless the context otherwise requires:

"the 1948 Act" means the Agricultural Holdings Act 1948;

"the 1977 Act" means the Agricultural Holdings (Notices to Quit) Act 1977;

"Case B", "Case D," "Case E" and Case I refer severally to the Cases set out and so named in section 2(3) of the 1977 Act;

"notice to remedy" means a notice served on the tenant of an agricultural holding for the purposes of Case D requiring him to remedy a breach of a term or condition of his tenancy;

"notice to do work" means a notice to remedy requiring the doing of any work of repair, maintenance or replacement;

"termination", in relation to an arbitration, means the date on which the arbitrator's award is delivered to the tenant.

(2) Any reference in this Order to any enactment or instrument shall, unless the context otherwise requires, be construed as a reference to that enactment or instrument as amended, extended or applied by any other enactment or instrument.

(3) The Interpretation Act 1889 shall apply to the interpretation of this Order as it applies to the interpretation of an Act of Parliament.

* amended by Agricultural Holdings (Arbitration on Notices) (Variation) Order 1984, art. 3.

Part II: NOTICES TO DO WORK

NOTICES REQUIRING ARBITRATION

Notice where arbitration is available at the notice to remedy stage only
3.—(1) Where a tenant on whom a notice to do work has been served wishes to have determined by arbitration under the 1948 Act any of the following questions, namely—

- (*a*) his liability under the terms or conditions of his tenancy to do any of the work specified in the notice;
- (*b*) the deletion from the notice of any item or part of an item of work on the ground that it is unnecessary or unjustified; or
- (*c*) the substitution, in the case of any item or part of an item of work, of a different method or material for the method or material which the notice would otherwise require to be followed or used,

he shall do so by service of a notice requiring the question or questions to be determined by arbitration under the 1948 Act.

(2) A notice under paragraph (1) shall be in writing, and shall be served on the landlord within one month after the service on the tenant of the notice to do work.

(3) A notice under paragraph (1) shall specify, as the case may be,—

- (*a*) any items in respect of which the tenant denies liability;
- (*b*) any items or parts of items which the tenant claims to be unnecessary or unjustified, and
- (*c*) any method or material in respect of which the tenant desires a substitution to be made.

Notice on other questions or in other cases
4.—(1) Where the tenant on whom a notice to do work has been served wishes to have determined by arbitration under the 1948 Act any question arising under that notice other than or in addition to any of those specified in Article 3(1), he shall do so by serving on the landlord within one month after the service of the notice to do work a notice in writing requiring the question to be so determined.

(2) A tenant who has not required arbitration under Article 3(1) or

paragraph (1) shall not be precluded from requiring arbitration under Article 9 in respect of any questions other than those specified in Article 3(1).

(3) Nothing in this Article shall preclude a tenant who has required arbitration under this Article and who has been found liable to comply with a notice to do work or with any part of it from subsequently requiring arbitration under Article 9 on the ground that, in consequence of anything happening before the expiration of the time for doing the work as extended by the arbitrator in pursuance of Article 6(2), it would have been unreasonable to require the tenant to do the work within that time.

POWERS OF ARBITRATOR

Power to modify notice

5. In addition to any powers otherwise available to him, an arbitrator may—

(a) in relation to any question specified in Article 3(1)(b), modify a notice to do work by deleting therefrom any item or part of an item of work specified in the notice as to which, having due regard to the interests of good husbandry as respects the agricultural holding to which the notice relates and of sound management of the estate of which that holding forms part or which that holding constitutes, the arbitrator is satisfied that it is unnecessary or unjustified, and

(b) in relation to a question specified in Article 3(1)(c), modify a notice to do work by substituting, in the case of any item or part of an item of work specified in the notice, a different method or material for the method or material which the notice would otherwise require to be followed or used where, having regard to the purpose which that item or part is intended to achieve, the arbitrator is satisfied that the last-mentioned method or material would involve undue difficulty or expense, that the first-mentioned method or material would be substantially as effective for that purpose, and that in all the circumstances the substitution is justified.

SUPPLEMENTARY

Extension of time for doing work

6.—(1) Where a tenant requires any question to be determined by arbitration under Articles 3 or 4, the time specified for doing the work which is the subject of the arbitration shall be extended until the termination of the arbitration.

(2) Where the arbitrator finds that the tenant is liable to comply with a notice to do work or with any part of it, he shall extend the time for doing that work by such further period as he thinks fit.

Date of termination of tenancy on failure to do work

7.—(1) Where the time specified for doing any work is extended under Article 6(2), the arbitrator may, either of his own motion or on the application of the landlord made not later than fourteen days after the termination of the arbitration, specify a date for the termination of the tenancy by notice to quit in the event of the tenant's failure to do the work within the extended time.

(2) A date specified under paragraph (1) shall not be earlier than—

(*a*) the date on which the tenancy could have been terminated by notice to quit served on the expiration of the time originally specified in the notice to do work, or

(*b*) six months after the expiration of the extended time,

whichever is the later.

(3) Where the landlord applies to the arbitrator under paragraph (1) he shall at the same time give written notice of the application to the tenant (except where the application is made at the arbitration) and the tenant shall be entitled to be heard on the application.

(4) A notice to quit on a date specified under paragraph (1) shall be served on the tenant within one month after the expiration of the extended time, and shall (subject to any right to contest its effectiveness available to the tenant) be valid notwithstanding that it is served less than twelve months before the date on which the tenancy is to be terminated or that that date is not the end of a year of the tenancy.

Recovery of cost of work

8. Where, on an arbitration relating in whole or in part to the question specified in Article 3(1)(*a*), it appears to the arbitrator that the tenant has done work required by a notice to do work which he was under no obligation to do, the arbitrator shall determine the reasonable cost of such work which shall be recoverable from the landlord by the tenant in accordance with section 71 of the 1948 Act.

Part III: NOTICES TO QUIT

Arbitration Concerning Notices to Quit

Notice requiring arbitration

*9. Where it is stated in a notice to quit an agricultural holding or part thereof that the notice is given for one or more of the reasons specified in Case B, D, E or I, and the tenant wishes to contest any of the reasons so stated, or any question arising under Schedule 1A to the 1977 Act, he shall within one month after the service of the notice serve on the landlord notice in writing requiring the question to be determined by arbitration under the 1948 Act.

* amended by Agricultural Holdings (Arbitration on Notices) (Variation) Order 1984, art. 4.

Appointment of arbitrator

*9A. A notice under article 9 above requiring arbitration under the 1948 Act shall cease to be effective for the purposes of that article 3 months after the date of the service of that notice unless before the expiry of those 3 months—

The Surveyor in Court

(*a*) an arbitrator has been appointed by agreement between the parties; or

(*b*) (in default of such an agreement) an application has been made by the tenant under paragraph 1 of Schedule 6 to that Act for the appointment of an arbitrator.

* inserted by Agricultural Holdings (Arbitration on Notices) (Variation) Order 1984, art. 5.

Service of counter-notice

10. Where there has been an arbitration under Article 9 in respect of a notice to quit which is capable of taking effect as a notice to quit to which section 2(1) of the 1977 Act applies and, in consequence of the arbitration, the notice to quit takes effect accordingly, the time within which a counter-notice may be served by the tenant on the landlord under that subsection shall be one month from the termination of the arbitration.

During arbitration

*11. Where a tenant requires a question arising out of a notice to quit to be determined by arbitration under Article 9, the operation of the notice shall be suspended until—

(*a*) the expiry of the time fixed in article 9A above for appointing an arbitrator or for making an application under paragraph 1 of Schedule 6 to the 1948 Act, or

(*b*) where any such appointment or application has been duly made, the termination of the arbitration.

* amended by Agricultural Holdings (Arbitration on Notices) (Variation) Order 1984, art. 6.

After arbitration or proceedings

12.—(1) Where—

(*a*) a notice to quit has effect in consequence of an arbitration under Article 9, or the Agricultural Land Tribunal has consented to the operation of the notice under the 1977 Act, and

(*b*) the notice would, but for the provisions of this Article, come into operation on or within six months after the termination of the arbitration, or the giving of the consent,

the arbitrator or the Tribunal may, either of his or their own motion or on the application of the tenant made not later than fourteen days after the termination of the arbitration or the giving of the consent, postpone the termination of the tenancy for a period not exceeding twelve months.

(2) Where the tenant applies to the arbitrator or the Tribunal under paragraph (1), he shall at the same time give written notice of the application to the landlord (except where the application is made at the arbitration or at the hearing before the Tribunal) and the landlord shall be entitled to be heard on the application.

EXTENSION OF TIME UNDER NOTICE TO REMEDY AFTER NOTICE TO QUIT

Extension by arbitrator
13. Where—

    (*a*) notice to quit is stated to be given by reason of the tenant's failure to remedy a breach of any term or condition of his tenancy—
        (i) within the time specified in a notice to remedy, or
        (ii) within that time as extended by the landlord, or in pursuance of Article 6 or of this Article, and
    (*b*) it appears to the arbitrator on an arbitration under Article 9 that, notwithstanding that the time originally specified or extended was reasonable, it would, in consequence of anything happening before the expiration of that time, have been unreasonable to require the tenant to remedy the breach within that time,

the arbitrator may treat the time as having been extended, or further extended, and may make his award as if the time had not expired; and where the breach has not been remedied at the date of the award, the arbitrator may extend the time by such period as he considers reasonable, having regard to the length of time which has elapsed since the service of the notice to remedy.

Termination of tenancy following extension
14.—(1) Where the time specified for doing any work is extended under Article 13, the arbitrator may, either of his own motion or on the application of the landlord made not later than fourteen days after the termination of the arbitration, specify a date for the termination of the tenancy by a subsequent notice to quit in the event of the tenant's failure to do the work within the extended time.

(2) A date specified under paragraph (1) shall not be earlier than—

    (*a*) the date on which the tenancy could have been terminated by the original notice to quit (that is, the notice which was the subject of the arbitration), or
    (*b*) six months after the expiration of the extended time.

whichever is the later.

(3) Where the landlord applies to the arbitrator under paragraph (1), he shall at the same time give written notice of the application to the tenant (except where the application is made at the arbitration) and the tenant shall be entitled to be heard on the application.

(4) A notice to quit on a date specified under paragraph (1) shall be served on the tenant within one month after the expiration of the extended time, and, subject to paragraph (5), shall be valid notwithstanding it is served less than twelve months before the date on which the tenancy is to be terminated or that that date is not the end of a year of the tenancy.

(5) Where a subsequent notice to quit is given in accordance with paragraph (1) in a case where the original notice to quit included a statement in accordance with Case D to the effect that it was given by reason of the tenant's failure to comply with a notice to do work, then, if the tenant serves on the

landlord a counter-notice in writing within one month after the giving of the subsequent notice to quit (or, if the date specified in that notice for the termination of the tenancy is earlier, before that date), the subsequent notice to quit shall not have effect unless the Agricultural Land Tribunal consent to the operation thereof.

*(6) On an application made for the consent of the Tribunal under paragraph (5) on the part of the landlord; the Tribunal shall consent to the operation of the notice to quit unless it appears to them, having regard—

(a) to the extent to which the tenant has failed to comply with the notice to do work;

(b) to the consequences of his failure to comply with it in any respect; and

(c) to the circumstances surrounding any such failure;

that a fair and reasonable landlord would not insist on possession.

* amended by Agricultural Holdings (Arbitration on Notices) (Variation) Order 1984, art. 7.

SUPPLEMENTARY

Notice to sub-tenants

15.—(1) Section 2(1) of the 1977 Act shall not apply where notice to quit an agricultural holding or part thereof is given to a sub-tenant by a tenant who has himself been given notice to quit that holding or part thereof and the fact that the tenant has been given such notice is stated in the notice given to the sub-tenant.

(2) Such a notice given to a sub-tenant shall have effect only if the notice to quit given to the tenant by the landlord itself has effect.

(3) Where a tenant accepts notice to quit part of a holding as notice to quit the whole under section 9 of the 1977 Act, then, for the purpose of this Article, the notice given by him shall be deemed to be a notice to quit the entire holding.

Service men

16.—(1) In any case to which, notwithstanding the existence of any such circumstances as are mentioned in the Cases set out in section 2(3) of the 1977 Act, subsection (1) thereof applied by virtue of the modification of that section by section 11(3) of that Act, the following provisions of this Article shall have effect.

(2) Where, on an application by the landlord for the consent of the Agricultural Land Tribunal to the operation of a notice to quit, it appears to the Tribunal that the notice to quit was given for one or more of the reasons specified in Case B, D or E, and that it is expedient that any question arising out of those reasons should be determined by arbitration between the landlord and tenant under the 1948 Act before the Tribunal consider whether to grant or withhold consent to the operation of the notice to quit, they may require that the question be determined accordingly.

(3) Article 9 shall apply with the addition of the following words:—

"so, however, that the tenant's failure to serve such a notice shall not affect his right to contest the reason in proceedings before the Agricultural Land Tribunal consequent upon the service of a counter-notice under section

2(1) of the 1977 Act or in any arbitration by which the Tribunal may require any question arising out of the reason to be determined."

(4) Article 10 shall not apply, but where a tenant requires a question to be determined by arbitration in pursuance of Article 9, the time within which a counter-notice under section 2(1) of the 1977 Act may be served by the tenant on the landlord under that subsection shall be one month from the termination of the arbitration.

Part IV: REVOCATION

Revocation of orders
17. The Agriculture (Notices to Remedy and Notices to Quit) Order 1964, and the Agriculture (Notices to Quit) (Miscellaneous Provisions) Order 1972 are hereby revoked, so, however, that those Orders shall continue to apply to notices to do work and notices to quit which have been served before the commencement of this Order, and to any proceedings relating to or consequent upon any such notices.

Rent Assessment Committees (England and Wales) (Rent Tribunal) Regulations 1980 (SI 1980 No. 1700)

Citation and commencement
1. These regulations may be cited as the Rent Assessment Committees (England and Wales) (Rent Tribunal) Regulations 1980 and shall come into operation on 28th November 1980.

Interpretation
2. In these regulations, unless the context otherwise requires, "the Act" means the Rent Act 1977 and "Chairman" means the person acting as chairman of the rent tribunal.

Proceedings before rent tribunals
3. Reference to a rent tribunal shall be by written notice. The notice shall specify the address of the house or part of a house to which the restricted contract relates, the names of the lessor and lessee, and the address of the lessor. The notice may be delivered at an office of the rent assessment panel, in which case it shall be deemed to have reached the rent tribunal on the day when it is so delivered, or may be posted to the rent assessment panel, in which case it shall be deemed to have reached the rent tribunal on the day when it would be delivered in the ordinary course of post.

The Surveyor in Court

*4. Where any reference is made to a rent tribunal, the rent tribunal shall give notice in writing to each party to the restricted contract informing him that he may within such time as the rent tribunal may allow (not being less than seven days from the date of the notice) give notice to the rent tribunal that he desires to be heard by them, or may send to the rent tribunal representations in writing;

Provided that the rent tribunal may extend the time stated in the notice.

*5.—(1) If any party to the restricted contract informs the rent tribunal that he desires to be heard, the rent tribunal shall give to each party not less than seven clear days' notice in writing of the time and place at which the parties will be heard.

(2) If the house to which the reference relates is one the general management whereof is vested in and exercisable by the local authority as housing authority, the said local authority shall be given an opportunity of being heard, or if they so desire, of submitting representations in writing.

* amended by Rent Assessment Committees (England and Wales) (Rent Tribunal) (Amendment) Regulations 1981.

6. At any hearing before a rent tribunal a party to the restricted contract may appear in person or by counsel or a solicitor or by any other representative or may be accompanied by any person whom he may wish to assist him thereat.

7.—(1) Subject to the provisions of these regulations the procedure at a hearing shall be such as the rent tribunal may determine, and the rent tribunal may if they think fit, and at the request of either party shall, unless for some special reason they consider it undesirable, allow the hearing to be held in public; but nothing in these regulations shall prevent a member of the Council on Tribunals in that capacity from attending any hearing.

(2) The rent tribunal may postpone or adjourn the hearing from time to time as they think fit.

8.—(1) The decision of the majority of a rent tribunal shall be the decision of the tribunal. The decision shall be in writing, signed by the chairman, and shall be sent as soon as may be to the parties to the restricted contract, and to the local authority in cases where the restricted contract was referred to the rent tribunal by the authority.

(2) The chairman shall have power, by certificate under his hand, to correct any clerical or accidental error or omission in the said decision.

9. Where any notice is required or authorised by the Act or by these regulations to be given by the rent tribunal it shall be sufficient compliance with the Act or the regulations if the notice is sent by post in a pre-paid letter addressed to the party for whom it is intended at his usual or last known address.

Rent Assessment Committee (England and Wales) (Leasehold Valuation Tribunal) Regulations 1981 (SI 1981 No. 271)

Citation and commencement

1. These regulations may be cited as the Rent Assessment Committee (England and Wales) (Leasehold Valuation Tribunal) Regulations 1981 and shall come into operation on 31st March 1981.

Interpretation

2. In these regulations, unless the context otherwise requires—
"application" means an application to a leasehold valuation tribunal under section 21(1) of the Leasehold Reform Act 1967, and
"tribunal" means a leasehold valuation tribunal.

Applications

3. The form of application prescribed under section 21(4A) of the Leasehold Reform Act 1967 is as follows:—

(a) in the case of an application under section 21(1)(a) of the 1967 Act, form number 1 in the Schedule hereto,
(b) in the case of an application under section 21(1)(b) of the 1967 Act, form number 2 in the Schedule hereto, and
(c) in the case of an application under section 21(1)(c) of the 1967 Act, form number 3 in the Schedule hereto,

or, in each case, a form substantially to the like effect.

4. On receipt of an application, the tribunal shall send a copy of the application and of each of the documents which accompanied it to each person named in it as a respondent.

Hearings

5.—(1) A hearing shall be on such date, and at such time and place as the tribunal shall appoint.

(2) Notice of such date, time and place shall be given by the tribunal to the parties to the proceedings not less than 14 days before the said date, and a copy of the notice shall be sent to any other person who is not already a party to the proceedings and gives notice to the tribunal of his intention to appear at the hearing.

(3) The notice referred to in paragraph (2) above shall contain a statement to the effect that an appeal to the Lands Tribunal from a decision of a tribunal may only be made by a person who appeared before the tribunal in proceedings to which he was a party.

(4) The tribunal may, where they consider it appropriate, arrange that a hearing in respect of one application shall be held together with the hearings in respect of one or more other applications.

(5) A hearing shall be in public unless, for special reasons, the tribunal

decide otherwise, but nothing in these regulations shall prevent a member of the Council on Tribunals in that capacity from attending any hearing.

6. At a hearing—

(*a*) the parties shall be heard in such order and, subject to the provisions of these regulations, the procedure shall be such as the tribunal shall determine;

(*b*) a party may call witnesses, give evidence on his own behalf and cross-examine any witnesses called by any other party; and

(*c*) a party may appear either in person or by a person authorised by him in that behalf whether or not that person is of counsel or a solicitor.

Non-appearance

7. If a party does not appear at a hearing, the tribunal, on being satisfied that the requirements of these regulations regarding the giving of notice of a hearing have been duly complied with, may proceed to deal with the application.

Adjournment

8.—(1) The tribunal at their discretion may of their own motion, or at the request of the parties, or one of them, at any time and from time to time, postpone or adjourn a hearing, but they shall not do so at the request of one party only unless, having regard to the grounds on which and the time at which such request is made and to the convenience of the parties, they deem it reasonable to do so.

(2) The tribunal shall give to the parties such notice of any postponed or adjourned hearing as is reasonable in the circumstances.

Documents

9.—(1) Before the date of a hearing, the tribunal shall take all reasonable steps to ensure that there is supplied to each of the parties—

(*a*) a copy of, or sufficient extracts from or particulars of, any document relevant to the application which has been received from a party (other than a document which is in the possession of such a party or of which he has previously been supplied with a copy); and

(*b*) a copy of any document which embodies the results of any enquiries made by or for the tribunal for the purposes of the application.

(2) Where at a hearing—

(i) any document relevant to the application is not in the possession of a party present at that hearing; and

(ii) that party has not been supplied with a copy of, or sufficient extracts from or particulars of, that document;

then unless—

(*a*) that party consents to the continuation of the hearing; or

(*b*) the tribunal consider that that party has a sufficient opportunity to deal with that document without an adjournment of the hearing;

the tribunal shall adjourn the hearing for a period which they consider will afford that party a sufficient opportunity for dealing with that document.

Inspections

10.—(1) The tribunal may, and shall at the request of any of the parties (subject in either case to any necessary consent being obtained), inspect the house and premises which are the subject of the application.

(2) An inspection may be made before, during or after the close of a hearing, as the tribunal may decide, and the tribunal shall give to the parties and their representatives an opportunity to attend.

(3) Notice of an inspection shall be given as though it were notice of a hearing, but the requirements for such notice may be dispensed with or relaxed in so far as the tribunal are satisfied that the parties have received sufficient notice.

(4) The provisions of this regulation shall apply, so far as is reasonable and practicable, to any comparable house or premises to which the attention of the tribunal is directed as they apply to the house and premises which are the subject of the application.

(5) Where an inspection is made after the close of a hearing, the tribunal shall, if they consider it expedient to do so on account of any matter arising from the inspection, reopen the hearing; and if the hearing is to be reopened paragraph (2) of regulation 5 of these regulations shall apply as it applied to the original hearing, save in so far as its requirements may be dispensed with or relaxed with the consent of the parties.

Decisions

11.—(1) The decision of a tribunal shall be recorded in a document signed by the chairman of the tribunal (or in the event of his absence or incapacity, by another member of the tribunal) which shall contain the reasons for the decision but shall contain no reference to the decision being by a majority (if that be the case) or to any opinion of a minority.

(2) The chairman (or in the event of his absence or incapacity, another member of the tribunal) shall have power, by certificate under his hand, to correct any clerical mistakes in the said document or any errors arising in it from an accidental slip or omission.

(3) A copy of the said document and of any such correction shall be sent by the tribunal to each party.

Provision of information

12. Where, under paragraph 7 of Schedule 22 to the Housing Act 1980 a tribunal by notice in writing require the giving of such information as the tribunal may reasonably require, the notice shall contain a statement to the effect that any person who fails without reasonable cause to comply with the notice is liable on summary conviction to a fine not exceeding £200.

Giving of notice

13. Where any notice or other written matter is required under the provisions of these regulations to be given or supplied by the tribunal it shall be sufficient compliance with these regulations if such notice or other matter is sent by post in pre-paid letter and addressed to the party for whom it is intended at his usual or last known address, or if that party has appointed an agent to act on his behalf, to that agent at the address of the agent supplied to the tribunal.

SCHEDULE

Form No. 1

Leasehold Reform Act 1967

Application for Determination by Leasehold Valuation Tribunal on acquisition of freehold

I/We apply for the determination by a Leasehold Valuation Tribunal of the price payable under section 9 of the Leasehold Reform Act 1967 for the house and premises named in paragraph 1 below and submit the following particulars. The respondents to this application are the persons (other than myself/ourselves) named in paragraphs 2 to 5 of those particulars.

*[I/We also apply to the Leasehold Valuation Tribunal for the determination under section 21(2) of the 1967 Act of the matters described in paragraph 12 below relating to the house and premises.]

* Cross out this paragraph if it does not apply.

THE PARTICULARS

1. Address of house and premises ....

2. Name and address of landlord to whom rent is payable by the tenant ......

3. Name of tenant (and address if different from 1 above) ....

4. Is the landlord mentioned in (2) above the freehold
owner of the premises?   Yes ☐   No. ☐
   If NO, give the names and addresses of
     (*a*) the freeholder ....
     (*b*) any additional, intermediate landlords standing between the land-
        lord mentioned in paragraph 2 and the freeholder   ....

5. Is anyone, to the applicant's knowledge, entitled to the
benefit of a charge on the freeholder's, or any other landlord's interest in the house and premises, such as a mortgagee (e.g. a building society)?   Yes ☐   No. ☐
   If YES, give names and addresses, if known ....

6. State the date on which notice was given by the tenant of his desire to
acquire the freehold ....
and enclose a copy of the notice.

7. Has the landlord given notice stating whether or not he
admits the tenant's right to have the freehold?   Yes ☐   No. ☐
   If YES, give the date of the notice .... and enclose a copy of it.

8. Has the landlord informed the tenant of the price he is
asking?   Yes ☐   No. ☐
   If YES, enclose a copy of the letter or notice from the landlord giving details
of it.

---

9. Have any other formal notices been given following the
notice by the tenant of his desire to have the freehold?   Yes ☐   No. ☐
   If YES, enclose copies of all the notices.

---

10. State the price which the applicant considers to be appropriate £ ......

---

11. Have the terms of the conveyance (other than the price)
been agreed?   Yes ☐   No. ☐
   If YES, enclose details or a copy of a draft conveyance.

---

12. Is this also an application under section 21(2) of the Leasehold Reform Act
1967:—
   (*a*) to determine what provisions ought to be contained
          in the conveyance?   Yes ☐   No. ☐
   If YES, give details on a separate sheet and enclose a copy
of the existing lease.
   (*b*) to apportion between the house and premises (or
          part of them) and other property, the rent payable
          under any tenancy?   Yes ☐   No. ☐
   If YES, give details on a separate sheet.

---

13. (*a*) Has any application been made to a Court to
            determine any question relating to this matter? Yes ☐   No. ☐
     (*b*) If YES, has the Court made an Order?   Yes ☐   No. ☐
   If YES, enclose a copy of the Order.

---

14. Is the applicant
    (*a*) the owner of the freehold?   Yes ☐   No. ☐
    (*b*) a landlord?   Yes ☐   No. ☐
    (*c*) the tenant?   Yes ☐   No. ☐

Signed ....
[On behalf of ....]
If signed by an agent, give name and address of agent ....
....
                              Date ....

FORM No. 2

LEASEHOLD REFORM ACT 1967

APPLICATION FOR DETERMINATION BY LEASEHOLD VALUATION TRIBUNAL OF
THE RENT TO BE PAYABLE

I/We apply for the determination by a Leasehold Valuation Tribunal of the
amount of the rent to be payable under section 15(2) of the Leasehold Reform
Act 1967 for the house and premises named in paragraph 1 below and submit

the following particulars. The respondents to this application are the persons (other than myself/ourselves) named in paragraphs 2 to 5 of those particulars.

*[I/We also apply to the Leasehold Valuation Tribunal for the determination under section 21(2) of the 1967 Act of the matters described in paragraph 11 below relating to the house and premises.]

* Cross out this paragraph if it does not apply.

THE PARTICULARS

1. Address of house and premises ....

2. Name and address of landlord to whom rent is payable by the tenant ...

3. Name of tenant (and address if different from 1 above).....................

4. Has a new tenancy, expiring 50 years after the original tenancy, already been granted for the house and premises?   Yes ☐   No. ☐
If YES, give the names and addresses of—
    (*a*) the landlord named in the new lease ....
    (*b*) any additional, intermediate landlords standing between the landlord named in the new lease and the tenant ....
Enclose a copy of the new lease and then GO TO QUESTION 10.

5. If a new tenancy has *not* yet been granted give the name and address of—
    (*a*) the person who will grant the new lease ....
    (*b*) any additional, intermediate landlords standing between that person and the tenant ....
and enclose a copy of the existing lease.

6. Have the terms (other than rent) for the new tenancy been agreed?   Yes ☐   No. ☐
If YES, enclose a copy.

7. Give the date of the notice by the tenant of his desire to have an extended lease..
....
and enclose a copy of the notice.

8. Has the landlord given notice stating whether or not he admits the tenant's right to have an extended lease?   Yes ☐   No. ☐
If YES, give the date of the notice ....
and enclose a copy of it.

9. Have any other formal notices been given following the notice by the tenant of his desire to have an extended lease?   Yes ☐   No. ☐
If YES, enclose copies of all the notices.

10. State the amount of rent the applicant considers appropriate—£.........

11. Is this also an application under section 21(2) of the Leasehold Reform Act 1967:—
    (*a*) to determine what provisions ought to be contained in the lease granting the new tenancy?   Yes ☐   No. ☐

If YES, give details on a separate sheet.

(*b*) to apportion between the house and premises (or part of them) and other property, the rent payable under any tenancy? Yes ☐ No. ☐

If YES, give details on a separate sheet.

12. (*a*) Has any application been made to a Court to determine any question relating to this matter? Yes ☐ No. ☐

(*b*) If YES, has the Court made an Order? Yes ☐ No. ☐

If YES, enclose a copy of the Order.

13. Is the applicant—

(*a*) the owner of the freehold? Yes ☐ No. ☐

(*b*) a landlord? Yes ☐ No. ☐

(*c*) the tenant? Yes ☐ No. ☐

Signed ....

[On behalf of ....]

If signed by an agent, give name and address of agent ....

....

Date ....

FORM No. 3

LEASEHOLD REFORM ACT 1967

APPLICATION FOR DETERMINATION BY LEASEHOLD VALUATION TRIBUNAL OF COMPENSATION PAYABLE TO A TENANT

I/We apply for the determination by a Leasehold Valuation Tribunal of the amount of the compensation payable under section 17 or 18 of the Leasehold Reform Act 1967 for the loss of the house and premises named in paragraph 1 below and submit the following particulars. The respondents to this application are the persons (other than myself/ourselves) named in paragraphs 2 to 4 of those particulars.

*[I/We also apply to the Leasehold Valuation Tribunal for the determination under section 21(2) of the 1967 Act of the amount of a sub-tenant's share under Schedule 2 to the Act of the compensation payable to the tenant.]

* Cross out this paragraph if it does not apply.

THE PARTICULARS

1. Address of house and premises ....

2. Name and Address of landlord by whom compensation is payable ......

3. Name of tenant (and address if different from 1 above) ....

4. Is this also an application under section 21(2) of the Leasehold Reform Act 1967 to determine the amount of a sub-tenant's share under Schedule 2 to the Act of the compensation payable to the tenant. Yes ☐ No. ☐

If YES, give the name and address of the sub-tenant ....

5. Give full details on a separate sheet of the circumstances under which the claim for compensation arises and enclose copies of—
    (*a*) the lease and of any agreements for sub-tenancies, and
    (*b*) all other relevant documents, applications to the Court and Court Orders, or notices.

6. State the amount of compensation which the applicant considers appropriate £ ....

7. Is the applicant—
    (*a*) the landlord?   Yes ☐ No. ☐
    (*b*) the tenant?   Yes ☐ No. ☐

Signed ....
[On behalf of ....]
If signed by an agent, give name and address of agent ....
....
Date ....

County Court Rules 1981 (SI 1981 No. 1687 (L. 20))

Order 20

Part V—Expert Evidence

Restrictions on adducing expert evidence

27.—(1) Except with the leave of the court or where all parties agree, no expert evidence may be adduced at the trial or hearing of an action or matter, unless the party seeking to adduce the evidence has applied to the court to determine whether a direction should be given under rule 37, 38 or 41 (whichever is appropriate) of R.S.C. Order 38, as applied by rule 28 of this Order, and has complied with any direction given on the application.

(2) Nothing in paragraph (1) shall apply to expert evidence which is permitted to be given by affidavit or which is to be adduced in an action or matter in which no defence or answer has been filed or in proceedings referred to arbitration under section 92 of the Act.

(3) Nothing in paragraph (1) shall affect the enforcement under any other provision of these rules (except Order 29, rule 1) of a direction given under this Part of this Order.

Application of R.S.C.

28. R.S.C. Order 38, rules 37 to 44 shall apply in relation to an application under rule 27 of this Order as they apply in relation to an application under rule 36(1) of the said Order 38.

Circulars

	Page
Circular No. 73/65	
The Award of Costs at Statutory Inquiries	555
Circular No. 38/81	
Planning and Enforcement Appeals, paras 1–25	561

Circular No. 73/65
The Award of Costs at Statutory Inquiries
(Circular 35/65 for Wales is in similar terms)

1. I am directed by the Minister of Housing and Local Government to refer to the report of the Council on Tribunals on the above-mentioned subject.

2. The Government has decided to accept the main recommendation in the report to the effect that costs should normally be awarded to successful objectors to compulsory purchase and analogous orders. Accordingly owners, lessees or occupiers of land on whom statutory notice of a compulsory purchase order has to be served will in appropriate circumstances qualify for such an award; in the analogous cases those who attend a local inquiry to defend their property may similarly, if successful, rank as qualified objectors.

Scope of this circular

3. This circular deals with the implementation of that recommendation so far as it affects inquiries held on behalf of the Minister of Housing and Local Government. These arrangements concerning compulsory purchase orders should be taken as applying to such orders submitted to other Ministers unless and until the responsible Minister indicates the contrary. It deals also with certain other recommendations, in the main those which it has been decided to accept and to put into effect by administrative action.

4. Legislation will be required to give effect to the recommendation, which has been accepted in principle, that the statutory provisions for the award of costs should be extended to cover hearings as well as local inquiries.

Award of costs to qualified objectors

5. The new practice with relation to the award of costs to successful objectors will be applied to inquiries held after the date of this circular on behalf of the Minister of Housing and Local Government, into the following types of orders or proposals submitted to him for confirmation or approval:

    (i) Compulsory acquisition of land;
    (ii) Clearance Orders (Housing Act 1957, Part III);
    (iii) Unfitness Orders (Land Compensation Act 1961, Second Schedule);
    (iv) Proposals under section 4(3) of the Town and Country Planning Act 1962 to designate land as subject to compulsory acquisition;
    (v) Orders under section 27 of the Town and Country Planning Act 1962, revoking or modifying a planning permission;
    (vi) Orders under section 28 of the Town and Country Planning Act 1962, requiring discontinuance of use, or alteration or removal of buildings or works.

Continued consideration will be given to the extension of this list to inquiries into further kinds of submissions that are of relatively infrequent occurrence, but may be considered as analogous in character, and further particulars may be issued by the Departments concerned, if necessary.

6. The Minister will normally make a favourable award of costs on application by a qualified objector who duly objected to an order or proposal concerning his property and who following a local inquiry had his objection sustained by the Minister's refusal to confirm the order or approve the proposal, or to do so in respect of the whole or part of the objector's property which was in question at the inquiry. The award will be made against the authority who made the order or proposal.

7. The Minister will consider making an *ex gratia* payment of costs to successful qualified objectors, following inquiries into similar orders or proposals initiated by himself (for example a revocation, modification or discontinuance order made by him in the exercise of his powers under section 207 of the Town and Country Planning Act 1962) and also following inquiries into orders under section 1 of the New Towns Act 1965, designating an area as the site of a proposed new town.

Award of costs in other cases

(a) Unsuccessful objectors

8. The council recommend that costs should not normally be awarded to unsuccessful objectors in compulsory purchase and analogous cases; but they qualified this by recommending that, when there was little or no merit in one objection over another and policy or chance was the determining factor as between one objector and another, the unsuccessful objector who had not behaved unreasonably, vexatiously or frivolously should be awarded his costs. In view of the impracticability of discriminating with obvious fairness between objectors in the manner proposed it has been decided not to make an award in cases of this kind.

(b) Unreasonable behaviour

9. In any case where it is alleged that a party has acted unreasonably, the Minister will in future have regard to the considerations set out in paragraphs 23–29 of the council's report before deciding whether to make an award of costs. This will apply to planning appeals and other types of proposals, many of which are not initiated by the authority concerned, as well as to cases of the kinds mentioned in paragraph 5 above. Awards of costs on grounds of unreasonable behaviour will, of course, arise only in very exceptional circumstances.

(c) Postponement and adjournment of inquiry

10. Where a postponement or adjournment of an inquiry is made necessary through the fault of any party, including a third party who has been allowed to appear at the inquiry, the Minister will be prepared to consider applications by the other parties appearing at the inquiry for their extra costs, so far as occasioned by the postponement or adjournment, to be paid by the party at fault.

(d) Re-opened inquiries

11. Any question of awarding costs following the re-opening of an inquiry by the Minister in cases where he has received new evidence which was not raised at the inquiry will be dealt with on the same basis as applied to the original inquiry.

Procedure

12. If representations about costs are made by parties at an inquiry, the Inspector will record the arguments for and against an award, but he will not normally make a recommendation on the subject. It is stressed that the making of an application for costs at the inquiry is not a necessary prerequisite of an award: successful objectors will where appropriate be asked whether they wish to submit an application to the Minister when his decision has been made. The question of an award will normally be dealt with by the Minister after the decision on the subject-matter of the inquiry.

Amount of award

13. Where the Minister has decided to accede to an application for costs, whether against or in favour of a local authority, he will in all cases give the parties concerned an opportunity to agree between themselves the amount which should be awarded and it is hoped that such agreement will in most cases be reached. Where the party receiving costs has been legally represented, the Minister will, without himself determining an amount, make an award for the payment of his costs of the inquiry, to be taxed (in the High Court) in default of agreement. Where the party receiving costs has not been legally represented, the Minister will be prepared to make an order in such amount as the parties may agree and request him to do; failing agreement in such a case, the disputed claim for costs will be referred to the Department for settlement, upon consideration of the arguments of the parties, and an order will be made in accordance with the Minister's determination.

Partly successful objectors

14. Where an objector is partly successful in opposing an order or proposal of the kind mentioned in paragraph 5 above, the Minister will make an award related to a proportion of the relevant costs. Such cases arise, for example, where the Minister, in confirming a compulsory purchase order, excludes part of the objector's land; or where an objector to a slum clearance compulsory purchase order can establish that his house is not unfit but he does not succeed in having it excluded from the order. (If, however, unfitness was the only issue on which he objected at the inquiry he would be regarded as wholly successful.)

Plural objections

15. Sometimes a single inquiry is held into two or more proposals, such as proposals to amend a development plan involving other alterations, as well as designation of land as subject to compulsory acquisition, and perhaps also an order for the compulsory acquisition of some or all of the land concerned; or an application for planning permission and an order for the compulsory acquisition of land included in the application. Where a qualified objector appears at such an inquiry in respect of more than one proposal and is successful in his objection in respect of a proposal of a kind mentioned in paragraph 5 above, he will be awarded costs in respect of that objection only.

Extracts from the Report of the Council on Tribunals on The Award of Costs at Statutory Inquiries (referred to in the above circular)

Award of costs in cases of unreasonable conduct

23. We recommend as a rule of general application that costs should normally be awarded against a party who behaves unreasonably, vexatiously or frivolously in favour of a party who, being legally entitled to appear at the inquiry, has duly appeared thereat and has not so behaved. Although "unreasonably" is a word wide enough to cover "vexatiously" or "frivolously," in stating this rule we have chosen to adopt the words "unreasonably, vexatiously or frivolously" because they are of familiar use in almost every branch of the law and have been judicially interpreted. This rule is intentionally worded in such a way that under it an award of costs could be made against a successful party, but we recognise that the circumstances in which such an order would be made will be rare. It is also intentionally confined to persons who are legally entitled to appear at the inquiry: we deal with the position of third parties in paragraphs 46 and 47.

24. The Ministry of Housing and Local Government have suggested that, in the field of planning appeals, the following general principles would seem to apply in considering whether an award of costs might be made on the ground of unreasonable behaviour:

> (i) The main criterion is whether one party has been put to unnecessary and unreasonable expense (*a*) because the matter should never have come to inquiry or (*b*) because, although the appeal

and inquiry could not reasonably have been avoided, the other party conducted their side of the procedure in such a way as to cause unnecessary trouble and expense.

(ii) It is reasonable to expect a higher standard of behaviour from planning authorities than from appellants, because the former ought to know more about the procedure and the strength of the arguments on both sides of a particular appeal.

Furthermore the Ministry take the view that these principles could be applied to other procedures subject to this important qualification that where a local authority initiated the proposal (for example, the compulsory acquisition of land by a local authority) it would generally be very difficult to make an award against an objector who was trying to retain his land or some right attaching to it.

25. We accept the principles put forward by the Ministry in the context of inquiries into planning appeals and recommend that they should be applied to all inquiries, subject to the qualification that it should be regarded as very exceptional to award costs against the citizen where a local authority or statutory undertaker initiated the proposal.

26. Obviously it is not possible to lay down cut and dried rules as to standards of reasonable behaviour where reasonableness (or the lack of it) is used as a criterion for deciding whether costs should be awarded. Each case necessarily will have to be judged in the light of its own particular circumstances. It is thought, however, that a few examples where an award might be justified would prove helpful.

27. The Ministry have suggested that cases coming within the category where an inquiry might have been avoided but for the unreasonable behaviour of one of the parties are as follows:

(i) Where a previous decision of the Minister has made it quite clear what his decision will be.

For example:

(*a*) where there has been a recent appeal in respect of the same site and the same or very similar development, and the Minister has made it plain that this development should not be allowed, conditions have not materially changed, but the appellant, despite warnings about the previous decision, has persisted in pressing his case to inquiry;

(*b*) where the Minister has dismissed a previous appeal, but indicated that he would see no objection to an application in a different form, such an application has been made, but the authority have persisted in refusing permission.

(ii) Where the planning authority have been unable to support their decision (or their failure to give one) by any substantial evidence.

(iii) Where the appeal could have been avoided if the parties had got together to discuss it, or more information had been provided, and either (*a*) one party had refused to discuss it, though asked to do so, or (*b*) one party had refused to provide information which they could reasonably be expected to provide.

(iv) Where the appeal or the authority decision was obviously prompted

by considerations which had little or nothing to do with planning—
for example, if an application were made as part of a publicity
campaign or a campaign against a neighbour or council, or if
permission were refused primarily because of prejudice.

(v) Where it must have been obvious from previous decisions well
publicised in official documents, or from official statements of law
or policy in circulars, handbooks or memoranda, than an appeal
was certain to be decided in a particular way.

28. The Ministry have also suggested that cases coming within the
category where, although the inquiry could not reasonably have been
avoided, one of the parties has put the other to unnecessary trouble and
expense by mishandling their side of the procedure, are as follows:

(i) Where a reason for refusal, or a ground of appeal is introduced at
a late stage in the proceedings, requiring an adjournment of the
inquiry so as to give an opportunity for consideration of the new
point or for finding a new witness or witnesses.

(ii) Where a reason for refusal or a ground of appeal is dropped in the
course of the proceedings after the opposing side have spent
money and effort in preparing themselves to meet it.

(iii) Where one party has refused to co-operate with the other in settling agreed facts or supplying relevant information before the
inquiry, thus unnecessarily prolonging the inquiry.

29. We consider that neither of the last two cases mentioned in paragraph
28 nor the third case in paragraph 27 should be regarded as unreasonable
behaviour on the part of the citizen. So far as the second case in paragraph
28 is concerned, it costs no more (probably less) if a ground of appeal is
dropped, even at a late stage, than if it is unsuccessfully persisted in, and the
latter is not a ground for awarding costs. With regard to the other two cases,
the rules of procedure impose no obligation on a citizen to discuss anything
or to provide any information or to co-operate in settling agreed facts in
advance of the inquiry. The parties are obliged to comply with the rules of
procedure and a failure to do so might well constitute unreasonableness, but
there is no obligation to go further than compliance with the rules demands.
This is of course as true of the local authority or statutory undertaker as it is
for the citizen, but for the reasons given in paragraph 24(ii) above it seems
to the Council that a local authority or statutory undertaker ought to be
expected when the occasion arises to go beyond the rules.

The position of third parties

46. We have referred in paragraph 23 to parties who are legally entitled
to appear at the inquiry and we have stated a general rule to apply to them.
In a local planning appeal, for example, the applicant for planning permission, the local planning authority and persons who have made representations on the application which is the subject of the appeal under section 37
of the Town and Country Planning Act 1959 (re-enacted in section 16 of the
1962 Act) or under section 36 of the Town and Country Planning (Scotland) Act 1959 are parties who have a legal right to appear at the inquiry.
Members of the public have no such right but may appear at the discretion

of the person appointed to hold the inquiry, and in practice any person who shows he has a genuine interest in the land which is the subject of the appeal and desires to be heard is permitted to appear. Thus, any person whose amenities may be spoilt or whose land may be diminished in value by reason of the proposed development may appear and be heard at the inquiry. Such persons are known as "third parties." We now turn to consider what their position is with regard to the award of costs at the inquiry.

47. At first sight it would seem right that there should be no award of costs against third parties since a third party has no legal right to be heard at the inquiry and is heard only at the discretion of the person holding the inquiry who may stop him if he considers that he is behaving unreasonably. In practice, however, it may often be difficult to know, until he has presented his case, whether a third party has behaved unreasonably or not. There may also be cases where the local planning authority take a neutral line and the real contest lies between the appellant and a third party. In such circumstances, should not the third party be eligible to receive and liable to be condemned in costs? We are aware of the danger of inhibiting persons who wish to put forward *bona fide* objections by being condemned in costs, and we are not in favour of the view, save in exceptional circumstances, that a third party should be liable to pay costs because he has put forward objections without reasonable cause or because he takes an unreasonable time to present his case. We consider that it is a logical consequence that save in exceptional circumstances third parties should not be eligible to receive costs even where another party has behaved unreasonably. An illustration of an exceptional case would be the case of an adjournment of the inquiry caused by the fault or default of one of the parties which we deal with in paragraph 44: in such cases a special award might be made in favour of or against a third party, as the case may be.

Circular No. 38/81
Planning and Enforcement Appeals

(Appeals under sections 36, 37, 88 or 97 of the Town and Country Planning Act 1971, determined by the Secretary of State or by an appointed person and proceeding by way of inquiry or written representations).

INTRODUCTION

1. DOE Circular 22/80 (Welsh Office Circular 40/80) emphasises the importance of a speedy and efficient development control system. This applies as much to appeals as to applications. Within the last two years much as been done to speed up appeal procedures; output and timescales have greatly improved. Local planning authorities (LPAs) have co-operated whole-heartedly and share the credit for the progress already achieved. But more can still be done and this Circular seeks further improvements in the handling of appeals, without disturbing the fundamental principles of fairness, thoroughness and consistency.

2. A speedy, efficient appeals system is of benefit to all. The community gains from earlier investment decisions and from the removal of uncertainty. The parties involved benefit from earlier release of the staff and other resources pre-empted by an appeal. There is disagreement over the merits of the case, or there would be no appeal, but there should be no dispute over the value of a rapid settlement. The key to achieving earlier decisions is more effective co-operation. This requires better communication between everyone involved in an appeal.

3. The Departments are taking a lead in this. The Planning Inspectorate has held meetings with 50 LPAs in England to discuss common problems and a similar limited programme of meetings with developers and agents is under way. The lessons already learned from this study are incorporated in this Circular. Representatives of the Inspectorate have begun to attend, from time to time, meetings of local development control forums. The explanatory booklet "Planning Appeals—A Guide to Procedure" is being revised to give clearer and fuller advice. Other means of making more information available are under study. These initiatives should go a long way to improve communications, but they will depend for their success upon the readiness of appellants and LPAs to co-operate between themselves and with the Departments.

4. Part I of this Circular contains advice on improved procedures for appeals generally. Part II presents a new edition of the timetable, first issued in 1965, for planning appeals dealt with by written representations. Part III explains how the regulations governing procedures for enforcement appeals, which will take effect on January 11, 1982, are intended to operate. The special problems posed by exceptionally large or complex appeals will be the subject of later advice.

PART I

THE CONDUCT OF APPEALS

The origins of an appeal
5. An appeal is an essential statutory safeguard within the development control system. But it is not to be embarked upon lightly. The process is costly to all the parties involved and also the taxpayers and ratepayers. Anyone considering an appeal should weigh the prospects carefully, perhaps taking professional advice.

6. Before a disappointed applicant for planning permission lodges a planning appeal, or a LPA issues an enforcement notice likely to result in an appeal, there should be consultation and negotiation between the parties and other bodies or individuals affected. Discussions of this kind can often resolve difficulties more quickly and cheaply than appealing. An appeal is intended to be, and should remain, a last resort.

7. Careful study of the policy background—in development plans,

Departmental circulars and advice notes and elsewhere—is essential; clearly stated policies which have been endorsed through the structure and local plan system, for example, are unlikely to be set aside lightly. Potential appellants can thus assess the merits of their case and the prospects of success, which they must balance against the costs and delays involved in an appeal. Conversely, LPAs' decisions to refuse a planning permission or issue an enforcement notice must take account of the possibility of a successful appeal. There is always a risk (in an inquiry case) that either party may be liable for costs if it can be shown that their behaviour has been unreasonable and has caused the other party unnecessary expense.

Improved appeal procedures

8. If negotiation fails and an appeal is made, experience in the Departments and the recent study (referred to in paragraph 3) suggest a number of steps which can be taken to ensure maximum economy in time and cost.

The choice of procedure

9. Many appeals still go to inquiry, generally at the request of the appellant, when the written representations procedure would be just as effective and save expense and time—for appeals decided by Inspectors, the average time saving in the six months up to October 1981 was about 2 months. Unnecessary inquiries therefore cause delay, especially in those areas where a LPA's capacity to hold or attend them is inadequate (see para. 15 below). The written method is already used in some 75 per cent of planning appeals and could be used in more, to the benefit of all concerned with the appeals system.

10. It remains the right of any appellant or LPA to be heard before a Planning Inspector. The inquiry procedure will always be appropriate for the most complex and contentious planning appeals and for a greater proportion of enforcement appeals where the need for cross-examination or evidence on oath may be more frequent. But appellants and LPAs could profitably give the written representations method their first and serious consideration, opting for an inquiry only when it is essential.

Written representations cases

Shorter statements

11. For *planning appeals*, too many statements by LPAs and appellants are excessively full and detailed. Elaborate and repetitive documents take much time and labour both to draft and to absorb. There are obvious benefits for Inspectors and the parties in shorter statements. Nothing is lost by a succinct statement of the material facts and policies and the grounds of the decision or appeal. Table 1 below gives guidance on the recommended format of a written statement, which should be concise, clear and relevant.

Table 1

Format of Written Statement

1. REFERENCES—Departmental and LPA reference numbers for appeal.

2. THE SITE AND ITS LOCATION—a description restricted to those features relevant to the appeal.

Avoid—describing characteristics of the site which are readily apparent from the plan.

3. POLICIES—a list, or other concise statement, of planning policies on which the decision or the appeal relies.

This should include *references* to relevant official documents (such as Departmental circulars or the Development Control Policy Notes) and *copies* of, or *extracts* from, appropriate published documents such as development plans; the status of the relevant plan (*e.g.* submitted or approved) should be given.

Avoid—lengthy rehearsals or interpretations of general planning policies in the text of the statement.

4. EXPLANATORY COMMENTS—additional statements, confined to the essence of the case, to augment where necessary the reasons for refusal or grounds of appeal.

For example, the relevant planning policies, and the way in which they have been applied, may need to be related to the proposed development and its surroundings; comment may be appropriate on points raised in other parties' statements; and there may be a need to include a brief history of the application, the site and the surrounding area, or a mention of personal circumstances.

> *Avoid*—a detailed history of the application where this is not relevant to the appeal;
>
> —repeating or interpreting at length, in the body of the statement, the comments of persons (other than the appellant and the LPA) adduced in support of the case. A copy of their views can be attached to the statement, with their consent;
>
> —quoting in the text relevant planning decisions. These can be readily set out in an annex.

---

12. For *enforcement appeals*, lengthier statements of the relevant facts, planning history and legal arguments may be essential, but they could often be marshalled and presented more clearly and concisely.

Repeated exchanges of representations

13. A common feature of many planning and enforcement appeals is a tendency to engage in repeated exchanges of representations where this is not warranted by the complexity of the case. Whether intended to reinforce points by repetition, to have the last word, or to save the best arguments to the end, such tactics are not helpful. They confer no advantage, encourage responses in kind, and serve only to prolong the appeal process.

Attendance at site visits

14. Site inspections are occasionally delayed when LPAs insist on waiting until their case officer is available. No discussion of the merits of an appeal is allowed at a site inspection, so that it is often unnecessary for the Inspector to be accompanied by either party. Where the Inspector has to enter on private property, and must therefore be accompanied, or where there are features of the site which need to be drawn to his attention, a junior member of staff can adequately represent the LPA.

Inquiry cases

Firm and early inquiry dates

15. A major factor in speeding up appeals has been the Department's greater firmness in fixing and keeping to inquiry dates. The Departments will continue to seek early dates for inquiries from the parties and will grant a postponement only where it is clearly justified. A few LPAs face a demand for inquiries which is sometimes greater than they can meet; backlogs develop, leading to queues and delays and a reduced service to appellants. Like the LPAs concerned the Secretaries of State wish to overcome such problems. Special arrangements are usually needed and the authorities should discuss the options with the Departments. In some cases a solution may be for the authority to re-allocate resources, at least temporarily, so as to increase its inquiry capacity.

Early clarification of inquiry issues

16. It is very helpful to isolate the principal issues and arguments in advance of the inquiry. This can shorten proceedings and save time in preparation by the appellant and LPA (and also the appointed Inspector). Appellants can play their part by stating their case in full on making an appeal and providing, in advance of the inquiry, any necessary additional explanation. The Secretaries of State will make greater use of their powers to require pre-inquiry statements in future.

General improvements

Conditions

17. The recent study by the Inspectorate (see para. 3 above) revealed that LPAs are sometimes concerned about the conditions attached (or not attached) to planning permissions granted on appeal, but are reluctant to offer views about conditions in advance, through fear that they might pre-judice their case. This fear is quite unfounded. The Secretaries of State would welcome LPAs' reasoned views, in their Rule 6 or 7 statements or in their written representations, on the conditions or limitations they would favour if the appeal were allowed; these views would always be open to comment by the appellant or to discussion at an inquiry.

Delays in forwarding documents

18. The study also revealed delays in forwarding appeal documents within some LPAs. Since local government re-organisation different departments within a LPA are, more often than before, in different buildings or towns. LPAs are asked to ensure that papers are not held up en route to their action officer. They are also asked that the Departments hold the most direct and practical address or addresses to use for correspondence on appeals.

Copying documents

19. The parties to an appeal can speed its progress by copying documents to each other, as many already do, instead of leaving all copying to the Departments. Such co-operation saves time otherwise lost in postal and handling processes and enables earlier consideration of the documents concerned and earlier action to take place. Examples of documents which the parties might usefully copy to each other are the appeal form itself (and its supporting documents) and the LPA's written statement.

Consultations

20. Some delays are caused by the failure of public bodies to reply promptly to consultations. The Secretaries of State will remind them of the importance of speeding handling of appeals.

Part II

A Timetable for Written Representations Planning Appeals

21. This Circular has stressed that a speedy, efficient appeals system is in both the parties' and the public interest. It contains advice designed to simplify procedures and improve communications to this end. The Secretaries of State believe that a standard timetable, closely observed by all parties, is essential to the improved handling of appeals. For *enforcement appeals* there will in future be statutory time limits, prescribed in regulations under section 88(5) of the 1971 Act (see Part III below). For *planning appeals* a timetable was first published in 1965. In issuing an updated version (Table 2 below) with this Circular, the Secretaries of State look for the co-operation of all parties in keeping to the time limits indicated as closely as possible.

22. This timetable embodies the basic concept of the written representations procedure, namely a *single* exchange of statements by the parties to the appeal. Thus the parties should make their main statements, containing all the material they consider relevant, in two key documents; the appellant's grounds of appeal (with supporting documents) and the LPA's written statement. Both parties have the chance to comment on these submissions; but, as the timetable makes clear, the time for further representations is strictly limited so as to avoid delay to the appeal.

23. The timetable indicates, as before, that the LPA should return its statement within 4 weeks of receiving a request from the Department. This request is now made with the notification of appeal. The appellant has 2 weeks to make any comments on the LPA statement. Each party can help to meet these deadlines by copying papers to the other. The timetable now also contains a request that a LPA should arrange for any third party comments to reach the Department within the period allowed for their own statement.

24. Late statements can seriously delay an appeal. A LPA or appellant who anticipates difficulty in submitting a statement on time should discuss this with the appeal's case officer in Bristol or Cardiff. Only where a good reason can be shown will the Department normally consider delaying a site visit or other action for the sake of a statement which is more than two weeks overdue.

25. The local authority associations, who agree that appeals should be determined as quickly as possible, have given their support to this approach.

Table 2

TARGET TIMETABLE FOR PLANNING APPEALS—WRITTEN REPRESENTATIONS

Appellant	Department	Local Planning Authority (LPA)
1 Submits statements of case to Department – the appeal form with any necessary documents		
	2 Receives appeal. Notifies LPA within one week, asking for completion of questionnaire – within 2 weeks – and a written statement of case in response to the appellant's – within 4 weeks	3 Receives notification of appeal from Department. Notifies local residents and others affected by the appeal, arranging for any comments to reach the Department within the period allowed for the LPA's own statement
		4 Returns questionnaire to Department (within 2 weeks*)
	5 Receives questionnaire from LPA. Consults other bodies if necessary	
		6 Submits written statement (within 4 weeks*)
	7 Receives any third party representations. Copies them to appellant and LPA within 3 days	
	8 Receives LPA's written statement. Copies it to appellant within 3 days	
9 Receives LPA's written statement.* Has 2 weeks* to submit any comments to Department		
	10 Receives appellant's comments (if any) on LPA's statement. Copies them to LPA within 3 days	

At this stage the Department should have sufficient evidence to decide the appeal and further representations will only be required in exceptional circumstances

| | 11 Site visit (arranged at earliest date possible for Inspector and, where appropriate, the parties) | |
| | 12 Inspector issues decision or reports to Department, within 4 weeks of site visit or conclusion of written exchanges | |

* All these periods run from the date of origin (e.g. the date of the Department's letter at stage 2) to the date of receipt by the Department, plus an allowance of 3 days for postage.

Index

A

Admiralty, Court of, 4
  assessors in, 59
Admissions, 50
  agreed facts as, 50
  expert evidence based on, 70, 77–81
  formal, 49, 50
  informal, 49
  valuation list entries as, 78
  without prejudice statements not, 49
Advocate (advocacy), 157–62
  arbitrators as, 277
  duties of, 157–8
  expert witness, distinguished from,
      155
  negligence, immunity from, 211, 221,
      249
  planning officer as, 155
  qualities needed by, 159–62
  style of, 158–9
Advocate-expert witness, 155–90
  consistency of roles, 156, 162
  criticisms of, 155–6
  cross-examination by, 184–7
  documents, preparation by, examples
      of, 172–7
  expert evidence by, examples of,
      177–80, 181–4
  factors against, 156–7
  final address by, example of, 187–9
  not permitted, where, 155
  opening address by, example of,
      168–70, 180–1
  qualities needed by, 162
  role, indication of, 157
  submissions and evidence,
      preparation by, 163–4
  valuation officer as, 156, 180–7
Affidavit see under Evidence
Affirmation
  arbitration, in, 312
  form of, 91
Agricultural arbitrations, 445–56
  Agricultural Holdings (Notices to
      Quit) Act 1977, under,
      454–6
    notice to quit, 454–5
    resumption of part, 455
    work, notice to do, 455–6
  Arbitration Acts do not apply to, 445
  arbitrator
    appointment of, 447–8
      agreement, by, 447

Agricultural arbitrations—*cont.*
  arbitrator—*cont.*
    appointment of—*cont.*
      Minister, by, 447
      Minister, transfer of functions
          from, 447
      prescribed fee, payment of, 448
      President, by, 447
      replacement, 448
      time limits for, 447
      time of, 447–8
      Wales, where land in, 448
      writing, to be in, 447
    death of, 448
    failure to act by, 448
    incapacity of, 448
    misconduct by, 448, 453
    removal of, 448
    remuneration of, 452–3
    revocation of appointment of, 448
    single, to be, 447
  award, 450–2
    appeal against, 454
    correction of, 453
    error of law on face of, 451, 453
    final and binding, 453
    form of, 451
    interest to be paid under, 452
    interim, 450
    matters to be included in, 452
    payment, date of, to be fixed in, 452
    reasons for, 451
    remission of, 453
    separate amounts to be stated in,
        451
    setting aside of, 453
    time for making, 450
    variation of, 453–4
  costs, 452–3
    arbitrator's discretion in, 452
    payment of, date for, 453
    taxation of, 452
    witness, may be disallowed, 452
  county courts, jurisdiction over, 11
  Court of Appeal, appeal to, 454
  general matters referred, 446–7
  High Court, no jurisdiction over, 454
  procedure in, 448–50
    affirmations, arbitrator may take,
        449
    Lord Chancellor, power to order,
        448
    oaths, arbitrator may administer,
        449

Agricultural arbitrations—*cont.*
  procedure in—*cont.*
    parties, obligations of, 449–50
    special case, question of law in form
      of, 450
    statement of case, 449
    witnesses, 450
  specific matters referred, 446
Agricultural Holdings Acts see
    Agricultural arbitrations
Arbitration
(see also Arbitration by order of court,
Arbitrator, Costs, Evidence,
Exclusion agreements, Statutory
arbitration)
  abandonment of, 382
  agreement, by, 261
  assessors, in, 307, 427
  commencement of, 273, 367
  court proceedings
    arbitration not terminated by,
      285–6
    interpleader summons, 286–7
    stay of, 285–8
  courts, relationship with, 260–1
  definition of, 259
  delay in, 281–2
  hearing, 308–12
    adjournment of, 308–9
    arbitrator's opening statement at,
      400–1
    arrangements for, 399–400
    attendance at, 309–10
    counsel at, 309–10
    ex parte, 310
    form of, 310
    need for, 308
    notes of, 311
    notice of, 308
    order of appearance at, 310–11,
      400–2
    parties at, 309–10
    shorthand writer at, 309, 311
    solicitor at, 309–10
    witnesses at, 309
  improperly procured, where, 377, 380
  injunction to restrain, 281–2
  law, issue of, 295, 304–8
    determination by
      arbitrator, 307, 427
      courts, 304–7, 427
      third party, 308, 427
  natural justice, rules of, apply to, 292
  procedure, 293–303
    applications by parties, 398
    arbitrator's powers as to, 293, 296
    consolidation, 297–8
    discovery of documents, 301
    ex parte, arbitrator's powers to
      proceed, 296, 300
    High Court, powers of, regarding,
      296

Arbitration—*cont.*
  procedure—*cont.*
    initial letter, 293
      example of, 390
    interrogatories, 301–2
    order for directions, 295–7
      contents of, 295–6, 297
      examples of, 393–5, 396–7
      peremptory, 296, 310
    ordinary rules of, 290
    pleadings, 298–301
      amendment of, 300
      arbitrator's power to order, 299
      contents of, 299
      delay in exchange of, 300
      further particular of, 299
      High Court, power to order, 300
      lists of, 298–9, 300–1
      purpose of, 298
      timetable for exchange of, 299
    pre-hearing documents, arbitrator's
      role regarding, 397–9
    preliminary meeting, 293–5
      example of, 392
      matters considered at, 279,
        294–5, 392
      notification of, 391
      purpose of, 293–4
    proofs and reports, exchange of,
      295, 394
    quality arbitrations, in, 291
    statement of agreed facts, 294, 301,
      341, 418–19
  special case, abolition of, 360
Arbitration Acts
  agricultural arbitrations, do not apply
    to, 445
  arbitration agreement, terms implied
    in, by, 200, 201, 266
  arbitrator, duties imposed on, by,
    291–2
  county court arbitrations, do not
    apply to, 264
  Crown, application to, 261
  independent expert, do not apply to,
    200
  judge-arbitrator, application to, 274
  statutory arbitrations, application to,
    261–2
Arbitration agreement, 264–8
  alteration of, 268
  appeal provisions in, 383
  arbitrator, duties imposed on by,
    289–91
  arbitrator's jurisdiction, contained in,
    267
  bankruptcy of party to, effect of, 265
  bilateral rights in, 266, 270–1
  binding force of, 265
  compliance with award, implied term
    as to, in, 385
  contract, governed by law of, 264

Arbitration agreement—*cont.*
costs, directions as to, in, 344–5
courts, ouster of jurisdiction by, 260, 285
death of party, effect of, 265, 283
definition of, 264–5
delay, not repudiated by, 281–2
domestic, 367
form of, 265
fraud, setting aside due to, 285
parol, effect of, 264
reference
    mode of, specified in, 276
    restriction of, in, 267
rights under, superceded by award, 385
Scott v Avery clause in
    setting aside of, 279–80
    stay of proceedings in respect of, 288
separate documents forming, 265
signatures to, 268
terms implied in
    Arbitration Acts, by, 200, 201, 266
    courts, by, 267
time limits in, 268–73
    extension of, 269–73
    Limitation Act, under, 273–4
    rent review clauses, 269, 272–3
    undue hardship, where caused by, 271–3
time of the essence in, 268
validity of, dispute as to, 281
Arbitration by order of court, 263–4
county court, in, 263–4
High Court, reference by, 263
Arbitration clause see Arbitration agreement
Arbitrator(s)
(see also Arbitration, Award and Umpire)
admitted mistake by, 373–4
advocate of appointor, as, 277
appointment, 274–80
    complete, when, 276, 277
    conditions on, 278
    court, by, 278–80
        agreement with parties, by, 280
        parties' failure to appoint, where, 278
        parties' failure to fill vacancy, where, 278
        replacement, where revocation or removal, 279–80
        third party, failure to appoint by, 278
        umpire or third arbitrator, not appointed or replaced, where, 278
    disqualification from, 274–5
    duty to check validity of, 289–90
    example of, 389

Arbitrator(s)—*cont.*
appointment—*cont.*
    form of, 276
    invalidity, waiver of, 290
    nature of, arbitrator or expert?
        indicia of
            clear words as to, 194
            dispute in existence, 196–7
            judicial role, 197–9
    parties, by, 276–7
    third party, by, 277–8
        failure to agree, meaning of, 277
        failure to appoint by, 277–8
        second appointment, power to make, 277
assistance to, 307, 325–6
bias of, injunction to restrain, 282
business connections of, 275
declaration regarding, 281–2
delay by
    misconduct, not, 284
    removal due to, 283–4
    remuneration lost by, 284
delegation by, 308, 325–6
fees of
    court, payment into, of, 350
    excessive, where, 350
    lien for, 350
    loss of, by delay, 284
    overpayment by party, 351
    taxation of, 350–1
functus officio after award, 358–9, 373
hearing, 308–12
    affirmations, taking of, at, 312
    form of, discretion as to, 310
    notes of, duty to take, 311
    oaths, administration of, at, 312
injunction to restrain, 281–2
inspection by
    powers regarding, 317–8
    receipt of evidence at, 318–9
judge as, 274
judicial role of, 197–9, 201
jurisdiction of
    arbitration agreement, set out in, 267, 377
    denial of, 302–3
    duty to ascertain, 290
    enlargement of, 377
    excess of, by, 376, 380
        action on award, effect of, 380
    may inquire as to, 302
    no power to decide own, 302
knowledge, use of own, 319–23
Lands Tribunal as, 14
law
    different view of, 323
    duty to apply fixed system of, 291
    issue of, determination by, 307
misconduct by
    adjournment, refusal of, 375

Arbitrator(s)—*cont.*
  misconduct by—*cont.*
    appointment in another capacity,
        where, 378
    award
      action on, no defence to, 387
      failure to state in enforceable
          form, 375
      inconsistency in, 371
      remission to, powers revived by,
          359, 373, 381
    bribe, acceptance of, 284, 378
    costs, regarding, 352–3
    evidence
      failure to receive, 323–4, 375
      receipt of after hearing, 378
      secret, receipt of, 284, 317–19,
          379
    examples of, 284–5, 375, 378–80
    ex parte, failure to make clear he will
        proceed, 375
    fact, error of, where, 379
    fees
      excessive demand for, 285, 379
      payment of, before award, 378
    hearing, in absence of parties, 378
    hospitality, acceptance of, 378
    inadmissible evidence, receipt of,
        316
    inspection, failure to make, 379
    law
      different view of, 375
      error of, 379
      meaning of, 374, 377–8
      numerous errors may constitute,
          285, 379
      old cases of, 378
    other remedies, and, 379
    remission due to, 374–5
    revocation due to, 284–5
    setting aside due to, 377–80
    submissions, failure to hear, 379
    without prejudice statements,
        receipt of, 314, 316
  negligence, immunity from, 206–10,
      211, 221, 249
  official referee as, 263
  procedural mishaps by, 376
  procedure
    discretion as to, 290, 293
    duty to ascertain, 290
    ordinary, to be followed, 290
    powers as to, 293, 296
    quality arbitrations, in, 291
  quasi-arbitrator, 208
  remission to, further evidence, receipt
      of, by, 381
  revocation of authority of, 280–5
    action on award, and, 386
    agreement of parties, by, 280
    bias, on grounds of, 283
    court, with leave of, 282

Arbitrator(s)—*cont.*
  revocation of authority of—*cont.*
    death of a party and, 265, 283
    delay, due to, 283
    fraud, due to, 285
    misconduct, due to, 283, 284–5
    replacement appointment, power of
        court as to, 283
    settlement of dispute, by, 280
    sole
      agreement silent, where, 276
      separate disputes, appointed to
          hear, 278–9
    two, reference to
      failure to appoint, where, 276, 283
      replacement appointments, 276, 283
    umpire
      appointment of, 276, 278, 279
      entry on the reference by, 276–7
Assessor(s), 59–60
  Admiralty Court, in, 59
  arbitration, in, 307, 427
  county courts, in, 59
  county court arbitration, in, 263–4
  function of, 59–60
  High Court, in, 59
  Lands Tribunal, in, 59
  Patent Court, in, 59
  planning inquiries, at, 27
Audi alteram partem rule see under
    Natural justice
Award
  (see also Arbitrator, Costs, Exclusion
  agreements, Interest)
    agreed facts in, 341
    alternative, 17, 328, 416–17
    amendment of, 358–9
    appeal against
      agreement, by, 383
      Court of Appeal, 367–8
      determination of, 360
      distinction fact and law in, 361
      exclusion agreement, effect of, on,
          367
      High Court, to, 360–6
      leave
        guidelines for, 361–6
        procedure for, 365–6
      Nema guidelines, 362–6
        doubts in lower courts regarding,
            363–4
        one-off clauses, application to,
            362, 366
        point of law, where new, 364
        reaffirmation of, 364–5
        standard clauses, application to,
            362–3, 366
      no exclusion of, 366
      remission to arbitrator, following,
          360
      rent review arbitrations, in,
          368–70

Award—*cont.*
 appeal against—*cont.*
  substantial effect on rights of parties
   necessary, 361–2, 366
  time limit for, 360
 certain, must be, 328
 challenge to, restrictions on right of,
  372
 complete, must be, 328
 consent, 280
 consistent, must be, 328–9
 correction of, 353, 359, 374
  example of, 423–4
 declaration as to, 382–3
 declaratory, 331
  enforcement of, 384
 defences to an action on, 386–7
 delegation of arbitrator's duties in,
  325–6
 delivery of, 353
 determination in, 329–31
 directions in, 329–31
  jurisdiction, where in excess of, 330
  payment, for, 330–1
  power to give, 329–30
 enforcement of, 383–7
  action, by, 385–7
   accord and satisfaction, where,
    387
   arbitrator's authority
    excess of, and, 386
    revocation of, and, 386
   attachment, where, 386
   bankruptcy, where, 387
   facts to be proved before, 385–6
   judgment estoppel, and, 387
   misconduct by arbitrator, where,
    387
   not binding, where award, 386
   performed, where award, 387
   specific performance, 387
   time limits for, 386
  attachment, by, 383
  judgment, as, 383–5
   clarity, where award lacking in,
    384
   declaratory award, and, 384
   doubtful validity, where award
    of, 384
   effect of, 383–4, 385
   foreign award, where, 385
   parol agreement, and, 384
   rent review award, and, 384
   statutory arbitration, where, 385
   time limits for, 385
   "to some effect", where judgment
    not possible, 385
  statutory arbitration, in, 262
 examples of
  with reasons, 403–18
  without reasons, 422–3
 facts in, effect on parties, 357

Award—*cont.*
 final, 326
  effect of, 355
  must be, 328
 immoral, must not be, 329
 interim, 326–7
  costs, final except as to, 327
  definition of, 327
  power to make, 326
  rent review arbitration, in, 327
 judgment estoppel, created by, 356–7
 law, submissions of, in, 335, 341
 legal assistance in preparation of,
  325–6
 natural justice, must not offend
  against, 329
 notification of publication of,
  example of, 423
 original tenant bound by, 358
 parol, validity of, 327
 performance of, 329
 property, cannot transfer, 357
 publication of, 353
 publication to the parties of, 353
 public policy, must not be contrary to,
  329
 reasons for
  arbitrator's knowledge, use of in,
   340, 341–2
  duty to give, 332–4
  exclusion agreement, effect of, on,
   332
  fact
   findings of, 340–1
   rejection of, 338, 341
  facts and problem, depend on, 336,
   341
  factual mistakes in, 337
  intelligible, must be, 336, 337, 341
  judicial guidance as to, 335–42
  lengthy, should not be too, 336
  opinion, rejection of, 338, 341
  order for, 332, 333
  some but insufficient, 333
  substantial points, must be dealt
   with in, 336, 338, 341
  "special reason", why not
   requested, 332–3
  valuation, need not be given, 338,
   339, 341
  when to be given, 334
  written representations, where
   used, 337, 342
 recitals in, 329, 341, 381, 403–5
 remission of, 370–7, 381–2
  admitted mistake, where, 373–4
  appeal
   in respect of, 382
   not alternative method of, 370–1
  arbitrator's powers revived by, 359,
   373, 381
  bad on the face, where award, 373

Award—*cont.*
  remission of—*cont.*
    costs, after, 382
    discretion of court as to, 371
    effect of, 371–2, 373
    error of fact or law, for, abolition of, 370
    evidence, receipt of, after, 381
    excess of authority, where, 376–7
    form of award, after, 381
    fresh evidence discovered, where, 375
    injustice, where necessary to avoid, 373
    misconduct by arbitrator, where, 352–3, 371, 374–5
    part only of award, 381
    procedural mishap, where, 376
    time for making award, after, 325, 381–2
    want of justice, where, 375–6
  setting aside of, 370–2, 377–80, 382
    admitted mistake, for, abolished, 370
    appeal
      in respect of, 382
      not alternative method of, 370–1, 378
    bad on face, where award, 380
    discretion of court in respect of, 371
    effect of, 371
    error of fact or law, for, abolition of, 370
    excess of authority, where, 380
    fresh evidence discovered, where, 380
    improperly procured, where, 380
    inherent jurisdiction of court as to, 377
    limitation period, effect on, 273–4, 382
    misconduct by arbitrator, where, 352–3, 377–80
    money payable, may be secured by court, 377
  signature(s) on, 331
  stamping of, 331
  strangers, effect on, 358
  submission, must comply with, 328
  three arbitrators, of, 326, 331
  time for making, 325
  two arbitrators, of, 326
  umpire, by, 326
  written, when required, 327

B

Barrister see Counsel
Birkett, Lord, *Six Great Advocates*, 160

C

Calderbank letter see under Costs

Champerty, law of, 102
Chancery Division, 4
Circuit judge
  county court, in, 11
  High Court, may be appointed to, 4
  official referee, as, 4
Circular 73/65 (The Award of Costs at Statutory Inquiries), 33–4, 555–61
Circular 38/81 (Planning and Enforcement Appeals), 32–3, 113, 561–8
Commercial Court, 4
  arbitrations, supervisory jurisdiction over, 4, 260
  judge of, as arbitrator, 274
Comparables
  agreement of, 50, 70
  Civil Evidence Act, notices under, for, 70, 99, 135
  hearsay evidence of, 67–71
  post-valuation date, admissibility of, 71–4
Construction see Interpretation
Costs
  arbitration, in, 344–53
    agreement by parties as to, 344–5
    Arbitration Acts, implied terms as to, 345
    arbitrator's discretion as to, 345–6
    arbitrary date, award of by reference to, 348
    award
      amendment of, where silent as to, 352, 359
      costs of the, 345, 349
      reasons for, in, 351–2
      remission of, where silent as to, 352–3
      setting aside of, where silent as to, 352–3
    Calderbank letter, and, 349
    follow the event, 346, 351
    misconduct as to, 352–3
    payment of, arbitrator's power to direct, 345, 349–51
    recovery of less than claim, where, 346
    reference, costs of the, 345, 349
    rent review, in, 347, 415–7
    sealed offer, effect of, 347–8
    security for, 298, 345
    shorthand writer, of, 311
    taxation of, 349–51
      arbitrator, by, 345, 349–50
      court, by, 350
      High Court scale, on, 350
      lump sum, in, 349–50
      party and party basis, on, 350
      solicitor and client basis, on, 345, 350
    without prejudice statements, and, 349

Costs—*cont.*
Calderbank letter, and, 81, 349
circular 73/65, 33–4, 555
county court, in, 13
discretion of tribunal regarding, 8,
345–6
follow the event, 8, 346, 351
High Court, in, 8–10
Lands Tribunal, in, 18–19, 348
liability for, 8
litigant in person, and, 10
local valuation courts, in, 22
meaning of, 8
payment into court, effect of, 8
planning inquiries, and, 33–4
rent assessment committees, in, 26
sealed offer, effect of, 18, 117, 347–8
security for, 16, 298, 345
taxation of, 9–10
arbitration, in, 349–51
basis of, 9–10
common fund, 9
indemnity, 10
party and party, 8, 9, 350
solicitor and client, 8, 10, 345,
350
trustee, 9
county court scale, 9
High Court scale, 9, 350
without prejudice statements, and, 81,
349
Counsel
arbitration, in
preliminary meeting, to be
consulted regarding, 294
hearing
attendance at, 309–10
attendance at, duty to notify, 294,
310
law, issue of, reference to, 217, 308,
427
negligence, immunity from, 211, 221,
249
role of, 115–16
County court(s)
agricultural arbitrations, powers in
respect of, 10–13, 448, 449, 452,
453
arbitration in, 11, 263–4
actions in, 11–12
appeals from, 13
assessors in, 59
business tenancies in, 11
commencement of proceedings,
correct court for, 11
constitution of, 10–11
costs in, 13
court expert in, 264
expert evidence in, 84–7
inquiry and report in, 13
jurisdiction of, 11
matters in, 11, 12

County court(s)—*cont.*
pre-trial procedure in, 12
pre-trial review in, 12
transfer of proceedings in, 12–13
trial and judgment in, 13
Court experts, 60
county court arbitration, appointment
in, 264
function of, 60
High Court, in, 60
Court of Appeal, appeal to
Agricultural Holdings Acts, under,
454
arbitration, in
award
against, 367–8
reasons, order for, 334
remission of, against, 382
setting aside of, against, 382
preliminary point of law, on, 305
county courts, from, 13
High Court, from, 10, 334
Lands Tribunal, from, 19
Cross-examination, 91, 119–20, 184–7
leading questions in, 186
own case, must be put in, 184
principles of, 184
purpose of, 184
techniques of, 185–6

D

Damages, 231–47
assessment of, 241–7
date of, 247
defective property, purchase of,
241–4
loan, valuation for, 245–7
sale, purchase or rental, valuation
for, 244–5
contract, in, 231
contributory negligence, effect of,
240–1
interest on, 247
joint defendants, apportionment of,
241
limitation of, 231
measure of, 231–3
basic rule regarding, 232
contract, in, 232
differences in, 232–3
tort, in, 232
mitigation, 235–7
benefits of, 237
expenses of, 236–7
plaintiff
duty of,
financial circumstances, and, 236
reasonableness in, 237
remoteness of loss, 233–40
causation, and, 234–9
certainty, and, 239–40

Damages—*cont.*
  remoteness of loss—*cont.*
    economic loss, and, 233
    intervening factors, in, 234–9
      external condition.or event, 239
      plaintiff
        conduct of, 234–7
        personal circumstances of,
          238–9
        third party, conduct of, 237–8
      lump sum award, and, 239–40
      vexation damages, and, 240, 244
  tort, in, 231
Declaration, 216
  arbitration, in, 281–2
Discovery of documents
  accounts, and, 74–5
  arbitration, in, 301
  county courts, in, 12
  High Court, in, 6
  Lands Tribunal, in, 15
du Cann, Richard, *The Art of the Advocate*,
  186

                      E

Estoppel, 53–6
  agreement, by, 56
  award, by, 356–7
  deed, by, 56
  general rule of, 53
  judgment estoppel, 53–5
    arbitration, application to, 356–7
    cause of action estoppel, 55
    effect on
      all persons, 53–4
      parties, 54–5
    issue estoppel, 55, 356
    Lands Tribunal, in, 54
  meaning of, 53
  representation or conduct, by, 55–6
  proprietary, 55
  promissory, 55–6
Evidence, 42–50
(see also Award, Comparables, Expert
evidence, Fact(s), Hearsay
evidence, Public policy, Privilege
and Without prejudice statements)
  admissibility of, 41, 315
  affidavit, by, 6, 8, 16, 43, 90, 312
  agreement with third parties,
    admissibility of, 70–1
  arbitrator, in, 312–24
    arbitrator
      own knowledge, use of, 319–23
      should hear all relevant, 323–4,
        375
    inadmissible
      arbitrator, from, 317–19, 379
      collateral matters, 316–17
      objection must be made to, 317
      outside sources, from, 319

Evidence—*cont.*
  arbitration, in—*cont.*
    inadmissible—*cont.*
      reception of, whether
        misconduct, 316
      tendered, must be, 317
    inspection, receipt of evidence, at,
      318–19
    rules of evidence
      application to, 313
      relaxation of, 313–15
    secret evidence, receipt of, 284,
      317–19, 379
  best evidence rule, 42
  county court arbitration, rules of,
    application to, 264
  diagram of, 39
  documentary, 43–4
  examiner, given before, 43, 312
  fact, of, examples of, 38
  law of
    function of, 37
    judicial proceedings, application to,
      37
    natural justice, not part of, 37–8
    need for, 37
    planning inquiries, application to,
      37–8
  meaning of, 42
  modern approach to, 42
  real, 44, 318
  relevant, 41
  rent returns, as, 20–1
  weight of, 41, 316
  witnesses, testimony of, 43
Evidence of Opinion and Expert Evidence
  (Cmnd 4489), 83, 86, 108
Examination-in-chief, 91, 118–19, 171
Exclusion agreement(s), 366–7
  award
    appeal against, effect of, on, 367
    reasons for, effect of, on, 332, 367
    preliminary point of law, effect of, on,
      305
  rent reviews, and, 370
  statutory arbitration, of no effect in,
    262, 367
Exclusion clause(s), 249–52
  consumer contracts, in, 251
  contract, must be included in, 250
  contra proferentem rule, and, 250, 439
  death or injury, application to, 250
  negligence, definition of, in respect of,
    250–1
  reasonableness, requirement of, 251–2
Expert evidence, 59–91
  accounts, admissibility of, 74–5
  admitted facts, based on, 50, 70, 77–81
  arbitration, in
    arbitrator may decline to hear, 323
    arbitrator not bound to accept, 323
    procedure for, 83, 315

Expert evidence—*cont.*
county courts, in, 84–7
facts, based on 68–82
proved by expert, 68–75
proved by others, 75–7
general professional knowledge, based
on, 67–8
hearsay, 85–6, 90
hearsay, and, 67–8, 68–71, 83
High Court, in, 84–7
hypothetical facts, based on, 81–2
judicial notice of, 51
Lands Tribunal, in, 15, 87–90
opinions of other experts, reference to,
77
post-valuation date facts,
admissibility of, 71–4
preparation of, 102–6
purpose of, 61–2
rejection of, 61
subjects of, 62–3
technical literature, reference to, 76–7,
91
third parties, agreement with, based
on, 70–1
Expert witness(es), 60–2, 95–122
advocate, distinguished from, 155
appeal, advice on, 121–2
bias of, 66
client, relationship with, 114
communication with, 91
compellability of, 65–6
competency of, 63–5
counsel
assistance to, 120–1
relationship with, 115–16
courage of his opinions, needed by, 99
cross-examination of, 91, 118, 119–20
definition of, 60–1
delegation by, 104
documents, preparation of, by, 106–14
duties of, 61, 95–7
evidence, preparation of, by, 102–6
evidence and procedure, knowledge
of, needed by, 98–9
examination-in-chief of, 91, 118–9
expertise of, 64, 97–8
expert report by, 86, 107–8, 110
fees of, 101–2, 122
fundamental rule for, 96–7
initial report by, 100, 101, 107
inspections, attendance at, 120
instructions to, 100–1
mistakes by, 120
negligence, immunity from, 64–5, 249
objective approach, needed by, 99
opinions by, 61
opposing expert, relationship with,
116
other experts, relationship with, 116
other witnesses, relationship with, 116
planning officer as, 96

Expert witness(es)—*cont.*
questions by tribunal to, 120
re-examination of, 118, 120
settlement, advice on, 116–7
solicitor, relationship with, 114–15
transcript, checking of, 121
witness of fact
as a, 68–75, 83
distinguished from, 61

F

Fact(s)
admissible, 41, 68
definition of, 38
expert as witness of, 68–75, 83
law, distinguished from, 38, 40
matrix of, 433
opinion, distinguished from, 38, 40
post-valuation date, admissibility of,
71–4
proof of, 41–2
relevant, 41
value a question of, 38, 40
weight of, 41
Family Division, 4

G

Gowers, Sir Ernest, *The Complete Plain
Words*, 160

H

Habeas corpus testificandum, arbitration,
issue of, in, 312
Hearsay evidence, 44–50
agreement, admissible by, 45–6, 70,
315
arbitration, in, 48, 314, 315
admissibility of, 315
procedure for, 315
relaxation of rules of evidence,
where, 314
Civil Evidence Acts
admissible under, 46–50
reformed by, 45
common law, formerly admissible at,
48–50
credibility of, 47–8
discretion of court regarding, 48, 70,
315
example of, 45
expert evidence, where based on,
67–8, 68–71
expert witness
by, 67–8, 68–71
problems for, 45
hypothetical facts, used to avoid rule
against, 82
Lands Tribunal, in, 48
meaning of, 44–5

Hearsay evidence—*cont.*
  rule against, 44
  rules of court regarding, 48, 315
  statute, admissible under, 46
  waiver, admissible by, 45–6, 315
  weight of, 47
High Court, 4–10
  agricultural arbitrations, no
    jurisdiction over, 454
  appeals
    from, 10
    to, 26, 34, 35, 360–6
  arbitration by order of, 263
  assessors in, 59
  commencement of proceedings in, 5
  costs in, 8–10
  court experts in, 60
  divisions of, 4
  expert evidence in, 84–7
  judges of, 4
  pleadings in, 5–6
  procedure in, 5, 7
  summons for directions in, 6–7, 85
  trial and judgment in, 7–8
House of Lords, 10

I

Independent expert, 193–220
  appointment of, 212–13
    implied terms in, 210–11
  nature of, expert or arbitrator?
    indicia of, 193–9
      clear words as to, 194
      costs, to be borne by parties, 199
      decision in absolute discretion of,
        199
      dispute, avoidance of, 196–7
      expertise required by, 196, 197–9
      investigatory role, 197–9, 201
    powers of court as to, 200–1
  Arbitration Acts do not apply to, 200
  costs, 199, 205–6
  decision of, 203–5
    challenge to, 203–5
    correction of, 205, 220
    enforcement of, 205
    examples of, 218–19
    reasons for, 204, 205
  delegation by, 213
  evidence, rules of, not applicable to,
    201, 216
  fees of, 206, 213
  inspection by, 217
  investigations by, 202
  judicial control over, 202–3
  law, question of, procedure on,
    216–17, 427
  letters by, 213–14, 215, 219–20
  negligence, liability for, 206–11, 249
    common law, at, 206–10
    examples of, 244, 245, 247

Independent expert—*cont.*
  negligence, liability for—*cont.*
    exclusion of, 210
    limitation, and, 249
    Supply of Goods and Services Act,
      under, 210–11
  revocation of authority of, 203
  without prejudice statements to, 216
  written representations to, 201, 205–6
Injunction
  arbitration, restraint of, by, 281–2
Inspections
  arbitrator, by, 317–18
  evidence, receipt of, at, 121, 318–19
  expert witness, attendance at, 121
  independent expert, by, 217
  Lands Tribunal, by, 17
  leasehold valuation tribunals, by, 25
  local valuation courts, by, 22, 190
  planning inquiry, following, 31
  real evidence, part of, 44, 318
  rent assessment committees, by, 25
  rent tribunals, by, 25
Interest
  arbitrator, award of, by, 342–4
    compound, no power to award, 343
    for period after award, 343–4
    for period before award, 342–3
    for period before proceedings, 342
    rent review, in, 344
  damages, on, 247
  Lands Tribunal, award of, by, 17
Interpretation, 427–41
(see also under Maps)
  all words, effect to be given to, 437
  contra proferentem rule, 250, 439
  exclusion clauses, 250, 439
  implication of a term, 428, 430–1
  intention of the parties, 193, 434
  law, a question of, 427
  lease, of a, 428
  literal approach to, 427, 431–3
  other clauses, by reference to, 194–5,
    436–7
  purposive approach to, 427–8, 433–6
    actions of parties irrelevant to, 434
    clear meaning, not altered by, 435
    matrix of facts, and, 433
    negotiations, irrelevant to, 434
    rent review clause, and, 434–5
    surrounding circumstances, and,
      193, 433
    valuation, in, 435–6
  reasonable result, should produce,
    437–9
  rectification, 428–30
  similar words, by reference to, 437
  whole document, by reference to, 193,
    436–7
  words used, meaning of, 427
Interrogatories
  arbitration, in, 301

Interrogatories—*cont.*
county courts, in, 12
High Court, in, 7, 302
Lands Tribunal, in, 15

J

Judges see under circuit judges, county courts and High Court
Judicial notice, 50–1

L

Lands Tribunal, 13–19
absent owners, compensation for, 14
appeals
from, 19
to, 14, 22, 26
applications to, 14
arbitrator, may act as, 14, 263, 308
assessors in, 16, 59
commencement of proceedings in, 14
constitution of, 13–14
costs in, 18–19
decisions by, 17
expert evidence in, 15, 87–90
hearing in, 16–17
hearsay evidence in, 48
High Court, and, 16
inspections by, 17
interlocutory applications in, 15–16
judgment estoppel in, 54
law, issue of, determination by, 308
pleadings in, 15
preliminary point of law in, 16
pre-trial review in, 16
references to, 14
sealed offer in, 18, 117
written representations to, 17–18, 89–90
Law
appeal against, award, on question of, 360–6
different view of, by arbitrator, 323
fact, distinguished from, 38
interpretation, a question of, 427
issue of
arbitration, in, 303–8
arbitrator, determination by, 307
courts, determination by, 304–7
early identification of, 303
third party, determination by, 308
independent expert, 216–17, 427
preliminary point of, 16
question of, meaning of, 361
submissions of, failure to hear, 323–4
valuation, error of, may be question of, 38, 40
Leasehold valuation tribunals, 23–6
(see also Rent assessment committees)
appeals from, 26
applications to, 24

Leasehold valuation tribunals—*cont.*
constitution of, 23
costs in, 26
decision by, 25–6
expert evidence in, 24, 84
hearing before, 24–5
inspection by, 25
jurisdiction of, 23
pre-hearing procedure in, 24
Limitation, 247–9
arbitration
award
enforcement of
action, by, 386
judgment, as, 385
where set aside, 274, 382
cause of, when arising, 273
commencement of, 273
Limitation Acts apply to, 273
statutory, application to, 274
cause of action, when arising, 248–9
contract, in, 248
economic loss, where, 248–9
rent review, in, 249
tort, in, 248
periods of
contract, in, 247, 273
deed, upon a, 273
land, to recover, 273
tort, in, 247, 273
Local valuation courts, 19–23
appeals
from, 22
to, 20
appearance, order of, in, 21–2, 166, 168
constitution of, 19
costs in, 22
decision, by, 22, 190
expert evidence in, 20, 84, 177–80, 181–4
hearing before, 21–2, 166–90
inspection by, 22, 190
jurisdiction of, 19
rent returns, use as evidence in, 20–1, 163, 178

M

Maps
agreement of, 49, 111
evidence of, 49
form and content of, 109
interpretation, aid to, 439–41
Masters
Chancery, 4
Queens Bench, 4
taxing, 10
Mitigation see under Damages

N

Natural justice, rules of, 292–3

Natural justice, rules of—*cont.*
  arbitration, application to, 292
  audi alteram partem rule of, 292, 317
  award, must not offend against, 329
  breach of, 292
  case, form of, no application to, 292
  evidence
    law of, not part of, 37–8
    secret, receipt of, breach of, 317
  law
    different view of, breach of, 323
    failure to hear submissions of,
      breach of, 324
    meaning of, 292
  planning inquiries, application to, 31
Negligence, 221–30
(see also Damages and Limitation)
  advocate, immunity from, 211, 221
  arbitrator, immunity from, 206–10,
    211, 221
  duty of care, 221–4
    to client, 221–3
    to third parties, 223–4
  exclusion of liability for, 249–55
    contract term, by, 249–52
    notice in tort, by, 253–5
    operation of law, by, 249
  expert witness, immunity from, 64–5
  implied term regarding, 210, 222
  independent expert, liability for,
    206–11, 221
  proof, burden of, 221
  standard of care, 224–30
    date for consideration of, 225–6
    general rule of, 224
    implied term regarding, 210, 222, 225
    instructions, acceptance of, imposes,
      225
    law, now a question of, 226
    valuation, in, 226–30
      defects, failure to recognise, 228
      incorrect, may not be evidence of
        lack of, 226–7
      inexperience, 229
      information, failure to collect,
        228–9
      instructions, failure to carry out,
        227
      judgment, errors of, 229–30
      law, lack of knowledge of, 227–8
      method used, 230
Notice in tort, 253–5
  death or injury, application to, 253
  negligence
    definition of, in respect of, 253
    exclusion of liability by, 253
  reasonableness, requirement of, 253–5

O

Oath
  arbitration, in, 312
  form of, 90

Official referee, 4
  arbitrator, as, 263, 308
  law, issue of, determination by, 308
  reference to, 263, 308
Official referee's schedule see Scott
  Schedule
Opinion
  distinguished from law and fact, 38
  expert witness, by, 60–1
  value, a question of, 40
  witness of fact, by, 61, 171
Originating application, 11
Originating summons, 5, 216

P

Patent Court, 4
  assessors in, 59
Planning hearings see Planning
  inquiries
Planning inquiries, 26–35
  administrative function of, 26
  appeals
    from, 34–5
    leading to, 27, 28
  assessors at, 27
  attendance and appearance at, 30
  costs, award of, 33–4
  evidence at, 26, 31, 37–8
  expert evidence at, 84
  inspection following, 31
  natural justice at, 31
  notification and publicity for, 29
  procedure at, 30–1
  report and decision following,
    31–2
  rules of procedure governing, 27–8
  statements at, 29–30
  third party representations at,
    28
  types of, 26–7
  views or directions at, 28–9
  written representations in place of,
    32–3
Planning officer
  advocate, as, 155
  expert witness, as, 96
Plans see Maps
Pleadings
  arbitration, in, 298–301
  county court, in, 12
  general points regarding, 299
  High Court, in, 5–6
  Lands Tribunal, in, 15
  purpose of, 5, 298
Presumptions, 51–2
Privilege, exclusion of evidence by,
  57–8
Procedure see under Arbitration or
  appropriate court or tribunal
Professional negligence see Negligence
Proof
  burden of, 7, 41–2, 170

Proof—*cont.*
  burden of—*cont.*
    local valuation court, in, 22
    presumptions, effect of, on, 51
    professional negligence, in, 221
  evidential burden of, 42
  legal burden of, 42
  meaning of, 41
  methods of, 42
  persuasive burden of, 42
  standard of, 42
Proof of evidence
  contents of, 108–9
  example of, 135–44
  reading of, 119
  reference to, 91
  supplementary, 145
Public policy, exclusion of evidence by,
    56–7, 312

Q

Quasi-arbitrator see under Arbitrator
Queens Bench Division, 4

R

Reasons
(see also under Award)
  arbitration, in, 332–42
  Lands Tribunal, by, 17
  local valuation court, by, 22
  planning inquiries, following, 32, 33
  rent assessment committee by, 26
Rectification see under Interpretation
Re-examination, 118, 120
Registrar(s)
  county court, arbitration conducted
    by, 264
  county courts, of, 11
  Family Division, of, 4
  Lands Tribunal, of, 13–14, 18, 19
Remoteness of loss see under Damages
Rent assessment committees, 23–6
  appeals from, 26
  constitution of, 23
  costs in, 26
  decision by, 25–6
  expert evidence in, 24, 84
  fair rent, objection to, 24
  hearing before, 24–5
  inspection by, 25
  jurisdiction of, 23
  pre-hearing procedure in, 24
  written representations to, 24
Rent tribunals, 23–6
(see also Rent assessment committees)
  appeals from, 26
  constitution of, 23
  costs in, 26
  decision by, 25–6

Rent tribunals—*cont.*
  expert evidence in, 24, 84
  hearing before, 24–5
  jurisdiction of, 23
  pre-hearing procedure in, 24
  restricted contract, reference to,
    24
  written representations to, 24
Reports
  expert
    contents of, 86, 107–8, 110
    county court, in, 86, 90
    High Court, in, 86, 90
      example of, 129–35
    production in evidence of, 90
  initial
    expert witness, by, 100, 101, 107
      example of, 123–6
Rule 42 documents
  contents of, 89, 110
  example of, 126–9
  production in evidence of, 90, 91

S

Scott Schedule, 111–12
Sealed offer see under Costs
Services, contract for supply of, implied
    terms, in, 210–11
Solicitor
  arbitration
    hearing, appearance at, 309–10
    preliminary meeting, attendance at,
      294
  law, issue of, reference to, 217, 308,
    427
  role of, 114–15
Special referee, 4, 263
Statement of agreed facts
  arbitration, in, 294, 301, 341, 418–19
  contents of, 110–11
  examples of, 165–6, 418–19
  Lands Tribunal, in, 15
  written representations, should be
    accompanied by, 112–13
Statutory arbitration(s), 261–3
  Arbitration Acts, application to,
    261–2
  award, enforcement of, 262
  examples of, 262–3
  exclusion agreement, of no effect in,
    262, 367
  Lands Tribunal proceedings, not, 263
  Limitation Acts, application to, 274
Subpoena ad testificandum
  arbitration, issue of, in, 311–12
  witnesses compelled to appear by, 43,
    65
Subpoena duces tecum
  arbitration, issue of, in, 301, 311–12
  documents, production of, compelled
    by, 43, 312

T

Taxation of costs see under Costs

U

Umpire
(see also under Arbitrator)
  appointment of
    failure to appoint, where, 276, 278
    two arbitrators, by, 276, 278
  award of, 326
  entry on reference by, 276–7

V

Valuation
(see also under Negligence)
  correct method of, interpretation to
    find, 435–6
  law, fact and opinion, illustrative of,
    38, 40
  law, may reveal error of, 38, 40
View see Inspections

W

Without prejudice statements, 78–81
  admissibility due to subsequent event,
    80–1

Without prejudice statements—*cont.*
  admissions, and, 49, 50
  application only to action in which
    made, 80
  arbitration, in, 314, 316
  costs, effect on, 81
  dispute, must be made in attempt to
    settle, 79
  express or implied, may be, 79–80
  independent expert, and, 216
  independent facts in, 80
  objection to, where no, 78
  persons made to, 79
  sequence of correspondence, in, 79
Writ, 5
Written representations, 112–14
  arbitration by
    order for directions, in, 297
      example of, 396–7
  circular 38/81, 32–3, 561–8
  example of, 145–54
  faults in, 112–13
  independent expert, to, 201
  Lands Tribunal, to, 17–18, 89–90
  planning appeals, in, 32–3
  rent assessment committees, to, 24
  rent tribunals, to, 24